ENCYCLOPEDIA OF
EARLY CHILDHOOD EDUCATION

GARLAND REFERENCE LIBRARY OF THE SOCIAL SCIENCES
(Vol. 504)

Editorial Board

ENCYCLOPEDIA OF
EARLY CHILDHOOD
EDUCATION

EDITED BY
LESLIE R. WILLIAMS
Teachers College
Columbia University

DORIS PRONIN FROMBERG
School of Education
Hofstra University

GARLAND PUBLISHING, INC.
New York & London
1992

Library of Congress Cataloging-in-Publication Data
Encyclopedia of early childhood education / edited by Leslie R.
Williams, Doris Fromberg.
    p. cm. — (Garland reference library of the social sciences; vol. 504)
    Includes bibliographic references and index.
    ISBN 0-8240-4626-9
    1. Early childhood education—Encyclopedias. I. Williams, Leslie R., 1944– .
II. Fromberg, Doris Pronin, 1937– . III. Title: Early childhood education. IV.
Series: Garland reference library of social science; v. 504.
LB1139.23.E53   1992
372.21'03—dc20   92–4579
                                                                 CIP

Printed on acid-free, 250-year-life paper
Manufactured in the United States of America

Dedication

With deepest appreciation, Leslie R. Williams dedicates this work to her family, who supported the sustained effort needed to produce the *Encyclopedia* with loving attention and encouragement.

Doris P. Fromberg dedicates this work to her mother, Rose Boris Pronin, who showed her the future, to the memories of her father, Samuel Pronin, who showed her the present, and to her husband Mel, and their family, who gave her the gift of time.

Table of Contents

Acknowledgments

We wish to acknowledge with gratitude Marie Ellen Larcada of Garland Publishing, who brought enthusiasm, confidence, and much good advice to this project. We are thankful as well to Kevin Bradley and the Garland editorial staff for their flexibility and hard work in making this project a reality. We have taken special pleasure in our association with the members of the *Encyclopedia*'s Editorial Board, who shared their wisdom, good humor, and concentrated energy with us during the past several years.

List of Contributors

Linah H. Albanna
Kennedy Institute and
Johns Hopkins University

K. Eileen Allen
University of Washington

Richard Ambrose
Kent State University

Louise Bates Ames
Gesell Institute

Alice Anderson
University of Houston

Mary Arnold
University of Houston

Annette Axtmann
*Teachers College
Columbia University*

William C. Ayers
University of Illinois, Chicago

Nita H. Barbour
University of Maryland, Baltimore County

Donna R. Barnes
Hofstra University

Arthur J. Baroody
University of Illinois, Urbana-Champaign

Rhoda Becher
Ohio State University, Marion

Susan F. Belgrad
Roosevelt University

Judith Berezin
Child Care Inc.

Doris Bergen
Miami University

Emily S. Berkowitz
ESB Grants Consulting

Carol Bersani
Kent State University

Carolyn Black
University of Houston, Clear Lake

Ann E. Boehm
*Teachers College
Columbia University*

Frances Bond
Towson State University

Roberta Wong Bouverat
*Western Washington University
Woodring College of Education*

Elizabeth Brady
California State University, Northridge

Sue Bredekamp
*National Association for the Education of
Young Children*

Susan Britsch
University of California, Berkeley

Carol Brownstein
DePelchin Children's Center

Brenda Bryant
University of California, Davis

Melva Burke
Teachers College
Columbia University

Christine B. Burton
University of Wisconsin

Cary A. Buzzelli
University of Alabama, Birmingham

Bettye M. Caldwell
University of Arkansas, Little Rock

Margorie A. Cambre
Ohio State University, Columbus

Janet C. Camp
Director of Day Care Services
Tennessee Department of Human Services

Philippa H. Campbell
Family Child Learning Center
Children's Hospital Medical Center of Akron
(Ohio)

Nancy Carlsson-Paige
Lesley College Graduate School

Suzanne C. Carothers
The City College of The City University of New
York

Joseph J. Caruso
Framingham State College

Kathryn Castle
Oklahoma State University

Christine Chaillé
Portland State University

Douglas H. Clements
State University of New York, Buffalo

Rhonda Clements
Hofstra University

Charles O. Collins
University of Northern Colorado

Bruce S. Cooper
Fordham University

William Corsaro
Indiana University

Kenneth P. Counselman
Wheelock College

Douglas E. Cruikshank
Linfield College

Susan B. Cruikshank
Central Connecticut State University

Harriet K. Cuffaro
Bank Street College of Education

Bernice E. Cullinan
New York University

Sandra R. Curtis
University of California, Berkeley

Michael D. Davis
Virginia Commonwealth University

David E. Day
Buffalo State College

Yvonne De Gaetano
United Way of New York City

June S. Delano
Carlow College

Louise Derman-Sparks
Pacific Oaks College

Rheta DeVries
Human Development Laboratory School
University of Houston

Bernardine Dohrn
Director of the Juvenile Court Project
Northwestern University School of Law

Anne G. Dorsey
University of Cincinnati

Anne Haas Dyson
University of California, Berkeley

Clifford E. Eberhardt
Oregon Department of Education

Carolyn Pope Edwards
University of Kentucky

Harriet Egertson
Nebraska Department of Education

Richard Elardo
University of Iowa

Debra Ersenio-Jenssen
Division of General Pediatrics
North Shore Hospital, Manhasset, NY

Eva L. Essa
University of Nevada

James Fagin
Division of General Pediatrics
North Shore Hospital
Manhasset, NY

Beverly Fagot
University of Oregon

Stephanie Feeney
University of Hawaii

Beatrice S. Fennimore
Indiana University of Pennsylvania

David Fernie
Ohio State University, Columbus

Kay A. Ferrell
University of Northern Colorado

Marjorie V. Fields
University of Alaska

Janis B. Fine
Loyola University

Eileen S. Flicker
Orange County Community College
(Middletown, NY)

George Forman
University of Massachusetts

Ruth Formanek
Hofstra University

Helen L. Freidus
Bank Street College of Education

Doris P. Fromberg
Hofstra University

Joe L. Frost
University of Texas, Austin

Peige Fuller
University of Houston

Eugene Garcia
University of California, Santa Cruz

Daniel Gartrell
Bemidji State University

Elsie W. Gee
California Association for the Education of Young
Children

Celia Genishi
Teachers College
Columbia University

Russell Gersten
University of Oregon

Susan H. Ginsberg
Bank Street College of Education

Elizabeth M. Goetz
University of Kansas, Lawrence

Stacie G. Goffin
University of Missouri, Kansas City

Ruth F. Gold
Hofstra University

Lazar Goldberg
Hofstra University

Donna M. Gollnick
National Council for the Accreditation of Teacher
Education

A. Lin Goodwin
Teachers College
Columbia University

Robert C. Granger
The Manpower Demonstration Research
Corporation

M. Elizabeth Graue
University of Colorado

Judith M. Gray
South Metropolitan Association
Flossmoor, IL

Polly Greenberg
National Association for the Education of Young
Children

Selma Greenberg
Hofstra University

Maxine Greene
Teachers College
Columbia University

Randall L. Gull
Alabama Department of Education

Dominic F. Gullo
University of Wisconsin

Violet J. Harris
University of Illinois, Urbana-Champaign

Verna Hart
University of Pittsburgh

Lendall L. Haskell
State University College
(Plattsburgh, NY)

Joan Herwig
Iowa State University

Dorothy W. Hewes
San Diego State University

Verna Hildebrand
Michigan State University

Asa G. Hilliard III
Georgia State University

N. Ray Hiner
University of Kansas, Lawrence

Rebecca Peña Hines
University of Houston

Randy Hitz
Montana State University

Walter L. Hodges
Georgia State University

Alice Sterling Honig
Syracuse University

Carollee Howes
University of California, Los Angeles

Karsten Hundeide
University of Norway
Oslo, Norway

Rebecca L. Huss
University of Houston, Clear Lake

Joan P. Isenberg
George Mason University

Heidi H. Jacobs
Teachers College
Columbia University

Mary Renck Jalongo
Indiana University of Pennsylvania

Mary A. Jensen
State University of New York, Geneseo

John M. Johnston
Memphis State University

Sharon Lynn Kagan
Yale University Bush Center in Child
Development and Social Policy

Constance Kamii
University of Alabama, Birmingham

Elaine Kanas
Spence School

Esin Kaya-Carton
Bureau of Educational Evaluation

Abby Shapiro Kendrick
Work/Family Directions

Doris Kertzner
Great Neck - Manhasset - BOCES
Parent-Child Home Program

Melanie Killen
Wesleyan University

Carol S. Klass
Cardinal Glennon Children's Hospital
St. Louis, MO

Pnina S. Klein
Bar Ilan University
Ramat-Gan, Israel

Edgar Klugman
Wheelock College

Susan J. Kontos
Purdue University

Gloria Williams Ladd
Sunshine Hill

Margaret Lay-Dopyera
Syracuse University

Phoebe W. Lazarus
North Shore Hospital
Manhasset, NY

Marvin Lazerson
University of Pennsylvania

Sarah Henry Lederman
Teachers College
Columbia University

Patrick C. Lee
Ontario Institute for Studies in Education
Toronto, Canada

Donna L. Legro
University of Houston

Hope J. Leichter
Teachers College
Columbia University

Phyllis Levenstein
Verbal Interaction Project, Inc.
The Mother-Child Home Program

Diane Levin
Wheelock College

Matthew Lipman
Montclair State College

Joan Lombardi
Early Childhood Specialist

Deborah Lonow
Fordham University

Jan McCarthy
Indiana University, Terre Haute

Kim McClennahan
University of Maryland

Mary Lou McCloskey
Florida Atlantic University

Joyce McGinn
Hewlett-Woodmere Public Schools

Lee McKay
Western States Leadership Network

Deborah L. McLean
Memphis State University

Robert Marcus
University of Maryland, College Park

Mavis O. Martin
University of New Mexico

Bryan D. Midgley
University of Kansas, Lawrence

Maureen Miletta
Hofstra University

Lamar P. Miller
New York University

Leslie B. Mitchel
National Committee for the Prevention of Child
Abuse

Anne W. Mitchell
Bank Street College of Education

Patricia Monighan-Nourot
Sonoma State University

Eva Moravcik
Honolulu, HI

Gilda A. Morelli
Boston College

Shirley K. Morgenthaler
Concordia University

Edward K. Morris
University of Kansas, Lawrence

Stephen R. Morris
Temple University

Lesley M. Morrow
Rutgers University

Joan E. Moyer
Arizona State University

Susan W. Nall
Southern Illinois University, Edwardsville

Natalie A. Naylor
Hofstra University

Harriet C. Neal
California State University, Sacramento

Alan E. Nelson
Indiana County Child Care Program, Inc.
(Indiana, PA)

Joanne R. Nurss
Georgia State University

Michael O'Loughlin
Hofstra University

Joanne Oppenheim
Bank Street College of Education

Carol H. Osteyee
Burke County Public Schools

Alice Paul
University of Arizona

Geraldine Pedrini
Sunshine Nursery School

Anthony D. Pellegrini
University of Georgia

Sylvia Cavazos Peña
University of Houston

Donald L. Peters
University of Delaware

Robert Pickett
Syracuse University

Phyllis Povell
Long Island University

Douglas Powell
Purdue University

Gary Glen Price
University of Wisconsin

Shirley Raines
George Mason University

Patricia G. Ramsey
Mt. Holyoke College

Marian Rauch
*Hawaii Association for the Education of Young
Children*

Adrienne Robb-Fund
*Wantagh Public Schools
(Wantagh, NY)*

Susan Rosen
United Cerebral Palsy, Nassau County (NY)

Martha Ross
James Madison University

Kenneth Rubin
*University of Waterloo
Waterloo, Canada*

Helen Ross Russell
Manhattan Country School

Frances O'C. Rust
New York University

June Sale
University of California, Los Angeles

Coreen Samuel
University of Houston

Barbara Scales
University of California, Berkeley

Helen Schotanus
New Hampshire Department of Education

Lawrence Schweinhart
High-Scope Educational Research Foundation

Carol Seefeldt
University of Maryland, College Park

Beverly Shaklee
Kent State University

Edna K. Shapiro
Bank Street College of Education

Susannah Sheffer
Holt Associates

Lorrie Shepard
University of Colorado, Boulder

Madeleine Sigman
Pennsylvania State University

Jonathan G. Silin
*Educational Consultant
Amagansett, NY*

Dorothy G. Singer
Yale University

Jerome L. Singer
Yale University

Patsy Skeen
University of Georgia

Robert Slavin
Johns Hopkins University

Carol E. Smith
*American Association of Colleges for Teacher
Education*

Doris O. Smith
California State University, Fresno

Joan K. Smith
Loyola University

Linda K. Smith
*Office of Family Policy & Support
Department of Defense*

Lourdes Diaz Soto
Lehigh University

Bernard Spodek
University of Illinois, Urbana-Champaign

Barbara Sprung
Education Equity Concepts

William J. Stewig
University of Wisconsin

Jim L. Stillwell
University of Alabama

Dorothy S. Strickland
Rutgers University

Elaine Surbeck
Arizona State University

Annette C. Swann
University of Northern Iowa

Cindy Woolford Symons
Kent State University

L. Christina Taharally
Hunter College

Lupita Montoya Tannatt
Santa Monica Community College

Janet B. Taylor
Auburn University

Mona Williams Thornton
Norfolk State University

James T. Todd
University of Kansas, Lawrence

Linda E. Todd
Ohio State University, Marion

Roberta Trachtman
Fordham University

Edward Z. Tronick
University of Massachusetts

Pamela Tuchscherer
Preschool Perspectives
Bend, OR

Roselva Rushton Ungar
Los Angeles Unified School District
Glen Alta Elementary School

Judith Van Hoorn
Stockton, CA

Anne van Kleeck
University of Texas

Edwina B. Vold
Indiana University of Pennsylvania

Dinah Volk
Cleveland State University

Maryann Waldon
Texas Southern University

Andrea Walton
Teachers College
Columbia University

Cynthia Warger
Association for Supervision and Curriculum
Development

Bernice Weissbourd
Family Focus

Marcy Whitebook
Child Care Employee Project

Leslie R. Williams
Teachers College
Columbia University

Marty Wilson
University of Houston

Phil Wishon
University of Northern Colorado

Elaine P. Witty
Norfolk State University

Haiyan Yang
Teachers College
Columbia University

Margaret Yonemura
State University of New York, Binghamton

Herbert Zimiles
Arizona State University

Karen B. Kepler Zumwalt
Teachers College
Columbia University

Chapter 1

INTRODUCTION

This *Encyclopedia* is a reference work about young children in the United States, designed for use by policy makers, community planners, parents of young children, teacher educators, early childhood educators, program and school administrators, and others. The field of early childhood education encompasses

- the education and care of children from birth through eight years of age;
- the preparation of adults who work with them (parents, teachers, caregivers, program or school administrators, and support personnel);
- engagement with policy issues that may affect the education and well-being of young children; and
- the nature of material resources.

The field of early childhood education is enormously varied because the tasks of teachers, caregivers, researchers, and policy makers cut across the concerns of families, and public and private agencies.

The field has been affected by changes taking place in the nation's economy, demographics, schools, communities, and families that influence political and professional decisions. It also has been affected by a history that is characterized by a plethora of movements, including the kindergarten movement, the nursery school movement, the parent education movement, the child study movement, and infancy studies. Each of these movements has its unique history arising from the period in our nation's development and practice that parented it. The disciplines of philosophy, psychology and anthropology, and the professions of medicine, law, social work, and elementary education have contributed insights and given direction to particular movements.

These diverse historical, political, economic, sociocultural, intellectual, and educational influences on early childhood education have hindered the development of a clear definition of the field. The *Encyclopedia* provides an opportunity to define the field of early childhood education against the background of these influences and sources of knowledge. The *Encyclopedia* relates the field of early childhood education to its diverse contexts and to the cultural and technological resources currently affecting it.

Over the past three decades, educational policy makers have become increasingly aware of the importance of early childhood education. The field has begun to establish unique traditions and has made contributions to the education, health, and welfare of young children.

Just as there are different models of family, teacher, community, and institution that interact with children in their early years, there is more than one model of childhood. There are likewise many perspectives for viewing early childhood education, and they influence how we define its subject matter. The first purpose of this volume is to bring together these varied perspectives in an informational way. It documents what early childhood practitioners and researchers know, how they apply it in educational practice, and how they can implement methods of investigation. There is also discussion of programs of professional preparation and the mutual impact of practice, theory, and research.

The volume also includes issues of child advocacy from the perspective of policies and practices that are sensitive to the nature of how young children experience their lives. While acknowledging the unique function of schools as a societal institution for the education of the mind, the *Encyclopedia* also recognizes the impact of other societal structures, such as families, agencies and communities, peer groups, industries, and the media. Within this societal context, the young child's mind develops through physical, aesthetic, social, and emotional means (Fromberg, 1987). There is a great distance between the forms through which adults understand knowledge and the conceptions of younger children. Educators of young children, therefore, have the complex task of translating the understanding of adults into the forms that young children are able to embrace.

Inasmuch as early childhood educators are concerned *with* the education of young children in a learning-and-caring field that is continually evolving and changing, they also are concerned *about* these forces. Therefore, a second major purpose of the *Encyclopedia* is an ethical one. This work is oriented toward developing the kind of citizen who is socially competent, critically constructive, ethically concerned, and intellectually able and curious.

To educate in effective and ethical ways, organizations and adults need to create environments that are adapted to young children. One such environment, for example, would introduce children to new skills and concepts within familiar contexts that are derived largely from children's cultural experiences (Williams, De Gaetano, Harrington, & Sutherland, 1985). The *Encyclopedia* discusses other culturally sensitive ways of working with young children.

A third major purpose of the *Encyclopedia* is to illuminate the ongoing forces of change and the frontier issues that affect and represent the development of the field of early childhood education. By providing readers with access to an array of philosophies, models, and approaches to early childhood education, this volume can serve as a forum to define and integrate the field of early childhood education. An additional purpose of the *Encyclopedia* is to serve as a catalyst required by the growth of the field to draw connections between its foundations, methods of investigation, educational applications, and professional preparation programs.

Intended as an informational and ethical work on the many areas of research, policy, and practice that now characterize the field, the *Encyclopedia* was created through interaction with early childhood educators, scholars, and practitioners from allied fields across the nation. In 1988 an editorial board of accomplished early childhood teacher educators and researchers met to initiate the *Encyclopedia* project at a symposium funded by the W. Alton Jones Foundation of Charlottesville, Virginia. A major purpose of the symposium was to further define the field of early childhood through discussion with invited speakers who were not themselves early childhood educators, but whose work represented provocative reflections on the field's inner structures.

Although any member of the editorial board as well as other early childhood scholars could have provided a significant and substantial definition of early childhood education, scholars from outside of early childhood education were asked to speak because it seemed advisable to try to move beyond the categories that ordinarily informed our efforts in our search for past, present, and possibly future delineations. The published proceedings that grew out of the symposium identified a heightened level of awareness about the multiplicity of perspectives that define early childhood education (Williams & Fromberg, 1988). The *Encyclopedia*'s editorial board members recognized the possibility that contributions of a few hundred authors, gathered within a single work, might extend the definition of the field in important and previously untapped ways.

The next step in the production of the work was the identification of possible contributors from all regions of the United States and across the wide variety of topics included in the initial table of contents. The contributors' interactions with members of the editorial board led to some expansions and alternatives so that the work has continually been informed by a large network of participants.

For the convenience of its readers, each chapter of the *Encyclopedia* is introduced by an essay that presents salient issues influencing the development and state of that aspect of the field. Articles are arranged within chapter sections by topic and generally are alphabetized.

Chapter 2 looks at the historical, intellectual, and philosophical sources from which early childhood theorists and practitioners have drawn. Historical contexts also are interspersed within other chapters.

Chapter 3 considers the many kinds of sociocultural contexts that deal with children's concerns. In addition to considering how early childhood education is sponsored, there is consideration for public and private variations in the forms that programs take, the roles of public policy and child advocacy, and sociocultural research.

Chapter 4 focuses on perspectives about young children and their development. This chapter deals with characteristics of children, their special learning needs, the varied theories that attempt to explain their development, environmental factors that influence their development, and assessment and evaluation trends and methods.

Chapter 5 is devoted to describing areas of curriculum, varied program offerings, the ways in which children with special learning needs have been taught, and how educators have used resources and technology. Because curriculum and child development make up the central substance and major tasks of the field of early childhood education, these chapters are longer than other chapters.

Chapter 6 discusses the knowledge base of early childhood teacher education and perspectives on early childhood educators, including how adults influence early childhood education. There is discussion about the availability, nature, and preparation of early childhood educators, and professional issues affecting them. Teacher education, parent education, and administrator education are considered along with the uses of support services.

A list of each author's affiliation appears in the front matter of the Encyclopedia. A general index of topics is included for rapid location of information.

The *Encyclopedia of Early Childhood Education* reflects a crosscut view of the field today as defined by the 25 scholars who serve as members of the Editorial Board and by the more than 200 scholars who authored articles. They have done so in ways that both embrace current circumstances and point toward ongoing issues. The contributors have made additional reference to resources that can extend and deepen the information available to the reader.

The authors regard the *Encyclopedia* as part of an evolving statement. It is our hope that it will enable others to continue the creation of

the field of early childhood education in ways
that best serve young children.

References

Fromberg, D. P. (1987). *The full-day kindergarten.*
New York: Teachers College Press.

Williams, L. R., De Gaetano, Y., Harrington, C. C.,
& Sutherland, I. R. (1985). *ALERTA: A
multicultural, bilingual approach to teaching young
children.* Reading, MA: Addison-Wesley.

Williams, L. R., & Fromberg, D. P. (1988). *Defining
the field of early childhood education.* Charlottesville,
VA: W. Alton Jones Foundation.

D. P. Fromberg & L. R. Williams

Chapter 2

HISTORICAL AND PHILOSOPHICAL ROOTS OF EARLY CHILDHOOD PRACTICE

Chapter *2*

HISTORICAL AND PHILOSOPHICAL ROOTS OF EARLY CHILDHOOD PRACTICE

Introduction

Early childhood practice as it is known in the United States today is generally understood to have originated in Europe less than 200 years ago. It is certainly true that many of the specific daily routines such as "circle time" and use of play as a medium of learning, as well as many common classroom materials such as blocks and paints were introduced in the European early childhood programs of the early 1800s. Especially influential was the Froebelian kindergarten, founded in Germany in 1837, and disseminated throughout much of Europe and the United States over the next 70 years. It is also true, however, that practices in the kindergarten and in other forms of early education were themselves suggested by far older understandings of and beliefs about the nature of childhood and of the ways children learn best.

Like all educational practice, early childhood education began as informal custom millennia ago in the accepted ways of child rearing. As child rearing and educational sys-tems became formalized over time, they came to embody the values of the societies of which they were a part. Thus, how children's essential nature was described, what they were seen as capable of doing, and the types of guidance and supervision they were expected to receive reflected larger societal trends. Social, political, intellectual, and religious currents all shaped child-rearing customs and, later, gave form to early childhood practice (Braun & Edwards, 1972).

During early eras, when the survival of a group depended on the productivity of all of its members and the average life span was less than half of what it is today, childhood was considered to be a relatively brief experi-ence. Once a child had become physically capable of work (at six or seven years of age), that child began to assume adult responsibili-ties and, in many instances, was viewed as an adult (Aries, 1962).

Over time, societies became differentiated by occupation and social caste; some children were trained to assume their specialized responsibilities through apprenticeship or a distinct period of schooling, during which they were taught the elements of their anticipated sphere of activity. In such circumstances, children tended to enter into adulthood at puberty (about 13 years of age). The period of "childhood" thus became more elongated than had previously been the case (Gutek, 1972). Adult responsibilities were not generally assumed until the period of training had been completed. It should be noted, however, that not all children experienced a schooling period. Their opportunity to do so depended on the affluence and social position of their families.

In recent centuries, as people from various parts of the world began to be in more frequent contact with one another, many different cultural traditions became apparent in relation to views of the nature and capability of the young child. In the midst of so much diversity, views on appropriate early childhood practice also varied. Decisions regarding who among all the children in a society was to be taught, by whom, when and where those children would be taught, and ultimately, for what purpose they were to be taught all depended on the particular configurations of the societies in which education was embedded.

By the turn of the present century in the United States, the original German form of the kindergarten was already being challenged by a distinctly North American view of democracy and its implications for the care and education of young children. At the same time, the growth of science inspired by Darwin's work in the mid-1800s accelerated at an extraordinary rate and expanded to encompass the human psyche, as well as the physical world (Kessen, 1965). In the field of education, theorists and practitioners began to abandon metaphysically and classically oriented courses of study in favor of scientifically based work. These trends took expression in the progressive movement in education, and the child study movement in psychology (Braun & Edwards, 1972).

During this period also, people of other than European ancestry—African-Americans, Asian-Americans, American Indians (Native Americans), and Hispanics or Latinos (who often represented European and American Indian, and sometimes African influences as well)—were continuing to use the traditions of which they were a part in the raising and education of their children. Thus, as early childhood education in the United States evolved, tensions between homes and schools developed that were partly rooted in ancient ways.

By the 1920s, the Froebelian system had been replaced by practices derived from the child study and progressive movements. These movements emphasized child observation as the foundation for curriculum making. Instead of being taught solely through a tradition of existing practices, new teachers learned to observe children at play and to examine the normal courses of children's development (Williams, 1992).

The following decades saw tremendous growth in the new science of psychology, and child development research was understood by some early childhood educators to be directly related to an evolving practice. As a result, a number of persons trained in child development rather than in education began to assume positions of leadership in the field; for many practitioners, child development literature came to be viewed as the primary source of curriculum for young children.

During the same period, what had previously been Froebelian kindergartens were being integrated into public elementary schools. The addition of the kindergartens to grades one through six progression often led to a reconceptualization of the content of the kindergarten curriculum in academic terms, with a focus on "readiness"—prereading, prewriting, and premath skills.

Consequently, a split developed in the early childhood community between persons assuming a "developmentalist" position and those who continued to use academic traditions as the sources of practice. While the work of developmental psychologists was strongly influencing the design of programs for children under five years of age toward the use of "process curricula," public schools were subsuming the kindergartens into their vision of schooling, a vision that revolved around transmission of specific knowledge and skills. Thus, the kindergartens for five-year-olds and the primary grades for six- to eight-year-olds came to reflect the educational emphases derived from analyses of subject matter. Children were prepared at each grade level to do the work of the grade level to come, and less attention was given in these settings to the growing body of knowledge regarding the developmental and learning characteristics of young children.

A development parallel to the movements in child development research and practice, and in kindergarten and primary school practice, was the passage of legislation directed at the care, protection, and education of young children. Spanning more than 80 years of effort, this legislation also influenced the direction of the field of early childhood education, as it interacted with emerging trends in child study, reform movements in education, and societal changes toward greater inclusion of women in the work force.

In the latter half of the twentieth century, and most particularly in the 1990s, all of these forces have begun to converge in a reassessment of a now broadened field that includes infant studies, child care, and early education. In some quarters, a renewed interest is emerging in multiple sources for program design for young children from birth through age eight. Advocates for this position emphasize that while child development literature speaks to the forms early education might best assume, it does not supply a full range of content. Analyses of the conceptions of knowledge underlying subject matter (Fromberg, 1977; 1987) and of the value systems that infuse selection of some content over others (Kessler, 1990) also are important sources.

At the present moment, political, social, economic, philosophical, and psychological concerns continue to influence the direction of early childhood research and practice. In this chapter the foundations for those involve-

ments are traced, both for their intrinsic interest, and as a prelude to understanding the many arenas of child care and early education today.

The chapter is divided into six major sections. The first section introduces ancient child-rearing values and practices that still have influence today on the diverse populations in the United States. The second section contains three essays that explore the overall history of the field in its philosophical, social, political, and educational contexts. The essays have been placed second because they provide a broad understanding of some of the movements that have given shape to child care and early education in the United States, and thus offer important perspectives on the specific information that follows in succeeding sections. It is recommended that they be read twice, once where they first appear, and then a second time at the conclusion of the reading of Chapter 2. The essays are rich with allusion to a wide variety of occurrences and, on second reading, may serve as panoramic views of the political, philosophical, and historical roots of the field.

The third section describes the early childhood programs and practices that originated and were commonly used prior to 1960, while the fourth provides a chronology of the legislation that has had a strong impact on child care and early education. The fifth section highlights the unique histories of some commonly used early childhood materials. The sixth and final section introduces some of the major figures who have contributed to the distinctive inheritance of the field.

References

Aries, P. (1962). *Centuries of childhood: A social history of family life.* New York: Vintage Books.

Braun S. J., & Edwards, E. P. (1972). *History and theory of early childhood education.* Belmont, CA: Wadsworth.

Fromberg, D. P. (1977). *Early childhood education: A perceptual models curriculum.* New York: Wiley.

Fromberg, D. P. (1987). *The full-day kindergarten.* New York: Teachers College Press.

Gutek, P. (1972). *A history of the western educational experience.* New York: Random House.

Kessen, W. (1965). *The child*. New York: Wiley.

Kessler, S. (1990). Early childhood education as caring. Paper presented at the Annual Meeting of the American Educational Research Association, Boston, MA.

Osborne, K. (1991). *Early childhood education in historical perspective*. Athens, GA: The Daye Press.

Williams, L. R. (1992). Determining the curriculum. In C. Seefeldt (ed.), *The early childhood curriculum: A review of current research* (2nd ed). New York: Teachers College Press.

L. R. Williams

2.1 Ancient Contributions to Child Care and Early Education (Prior to A.D. 1750)

While early childhood education and child care have existed as a recognized field of study and practice in the United States for fewer than 200 years, many far older influences can be seen in their present form and content. From ancient times, each society around the world has had its distinctive child-rearing practices, traditions that were tied to that society's larger culture. Such practices reflected the deep structures or values of the society and evolved over time as those values evolved.

The articles that follow are divided into two groups. The first group describes some of the cultural influences on present practices in the United States that originated prior to A.D. 1750. Current expressions of child rearing and early childhood education practices show the complexity resulting from the contact and interaction of many groups within our multicultural society.

The second group of articles traces child rearing and early educational practices through the periods of European history that directly informed the early childhood programs imported into the United States during the latter half of the nineteenth century. Major figures associated with various eras are discussed directly after an overview of the period.

L. R. Williams

African Influences

Africa is a large continent, yet there were (and continue to be today) profound cultural similarities among traditional people on the continent and even among the descendants of African people throughout the African world diaspora (Diop, 1978). Social and spiritual values and aims were at the very core of African culture (Mbiti, 1979; Griaul & Dieterian, 1986). Beliefs about and attitudes toward young children and their development today must be understood against the backdrop of these ancient social and spiritual values and aims.

African children were regarded by their parents and communities universally as "the reward of life." They were born with an honored place in a society that included within it the ancestors, the living, and those yet to be born. Therefore, the central question that was asked in Africa was not "What is a child?" but "Who is that child?" Since the child actually had an identity before birth, the nurturance of the pregnant mother and the fetus should be seen as the beginning of the early education of the child (Ainsworth, 1967; Evans, 1970; Gerber, 1958; Pearce, 1977; Pearce, 1985; Semaj, 1980).

For the first few years of life, the child was the almost constant companion of its mother. Close relatives and, in particular, older siblings relieved the mother of child care from time to time. The child was immersed in the day-to-day activity of adults. He or she was a secure and protected observer, with few limits on the opportunity to explore and to socialize. As maturity dictated, the child gradually learned through observation, imitation, and participation. Though carefully monitored and supervised by a growing variety of adults and older siblings, the child was encouraged to develop its own initiative without rigid direction.

African parents and communities nurtured the child so as to establish close bonds, first to the mother, then to the family, to the extended family, to the tribe or nation, to the natural world, and to the particular group's beliefs about God. Thus, African early childhood education was a shared community responsibility. Through play, participation in the rich community environment of work, ceremonies, proverbs, stories, songs, dances, and (recently) through formal schooling, the young child developed in a secure, loving, and purposeful way. The young child gradually was required to assume serious work tasks and responsibilities and, as it grew older, to assume child care responsibilities for younger siblings.

These activities prepared the child to join later in cooperative living and learning activities with age mates of the same sex who became bonded as closely as the family itself. With this peer group, the child embarked upon a cooperative learning career. This cooperative learning in formal and informal education and socialization was part of a broader cooperative community philosophy.

African educational systems can be viewed today through the study of the ancient African cultures of Kemet (Egypt), Cush (Nubia and Ethiopia), Punt (Somaliland), Kenya, Mali, and many others. All shared similar systems of formal and informal education and socialization. These were open enrollment systems built on universal primary and secondary schooling. There was a saying in ancient Kemet (Egypt) that "There is no son for the chief of the Double White House." Put another way, there is no royal road to knowledge. African people regarded the education and social development of their children as central to their group's survival.

The highest goals of adult education were either spiritual or political leadership. Therefore, early childhood education must be seen not only in the context of the activities of young children in the early years but also as part of a continuum leading to ultimate ends that included living in harmony with the natural and human environment, and with the group's beliefs about the will of God.

Serious students of African educational systems only now are beginning to appreciate the profound complexity and powerful consequences of traditional African education. In fact, we now see some of the more important elements of African systems in some of the systems of the Western world. For example, cooperative learning and strategies that support bonding and attachment are very close to African systems. Some scholars have even traced the impetus for the emphasis on such things as bonding and attachment to lessons from research on African children and families in traditional societies (Ainsworth, 1967).

References

Ainsworth, M. D. S. (1967). *Infancy in Uganda: Infant care and the growth of love*. Baltimore: Johns Hopkins University Press.

Diop, C. A. (1978/1959). *Cultural unity of Black Africa*. Chicago: Third World Press.

Evans, J. L. (1970). *Children in Africa: A review of psychological research*. New York: Teachers College Press.

Gerber, M. (1958). The psycho-motor development of African children in the first year, and the influence of maternal behavior: Medical Research Council's Infantile Malnutrition Unit, Mulago Hospital, Kampala, Uganda. *Journal of Social Psychology, 47* (1), 185–195.

Gerber, M., & Dean, R. F. A. (1958). Psychomotor development in African children: The effects of social class and the need for improved tests. *Bulletin of the World Health Organization, 18*, 471–476.

Griaule, M., & Dieterien, G. (1986/1965). *The pale fox*. Chino Valley, AZ: Continuim Foundation, P.O. Box 636, Chino Valley, Arizona, 86323.

Mbiti, J. S. (1979). *African religion and philosophy*. New York: Praeger.

Pearce, J. C. (1977). *Magical child*. New York: E. P. Dutton.

Pearce, J. C. (1985). *Magical child matures*. New York: E. P. Dutton.

Semaj, L. T. (1980). Rastafari: From religion to special theory. *Caribbean Quarterly, 26* (4), 22–31.

A. G. Hilliard III

American Indian (Native American) Influences

Throughout their existence, American Indian tribes indigenous to the United States (including Alaska) have valued the birth of a child. Adults consider each child to be a special gift and see the child as a sign of the survival of the tribe into the future. Every tribe has social, cultural, and spiritual priorities. Each tribe is unique in the aspects of its culture, such as language, traditional practices, and child-rearing relationships. While the spectrum of Native peoples and their cultures is diverse and dynamic, there are commonalities among many tribes relating to the rearing of children.

The extended family is a strong element in child rearing, as the child is seen as belonging to the family group. The type of Indian community may vary and the kinship patterns followed may be different, but every child has a place in the identified structure of the tribe. The extended family grounds a child's relationships between his or her family and other families. Certain members, such as the mother, may have special responsibilities for rearing and care, but discipline may be left to other members of the clan. In a matriarchal society, it is sometimes the case that the most influential male for the child is not the child's father, but may be an uncle, a brother of the child's mother.

The "old ways" among Indian tribal elders reflected a sophistication of conscience through the extended family that left no orphans to be placed outside the family system. Indian children had many parents and teachers to guide them and from whom they could learn. The participation in a clan structure led children to understand their reciprocal duties to each other and the kinship system. This in turn led to a broader communal responsibility.

Much of the Indian child's learning is experientially based. To learn by doing is a long-held practice of Native Americans. Adults often make miniature tools through which they teach the children utilitarian crafts, creating items for family use. Adults include the children in each step of the preparation, teaching criteria for selection and gathering of materials as the step is experienced. The hands-on process followed is relevant, functional, and meaningful. The adult tells the child the reasons for following each step when he or she feels the child is ready for information.

There is a long history of the use of an oral tradition among the tribes. It is often an elder, such as a grandmother or grandfather, who has the responsibility for sharing tribal values. Legends are often the means of this transmission as they are told and retold to children to pass on the tribe's values, mores, and practices. This tradition, however, fosters a listening role for the child, not an interactive one.

As the child grows, his or her responsibility for the family's welfare increases. Children are included in all types of family and community gatherings. The expectation is that through early exposure, children will have a fuller understanding of practices of their family and tribal community.

Indian child rearing is more self-exploratory than it is restrictive and may be labeled as "permissive" in contrast to majority standards. The American Indian perspective is to let a child be a child for as long as possible. Most Indians, however, also give a greater responsibility to their children at an early age. For example, a Navajo child may herd sheep alone as early as six years of age.

The focus of a child's upbringing is in terms of where and how each will participate as a group member rather than as an individual. This process also builds for the individual a rightful place within the tribe and develops a strong tribal identity and self-concept.

Survival over time for Native Americans, however, has partially been because they have had to work cooperatively. Educating children was a collaborative and holistic process involving family and peers in a supportive environment. The process was not like the European-American education model, which is highly structured, independent, and competitive. Traditional Native American education emphasized acquiring language, cultural knowledge, values, and perspectives that served particular purposes within the tribal practices.

Bridging the gap between two worlds for Indian children begins with understanding the multiple realities that exist. People from different vantage points perceive reality differently. Children will be successful when educators accept their perceptions as equally valid.

References

Butterfield, R., & Pepper, F. (In press). Improving parental involvement in elementary and secondary education for American Indian and Alaska Native students. In G. M. Charleston (ed.), *Indian nations at risk: Solutions for the 1990s* (Chapter 11). Washington, DC: U.S. Department of Education.

Charleston, G. M. (In press). *Indian nations at risk task force—A time for change: Native education in the year 2000.* Washington, DC: U.S. Department of Education.

Deloria, V., Jr. (1978). The Indian student amid American inconsistencies. In Thompson, T. (ed.), *The schooling of Native America* (pp. 9–27). Washington, DC: American Association of Colleges of Teacher Education.

Lake, R. (Medicine Grizzlybear). (1990). An Indian father's plea. *Teacher Magazine, 2* (1), 48–53.

National Education Association. (1983). *American Indian/Alaska Native education: Quality in the classroom.* Washington, DC: Author.

Paul, A. S. (In press). Early childhood education in American Indian and Alaska Native communities. In G. M. Charleston (ed.), *Indian nations at risk: Solutions for the 1990s* (Chapter 9). Washington, DC: U.S. Department of Education.

Thompson, T. (1978). Preface. In T. Thompson (ed.), *The schooling of Native America* (pp. 1–8). Washington, DC: American Association of Colleges for Teacher Education.

A. S. Paul

Asian Influences

The civilizations of Asia are ancient and widespread, encompassing those of China, Japan, Korea, Mongolia, the Philippines, Southeast Asia (Cambodia, Laos, Malaysia, Singapore, Thailand, and Vietnam), and Tibet. While there are substantial differences among those cultures, there are also certain similarities due to contact and cultural diffusion (Hoffman, 1988).

In the Asian lands that were influenced by the philosophy of Confucius (550–479 B.C.), a primary tenet governing behavior was recognition of the duties of individuals to one another. There were considered to be five relationships—son to father, wife to husband, younger brother to elder brother, subjects to sovereign, and friend to friend (Kenworthy, 1975). These five relationships formed the basis of Chinese (and many other Asian cultures') family structure. The major characteristic of that structure was subordination (known as "filial piety") of the young to the aged. Elders held supreme authority in this structure.

A significant feature of the Asian family structure was the extended kinship network. It was not uncommon for three generations of the paternal lineage to live in the same household. Married sons lived in their parents' home, with property and income managed in common under the leadership and authority of the father (Kenworthy, 1975).

Because of the strongly patriarchal nature of the society, male children were highly valued. A family's wealth was calculated partly in terms of the number of sons. Attitudes stemming from this preference persist in some Asian families to the present day.

Traditionally, Asian parents tended to be very benevolent to young children. During the first four or five years of life, children usually slept with their mothers. They were frequently in the company of a nurturing family member and were largely indulged in their inclinations (Bond, 1986; Kenworthy, 1975; Kojima, 1986; Yamamura, 1986).

Around the age of six, when they entered a situation of formal schooling, the indulgence could abruptly stop. The children were held to strict standards of behavior in order to ensure that they responded to and reflected the strict hierarchy of the culture. Children experienced themselves as embedded in a net of emotionally close relationships. This circumstance promoted the feeling that what shamed the child, shamed the family. The prospect of shame was thus a strong deterrent to "bad" behavior (Bond, 1986; Kenworthy, 1975).

Children began the practice of filial piety at an early age. They were taught to obey and respect their parents and other elders in the family under any circumstance. In addition, as parents aged, children had the obligation to live with and care for them. The only way that one could properly repay one's parents for the care they had provided was by being a dutiful child.

In the past (and for some families still today), some Asian families were more concerned with impulse control and less tolerant of aggressive or independent behaviors than were families of European derivation. Children were not encouraged to become fully independent from their parents. Because parents were understood to have absolute authority, children generally were not expected to express opinions different from those of their parents (Bond, 1986).

Many Asian parents today still hold education in great esteem and have high expectations for their children's academic achievement. Historically, in Chinese society, intellectuals had high social and political status. Some modern-day parents feel that underachieving children bring disgrace not only to themselves but to the whole family.

References

Bond, M. H. (ed.). (1986). *The psychology of Chinese people*. New York: Oxford University Press.

Kenworthy, L. (1975). *Studying China*. New York: Teachers College Press.

Hoffman, L. W. (1988). Cross cultural differences in childrearing goals. In R. A. Levine, P. M. Miller, & M. M. West (eds.). *Parental behavior in diverse societies. New Directions for Child Development*, No. 40, (pp. 99–122). San Francisco: Jossey-Bass.

Kojima, H. (1986). Child rearing concepts as a belief-value system of the society and the individual. In H. Stevenson, H. Azuma, & K. Hakuta (eds.). *Child development and education in Japan*, (pp. 39–54). New York: W.H. Freeman.

Yamamura, Y. (1986). The child in Japanese society. In H. Stevenson, H. Azuma, & K. Hakuta (eds.). *Child development and education in Japan*, (pp. 28–38). New York: W.H. Freeman.

H. Yang

Biblical (Jewish/Christian) Influences

Biblical influences on child rearing and early education in the United States were of two sorts—those derived from the Jewish scriptures and those derived from the Christian scriptures. The Jewish scriptures include the Torah, or first five books of the Jewish Bible, and the "wisdom literature," including Proverbs, the Book of Job, the Song of Songs, Ecclesiastes, and the Wisdom of Solomon and of Ben-Sirach or Ecclesiaticus. The Christian scriptures include the Jewish Bible (known by Christians as the Old Testament), and the Gospels, the Acts, the Epistles, and the Book of Revelation (collectively known by Christians as the New Testament).

Ancient Jewish Educational Practices

The Jews of biblical times considered themselves a people with a special destiny. They saw themselves as called upon by their belief in one God to worship and obey the Divine Word and to testify to their God's existence, omnipotence, and omnipresence. As such, the Jews had obligations that differed from those of other peoples living in the deserts and mountains of Egypt, Babylonia, Syria, and Palestine.

In some ways, of course, the Jews shared certain ways of life with their neighbors. Like them, they tended sheep, ground grain to bake bread, shaped clay into cooking and storage pots, spun wool to make yarn to be woven into garments, tanned animal hides to make leather, roasted birds over open fires, and sought honey from beehives. Learning to perform those tasks was part of what growing up involved for young Jewish boys and girls, who learned by carefully observing their elders and imitating them.

The ancient Jewish teachers (the prophets and priests of the people of Israel and Judah), however, had made it clear that families also had religious and moral responsibilities, as did the entire community. Those responsibilities were teaching children the central religious beliefs that differentiated them from others.

Jews were expected to be personally faithful to God in their beliefs and their actions. They learned about their dependence upon God and their limitations as human beings from both prophets and psalmists, and later, from sages or wisemen ("Hakamin") who produced the wisdom literature of their Bible. As

Jews linked religion with morality, it was not enough to worship and pray. Behavior toward others also became a measure of adherence to God's commandments and laws.

Jewish people valued children, seeing them as a blessing from God; but children, too, were expected to keep the commandments and "fear the Lord." Jewish children did not attend school, as there were no schools in biblical times in Palestine. The children learned through participation in family rituals, by listening to and questioning their parents and other elders in the community, and by worshipping in the Temple.

With the Babylonian exile (586 B.C.), the synagogue came into being as a place where scribes devoted themselves to interpreting the sacred books, and teaching the Law to the people. The adults who studied there were expected to pass the teaching on to their children. That practice persisted when the Jews returned to Palestine.

In time, the Jews came into increasing contact with the Greeks. Greek thought influenced the Jews, and Hellenized Jews found themselves attracted to some of the features of Greek life and education. Some Jewish boys studied at the gymnasium and undertook the physical sports and training that were antithetical to traditional Jewish notions of modesty. This trend continued under the later occupation by the Romans.

The uneasy accommodation between Jews, Greeks, and Romans ended with the revolt of the Maccabees in 168 B.C. By then, it had become clear to the Jews that they would need to separate from the Greco-Roman world to preserve their identity. After reclaiming their Temple, the Jews provided schools for adolescent boys to promote study of the scriptures. The chief instructors were conservative, orthodox, strictly observant Pharisees, who stressed the ancestral religion's commitment to monotheism in the midst of a "pagan" world.

Early Christian Educational Practices

A number of Palestinians and Syrians who encountered Jesus of Nazareth in Palestine while it was still under Roman occupation became convinced by his teachings to adopt a new orientation toward their religion. Retaining many elements from their Judeo-Greco heritage, the "Christians," as they came to be known, taught these as well as their new tenets to their children and to converts to their religion.

Early Christians believed they had a religious and educational mission to "spread the word" of God's redemptive power through acceptance of Jesus as one with God. Jesus became known as "the Christ" (the Anointed One). Christians expected that Christ would return at some not-too-distant time to judge those who had followed the tenets of the faith and those that were found wanting. Central to the Christian experience were beliefs in the birth, life, death, resurrection, and divinity of Jesus; in the miracles he performed; and in his moral, as well as religious teachings.

Jesus amended the Ten Commandments (fundamental to the Jews) by proclaiming a new commandment—that the faithful must love one another and treat their neighbors as they themselves would choose to be treated. Moreover, he taught that the first commandment that undergirded all the law was the requirement that people love God without reservation. In the Beatitudes, Jesus preached a new set of moral values. The poor, meek, merciful, pure in heart, those who mourned, those who were persecuted for the sake of righteousness or reviled for Jesus' sake would be the inheritors of God's favor, rather than the rich and proud, or those who sought to enhance their power and influence.

People became Christians through the rite of baptism, paralleling the experience of Jesus who received heavenly recognition through the purifying power of water. Preparation for baptism required studying and adopting the beliefs and the moral practices of the Christian community. Essentially, that preparation depended upon the oral tradition that included the telling of Christian stories, the preaching and "witnessing" of the apostles, and the reading and sharing of the letters written by some of the apostles to the various communities of believers.

Jesus was quoted by the apostle Mark as saying that little children should "come unto [him]." His disciples and early followers understood that injunction to mean that even small children should be prepared for baptism, and that initial instruction should be provided by their families, with fathers assuming the central educational role. While the apostle Paul urged the importance of instruction and parental discipline of children, he also stressed a reciprocal need for children to love and respect their parents, and for parents to be deserving of that love and respect.

Initially, the Christian faith attracted simple working people. It was later that the intellectually and economically powerful began to join the group. Two to three centuries after the death of Jesus, the Christians began to develop a priestly cadre who established churches, codified Christian religious beliefs, and oversaw the education of boys who were selected to promulgate the teachings of the church. Most young girls and boys continued to be educated to their Christian beliefs and responsibilities in the home, but those families who could afford to do so would send a son to be schooled as a cleric, and thus contribute to the perpetuation of the Christian faith.

References

Barclay, W. (1959). *Train up a child: Educational ideals in the ancient world*. Philadelphia: Westminster Press.

Bouquet, A. C. (1953). *Everyday life in New Testament times*. New York: Scribner.

Castle, E. B. (1962/1958). *Educating the good man: Moral education in Christian times*. New York: Collier Books.

Chouragi, A. (1975). *The people and faith of the Bible*. (Trans. Gugli, W. V.) Amherst: University of Massachusetts Press.

Clements, R. E. (ed.). (1989). *The world of ancient Israel: Sociological, anthropological, and political perspectives*. New York: Cambridge University Press.

Daniel-Rops, H. (1962). *Daily life in the time of Jesus*. (Trans. O'Brian, P.) New York: Hawthorne Books.

Davies, J. G. (1967). *The early Christian church: A history of its first five centuries*. Garden City, NY: Doubleday.

Gottwald, N. K. (1979). *The tribes of Yahweh: A sociology of the religion of liberated Israel, 1250–1050 B.C.* Maryknoll, NY: Orbis Books.

Grant, M. (1973). *The Jews in the Roman world*. New York: Scribner.

Halpern, B. *The emergence of Israel in Canaan*. Chico, CA: Scholars Press.

Oesterley, W. O. E. (1970/1941). *The Jews and Judaism during the Greek period: The background of Christianity*. Port Washington, NY: Kennikat Press.

D. R. Barnes

Greeks, Ancient, Influences of

The education provided to young children in ancient Greece depended upon family status and upon the family's city-state. Athens and Sparta had different conceptions of what citizenship required and placed different emphases on various components of education. Both envisioned citizenship as involving male participation in civic activities.

Slave children had different experiences and expectations from citizens' children. Slave children were expected to learn to fulfill adult roles by imitating the behaviors of adult men and women slaves. They were expected to learn their "place" in the social order; to perform household tasks, field work, craft work, or manual labor; to show allegiance to their masters; and to earn what entitlements they had to food, shelter, and clothing. Slave children tended to learn these lessons at a relatively young age.

The children of citizens also began their training and education at a young age. In Sparta, young boys learned through example that they, too, would be expected to defend their city militarily and enter into battle to secure honor, glory, riches, foods, and lands. Emphasis was placed on bodily strength and endurance, and on physical skills and agility. Boys also were expected to memorize heroic legends. Moreover, they were taught that direct, straightforward speech was the mark of Spartan men.

Young Spartan girls learned to take on the tasks performed by their elders. They grew up eating plain food, simply prepared, and later learned to prepare those foods. They also learned to wash clothes, tend the hearth, spin and weave, and help raise children. Spartan girls grew up knowing that women were expected to produce strong, healthy babies. They knew fathers were expected to look closely at their newborns for signs of deformity. Disability would not be tolerated in the Spartan population, and deformed infants would be exposed and left to die.

Athenian girls exercised and participated in dances that strengthened their bodies. Attendant values of womanly virtue and modesty, however, restricted their physical activities later. Early play with dolls and other toys soon gave way to learning about household tasks.

Athenian boys also developed their physical capacities and abilities through exercise and sport. During their earliest years, boys played with hoops, balls, and knucklebones. They participated in competitive physical training programs in the "palaestra" (wrestling school) and later in the gymnasium, where they practiced running relay races, hurling the javelin, and throwing the discus.

Military training was required of adolescent male Athenians. Young boys anticipated that they would learn to handle the spear, shield, and sword, march in military formation, and handle armor. However, Athenians also emphasized the participation of citizens in the deliberative and judicial aspects of political life. Young boys were brought to the forum to hear the issues of the day discussed and court decisions explained.

Music and poetry were important parts of the education of young Athenians. These arts were understood to contribute to children's sense of rhythm, and to their physical as well as verbal agility. Music and poetry also reinforced cultural values. Homeric ideals of "arete" (perfection or excellence) as exhibited in valor were initially taught through the oral recitations of the poet. Religious observances often made use of music and poetry.

City-sponsored drama contests featured poetry and music performed by a chorus and masked actors who taught Athenians about their history and destiny.

Athenian citizens sent their sons to school at approximately age seven to learn instrumental music and singing from "citharistes," and reading, writing, and poetry from "grammatistes." Schooling was essentially a matter of literacy. Perhaps Greek parents thought literacy valuable, but not as valuable as participation in the discussion of public events. Athenian parents, therefore, did not have an especially high regard for the schoolmasters and "pedagogus" slaves, and school pupils often behaved disrespectfully toward their teachers (Marrou, 1956; Castle, 1961).

Nonetheless, there was discussion about what form of education was most appropriate. Two major avenues of thought developed. In one, represented by Socrates, Plato, and Aristotle, a close relationship was seen between the cultivation of principles of good conduct in public and private life, and the search for wisdom and knowledge through philosophy, dialectic, and science. The second avenue, represented by Isocrates and the sophists, argued that the exercise of citizenship relied most heavily upon the citizens' abilities to discuss and debate public affairs. Cultivation of analytical and rhetorical capacities through training in public speaking was offered by the sophists, who taught young men to argue all sides of an issue.

Whether slave or citizen, Athenian or Spartan, most Greek youngsters were expected to follow in their parents' footsteps. All children turned to their families first for models of behavior, in terms of economic activities, religious beliefs and practices, and participation in community life. They saw their families as embodying the values that were at the center of their society.

References

Barclay, W. *Train up a child: Educational ideals in the ancient world*. Philadelphia: Westminster Press.

Beck, F. A. G. (1964). *Greek education, 450–350 B.C.* New York: Barnes & Noble.

Bowra, C. M. (1957). *The Greek way*. New York: World Publishing Company.

Castle, E. B. (1964, 1961). *Ancient education and today*. Baltimore: Penguin Books.

Finley, M. I. (1964, 1963). *The ancient Greeks: An introduction to their life and thought*. New York: Viking Press.

Jarrett, J. L. (1969). *The educational theories of the Sophists*. New York: Teachers College Press.

Kaster, R. A. (1986). *Guardians of the language: The grammarian and society in late antiquity*. Los Angeles: University of California Press.

Marrou, H. I. (1982, 1956). *A history of education in antiquity*. New York: Sheed and Ward.

D. R. Barnes

Aristotle

Born in Stagira in Chalcidice, Aristotle (384–322 B.C.) entered Plato's Academy in Athens at the age of 17 and remained there until Plato's death in 348–347 B.C. In 343–342 B.C., Philip of Macedonia appointed him tutor to his son, Alexander. Subsequently, Aristotle returned to Athens, where he worked for most of his remaining years as head of the Lyceum.

The animating principle of Aristotle's thinking about the education of children is contained in an often cited dictum of the *Nicomachean Ethics*. "The things we have to learn before we can do," Aristotle writes, "we learn by doing—for example, people become builders by building, and lyre players by playing the lyre; so too we become just by doing just acts, temperate by doing temperate acts, brave by doing brave acts" (Ostwald, 1958, pp. 1103a32–1103b2).

Since the object of education is to make virtuous people—people whose desires always aim at virtuous activity—it follows from Aristotle's dictum that the education of young children is an ongoing process of habituation. Children will become virtuous by first having the habits of virtue instilled in them. Like Plato, Aristotle emphasizes the efficacy of children's play for the development of good habits; for in play, he says, children engage in "imitations of what will later be in earnest" (Barker, 1962, pp. 1336a32–33).

Aristotle firmly believed, as his teacher did, in the censorship of children's educational materials for didactic purposes. He conceives of early education as "the chief and foremost concern" of the legislator of a good state (*Ibid.*, pp. 1337a11–12). Thus, he insists that the state's system of education "must be a matter of public action (*Ibid.*, pp. 1337a22–23). Since the good of all citizens as a group depends on the virtue of each one separately, there is no sense in risking the character and welfare of a child on public vagary. So, exposure of the young to the arts and sciences must be carefully calculated to improve character. (Aristotle discouraged use of the flute because of its association with the catharsis of Dionysiac frenzy; he commended the solemn Doric mode, favored by the Spartans.)

For Aristotle, the crucial fact about children is that they have not yet attained their potential, which is, most fully stated, to be rational, systematic understanders of the world. Thus, they will not benefit from the sorts of arguments and lectures that would persuade and move a rational adult. Instead, they must be appealed to through the nonrational incentives of pleasure and pain to make them like and dislike what they should, so that they acquire the habits of liking good things and disliking bad ones.

When good habits have settled firmly into character (so that one always wants to do what one should do), and the rational capacities have been fully developed, one is ready for the rational stage of ethical education (in which one acquires knowledge of what constitutes ethical action, as well as the proper motivation for engaging in it, namely for its own sake). Before this final stage, however, moral education "is concerned with pleasures and pains; for it is on account of pleasure that we do bad things, and on account of pain that we abstain from noble ones" (Ostwald, 1958, 1104b8–11). Such, at any rate, are the natural inclinations of children. For Aristotle, it is by accepting and channelling these inclinations, rather than suppressing them, that education works best.

References

Barker, E. (ed. and trans.). (1962). *The politics of Aristotle*. Oxford: Oxford University Press.

Ostwald, M. (trans.). (1958). *Aristotle: The Nicomachean ethics*. Indianapolis: Bobbs-Merrill.

S. R. Morris

Plato

The Athenian philosopher Plato's (c. 429–347 B.C.) thoughts on the education of young children are contained in his two longest works, *The Republic* and *The Laws*. His theory of knowledge and his conception of the soul dictated a firm belief in the efficacy of education: the tales children hear and the games children play are both, in Plato's eyes, decisive in the shaping of young minds. In his Good City, the creators of children's tales are closely supervised, while the two pillars of the traditional curriculum, Homer and Hesiod, are bowdlerized with a free hand (Plato, *The Republic*, 1974).

It is tempting to regard Plato as the first opponent of corporal punishment. In any case, he did not believe it possible to compel a child to learn, and insisted that games and structured play be incorporated into early curricula. (In *Laws* 819, he suggests using "apples or garlands" to teach infants arithmetic.) He spoke against rebuking children to instill respect, stating that only by being consistently shown respect would children ever learn it (*Laws*, 729bc). Discipline and indulgence should be balanced, but discipline must never extend to humiliation (Ibid., 729de).

"Of all wild things," Plato writes, "a child is hardest to handle" (*Laws*, 808d). Children's education must be placed in the hands of skilled trainers and guardians, whose task in turn is to make them "guardians of themselves" (*Republic*, 591a). Classes for young children emphasize physical training, but always with a pronounced didactic end. Their structure, one gathers, is loose, since it is in play, Plato believes, that a child's natural proclivities and virtues emerge most clearly.

Plato alone among educators of the ancient world insisted that boys and girls receive the same training. Otherwise, he writes, a city is only half a city, and "becomes only half of what it might be" (*Laws*, 805ab).

References

Grube, G. M. A. (trans.). (1974). *Plato's republic*. Indianapolis: Hackett.

Lodge, R. C. (1947). *Plato's theory of education*. London: K. Paul, Trench & Trubner.

Saunders, T. J. (trans.). (1975). *Plato: The laws*. New York: Penguin.

S. R. Morris

Islamic (Muslim) Influences

The religion and culture of Islam includes 900 million people. They identify themselves as Basule, Houssa, Ibo, Swahili, Arabs, Imazighen, Nubians, Shensi, Karsa, Albanians, Bulgarians, Yugoslavs, Turks, Kurds, Circassians, Iranians, Afghanis, Biharis, Indians, Pakistanis, Bangladeshis, Indonesians, Moghuls, Russians, Chinese, and more recently, Latin Americans, North Americans, and others. Diverse in ethnicity and separate and dispersed geographically and nationally, the people of Islam offer their individual ritual "salat" (prayer) five times each day in Arabic, facing the holy city of Mecca in Saudi Arabia, the birthplace of the prophet Muhammad. The Qur'an, revealed to Muhammad in the Arabic language during the month of Ramadan, is probably the most often read book in the world, the most often memorized, and the most influential in the daily life of the Muslim people.

In spite of difference and diversity, Muslim family life all over the world is patterned as closely as possible to the Prophet's family life (Ammar, 1954; Farghal, 1978). The Prophet Muhammad lived as a man, was married, had children, earned a living, died, and was buried in a grave. In doing so, he provided a model for Muslims to follow. The different Islamic "madhahab" (sects) attempt to adhere to the same family rites and traditions codified in the life of the Prophet Muhammad.

The rite of marriage to a Muslim is a call reminding the single of their duty to marry and multiply. The community of Muslims bid the faithful servant of Allah, the Muslim, to marry, for "He who marries has perfected half his religious requirements, and he has only to fear God in the other half" (Ammar, 1954, p. 75). Allah, according to tradition, would then bless the newly married with a child.

The first child, especially a male child, is received with tremendous rejoicing and is an occasion for celebration for the entire clan. The name of the child is usually chosen by the parents or the eldest member of the family. With the first child, the name is that of the grandfather for a boy, or grandmother for a girl. The majority of the names of both boys and girls are names of a religious personality or suggest a religious meaning. If born in the Middle East, the child would then be referred to by that name followed by 'Ben'/'Bint' or 'Ibn' (meaning the son/daughter) and the father's name. According to custom the parents would then be called "Abu" (father of) or "Umm" (mother of), followed by the name of the first child. The family affiliation is, therefore, announced.

The child during its early years is in the care of the mother. Muslim law prohibits the separation of a child from the mother. In case of divorce, the boy is to remain with his mother until the age of seven and the girl until the age of nine. The Qur'an urges that "mothers shall give suck to their children for two whole years" (Qur'an, 2:234), but still provides the choice that "If both should agree by mutual consultation and consent upon weaning the child, there shall be no blame on them" (Qur'an, 2:234). The period of nursing, then, varies from child to child and from mother to mother. By tradition boys are usually nursed less than girls. In cases of mothers who are unable to nurse, the Qur'an says, "Should you desire to engage a wetnurse for your children, there shall be no blame on you" (Qur'an, 2:234). The Qur'an is resolute, however, in prohibiting marriage between boys and girls who have been nursed from the same breast, for they have become "Ikhwa bil Rda'a" (brother and sister by breast feeding).

Orphaned in the early years of his life, Prophet Muhammad wove a detailed code of conduct specifying the role and relationships of Muslim adult and the Muslim community to the child. Through the "Shari'a" (law of God), his "Hadith" (sayings and deeds) and teachings, he instructed the individual Muslim and the community of Muslims to be the overseers and protectors of the well-being of the children, especially the sick and the orphaned. Known to have loved children immensely, Muhammad desired the community of Muslims to become distinguished among other communities for its kindness to children.

Parents are responsible for the development of the child, the mother for the day-to-day care and teaching of the child, and the father for supplying the material needs of shelter and food. Children are the responsibility of their "wali" (guardian), who would normally be the father or other legally appointed male, until they reach maturity at age 18.

The religious education of a child is the duty of every parent or wali to pursue. The Qur'an was sent down as a "Book to be repeatedly read, easily comprehensible, that you may understand. It forms part of Our Eternal Guidance, exalted and full of wisdom" (Qur'an, 43:3). To study and memorize the Book is the duty of all Muslims. Muslims are to search for and acquire the knowledge and the word of Allah, and the student of knowledge is the "talib'" (literally, in Arabic, the searcher) for knowledge. Muslim scholars, the "ulema," who are also the leaders of the Muslim community, are entrusted with the duty of transmitting to others the religious knowledge of the Holy Book and the pious ancestors.

Traditionally, at the age of six the child was sent to the "kuttab," the Qur'anic school, usually situated near a mosque. Kuttab is an Arabic word derived from the word "kitab" (book). It is the place where the Holy Book was learned, and the skills of reading and writing were acquired to facilitate the perfection of the Islamic traditions of learning. The kuttabs were confined to boys. Only recently have girls been able to attend the kuttab. Even with the introduction of modern systems of education throughout various Muslim countries, the institution of the kuttab has persisted in some countries. Religious education and instruction in most countries, however, has been transferred to a government-supported system of education.

The "aila" is the basic social unit from which the children are to construct their understanding of the world. The aila (the family, or literally in Arabic "the social unit that supports its members"), consists of all those related to the child either by "asaba" (patrilineal), "lahma" (matrilineal) and "nasab" (through in-laws), or any other intimate ties (Ammar, 1954, p. 56). The child, at an early age, maps out the intricate relationships existing among the various family members. The child's understanding of the responsibility and meaning of the aila develops by actively experiencing the world of the family through gradual exploration of, experimenting with, and manipulating of the relationships.

The Muslim aila, then, is entrusted with the mission of raising the children to be pious believers. It is also the aila's responsibility publicly to address the conduct, discipline, behavior, performance and well-being of all its individual members, especially the children.

The Muslim child, on the other hand, must recognize the social sanctions that constitute what is acceptable as the "ibn salih/bint salha" (good son/good daughter). Islamic tradition is explicit in the duties and obligations that a child needs to fulfill to be a member of the aila. Foremost among the social sanctions is the command to accord "adab'" (respect) to the family, for "We have enjoined on man to act benevolently towards his parents" (Qur'an, 46:16). Acquiring the qualities of being polite ("muaddab"), "envisaged as a way of disciplining the child to conform to the adults' standards" (Ammar, 1954, p. 126), is considered essential in learning the prescribed Islamic code of conduct expected of the members of the community of Muslims.

Child rearing in Islam, then, is directed toward the process of becoming a pious believer, knowledgeable of Qur'anic studies and observing religious duties as dictated by Allah to Muhammad in the Qur'an. To the family, Islam entrusted the duty of teaching the moral and ethical dictates of Islam, the religion and tradition; and, to the child, Islam gave the duty of readiness to learn and accept its teachings.

References

Ammar, H. (1954). *Growing up in an Egyptian village: Sikwa, Province of Aswan.* London: Routledge & Kegan Paul.

Farghal, M. H. (1978). *The theory of modernization in the Qur'an and some implications for the Arab world.* Unpublished doctoral dissertation. New York: New York University, ERIC 782 4212.

The Qur'an (1981). (Muhammad Zafrulla Khan, trans.). London: Curzon Press.

L. Al-Banna

Latino (Hispanic) Influences

Hispanic families comprise an increasing percentage of the population of the United States. The number of Hispanic children has increased by 34 percent since 1980, and Hispanics have a birthrate that is 50 percent higher than the U.S. average (Valdivieso & Davis, 1988). Hispanics are diverse, originating from a variety of rich cultural traditions. Of the Hispanics currently living in the United States, 62 percent are Mexican-American, 13 percent are Puerto Rican, 5 percent are Cuban-American, 12 percent come from Central or South America, and 8 percent come from other areas. Hispanics may comprise the largest minority within the United States by the twenty-first century.

The brief description below emphasizes some common child-rearing practices observed across Hispanic groups. Sweeping generalizations are not intended, and it should be kept in mind that there are also differences in practice across the groups mentioned above, as well as within groups.

Salient cultural features that affect child-rearing practices include a child-centered philosophy, an extended family system, an appreciation for "consejos" (advice), the valuing of "respeto" (respect for elders or those perceived as worthy of respect), the valuing of group norms and opinions, "personalismo" (the valuing of personal contact with and knowledge of individuals), and an expectation of mutual help. Many Hispanic families continue selectively to retain ethnic values and identities in spite of generational differences in culture and an impetus toward assimilation into the dominant culture (Soto & Negron, 1991).

The child-centered philosophy is exemplified by the acceptance of youngsters at most social occasions. Children are expected at weddings, dinner parties, birthdays, and most daily activities. Grandparents and extended family members are trusted and preferred for child care. The term "hijos de crianza" (children by upbringing) denotes the willingness of families to care for non-nuclear family members. Sending a child to an orphanage is thought of as heartbreaking, cruel, and unnecessary.

Hispanic families tend to value the extended family system, with grandparents living nearby or within the family home. Grandparents and other relatives usually are seen as rich sources of stories and traditions for young children at home. Many families value children's retention of the Spanish language, in addition to the acquisition of English. This is especially true in areas of the country where the older generation is more fluent in Spanish than in English, or does not speak English at all. For such families, confusion and distress result when educators advise them to speak only English at home "for the good of the child." Home-school communication, as well as educational possibilities between parents and children, can be adversely affected by such school practices.

Many Hispanic families place great trust in educators. Among some Hispanic families, the expression "La missy nos dijo que . . ." (Teacher told us that . . .) is evidence of that trust. Advice given by caregivers or teachers is deeply valued, and such "consejos" may be followed almost religiously.

Motherhood is regarded as a highly respected position within the family system. Mothers impart a tremendous amount of physical and emotional care on a daily basis. The Mother's Day celebrations in Puerto Rico, one example of demonstrations of "respeto," shower mothers with love, affection, gifts, flowers, and outings. Mothers tend to take on an almost sacrificial role if their children do not follow the accepted norms of their society.

Group norms and opinions are highly valued by many Hispanic families. A self-differentiated or individualized perspective has less worth in such families than a group-oriented or family-shared goal. The weight placed on public opinion can be seen in comments that include the expression "Que diran la gente?" (What will people say?).

"Personalismo" and mutual help are concepts that also affect child-rearing practices. The idea behind "personalismo" is that the inner worth of the person is valued more highly than material wealth or the accumulation of goods. Children reared with "personalismo" will value social experiences more than materialistic gains. Mutual help can be compared to the "good neighbor" concept, but extends beyond traditional neighborhood boundaries. The willingness to help family and nonfamily members alike is exemplified by the term "servicial" (service oriented).

Hispanic families share the same hopes, dreams, and aspirations for their children as all families. The child-rearing practices of Hispanic families mirror both present and traditional cultural values. Variation in practice both across and within Hispanic groups is therefore to be expected.

References

Soto, L. D., & Negron, L. (1991). Educational issues and practices affecting Hispanic children's play. In J. Roopnarine (ed.). *Children's play in diverse cultures*. New York: State University of New York Press.

Valdivieso, R., & Davis, C. (1988). U.S. Hispanics: Challenging issues for the 1990's. Washington, DC: Hispanic Development Project.

L. D. Soto

Romans, Ancient, Influences of

Early Roman society placed great emphasis upon the family as the basic educational entity. Within the family, the role of the father was that of "paterfamilias," whose unquestioned right and obligation was to make all decisions for his wife, children, and slaves.

Two values were especially strong within Roman families, those of "gravitas" (sobriety or gravity) and "pietas" (piety). Children were expected to learn to behave in ways that would bring honor and avoid family disgrace. Children also were expected to be modest, serious, and judicious in speech and actions. They were to avoid boisterous behavior and dishonorable companions. They were taught to perform the rituals at the hearth that assured the divinities' blessings upon the household. Labor was respected by the early Romans, who were essentially farmers. Their sons and daughters learned the rhythms of work on the family farm and in the household.

Sons were expected to learn from their fathers how to fertilize and till, schedules for planting and harvesting, ways to flail grain and store it, when and how to prune vines, and how to deliver piglets from brood sows. Daughters learned by observing and helping their mothers to prepare all types of food and to offer a salted cake to Vesta and the deities of the hearth. They also learned to light wicks and fill lamps, just as they learned to feed sheep and goats, wash the family togas, and sweep out the households. Some of this learning began at an early age.

The earliest training of Roman children was, for the most part, in the hands of their mothers. Their mothers taught them to speak in the quiet tone of voice seen as appropriate to "gravitas," and reminded them of their continuing obligations toward their father and to the gods. Tacitus and others acknowledge the early Roman belief in the importance of maternal guidance and molding of children.

Girls continued instruction with their mothers, while boys learned from their fathers from about seven years of age onward. Fathers taught their sons the moral principles involved in "vir bonus" (the good man). These included not only piety and gravity, but also prudence, justice, manliness, moderation, and constancy. Actions based on these values would bring honor to the family. Roman fathers stressed the virtues of family ancestors as models to be emulated. Fathers also taught their sons the rudiments of fighting.

Later, Roman society adopted certain elements of Greek education. The Hellenizing of Roman education put greater emphasis upon schooling and a decreased emphasis upon the educational role of the family. The Greek language became the symbol of civilized status in Rome and began being used for diplomacy and international trade. Schools were founded to teach Greek to Roman youngsters from the ruling classes. Old values and forms of social organization gave way to Greek influence. The Greek theater came to Rome and Greek emphases upon city life prompted wealthy Roman landowners to entrust their farms to managers and to move to city villas. Roman boys who attended school encountered the Greek educational model.

The Greek model emphasized elementary instruction for seven- to twelve-year-old boys in reading, writing, and arithmetic. Such rudimentary instruction was followed for some adolescent boys by scholarly study of the Greek and Latin languages and literature at the hands of a "grammaticus," and concluded at the hands of a "rhetor" for those young men seeking careers requiring skills as public speakers.

The "magister ludi" (elementary schoolmaster) was similar to his Greek counterpart in that he was generally poorly educated and not well paid or respected. Contemporary critics of the shift in emphasis from traditional Roman values pointed out the failure to hire men of quality as teachers. The Roman writer Juvenal ranked these schoolteachers in the same category as "bath attendants, fortune tellers, and tight-rope dancers" (Castle, 1961, p. 126, citing Juvenal III, 76).

Unlike the Greeks, the Romans did not debate the purposes of education or appropriate curriculum content for the instruction of children so that they might become learned and virtuous adults. Aside from Cicero and Quintilian, there were few theorists of Roman education.

One consequence of the growth of the Roman Empire was that few children went to school for extended periods of time. The diminished importance given to family education further weakened what was once a unified social fabric based on shared familial values. The children of wealthy Romans pursued private ambition, power, and luxury, while low income children had few options. For them, education had become learning to survive in a harsh, exploitive environment. (See also, **Greeks, Ancient, Influences of.**)

References

Barclay, W. (1959). *Train up a child: Educational ideals in the ancient world.* Philadelphia: Westminster Press.

Bonner, S. P. (1977). *Education in ancient Rome, from the elder Cato to the younger Pliny.* Berkeley: University of California Press.

Castle, E. B. (1964). *Ancient education and today.* Baltimore: Penguin Books.

Dilke, O. A. W. (1975). *The Ancient Romans, how they lived and worked.* Newton Abbot, Devon: David & Charles

Kaster, R. A. (1986). *Guardians of the language: The grammarian and society in late antiquity.* Los Angeles: University of California Press.

Marrou, H. I. (1982, 1956). *A history of education of antiquity.* New York: Sheed and Ward.

D. R. Barnes

Quintilian

The Roman educator Quintilian (A.D. c. 35–c. 95) became widely known and respected for his oratorical model of education. Born in Rome's Spanish provinces, Quintilian was raised in the ancient Roman traditions that emphasized practicality and loyalty to family, duty, and nation. An extended period of work in Rome during a time when it was being strongly influenced by Greek culture, however, broadened his view to encompass the Greek understanding of the educated person as one whose powers of reason were highly refined. Subsequently, he developed a system of oratory that embodied both Roman

and Greek values and expectations (Gutek, 1972).

Quintilian articulated one of the first recorded understandings of human development as proceeding through distinct stages and argued that those stages had clear implications for educational practice. He saw children from birth to seven years of age as being subject to strong impulses and directed by their own needs and desires. For that reason, Quintilian warned, proper role models are extremely important for young children, who must constantly be guided by example.

Quintilian was one of the earliest European educators to recognize the effectiveness of the use of manipulative materials in the teaching of literacy. He designed sets of ivory letters that the boys in his school could handle and trace as part of the process of learning to write. He also wrote against the use of corporal punishment, believing that early learning should be motivated by interest, and that teachers should strive to make learning activities attractive to young children (Braun & Edwards, 1972; Gutek, 1972). (See also **Greeks, Ancient, Influences of;** and **Romans, Ancient, Influences of.**)

References

Braun, S. J., & Edwards, E. P. (1972). *History and theory of early childhood education.* Belmont, CA: Wadsworth.

Gutek, G. L. (1972). *A history of the western educational experience.* New York: Random House.

L. R. Williams

Medieval Education

The medieval era (including both the "Dark Ages" and the "Middle Ages") in western Europe spanned almost 1,000 years (from approximately A.D. 500 to approximately A.D. 1500) and was characterized by considerable diversity across various time periods, geographical locations, and social class. Not surprisingly, then, young children's educational experiences during the medieval period varied considerably depending on the social class of the children's family and the time and place in which they lived.

Moreover, children's education was strongly influenced by their religious background. While most Europeans were Christian during the Middle Ages, some children were Jewish, and others were Muslim. The experience of Jewish and Muslim children differed profoundly from those of their Christian counterparts. (See also **Biblical (Jewish/ Christian) Influences** and **Islamic (Muslim) Influences**.) The description below pertains to the experience of the majority of children in Europe during the period, who were Christian.

For most of its history medieval Europe was fundamentally a two-class society, consisting of the aristocracy (the feudal lords or landowners) and the peasantry (those who worked the land). Peasants were either serfs or freemen. Those who were serfs were subject to the feudal lords in virtually every aspect of their lives. There was, in fact, a third class of people consisting of the artists, artisans, and merchants. Their numbers were greatly outweighed by the peasantry, and it was not until the decline of the feudal system that they became more prominent by gathering in the growing cities, where they could find markets for their specialized skills and products. Each of the three classes had its own way of educating its children.

Children of the Aristocracy

The sons and daughters born to members of the nobility (kings, princes, dukes, earls, barons), provided they were legitimate and healthy, were expected to learn the courtly behaviors required of knights and ladies. Life at court required courtesy in actions and speech, table manners, the ability to sing and dance with grace, refinement in choice of entertainment, diplomacy, and knowledge of the family's history and relationships fostered through marriage, alliance, treaty, or warfare. Furthermore, members of noble households needed to understand how laws, decrees, and court judgments were reached and recorded. In addition, the nobility was expected to patronize the church and defend the Christian faith (militarily, if necessary). Some boys, particularly those who were expected to have close connection with the church, were taught to read and write in Latin.

Warfare was a way of life for the nobility. Young aristocratic boys anticipated that they would become knights, defending the faith and their family honor. Chivalric training began early with preparation in use of all manner of weaponry, horsemanship, hunting and hawking, and military strategy (taught partly through the game of chess). The children learned these skills both through intensive observation and as a result of instruction and coaching from older men. Boys could anticipate learning the arts of war by becoming pages at age 7, squires at 14, and being dubbed knights at about 21 years of age.

Young girls knew that they would eventually be responsible for managing large households. They needed to understand the requirements of hospitality and provide it for large numbers of people, manage production of food and clothing, oversee the movement of the household whenever required by military campaigns, supervise child rearing and ensure the presence of piety in the household. They learned these tasks by observing the behavior of women in the court and participating in the tasks themselves.

Over the span of the medieval period, a system of chivalrous honor and courtly love developed with elaborate codes of behavior that adolescent boys and girls learned would be expected of them as adults. By the twelfth century, didactic "courtesy books" were in vogue, providing mannerly codes of proper behavior for noble children, especially for the boys.

Children of the Peasantry

Most children were the sons and daughters of peasants, who earned their living from the land. Children of serfs and freemen alike learned that they had obligations to their secular and religious overlords, typically including the payment of rents, performance of labor, and deference to the lord's authority.

Girls learned food preparation, animal husbandry, the making of clothing, and child rearing through observation and imitation of their mothers. Boys learned agriculture, fence and house construction, roof thatching, and peat digging from observing and imitating their fathers. Both girls and boys learned forms of worship from their elders and the village priest. Generally they could recite certain prayers, although they usually could not read. They also learned herbal medicine from their parents. Parental example was the primary educational influence in their lives.

Children of Artists, Artisans, and Merchants

Children born to artists, artisans, and merchants learned to live in developing cities, where the rhythm of life was different from that of the peasantry. Often their homes were in close proximity to one another, with shops on the lower floor and living quarters above. The noises of work and city life were in children's ears from birth.

Children learned early that they would probably follow the same trades as their parents. They learned the particulars of that trade from observing and imitating their parents at work. Sometimes boys were apprenticed to other craftsmen so that they could learn the "mysteries" of those trades.

Children whose fathers belonged to crafts or merchant guilds learned that guildsmen attended the same parish church, set aside money for burying guildsmen and to support their widows and orphans, and met to discuss prices and competition within the city. The guildsmen also set the prevailing conditions for apprenticeship and determined what would constitute an acceptable display of skills in the creation of a "masterpiece," so that young people could conclude their apprenticeship and become journeymen and then, eventually, masters themselves.

Occasionally girls were apprenticed. Far more frequently, it was their brothers who were apprenticed, and when they left the family household to serve their apprenticeship, they were likely to move to another section of the city or even to a distant city. Chances for visits home were limited. The period of apprenticeship typically lasted from three to seven years, depending on the complexity of the skills to be mastered.

Most girls, however, were expected to marry, and consequently spent their early years learning domestic arts. They learned the special problems of keeping a household clean and vermin free in a city, as well as all the usual tasks of cooking, making clothing and child rearing. As in most other circumstances described above, they learned these skills through observation, imitation, and direct participation under their mother's tutelage.

Across all three social classes, childhood was seen as a relatively short period, followed at approximately age seven by the assumption of some degree of adult responsibilities. Among noble families, it was not unusual for couples to be betrothed or even married while very young in fulfillment of family arrangements. In the other classes girls as young as 12 were married and expected to assume responsibility for running their households.

The role of the church was pervasive in medieval life. The rhythm of life revolved around church fast days and holy days on both the feudal estates and in the cities, where the great cathedrals were located. Consequently, the tenets of the church underlay much of the moral instruction provided, while the practical instruction sprang largely from the day-to-day tasks of living within a particular social class.

References

Aries, P. (1962). *Centuries of childhood.* New York: Random House.

Bagley, J. J. (1960). *Life in medieval England.* New York: Putnam.

Barnes, D. R. (ed.). (1971). *For court, manor, and church: Education in medieval Europe.* Minneapolis: Burgess Publishing.

Coulton, G. G. (trans.). (1967/1910). *Life in the middle ages.* New York: Cambridge University Press.

Evans, J. (ed.). (1966). *The flowering of the middle ages.* New York: McGraw-Hill.

Glick, T. F. (1979). *Islamic and Christian Spain in the early middle ages*. Princeton, NJ: Princeton University Press.

Holmes, U. T., Jr. (1964, 1952). *Daily living in the twelfth century*. Madison: University of Wisconsin Press.

Mundy, J. H., & Riesenberg, P. (1958). *The medieval town*. Princeton, NJ: Van Nostrand.

Orme, N. (1984). *From childhood to chivalry: The education of the English kings and aristocracy 1055–1530*. New York: Methuen.

Riche, P. (1978). *Daily life in the world of Charlemagne*. Philadelphia: University of Philadelphia Press.

D. R. Barnes

Renaissance Education

The Renaissance period in Europe lasted approximately 200 years, overlapping at its beginning with the end of the Middle Ages, and at its conclusion with the period of Reformation. The Renaissance began in Italy in the 1400s and moved slowly westward through the next century and into the early 1600s.

As the feudal system started to disintegrate, the cities of Europe began to grow and became powerful centers for trade and for the promulgation of the arts. The massive movements of populations that had resulted from the succession of Crusades during the medieval period had brought scholars again into contact with the arts and literature of ancient Greece and Rome (Fowler, 1983; Gutek, 1972).

Exposure to classical arts turned the attention of Italian artists and intellectuals away from total absorption with the church, its history, traditions, and art forms, to a focus on the individual. A movement toward Humanism spread from Italy in the 1400s, to Spain, France, the Netherlands, and England in the 1500s and 1600s. It also moved slowly eastward into Eastern Europe. The Renaissance period influenced not only arts and letters, but also some of the educational forms available to children of the elite, which became more varied. Children of the merchant, artisan, and peasant classes continued to be educated much as they had been during the me-

dieval period (Fowler, 1983). (See also **Medieval Education**.)

References

Fowler, W. (1983). *Potentials of childhood*. (Vol. 1). Lexington, MA: D.C. Heath.

Gutek, G. L. (1972). *A history of the western educational experience*. New York: Random House.

L. R. Williams

Comenius (Jan Ámos Komenský)

Comenius (1592–1670) has been called by some scholars "the lost founder of early education" (Fowler, 1983, p. 67). Born and raised in what is now Czechoslovakia, Comenius became a bishop in the Protestant Moravian Church of the Brethern. Although his life and career were severely disrupted by the Thirty Years' War, Comenius managed to write a variety of educational treatises and produce some of the earliest materials specifically designed to teach young children (Gutek, 1972).

He himself was a teacher who demonstrated a sophisticated understanding of the characteristics of young learners, considerably before the articulation of modern-day theories of child development and learning. Believing that language provided the foundation for all subsequent learning, Comenius designed programs for language and concept acquisition that were intended to begin in infancy and to carry on through the childhood years. He advocated teaching in the vernacular, as well as in the Latin needed for written transactions. To aid in the development of literacy, he designed books especially for young children. The best known of these was the *Orbis sensualium pictus*, a book introducing vocabulary in Latin and the vernacular, with woodcuts illustrating particular words and concepts (Gutek, 1972).

His educational theories appeared in his comprehensive work *The Great Didactic*, first published in 1628. In this treatise, he described the course of child development in ways that presaged the work of Piaget, as well as that of later educators such as Pestalozzi, Froebel, Montessori, and Dewey. Additionally, he emphasized the role of activity and play in learning, a concept foreign to the thinking of the educators of his day (Fowler, 1983; Braun & Edwards, 1972). The work combined Comenius's thoughts on education with expression of his particular religious beliefs, as he saw each to be the reflection of the other (Gutek, 1972).

Comenius was distinguished not only for his teaching methods and materials that anticipated the elements of modern practice of early childhood education, but also for advocating universal education. He believed that both boys and girls of all social classes should experience at least the first two phases of education, the "Mother's Knee" (birth through age six) and the Vernacular School (approximately seven to ten years of age). Subsequent phases (the Latin School for later childhood, and university and travel for youth) were recommended for those who had need of more advanced education (Fowler, 1983). (See also **Dewey, John; Froebel, Friedrich Wilhelm; Montessori, Maria; Pestalozzi, Johann; Piaget, Jean.**)

References

Braun, S. J., & Edwards, E. P. (1972). *History and theory of early childhood education*. Belmont, CA: Wadsworth.

Fowler, W. (1983). *Potentials of childhood.* (Vol. 1). Lexington, MA: D.C. Heath.

Gutek, G. L. (1972). *A history of the western educational experience*. New York: Random House.

L. R. Williams

da Feltre, Vittorino

One of the most important Humanist educators during the fourteenth-century Renaissance in Italy, Vittorino da Feltre (1378–1446) attended the University of Padua, entering it at age 18 to study grammar and Latin letters, and remained there as a student and teacher for some 20 years.

Because his own family was impoverished, although respected, de Feltre had to take on private assignments teaching grammar. Even after earning his doctorate, he had to continue to support himself by working as a household employee (famulus) and tutor. While at Padua, he took into his own home a limited number of young male students who lived a distance from the city. Some of those he charged fees— if they came from landed patrician or wealthy merchant families; others he charged nothing if they were very able but poor. He supervised their studies and moral behavior carefully.

That pattern could also be seen in da Feltre's most important instructional undertaking. In 1423, Vittorino accepted the invitation of Gianfrancesco Gonzaga, the head of the ruling family of Mantua, to come to his court to open a school there. Initially, da Feltre provided instruction for the five Gonzaga children, including one daughter. Later, others were included among the students, some who paid for their instruction, and others who required financial support for their food, clothing, and books. Da Feltre spent the rest of his life in the school he called "La Giacosa" ("The Pleasant House"), located in a villa belonging to the Gonzaga family.

Some students as young as four or five attended the school. Others entered at age six or seven, and some stayed until they were twenty-five. Students eventually numbered 60 to 70 at a time. Da Feltre trained other teachers to work with him. He combined an emphasis upon Latin and Greek literature with study of ancient history, physical exercise and games, moral philosophy, and Christian piety, all with the view of educating students, primarily boys, to roles as responsible, adult leaders.

Particularly noteworthy was da Feltre's practice of ascertaining the interests and abilities of individual learners and tailoring instruction to those capacities. In an age when flogging was a common way of beating learning into children, da Feltre believed in encouraging children to learn, rather than punishing them for failing to learn. With the youngest pupils, da Feltre utilized games, activities, and stories as a way of interesting the children in classical literature. The children learned to read through letter games and speech exercises, and later learned to recite increasingly difficult passages of Latin literature from memory.

Revered as a teacher who set an example through his own rigorous exercises, moderate diet, modest attire, moral concerns, command of Latin and Greek, and adherence to Christian religious practices, da Feltre was remembered by his students long after he died in 1446.

Reference

Woodward, W. H. (1897/1963). *Vittorino da Feltre and other humanist educators*. New York: Teachers College Press.

D. R. Barnes

Reformation, Education in the

The Protestant Reformation in Europe began in 1517, the year that the Catholic monk Martin Luther nailed his ninety-five theses against the sale of indulgences to the Castle Church door in Wittenberg, Germany. In fact, Luther's theses and subsequent writings contributed strongly to extensive theologial and philosophical debates that were already spreading throughout Europe and challenging the political and social structures of the day (Dillenberger, 1961). Within a century, Europe had become divided between Protestant and Catholic factions, each seeking to consolidate its power and influence.

Leaders of the growing Protestant denominations, such as Calvin, Knox, Zwingli, Huss, and Fox, preached and wrote about the part individuals play in their own salvation, with particular emphasis on immediate access to the Scriptures. There were two direct implications that came from this way of thinking. First, the Scriptures had to be published in the vernacular; and second, ordinary men and women had to become literate enough to read them (Fowler, 1983). In many Protestant communities, village schools were established for this purpose.

Another influence during this period was the Humanism that appeared earlier, at the beginning of the Renaissance. This movement renewed interest in the aesthetic, intellectual, and political ideals of classical Greece and Rome, in an effort to move away from the "studied subtleties" that had characterized the scholastic movement of the medieval Roman Catholic church (Dillenberger, 1961, p. xi).

The collective result of so much activity was an extension of opportunities for literacy beyond the upper classes to at least the rising middle class, and in some instances, the opening of primary education to females.

References

Dillenberger, J. (ed.). (1961). *Martin Luther: Selections from his writings*. Garden City, NY: Doubleday.

Fowler, W. (1983). *Potentials of childhood, Volume 1*. Lexington, MA: D.C. Heath.

Gutek, G. L. (1972). *A History of the Western educational experience*. New York: Random House.

L. R. Williams

Luther, Martin

In 1517, Martin Luther (1483–1546) affixed his ninety-five theses to the Castle Church door in Germany. He probably had no idea that, in so doing, he would create the Protestant Reformation and support humanistic thinking in Europe.

Luther refuted the medieval idea that clergy were necessary representatives for the prayers of ordinary folk. He challenged people to develop their goodness through the reading of the Scriptures and the leading of a thoughtful life.

Luther called for town councils to create public libraries and educate their children, thereby reinventing childhood as a special period in human development. He urged that children be taught to read and write in their native language rather than in Latin, and championed the publication of the Scriptures in German so that they could be read by ordinary people. He also encouraged the education of girls as well as boys. (See also **Reformation, Education in the**.)

References

Braun, S. J., & Edwards, E. P. (1972). *History and theory of early childhood education*. Belmont, CA: Wadsworth.

Luther, M. (Smith, P., trans. & ed.). (1913–18). *Luther's correspondence and other contemporary letters*, 2: 487–88. United Lutheran Publication House.

S. F. Belgrad

Enlightenment, Education in the

The Enlightenment is the general term given to the spirit of the times revealed in the philosophy, science, and arts of the late seventeenth and the eighteenth centuries in Europe, and to that of the eighteenth century in the United States. While the movement took somewhat different forms in different regions (thus, one can speak of the German Enlightenment, the French Enlightenment, or the English Enlightenment), it generally may be characterized by a turning away from a theocentric world view to a humanistic one. The personal God who was so much the focus of earlier interactions in the development of European society gave way in some circles to an impersonal conception of a clockwork creator, who had set the universe in motion and now left it to its own devices. The perfection of human beings through the acquisition of knowledge became a major theme of the period.

Renewal of interest in the writings and ideals of ancient Greece and Rome appeared in the arts and architecture of the day, and in the courses of study defined for the children of the upper classes. Following classical custom, most sons of the well-to-do were tutored in writing, rhetoric and debate, languages, history, mathematics, and sciences at home or at private preparatory schools until they reached the age of university entrance (middle to late teens). Their study at university was capped with a "Grand Tour," when they visited the major capitals and saw the famous sights of Europe.

Girls of the upper classes usually continued to be educated at home, with an emphasis on the arts and music, languages, and domestic accomplishments such as fine embroidery, until they reached marriageable age. Middle-class families aspired to have their sons

and daughters educated in a similar manner. Working-class families, on the other hand, continued to have little access to any education beyond the rudiments of literacy provided through village or church-related schools.

References

Fowler, W. (1983). *Potentials of childhood, Volume 1.* Lexington, MA: D.C. Heath.

Gutek, G. L. (1972). *A history of the Western educational experience.* New York: Random House.

L. R. Williams

Locke, John

One of the most influential philosophers of the English Enlightenment, John Locke (1632–1704) completed his B.A. and M.A. degrees in philosophy at Oxford University in 1659. Locke taught philosophy, Greek, and rhetoric at the same university until, in 1665, he undertook a diplomatic mission to the German principality of Brandenburg. Although he completed a medical degree and obtained a license to practice in 1674, he never practiced medicine as his major occupation. His political career continued in various forms through the installation of William of Orange as King of England in 1688, until his health forced retirement in 1700. In his last years, he lived as a guest of a family that reflected his intellectual interests (Copelston, 1964).

Locke's best-known educational work is his *Essay Concerning Human Understanding*, first published in 1690. In it, he discusses the empiricist view that all knowledge comes to us through the senses. The ideas that result from this sense experience then are molded into understanding through introspection, or the application of reason to common experience. To achieve this position, he rejects the possibility of innate ideas and sets the stage for the argument that environment and experience are the determinants of the human intellect.

Locke's work anticipated the position assumed 200 years later in the new science of psychology by the early behaviorists and connectionists such as Waston, and more recently, by Skinner. He articulated the importance of "nurture" over "nature" in the proper upbringing and education of children, and thus can be seen as in a direct line of connection to the behavioral early childhood programs and teaching strategies of the 1960s, 1970s, and 1980s. (See Chapter 3, Section 3.2, **Primary School Follow Through Programs,** Chapter 4, Section 4.3, **Theories of Child Development and Learning, Behaviorist,** and Chapter 5, Section 5.7, **Strategies of Teaching, Behavior Modification.**)

Reference

Copleston, F. (1964). *A history of philosophy. Volume 5, Modern philosophy: The British philosophers (Part I Hobbes to Paley)*. Garden City, NY: Image Books of Doubleday & Company, Inc.

L. R. Williams

2.2 Philosophical, Political, and Educational Contexts in the United States

Early childhood education in the United States today can be understood in part through reviewing intellectual, social, economic, political, and educational contexts that have influenced the evolution of the field over the past 200 years. Philosophical leanings popular at the time of the birth of the kindergarten in Germany in the early 1830s, for example, were reflected in the design of the program, as was the increasingly rapid change from an agrarian to an industrial society. With the profound changes in the economic base, the political base had to assume different forms for governance of new societies. As societies elaborated their new directions, their visions of education also changed, as did their understandings of the capabilities and needs of young children. All of these parameters influenced the direction of child care and early childhood education in the United States.

The three essays below offer perspectives on the broader contexts from which child care and early education have emerged. In the first, Maxine Greene suggests that we must acknowledge the multiple realities of early childhood before we can respond intelligently and responsibly to the needs of young children and their families. Marvin Lazerson in the second essay discusses why public versus private responsibility for the nurturance of young children remains controversial within our society today. Finally, Sarah Lederman traces the transformation of the common school as it intersected with the presence of young children in a rapidly changing world.

Each essay may achieve its greatest effect if read twice, once as the second section of this chapter to provide a background for the material that follows, and again as a reflective summary of the major currents of the chapter as a whole.

L. R. Williams

Beyond the Predictable: A Viewing of the History of Early Childhood Education

At a moment when the lives and voices of children are being discovered and rediscovered, there is a fearful irony in the continuing tendency to reduce the problems of early childhood to technical problems. There is an irony too in the unreflective habit of treating the very young as resources or consumers or audiences or mere "objects" of custodianship and (on occasion) care. Scholars like Brian Sutton-Smith, Kieran Egan, Valerie Polakow, Patricia Carini, and the many practitioners dealing with "whole language" teaching, children's writing, journals, and the rest are opening all sorts of new perspectives on children's capacity to tell stories, to make meanings, to explore imaginary worlds. We know more than we ever have about children's vantage points and perspectives; we are beginning to resonate to the "truths" they come upon, the spurts they make, the surprises they hold in store. For many of us, this makes all the more painful, all the more inconceivable the violations of children in our culture—the child abuse, the illnesses, the homelessness, the neglect, and, always and always, the unforgivable poverty.

Openings on the one hand, closings on the other; the so-called educational reforms have meant too often, we are told, increases in mandates, tests, packaged curricula, and even the categorization that tracks and boxes and alienates children from their lived lives. There is still official talk about objective states of affairs, susceptible to predictions and calculations that (it is implied) cannot be gainsaid by people with alternative views of what is possible. Yet for many thinkers, including John Dewey and the phenomenologists and modern philosophers like Richard Rorty, "reality" signifies interpreted experience. If there are indeed a range of conceivable interpretations, each with its own integrity, we have to acknowledge the existence of what have been called multiple realities.

There are formal and empirical explanations in the natural and social sciences; there are also qualitative, particularistic interpretations. We understand by now that the lived reality of the child or the teacher in the classroom is quite different from the reality of a school administrator, an evaluator, or a curriculum designer. And what of the lived reality of the family on the drug-endangered street, the foster child entangled in the system, and the agency head? To avoid the multiplicity of reality is to take refuge in the measurable, the testable, and the fixed. To come to terms with it is to open the way to new kinds of dialogue and conversation. It is to allow for novelty and fresh initiatives; it is to go beyond the predictable toward untapped possibilities.

Hannah Arendt has written that things are always assumed to be predictable and determined when they are viewed from the standpoint of any system (1961, pp. 169–171). From a distant and detached point of view, it is always easy to speak in terms of trends and probabilities. From the vantage point of a person about to take action in a lived situation, however, initiatives and new beginnings are always conceivable. There are always possibilities, many of them beyond anticipation. It seems to be deeply important to experience an ongoing dissonance between the predictable and the possible, between the view from

without and the view from within a lived situation of choice.

For Arendt, the newcomer, or the child viewed as newcomer, was central to the conception of an enduring polity. The birth of every individual, she points out, promises a new beginning; and this "natality" is as important a feature of human existence as are the features of plurality and communication. Plurality signifies the distinctiveness of human beings, the fact that no single one duplicates the other. It also refers to the multiple perspectives through which distinctive beings look out upon what they share, perspectives that differ according to life story and location, but which may become connected as persons act in concert and attain a reciprocity. This does not exclude the social construction of the meanings persons make; nor does it exclude the different cultural contexts through which their understandings are mediated. It simply places emphasis upon point of view, perspective, and difference. It informs the very idea of communication with profound and palpable significance, since it is through communication that individuals convey their stories to one another and recognize each other in their ongoing efforts to generate something in common among themselves. This may be how we understand what education ought to be, how we grasp the efforts to initiate children into webs of shared meanings, into what is called the "conversation" going on over time. Natality is the innovative potential in all of this, since every newcomer brings with her or him another way of being and seeing. Natality allows for the unanticipated and the unforeseen—as well as for renewals.

To say this is to affirm that there can be no definition—there is no way of determining with any assurance the essence of any child. Indeed, philosophers of many persuasions agree on this. For Jean-Paul Sartre (1947) the human being is what she or he makes of herself or himself. The child must be understood as a "project" propelling herself or himself toward an awareness of his or her future. In *The Words* (1964) Sartre wrote about himself that he was born (and reborn) "out of a future expectation. . . . I was often told that the past drives us forward, but I was convinced that I was being drawn by the future. I would have hated to feel quiet forces at work within me, the slow development of my natural attitude" (p. 237). For Paulo Freire (1970), such futuring might be conceived of as his vocation, one Freire describes as "humanization" (p. 28), which is always in danger of being thwarted by injustice, exploitation, and (we would add) abuse and violations. The whole notion of futuring, of a life story in some way written by the person living it, was anticipated by John Dewey in another context (1916), writing that "the self is not something ready-made, but something in continuous formation through choice of action" (p. 408).

Even the analytic philosopher Israel Scheffler (1960) wrote about the difficulty of defining the human being and the multiple alternative definitions there are (p. 33). He prefers a "programmatic definition," which singles out things toward which social practice "is oriented in a certain way" (p. 19). If we single out aspects of observable behavior in a Skinnerian manner, we would orient our practice toward a type of control. If we single out those aspects of a child's fascination with "transitional objects" (Winnicott, 1971), we might devise a practice grounded in play, moving to "shared playing, and from this to cultural experiences" (p. 51). If we single out the symbolic or communicative capacity, we might focus on "whole language," on children talking, writing, and reading in a classroom community. Whatever the orientation, however, if we allow for a child's sense of agency in futuring and in creating a self, the consequences are in some significant way unpredictable.

All the above thinkers, nevertheless, acknowledge what Philippe Aries called "the ideal of childhood" (1962). Aries enabled numbers of us to understand that childhood itself is a construct as was the social space that made it possible for childhood to emerge. What a child signified depended then and now on adults' viewing of the world. As most people know from acquaintance with medieval and Renaissance paintings, there was a long period when the child, once past infancy, was pictured as a miniature adult—and, in most cases, treated that way. It took generations before the idea of the child and her or his particular nature had any place in European thinking at all. Only when it did could there be any attempt to take note of the child's distinctive and fruitful dependency, special needs, and vulnerabilities.

For Aries and others, people could not allow themselves to become too attached to anything as frail and vulnerable as a child until the seventeenth century because of the near certainty they might lose that child. Children were simply absorbed into the adult working community and made susceptible to the same dangers and contingencies shadowing most common men and women at the time. It was with the emergence of the middle class and the beginnings of what we know as individualism in the seventeenth and eighteenth centuries that children were allowed a "childhood." They were primarily young boys, either young gentlemen or the little sons of burghers, separated out from the adult world and sent to tutors after their days with nurses, or to schools where they would be reared as properly moral, rational beings, nurtured in their "natural" development, or prepared for a world of property and dignified work. John Locke, at the end of the seventeenth century, wrote an essay about education in "right reason" for the gentleman who was his prime concern, a person whose character (even when very young) had to be assured (1964, p. 70). Locke wrote about the lasting consequences of the "little, or almost insensible impressions on our tender infancies" and about how much of what men became depended upon their education (p. 20).

Jean-Jacques Rousseau, who made one of the major contributions to the recognition of childhood as a stage of life, believed that social institutions might corrupt the child if the child's nature were not taken into account in the course of his growing, if the child were not to be allowed to grow in accord with "nature." Knowing well, Rousseau wrote, how few young people live out a full span of life, it seemed barbarous to "sacrifice the present to an uncertain future" and make the child "miserable in order to prepare him for a remote happiness which he will probably not live to enjoy" (1962, p. 33). He went on to say that social servitude would come with the age of reason. "Why anticipate it by a domestic servitude? Let one moment of life be free from this yoke which nature has not imposed, and leave the child to the enjoyment of his natural liberty" (p. 37). We recognize now that Rousseau's Emile inhabited a harmonious, law-governed, rational universe or a world of nature that could be relied upon to counterbalance body and mind, power and desire. Later Johann Pestalozzi, working during the Napoleonic Wars, put into practice some of Rousseau's ideas with destitute children whom he tried to love and for whom he tried to "do everything." He made use, he wrote,

> of the impressions and experiences of their daily life to give my children a true and exact idea of right and duty.... I shall never forget how strong and true I generally found their sense of justice and reason, and how this sense increased and, as it were, established their good will (1962, p. 74).

By the end of the eighteenth century, Immanuel Kant (much influenced by Rousseau) became interested in education for the sake of overcoming "the unruliness" of children. He wrote that "if a man be allowed to follow his own will in his youth without opposition, a certain lawlessness will cling to him throughout his life" (1960, p. 4). Education meant discipline and instruction, both needed if children were to become cultured and restrained enough to exercise their free will, to become fully dutiful, rational beings. It is not difficult to see that his view of children was closely related to other views becoming institutionalized in the nineteenth century, at length applying to children other than those of the middle class. More and more children became separated from the world of adultness, most often to be prepared (with a mingling of benevolence and severity) to perform allotted roles.

In the nineteenth century, the images of childhood multiply and conflict. We need only compare, for example, Horace Mann's viewing with Emerson's and Hawthorne's, or the vision of schooling itself with the visions of romantic poets, such as Blake and Wordsworth. Mann (1959) wrote that "children, without some favoring influences to woo out and cheer their faculties, may remain mere inanimate forms, while surrounded by the paradise of knowledge" (p. 30). At other times, he wrote of children becoming "intoxicated and delirious with the highly stimulating air of freedom; and thus ... they remain unfitted, unless they have become morally acclimated to our institutions, to exercise the rights of a freeman" (p. 58). He used words like "anarchy" and "vengeance"; he compared unschooled children with baby vultures. All this was to support the argument for schools as a means of guaranteeing "self-control" and "voluntary compliance" with the laws of righteousness, virtues that would be rewarded by upward mobility and the opportunity to pursue success.

Emerson's images were of children endowed with the capacity to wonder, to imagine, to move freely and affirm themselves until they were confined.

> Do not think youth has no force, because he cannot speak to you and me. Hark! In the next room his voice is sufficiently clear and emphatic. It seems he knows how to speak to his contemporaries. Bashful or bold, then, he will know how to make us seniors very unnecessary (1966, p. 105).

This is the transcendental romantic notion of the values of spontaneity and expressiveness, values that ought not to be tampered with by adults. Emerson came before the moment of realization that children could only become human by means of communication in social contexts. His spiritual conception, linking the soul of the child to the Divine, was much like that of his contemporary Bronson Alcott. Together, intentionally or not, they shaped the question having to do with the meaning of "self" and the possibility of self-fulfillment in an industrializing society bent on making children the means to further ends.

We can recall Hawthorne's little Pearl in The Scarlet Letter, the embodiment of the elfin, the "natural," the disruptive—until at the end she is acknowledged by her father and liberated, in some way, to love. We can think of Blake's children in *Songs of Innocence and Experience*, exploited as chimney sweeps, pressed down by the authority of church and family and school.

> How can the bird that is born for joy
> Sit in a cage and sing?
> How can a child, when fears annoy,
> But drop his tender wing, and forget his
> youthful spring?" (1958, p. 58).

That, after all, was suggested by Blake's vision of a schoolboy! And that might in turn recall Wordsworth's Lucy "sportive as the fawn / That wild with glee across the lawn / Or up the mountain spring: / And hers shall be the breathing balm, / and hers the silence and the calm / Of mute insensate things" (1962, p. 10). There are intimations of what Friedrich Froebel seized upon here, the German idealist with radiant views of spontaneity and play, of growth in a "kindergarten." There are intimations of the work of Francis Parker, applying similar values to elementary education as the nineteenth century moved to its end. The idea of childhood, as we see, summons up the most fundamental fears and delights in the adults who can remember tensions between freedom and control, sustaining and leaving.

Always there have been ambiguities and dread uncertainties. We can read Friedrich Engels even today and feel horrified by his accounts of children in the British potteries— the illness, rheumatism, the stunted growth, the vomiting (1974, p. 219). We can return to Dickens's *Oliver Twist* and *Nicholas Nickleby* and rediscover personally the child as victim, the child as plaything or slave. We can read accounts of American factories and mills at the same moments of time, look at fading photographs of mill girls, mine boys, ragpickers. The literary artist has the capacity, of course, to uncover individual experiences; but that does not totally overcome the tendency to aggregate and to categorize, especially when it comes to the suffering and the oppressed. To classify (as writers often do with regard to child mineworkers or those working at the looms) may be to force a special kind of invisibility on children, rendering them all the more helpless and speechless— like Herman Melville's Bartleby the scrivener who is compared with a "bit of wreckage in the mid Atlantic," and who can only murmur, "I know where I am" (1986, p. 127). This may be the case even today when we aggregate too much in terms of class and color and even gender, important as it is to expose the context, and especially when it demeans. When we do so, however, we are sometimes in danger of abandoning the existing person, of refusing her or him what has been called natality.

The lenses change, as they must in studies of children. The images shift and change as well. We have to be aware of this whenever we look through perspectives as time tested as those offered by developmental or cognitive psychology, by psychoanalysis, by child study in one or another of its many forms. When children are viewed as oppressed, is it because they are children, or because they are members of a minority group or a class? When they are loved, is it for themselves? Are more privileged children spared containment and abandonment? Are they left in sustaining situations where they can become? What of children from other cultures, who have to mediate what they hear and see through ideas and beliefs often at odds with the culture's mainstream? How do we pay heed? How do we enable them to speak in their own voices, to choose themselves in their own contexts, and at once to enter into the larger community? How do we sustain their families and involve their families in moving little children to learn to learn?

We may have to manifest more concern for the effects of a diffused power of the kind Michel Foucault has described (1984). He warned against a homogeneity continually imposed by the rules we devise, by measurements that weigh all differences against a given norm. He said that, for signs of privilege and status we have substituted a whole range "of degrees of normality indicating membership in a homogenous social body, but also playing a part in classification, hierarchization" (p. 196). We see the effects when the process of what Foucault called "normalization" works too indifferently. We also can see some of those effects in classrooms where children are refused opportunities to choose themselves, to express themselves, to be.

For all the occasional visions of emancipation, for all the poetic and normative visions of the young set free to be, the history of childhood, marked as it is by normalization and confinements, is often fearful. It challenges scholars and practitioners to choose and choose again to find out what it signifies in our own time, to find out what we truly see. Can we socialize without destroying distinctiveness? Can we initiate without silencing? Can we who deal with children (teaching them, doing research into their lives, engaging with them) at once effect connections with them as living, searching beings? Can we trust ourselves to care?

There may be a sense in which our whole enterprise depends for its worth on the capacity to love our children enough, even as we love our world. One of the most significant works in the history of childhood, Dostoyevsky's *The Brothers Karamasov*, becomes painfully relevant as violations and abuses of children increase. You may recall Ivan Karamasov telling his brother Alyosha that he loves life more than the meaning of it, "regardless of logic." But he is preoccupied with the suffering of children, which (with his Euclidean mind) he cannot reconcile with the goodness of God. He tells story after story of the torture of children, punishments carried out by the well educated and the cultivated to "correct" their young, the murder of a child by a general for throwing a stone at his dog. He says that he cannot accept any eternal harmony if children's sufferings must pay for it. Whatever the truth is, it is not worth the price, he says.

I don't want the mother to embrace the oppressor who threw her son to the dog! She dare not forgive him . . . Is there in the whole world a being who would have the right to forgive and could forgive? I don't want harmony. For love of humanity I don't want it. I would rather be left with the unavenged suffering and unsatisfied indignation, even if I were wrong (p. 29).

We would not talk of "eternal harmony" today; but we nonetheless are tempted to smooth out the suffering, even to adjust to it by means of technical explanation, categorization, aggregation. How often do we react with Ivan's indignation to the plight of a child living in a shelter, a child whose brother has been shot on the street, a young woman with an AIDS baby? How often are we moved by the predicament of a child obviously being manipulated to grow into consumerism and material success? Educators on all levels still have to break through the folding screens and denials that obscure the unresolved and the desperate with pieties and slogans. We still have to *decide*, I think, the purpose of our inquiries, the actual possibilities for children we can open with our work.

It is so important to hear the forlorn voices of children confronting the terror of our times: not only those suffering the damages of *apartheid* or carnage, but the children begging in the city streets, the children compelled to peddle for drug-dealers, the children made to sell themselves. Early childhood education studies cannot leave them out, nor can those who deal directly with the young in classrooms, corridors, administrative offices. Like Ivan's tormented little ones, they may be the test of what we do, the test of our "success."

Robert Coles's work during the civil rights struggles and today is still suggestive, especially his account of children like Ruby in his book called *Children of Crisis* (1967, pp. 37–71). Coles tried to enter the world of such children when they were caught in the dangerous endeavor of integrating the southern schools. He had them draw pictures for him; he had them talk informally with him. Laying aside his theoretical glasses, avoiding labels and "heavily intellectualized speculations," he tried to commune somehow with their worlds. He tried not to treat them as cases; he refused to see pathology when they were risking their lives; he did not "treat," even when treatment seemed to be called for. He tried to empower the children to name, to reflect, to affirm themselves. In so doing, he was moved to redefine himself.

The point, of course, is not that the cognitive sciences or developmental psychology or psychoanalytic theory or social psychology ought to be replaced by qualitative or interpretive research under all circumstances. It is simply that the spheres of inquiry may require much more deepening and widening until they open to the full stories of human incompleteness and fragility. Only then are we likely to experience the tension between the need to initiate and the need to release, the need *not* to expel even as we renew.

We have to allow, as we never have in the past, for the unexpected, even the shocking. There is an example in Don De Lillo's *White Noise*, a novel having to do with an "airborne toxic event," the sudden leak of a noxious gas in an American college town. The novel tells of the clash between statistical diagnoses and prescriptions and lived experiences with the fear of death. Children are central to the work. They respond variously—technically, in media language, in total literalism, in the stutter of incomprehension. Wilder, the smallest child, cries inexplicably for four hours one day. The weeping, which no one can understand and no one can assuage, goes on until it mysteriously dies out; but there is something metaphorically significant in the sound. It is one that must be heeded in the midst of measurements and calculations, in the quiet of the observation room, in the concentration of the laboratory, among the clicking noises of our technical tools.

Aware as we are of idiomatic ways of parenting, of being poor, of expressing despair, we know that maturation does not proceed in accord with unchanging norms. Still, we are taken up with recurrences and uniformities, with the persistent need to generalize. That makes us inattentive to the irregulari-

ties or unwilling to deal with them—the revelations of an Ivan, Wilder's weeping, the unexpected leaps ahead in certain cases, the fallbacks in places where no one seems to know the way.

Most of us do realize, of course, that generalizations about stages and structures never capture all the nuances of child development, and that the possibilities often do outrun the predictions. Vygotsky (1978) knew, for example, that measured achievement seldom tells enough about what is happening or what might happen when children work with others in a distinctively social world. He spoke about the "zone of proximal development" and about the phenomenon that "learning awakens a variety of internal developmental processes that are able to operate only when the child is interacting with people in his environment and in cooperation with his peers" (p. 85). Clearly, those processes do not operate to one end-point; predictions have to give way.

Such discoveries, like many of Dewey's, lead many to wonder how much we do understand with regard to the ways in which children deal "consciously and expressly; with the situations in which they find themselves" (1934, p. 263). What repertoires do they use? What scripts do they have in hand? Does research conducted according to the norms of technical rationality help us penetrate what it means to be mindful in specific cases, to attend to lived actualities that can never be generalized? We all realize that children must be viewed as speaking and acting subjects in a social world, beings striving to make meanings, not all of whose activities can be scientifically understood. Indeed, much of the meaning construction that goes on is excluded from empirical and statistical description. The identification of "storytelling" as a mode of knowing seems to be taking place in a channel parallel to but separate from the technicist one (Bruner, 1986; Egan, 1988). For many, Robert Coles's Ruby, with her desire to draw God as "a real big man," and Wilder, with his prophetic weeping, need to be dismissed because they cannot be "explained."

In an essay called "Eye and Mind," the philosopher Maurice Merleau-Ponty characterized scientific thinking as the kind of thinking that focuses on the "object-in-general." He said that thinking ought to return now and then to the "there is" underlying it "to the site, the soil of the sensible and opened world such as it is in our life and for our body—not that possible body which I may legitimately think of as an information machine but that actual body I call mine, this sentinel standing quietly at the command of my words and my acts" (1964, p. 160). Merleau-Ponty reminded us continually of embodiment, of the embodied consciousness involved intersubjectively with others. It may be that the presentness and potentiality of the body are ignored in too much early childhood education literature—and by that I mean the body of the inquirer, the body of the practitioner, through which consciousness expresses itself in so many ways. Consciousness, for Merleau-Ponty, originates in a perceived landscape that children pattern from their own situated vantage points, as they move about and smell and touch and listen to aspects of the appearing, sounding world. Informing their experiences through such perceptual ordering, children establish their relations to the fields opening before them and to their personal and social surroundings. This happens *beneath* the relationship of the knower to the known later on, as the child grows. Perceived and imaginary landscapes remain foundational to rationality, the ground of meanings that become layered as children move into the life of language and begin thematizing, symbolizing, making conceptual sense. Merleau-Ponty was describing a being at home in the world, as body/mind in lived time.

The most authentic way in which adults can grasp the moments of initiating relationships is by reflecting back. To recapture some of the origins of rationality is important for every early childhood teacher. To reach back to become present to oneself may be to come much closer to the interpretive awareness of children's lives, as they are pulled forward by their futures, making something of what they are made. This may be one of the ways of opening pathways to conversations with children, to the kinds of dialogue that may clear the way to understanding who those children are. Merleau-Ponty (1964) wrote of perception as a nascent logos, suggesting that children (perceiving incompleteness, wondering what it is like where the road turns, where their parents go in the morning, what the indistinct voices are really saying, what the darkness holds) keep reaching beyond what they perceive if they are released—perhaps taught —to do so. They make new connections in their experience; they weave networks, and, in time, they begin, as Dewey said, to "fund" meanings as they grow.

There is no question but that informed encounters with works of art often make it possible for teachers to recover a lost spontaneity in this way. I am much involved in opening teachers to such encounters—to their opening works of art as aesthetic objects, objects of *their* experience. I am eager to enable as many as possible to transmute the painted strokes they see on canvases into complex worlds of shape, form, nuances of light. I should like more and more for teachers to begin dancing and, through dancing, open themselves to their own and other's bodies in motion, making shapes, displaying energy in time and space. And, clearly, I want to enable teachers to lend their lives more and more passionately to poems and novels and stories, viewed as works of art to be discovered through leaps of imagination, through allowing imagination to play over what is perceived.

Experiencing this ourselves, we may become more attuned to what it signifies to awaken children to become the imaginative beings they can and ought to be. There is more to understand when it comes to the capacities that allow even little children to look beyond the actual, to realize that experience holds more than it seems. Interest in children's imaginations on our part depends on how we perceive children in this culture, how the public comes to perceive them, what we value, what we are visibly striving to attain. Clearly, I am concerned lest this very dimension be excluded as we focus on assessments of cognitive performance, achievement, and success. Like the philosopher Gadamer (1975) I want to keep pointing to the "peculiar falsehood of modern consciousness: the idolatry of scientific method and of the anonymous authority of the sciences" (p. 307).

My preoccupation with all this—and with reflectiveness, imagination, and dialogue—is not meant to exclude empirical and logical modes of sense-making, nor the structural, nor the linguistic, nor the semiotic. I simply want to argue against anonymity as we regard the lives of children now and in the past. I want to argue against the decontextualization of those lives. I want to resist the temptation to accommodate to the demands of a system more interested in technological growth than in the growth of diverse children. I want to think about flexibility and relationship and the conversational reconciling of a multiplicity of voices as we strive for a decent and humane world. It will only be decent and humane if the violations cease, if we can support at last and take responsibility for newcomers and love our children as much as we love the world.

References

Arendt, H. (1958). *The human condition.* Chicago: University of Chicago Press.

Arendt, H. (1961). *Between past and future.* New York: Viking Press.

Aries, P. (1962). *Centuries of childhood.* New York: Knopf.

Blake, W. (1958). *Collected poems.* Baltimore, MD: Penguin Books.

Bruner, J. (1986). *Actual minds, possible worlds.* Cambridge: Harvard University Press.

Coles, R. (1967). *Children of crisis.* Boston: Little, Brown.

De Lillo, D. (1985). *White noise.* New York: Viking Press.

Dewey, J. (1916). *Democracy and education.* New York: Macmillan.

Dewey, J. (1934). *Art as experience.* New York: Minton, Balch.

Dostoyevsky, F. (1945). *The brothers Karamasov.* New York: Modern Library.

Egan, K. (1988). Education and the mental life of young children. In L. R. Williams & D. P. Fromberg (eds.). *Defining the field of early childhood education: An invitational symposium.* Charlottesville, VA: W. Alton Jones Foundation.

Emerson, R. W. (1966). *Emerson on education.* In H. M. Jones (ed.) New York: Teachers College Press.

Engels, F. (1974). The condition of the working class. In Steven Marcus (ed.). *Engels, Manchester & the working class.* New York: Vintage Books.

Foucault, M. (1984). Politics and ethics: An interview. In P. Rabinow (ed.), *The Foucault reader.* New York: Pantheon Books.

Freire, P. (1970). *Pedagogy of the oppressed.* New York: Herder and Herder.

Gadamer, H. G. (1975). Hermeneutics and social science. *Cultural Hermeneutics, 2* (2), p. 307–316.

Kant, I. (1960). *Education.* Ann Arbor, MI: Ann Arbor Paper Books.

Locke, J. (1964). *John Locke on education* (Peter Gay, ed.). New York: Teachers College Press.

Mann, H. (1959). *The republic and the school: Horace Mann on the education of free men* (L. A. Cremin, ed.). New York: Teachers College Press.

Melville, H. (1986). Bartlelby the scrivener. *Billy Budd, sailor and other stories.* New York: Bantam Classics.

Merleau-Ponty, M. (1964). Eye and mind. *The primacy of perception.* Evanston, IL: Northwestern University Press.

Pestalozzi, J. H. (1915). *How Gertrude teaches her children.* Syracuse, NY: C. W. Bardeen.

Rousseau, J.-J. (1962). *The Emile of Jean Jacques Rousseau: selections* (W. Boyd, ed.). New York: Teachers College Press.

Sartre, J.-P. (1947). *Existentialism.* New York: Philosophical Library.

Sartre, J.-P. (1964). *The words.* New York: George Braziller.

Scheffler, I. (1960). *The language of education.* Springfield, IL: Charles C. Thomas.

Vygotsky, L. S. (1978). *Mind in society.* Cambridge: Harvard University Press.

Winnicott, D. S. (1971). *Playing and reality.* New York: Basic Books.

Wordsworth, W. (1962). The Lucy Poems. In C. Baker, ed., *Wordsworth: The prelude and selected poems and sonnets.* New York: Holt, Rinehart, and Winston.

M. Greene

Historic Tensions and Future Opportunities: Public Responsibility and Early Childhood Education

Redefining our national conception of public responsibility toward children and providing a basis for an equitable and rational national policy toward families is a central issue in early childhood education (broadly conceived to include such areas as child care, preschooling, kindergarten, and parent education serving children from birth through age eight).

There are a number of reasons for this. Educational reform remains high on the public agenda, including growing support for an expansion of educational services to the young. The welfare system, especially the Aid to Dependent Children program, may be overhauled as we grapple with the possibilities of a national policy toward families. All the demographic projections suggest that the forces driving toward greater commitments to early childhood education—working mothers, single parent families, labor shortages in the private sector, greater emphasis on academic achievement—are likely to grow. They certainly will not diminish.

My concern here, however, is not so much whether the efforts to increase the provision of early childhood education through national and state policies will be successful, but rather with the possibilities that a fuller conception of early childhood education can alter how we think about children and families. Of interest, for example, is how rethinking our social responsibilities toward children will allow us to develop richer conceptions of family life by opening up the boundaries of the closed nuclear family, and by revising our longstanding hostility toward maternal employment. If properly conceived and implemented, a fuller conception of early childhood education can generate a more positive vision of public programs, rather than viewing them as necessary only for those who fail or who are the victims of tragedy.

These are all possibilities, but they will not come easily. Opposition to an enlarged conception of early childhood education and public responsibility for children remains strong—even as an unusual coalition of conservatives and liberals seeks to develop a national policy toward families and children. Many continue to believe that the best public policy toward families is no policy at all. Others remain opposed to maternal employment or at least hold to the ideology that children are seriously at risk when mothers work, even as large numbers of mothers are working and will continue to work. Moreover, family and child professionals are continually at odds over who should be involved most directly with children and what kinds of programs should be offered. The current debate over the efficacy of preschooling within the public schools is an example of this. But beyond these fields of battles is a larger set of historic assumptions about the relationship of public policy toward families and young children that needs to be revised.

Revising Historic Assumptions

At least three historic assumptions have been crucial to the evolution of public policies toward families and children:

- The myth of the private family
- The doctrine of *parens patriae*
- The view of parents as determiners of their children's fate.

The *myth of the private family* begins with a view of the family as a separate entity, largely autonomous in an embattled and difficult world. But families are not autonomous. They are special places. In them intimacy and love are shared, emotions are expressed, and children are socialized more openly and in more intensive ways than occurs elsewhere. When families work well, they are havens in a heartless world, places of refuge, as well as the jumping off place for entry into the wider society. But that is not the same thing as viewing the family as somehow independent of the wider world. Our wishfulness to see the family as separate from the outside world, as a place where we can be protected from the world, is simple-minded, incomplete, and self-deceiving. And, it has terribly undermined our ability to forge effective and humane public policies for young children.

In fact, families are extraordinarily open places, subject to all sorts of external influences. Interest rates on mortgages, levels of unemployment, tax policy, government expenditures, the price of oil and gas, food and housing, environmental protection—these and countless other issues over which families have no control and hardly any influence affect children's lives as much as individual family decisions. Even in the area that appears most sacrosanct and private, the practice of child rearing, families are only one of many powerful agencies that influence children, agencies that include child care facilities, schools, the health care system, television, peer groups, and the professionals who interact with them on a regular basis. Holding on to the myth of the private family as if these external circumstances were not crucial to the young denies reality. With that denial, we segment our public policies into those that are about and for children, and those that are about the economy, defense, transportation, or the environment, without explicitly asking what these policies mean for children.

The second assumption that has powerfully and adversely affected public policy toward the young has been the continuing commitment to the doctrine of *parens patriae*. During the nineteenth century, the English legal doctrine of *parens patriae*, which gives the state ultimate parental powers, was refashioned into a conception of limited public responsibility. While the state had the authority to intervene, it was supposed to supersede private responsibility only under conditions of family disorganization and pathology. That is, the doctrine as it emerged in the nineteenth-century United States made public responsibility dependent upon findings of familial or parental failure, whether because of parents' own behavior, or because social conditions overwhelmed parents.

Public action, then, became seen as a second-best resort, most often targeted at those who were coming out second best in the race for success and security. It was not something the state wanted to do, citizenry were supposed to want, or individuals could feel good about accepting. *Parens patriae* meant that public intervention was seen as an abnormal activity, temporary and parsimonious. This limited the scope of public responsibility and kept public funds low. The presumption of parental failure built into this formulation of public policy meant that children in public institutions or those receiving public supports were labeled as potential failures, adding yet a further stigma to those who received special government support. (The one major exception to this has been the public schools. Since public education came to be seen as an avenue of individual mobility and personal gain, and as an avenue toward children's growth, it was able to escape the stigmatizing impact of public supports.)

The doctrine of *parens patriae* was intimately linked to the myth of the private family. If one assumes that families exist largely on their own, then providing public services to children depends upon demonstrating that families cannot provide those services or are failing as parents. In its most conservative manifestations, this gets phrased as government should give only to those who cannot help themselves, and only until those who are the object of government charity can "stand on their own." Even in its more liberal manifestation, there is the view that families would be better off if the state stayed away. The political and ideological differences often come down to arguments about how poor are the poor, how discriminated against are minorities, how low a test score entitles one to tutoring, how many weeks of unemployment constitute a legitimate need for retraining.

There is nothing inherently wrong with such questions. Being concerned about economic self-sufficiency or points of access to government services is a legitimate part of the political process. The trouble has been that the myth of private family and the doctrine of *parens patriae* have combined to prevent us from conceptualizing alternative notions of public policy that emphasize broad government responsibility for the ability of families and children to flourish, notions that begin with the assumption that the state has responsibilities before tragedy strikes or parents fail. At a minimum, then, we need a conception of public responsibility that begins by recognizing, as Kenneth Keniston and the Carnegie Council on Children put it some years ago, that, "family self-sufficiency is a false myth," and that "all today's families need help in raising children" (Grubb & Lazerson, 1988, p. 49).

The third assumption that has bedeviled public policies toward families and children has been the notion of *parental determinism*. Americans have tended to believe that parents make their children, that they determine their children's futures. As adults, many of us define our success by whether our children have succeeded. Again, there is a certain rationality to that. Taking credit for one's children is a well-earned reward for the travails of child rearing. However, the other side of the coin is not so positive; for under the assumption of parental determinism, when children do not do well, parents are quick to chastise themselves or to be blamed by others for the failure.

Like the myth of the private family to which it is related, parental determinism is a simple-minded and incomplete truth. It seems much more realistic to recognize that parents are more guides and managers, at best promoters, of their children's activities in a world of a myriad of institutions and influences. Parents play important roles in choosing child care, schools, neighborhoods, churches, television programs. They may also be active in school reform, parent education, or their children's social organizations. Parents as individuals, however, have very little capacity to change the content of television programs, even as they try to determine which individual program their child watches. Parents are virtually powerless to affect the health care system, even as they choose a particular health care professional for their child. Even the most powerful and authoritative parent feels powerless in the face of institutions that are national in scope, that depend for their legitimacy upon professional experts, and that have attained the size and power of many modern institutions. At best, parents are guides for their children through institutions that they cannot control.

Recognizing this, it becomes imperative for parents to stop thinking of themselves simply as individuals acting to determine their children's futures, and to adopt a much broader sense of collective responsibility. Recognizing that the issues that face all children are inadequate schools, unsafe streets, unavailable and inappropriate medical care, exploitative television programs, and an economy that is failing millions, allows parents to recognize that they can do little as individual parents. By redefining the issues in public and social terms, rather than in private and personal ones, we can all look outside the family and turn away from individualistic approaches to families and children.

Tensions in Early Childhood Education

These three assumptions—the myth of the private family, the doctrine of *parens patriae*, and the ideology of parental determinism— and their consequences—the failure to take the social conditions of family life seriously, the blaming of parents, the generation of public programs primarily on the basis of parental failure or tragedy, and individualistic rather than collective responses to child-rearing issues—have all influenced our approaches to public policies toward children. Without understanding and revising these assumptions, the possibilities inherent in the present moment for developing better, more rational, and more equitable public supports for the young and their families are not likely to be successful.

But there are other tensions more specific to early childhood education that need to be addressed. They include the ongoing central dilemmas of mothers' working and purposes of early childhood education. The first centers on the tension between the dogma of domesticity, that mothers are responsible for young children, and the notion that the rearing of the very young can be shared with other individuals, particularly in support of mothers who work outside of the home.

To resolve this tension, supporters of early childhood education have had to claim familial disorganization and excessive returns to their programs. Early childhood education becomes justified by showing that families are too poor or too disorganized to raise their children adequately. Thus, one line of early childhood education has been rooted in welfare, whether one talks of the day nurseries in settlement houses at the turn of the century, or the welfare-based child care centers of more recent times. The second related theme, with important public consequences, has been the provision of public supports during periods of national emergency. The two most obvious instances have been the Depression of the 1930s, when federal funds became available for preschools as part of the unemployment relief programs of the New Deal, and the Lanham Act investments during World War II to provide child care in areas of high labor needs in national defense industries.

The themes of national crisis and familial disorganization came together in the 1960s War on Poverty with a third dimension—that appropriate kinds of early childhood education could provide educational benefits. In the absence of such "emergencies," or a public perception that families cannot cope, it has been extremely difficult to generate a sustained commitment to early childhood education. The result has been to keep early childhood education underfunded, chaotic, and suspect.

There has been another tension in the history of early childhood education, one between welfare care and educational development. At the turn of the century, much of what we now think of as early childhood education (in contrast to the placement of young children with neighbors or family members) occurred in day nurseries that were extensions of private philanthropy associated with settlement houses and directed at children from low-income families whose mothers worked. They provided care for children under the often expressed view that their parents were neglectful, and, because many of the families were immigrants, that the children (and their par-

ents) needed to be taught American ways. The families in day nurseries were often considered inadequate, as summed up by one nursery worker who noted, "We gave many of them more abundant food and much better care than their poor homes could afford" (Grubb & Lazerson, 1988, p. 211). The ideology of domesticity reinforced the view that mothers who could not or chose not to rear their children full-time were by definition inadequate.

It is thus not surprising that the major public efforts on behalf of families during the late nineteenth and early twentieth centuries were to aid mothers in keeping their children at home. The most obvious of these were the efforts to establish mothers' pensions, an early version of aid to dependent children. The day nurseries never succeeded in overcoming their association with poor people and with mothers who placed their children "out" in order to work. By the 1920s, the day nurseries suffered from poor funding, undersubscription, high turnover, and poor care.

The developmental and educational themes in early childhood education have had a somewhat different history. Originally based in infant schools of the nineteenth century, but more importantly in the nursery schools and child development research that emerged in the first half of the twentieth century, the developmental theme stressed socioemotional development, and to a lesser extent, cognitive growth of the child—in contrast to the care of working mothers and the poor. As they evolved in the 1920s, nursery schools were part day rather than full day, and were directed at the environmental enrichment of middle-class children. Many such schools were established in university communities, often as part of child study and child development programs. Conceived as extensions of the home and complements to mothering rather than as "mother substitutes," nursery schools assumed that mothers were available full-time, or most of the time, and they assumed that homes and families from which the children came were adequate.

These assumptions allowed the nursery schools and child development programs to avoid at least some of the conflicts over the appropriate social role of women as mothers. And, because they were in the private sector or were part of university and college programs, the nursery school also avoided the stigma associated with poor and disorganized families. Within an emerging early childhood and child care profession, the nursery schools' founders and teachers well into the 1960s regarded the day nursery schools as providing a strong institutional image of what the education of young children ought to be.

Such day nurseries and nursery schools were private and philanthropic entities. Public funding did not really come into play until the 1930s, when WPA funds were provided to give employment to unemployed teachers in kindergartens and preschool programs. Since these programs were administered by state departments of education and local school boards, they reflected the educational orientation of the schools. During World War II, the Lanham Act provided funds for day care centers to facilitate the employment of women in defense-related industries. In both of these cases, however, public support was tied to emergency conditions. By 1946 the federal government had withdrawn almost all of its support for early childhood education and child care programs.

By the 1960s the surge in women's employment, new research in child development asserting the importance of the preschool years, and racial and social pressures that gave rise to the War on Poverty, provided a new impetus to the education of young children. Head Start quickly became the centerpiece of those concerns, although a number of efforts to expand and modify welfare programs directed at young children also occurred. Head Start is particularly important, however, because it implicitly sought to merge the historically divergent elements of early childhood education. It aimed at poor children and families in need of welfare support, but it focused on cognitive development and educational gains.

The many ups and downs of Head Start since the late 1960s will not presently be ad-

dressed, except to say that the rising concern with educational achievement played a major role in simply allowing Head Start to survive, even after the initial findings that Head Start made little difference to poor children's school success (see Chapter 3, Section 3.3 **Early Childhood Settings in the Public Sector**). But neither Head Start nor the other programs directed at young children and families have been able to overcome the continuing antagonism to mothers' working, to providing for young children on a basis other than *parens patriae*, or to overcoming the reluctance to evaluate public policies in terms of their potential effect on children and families. The result has been that early childhood education has been provided by a welter of different organizations, uncoordinated and often contradictory in their goals, with insufficient funding. It has also meant the emergence of an early childhood education system sharply class divided between those young children in high tuition programs and those in subsidized care or in settings of low cost and little supervision.

Future Promises

There are some promises for the future, for clearly the pressure to expand our commitments to young children is going to grow. There are at least four reasons for this.

First, the trend of mothers' working in paid employment appears irresistible. More than half of the women with children under six years of age are now in the work force. That proportion has been rising since the 1960s. Working mothers are no longer an aberrant or deviant phenomenon. This phenomenon certainly is not limited to low-income mothers. While the rate of entry into the labor market may be slowing down, it is clear that the dilemma of what to do with young children while mothers work is not going to go away.

Indeed, labor market pressures are likely to increase further the proportion of mothers in paid employment; and in all likelihood, some of the push to provide early childhood education programs is going to come from the private sector. Major corporations like ARA

Services are already involved in offering child care programs in areas where labor markets are tight. Other employers either have child care programs or are considering them in order to assure themselves of an adequate and stable supply of workers.

Second, the emphasis on academic achievement is unlikely to decline in the near future, and will probably increase. While too much is undoubtedly made of research findings that suggest that preschooling helps children succeed academically, every study that purports to show such findings furthers the intensity with which parents seek early childhood education programs. Early childhood education is likely to continue to be seen as an opportunity to move more quickly and more successfully up the academic achievement ladder, and the proportion of parents seeking it for their children will go up.

Third, the educational system is looking for ways to incorporate preschooling into its mandate. The broad array of social problems suggest the need for closer collaboration between schools and families with young children. The educational profession itself now sees that unfilled classrooms might be used for the schooling of three-and four-year-olds, as well as for all-day kindergartens. Whatever the results of the current debate about the efficacy of preschooling in the public schools—and the strongest claim is the greater universality of public education—the competition for young children is likely to result in more spaces available to them and greater efforts to get them into early childhood education programs.

Finally, it seems likely that the social and political concerns linked to poverty also will increase. After the serious deterioration in the economic status of children during the 1980s that left one in four children living in poverty, some shifts are pending. Given the propensity of the American populace to prefer educational solutions to the economic problems, rather than to undertake income redistribution, and given the pressure to tie educational and care programs for poor children to job training and employment, public and private initiatives will probably be heavily focused on early childhood education.

The likely expansion of investments in young children indicated by these four trends does not mean that we will see nirvana in regard to the young. Indeed, the arguments just sketched to lay out the potential growth in early childhood education say nothing about quality, sufficient support, rationality, or even greater sensitivity to the broad range of children's needs. But there is an opportunity to take advantage of public debate about the family and children, a debate that suggests that the family is not a private and autonomous institution, that government is responsible for aiding all children, not simply those whose parents are defined as too poor or too disorganized to help, and that while all parents need to be involved in guiding their children through children's institutions, most of the major issues that confront the young are broad public issues that need to be faced collectively. Unless we recognize our collective responsibility for all children, our public and social love for children, rather than simply emphasizing the private and personal love we give as family members, the promise of the future will be broken. All our children will be left at risk once again.

Reference

Grubb, W. N., & Lazerson, M. (1988). *Broken promises: How Americans fail their children*. Chicago: University of Chicago Press.

M. Lazerson

Educational Contexts: The Common School in Relation to Early Childhood Education

During the nineteenth century common schools provided instruction in reading, writing, and arithmetic and inculcated democratic ideas in white children in the northern United States. Locally controlled and supported, these public, nonsectarian Protestant, educational institutions varied significantly in teacher competence, facilities, and student attendance. In the 1830s the lack of uniform standards promoted a common school reform movement that lasted until after the Civil War and altered the fundamental form and content of public education for children aged five to fifteen. Ironically, reformers' efforts to centralize schools at the state level resulted in the eventual replacement of common schools by graded elementary, junior high, and high schools.

Prior to 1776, common schools (also known as petty or grammar schools) were one of several options available to colonists who viewed schooling as the key to literacy and literacy as the key to religious salvation. A Massachusetts law of 1647 mandated that communities of fifty households or more offer instruction in reading and writing for six months a year. Though this statute was never strictly enforced, it was usually respected and later emulated by neighboring colonies. Common schools were less popular in the mid-Atlantic colonies, where charity schools and private schools predominated, and were virtually nonexistent in the South, where private tutors and itinerant school teachers were the norm.

After the American Revolution common schools became the repository of the new nation's political aspirations. Schools proliferated and enrollment soared throughout the first decades of the nineteenth century in response to demographic changes and increased interest in education. For example, in New York State the percentage of children aged 2 to 19 enrolled in public schools jumped from 37.1 percent in 1798 to 60.2 percent in 1830 (Kaestle and Vinovskis, 1983).

Despite differences from one district to the next, a few generalizations about physical facilities, teachers, and the curriculum are possible. During the Colonial era, instruction in reading and arithmetic was as likely to occur in the teacher's or a local resident's dwelling as in a separate building. After the American Revolution, teachers taught in schoolhouses of one or more rooms. Typically located on a barren plot of land, by a highway or a swamp, schools were roughly built, poorly ventilated, dark, and drafty. Students sat for endless hours on backless benches with their legs dangling above the floor, and they either froze or roasted depending on their proximity to the school stove.

Teachers, predominantly male prior to the 1820s, were considered above all else to be drill masters and disciplinarians. Commencing their careers as early as age 14, a teacher was often qualified merely by completing the course of instruction at the local school. When female teachers began to dominate the educational work force, not only was their labor cheaper (they earned 50 percent or less than their male counterparts), but in general it was found that they resorted less often to corporal punishment and were more patient and dedicated.

In addition to their inexperience and the hostile school environment, teachers confronted great challenges with their students. Prior to the 1840s, pupils in a single classroom ranged in age from 2 to 19 years old. Accommodating these unruly groups proved challenging at best, particularly when each student had a different textbook. Usually teachers assigned rote memorization of the alphabet, syllabarium, catechisms, and of "sums" involving addition, multiplication, and division. Students were called individually or in groups to recite the lessons. Advanced students copied words in copy books with quill and ink, while novices used slates and chalk to form their letters. Diversions such as spelling bees were a highlight of the exercises.

The length of time that a student spent in school varied from six weeks to six months through the mid-nineteenth century, with many variables such as the location of the school in a rural or urban community, the demography of the students, and the socioeconomic status of local voters, affecting school attendance. In Massachusetts the average number of school days rose from 150 in 1840 to 192 in 1880. During this time students' average attendance rose from 60 to 72 days a year (Kaestle and Vinovskis, 1983). Considering the boredom and discomfort that most students endured it is little wonder that attendance was erratic at best.

Overcrowding in urban schools became a serious problem as the nineteenth century progressed. One solution was the Lancaster monitorial system, invented by Joseph Lancaster in the 1820s. The system required advanced students to instruct less advanced students. It emphasized rote memorization and recitation, and was lauded for efficiency. The Lancaster system's popularity waned as a higher premium was placed on qualified teachers.

Overcrowding was only one of many problems, however. Reformers of the early nineteenth century, such as Horace Mann and Henry Barnard, demonstrated that most common schools were hovels of discomfort, darkness, and ill health, where students failed to learn the rudiments of American democracy. The reformers campaigned to guarantee fully tax supported schooling, to establish the first normal school for teachers, to lengthen the school year, to win legislation for compulsory attendance, and to improve pedagogical materials. Their innovations significantly led the way for the transformation of the school from a locally controlled and supported entity, to one that was sponsored and controlled by the state. In conjunction with the lengthening of the school year, reformers narrowed the age range of students attending school. Though an infant school promoting the enrollment of children at age two gained momentum in the early nineteenth century, by the 1840s the idea was discouraged. For disciplinary as well as developmental reasons, school reformers urged parents to keep their children home until they reached age five or six.

In the history of the common school may be found many of the origins of the twentieth century's system of public education. The numerous innovations promoted by Mann, Barnard, and their successors, and generally endorsed by voters, solidified trends toward centralized school systems with uniform standards. The reformation of the common schools from roughly 1840 to 1880 marks the transition from the fragmentary arrangements of the Colonial era, where public schooling was hap-

hazard at best, to the bureaucratized public school systems of the late twentieth century.

References

Cremin, L. A. (ed.). (1957). *The Republic and the school: Horace Mann on the education of free men.* New York: Teachers College Press.

Finkelstein, B. (1989). *Governing the young: Teacher behavior in popular primary schools in nineteenth-century United States.* New York: Falmer Press.

Kaestle, C. F. (1983). *Pillars of the Republic: Common schools and American society, 1780–1860.* New York: Hill and Wang.

Kaestle, C. F., & Vinovskis, M. A. (1983). *Education and social change in nineteenth century Massachusetts.* Cambridge, England: Cambridge University Press.

Macmullen, E. (1991). *In the cause of true education: Henry Barnard and nineteenth-century school reform.* New Haven: Yale University Press.

S. H. Lederman

2.3 History of Early Childhood Programs and Practices (Prior to 1960)

For more than a century after the inception of the first kindergarten in 1837, child care and early education, and the parent education associated with it, remained limited endeavors. Several different approaches to early education and child care were developed, most of them independently of one another, in response to particular societal needs. Some of those approaches were eventually transformed into more modern expressions, while others have remained a part of early childhood practice to the present day.

Dissemination of early childhood theory and practice was limited by lack of funds for large-scale implementations. The public was not convinced that child care and early education outside of the home had substantial benefits, and women had not yet entered the work force in large numbers. In spite of those difficulties, the pioneer early childhood practices persisted to create the foundations that supported rapid growth of the field in the mid-1960s, when federal monies for program research, development, and implementation finally became available. The articles below describe the early practices that, in various ways, still influence child care and early education today.

L. R. Williams

Bureau of Educational Experiments (Bank Street)

The Bureau of Educational Experiments, now known as the Bank Street College of Education, was founded in 1916 in New York City by Lucy Sprague Mitchell. The first years of the Bureau were characterized by a wide range of projects and interests, among them studies on rural schools, surveys of experimental school programs, psychological testing, public school nutrition, day nurseries, materials in early education programs, and a farm labor camp. Binding this diversity was a commitment to a spirit of experimentation and the social vision of the progressive movement. Within a few years, a focused research perspective evolved in the Bureau's work—"the scientific study of children and the way they react to different environments in order to plan intelligently an appropriate environment" (Antler, 1987, p. 224).

To study the total development of children and the materials, curriculum, and environments that would be responsive to children's needs, a nursery school headed by Harriet M. Johnson was established in 1919, for children aged fifteen months to three years. Collaboration with the Play School founded by Caroline Pratt in 1914 (later named the City and Country School) permitted Bureau researchers to extend their studies to children through the age of eight.

Into the next decade a massive collection of data about development and early education was accumulated, and the Bureau occupied "a unique place at the intersection of the child development and progressive education movements" (Antler, 1987, p. 290). The research perspective and educational programs of the Bureau were strongly influenced by John Dewey's philosophy concerning the relationship between the child and the curriculum and education in a democratic society. It is in the writings of Barbara Biber, who joined the Bureau staff in 1928, that this "intersection" of developmental and educational perspectives is illustrated dynamically.

In 1930 the Bureau began a new experiment with the establishment of the Cooperative School for Student Teachers, a joint creation of eight experimental schools and the Bureau as a means to prepare teaching faculty for these progressive schools. From this initial venture, the Bureau expanded its teacher education program to include the preparation of teachers for a variety of private and public schools. To house the new teacher education program, the research studies, and the expanded nursery school, the Bureau moved to larger quarters on Bank Street in Greenwich Village (New York City) and became known informally as "Bank Street." In 1951 the institution was authorized to grant the Master of Science degree and was renamed the Bank Street College of Education.

The Bureau's initial interest in the scientific study of children and the learning environments that supported growth, and its commitment to the social vision of the progressive movement, continued in the decades that followed. Bank Street has played a prominent role in early childhood education in a variety of national programs, including Head Start, Follow Through, and the Child Development Associate Program.

The spirit of experimentation and the dynamic interests of Lucy Sprague Mitchell that shaped the work and direction of the Bureau are still evident presently in the various divisions that make up the Bank Street College of Education. At this writing, the various college divisions include the School for Children and Family Center (nine months to thirteen years); Publications; Research, including a Center for Children and Technology; Continuing Education, with a variety of outreach projects; and the Graduate School's programs in teacher education and educational leadership.

References

Antler, J. (1987). *Lucy Sprague Mitchell: The making of a modern woman.* New Haven: Yale University Press.

Biber, B. (1984). *Early education and psychological development.* New Haven: Yale University Press.

Cooperative School for Student Teachers. Annual Report 1934–35. Bank Street College of Education Archives.

Johnson, H. M. (1972). *Children in "the nursery school."* New York: Agathon Press. (Originally published in 1928.)

Mitchell, L. S. (1953). *Two lives: The story of Wesley Clair Mitchell and myself.* New York: Simon & Schuster.

Mitchell, L. S. (1950). *Our children and our schools.* New York: Simon & Schuster.

H. K. Cuffaro

Froebelian Kindergarten, The*

The Froebelian kindergarten represents the first attempt by Western European educators to carry out an educational program reflecting the learning characteristics of young children (4 to 6 years of age). For that reason, the appearance of the kindergarten in Germany in 1837 can be considered the beginnings of early childhood education as it is practiced today in Europe, the Americas, and portions of Africa and Asia.

Prior to the establishment of the kindergarten, education of children too young for formal schools has been carried out in Europe much as it was in the rest of the world—through the children's observation of, and participation in, the activities of the home. As a rule, adults were not particularly aware that young children had ways of learning that were different from those of older children or adults. On the occasions when young children actually were sent to schools to begin the process of learning to read, write, and cipher, they generally were expected to respond in the same ways as older children to the formal demands of the classroom. The fact that young children usually did not make rapid progress in meeting these expectations was not considered to be important. It was commonly understood that "real" learning began at a later age (Gutek, 1972).

Friedrich Wilhelm Froebel's work revolutionized that concept by showing that young children were capable of rapid skill acquisition if they were taught through use of materials that allowed them to exercise their tendency toward active play while they developed their minds. Although Froebel's program is no longer in use today in its original form, it so profoundly influenced the course of early education that some teacher educators continue to include its discussion in teacher preparation programs.

Underlying Theory

Review of Froebel's major writings reveals several dominant themes: a strong belief in the unity of all creation and a subsequent vision of an interconnectedness of all that makes up the world; a belief that a part of anything reflects the structure and organization of the whole (the doctrine of Gleidganzes); an acceptance of the idea that all that a being (plant, animal, or human) is to become is germinally present at the moment of birth (the doctrine of preformation); an understanding that latent powers and knowledge unfold with exposure to materials and experiences that make "the inner become outer"; and a view of mathematics as the language of the universal laws stemming from a supreme being and governing all creation (Froebel, 1887, 1895).

Froebel was a deeply religious man whose mystical, pantheistic bent was strongly influenced by the romanticism prominent in the philosophy of his day. German romanticism espoused a concept of all manifestation (all that makes up the cosmos) as being the expression of certain eternal laws. Humankind, reflecting those laws, was thought to contain within itself the potentialities for perfection of body, mind, and spirit. Froebel's view was that exercise of their emerging capabilities could lead children to higher and higher levels of physical, intellectual, and moral development (Downs, 1978).

Also prominent in Froebel's theory was the belief that recognition of "first principles" could be brought about in young children by encouraging them to observe, imitate, and reconstruct examples of the operation of universal (mathematical) laws through use of directly manipulable materials. Finally, Froebel had a vision of the mother-teacher as loving mentor to the child's awakening powers. The mother whom Froebel had never had became the channel that nurtured the infant "seeds" in his "garden of children" (Woodham-Smith 1969).

Froebelian Materials and Classroom Practice

The materials which Froebel designed as vehicles for promoting children's intuitive understanding of universal first principles consisted of ten "gifts" and an associated set of exercises that became known as the "occupations." The gifts were all made of natural materials (chiefly wood), carefully constructed in exact mathematical relation to one another. The first gift was a set of six worsted colored balls that could be suspended from string and thus moved in many different ways. The second gift was a wooden sphere, cube, and cylinder, likewise able to be suspended and variously manipulated. The third through sixth gifts consisted of increasingly complex one-inch cubes, fractions of cubes, and oblongs that could be fitted together precisely to form larger cubes. The seventh and eighth gifts moved from solids to surfaces with wooden squares and triangles, splints, and metal rings. The ninth gift progressed to points with manipulation of seeds, beans, and pebbles; while the tenth used softened peas or pellets of wax with straw to reconstruct surfaces and solids from the point (Weber, 1969).

The occupations, in contrast, were "handwork" activities—clay modeling, cardboard work, woodcarving, paper folding and cutting, parquetry, painting, interlacing, weaving, embroidery, drawing, bead stringing, and paper perforating (Weber, 1969).

Under the teacher's careful direction, children moved through the sequence of gifts, spending many days or even weeks examining all the possibilities of one before going on to the next. Work with the occupations completed study of the gifts, giving the children concrete examples of how the relationships they had sensed in the relatively fixed gifts could be translated into construction using malleable materials (Weber, 1969).

Children came to kindergarten for two to three hours each day. A typical work plan included an initial meeting of the whole class in a circle for introduction of the morning's work, songs and finger plays, guided use of a selected gift, time outside for care of the school garden and pets and for playing circle games, and work on an occupation, usually resulting in a product that could be taken home (Weber, 1969).

Interactions of all types in the course of the morning were highly teacher oriented. Much of the teachers' talk was designed to make explicit the principles contained in the gifts and occupations, such as the appearance of unbroken unities, wholeness formed from parts, the relationship of one gift or occupation to another, and the discovery of the nature of a material through examination of opposites. Grasp of the inner harmony of the materials, games, and songs was thought to develop the children's own sense of balance in all aspects of their lives (Downs, 1978).

Issues and Problems Affecting the Program

Froebel had a charismatic personality as well as an educational system of great aesthetic appeal and power. Consequently, many disciples continued his work after his death. In 1861 his teacher-training institute (closed in 1852 by the government of the principality due to charges of subversive political activity) reopened, and a stream of educators came from various parts of Europe and the United States to learn the method. In England, the Froebel Society sponsored kindergartens established by Bertha Ronge, Adele von Portugall, and Eleanor Heerwort (Woodham-Smith, 1969), Henriette Breyman in Switzerland, Uno Cygnaeus in Finland, and Otto Salomon in Sweden disseminated the system through private organizations or government-sponsored schools; and Baroness Bertha von Marenholtz Bulow-Wendhausen lectured on the kindergarten in Germany, England, France, Italy, and the Netherlands (Gutek, 1972).

In the United States, Elizabeth Peabody, Caroline Luis Frankenburg, Kate Douglas Wiggin, John Kraus and his wife Maria Boelte-Kraus, and Susan Blow were among the many enthusiastic workers who established kindergartens and developed institutes for the training of "kindergarteners" (i.e., kindergarten teachers) (Weber, 1969).

Originally the kindergarten had been designed for the children of the middle-class parents who were Froebel's patrons. As the century moved to a close, however, and educators became more conscious of the need to serve children of less affluent social classes, many Froebelian kindergartens were established as agencies for social reform, often in conjunction with other social services offered by settlement houses (Weber 1969).

National school systems began to institutionalize the kindergarten, and a teacher preparation network was established. The once innovative and "revolutionary" program became a new form of orthodoxy and began to suffer from a growing rigidity and sterility. The influences of modern science started to detach teachers from the mystical theory that had grounded their practice, and meaningless repetitions of formulae moved a new generation of early childhood educators to reconsider the relevance of "outdated" symbolism to children destined to become citizens of growing democracies (Braun and Edwards, 1972).

At the turn of the century, the Froebelian system was challenged by the new "progressives" who believed that curricula for young children should reflect the materials and experiences of their daily lives. At the same time, a growing "child study" movement was urging the freeing of children from "excessive" teacher direction, so that they might have greater scope for the development of their own sense of initiative (Weber, 1969).

By 1920 the confluence of the progressive and the child study movements served to eliminate the purely Froebelian kindergarten from the educational scene. Those programs that remained adapted to the new vision, dis-

carding many of the traditional gifts and occupations and the strict sequence of their use. Teacher behaviors also changed, moving from teacher initiation to teacher observation and facilitation of child-initiated work. Still, vestiges of the Froebelian method have remained in some of the materials that children today continue to find appealing—cube blocks and parquetry, painting, clay work, sewing cards, paper weaving, "tinker toys," and drawing; as well as in many of the songs, finger plays, and circle games so common to present-day early childhood classrooms (Weber, 1969). (See also **Blow, Susan; Froebel, Friedrich Wilhelm; and Peabody, Elizabeth.**)

References

Braun, S. J., & Edwards, E. P. (1972). *History and theory of early childhood education.* Worthington, OH: Jones.

Downs, R.B. (1978). *Friedrich Froebel.* Boston, MA: Twayne.

Froebel, F. W. A. (1887). *The education of man.* (Translated by W. N. Hailmann). New York: Appleton.

Froebel, F. W. A. (1895). *Education by development: The second part of the pedagogics of the kindergarten.* (Translated by J. Jarvis). New York: Appleton.

Gutek, G. L. (1972). *A history of the western educational experience.* New York: Random House.

Weber, E. (1969). *The kindergarten: Its encounter with educational thought in America.* New York: Teachers College Press.

Woodham-Smith, P. (1969). The origin of the kindergarten. History of the Froebel movement in England. In E. L. Lawrence (ed.). (1969). *Froebel and English education: Perspectives on the founder of the kindergarten* (pp. 15–33 and 34–94). New York: Schocken Books.

L. R. Williams

*Reprinted from the *International Encyclopedia of Education* with permission of Pergamon Press, Ltd., Headington Hill Hall, Oxford OX3 OBW, England.

Laboratory Schools

Laboratory schools for teacher training focused on the early childhood years were established in the United States first in the form of practice schools associated with Froebelian teacher training institutions. The first such practice school was established by Matilde Kriege in Boston in 1868. Other schools soon followed in New York (1872, John Kraus and Maria Kraus-Boelte), Washington (1872, Emma Marwedel), and Milwaukee (1873, William and Eudora Hailmann).

In a parallel system, teacher training laboratory schools for African-American kindergarten teachers were established at the Hampton Institute in 1893, and at Tuskegee Institute by the turn of the century. Atlanta University made use of kindergartens in Atlanta for practice teaching experiences. Howard University awarded 13 kindergarten diplomas in 1902. Most of these institutions were oriented toward the Froebelian system, although some (for example, Hampton and Tuskegee) incorporated elements of Montessori's practical life" concerns, parent programs, and infant child-rearing practices.

In the early part of the twentieth century, the rapid growth of the child study movement encouraged philanthropists to establish a system of research institutes and laboratory nursery schools associated with schools of higher education throughout the country. These schools were designed to combine three functions, namely, teaching, research, and service. Among the first of these were the Institute of Child Welfare Research and the Manhattanville Day Nursery, directed by Patty Smith Hill, both in New York City; the Institute of Child Welfare at the University of Minnesota in Minneapolis; the Iowa Child Welfare Research Station at the State University of Iowa in Iowa City; the Merrill Palmer Institute, directed by Edna Noble White, in Detroit; and the Institute of Psychology, directed by Arnold Gesell, at Yale University in New Haven, Connecticut.

A second wave included at the University Elementary School at UCLA, directed by Barbara Greenwood, and the establishment of nursery schools in connection with home economics departments at the University of Georgia, Purdue University, Kansas State University, the University of Nebraska, the University of Cincinnati, Oklahoma A. and M. at Stillwater, Oregon State University at Corvallis, Iowa State University at Ames, Ohio State University, and Cornell University. Soon afterward, women's liberal arts colleges joined the ranks with laboratory nursery schools at Vassar, Mills, Smith, Wellesley, Stephens, and Antioch.

Again in a parallel movement, the first two African-American laboratory nursery schools were opened in 1929 and 1930, respectively. These were the nursery school directed by Phyllis Jones Tilly within the School of Home Economics at Hampton, and the nursery school directed by Pearlie Reed at Spelman College. Bennett College followed their lead in 1931.

Unlike the earlier Froebelian teacher training laboratory schools, the research institutes and the laboratory nursery schools focused on child growth and development, rather than on educational theory and tradition, to set the parameters of program design. They made use of the principles of the progressive movement and considered themselves scientific in their incorporation of the most currently available information on the ways young children learn. They also actively involved parents in their programs and sought ways to strengthen families as the primary educators of young children. (See also Section 2.3, **Froebelian Kindergarten, The; Montessori Method, The;** and Chapter 3, Section 3.4, **Nursery School [Prekindergarten].**)

References

Cunningham, C. E., & Osborn, D. K. (1979). A historical examination of blacks in early childhood educaiton. *Young Children 34* (3), pp. 20–29.

Johnson, H. (1972). *Children in the nursery school.* New York: Schocken. (Originally published 1928).

Osborn, D. K. (1991). *Early childhood education in historical perspective.* (3rd edition). Athens, GA: The Daye Press.

Snyder, A. (1972). *Dauntless women in childhood education, 1856–1931.* Washington, DC: Association for Childhood Education International.

L. R. Williams

McMillan Nursery School, The

The McMillan Nursery School originated at the turn of the century in Britain through the efforts of two remarkable sisters, Margaret and Rachel McMillan. The McMillans were Christian Socialists who responded to the desperate situation of women and children who were being exploited by the demands of industrialization.

Margaret McMillan in particular became an outspoken advocate for children, drawing the attention of a nation to the lack of labor regulation and abysmal health conditions that kept many British children from attending school. Margaret managed election to the Bradford (England) School Board at the age of 33, and through that agency worked to make medical examinations and treatment available to school children (Braun & Edwards, 1972).

The speed with which children became reinfected in their unsanitary homes after being treated, however, led the McMillans to see that additional steps were necessary. They first established an open air camp school for boys, and then one for girls. Shortly before the outbreak of World War I, Rachel and Margaret turned their attention to younger children and established the Deptford Open Air Nursery that became synonymous with their name. The program expanded rapidly during the war years as a nursery school for the children of mothers working in munitions factories. In spite of the premature and deeply felt death of Rachel in 1917, Margaret continued to run the school; and in 1919, the school was officially recognized by the British government for its excellence (McMillan, 1919).

The school became a center of educational activity, disseminating the McMillans' educational theory and practice, and preparing teachers until Margaret's death in 1931. She lived to see the institution of the Rachel McMillan Training College for Nursery School Teachers in 1930, and her publications (notably, *Early Childhood* [1900], *Education Through the Imagination* [1903], and *The Nursery School* [1919]) continued to influence nursery school practice for decades.

Margaret McMillan felt that the education of young children must stem from their "sense of wonder." The teacher must know what attracts and absorbs the child's spontaneous attention, so that concentration becomes voluntary. The teacher's first efforts should be directed toward nurturing children's emotional life and development of their imaginations. The McMillans' program for young children focused on many opportunities for play, movement, nutritious food and rest, music, dancing, use of language, and storytelling. Whenever the weather permitted, they had the children do as many activities as possible outdoors, as they believed that this was the most healthful setting for growing children.

The legacy of the McMillans was evident in the work of those who followed them, notably Susan Isaacs and other proponents of "open education." Their integration of health with educational services became a model for such latter-day efforts as Project Head Start; and the designation of "nursery school" that they chose to characterize their work has been adopted almost universally to describe early childhood programs focusing on the social and emotional development of three- and four-year-olds. (See also **McMillan, Margaret and Rachel**.)

References

Braun, S. J., & Edwards, E. P. (1972). *History and theory of early childhood education*. Belmont, CA: Wadsworth.

Fowler, W. (1983). *Potentials of childhood*. (Vol. 1). Lexington, MA: D.C. Heath.

McMillan, M. (1900). *Early childhood*. London: The Gresham Press.

McMillan, M. (1903). *Education through the imagination*. London: The Gresham Press.

McMillan, M. (1919). *The nursery school*. New York: E. O. Dutton.

L. R. Williams

Montessori Method, The

The Montessori Method began in Italy's State Orthophrenic School for the "mentally deficient" in 1898. (It should be noted that intelligence tests were not yet in use, and the exact nature of these children's "deficiency" is not presently known.) Using the methods of French physicians Jean-Marc-Gaspard Itard and Édouard Séguin, Maria Montessori (also a physician) developed didactic materials for children that relied heavily on sensory experiences. Even though they had been identified as "feeble minded," the children were able to pass Italy's State National Examination after having worked with Montessori's materials.

Montessori broadened her own medical background by studying experimental psychology and pedagogical anthropology at the University of Rome. She utilized her theoretical and practical ideas to begin her work in 1906, in the model tenements built for the low-income residents of the San Lorenzo district of Rome.

In 1907 Montessori opened the "Casa dei Bambini," or "Children's House," in San Lorenzo, a setting that featured an innovative prepared environment specifically adapted for children rather than adults. All furniture was child sized, light, and of a light color, in order to make washing and otherwise handling it easy for the children. The children were grouped in a family style or vertical grouping, with children from three to seven years in the same room.

Montessori designed her program with several predetermined principles in mind. One of these came from the German psychologist Wilhelm Wundt's child observations. She used Wundt's technique to study the children and to individualize programs for them within the prepared environment. This observation required a "neutral character of the adults." In the environment the children "were left pretty much to their own resources" as they worked with the special materials (Montessori, 1966, p. 167).

She began her experiment by equipping the classroom with a little bit of everything and allowing the children to choose for themselves what they wished. She noted which equipment they selected and which they did not use. The latter was eliminated from the environment. Initially the material was kept

out of reach of the children until the directress (Montessori's term for teacher) distributed it. Gradually the children demonstrated a sense of care for the materials. At that point she added open cabinets (now indispensable to any Montessori school), and the directress permitted the children to get their own materials. Many of the original materials for the "feeble minded" were either eliminated or adapted to "normal" children by providing "auto-education" or self-correction in the materials themselves (Montessori, 1964, p. 169).

Montessori emphasized sensitive periods in children's development. She called the period from birth to three years old the "unconscious absorbent mind." This is the period in which children take in everything from their environment. From three to seven years old was termed the "conscious absorbent mind," when children made order out of acquired information. The children refined their language in this process of ordering. In recognition of these periods, Montessori divided her method into three parts: Motor Education, Sensory Education, and Language.

Montessori noted, "The care and management of the environment itself afford the principal means of motor education, while sensory education and the education of language [are] provided by my didactic material" (Montessori, 1965, p. 50). The materials consist of a wide variety of objects for the training of the senses, including materials for the preparation of writing and arithmetic. In general, the directress presents the didactic materials in a predetermined order that is more important, according to Montessori, than the actual content. The order is the following:

1. Recognition of identities.
2. Recognition of contrasts.
3. Discrimination between objects very similar to one another (Montessori, 1965).

Montessori based the Method on the premise that the control of error "lies in the material itself, and the child has concrete evidence of it" (Montessori, 1965, p. 71). The child recognizes his or her own errors and is able to correct them. The goal is for the child to learn to observe, make comparisons, form judgments, and to reason and decide. The success of the Method is dependent on little intervention from the directress. She must wait while observing.

Montessori believed a child's work is his or her play. She also eliminated rewards and punishments. She believed that children desired an inner sense of accomplishment, rather than external prizes. The "exercise of silence," now an integral part of the Montessori classroom, developed from a practical experience. Montessori once brought a four-month-old baby into the classroom. She remarked to the class that they could not breathe as silently as the child. The children became enthralled with the silence. She later created a lesson in which she called the children individually, and they came to her as quietly as possible so as not to disturb the silence.

Montessori added writing and reading to her Method when the children demanded to be taught how to write and read. There are specific materials to prepare the hand for writing, and sandpaper and movable letters to develop phonetic associations.

The Method, however, moves beyond the didactic materials to areas of prime importance. Respect for the child and the child's privacy is a key component of Montessori's beliefs. Individuality, too, is important. "Children reach the goal of self-fulfillment and self-control by different roads, indirectly, prepared by the perceptive adult" (Rambush in Montessori, 1965, p. 18).

Liberty or freedom (terms Montessori uses interchangeably) is another major element of her Method. Montessori observed that the child is seeking to expand his/her own personality, has initiative, is able to choose his/her own work, persists in it, changes it to meet individual needs and seeks to overcome obstacles to success. She further noted that "It is the teacher who calls into being that liberty . . . the birth-right of every child. It is the teacher who frees the child to learn. Freeing a child to learn through his own efforts is a true

beginning and end of early education" (Rambusch in Montessori, 1965, pp. 25–26). (See also **Montessori, Maria**, and **Séguin, Édouard**.)

References

Montessori, M. (1948). *The discovery of the child.* Adyar, Madras, India: Kalakshetra Publications.

Montessori, M. (1964). *The Montessori method.* New York: Schocken Books.

Montessori, M. (1965). *Dr. Montessori's own handbook.* New York: Schocken Books.

Montessori, M. (1965). *Spontaneous activity in education.* New York: Schocken Books.

Montessori, M. (1966). *The secret of childhood.* Notre Dame, IN: Fides Publishers.

Montessori, M. (1967). *The absorbent mind.* Adyar, Madras, India: Kalekshetra Publications.

P. Povell

Parent Education, History of

The earliest record of group meetings of parents in America dates back to 1815 in Portland, Maine (Croake and Glover, 1977). These were study groups called maternal associations that met to talk about their children's moral and religious development.

One commentator considers the work of G. Stanley Hall and the child study movement of the 1880s to be the genesis of what is now called parent education (Schlossman, 1976). Hall, the president of Clark University and a prominent psychologist, instituted the study of child development in the university. He also was influential in creating the agenda for a large meeting in 1897, which was to form the National Congress of Mothers, subsequently known as the Parent-Teacher Association.

Soon after, the federal government gave support to parent education through the first White House Conference on Children (1909), the opening of the Children's Bureau in 1912, the funding of a large number of county demonstration agents in 1914, and parenting programs focused on health issues offered by the U.S. Public Health Service. During this progressive era, parent education was seen as a means to reform policies that affected children and families, such as child labor laws and housing codes.

In the 1920s the constituency and the focus of parent education shifted. Programs dropped advocacy and social reform and focused on middle-class women seeking advice on child rearing. The emphasis changed from adolescence to preschool children, and the nursery school became increasingly important in offering parent education. Psychologists, educators, psychiatrists, and sociologists joined lay supporters of parent education. The Child Study Association led the movement and created the first university course on parent education, given at Teachers College, Columbia University, in 1925.

Interest in parent education declined in the 1930s and 1940s but revived in the early 1950s in both the public and private sectors. This was stimulated by research on the significance of the early childhood years and the role of parents in facilitating children's development. Parent education was given an enormous impetus by the Head Start program beginning in 1965, a movement that broadened the constituency for parent education by focusing on low-income parents.

There was a major proliferation of parent education programs in the 1970s and 1980s, perhaps due to increased mobility, divorce, teenaged pregnancy, and the number of women in the work force. Parents of all socioeconomic levels now seek help in the rearing of their children. Many sources, including hospitals, religious institutions, community groups, social service agencies, and corporations, generate and fund programs geared to a wide range of participants. (See also Chapter 4, Section 4.2, **Hall, G. Stanley;** and Chapter 6, Section 6.8, **Parent Education in the United States, Emergence of.**)

References

Croake, J. W., & Glover, K. E. (1977, April). A history and evaluation of parent education. *The Family Coordinator, 26* (2), pp. 151–158.

Powell, D. R. (1986, March). Parent education and support programs. *Young Children, 41* (3), pp. 47–53.

Schlossman, S. L. A. (1976). Before Head Start: Notes towards a history of parent education in America, 1897–1929. *Harvard Educational Review, 46* (3), pp. 436–467.

S. H. Ginsberg

Progressive Movement, The

Although John Dewey's name is most frequently associated with the progressive movement in the United States, he was not the movement's originator. The movement itself dated back to the late eighteenth century with the influence of such thinkers as Rousseau and Pestalozzi on conceptions of education. Initiatives toward reform in education were joined in the nineteenth century by social reform movements seeking to better the human condition through application of science and reason.

In the United States, the movement began gaining strength in the 1880s through the confluence of political, social, judicial, and journalistic attention to the effects of monopoly and corruption on the quality of life. Reformers viewed the old ways as being in a state of decay and urged "progress" toward a new vision, a "progressive" society where each individual could develop his or her fullest potential.

Educational progressivism received a push forward through the work of the journalist Joseph Mayer Rice in 1892. Rice traveled throughout the country reporting on the state of the nation's schools and was appalled by the sterility and rigidity of the instruction he encountered in many classrooms. His vivid newspaper accounts of the worst in American education lent support to the critique of existing educational systems arising from such disparate sources as Sigmund Freud's psychoanalytic psychology, John Dewey's pragmatic philosophy, and Jane Addams's social vision.

Essentially the critics charged that schools had ignored the total development of the child in favor of nurturing the intellect alone, thus denying a significant portion of human experience. Further, they postulated that the true beginning of instruction lay in direct experience with the environment, and that learners should be seen as having individual differences in part reflective of their experience.

The implications of these understandings were that (1) the "whole child" was the proper subject of education, and (2) the curriculum should originate through observation and study of children's interests and needs, rather than through analysis of subject matter. The teacher's role should change from that of disseminator of information to facilitator or guide to the children's learning. Correlates of these principles were to encourage cooperation rather than competition in the classroom as most facilitative of children's learning, and to urge home/school cooperation to further the child's overall development.

John Dewey became deeply involved in this line of thought first at the University of Chicago and then at Teachers College, Columbia University, and soon became a major spokesman for the movement. At the same time G. Stanley Hall at Clark University was beginning the child study movement that examined the development of young children through observation of their interaction in nursery school classes. Edward Thorndike at Teachers College added another prong to the movement by applying science to definitions of intelligence and achievement.

By the turn of the century, the kindergarten movement in the United States that had been almost exclusively derived from Froebel's idealistic and mystical educational system, came under progressive attack. At the same time, a new movement toward nursery education, inspired by the work of the McMillan sisters in England, was gaining popularity in the United States. A new generation of kindergarten and nursery school teachers was being prepared in progressive courses of study with Dewey, Hall, Kilpatrick, and their followers. The last Froebelian teacher training institution in the United States closed in 1918, effectively leaving the field of early childhood education and child care in the hands of progressive educators.

From the 1920s through the mid-1950s, progressivism was the strongest movement in early education, child care, and parent education. There were developments that did not subscribe to its principles, such as the continuation of the day nurseries founded for custodial care of the children of working parents. In most settings for young children where learning was understood to be taking place, however, the progressive vision dominated the thinking of educational innovators.

By the late 1950s, the engagement of the United States in the Cold War with the Soviet Union created a feeling of crisis in American education. Educational critics of the period saw progressivism as having weakened the curriculum and urged a return to the "rigor" of study of disciplines. In programs for young children, this shift meant intensified attention to the acquisition of concepts and skills, often through various forms of direct instruction.

Not all early education and child care programs in the succeeding 25 years abandoned progressive principles, however; and in recent years the "child-centered" approaches of progressivism have joined with awareness of children's developmental sequences in definition of "developmentally appropriate" practice. (See also **Dewey, John.**)

References

Cremin, A. A. (1964). *The transformation of the school: Progressivism in American education, 1876–1957.* New York: Vintage Books.

Gutek, G. L. (1972). *A history of the Western educational experience.* New York: Random House.

Williams, L. R. (1992). Determining the curriculum. In C. Seefeldt (ed.) *The early childhood curriculum: A review of current research*, 2nd. ed. New York: Teachers College Press.

L. R. Williams

Traditional Nursery School, The

(See **McMillan Nursery School, The**; and Chapter 3, Section 3.4, **Early Childhood Settings in the Private Sector, Nursery School.**)

2.4 History of Child Care and Early Childhood Education Legislation

Legislation directed toward the care and education of young children has exerted an increasingly strong influence on the field over the past 80 years. Passage of such legislation often has required protracted struggles with public perceptions and a gradual shift of those perceptions toward acceptance of public responsibility for the well being of young children. Some advocates of young children in the United States argue that the country as a whole is a long way from offering the kinds of support and protection of children that are actually needed, given the radically changing social and physical environments of the present day. The article below chronicles the development of legislation on child care and early education from its inception in this country to its current status, with commentary on some of the trends that have influenced its direction.

L. R. Williams

Federal Legislation of Importance to Early Childhood Education: A Chronology

The federal government formalized its involvement with programs affecting children in 1912 with the formation of the Children's Bureau. In 1989, there were 93 programs operated by 13 federal agencies that provide services to children (early childhood and beyond) and their families (Garwood, Phillips, Hartman, & Zigler, 1989). Of these, at least 22 programs provide some form of child care assistance (Robins, 1988).

The range of federal agencies providing programs and services to children and their families highlights not only the absence of a centralized, coordinating agency for children's programs, but also the diversity of needs and services that fall within the purview of early childhood education. Perhaps it is because of the diversity of programs and the fragmentation of responsibility, that no single, comprehensive source of federal legislation important to early childhood educators appears to exist.

Consequently, this chronology was compiled from a variety of sources, the most significant of which are listed at the end of this article. As a result, this legislative history represents selected highlights of federal legislation passed on behalf of young children through 1990. It focuses on legislation specific to the care and education, health, and general welfare of young children, plus support services is to their families. Legislation focused on foster care, adoption, child custody, and child protective services is not described unless a part of the legislation also addresses early childhood care and education. The chronology begins with the convening of the first White House Conference on Children, because this event can be viewed as a first symbol of the federal government's formal commitment to involvement in child policy.

Because unsuccessful legislative proposals can also be informative for understanding the history of early childhood education in the United States, those of historical significance also are included. It is noteworthy, for example, that the One Hundredth Congress (1986–1988) considered over 100 pieces of legislation pertaining to child care—none of which passed. This statistic reveals not only the degree of current national interest in the child care issue, but it also exposes the lack of national consensus about how the issue might best be resolved and the role of the federal government in this debate. This uncertainty has been a constant companion of the federal government's involvement in issues related to children and families.

1909 First White House Conference on Children: The Care of Dependent Children, was convened to discuss and marshal support of governmental planning and protection of the nation's children (in effect, the conference was a planning body for creation of the Children's Bureau). The conference has been reconvened every ten years, excepting 1980.

1912 Law creating the U.S. Children's Bureau as part of the U.S. Department of Commerce and Labor signed by President William Taft "to investigate and report upon all matters pertaining to the welfare of children and child life among all classes of our people."

1919 Second White House Conference on Children: Child Welfare Standards, was convened.

1921 Sheppard-Towner Act signed by President Warren Harding created a federal-state program to provide infant and maternal hygiene and welfare programs; its renewal was defeated in 1929.

1922 Passage of the Mother's Pension Act (forerunner to Aid to Families with Dependent Children [AFDC]) to support widowed, divorced, or abandoned mothers so they could attend to parenting.

1925 President Herbert Hoover proposed a children's Bill of Rights arguing that "there shall be no child in America that has not been born under proper conditions."

1930 Third White House Conference on Children: Child Health and Protection, was convened.

1933 President Franklin Roosevelt signed the Federal Emergency Relief Act providing funds for nursery schools and child care programs administered under the Works Progress Administration. The funding was provided primarily to sponsor jobs for unemployed workers as child care providers in programs for "children of needy, unemployed families or neglected or underprivileged homes where preschool-age children [would] benefit from the program offered." Funding ceased at the end of the Depression in 1943.

1935 Title V, Social Security Act of 1935 (known as Title IV-B since 1967) was signed into law by President Roosevelt; provided grants-in-aid for child welfare services, including child care (ADC, later AFDC) and grants for child care research and unemployment compensation.

1938 Passage of a child labor law; the National Child Labor committee was formed to investigate child labor in 1904; the first federal legislative attempt to bar child labor was introduced in 1906.

1940 Fourth White House Conference on Children: Children in a Democracy, was convened.

1942 Lanham Act (the Community Services Act of 1941) was signed into law by President Roosevelt; it supplied federal funding to war-impacted areas to provide child care for children whose parents were employed in wartime industries during WWII. Funding ceased shortly after the war's end in 1946. At its peak, 1.6 million children were enrolled in over 3,000 centers. The Act represented one of the first cooperative arrangements between the federal and state governments in child care.

1946 National School Lunch Act is signed by President Harry Truman, providing food for licensed child care facilities (Child Care Food Program).

1950 Fifth White House Conference on Children: The Midcentury, was convened.

1954 President Dwight Eisenhower signed amendments allowing tax deductions for work-related child care expenses from gross income.

1960 Sixth White House Conference on Children: The Golden Anniversary of Children and Youth, was convened.

1961 President John Kennedy signed a law (Title IV-A, Social Security Act Amendments of 1962) creating the AFDC–Unemployed Parent Program for two-parent families, which provided work-expense benefits for child care.

1962 The Child Welfare Services Program (Title V, Social Security Act Amendments of 1962 [known as Title IV-B since 1967]) was passed to help state public welfare agencies improve their child welfare services; the Child Welfare Training Program, which is part of the same program, provides funds for training child care workers.

1964 Passage of the Food Stamp Act, which also subsidizes work-expense benefits for child care.

1964 President Lyndon Johnson signed the Economic Opportunity Act, which led to the creation of Head Start (initially developed as part of the Community Action Programs, with an emphasis on parents as activists), Job Corps, and other educational and occupational training programs for children from families living within the poverty guidelines.

1965 Area Economic and Human Resource Development Program (Appalachian Regional Development Act) was created. It provided child care services for children living within the poverty guidelines in the Appalachian region. The act expired in Fiscal Year (FY) 82. Program extension has occurred through appropriations legislation.

1965 President Johnson signed the Medicare and Medicaid law authorizing the Early and Periodic Screening, Diagnosis and Treatment program.

1965 The Elementary and Secondary Education Act was passed, which provided funding for school programs, including compensatory preschool education (formerly Title I, now Chapter I) for children living in low-income families.

1966 Enactment of the Child Nutrition Act of 1966 (P.L. 89-642), which supported the School Breakfast Program and the Special Milk Program to address the needs of working mothers in areas with a significant number of low-income children (the precursor to the Child Care Food Program).

1967 Work Incentive Program (WIN; Title IV-C, Social Security Act Amendments) extended federal funding for child care to low-income families in jobs or in job training; participation was required as a condition of eligibility for AFDC benefits except for mothers with children under the age of six.

1967 Funding was authorized for Follow Through programs that were initiated to extend Head Start's efforts into kindergarten and the primary grades.

1968 Federal Interagency Day Care Regulations (FIDCR) issued, specifying strict staff-child care ratios and other requirements for child care programs receiving federal funding. Enmeshed in political quagmire for 12 years, the regulations were allowed to "die" in 1980.

1968 P.L. 90-302 amended the Child Nutrition Act of 1966 to create Special Food Service Program for Children: the Summer Food Program and the Child Care Food Program.

1969 The Office of Child Development, which incorporated the Children's Bureau, was established; the Bureau was organized to serve as a focal point for children's programs within the federal government; no separate funding was appropriated for program services.

1970 Seventh (and last held) White House Conference on Children and Youth was convened.

1970 Congress passed the Comprehensive Child Care Act, which would have legislated approximately $2 billion to fund comprehensive child development services.

1971 President Richard Nixon vetoed the Comprehensive Child Care Act stating that the legislation "would commit the vast moral authority of the national government to the side of communal approaches to child rearing over and against the family centered approach."

1972 Passage of the Special Supplemental Food Program for Women, Infants, and Children (WIC). The program is designed to provide food supplements to pregnant women, lactating mothers, infants, and preschool children who are diagnosed by health clinics to be nutritionally "at risk."

1973 Revision of the Internal Revenue Code allowed tax deductions for businesses providing child care services. Revision recognized child care as a legitimate business expense.

1974 Amendments to the Social Security Act (Social Security Amendments of 1974) created Title XX (Social Services Block Grant since 1981), which provided funding to the states, based on population, to provide social services, including "child care services, protective services for children, services for children in foster care, services related to the management and maintenance of the home, and appropriate combinations of services designed to meet the special needs of children" who fall within the poverty guidelines.

1974 Community Development Block Grant (Title I), which is a part of the Housing and Community Development Act, subsidizes the cost of child care services to families living in public housing projects.

1975 The Child and Family Services Act, with which Senator Walter Mondale attempted to create a comprehensive program of children's service, is overwhelmingly defeated by conservative opposition.

1975 President Nixon signed the Education of the Handicapped Act (P.L. 94-142) guaranteeing school-age children with handicapping conditions "free and appropriate education" and providing direct service funds for children as young as three years.

1975 The Child Nutrition Amendments of 1975 (P.L. 94-105) permanently authorized the Child Care Food Program that provides financial reimbursements for the meals served in home and center child care.

1976 Public Law 94-401 amended sections of Title XX; it waived the Federal Interagency Day Care Regulations (FIDCR), permitted the use of group eligibility for services, and provided a tax incentive for the hiring of mothers on welfare in child care centers.

1976 Enactment of the Child and Dependent Care Tax credit, which was part of the Tax Reform Act of 1976 (Section 21, Internal Revenue Code), provides tax benefits for families using child care. It extended benefits to upper-income families and eliminated the prerequisite that families itemize deductions on their tax returns.

1978 Indian Child Welfare Act was enacted (Title II, Indian Child Welfare Act of 1978). It subsidizes child care services to Native Americans as well as child custody, foster care, and adoption assistance.

1980 FY 1980 Appropriations Bill delayed implementation of the Federal Interagency Day Care Regulations (FIDCR) for one year.

1980 Theme of White House Conference on Children and Youth expanded to include families. Following debate on the definition of family at state and regional meetings, the national conference was not held.

1981 Dependent Care Assistance Programs (Section 129, Internal Revenue Code) expanded tax benefits for child care and created a sliding fee scale.

1981 Revision to the Internal Revenue Code by the Economic Recovery Tax Act of 1981 makes business-provided child care centers eligible for accelerated depreciation.

1981 The Omnibus Budget Reconciliation Act enacted by the Ronald Reagan administration restructured support for many children's programs, including Medicaid, AFDC, Title XX social services, child nutrition programs, and education programs, by restrictions in eligibility criteria or service coverage. The Community Services Block Grant, which is part of the Omnibus Budget Reconciliation Act, amended Title XX to create the Title XX Block Grant. As a result, federal funding for the Title XX was cut by 20%, increases scheduled for future years were cancelled, $75 million earmarked for training for social service providers was cancelled, $200 million targeted for child care was eliminated, the Child Care Food Program's funding was cut by one third, and the Federal Interagency Child Care Regulations were abolished.

1981 The Omnibus Budget Reconciliation Act of 1981 reauthorized Head Start (Head Start Act of 1981).

1982 The Dislocated Workers Program, a title of the Job Training Partnership Act, permits funding for child care services for dislocated workers in need.

1983 A temporary increase of $225 million is given to Title XX as part of an emergency jobs bill (P.L. 98-8).

1984 Head Start is reauthorized with provisions to ensure the delivery of comprehensive services. Authorization for grants to the states for school-age child care and Resource and Referral programs is enacted.

1985 FY 1986 appropriations bill provides a permanent $225 million increase to Title XX; $25 million is appropriated for training child care workers.

1986 The Child Development Associate Scholarship Program, part of the Human Services Reauthorization Act, authorized scholarships to candidates for the Child Development Associate credential. Dependent Care Planning and Development, also part of the Human Services Reauthorization Act, reauthorized grants to the states for school-age child care and Resource and Referral programs. Head Start reauthorized.

1986 Passage of the Education of the Handicapped Act Amendments (P.L. 99-457) directed the states to provide "free and appropriate education" for all children three through five years of age with handicapping conditions; also provided incentive funds for states to provide family-centered programs for infants and toddlers with handicapping conditions.

1986 P.L. 99-591 allowed an additional three cents reimbursement per child for breakfast programs in child care homes and centers.

1986 The Higher Education Act authorized $10 million for child care for low-income college students.

1988 The Hunger Prevention Act, beginning in July 1989, allocated an additional three cents per child in center and home child care breakfast programs; for child care centers only, federal reimbursement was allowed for an additional meal or snack.

1988 Passage of the Elementary and Secondary School Improvement Amendments of 1988 created Even Start, a joint parent-child education program aimed at improving adult literacy and offering early childhood education to children between one and seven years of age; also officially extended the Chapter 1 migrant education program to include three- and four-year-olds.

1988 Passage of the Family Support Act (welfare reform legislation), which provides child care financial support for parents who are required to participate in job training or education, including training as a child care provider; "transitional" child care assistance provided for mothers whose income makes them ineligible for welfare payments.

1990 Passage of the Family and Medical Leave Act, which would entitle employees in firms with greater than 50 employees to take up to 12 weeks total per year for any combination of medical and family leave for the birth, adoption, or serious illness of a child, spouse or parent, and to recover from an employee's own serious health condition. The bill was vetoed by President George Bush; Congress failed to override the veto.

1990 Passage of federal child care legislation, "Child Care and Development Block Grant," as part of the Omnibus Budget Reconciliation Act. First introduced as the the Act for Better Child Care in 1987, advocacy efforts spawned a national network of early childhood advocates and succeeded in thwarting a threatened veto by President Bush. The bill is the first successful attempt, since the Comprehensive Child Care Act was vetoed by President Nixon in 1970, to construct a comprehensive federal child care policy that addresses the availability and affordability of quality child care. Funds help subsidize the cost of child care for low-income families, ensure additional income support through new and expanded tax credits, and begin to address the issue of quality, including staff compensation.

1990 Passage of "The Augustus F. Hawkins Human Services Reauthorization Act of 1990" reauthorized Head Start, Follow Through, the Community Services Block Grant, and the CDA Scholarship Assistance Act. The Head Start reauthorization set aside 10 percent of the total funding for quality improvements, including staff compensation; it also set goals to ensure that all eligible, low-income children receive services by 1994. Congress also passed a resolution to permit each Head Start program to provide full-day, full-year services to eligible children in families who have full-time work, education, or training responsibilities.

1990 Passage of the Claude Pepper Young Americans Act; provides the monies to states for increasing awareness of the value and needs of young children and of the extent to which services currently are provided and/or needed; established a Federal Council on Children, Youth, and Families to advise the President and Congress on matters related to the special needs of young Americans; and authorized (without appropriations) White House Conference on Young Americans to be held in 1993, for the purpose of, among other things, arriving at a statement of a comprehensive, coherent, national policy on children, youth, and families.

The history of federal involvement in child policy is a history of changing perceptions of childhood and the impact of changing social and economic contexts on child and family policies. It is also a story about the constancy and tensions among assumptions and beliefs about the kinds of relationships that should exist among families, children, and various levels of government.

A focus on the period of childhood as an issue of social concern is little more than 100 years old. It is linked to the conceptualization of childhood as a distinctive, developmental phase of special vulnerability, and to dramatic social and economic changes in society (Pence, 1987; Ross, 1982; Takanishi, 1978; Zelizer, 1985).

Before the 1850s, governments at any level played a minor role in responding to the needs of children and their families. Services to needy children and families were primarily the responsibility of religious organizations and private philanthropic groups (Abner, 1983; Grubb & Lazerson, 1988; Pence, 1987).

Economic and social changes during the second half of the nineteenth century, however, transformed families and American society. Urbanization, industrialization, and the arrival of millions of immigrants created social turmoil, separated the world of work from that of the home, and created separate roles and responsibilities for men, women, and children. Home and families changed into havens from the "cruel" world of work; women became symbols of goodness and warmth; childhood became sentimentalized, and children "developed needs" for special nurturing (Grubb & Lazerson, 1988; Kessen, 1979; Pence, 1987; Strickland, 1982; Zelizer, 1985).

At the same time, rapid growth in new scientific knowledge accompanied industrialization. Social reformers argued that this new knowledge could also be applied to understanding children and to solving the problems of society. Together, these changes helped create the context for beliefs and attitudes that continue to influence the debate on child and family policies, a debate that includes such issues as the privacy and self-sufficiency of the family in its child-rearing role, the special vulnerability of children and the importance of their early years, and the need to nurture children in the interests of society's future well-being.

Because of strong beliefs in the self-sufficiency of families, and more recently, confidence in the capability of local communities and private enterprise to meet the needs of the neediest families, some have perceived government involvement, especially at the federal level, as intrusive. When federal support has been made available, it has traditionally been in response to a crisis situation (e.g., the programs of the Works Progress Administration, the Lanham Act), or focused on children and families "in need" rather than the needs of all children (e.g., Head Start, the Education of all Handicapped Children Act). As a result, federal programs have tended to be fragmented, categorical, and crisis oriented (Goffin, 1983).

Furthermore, no one is clearly in charge of early childhood programs. The results of this piecemeal approach to early childhood policy have finally reached a crescendo, and some advocates are demanding responses that address the infrastructural needs of the field (Kagan, 1989; Kahn & Kamerman, 1987).

During the 1980s, the federal government has dramatically decreased its financial support for services and programs to children. These changes are, in part, reflective of a resurgence in attitudes about the family's self-sufficiency and solitary responsibility for child rearing.

There also has been a change in the focus of funding efforts. Federal monies have been moved from the provision of direct services to children (supply subsidies) to indirect assistance (demand subsidies) (Garwood et al., 1989; Robins, 1988). Whereas the funding of direct services, such as Head Start and child care programs under Title XX, tend to benefit poor families, indirect subsidies, such as the tax deduction allowed for dependent care, primarily benefit middle- and upper-income families. "This funding shift constitutes a comprehensive reform in the structure of federal support for children" (Garwood et al., 1989, p. 437).

Early childhood educators are becoming increasingly aware of the impact of federal policies on the lives of children, families, and the early childhood professions. As early childhood advocates, they are becoming more involved in trying to assure that these policies are supportive of families' child-rearing responsibilities and children's development. Passage of federal child care legislation in 1990 was historic in part because it galvanized the early childhood community and symbolized an acknowledgement by the federal government that it does, in fact, have a role in supporting early childhood care and education.

References

(Significant sources for chronology of federal legislation)

Grubb, W. N., & Lazerson, M. W. (1988). *Broken promises: How Americans fail their children* (rev. ed.). Chicago: University of Chicago Press.

Marver, J. S., & Larson, M. A. (1978). Public policy toward child care in America: A historical perspective. In P. K. Robins & S. Weiner (eds.). *Child care and public policy* (pp. 17–42). Lexington, MA: D.C. Heath.

Robins, P. K. (1988, Summer) Federal support for child care: Current policies and a proposed new system. *Focus, 11* (2), 1–9. A newsletter by the Institute for Research on Poverty, University of Wisconsin, Madison, WI.

Zigler, E. F., Kagan, S. L., & Klugman, E. (eds.). (1983). *Children, families, and government: Perspectives on American social policy* (pp. 96–116). New York: Cambridge University Press.

Additional References:

Abner, J. L. (1983). The role of state government in child and family policy. In E. F. Zigler, S.L. Kagen, E. Klugman (eds.), *Children, families, and government: Perspectives on American social policy* (pp. 96–116). New York: Cambridge University Press.

Garwood, S. G., Phillips, D., Harman, A., & Zigler, E. F. (1989). As the pendulum swings: Federal agency programs for children. *American Psychologist, 44* (2), 434–440.

Goffin, S. G. (1983). A framework for conceptualizing children's services. *American Journal of Orthopsychiatry, 53* (2), 282–290.

Kagan, S. L. (1989). Early care and education: Tackling the tough issues. *Phi Delta Kappan, 70* (6), 433–439.

Kahn, A. J., & Kamerman, S. B. (1987). *Child care: Facing the hard choices.* Auburn House.

Kessen, W. (1979). The American child and other cultural inventions. *American Psychologist, 34* (10), 815–820.

Pence, A. R. (1987). Child care's family tree: Toward a history of the child and youth care profession in North America. *Child and Youth Care Quarterly, 16* (2), 151–165.

Ross, C. J. (1982). Of children and liberty: An historian's view. *American Journal of Orthopsychiatry, 52* (2), 470–480.

Strickland, C. E. (1982). Paths not taken: Seminal models of early childhood education in Jacksonian America. In B. Spodek (ed.), *Handbook of research in early childhood education* (pp. 321–334). New York: The Free Press.

Takanishi, R. (1978). Childhood as a social issue: Historical roots of contemporary child advocacy movements. *Journal of Social Issues, 34* (2), 8–28.

Zelizer, V. A. (1985). *Pricing the priceless child: The changing social value of children.* New York: Basic Books.

S. G. Goffin

2.5 Evolution of Unique Early Childhood Curriculum Materials

The materials used in early childhood classrooms vary according to the philosophical orientation and goals of particular programs. In classrooms subscribing to what has been termed "developmentally appropriate practice" (DAP), the materials generally are manipulatives used for construction or for the development of other kinds of thinking skills, malleable materials such as paint, clay and sand, props for sociodramatic play and many types of children's books. Classrooms subscribing to a formal, academic approach also may use workbooks. Descriptions of the present forms of all of these materials are found in Chapter 5.

Blocks and children's literature, however, are two types of early childhood materials that have had unique histories, showing a remarkable degree of development and transformation over time. The articles below review the histories of these materials.

L. R. Williams

Blocks, The Development of, in the United States

The first wooden blocks to be used intentionally as tools for learning were created by Freidrich Wilhelm Froebel (1782–1852), the founder of the kindergarten. These wooden blocks, which he called "gifts," served a central function in realizing Froebel's educational vision and spiritual philosophy. It is the third through sixth gifts from a larger series of gifts and occupations of the Froebelian kindergarten that have served as prototypes for the extensive number and variety of blocks that have been produced since the 1830s. While Froebel experimented with different sized blocks in his educational work (Liebschner, 1975, pp. 225, 229), a standard form evolved over time.

Enclosed in wooden boxes with covers, the third and fourth gifts consisted of two-inch divided wooden cubes. In the former gift, the division produced eight equal smaller cubes; in the latter, the division created eight equal oblongs. In the fifth and sixth gifts the wooden cubes were enlarged to three inches. Triangles were introduced in the fifth gift by adding diagonal cuts to some of the smaller cubes. The division of the sixth gift produced rectangles and two sizes of oblongs. The geometric shapes produced by the vertical, horizontal, and diagonal division of a simple cube were used in a variety of activities on child-sized tables with one-inch grid tops.

In manipulating the divided cubes and experiencing the part-whole relationships of the gifts, the ideals and divine principles central to Froebel's spiritual philosophy would be intuited by the child. Those ideals and principles were unity, diversity, and harmony; the interconnectedness of the universe; and the divine presence that Froebel considered was the essence of all things. In activities that focused on mathematical, representational, and aesthetic forms and knowledge, the child's spiritual, mental and social development would be unfolded and, with guidance, realized (Lilley, 1967).

Froebelian kindergartens were introduced in the United States in 1859, and rapidly gained popularity. In the decades that followed, the influence of societal changes occurring in the United States in the late nineteenth and early twentieth centuries, plus the impact of the child study movement of G. S. Hall and the philosophy of John Dewey, altered profoundly the aims and activities of the Froebelian kindergartens. As educational aims changed, so did the use and appearance of the wooden gifts.

The first change, an enlargement of the blocks, may have been the work of Anna E. Bryan (1858–1901) of Louisville, Kentucky. Such experimentation would have been consonant with her rejection of the rigid, formalized practices of some Froebelians. The enlargement of the blocks moved them from table tops to the floor where children could use their bodies and imagination with greater freedom.

Patty Smith Hill (1868–1946), Bryan's assistant in Louisville, continued experimenting with the size and shape of blocks. In a 1900 article, Hill mentions the dimensions of an enlarged unit block as 6" x 3" x 1 ¹/2". In the 1918 catalogue of the Bureau of Educational Experiments, there is a listing for Hill Floor Blocks as a set of seven shapes based on the 6-inch unit with the longest block 24 inches in length. Continued experimentation altered this original set both in its dimensions and use. Grooved corner pillar blocks were added in heights of 15 inches to 17 inches into which blocks varying in length from 6 inches to 36 inches would fit. The large structures were stabilized through the use of pegs and holes, copper wire rods, and girders. Children entered directly into these large stabilized structures and enacted their roles as family members, postal workers, and customers in the homes, post offices, and restaurants they built. The growing influence of the progressive movement was evident in curriculum content that focused on understanding the interdependent nature of community life. Froebel's symbolism and universal truths gave way to the detail and connections to be found in everyday experience.

The blocks that have proven to be the most enduring in popularity and have become standard equipment in early childhood classrooms are those designed by Caroline Pratt (1867–1954) who founded the City and Country School in New York City in 1914. The 1918 catalogue of the Bureau of Educational Experiments describes the Pratt unit block as 1 ³/8" x 2 ³/4" x 5 ¹/2", measurements that remain to the present. In addition to the basic unit there were half units, triangles, and multiples of the unit with the longest block a length of 22 inches. The 1924 catalogue also lists pillars, cylinders, curves, and switches. In contrast to the Hill Floor Blocks, the smaller sized Pratt blocks evoked a different form of dramatic play, a form encouraged intentionally by Pratt through the accessories she created. These were the "Do Withs," a series of people and animals scaled to the blocks she had designed. Working with blocks and accessories, children symbolically represented and reconstructed their experiences and un-derstanding of self and their social and physical world.

From the mid-1800s to the last decade of the twentieth century, wooden building blocks have continued to be a part of the early childhood curriculum. Like textbooks that are revised periodically, blocks as tools for learning have been changed to match the educational aims and vision of different periods. (See also **Bryan, Anna; Hill, Patty Smith; Froebel, Friedrich Wilhelm; Froebelian Kindergarten, The;** and **Progressive Movement, The;** Chapter 5, sections 5.3 and 5.4, **Blocks.**)

References

Hill, P. S. (March, 1900). A statement of my views of present kindergarten methods and materials. *Kindergarten Magazine, XII,* (7), pp. 406–410.

Hunt, J. L. (1918). *A catalogue of play equipment.* New York: Bureau of Educational Experiments.

Hunt, J. L. (1924). *A catalogue of play equipment* (Third edition, revised). New York: Bureau of Educational Experiments.

Liebschner, H. P. J. (1975). *Freedom and play in Froebel's theory and practice.* University of Leicester, England. Unpublished M. Ed. thesis.

Lilley, I. M. (1967). *Freidrich Froebel: A selection from his writings.* Cambridge: Cambridge University Press.

Pratt, C. (1971/1948). *I learn from children.* New York: Corner-Stone Library.

H.K. Cuffaro

Children's Literature in the United States, Evolution of

Conceptions and definitions of children's literature have fluctuated throughout the centuries. Some view children's literature as those books written specifically for all children, such as Margaret Wise Brown's *Goodnight Moon.* Others perceive children's literature as a special offering to a special child or children, such as Kenneth Grahame's *The Wind in the Willows.* Still others regard children's literature as works, such as Jonathan Swift's *Gulliver's Travels,* that were intended for adults but appropriated by children. A new category has appeared with greater frequency; children's literature created by those who believe that a particular story is best related through children's literature, such as Alice Walker's *To Hell With Dying.* The authors within this newest category are generally associated with adult literature. Regardless of the labels or conceptions, children's literature has become an integral component of childhood and schooling.

The new centrality of literature in the lives of children was achieved after centuries of development, support, and contestation. Debates about appropriateness of content continue to rage today. Other issues—the role of series fiction, the connections between children's books and electronic media, and censorship—appear and reappear throughout the decades. The following sections detail the myriad of changes.

Oral Tradition Roots of Children's Literature

Each culture fosters the development of stories, tales, myths, legends, poetry, ballads, and other verbal creations that are shared and bequeathed to younger and future generations. These created stories ensure that the culture's beliefs, achievements, history, and religion continue to unify the people. Verbal transmission of culture predominated for the majority of people until the 1400s. Adults and children heard the same tales, legends and myths, even though some contained violence, references to lovemaking, and lewd language. Class divisions determined the types of stories available to citizens. The aristocracy had professional bards and minstrels at its command; the peasantry and trade classes told their stories to each other.

The invention of the printing press by the 1400s and the subsequent availability of mechanically printed texts altered storytelling and learning in fundamental ways. Originally available only to the wealthy and clergy, books were precious, rare commodities. The earliest printed materials were written primarily in Latin and featured religious or didactic stories. Some of their exclusivity, however, lessened as mechanically printed texts became more available in Europe. Books written in the vernacular of a particular country or re-

gion appeared as the new technology spread. For example, William Caxton, a major printer in England, published books used with children such as *Caxton's Book of Courtseye, Aesop's Fables, Reynart the Fox,* and *Le Morte d'Arthur. Caxton's Book of Common Courtseye* included the following admonitions: "comb your hair, clean your ears, clean your nose but don't pick it, and do not undo your girdle at the table." The works that he published set a foundational standard that would continue throughout the sixteenth and seventeenth centuries.

As the availability of printing presses grew and opportunities for education increased among the middle class, less expensive children's books, or hornbooks, appeared. The content remained religious, but some included alphabets and other secular materials. More significant changes in content would occur in the seventeenth century. Children's literature published in the United States had its roots in European oral tradition and published literature.

Seventeenth Century: Religion and Didacticism

Tremendous economic, social, and political changes engulfed the empires, feudal states, city states, and nations of the world during the seventeenth century. In religious and political spheres, the influence of the Puritans expanded in England and the American colonies. The Puritans considered children little adults needing rescue and salvation from sin. Many Puritans believed that one way of rescuing children involved eliminating reading materials that were fanciful and nonreligious, that is, literature that featured giants, fairies, and witches.

The number and types of books available to children expanded and improved. Hornbooks, ABCs, primers, and chapbooks augmented children's choices. Books devoted to literacy instruction received the approval of watchful adults if they featured the appropriate religious content. Adults reserved their special ire for chapbooks—crudely printed and illustrated books replete with tales of action, adventure, and lightheartedness. Despite the disapproval of some adults, chapbooks were popular and sold well. Many consider chapbooks the forerunners of comic books.

Books of note published during the period include *Orbis Pictus*, a precursor of today's encyclopedias, *Pilgrim's Progress, Spiritual Milk for Boston Babes*, and the *New England Primer*. Each book continued the fight waged by Puritans for the souls of children. These weighty, somber tomes proved popular. Nearly 3 million copies of *New England Primer* were sold in the United States in a period of 100 years, a remarkable achievement for a nation without universal literacy or primary education. Less somber books made some headway among adults and children, including Charles Perrault's tales, including *Tales of Mother Goose, Cinderella, Sleeping Beauty, Puss in Boots, Little Red Riding Hood,* and *Blue Beard.* Fables written by Jean de la Fontaine engaged children as well. The publication of these books at the end of the century suggested that gaiety might enter into children's books despite the watchful eyes of clerics.

Eighteenth Century: Entertainment and Moralism

Changing attitudes about children, their development, and needs resulted in changing conceptions of childhood. Children were no longer miniature adults but individuals who needed the nurturance, guidance, and help of adults. Their literature reflected these changing mores. Didacticism slipped on a new form; overt religious instruction gave way to guidance in moral development.

In the 1760s, John Newbery garnered acclaim as the publisher in the United States who ushered in the field of children's literature. His first book, *A Little Pretty Pocket*, featured illustrations and highlighted love and fair play, games, fables, rhymes, lessons, and the alphabet. Children began asserting their independence and appropriated books originally intended as adult fare, for example, *Robinson Crusoe* and *Gulliver's Travels.* These books contained elements of fantasy and adventure, and a sense of challenge and accomplishment that appealed to children. Poetry emerged as an important genre. Exemplars

included William Blake's *Songs of Innocence* and *Songs of Experience.* Women writers entered the field with the special purpose of providing models of moral responsibility and development.

A number of factors account for the shift in children's books that would flower in the next century. The number of authors increased. Changes in attitudes about children and childhood prompted beliefs that children needed materials suited to their development. Publishing houses founded in Philadelphia, New York, and Boston increased the selection of books available to greater numbers of people. Children's delight in the adult books they appropriated signalled a need for a similar body of child characters in the literature. The combination of these resulted in a "golden age" of children's literature during the nineteenth century, the Victorian age.

Nineteenth Century: A Golden Age

The Victorian age, evoking images of repressed individuals obsessed with appropriate social and moral behavior, work ethics, religious piety, and correct manners, seems an unlikely and inhospitable century for the nurturance of literature that emphasized humor, fantasy, pleasure, and entertainment.

Lewis Carroll, Robert Louis Stevenson, Clement Moore, the Grimm brothers, Hans Christian Andersen, Louisa May Alcott, Walter Crane, Randolph Caldecott, and Kate Greenaway are a few of the authors and illustrators who provide justification for labelling the period a golden age. Didacticism and moralism continued to pervade the pages of some children's books, for example, in the stories of Maria Edgeworth, Martha Finley's *Elsie Dinsmore* series, Samuel Goodrich's *Peter Parley* series, and Jacob Abbots' *Rollo stories.* Realism, fairy tales, fantasy, and lavishly illustrated texts delighted children for decades, however.

Several trends characterized the century. Fairy and folk tales, given renewed vitality by the Grimm brothers and Hans Christian Andersen, engaged children in ways that would have caused Puritans disapproval. Textbooks became essential curricula material, especially the *McGuffey Readers* and Webster's *Blue Back Speller* with their emphasis on nationalism, morals, and good literature. Women began writing more family stories. Books set outside the United States, for example, *Sara Crewe, The Little Princess, Little Lord Fauntleroy, The Secret Garden, Hans Brinker,* and *Heidi,* informed children of other lands and provided examples of feisty heroes and heroines. Adventure stories such as *Treasure Island* and *The Last of the Mohicans* enabled children to test the limits of home and hearth without leaving either. For those children who needed tales of personal uplift and achievement, the Horatio Alger series provided stories of triumph. As unlikely as it seems, science fiction debuted to enthusiastic reception. *Journey to the Center of the Earth* and *Twenty Thousand Leagues Under the Sea* seem almost contemporary, but they are phenomena of the nineteenth century. Other story types of importance included animal, humorous, and fantasy, *Alice's Adventures in Wonderland* being but one example. Poetry continued its ascendance with Robert Louis Stevenson's *A Child's Garden of Verses.*

While always important, children's magazines and book illustrations reflected new levels of excellence. *The Youth's Companion, The Riverside Magazine,* and *St. Nicholas* were just three examples of the scores of magazines for children. Although they conveyed upper-class sensibilities and values, they managed to appeal to a broad cross section of children with stories, songs, games, puzzles, and information selections. Illustrators Walter Crane and his trademark elaborate borders, Randolph Caldecott with his joyous, carefree scenes, and Kate Greenaway with her gardens of prim and proper children, garnered well-deserved recognition.

Without a doubt, the nineteenth century represented a golden age in children's literature. Future decades would continue the innovations and excellence in writing and illustration.

Twentieth Century: Alternating Stability and Upheaval

Many of the trends that emerged during the nineteenth century continued into the twentieth. Tremendous political and economic upheavels and changes in sociocultural values affected children and their literature. Adults demanded didacticism, education, entertainment, and quality in children's books. Children gravitated to some books that would become classics, but exerted their independence in their selection of series books, pulp fiction, comics, and dime novels early in the century and throughout the decades. Occasionally children and adults agreed upon a book, for instance, Beatrix Potter's *The Tale of Peter Rabbit;* more typically, their selections diverged from adults.

Adults exerted a new kind of influence on children's literature. Dedicated and capable women became children's books editors at major publishing companies. They lobbied for consistent quality in the writing, illustrations, and book production. These editors won acceptance for children's literature in publishing in a manner heretofore unseen. Children's librarians, for the most part women, supported the efforts of the editors to provide children with literature that would affect their lives in meaningful and positive ways. They fought for and won separate children's departments in public libraries staffed by trained, competent, and caring individuals.

Other examples of adult support and critical acclaim is evident in the number of awards and promotions created: the Newbery Medal (1922) for fiction; the Caldecott Medal (1938) for illustrations; Children's Book Week (1919), and the Children's Book Council (1945) heralded a new era of acclaim. In addition, journals devoted to children's literature, the *Horn Book Magazine* (1924), for instance, provided informed criticism and information.

Various expansions of genre and subgenre occurred. Picture books conveyed the innocence, whimsy, curiosity, and uncertainty of childhood in books that appealed to children such as *Millions of Cats,* the Dr. Seuss books, *Where the Wild Things Are,* and *Make Way for*

Ducklings. These books tapped an essential emotional core in many children. Series books' popularity remained constant from the *Bobbsey Twins*, the *Hardy Boys*, and *Nancy Drew* to today's series such as the *Berenstain Bears*, the *Baby-sitters Club*, and *Sweet Valley High.*

Inexpensive literature received another boost from the establishment of Golden Books. Toy books reemerged as popular manipulatives. Books for infants and beginning readers were also important during the latter half of the century. The pairing of children's books with media characters, for example, the Sesame Street characters and movie characters such as the Teenage Mutant Ninja Turtles, proved extremely popular. Few books, however, have equaled the success of the *Where's Waldo* series; but classics such as E. B. White's *Charlotte's Web* remain perennial favorites among children.

Experimentation with form and content in books such as *Dear Mr. Henshaw, The Magical Adventures of Pretty Pearl, Bridge to Terebithia, Up a Road Slowly, Number the Stars,* and *Sarah, Plain and Tall* expanded traditional creative limits. Artistic limits gave way as illustrators such as Chris van Allsburg added elements of fantasy to their works. Information books, notably the works of David McCauley, Millicent Selsam, Patricia Lauber, Milton Meltzer, Johanna Cole, James Haskins, Patricia McKissack, and others, fed children's desires for knowledge. Science fiction and fantasy, for example, *A Wrinkle in Time,* enjoyed even greater popularity. Poetry, too, was revived with the works of Shel Silverstein, Myra Cohn Livingston, David McCord, Jack Prelutsky, Arnold Adoff, Eve Merriam, and Eloise Greenfield.

One significant aspect of publishing was the acceptance of children's literature about minorities or people of color—African, Asian, Hispanic, and Native Americans. Members of these groups had created and published literature in previous decades, even centuries, but that literature, for example, Paul Laurence Dunbar's *Little Brown Baby* published in the nineteenth century and *The Brownies' Book* (1920–1921), were all but ignored in mainstream publishing and reading circles. A few authors, Arna Bontemps and Pura Belpré, for example, acquired some critical acceptance and popularity. Most, however, labored in obscurity.

That obscurity would end in the mid-1960s with the publication of an article by Nancy Larrick entitled "The All-White World of Children's Books" and a book, Ezra Keats's *The Snowy Day.* These efforts, in conjunction to those waged by people of color, such as librarian Augusta Baker and organizations such as the Council on Interracial Books for Children, resulted in a veritable flood of books about minorities. Authors such as Virginia Hamilton, Walter Dean Myers, John Steptoe, Lucille Clifton, Yoshiko Uchida, Laurence Yep, Virginia Driving Hawk Sneve, and Nicholasa Mohr wove fantasies and stories that celebrated the people and cultures portrayed. Despite promising acceptance through the mid-1970s, children's books about people of color fluctuate dramatically in terms of numbers even though quality, in many instances, is exceptional; for example, Hamilton's *M. C. Higgins, the Great* won the Newbery Medal, a National Book Award, and the Boston Globe–Horn Book Award.

Other signs of the importance and prominence of children's literature exist in sales figures and in the number of bookstores devoted exclusively to children's books. Nearly 5,000 children's books were published in 1990. One billion dollars in children's books were sold in 1990; projections are for sales of one and a half billion by mid-decade. The existence of more than 300 bookstores devoted to children and their literature further underscore its value.

Unquestionably, these trends indicate a second golden age that continues through the later stages of the twentieth century. Some cause for concern exists despite the rosy picture. Rising book prices prevent many from enjoying lavishly illustrated and well-written books. Censorship remains a critical problem; Judy Blume is still the most frequently attacked author. Nonetheless, past and current history suggests that children's literature will continue its third, fourth, and more golden ages.

References

The history detailed in this essay is based on information contained in the following.

Field, W. (ed.). (1969). *Horn Book reflections*. Boston: The Horn Book, Inc.

Heins, P. (ed.). (1977). *Crosscurrents of Criticism*. Boston: The Horn Book, Inc.

Huck, C., Hepler, S., and Hickman, J. (1987). *Children's literature in the elementary school*. New York: Holt, Rinehart and Winston.

Kelly, R. (1984). *Children's periodicals of the United States*. Westport, CT: Greenwood Press.

Larrick, N. (1965). The All-White World of Children's Books. *Saturday Review, 48*, 63–65, 84–85.

Lukens, R. (1990). *A critical handbook of children's literature*. Glenview, IL: Scott, Foresman.

McElderry, M. (1974). The best of times, the worst of times: Children's book publishing, 1924–1974. *The Horn Book Magazine, 50*, 85–94.

Reid, C., & Reuter, M. (1990, July 13). Confounding doomsayers, industry figures see rosy present and future. *Publishers Weekly, 237*, 13–15.

Roback, D. (1990, March 8). Commercial books scored big with kids. *Publishers Weekly, 238*, 30–35.

Sims, R. (1982). *Shadow and substance: Afro-American experience in contemporary children's fiction*. Urbana, IL: NCTE.

Sutherland, Z., & Arbuthnot, M. (1991). *Children and books*, 8th ed. Glenview, IL: Harper Collins.

V. J. Harris

2.6 Pioneers in Child Care and Early Childhood Education (After A.D. 1750)

The first pioneers in early childhood education were men. These included theoreticians, like Robert Owen and Friedrich Froebel, as well as practitioners. Owen's first teacher was a man, as was Froebel's. Bronson Alcott taught in his own infant school in Boston during the 1820s.

By the latter half of the nineteenth century, when kindergarten had become established in the United States, early childhood education had become a women's profession, and leadership in the field also had shifted to women. There were a number of reasons for this shift. Among them was the changing role of women in the society as a whole, and the perceived importance of women's role in maintaining families and nurturing children. The nurturing image had been promulgated as part of the movement known as "Fireside Education."

Teaching kindergarten and primary grade children or serving as a child care worker were exclusively women's occupations by the turn of the century. In some ways, this was an unfortunate situation as it denied young children the advantages of having direct contact with adults of both sexes. On the other hand, the circumstance did serve to provide an area for the career development of women. Leadership roles that would otherwise have been reserved for men became available to women in the kindergarten movement and, later, in the child study movement.

Early in the twentieth century, the only faculty positions available to women in many universities were in the area of home economics. Often child study and early childhood education as areas of concentration were housed within departments of home economics, providing women with both academic opportunities and opportunities within fields of practice.

Today, the number of men in the field of child care and early education is increasing, though it is still small. Career patterns in the field tend to be different for men than for women, however. Men are more likely than women to move out of the classroom into administrative, research, or teacher education positions. This tendency parallels career patterns in other professional fields in the nation.

The preponderance of women in the field was seen not only in individuals who chose to become early childhood educators, but in the professional associations that were established to promote child care and early education. While the leadership of those organizations was disproportionately in the hands of men, the broader endeavor of the work of the associations was undertaken largely by women. In recent decades, leadership has been assumed by women as well as by men, and the membership is seeking to attract more male teachers and caregivers into the organizations.

The articles that follow introduce the pioneer individuals and organizations whose work from 1750 to 1960 gave shape to the child care and early education programs that exist today. The entries are arranged alphabetically.

References

Seifert, K. (1988). Men in early childhood education. In Spodek, B., Saracho, O., and Peters, D. L. (eds.), *Professionalism and the early childhood practitioner.* New York: Teachers College Press.

Shapiro, M. S. (1983). *Child's garden: The kindergarten movement from Froebel to Dewey.* University Park: Pennsylvania State University Press.

B. Spodek

Addams, Jane

A leader in the social settlement movement, Jane Addams (1860–1935) was a progressive reformer, a social worker, and a pacifist. She was born and raised in Cedarville, Illinois, and attended Rockford Seminary in 1877. Like many of her educated female contemporaries, Addams struggled to reconcile her vocational ambitions with the constraints of domesticity. This inner turmoil and her father's untimely death in 1881 left the idealistic Addams depressed and undirected. While traveling in Europe in 1887, however, Addams and her companion, Ellen Gates Starr, visited London's Toynbee Hall, a settlement house run by Oxford men. Inspired by this social experiment, they established Hull House in Chicago's Nineteenth Ward in 1889.

During the ensuing years, Addams pioneered in the field of social work. Along with her colleagues at Hull House (among them, Florence Kelley, Julia Lathrop, Alice Hamilton, and Edith and Grace Abbott), Addams underscored the relationship between social research and reform.

Her writings (Addams, 1970/1895; 1981/1910) depicted Chicago's poor tenement conditions and illustrated the need for universal education, child labor legislation, day nurseries, and other reforms to meliorate urban life.

Addams's writings conveyed her respect for cultural pluralism, her awareness of tensions experienced by immigrant families, her commitment to social justice, and her affirmation of democracy and community life. (See also **Progressive Movement, The.**)

References

Addams, J. (1970/1895). *Hull-House maps and papers.* New York: Arno Press.

Addams, J. (1981/1910). *Twenty years at Hull-House.* New York: New American Library.

Davis, A. (1973). *American heroine.* New York: Oxford University Press.

Lagemann, E. C. (ed.). (1985). *Jane Addams on education.* New York: Teachers College Press.

A. Walton

Adler, Felix

Born in Germany, Felix Adler (1851–1933) was the son of a leader in Reformed Judaism. He moved to New York City as a child, and in 1876 founded the Ethical Culture Society as a nondenominational organization to unite those with religious feelings and needs with those who simply cared for moral betterment. His major idea, considered radical at the time, was that one could be moral without being religious.

The Free Kindergarten sponsored by the Ethical Culture Society was opened in 1881 at the corner of 45th Street and Broadway in New York City, to provide a model of instruction for children from three to six years of age. Kindergarten graduates attended the Workingman's School until they were 13 or 14 years old. Attendance at the Workingman's School could be followed by evening technical classes, including instruction and supervised work for kindergarten teachers.

Adler adopted many ideas from Froebel, including the need to have continuity in education, and the honor of menial work if it is performed with pride and dignity. In campaigning against child labor, he traveled widely in the United States and helped to establish free kindergartens in San Francisco, Los Angeles, and Denver. His ideas spread to England, where he helped start the London Ethical Society. After 1902, Adler was a professor of social ethics at Columbia University. (See also **Froebelian Kindergarten, The.**)

References

Adler, F. (1892). *The moral instruction of children.* New York: Appleton.

Barnard, H. (1884). *Kindergarten and Child Culture papers.* Hartford, CT: American Journal of Education.

Osborn, D. K. (1991). *Early childhood education in historical perspective.* Athens, GA: The Dye Press.

D. W. Hewes

Barnard, Henry

Born in Hartford, Connecticut, Henry Barnard (1811–1900) was one of the most influential of the educational reformers of the nineteenth century. His long and diversified career encompassed successively work as a Whig reformer (aimed at maintaining that political party's ideals of promoting effort and discipline in individuals and order and harmony in society), a school administrator, teacher educator, college president, national educator, and educational historian (MacMullen, 1991).

His early work focused on reform of the common schools through upgrading the education and qualifications of teachers. He was especially interested in fostering attention to pedagogy or the art of teaching, so that ways could be found to engage children's interest in learning. He found the practices of the common school of his day to be sterile and uninspiring; and he was looking for ways to motivate children to greater intellectual accomplishment.

As early as 1939, he was attracted to the work of Johann Pestalozzi and promoted use of Pestalozzi's teaching principles in schools throughout southern New England. His particular enthusiasm for that work stemmed from "Pestalozzi's emphasis on the child, and on the role of the environment in the education of children, his insistence on the importance of the real and the immediate as sources for the teaching of children, and his elevation of

the teacher as the moral as well as the intellectual guide for children" (MacMullen, 1991, p. 316), all of which fit Barnard's vision of a more humane and pertinent way to teach.

In his later work as an educational historian, he became interested in the Froebelian kindergarten movement and lent it support by publishing essays of Elizabeth Peabody, a leading kindergarten proponent. As editor of the *American Journal of Education*, he devoted a whole volume to the "Kindergarten and Child Culture Papers" in 1884; and, in 1894, toward the end of his life, he took special pleasure in accepting an invitation to award the diplomas to the graduates of the Chauncey Hall Kindergarten Training Program in Boston. (See also **Froebelian Kindergarten, The; Pestalozzi, Johann;** and Section 2.2, **Educational Contexts: The Common School in Relation to Early Childhood Education.**)

References

Barnard, H. (1884). *Kindergarten and child culture papers.* Hartford, CT: American Journal of Education.

MacMullen, E. N. (1991). *In the cause of true education: Henry Barnard and nineteenth-century school reform.* New Haven: Yale University Press.

L. R. Williams

Blow, Susan

One of the more controversial Americans who studied the Froebelian kindergarten in Europe, Susan Blow (1843–1916) was introduced to the kindergarten idea while traveling with her ambassador father. Before opening the first public school kindergarten in St. Louis in 1873, she took an intensive training course with Maria Kraus-Boelte in New York. She also studied in Dresden with the Baroness von Marenholtz-Bulow in 1877.

Until well into the 1900s, she was a prolific writer, translator, and professor of education at Teachers College, Columbia University, despite recurring physical problems. During a period at the turn of the century, Blow tried unsuccessfully to retain what she believed to be the true kindergarten system. She felt that all children were the same and that Froebel's system needed no modification for different cultures or for different locations. (See also **Froebel, Friedrich Wilhelm; Froebelian Kindergarten, The.**)

References

Barnard, H. (1884). *Kindergarten and child culture papers*. Hartford, CT: American Journal of Education.

Blow, S. (1894). *Symbolic education: A commentary on Froebel's "Mother Play."* New York: Appleton.

Hewes, D. W. (1985). Compensatory early childhood education: Froebelian origins and outcomes. ERIC ED264980 PSO15596.

Synder, A. (1972). *Dauntless Women in Childhood Education 1856–1931*. Washington, DC: Association for Childhood Education International.

D. W. Hewes

Bryan, Anna E.

Born in Louisville, Kentucky, as the second of three children of Parish G. and Eliza H. Belle Bryan, Anna E. Bryan (1858–1901) began her career as a kindergarten teacher by studying at the Chicago Free Kindergarten Association's training school for teachers, where she was strictly trained in Froebelian method. Upon completing her instruction in 1884, Bryan accepted a teaching job in Chicago at Marie Chapel Charity Kindergarten. She remained there until 1887, when she was asked to return to Louisville to direct the development of a new training school and form a Free Kindergarten Association.

Bryan regarded her return to Kentucky as an opportunity to break with kindergarten teaching methods based on what she considered to have been Froebelian "indoctrination." Within the confines of her own school, Bryan developed a unique program based on progressive, child-centered thinking that included respect for experimentation, recognition of individual differences in children, and acceptance of a need for spontaneity.

Bryan's alternative kindergarten, with its tolerant and experimental environment, became the focus of attention of educators from all over the United States. Among the more than 3,000 visitors to the program in 1890 were Colonel Francis Parker and William Hailmann, who had organized the first German kindergartens in Kentucky. Emphatically supporting what they observed, Parker and Hailmann spread the word of Bryan's work. With such recognition of her efforts, Bryan accepted an invitation to write a series of articles about her anti-Froebelian methods for the *Kindergarten Magazine* between 1890 and 1893.

One of the first graduates of the teacher training program associated with Bryan's school was Patty Smith Hill. Hill joined Bryan's staff upon her graduation from the program; Bryan and her capable assistant attended numerous meetings together in their search for alternative ways to reform kindergarten theory and practice. When Bryan left Louisville in 1893 for further study at the University of Chicago with John Dewey, Hill became the acting director of Bryan's program.

When Bryan returned to Chicago, John Dewey sought her advice in establishing the kindergarten section of his new experimental school at the University of Chicago. In 1893, Bryan became the director of the Chicago Free Kindergarten Association, and in 1894, the principal of the kindergarten normal department at Armour Institute in Chicago. In both settings, she applied the findings of G. Stanley Hall, as well as those of John Dewey, to kindergarten education. Alice Temple trained under Bryan's tutelage, beginning there her lifelong support of Bryan's progressive views.

Anna Bryan's distinction lay in her ability to guide and inspire others. She continued to provide leadership through her work in the International Kindergarten Union as Chairman of its Child Study Committee and as a member of its Teacher Training Committee. Bryan died of heart disease in Chicago at the age of 42. (See also **Dewey, John; Froebelian Kindergarten, The; Hailmann, William; Hill, Patty Smith; Progressive Movement, The; and Temple, Alice.**)

References

Bryan, A. E. (1890). The letter killeth. *National Educational Association's Journal of Proceedings and Addresses*, pp. 573–581.

Committee of Nineteen. (1924). *Pioneers of the kindergarten in America.* New York: Century.

Snyder, A. (1972). *Dauntless women in childhood education, 1856–1931.* Washington, DC: Association for Childhood Education International.

Stockton, C. L. (1890). A glimpse of Louisville kindergartens. *Kindergarten Magazine*, 3, pp. 29-33.

J. B. Fine

Clapp, Elsie R.

A progressive educator who brought the principles of John Dewey to rural education, Elsie Ripley Clapp is best known for her work at the Arthurdale School in Arthurdale, West Virginia. There in the 1930s, Clapp established an elaborated community school system that included an elementary school and a high school, each drawing extensively upon community resources, the local traditional culture, and parental involvement in the creation of the curriculum.

Clapp founded the Arthurdale Nursery School in 1934. The Nursery School's first concerns were dealing with problems of health, malnutrition, and adjustment of the children, and it soon became a center of community activity around its baby clinics, health promotion work, and parent education programs.

Clapp built the curriculum around the everyday life of the children in their rural community, using the children's enactment of day-to-day chores and the widely shared interests in farming as ways to extend their concepts and skills. She encouraged parents to visit the school frequently and to contribute whatever they could by way of "odds and ends" to augment the classroom materials.

Clapp was a great admirer of Dewey's work, and designed her schools as exemplars of his philosophy. Seeing the Arthurdale schools as a nexus of social action, she anticipated that the ways of coping learned there would help the community as a whole to survive and move beyond the Great Depression. (See also **Dewey, John;** and Section 2.3, **Progressive Movement, The.**)

References

Clapp, Elsie R. (1939). *Community schools in action.* New York: Viking Press.

Clapp, Elsie R. (1952). *The use of resources in education.* New York: Harper.

L. R. Williams

Committee of Nineteen

The International Kindergarten Union (IKU), established at the 1892 meeting of the National Education Association at Saratoga Springs, included a variety of approaches to Froebelian methodology. At the IKU meeting in 1903, Susan Blow, Lucy Wheelock, and Alice Putnam were asked to select 12 other members to write a mutually agreed upon statement about contemporary kindergarten thought. This group was later expanded to become a Committee of Nineteen, but instead of mutual agreement there emerged the Progressive, the Conservative, and the Conservative-Liberal subcommittees.

Annual IKU reports show that committee members shifted from one subcommittee to another, or served on two simultaneously. To further complicate the situation, those termed "Progressives" actually reflected the philosophy of the original German kindergartens while minimizing the dictated use of sequenced Gifts and Occupations and experimenting to see what seemed to work best in actual classroom practice. Their incorporation of new psychological and physiological research followed directives given by Froebel to his coworkers during the 1840s. The Conservatives tended to advocate authoritarian but loving control by the teacher, while the Conservative-Liberal group attempted to combine Americanized Froebelian philosophy with scientific appreciation.

For its final document in 1909, these labels were dropped, and signatures were attached to the First, Second, and Third Reports. Some members continued to identify with two subcommittees and signed two reports. All three were published as *The Kindergarten* in 1913. The committee continued to function for special projects, such as work on behalf of French refugee children after 1917, efforts to help American children cope during World War I, sponsorship of international tours in 1923 and 1927, and the writing of a 1924 book about kindergarten pioneers.

References

Annual proceeding of the International Kindergarten Union, 1892 to 1929.

Committee of Nineteen. (1913). *The kindergarten.* Boston: New York: Houghton Mifflin.

Committee of Nineteen. (1924). *Pioneers of the kindergarten in America.* New York: Century.

Snyder, A. (1972). *Dauntless women in childhood education 1856–1931.* Washington, DC: Association for Childhood Education International.

D. W. Hewes

Darwin, Charles

English naturalist Charles Darwin's (1809–1882) theory of evolution, published in the *Origin of the Species* (1859), revolutionized how scientists viewed human nature and had a pervasive influence on social thought. Other thinkers had argued that evolutionary variation occurs, but Darwin's field observations, made during his voyage aboard the HMS *Beagle* (1831–1836), enabled him to explain the mechanism of change.

Darwin's interpretation of his evidence (informed by his reading of Malthus's *Essay on the Principle of Population*) led him to question the immutability of the species. Though he formulated his ideas in writing as early as 1842, he delayed publishing his theory, given its implications, for nearly 20 years. It was Alfred Russel Wallace's independent formulation of evolution and natural selection in 1858 that prompted Darwin to publish his *Origins*. Two later texts by Darwin (1871; 1872) further applied the principle of natural selection to human development, thereby asserting scientific authority over Christian orthodoxy.

Darwin's writings, including his biographical sketch of his infant son, initiated comparative and developmental studies of the child and heightened interest in scientific pedagogy. Leaders during the early years of the child study movement, most notably psychologist G. Stanley Hall, drew inspiration from Darwinian thought, as did pragmatist John Dewey and later progressive educators and educational psychologists (Cremin, 1961). (See also Chapter 4, Section 4.1, **History of Child Development and Learning Theory;** and Section 4.2, **Hall, G. Stanley;** Chapter 2, Section 2.3, **Progressive Movement, The;** and Section 2.6, **Dewey, John.**)

References

Cremin, L. A. (1961). *The transformation of the schools: Progressivism in American Education 1876–1957.* New York: Knopf.

Darwin, C. (1859). *The origin of species.* London: J. Murray.

Darwin, C. (1871). *The descent of man.* London: J. Murray.

Darwin, C. (1872). *The expression of the emotions in man and animals.* London: J. Murray.

Howard, J. (1982). *Darwin.* New York: Oxford University Press.

Kohn, D. (ed.). (1985). *The Darwinian heritage.* Princeton, NJ: Princeton University Press.

Malthus, T. R. (1798). *An essay on the principle of population.* London: Reeves and Turner.

A. Walton

Dewey, John

Philosopher, psychologist, and educator John Dewey (1859–1952) was born in Burlington, Vermont. He received his doctorate from Johns Hopkins University in 1884 and for the following decade taught at the University of Michigan. In 1894, he moved to the University of Chicago, where he headed the newly created Department of Psychology, Philosophy, and Education, and where, in 1896, he founded the Laboratory School. He left Chicago in 1904 to join the faculty of Teachers College, Columbia University, where he remained until his retirement in 1930. Dewey was known as the foremost educator and major theorist of the progressive movement in the United States, and his contributions to philosophy were internationally acclaimed. Dewey only infrequently addressed early childhood education specifically in his writings, but his philosophical concerns and the questions he raised greatly influenced the growth and direction of the field. Many of the guiding principles as well as much of the language of early childhood as an area of study and practice are rooted in Dewey's philosophy.

Throughout his life, Dewey sought to awaken the vision of educators to connections denied by traditional mindsets. As the titles of many of his books illustrate (*The School and Society*, *The Child and the Curriculum*, *Democracy and Education*, *Experience and Education*), Dewey joined what others separated. In Dewey's view, the development of the curriculum is a collaborative effort, a partnership in which children's interests and their questions become entry points into the established domain of schooling. The teacher's concern is "not with subject matter as such, but with the subject matter as a related factor in a total and growing experience" (Dewey, 1956, p. 23).

Learning becomes a "total and growing" affair when there is continuity in experience, when the child's experiencing "arouses curiosity [and] strengthens initiative," and when it becomes a "moving force" that pushes toward further learning and experiencing. The child and the curriculum become connected when established subject matter is permeable to and shaped by the child's interests. In the same way, experience and education are connected intrinsically when there is continuity in experience, and interaction between the child and the environment. Embedded within the word "interaction" are images of the child engaged fully in activity, making discoveries and connections, and responding to the challenge of problems to be solved and meanings to be constructed.

In such interaction, Dewey presents an idea central to his thought—that is, that education "is essentially a social process." He sees the child as a social individual, one who is related, connected, and contextualized. From this nucleus grow the ideas of community, group membership, and organization "in which all the individuals have an opportunity to contribute something, and . . . in which all participants are the chief carriers of control" (Dewey, 1963, p. 56). Dewey envisions the community created out of shared work, interests, and communication as a microcosm of a larger democratic society.

The Deweyan legacy to early childhood education includes such principles as children's learning from experience through action and reflection; welcoming, supporting, and enlarging the interests and activity of children; participating in a community of shared work and responsibility; transforming impulse into purpose; creating an environment that invites interaction, experimentation, and communication; and understanding teaching as a mindful, moral undertaking, in which promoting and supporting the democratic ideal is central to the teacher's task. (See also **Bryan, Anna**; **Darwin, Charles**; **Johnson, Harriet**; **Hill, Patty Smith**; **Mitchell, Lucy Sprague**; **Progressive Movement, The**; and Chapter 5, Section 5.1, **History of Curriculum Trends in the United States**.)

References

Dewey, J. (1956/1900). *The school and society*. Chicago: University of Chicago Press.

Dewey, J. (1956/1902). *The child and the curriculum*. Chicago: University of Chicago Press.

Dewey, J. (1966/1916). *Democracy and education*. New York: The Free Press.

Dewey, J. (1963/1938). *Experience and education*. New York: Collier Books.

H. K. Cuffaro

Eliot, Abigail

Generally credited with introducing the nursery school into the United States from England, Abigail Adams Eliot (1892–) conducted most of her early work in nursery education in and around Boston, Massachusetts.

A social worker by training, Eliot studied with Arnold Gesell at the Clinic of Child Development at Yale University and was encouraged by him in 1921 to go to England to study with Margaret McMillan. While McMillan focused on the growth and development of children in the school or center, Eliot was primarily interested in the interaction of children with their parents. She thus extended current thinking in early childhood education to include the family, with a vision of parents as active partners in the educational enterprise.

Eliot helped the American nursery school movement to encourage home/school partnerships. In 1922 she opened the Ruggles Street Nursery in Roxbury (adjacent to Boston), Massachusetts, where she incorporated the principles of nursery practice she had learned in England. In addition to her strong emphasis on parent involvement, she fostered interest in focusing on the child's present experience and stage of development, rather than always preparing him or her for the next experience or stage of schooling.

Throughout the 1920s, Eliot (with Arnold Gesell and Patty Smith Hill) was a major leader of the nursery school movement in the United States. In later decades, she built up the teacher training school associated with the Ruggles Street Nursery, and in 1951, she finalized the location of the teacher preparation program at the Eliot-Pearson Department of Child Study at Tufts University. She moved to Pasadena, California, one year later to help establish Pacific Oaks College. She then returned to Massachusetts to continue work in nursery school education until her retirement in 1962. (See also **Hill, Patty Smith; McMillan, Margaret and Rachel;** and Chapter 4, Section 4.2, **Gesell, Arnold.**)

References

Eliot, A. (1972). Nursery schools fifty years ago. *Young Children*, 27 (4), 208–213.

Hymes, J. (1972). *Living history of early childhood education* (Eight audio cassettes). Washington, DC: Childhood Resources.

Osborn, D. K. (1990). *Early childhood education in historical perspective* (3rd edition). Athens, GA: The Daye Press.

L. R. Williams

Froebel, Friedrich Wilhelm*

Born in Oberweissbach in the German principality of Schwarzburg-Rudolstadt, Friedrich Froebel (1782–1852) himself had an unhappy childhood. He lost his mother at an early age; and unable to live harmoniously with his father, he lived away from home from the age of ten, attending school in his uncle's village, working with a forester to whom he was later apprenticed and, finally, sharing lodgings with his brother at the University of Jena. He took classes in mathematics, philosophy, and science at the university for 19 months, before beginning his working life (Downs, 1978).

During the years that followed, Froebel worked at occupations that exercised his mathematical and scientific knowledge. In 1805 he went to Frankfurt to train as an architect and was thereby exposed to the relationship between form and function. A fortuitous meeting with Gruener (the head of a new Model School) led him to leave his work in architecture to begin teaching, a profession for which he had a talent and, he discovered, an enormous liking. Desire to refine his teaching skills brought him to Yverdun, where for the first time he was exposed to the work of Johann Pestalozzi, a remarkable educator then advancing a theory of education through systematic use of sense impressions as avenues to knowledge. This experience encouraged Froebel to return to university to continue intensive study in the sciences and in linguistics (Downs, 1978; Woodham-Smith, 1969). In 1813 he joined the army to resist Napoleon and there met two contemporaries, Langethal and Midendorf, with whom he found he shared a vision for the creation of a new educational system. The two men stayed with Froebel for many years as companions and colleagues in his work (Braun and Edwards, 1972).

The years between 1816 and 1849 were rich in the opportunities they presented for the maturing of Froebel's thought and practice. Moving steadily from posts as tutor to work as founder of several innovative schools, to the position of director of the orphanage school at Burgdorf, Froebel integrated his experiences into an articulated philosophy of education and developed a set of materials and teaching procedures remarkable in their originality (Froebel 1887, 1895). By 1840 he was ready to begin the dissemination of his program, and for that purpose established his officially named "kindergarten" ("children's garden") in conjunction with a modest teacher training institute at Blankenburg (Downs, 1978).

The remaining years of his life were spent in pursuit of funds to expand his work and in avoidance of the political currents that interpreted his educational work as dangerously revolutionary. In 1851 his school was ordered closed. He died in 1852 without the satisfaction of seeing it reopened (Woodham-Smith, 1969). (See also **Blow, Susan; Froebelian Kindergarten, The; Harrison, Elizabeth; Marwedel, Emma; Peabody, Elizabeth; Schurz, Margarethe; Wiggin, Kate Douglas**; and Chapter 5, Section 5.1, **History of Curriculum Trends in the United States**.)

References

Braun S. J., & Edwards, E. P. (1972). *History and theory of early childhood education*. Worthington, OH: Jones.

Downs, R. B. (1978). *Friedrich Froebel*. Boston: Twayne.

Froebel, F. W. A. (1887). *The education of man*. (trans. by W. N. Hailmann). New York: Appleton.

Froebel, F. W. A. (1875). *Education by development: The second part of the pedagogics of the kindergarten* (Trans. by J. Jarvis). New York: Appleton.

Woodham-Smith, P. (1969). The origin of the kindergarten. History of the Froebel movement in England. In Lawrence, E. L. (ed.). *Froebel and English education: Perspectives on the founder of the kindergarten*. (pp. 15–33 and 34–94). New York: Schocken Books.

L. R. Williams

*Reprinted from the *International Encyclopedia of Education* with permission of Pergamon Press, Ltd., Headington Hill Hall, Oxford OX3 OBW, England.

Hailmann, Eudora

Born to an established American family, Eudora Hailmann (1835–1904) was strongly involved in the movement to abolish black slavery and to allow women full political and legal rights. She became interested in the kindergarten while working as a volunteer mother in the Louisville German-American school with a German-trained teacher. She studied in Europe in 1866 and 1871, where in the words of her husband, William Hailmann, she "gleaned a rich harvest which enabled her to become a progressive leader in the field." Until the mid-1890s, she educated teachers, established training schools, worked with associations opening charity kindergartens, designed exhibits for world's fairs, and taught in many other capacities. (See also **Hailmann, William; Froebelian Kindergarten, The**.)

References

Hewes, D. W. (1975). *W. N. Hailmann: Defender of Froebel*. (Publication #75-15, 939). Ann Arbor, MI: University Microfilms.

Hewes, D. H. (1990). *The egalitarian marriages of six leading educators of late nineteenth century America*. [presently being assigned an ERIC number]

Hewes, D. W. (1988). *Kindergarten teacher training in the United States from 1870 to 1920*. ERIC ED299031 PSO17549.

D. H. Hewes

Hailmann, William

Educated in Switzerland, William Hailmann (1836–1920) moved to the United States in 1852 as a youth of 16. He discovered Froebelian kindergartens while visiting his parents in Zurich in 1860. As administrator of German-American schools, of public school districts, and of the Federal Indian schools from 1893 to 1898, he developed Froebelian education at all levels from kindergarten to vocational schools for adults. By the time of his death, Hailmann had translated an authoritative edition of Friedrich Froebel's "The Education of Man" and had written a dozen books. He had taught in colleges, given countless lectures, and had coedited with his wife the periodical that bound the national kindergarten organization into a cohesive group. His work was primarily in the mid-western region of the United States. (See also **Hailmann, Eudora; Progressive Movement, The**.)

References

Hewes, D. W. (1975). *W. N. Hailmann: Defender of Froebel* (Publication #75-15, 939) Ann Arbor, MI: University Microfilms.

Hewes, D. W. (1988). *Organic education in public schools of late nineteenth century America.* ERIC ED299048 PSO17570.

Hewes, D. W. (1990). *The egalitarian marriages of six leading educators of late nineteenth century America.* [presently being assigned an ERIC number]

D. W. Hewes

Harris, William T.

Born in Connecticut, William Torrey Harris (1835–1909) served as Superintendent of Schools in St. Louis from 1857 to 1880. In addition to his master's degree from Yale and a doctorate from Missouri State University, Harris had honorary doctorates in recognition of his outstanding contributions to education and Hegelian philosophy.

As a Hegelian, he had an optimistic belief that civilization would improve despite inevitable conflicts, but that all groups and institutions, including kindergarten classrooms, could achieve their goals only through discipline and orderly behavior. Since this philosophical orientation led him to believe that kindergartens could salvage both the "pampered" children of the rich and the "weaklings" living in poverty, he was an advocate of one version of Froebelian methodology.

Harris was characterized as a kind and gentle man, but one could speculate that his particularly solicitous concern for young children also related to the early deaths of his daughter and son. He recommended in 1870 that the St. Louis schools should include subprimary classes; and in 1873 he provided a room at the Des Peres School for Susan Blow to open the first public school kindergarten in the United States.

Harris became one of the most influential and prestigious educators in the United States in the formative years of public schools during the late nineteenth century. During this time, he consistently supported public school kindergartens. As participant and elected officer of the National Education Association, many of his 145 recorded speeches dealt with recommendations for kindergarten level classes. As the federal Commissioner of Education from 1889 to 1906, he promoted incorporation of kindergartens into public schools by subsidizing reports and publications justifying their adoption. As editor of Appleton's Education Series, he was responsible for the publication of seven books about Froebelian methods.

References

Curti, M. E. (ed.). (1935). *William T. Harris, the conservator. Social ideas of American educators.* (pp. 310–347). New York: Scribner.

Hewes, D. W. (1975). *W. N. Hailmann: Defender of Froebel* (Publication #75-15, 939). Ann Arbor: University Microfilms.

Leidecker, K. F. (1946). *Yankee teacher: The life of William Torrey Harris.* New York: Philosophical Library.

D. W. Hewes

Harrison, Elizabeth

A kindergarten educator, an author, and a lecturer, Elizabeth Harrison founded the Chicago Kindergarten Training School in 1887 (now National-Louis College of Education). Always in search of new insights into Froebel's theory and practice, she studied with Alice Harvey Putnam, Susan Blow, and Maria Kraus-Boelte, and eventually traveled to Germany to interview Frau Henriette Breymann Schrader and Baroness Bertha von Marenholz-Buelow.

Harrison wrote books for children, teachers, and parents, and took a leadership role in the International Kindergarten Union (IKU). Harrison's open-mindedness toward the new scientific study of children, as well as her respect for Froebel's philosophy, enabled her to write the compromise report for the IKU's Committee of Nineteen.

Harrison went to Italy in 1912 to study the work of Maria Montessori. Upon her return she wrote a report of her observations, *The Montessori Method and the Kindergarten*, a description of the Montessori Method from the Froebelian point of view. The report was published and distributed by the U.S. Bureau of Education in 1914. (See also **Blow, Susan; Committee of Nineteen; Froebelian Kindergarten, The; International Kindergarten Union, The; Montessori Method, The.**)

Reference

Snyder, A. (1972). *Dauntless women in childhood education 1856–1931*. Washington, DC: Association for Childhood Education International.

G. W. Ladd

Hill, Patty Smith

Born to a family devoted to the education of women and the pursuit of educational means for improving the human condition, Patty Smith Hill (1868–1946) came naturally to her lifelong interest in fostering learning in young children. She was raised in Kentucky, Missouri, and Texas, where, just after the Civil War, she had the opportunity to observe educational processes in the schools her parents ran.

After her father's death, Hill returned with her family to Louisville. There in 1887 she became one of the first five graduates of the kindergarten training school established by Anna E. Bryan. Bryan was already professionally established in her career unlike the young Hill, but she found in Hill a lively intellect and vigor that promoted a mutually beneficial colleagueship. When Bryan took a leave from her directorship of the Louisville Free Kindergarten Association in 1893 to assume other responsibilities, she named Hill as her temporary successor.

Hill's work with the Louisville kindergartens came to national attention that same year through her participation in the Columbia Exhibition in Chicago. Both John Dewey's and Colonel Francis Parker's subsequent visit to Louisville encouraged Hill to go to Chicago to study with Dewey that summer, before returning to Louisville to assume the full directorship of the Free Kindergarten Association. She held that position for the next 12 years.

During this period, Hill continued to modify her originally Froebelian orientation through her increasing attraction to the work of Dewey and the progressive movement, and through periodic study with G. Stanley Hall. She moved from Louisville to New York City in 1905, when she accepted the invitation of Dean James Earl Russell at Teachers College, Columbia University to teach a course in early childhood education jointly with the famous Froebelian advocate, Susan Blow. Subsequently, she joined the faculty of Teachers College, and, in 1910, became the head of the kindergarten department.

During her time at Teachers College, Hill continued and deepened her interest in progressive thinking in the design and implementation of her laboratory kindergarten and nursery schools, and her teacher training program. In time, she also studied the work of Thorndike and other psychologists and saw immediate applications of their research to the education of young children. She understood design of programs for young children to be an experimental activity, scientifically based and philosophically open to new waves in educational thought.

Hill expanded her work in 1921 to include direction of the newly established Institute for Child Welfare Research. She also continued the work she had begun in the early part of the century with the Association for Childhood Education International (formerly the International Kindergarten Union, where she had chaired the liberal faction of the Committee of Nineteen) and also helped to establish a new professional organization, the National Association of Nursery Educators, in 1925. During the same period, she developed international interests and was influential in promoting dialogue between American and Soviet educators in the late 1920s.

After her retirement from Teachers College in 1935, Hill devoted her energies to social action around the Manhattanville Nursery School project. She had originally established that project to address the appalling conditions of poverty in the neighborhoods bordering Teachers College; and during the Great Depression, the need for her services in that area were more pronounced than ever. (See also **Bryan, Anna E., Committee of Nineteen; Dewey, John;** Section 2.3, **Progressive Movement, The;** and Chapter 4, Section 4.1, **Hall, G. Stanley.**)

References

Osborn, D. K. (1991). *Early childhood education in historical perspective*, 3rd ed. Athens, GA: The Daye Press.

Snyder, A. (1972). *Dauntless women in childhood education: 1856–1931*. Washington, DC: Association for Childhood International.

L. R. Williams

International Kindergarten Union

Founded in 1892, the International Kindergarten Union (IKU), the professional organization of the kindergarten movement, worked to promote the kindergarten and to improve the standard of teacher training.

From its inception, the IKU provided an arena for the debate about new educational ideas and practices derived from the beginnings of child study by G. Stanley Hall at Clark University and discussion of the practice in John Dewey's laboratory school at the University of Chicago. The last major document concerned with this debate was the 1913 report of the Committee of Nineteen, in which the Froebelian point of view was presented by Susan Blow, the progressive point of view by Patty Smith Hill, and a compromise position by Elizabeth Harrison.

The IKU established its permanent headquarters in Washington, D.C., in 1924 and began publishing *Childhood Education*, the first professional journal of its kind. The kindergarten movement broadened into early childhood education; and in 1930 the IKU merged into the National Council of Primary Education to become the Association for Childhood Education International. (See also **Blow, Susan; Dewey, John; Froebelian Kindergarten, The; Hall, G. Stanley; Harrison, Elizabeth; Hill, Patty Smith;** Section 2.3 **Progressive Movement, The;** and Chapter 3,

Section 3.2, **History of Sponsorships and Interest Groups.**)

Reference

Weber, E. (1969). *The kindergarten: Its encounter with educational thought in America*. New York: Teachers College Press.

G. W. Ladd

Johnson, Harriet

A fervent progressive educator, Harriet Johnson (1867–1934) began her career as a teacher and later became a nurse and staff worker at the Henry Street Settlement House in New York City. There she began to consider alternatives to the existing public schools that, to her mind, stifled children's natural curiosity and creativity. Most particularly, she became interested in the nursery school movement that was building momentum across the United States and saw it as one way to actualize her vision of education for children from 14 to 36 months of age.

In 1919, Johnson founded an experimental nursery school as part of the Bureau of Educational Experiments (later the Bank Street College of Education) in New York. She designed the school to serve children younger than those accepted at the City and Country School, the primary laboratory school of the Bureau of Educational Experiments, feeling that for best effect, early childhood programs had to address the needs of the very young.

Johnson built her curriculum not only on the elements of practice learned from the McMillan sisters in England, but around the principles of child growth and development enjoying currency as a result of the child study movement in the United States. Johnson was one of the early advocates of play in early childhood education, understanding it to be the most natural form of children's activities. Through observation of play, Johnson and her student teachers learned how to plan a program for very young children that supported their growth and development. (See also **McMillan, Margaret and Rachel; Pratt,**

Caroline; and Section 2.3, **Bureau of Educational Experiments.**)

References

Johnson, H. (1972). *Children in the nursery school.* New York: Schocken. (Originally published 1928).

Osborn, D. K. (1990). *Early childhood educaiton in historical perspective* (3rd edition). Athens, GA: The Daye Press.

L. R. Williams

Marwedel, Emma

An ardent feminist who had studied with Froebel, Emma Marwedel (1822–1893) was the directress of the Girls' Industrial School in Hamburg when Elizabeth Peabody persuaded her to move to the United States. After an unsuccessful year in Washington, D.C., she opened the first Pacific Coast kindergarten and training school in 1876. She remained dedicated to "the cause" until her death. For instance, at age 64, when she had no money for a regular ticket, she rode almost 2,000 miles in the caboose car attached to the end of a freight train in order to attend the 1882 Friends of Froebel meeting in Detroit. She had many outstanding students, including Nora Smith, Kate Douglas Wiggin, and others who contributed to making the California kindergartens outstanding. (See also **Froebelian Kindergarten, The; Wiggin, Kate Douglas.**)

References

Hewes, D. W. (1975). *W. N. Hailmann: Defender of Froebel.* (Publication #75-15, 939). Ann Arbor, MI: University Microfilms.

National Education Association. (1894). Emma Marwedel In Necrologies, *Annual Proceedings.* Washington, DC: Author.

Swift, F. H. (1931). Emma Marwedel, 1818–1893, Pioneer of the kindergarten in California. *Publications in Education, 6* (3), 139–216.

D. W. Hewes

McMillan, Margaret and Rachel

Margaret and Rachel McMillan were the daughters of Scottish immigrants to the United States. Margaret (1860–1931) was younger than Rachel (1859–1917) by only one year. The two sisters remained close companions and colleagues as long as they lived. Margaret's mother, widowed suddenly when Margaret was five years old, returned to Scotland and raised her two daughters there. Even though Margaret was deaf from childhood (she suddenly gained her hearing at age 14), she and her sister were brilliant young scholars who completed an academy education with distinction.

The death of their grandfather and their mother when Rachel was 17 and Margaret 16 altered their circumstances. Both young women began the upward struggle to complete their educations through a series of positions as governesses and student teachers in Britain and on the Continent. Rachel became converted to Christian Socialism in 1887 through the sermons of Dr. John Glasse. Margaret, equally horrified by the stark poverty that attended the advance of the industrial revolution in Britain, followed suit shortly thereafter.

After initial work as promoters of the Socialist cause, they became noted advocates speaking against child labor and other abuses of the system. Margaret at the age of 33 became the only woman member of the Bradford (England) school board, and in that position continued her campaign to remove child workers from the factories so that they could attend school. She also persuaded the school board to appoint a School Medical Officer to address some of the appalling health conditions that poverty had engendered.

At the turn of the century, two of Margaret's books, *Early Childhood* (1900) and *Education Through the Imagination* (1903), established her reputation as an educator. Financed by Joseph Fells, an American philanthropist, the two sisters opened their first (which failed) and then a second school clinic in London. This endeavor evolved into the McMillan

Nursery School, for which the sisters became famous.

Rachel died suddenly in 1917, leaving Margaret desolate. With her characteristic strength, however, she recovered from the shock and went on to continue to fight for children's and women's rights. She completed and published her best known book, *The Nursery School*, in 1919, and continued to exert great influence on British and later American educators until her death in 1931. (See also **McMillan Nursery School, The**; and Chapter 5, Section 5.1, **History of Curriculum Trends in the United States.**)

References

Braun, S. J., & Edwards, E. P. (1972). *History and theory of early childhood education*. Belmont, CA: Wadsworth.

McMillan, M. (1900). *Early childhood*. London: The Gresham Press.

McMillan, M. (1903). *Education through the imagination*. London: The Gresham Press.

McMillan, M. (1919). *The nursery school*. New York: E. P. Dutton.

Osborne, D. K. (1991). *Early childhood education in historical perspective*. Athens, GA: The Daye Press.

L. R. Willliams

Mitchell, Lucy Sprague

Born in Chicago, Lucy Sprague Mitchell (1878–1967) was the fourth of six children of a well-to-do, entrepreneurial family that lived its New England heritage in its household organization and child-rearing practices. Mitchell was unhappy as a child due in part, she later felt, to her father's rigid nature and her mother's acquiescence to masculine dominance. Her father's poor health brought the family to California, where Mitchell spent most of her adolescence.

At age 17, she made the decision to move away from her family's sphere and to create a life of substance for herself. Recognizing that educated women of the day usually had to forfeit marriage, she decided nevertheless to attend Radcliffe College. There she was an exceptionally fine student, graduating in 1900 with honors in philosophy.

After another painful period of dealing with family illness, Mitchell accepted an invitation in 1903 first to join the faculty of the University of California at Berkeley and then to become its Dean of Women. There she gained the administrative experience that was to serve her in later years.

In 1912 she married Wesley Clair Mitchell, creating with him a marriage very different from the model provided by her parents. Between 1913 and 1918, the Mitchells adopted two children and gave birth to two more, and Lucy Mitchell worked to provide a loving home for her family. At the same time, however, she developed a fully articulated career as an educator. Though her husband was a supportive partner in her endeavors, the tension caused by balancing the needs of family and career remained a powerful motif throughout her life.

The Mitchells settled in New York City in 1912. In pursuit of a new focus for her career, Mitchell began studies at Teachers College, Columbia University with John Dewey and Edward Thorndike, two of the primary leaders of the progressive movement. In subsequent years, she remained a social friend of Dewey's and was able to observe firsthand the continuing development of his work. Through that influence, Mitchell began to develop her idea of the school as a community center.

Over the next several years, Mitchell and a group of associates, which included Evelyn Dewey, Caroline Pratt, and Harriet Johnson, conceived a plan in 1916 for the Bureau of Educational Experiments in New York, intended to coordinate and sponsor educational innovations. Financial support from a cousin enabled the plan to become a reality, and Caroline Pratt's Play School (later City and Country School) became the Bureau's major laboratory school.

Between 1916 and 1930 the Bureau undertook a wide variety of educational experiments, including study of individual differences in children, promotion of a sex education program, design of parent involvement programs, the addition of Harriet Johnson's nursery school as a laboratory setting, and collaboration with various public schools on implementing progressive teaching principles in the classroom.

In 1930 Mitchell and the Bureau began a new venture, the Cooperative School for Student Teachers. The same year, the Bureau moved to 69 Bank Street in Greenwich Village in New York. The Bureau acquired the informal name of "Bank Street," and eventually the formal name of the organization became the Bank Street College of Education.

Over the next 25 years, Mitchell led Bank Street's development and taught at the College. She became especially well known for her interest in unifying the arts and the sciences, her insistence on direct experience as a requirement of learning in young children, and her development of an experiential program for "young geographers" that made immediate study of the community the basis of the early childhood curriculum.

Mitchell devoted her later years to writing that included reexamination of her professional life. She died of a heart attack at age 89. (See also **Dewey, John; Johnson, Harriet; Pratt, Caroline;** Section 2.3, **Bureau of Educational Experiments (Bank Street College),** and Section 2.3, **Progressive Movement, The.**)

References

Antler, J. (1987) *Lucy Sprague Mitchell.* New Haven: Yale University Press.

Mitchell, L. S. (1953). *Two lives: The story of Wesley Clair Mitchell and myself.* New York: Simon & Schuster.

L. R. Williams

Montessori, Maria

Born in the year of Italy's unification, Maria Montessori (1870–1952) began her life in Chiaravalle, Italy, a small town on the Adriatic Sea, in the province of Ancona. Her father, Alessandro, was a military man descended from a noble Bolognese family. Later in his life, he became a civil servant. Her mother, Renilde Stoppani, was the niece of the famous Italian philosopher-scientist Antonio Stoppani. Her mother believed in rigid discipline and raised her only child in accordance with these beliefs. Montessori lived with her family in Chiaravalle until she was three years old, when the family moved to Florence. When she was five years old, the family moved to Rome, where she had access to a better education.

Her interest and aptitude in mathematics led her to choose a course in engineering at a boys' school, in spite of her parents' wishes that she apply her talents to a teaching career. While attending that school, she realized it was biology that she liked and a career in medicine that she wanted. Once again, she fought strong opposition from her family to become the first woman medical student in her country. It is reported that she appealed to Pope Leo XIII to support her admission to medical school (Kramer, 1976). She was graduated in 1896 as the first woman physician in Rome. That same year, she was chosen as the Italian representative of the feminist congress in Berlin.

After her internship, she began to study children's diseases and became interested in the "mentally deficient." She believed that the problem of "mental deficiency" was pedagogical, not medical (Montessori, 1964). In an address to the Pedagogical Congress of Turin in 1898, she called for "a union between medicine and pedagogy" (Montessori, 1913, p. 15).

Following this address, she was asked to give a course on the education of "feeble minded" children to Rome's elementary school teachers. As a result, the state Orthophrenic School was founded. Children who attended this school had severe learning problems. Montessori spent two years working with these children, an experience that prepared her for her future work.

Montessori's studies led her to the works of Jean-Marc-Gaspard Itard and Édouard Séguin; she credited many of her ideas to their earlier research. Guided by their work, she manufactured a great variety of didactic materials through which the children succeeded in passing the Italian state examinations for the public schools.

Desiring to study what she termed "normal pedagogy," Montessori went to the University of Rome, where she took courses in experimental psychology and pedagogical anthropology. Having decided that it was theoretically possible to transform the schools for "normal" children, as she had successfully done with those who were then termed "mentally deficient," she looked for an opportunity to work with them. Her chance came at the end of 1906, when she was invited to organize infant schools in a model tenement. In this institution, later named "Casa dei Bambini," or "The Children's House," Montessori began in January 1907 the experiments that later would be called "The Montessori Method." Montessori actively worked with children and teachers until her death. (See also, **Montessori Method, The**; and **Séguin, Édouard**; and Chapter 5, Section 5.1, **History of Curriculum Trends in the United States.**)

References

Kramer, R. (1976). *Maria Montessori: A biography.* New York: Putnam.

Montessori, M. (1913). *Pedagogical anthropology.* Trans. by F. T. Cooper. New York: Frederick A. Stokes Co.

Montessori, M. (1948). *The discovery of the child.* Trans. by M. A. Johnstone. Adyar, Madras, India: Kalakshetra Publications.

Montessori, M. (1964, 1912). *The Montessori method.* Trans. by A. E. George. New York: Schocken Books.

P. Povell

National Association of Nursery Educators (NANE)

Officially begun at the Chicago meeting of the National Committee on Nursery Schools in 1926, NANE had been organized at a time when the English idea of nursery schools was being introduced to the United States with a wide variety of program approaches.

Patty Smith Hill, an influential professor at Teachers College, Columbia University, had worked in 1895 with G. Stanley Hall and a group of progressive Froebelians on what she later called "an ideal scheme of education for child welfare in early life." She believed that the nursery school movement could implement that plan. She therefore carefully selected members of a committee to promote nursery schools in 1925. The committee's formal organization in 1926 took place at a conference in Washington, D.C. At the committee's 1929 business meeting in Chicago, the name NANE was chosen, with the original committee members continuing as an executive committee until elections in 1931.

From the group's inception, Hill and other members of the association had a "whole child" emphasis that included families in its scope. Close liaison with other professional groups was important. Members were also involved with establishing standards for the Works Progress Administration (WPA) nursery schools in 1933, in setting up Lanham Act child care centers during World War II, in providing guidelines for the influx of preschool programs during the "baby boom" years of the 1950s, and in setting up Head Start in 1965. National conferences were held every other year financed by contributions from interested members until the conference made a profit for the first time in 1957.

Beginning in 1945, the NANE *Bulletin* was published quarterly in mimeographed form. It changed its name in 1956 to the *Journal of Nursery Education*, and in 1964 it became *Young Children*. Membership in the association went from a low of less than 100 in the early 1940s to over 6,000 by 1966, and 75,000 in 1991. Its name was changed to the National Association for the Education of Young Children in 1966, and a permanent Washington, D.C., address was established. (See also Chapter 3, Section 3.2, **History of Sponsorships and Interest Groups**; and Chapter 6, Section 6.3, **National Association for the Education of Young Children, The.**)

References

Davis, M. D. (1964). How NANE began. *Young Children*, *20* (2), 106–109.

Hewes, D. W. (1976). NAEYC's first half century in Young Children:1926–1976. *Young Children*, *31* (6), 461–476.

Hewes, D. W. (1976). Patty Smith Hill: Pioneer for young children. *Young Children*, *31* (4), 297–306.

D. W. Hewes

National Kindergarten Association

A philanthropic organization that promoted universal acceptance of the public school kindergarten, the National Kindergarten Association (NKA) was founded in 1909 by Bessie Locke and functioned on local, state, and national levels until 1976.

The NKA's affiliations with organized women, such as the General Federation of Women's Clubs and the National Congress of Mothers (later the PTA), provided an important means of working on the state and local levels. The NKA's field secretaries in each state acted as liaisons between its New York office and the women's clubs. Together the field secretaries and the women's clubs worked to inform the public about the kindergarten's value and to promote state legislation concerning kindergartens.

On the national level, from 1913 to 1919, the NKA cooperated with the United States Bureau of Education to promote the kindergarten. In the 1930s and 1940s, the NKA lobbied in Washington for a permanent form of federal aid for kindergartens.

Aside from publicizing the kindergarten and lobbying for it, the NKA attempted to reach families in areas where no kindergarten existed through its parent education materials. These materials were published from 1917 to 1954.

With the kindergarten's universal acceptance, the NKA's principal goal was accomplished. The organization became increasingly isolated from the mainstream of early childhood education until it eventually ceased to exist in 1976.

Reference

Ladd, G. W. (1982). The National Kindergarten Association: Its place in early childhood education. Unpublished doctoral dissertation, Teachers College, Columbia University.

G. W. Ladd

Owen, Robert

A social reformer who founded the infant school, Robert Owen (1771–1850) abolished child labor in his textile factory and made New Lanark, Scotland, a model industrial community. He opened the Institution for the Formation of Character in New Lanark in 1816, with classes for both infants and children, and an adult education center.

Owen emphasized using kindness, deplored punishments, and wanted to train children in good habits. Two- to five-year-olds in the infant classes spent half their time in supervised play. His school used visual aids and stressed physical exercise, singing, music, dance, and outdoor nature study. After visiting Johann Pestalozzi and Friedrich Froebel in 1818, Owen adopted some of their ideas.

Owen founded New Harmony, Indiana, in 1824 to further implement his visionary ideas. The first infant school in the United States was established there under Pestalozzian teachers. However, the New Harmony communitarian experiment floundered, and Owen returned to Britain in 1827.

In a time when most working-class children had little opportunity for formal education and rote instruction and the monitorial system were prevalent, Owen's schools were models inspiring others. His direct influence on educational practice, however, was somewhat limited in his own day. Nevertheless, Robert Owen's pioneering role in demonstrating the feasibility and importance of nursery and infant schools has been acknowledged in the twentieth century. (See also **Froebel, Friedrich; Pestalozzi, Johann;** and Chapter 3, Section 3.2, **History of Sponsorships and Interest Groups.**)

References

Altfest, K. C. (1977). *Robert Owen as educator.* Boston: Twayne.

Silver, H. (ed.). (1969). *Robert Owen on education.* Cambridge: Cambridge University Press.

N. A. Naylor

Peabody, Elizabeth

Well described by the epitaph on her tombstone as "a teacher of three generations of children and a founder of the Kindergarten in America," Elizabeth Palmer Peabody (1804–1894) had little regard for the tangibles that money could buy. One of the largely self-educated Bostonian intellectuals, she was active in the Unitarian church, Hegelianism, and Transcendentalism. Since childhood, she had been involved with various endeavors related to education, from the private school in her parents' home, to working as a governess, assisting Bronson Alcott in the Temple School, and running Pestalozzi-based infant schools.

Frequently referred to as the apostle who led the kindergarten crusade, Peabody was inspired by a Froebelian pamphlet to open America's first kindergarten for English-speaking children in 1860. Until about 1882, when her attention was diverted to the plight of the Piute Indians, she was constantly writing, fundraising, lecturing, and traveling on behalf of the kindergartens. She was president of the Friends of Froebel and the subsequent American Froebel Union. She published the *Kindergarten Messenger* between 1873 and 1875. In 1877–1878, Peabody spent 15 months visiting European kindergartens, where she became convinced that the essence of the system was strict adherence to use of materials and games attributed to Froebel.

Peabody introduced radical ideas about humane discipline, postponement of reading instruction until age seven, and the importance of joyous play as the basis of later creative and intellectual attainments. Peabody's emphasis upon the innate spirituality of young children provided the inspirational rationale behind the spectacular increase of kindergartens, from perhaps 10 in 1870, to over 400 by 1880, and 4,000 by 1890. (See also **Froebel, Friedrich Wilhelm,** and **Froebelian Kindergarten, The.**)

References

Barnard, H. (ed.). (1890). Letter from Miss Peabody to the Editor. *Froebel, Kindergarten, and Child Culture Papers.* Hartford: American Journal of Education.

Baylor, R. M. (1965). *Elizabeth Palmer Peabody: Kindergarten pioneer.* Philadelphia: University of Pennsylvania Press.

Peabody, E. P. (ed.). (1873–1877). *Kindergarten Messenger.* newsletter published and disseminated by Elizabeth Peabody.

Peabody, E. P. (1893). *Lectures in the training schools for the kindergartners.* Boston: D.C. Heath.

Tharp, L. H. (1950). *The Peabody sisters of Salem.* Boston: Little, Brown

D. W. Hewes

Pestalozzi, Johann

An Italian-Swiss teacher, Johann Pestalozzi (1746–1827) was intellectual heir to both Rousseau and the Enlightenment. He saw the child as pliant and pure, whereas a corrupt society was responsible for the loss of "natural innocence." Appropriate education would enable the innate potential of childhood to be realized and, ultimately, would lead to social reform. He believed that effective education must acknowledge the developmental characteristics of children and address moral, physical, and intellectual needs.

In the novel *How Gertrude Teaches Her Children*, published in 1801, Pestalozzi articulated his belief that roots of moral education lie in the parent-child relationship. Education begins in the home; emotional security and moral instruction coupled with a well-established work ethic enable children to resist the evils of society. Children with this strong moral foundation are prepared to master skills necessary for economic self-sufficiency. The true road to social reform lies in educating people to help themselves.

Intellectual growth is rooted in *Anschauung*, a process through which cognitive development takes place. Presaging Jean Piaget,

Pestallozzi believed learning must be active and interactive. *Anschauung* begins as the child translates sensory impressions received from interaction with the external environment into mental images. Through mental concentration, the child combines these mental images to form ideas or concepts. The process culminates as the child abstracts these ideas or concepts from concrete experience and internalizes them. While *Anschauung* is innate and intuitive, education that activates this process requires the type of systematic observation espoused in the philosophy of the Enlightenment.

Pestalozzi applied his philosophy at schools in Stans, Burgdorf, and Yverdon. Assuming the role of a father figure more than that of a traditional schoolmaster, Pestalozzi implemented a child-centered curriculum. Underlying all was a belief in the interrelationship of humankind and the environment. (See also **Froebel, Friedrich Wilhelm; Owen, Robert; Rousseau, Jean-Jacques;** and Section 2.1, **Enlightenment, Education in the.**)

References

Kessen, W. (1965). *The child.* New York: Wiley.

Pestalozzi, J. H. (1801/1894) *How Gertrude teaches her children.* Trans. by Holland, L. & Turner, F.) London: George Allen and Unwin.

Weber, E. (1984). *Ideas influencing early childhood education.* New York: Teachers College Press.

H. Freidus

Pratt, Caroline

Known for her inventive extensions of children's play and learning materials, the progressive educator Caroline Pratt (1867–1954) was born and raised in Fayetteville, New York. She began her career in 1884 as a teacher in a one-room schoolhouse prior to her own graduation from high school. After she received her diploma, she taught in a village school for five years before moving on in 1892 to study at Teachers College in New York City.

At the College, Pratt changed her specialization from kindergarten methods to manual arts, then the new wave in addressing the educational needs of recent immigrants and other groups struggling for economic survival. She subsequently taught carpentry for seven years. During this period, she became interested in the construction of children's playthings; in 1908, she turned her attention to design.

Between 1908 and 1913 Pratt designed a variety of manipulable learning materials for young children. Notable among these were her adaptations of the blocks used in early childhood classrooms. She changed the dimensions and added variety in shape to those then in use to create the Pratt (or standard) unit blocks now found in blockbuilding areas in most early childhood centers and classrooms today.

From 1913 to 1914, Pratt organized and then initiated the Play School, where she tried out her new materials in the context of a progressive educational environment. Coming to the attention of John Dewey in 1915, the Play School soon gained an excellent reputation for progressive practice. Pratt changed its name to the City and Country School in 1919, when it became formally affiliated with the Bureau of Educational Experiments (now Bank Street College of Education) as the Bureau's Laboratory School.

In City and Country, Pratt built a curriculum around blockbuilding for younger children, and a "jobs" program for older ones. She was especially interested in children's uses of symbolic play as vehicles for their development and learning. Like Dewey, Pratt felt that learning was most effective when it proceeded out of the children's immediate experience coupled with reflection on that experience.

Pratt directed the City and Country School from 1919 until her retirement in 1945. She devoted a portion of her remaining years to writing her autobiography, *I Learn from Children.*

References

Carlton, M. Patricia. (1986). *Caroline Pratt.* Unpublished doctoral dissertation, Teachers College, Columbia University.

Pratt, Caroline. (1948). *I learn from children: An adventure in progressive education*. New York: Simon & Schuster.

L. R. Williams

Rousseau, Jean-Jacques

A French philosopher and author, Jean-Jacques Rousseau (1712–1778) had a childhood marked by little that might have foretold his illustrious accomplishments later in life. The privileges ordinarily afforded children born into upper-class families in eighteenth-century Geneva were never realized by Rousseau. Barely a week after his birth on June 28, 1712, his mother died, leaving Rousseau to the care of his father Isaac, a watchmaker by trade, and to his aunts. His kind but wandering father eventually abandoned Rousseau, effectively disintegrating the ten-year-old boy's family. After apprenticing for five years as an engraver, Rousseau left Geneva, and as a footman, seminarist, music teacher or tutor, wandered Europe in a vain search for happiness. In 1732 he settled for eight years at Chambery or at Les Charmettes, the country house of Madame de Warens, a woman who served Rousseau as a sponsor, surrogate mother, and mistress.

In Paris in 1741 Rousseau met Denis Diderot who commissioned him to contribute articles for the *Encyclopedia*, the most significant literary enterprise of eighteenth-century France. It was his friend Diderot who encouraged Rousseau to proceed with what eventually became a prize-winning essay in response to a question set by the Academy of Dijon in 1749: "Has the revival of sciences and the arts helped to purify or to corrupt morals?" In his celebrated *Discourse*, which laid the foundations of his literary fame, Rousseau assailed the corruption, hypocrisy, oppression and baseness he saw in the social, cultural, and political institutions of his time. Rousseau made a powerful denunciation of his century of Enlightenment and, in so doing, applied himself boldly and with indelible social consciousness to the important questions of human betterment.

Throughout all of his writings (and especially in two of his books *The Social Contract* and *Emile*), Rousseau displayed a genuine concern for the individual and for a social environment that would both facilitate and preserve the emergence of the best in the individual. In view of an insincere and decadent society, Rousseau conceived in *Emile* a hypothetical child who is deposited in the hands of a sage who takes the child "back to nature" to inspire him with wisdom, moderation, self-control, and the power of reflection. The purposes of *Emile* were to (1) refute the contention that people were originally evil, or base, or ignorant, and (2) show that their misery and conflict had come about because of the manner and utilization of knowledge acquired through the study of the sciences as they were taught and made use of according to the dictates of fashion, pretense, and artifice.

In his description of the education of Emile, Rousseau was the first of his generation to view the child as a child rather than as a miniature adult. His views represented a reaction against what he considered to be a passive, artificial, and largely irrelevant education that turned children into shallow and mindless little puppets. He believed that by returning the child to "nature" there would be liberation from the constraints, influences, and inhibitions of a base and self-absorbed society. By allowing nature and experience time to interact, Rousseau believed that children would become capable of finding their own routes to overcoming alienation and integrating nature and culture (society).

In *Emile*, with its focus on the child as an active learner and its emphasis on learning experiences for the child that are relevant in terms of the child's conceptual ability and interest, Rousseau set forth the basic tenets of what is now called "progressive education." Rather than simply reflecting adult sensibilities, Rousseau held that education should respond to the abilities and needs of children. The role of the adults in the child's life was to provide opportunities to explore, learn, and solve problems.

Respect for childhood, the insistence upon active learning and physical freedom, the avoidance of inhibitions, the full use of the child's senses, the exposure to objects and things were among Rousseau's ideas that were to influence the modern schools of education. The ideas of Johann Pestalozzi, Friedrich Froebel, Maria Montessori, and John Dewey also were influenced by *Emile*. In all of his works, Rousseau invoked the sacredness of individual ideals against the powers of the state and the pressures of society. His last years were spent largely in Paris.

References

Bloom, H. (1988). *Jean-Jacques Rousseau*. New York: Chelsea House.

Claydon, L. F. (ed.). (1969). *Rousseau on education*. London: Macmillan.

Hendel, C. W. (1934). *Jean-Jacques Rousseau: Moralist*. New York: Bobbs-Merrill.

Rousseau, J.-J. (1883). *Emile: Or concerning education*. Trans. by E. Worthington. New York: D.C. Heath.

P. Wishon

Schurz, Margarethe Meyer

The first active Froebelian educator in the United States, Margarethe Meyer Schurz (1832–1876) and her husband Carl Schurz immigrated to the United States in 1852, as a result of the German Revolution of 1848. While still in Germany and prior to her marriage, Margarethe and her brother Adolf, her sister Bertha Meyer Ronge, and brother-in-law Johannes Ronge had become strong supporters and advocates of Froebel's new type of education for young children—the kindergarten.

Bertha Meyer Ronge and Johannes Ronge had left Germany in 1851 to go to England, where they founded an "infant garden" in Hampstead. Bertha Ronge was responsible for the kindergarten exhibit that caught the American educator Henry Barnard's eye at the Educational Exhibition in London in 1854.

While poor health prevented Margarethe from becoming immediately involved in Froebelian education in the United States, she remained eager to put her training to practical use. In the summer of 1856, Margarethe and her husband settled in Watertown, Wisconsin. Having become the mother of a daughter, Agathe, Margarethe decided to run a small program for Agathe and four cousins living nearby. She entertained the five children with Froebelian songs, games, "gifts," and "occupations." Soon, other relatives and friends asked that their children might join the group. The expansion in class size caused Margarethe to move the program from her home to a small building in the town in the late fall of 1856, the date usually given for the establishment of her kindergarten. The program, conducted in German, is generally regarded to have been the first kindergarten in the United States.

Margarethe Schurz's contribution to the kindergarten movement did not end in Watertown. During a visit to Boston in 1859, Margarethe met Elizabeth Palmer Peabody and convinced her of the value of kindergarten education. Elizabeth was fascinated by Agathe's behavior, noting that the girl was "a miracle—so child-like and unconscious, and yet so wise and able, attracting and ruling the children who seem nothing short of enchanted" (Baylor, 1965, p. 35). Margarethe replied that it was no miracle; it was a kindergarten education. She then explained some of Froebel's ideas, and followed up by sending Elizabeth Peabody a copy of the preface to Froebel's *Education of Man*. Elizabeth Peabody was so influenced by this encounter that she made her own first attempt to establish a kindergarten in 1860.

Ill health continued to haunt Margarethe, making her more and more of an invalid. After giving birth to a second daughter, who died, Margarethe returned to Hamburg, Germany, in 1876. She died there at the age of 43. (See also **Barnard, Henry; Froebelian Kindergarten, The;** and **Peabody, Elizabeth.**)

References

Baylor, R. M. (1965). *Elizabeth Palmer Peabody, kindergarten pioneer*. Philadelphia: University of Pennsylvania Press.

Snyder, A. (1972). *Dauntless women in childhood education 1856–1931*. Washington, DC: Association for Childhood Education International.

J. K. Smith

Séguin, Édouard

Born in Clamecy, France, to a family long associated with the medical profession, Édouard Séguin's (1812–1880) upbringing, which followed the principles of Rousseau, influenced his subsequent approach to education. His entire career revolved around the treatment and training of the mentally retarded.

Séguin worked with Jean-Marc-Gaspard Itard, who was famous for his attempts to educate a young boy found living wild in the forests of Aveyron, France. Séguin initially incorporated Itard's emphasis on sense development into his own system. Later, however, he expanded his program to include the "physiological method" involving training of the muscles.

Maria Montessori credits Séguin with "having completed a genuine educational system for 'deficient' children" (Montessori, 1964, p. 34). Séguin applied his ideas in France, where he successfully established the first school for the mentally retarded. Principles derived from his practice that have provided a basis for the education of the mentally retarded in the United States include recognition of child observation as the infrastructure of education, attention to the whole child as the focus of education, recognition that the child learns best from use of concrete objects, insistence that all concept learning be preceded by sense training beginning with the sense of touch, and recognition that all children have some capacity for learning.

Séguin first described his method in 1846 in a French publication. Shortly thereafter, he immigrated to the United States, where he practiced medicine, served as director of the Pennsylvania Training School, and acted as consultant to many state institutions. He helped to organize the School for Defectives on Randalls Island, New York City, and for the next 20 years worked for the improvement of training techniques for the mentally retarded.

With the assistance of his son, Edward C. Séguin, a distinguished neurologist, Séguin published another book on his method in 1866. That work, entitled *Idiocy and Its Treatment by the Physiological Method*, was followed by *Medical Thermometry and Human Temperature* (1876) and *Report on Education* (1875), which Séguin wrote as a member of the delegation to the Vienna International Exhibition of 1873. That volume contained a comprehensive review of the work of both foreign and American schools with retarded children.

Séguin died in Mount Vernon, New York, in 1880, but his influence on special education has endured. Samuel Gridley Howe utilized Séguin's methods in the establishment of the first state school for the mentally retarded in the United States. Maria Montessori also acknowledged her indebtedness by saying, "my ten years of work may in a sense be considered as a summing up of the forty years of work done by Itard and Séguin" (Montessori, 1964, p. 46). More than a century after his death, Séguin's influence can still be seen in current methods of instruction for children with special needs. (See also **Montessori Method, The.**)

References

Ball, T. S. (1971). *Itard, Séguin and Kephart: Sensory education—A learning interpretation*. Columbus, OH: Charles E. Merrill.

Bero, F. (1983). Teaching the "ineducable": The impact of the sensationalist philosophy on educational thought and practice. Paper presented at the Annual Meeting of the American Educational Research Association, Montreal, Canada, April, 1983.

Meyers, K. (1913). Séguin's principles of education as related to the Montessori method. *Journal of Education, 77*, 538–541.

Montessori, M. (1964). *The Montessori method*. New York: Schocken Books.

Reynolds, C. R., & Mann, L. (eds.). (1987). *Encyclopedia of Special Education. Vol. 3*. New York: Wiley.

Séguin, E. (1971/1866). *Idiocy and its treatment by the physiological method*. New York: Augustus M. Kelley.

Wolman, B. (ed.). (1977). *International Encyclopedia of Psychiatry, Psychology, Psychoanalysis and Neurology*. Vol. 10 (pp. 94–95). New York: Aesculapius Publishers.

Zusne, L. (ed.). (1984). *Biographical Dictionary of Psychology* (pp. 390–99). Westport, CT: Greenwood Press.

P. Povell

Temple, Alice

Born in Chicago, Illinois, as the youngest daughter of John F. and Eliza Ann Bryan, Alice Temple (1871–1946) was raised in a family that possessed a broad, social consciousness. Not surprisingly, Temple's first teaching experience was in a kindergarten run by a church in a poor neighborhood.

Temple trained and did her practice teaching from 1894 to 1896 at the Chicago Free Kindergarten Association under the tutelage of Anna E. Bryan, a detractor of the widely followed Froebelian method. Following Bryan's death in 1901, Temple became the principal at the Free Kindergarten Association and remained there until 1904, when she left to study at the University of Chicago. There she attended lectures by John Dewey and became a strong proponent of applying Deweyan philosophy to early childhood education.

After four years of teaching at the University of Chicago's Department of Kindergarten Education, Temple became the director of the department, a position she held from 1909 until her retirement in 1932. During her tenure at that institution, Temple employed G. Stanley Hall's techniques in child study and became a principal force in turning Dewey's theory into practice.

As department director, Temple organized the Kindergarten-Primary Department in 1913. The new organization was based on her concurrence with Dewey that for education to be effective, it must be continuous and follow a developmental pattern. Hers was the first university department to articulate kindergarten with the primary grades and grant a Kindergarten-Primary certificate. Through first a two-year program and then a four-year bachelor's degree in education, Temple's program featured a Deweyan child-centered philosophy, with classrooms reflecting democratic society in miniature. There she used Hall's techniques of observation, survey, and questionnaires to enable her teachers to evaluate strengths and weaknesses of the program.

Temple was active in the International Kindergarten Union (IKU) and its successor, the Association for Childhood Education International (ACEI), serving on a variety of committees over her many years of service. On her recommendation the Committee on Cooperation with the National Education Association was formed in 1911, formally establishing cooperative relations between the two kindergarten groups. Her arduous efforts for the inclusion of an early childhood education division in the United States Bureau of Education finally came to fruition during her term as president of the IKU (1925–1927).

Temple was a frequent author of articles in professional journals and bulletins published by the University of Chicago and the United States Bureau (later Office) of Education. Notable among these was *Unified Kindergarten and First Grade Teaching*, coauthored in 1928 with Samuel C. Parker. While she was president of the IKU, the journal *Childhood Education* came into existence. Temple regarded the journal as a vehicle for addressing the needs of children from three to eight years of age, thereby strengthening the argument for articulated continuity in childhood education. Alice Temple died in New York at the age of 75. (See also **Bryan, Anna; Dewey, John;** and Chapter 4, Section 4.2, **Hall, G. Stanley.**)

References

Chicago Tribune. (January 7, 1946). *Alice Temple*. p. 16.

Marquis, A.N. (Ed.) (1931). *Who's who in Chicago* (5th edition). Chicago: Marquis.

New York Times. (January 7, 1946). *Alice Temple*. p. 19.

Snyder, A. (1972). *Dauntless women in childhood education, 1856–1931*. Washington, DC: Association for Childhood Education International.

J. B. Fine

Wiggin, Kate Douglas

An artist, author, and educator, Kate Douglas Wiggin's (1856–1923) endeavors stemmed from her love for and understanding of young children. Born in rural Maine, her early years growing up on a farm gave Wiggin a sense of oneness with nature that she carried with her throughout her life. Her numerous books, including *Rebecca of Sunnybrook Farm* and *The Birds' Christmas Carol*, reflect this life view, as does her extensive work with the kindergarten movement.

At the Abbot Academy in Andover, Massachusetts, Wiggin was first introduced to the work and writings of Friedrich Froebel and Elizabeth Peabody. Upon completion of her studies at Abbot Academy, Wiggin joined her family who had relocated to California and became a student in the first Froebelian training school for kindergarten teachers on the West Coast.

Wiggin, like Froebel, believed that good education must seek to bring children into harmony with their environment. She understood that, if kindergartens were to be successful in the United States, modifications needed to be made in many Froebelian methods and materials. She held true, however, to the Froebelian philosophy that the instruction of young children must take place in a specific order—imitation, direction, free expression. She noted that "[t]he greater the freedom given to the child, the greater the necessity of teaching him to use that liberty in and through law" (Wiggin and Smith in Snyder, 1972, p. 118).

Wiggin was involved in the free kindergarten movement that, foreshadowing the philosophy of Head Start, sought to improve the life course of low-income children by providing them with early childhood education. She believed that society might be reformed, and the "American Dream" might become a reality through the education of these children.

Wiggin started the Silver Street Kindergarten in 1878 in one of the worst slum sections of San Francisco. As many as 50 children aged 3 to 7 years attended daily. The school was a success and contributed to efforts to incorporate kindergarten into the public school system. (See also **Froebelian Kindergarten, The**.)

Reference

Snyder, A. (1972). *Dauntless women in childhood education 1856–1931*. Washington, DC: Association for Childhood Education International.

H. Freidus

Yates, Josephine S.

Professionally active during the late nineteenth and early twentieth centuries, Josephine Yates was a college teacher and writer in the field of education who gave special attention to the history and progress of the African-American kindergarten and nursery school movements in the United States.

In her column in the *Colored American Magazine*, Yates was an advocate for Froebel's system of kindergarten education and for the value of play in curricula for young children. The African-American community, like other educational communities in the United States at that period, was questioning the value of play. Yates believed that providing opportunities for play as an important aspect of early education created part of the constructive environment needed for social change toward equal opportunity for African-Americans.

References

Cunningham, C. E., & Osborn, D. K. (1979). A historical examination of blacks in early childhood education. *Young Children, 24* (3), pp. 20–29.

Yates, J. S. (1905). Kindergarten and mother's clubs. *Colored American Magazine 10* (6), pp. 304–311.

Yates, J. S. (1906). Education and genetic psychology. *Colored American Magazine, 10* (5), pp. 293–297.

L. R. Williams

Young, Ella Flagg

The first female superintendent of a major city in the United States (Chicago), Ella Flagg Young (1845–1918) started her career in that city as an elementary school teacher in 1862 at the age of 17. The following year, she was made a head assistant of a larger elementary school; and two years later, she was appointed principal of the city's first practice teaching school. By 1876, she was the principal of a regular elementary school; and ten years later, she was in the school's central office as a district superintendent.

Feeling a need for extending her education, she matriculated in a Ph.D. program under the direction of John Dewey at the University of Chicago. After receiving her doctoral degree, she taught at the university until 1904, when she became the principal of the Chicago Normal School and finally superintendent of Chicago's schools (1909–1915).

It was during her eight years at the University of Chicago that she was most directly involved in early childhood education. There she helped Dewey reorganize and run his lab school when certain weaknesses became apparent. She suggested the title of "laboratory school" to signify a place where the latest educational practices could be tested and verified. Dewey credited Young with helping him to translate his philosophical conceptions into their empirical equivalents. Young tried to organize the curriculum in true pragmatic fashion, believing as Dewey did that what we know is embedded in what we experience.

In the laboratory school all learning was centered around projects in a socially cooperative setting. The four- to five-year-olds learned household occupations, and six-year-olds engaged in social occupations (such as those of the baker, the grocer, or the farmer) that served the household, actually running a small "store," planting crops, or cooking.

From the ages of seven to thirteen, the children studied units that focused on "human progress through discovery." The seven-year-old children related first inventions to primitive societies. They built shelters and vessels and made weapons and utensils. The eight-year-olds studied the Phoenician culture and focused on activities related to trading, mercantile developments, and mapmaking.

History was the curriculum for nine- to eleven-year-olds. The nine-year-old children studied local history. They took field trips to museums and to city hall to watch government in action, wrote stories, and read about the development of the city. The ten-year-olds studied Colonial history (including the American Revolution) by building colonial furniture, sewing, and weaving. The eleven-year-old students learned about the European backgrounds of the colonists by, for example, engaging in activities necessary to run an English village. Twelve- and thirteen-year-olds engaged in social experiments that lasted for longer periods of time. They formed clubs and built club houses.

Young left the university in 1904, but continued to practice the educational tenets of pragmatism. In training teachers at the normal school she stressed the scientific method as applied to the art of teaching, and she cautioned teachers to be "less concerned with obedience and more concerned with understanding individual patterns." She noted, "No one would be so rash as to claim that it makes no difference what food a child has, that the only question is how does the stomach attack the food. Yet certain educators maintain that the significant question in education is how children learn and not what they learn" (Young, 1903, p. 147).

As superintendent Ella Flagg Young continued to reorganize the schools to meet individual differences and to be more progressive in general. She retired in 1915 at the age of 70. Although she had planned to write, she instead devoted herself to raising money for World War I. She died of complications related to the Spanish influenza epidemic in October 1918. (See also, **Dewey, John;** and **Progressive Movement, The.**)

References

Smith, J. K. (1979). *Ella Flagg Young: Portrait of a leader*. Ames, IA: Educational Studies Press.

Young, E. F. (1902). *Isolation in the schools*. Chicago: University of Chicago Press.

Young, E. F. (1903). *The scientific method in education*. Decennial Publication Series. Chicago: University of Chicago Press.

J. K. Smith

Chapter 3

SOCIOCULTURAL, POLITICAL, AND ECONOMIC CONTEXTS OF CHILD CARE AND EARLY EDUCATION

Chapter *3*

SOCIOCULTURAL, POLITICAL, AND ECONOMIC CONTEXTS OF CHILD CARE AND EARLY EDUCATION

Introduction

Early childhood education, like education in general, is carried out within distinct settings and is subject to influence from a host of social, cultural, economic and political forces. The range of possible settings tends to vary more widely than that associated with other forms or levels of education, however, because of the broad nature of the involvement of early childhood education with young children and their families. For the same reason, the influence of societal forces on early educational practice, policy, theory, and research tends to be far-reaching. This chapter provides information on the demographics and diversity of the populations served, the history of program sponsorship and sources of program funding, public and private settings for child care and early education, and the status of public policy, funding, and advocacy affecting programs for young children. It also includes analyses of several of the issues that historically have had, and today continue to have, a strong impact upon the form, content, and study of early

education and child care. Those issues are summarized briefly below.

The Individual and Society

A perennial question in the field of education is that of whose interests are to be served, the individual's or the larger society of which the individual is a part. In early childhood education and child care, the tension between the needs of individual children and the society has played itself out in many ways. Most particularly, it has affected assumptions made about what children bring with them to early childhood settings and the nature of the settings themselves. It also has affected the possibilities for articulation among various forms and levels of child care and early education. While Chapter 4 of the *Encyclopedia* provides detailed descriptions of the development of the child as an individual, it is very important to recognize that development may be affected by the broader social, political, and cultural issues treated in the present chapter.

It is well known that child care and early education begin before, and continue outside of, children's experience in group settings. Young children arrive at centers, schools, or other early childhood settings with a variety of strengths and different types of readiness for group life and school learning. Family and community influences have contributed to these conditions in many ways (Heath, 1983; Teale, 1988; Whiting, Edwards et al., 1988). Young children also bring preliterate and oral capabilities that have been shaped by early experiences in their families and communities, and these structures are a significant foundation upon which educators can build (Egan, 1988; Heath, 1983).

When group settings do build on these strengths, there is greater continuity between the experiences of home, school, and community. Early educators argue that such continuity provides young children with feelings of success that contribute to their continuing accomplishment in group settings. It is likewise thought that children's familial and community experience with uses of space and time, interaction with people of different generations and cultural and/or linguistic groups, practice with language that increases the use of metaphor and other symbolic applications, exercise of responsibility for other people and for materials, and the content of available materials are all influences upon children's readiness for constructive functioning within group care and educational settings.

The nature and quality of these experiences differ according to the unique elements of the cultures in which children are raised, the economic situation of their families and community, and any experience they or their families might have with racism, classism, sexism, handicapism, and ageism.

All children are members of cultures and socioeconomic groups that reflect variation in beliefs and customs, linguistic behavior, cognitive styles and motivation. Such pluralism can be an asset in early childhood settings, for this diversity brings a vitality to teaching and learning as the children absorb both the rudiments of the common culture and those of other cultures.

For many middle-class European-American children, the values of the school and other early childhood settings may be quite similar to and compatible with the values of their homes. For children of some other groups, however, the values of the school may be incongruent with their own. Those children's ways of coping with school structures and organized ways of learning may not be valued in the school or early education setting.

Many of these children are from African-American, American Indian (Native American), Asian-American, and Latino (Hispanic) groups. Teachers and other child caregivers traditionally have seen education as a way that children might assimilate the dominant cultural and social heritage of the United States. As children from these groups cannot assimilate in ways that decrease their visibility, they may be seen as a threat to cultural homogeneity and be prejudged to be lacking the traditional values of individualism, self-reliance, and discipline, as well as lacking the work ethic. Such racial prejudice has deleterious effects on the children's self-confidence and self-esteem and ultimately, it is now believed, on their academic achievement.

Many children from particular cultural groups also enter early childhood settings speaking a language other than English. This circumstance requires careful attention to bilingual educational approaches built on the premises that bilingualism is an asset, and that linguistically different children are not deficient in their ability to learn.

The dilemma of cultural pluralism is one current manifestation of the tension between serving the interests of individuals and those of the larger society. The influence of children's early cultural and social experience on their subsequent development is now only beginning to be understood. Protection of a high quality of children's early experiences has subsequently become the focus of much debate in the arena of public policy in the United States.

Status of Public Policy, Funding, and Advocacy

The nature and quality of children's experiences may be affected by governmental funding and regulation of child care and early education programs. Family participation in programs that provide nutritional and other health care services, social services, or other interventions before or at the same time as group child care and early education may have profound effects on children's subsequent development. Availability of such opportunities, however, is dependent upon public recognition of the serious problems faced by many young children in the United States today and upon public support for finding their solutions.

By the turn of the next century, a decline in population growth will result in fewer young adults entering the work force. In educational, governmental, and corporate circles, there is deep concern about the current status and future ability of children who are experiencing serious economic, familial, educational, and health and welfare problems to support the future economy. Questions arise about the likelihood of there being a viable work force because of intensifying health problems such as addiction to drugs at birth, fetal alcohol syndrome, and pediatric AIDS, as well as ongoing concerns about high infant mortality rates (particularly among African-American and American Indian/Native American children). Future projections are further confounded by such issues as rising numbers of homeless families, the possible effects of children's exposure to violence in television programming (Hymes, 1990), and parental pressure on children to attain early academic skills regardless of resulting experience of high stress (Elkind, 1981). These considerations affect current policy, funding, and advocacy issues, which are discussed below.

Policy. Social policy on the local, state, and national level has been and will continue to be developed to deal with the ramifications of these problems. Examples are the Stewart B. McKinney Homeless Assistance Act (P.L. 100–77), designed to ensure the guarantee of states to educational access for all homeless children (Eddowes & Hranitz, 1989), and the Education of the Handicapped Act Amendment of 1986 (P.L. 99–457) that extends funds for mainstreaming into early childhood programs (Smith & Strain, 1988).

Educational policy that affects young children is another current concern at the national, state, and local levels. While the National Association for the Education of Young Children has promoted "developmentally appropriate practice" (see Chapters 4 and 5) both in the classroom and in all testing of young children (Bredekamp, 1987; Meisels, 1987), there is a discrepancy between professional policies and educational practices. An increasing number of states, for example, are administering academic readiness testing prior to kindergarten or first grade (see Chapter 4) and are implementing "developmental kindergartens" or "transitional first grades" (Schultz, 1989). Despite their use of the term "developmental," these programs generally are designed to retain children at a level lower than first grade until they are "ready" to do formal academic work, rather than to enable children to succeed in first grade through use of a developmentally appropriate first grade curriculum.

The discrepancy between research and practice is another issue to take into account. At the same time that researchers have identified a variety of early interventions with long-term payoff for economically disadvantaged children (Schorr, 1988), little attention is being given to clarifying which elements or combination of elements of practice make significant differences, nor are the proven practices being supported and extended.

Funding. Funding continues to be a challenge in the implementation of improved policies that can influence the care and education of young children. Corporate sponsorship of child care is increasing slowly. Government funding generally is supported in theory; but policy questions concerning the separation of church and state and the value of public versus private child care and early education continue to create dilemmas.

Advocacy. The massive social, economic, and educational policy difficulties described briefly above have continued to challenge those deeply concerned about young children to become advocates on their behalf. Advocacy is defined as active involvement, beyond paid remuneration, in the lives of young children with the goal of enhancing equal opportunities for optimal growth and development (Fennimore, 1989). Current legislative initiatives for increased child care and related educational services have required child advocates to demonstrate an understanding of the intricate workings of the United States Congress and the legislative process (Goffin & Lombardi, 1988). Advocates support ongoing child care and early education initiatives by making personal visits to members of Congress, engaging in letter writing and telephone campaigns, and through public speaking and publication, encouraging many other people to do the same.

Ultimately, much of the advocacy effort must address the distribution of resources and the politics of sponsorship. Complex political dimensions affect the increasing public, private, and corporate financial sponsorship of early education programs. An inconsistent relationship, however, has existed between social and economic policy for children in the United States at a time when far-reaching social, economic, and demographic changes have created the need for extensive programs (Edelman, 1989).

Current policy initiatives (such as over 200 bills with child care provisions introduced in the 1988 session of Congress) indicate potential for large increases in resources for children (Mitchell, Seligson, & Marx, 1989). While funding of programs for children over five years of age is governed by a generally compatible coexistence between public (90 percent of children involved) and private (10 percent of children involved), the funding of programs for children under five years of age is affected by a diverse array of public and private financial and political interests (Mitchell, Seligson, & Marx, 1989). In the case of programs for children under five years of age, 37 percent of the services provided are publicly

funded, and 63 percent are privately funded (U.S. Bureau of the Census, 1980).

Legislative debates over child care revolve around the value of income tax credits for low-income families, contrasted with a mixture of tax credits for families and grants to states (Hymes, 1990). Policy decisions, on the other hand, address the relative merits of ongoing categorical funding streams such as Head Start, Chapter I (which provides funds for compensatory programs), and subsidized day care, versus new initiatives such as universal availability of prekindergarten programs in the public schools (Children's Defense Fund, 1989). Central to the politics of sponsorship are decisions regarding whether to expand services to the most children possible at the lowest possible cost, or to preserve quality and protect options for children and their families (Children's Defense Fund, 1989).

Future Alternatives

Future alternatives in each of the areas described above will depend upon the interaction of several potent factors, including the continuing shift in demographics, with possibly even greater diversity and shifts in the cultural and economic makeup of the United States; concomitant shifts in the bases of power governing political and social interaction; changes in sponsorship of child care and early education programs to reflect changing societal needs; and publicizing the results of research on the effects of early education and child care.

There are challenges to previously accepted ideas about the content and forms of early education that may stimulate still further the diversification of settings for child care and early education. These challenges include the growing presence of women in the work force, which creates a demand for child care outside of the home, and the development of cultural pluralism. Financial resources may have to be distributed very differently as the public and private balance in sponsorship changes in response to the new configurations. Research is likely to turn more and more attention to unraveling the complexities of the interactions between individual development of children and the development of their social selves, and to discovering how the dynamics of particular settings affect one another and the ultimate outcomes of child care and early education.

The articles appearing below are grouped in sections according to the progression of topics and issues that have been outlined in this introduction. Within each section, articles generally are arranged alphabetically, except when a topic is so related to one that precedes it that it must follow logically as an amplification.

References

Bredekamp, S. (ed.). (1987). *Developmentally appropriate practice in early childhood programs serving children from birth through age 8*. Washington, DC: National Association for the Education of Young Children.

Children's Defense Fund. (1989). *The nation's investment in children: An analysis of the President's FY 1990 budget proposals*. Washington, DC: Author.

Eddowes, E. A., & Hranitz, J. R. (1989). Educating children of the homeless. *Childhood Education*, *65* (4): 197–200.

Edelman, M. W. (1989). Economic issues related to child care and early childhood education. In Rust, F. O'C., & Williams, L. R. (eds.), *The care and education of young children: Expanding contexts, sharpening focus*. New York: Teachers College Press.

Egan, K. (1988). The origins of imagination and the curriculum. In Egan, K., & Nadaner D. (eds.), *Imagination and education* (pp. 91–127). New York: Cambridge University Press.

Elkind, D. (1981). *The hurried child: Growing up too fast too soon*. Reading, MA: Addison-Wesley.

Fennimore, B. S. (1989). *Child advocacy for early childhood educators*. New York: Teachers College Press.

Goffin, S. G., & Lombardi, J. (1988). *Speaking out: Early childhood advocacy*. Washington, DC: National Association for the Education of Young Children.

Heath, S. B. (1983). *Ways with words: Language, life, and work in communities and classrooms*. New York: Cambridge University Press.

Hymes, J. (1990). *Early childhood education: The year in review. A look at 1989*. Washington, DC: National Association for the Education of Young Children.

Meisels, S. J. (1987). *Developmental screening in early childhood education: A guide*. Washington, DC: National Association for the Education of Young Children.

Mitchell, A., Seligson, M., & Marx, F. (1989). *Early childhood programs and the public school: Between promise and practice*. Dover, MA: Auburn House.

Schorr, L. (1988). *Within our reach: Breaking the cycle of disadvantage*. New York: Doubleday.

Schultz, T. (1989). Testing and retention of young children: Moving from controversy to reform. *Phi Delta Kappan*, *71*(2): 125–129.

Smith, B. J., & Strain, P. S. (1988). Early childhood special education in the next decade: Implementing and expanding PL 99–457. In Smith, B.J., & Strain, P.S. (eds.), *Topics in early childhood special education*, *8* (1): 37–47.

Teale, W. H. (1988, November). Developmentally appropriate assessment of reading and writing in the early childhood classroom. *Elementary School Journal*, *89* (6): 173–183.

United States Bureau of the Census. (1980). Census of Population PO80–1–B1. Washington, DC: U.S. Government Printing Office.

Whiting, B. B., & Edwards, C. P., et al. (1988). *Children of different worlds: The formation of social behavior*. Cambridge, MA: Harvard University Press.

B. S. Fennimore, D. P. Fromberg, E. B. Vold, & L. R. Williams

3.1 Demographics and Diversity

The demographics reported below cover a variety of areas affecting the provision of child care and early childhood education. Population trends, the presence of women in the work force, changing family configurations, the distribution of financial resources, and concentrations of populations of particular cultural and ethnic groups all may have an impact upon the forms and content of early childhood programs. Most of the sources of such statistics report national trends. Some information is available on regional trends, however, allowing a closer look at the changes occurring in specific parts of the country and a comparison with the national figures. As each state has its own system for data collection and its own set of priorities in reporting, there is a concomitant degree of uniqueness in the topics addressed from region to region.

L. R. Williams

National Demographic Trends

Population trends will have important effects on early childhood education in the United States during the 1990s. The population of children under the age of five has been predicted to rise from its 1983 level of 17.8 million to 19.2 million by 1990, and to begin to drop and level off to between 17.5 million and 18 million after the year 2000. Smaller increases are projected for the elementary school population. Although nearly all states have contributed to the currently growing early childhood population, the largest gains are occurring in the southern and the western parts of the country. Since 1980, California and Texas together have accounted for 40 percent of the nation's growth in the total population (U.S. Bureau of the Census, 1985; 1988a).

About half of all women having babies are in the work force. This figure reflects a long-term trend. The number of women with children under the age of five has increased from 12 percent in 1950 to 45 percent in 1980, exceeded 50 percent in 1990, and is expected to continue to increase through the 1990s. The older their children, the larger the percentage of working mothers. Women in the work force with children six years of age and older increased from 28 percent in 1950 to 62 percent in 1980 (U.S. Bureau of the Census, 1988b).

Birth rates differ for white, black, and Hispanic populations. In 1987 white women had 68.5 births, black women had 83.2 births, and Hispanic women had 95.8 births per 1,000 women. The highest overall birth rate occurred in the western part of the country, with 77.4 births per 1,000 women. The next highest rate was in the south, with 69.5 births per 1,000 women. The states on the southern border of the United States have proportionately larger Hispanic populations than other regions of the country, resulting in a larger growth of the early childhood population in those areas.

Family configurations vary across groups. In 1984 children lived with both of their parents in 81 percent of white families, 70 percent of Hispanic families, and 41 percent of black families. Among all families, one out of four children lived with one parent. A sizable population of young children was supported by a single parent because of a high divorce rate and a large number of births to unmarried mothers. For the general population, close to one out of every five families was maintained by a single mother. Of these families headed by a mother, 15 percent were white, 25 percent were Hispanic, and 50 percent were black (U.S. Bureau of the Census, 1986). Only from 1 percent to 3 percent of white, black, or Hispanic families were headed by a single father or by other relatives.

The general population trends have been reflected in school enrollments. During the five years from 1981 to 1986, preprimary enrollment grew by 25 percent, but elementary school enrollment declined by 3 percent. The decline was less for black children; and, in fact, elementary school enrollment for black children is expected to increase by 24 percent between 1986 and 1998, when enrollment will peak. Even greater increases in enrollment may be expected for Hispanic children, especially in the southern border states (U.S. Bureau of the Census, 1988b). From these population trends, it is clear that the demand for child care and early childhood education will grow markedly from the present until at least the year 2000.

References

United States Bureau of the Census. (September 1985). Population profile of the United States 1983/84. *Current Population Reports,* Series P-23, No. 145. Washington, DC: U.S. Government Printing Office.

United States Bureau of the Census. (November 1986). Women in the American economy. *Current Population Reports,* Series P-23, No. 146. Washington, DC: U.S. Government Printing Office.

United States Bureau of the Census. (May 1988a). Fertility of American women: June, 1987. *Current Population Reports,* Series P-20, No. 427.

Washington, DC: U.S. Government Printing Office.

United States Bureau of the Census. (August 1988b). School enrollment—social and economic characteristics of students: October, 1986. *Current Population Reports*, Series P-20, No. 429. Washington, DC: U.S. Government Printing Office.

C. Brownstein

Regional Demographic Trends

The 50 states of the Union are divided informally into regions that are not only geographical but also tend to be reflective of a shared history and economy. At one time, the regions also retained distinctive cultural patterns (including regional inflection in language). Recently, however, such distinctions between regions have begun to diminish as cultural pluralism has become more widespread throughout the United States and as increased mobility has moved populations from one region to another.

L. R. Williams

Midwest

The Midwest of the United States, also recognized as the North Central Region, includes 12 states: Illinois, Indiana, Iowa, Kansas, Michigan, Minnesota, Missouri, Nebraska, North Dakota, Ohio, South Dakota, and Wisconsin. These states exhibit a wide diversity in size and population. The chart below indicates the density of population, which ranges from 9.4 persons per square mile (South Dakota) to 264.7 persons per square mile (Ohio).

Density of Population of Midwest States

(persons per square mile)

South Dakota	9.4
North Dakota	9.6
Nebraska	20.9
Kansas	30.6
Iowa	50.6
Minnesota	54.1
Missouri	74.6
Wisconsin	89.2
Indiana	154.6
Michigan	162.2
Illinois	208.7
Ohio	264.7

The Midwest is experiencing growth in its population. Since 1980 only two states have indicated a decline in their populations. Michigan's population declined by 0.2 percent, and Iowa's population declined by 2.7 percent. The chart below indicates populations by state and the percentage of change in population since 1980 (*The World Almanac*, 1990).

	Population (in thousands)	Percentage of Change from 1980
Illinois	11,614	6.0
Ohio	10,855	0.5
Michigan	9,240	-0.2
Indiana	5,556	1.2
Missouri	5,141	4.6
Wisconsin	4,855	3.2
Minnesota	4,307	5.7
Iowa	2,834	-2.7
Kansas	2,495	5.6
Nebraska	1,602	2.1
South Dakota	713	3.2
North Dakota	667	2.2

One way of examining the manner in which services are provided to children and families is to look at the program known as Aid to Families with Dependent Children. The most recent information from the Office of Research and Statistics (*The World Almanac*, 1990) is contained in the chart below. It includes average monthly caseloads (families) by state, the average number of children served on a monthly basis in that state, and the average monthly payment per person and per family.

The chart indicates the wide range of caseloads, from a high in Ohio of 225,541 to a low in North Dakota of 5,219. Illinois served an average of 456,691 children each month, while North Dakota served 9,580 children through Aid to Families with Dependent Children. Those payments ranged from a low of $88 per person in Missouri to a high of $172 in Minnesota.

All states in the region showed a decrease in the rate of births to teenaged mothers from 1980 to 1987. The 1987 figures show that teenaged mothers account for 7.3 percent to 14 percent of births in this region. This percentage is down from the 1980 figures, which in-

	Average Monthly Caseload	Average Number of Children	Average Monthly Payment per Served Person/Family
Ohio	225,541	418,902	$104/$298
Illinois	220,071	456,691	$101/$308
Michigan	213,163	416,208	$159/$481
Wisconsin	89,109	174,141	$156/$473
Missouri	67,778	133,665	$88/$264
Minnesota	54,696	104,402	$172/$515
Indiana	52,975	102,734	$92/$263
Iowa	37,082	66,365	$124/$348
Kansas	23,996	46,745	$115/$338
Nebraska	14,677	29,013	$110/$320
South Dakota	6,495	12,966	$94/$270
North Dakota	5,219	9,580	$126/$350

dicated that births to teenaged mothers ranged from 10.4 percent to 17.3 percent. The states in the Midwest with the lowest percentage of births to teenaged mothers in 1987 were Minnesota, North Dakota, and Nebraska. The highest percentages of births to teenaged mothers were in Indiana, Missouri, and Ohio. The largest rate of decrease in births to teenaged mothers occurred in South Dakota (a 3.8 percent decrease from 13.5 percent to 9.7 percent), Missouri (a 3.5 percent decrease from 16.9 percent to 13.4 percent), and Kansas (a 3.5 percent decrease from 15.0 percent to 11.5 percent) (U.S. Bureau of the Census, 1989).

Nationwide, the numbers of children enrolled in nursery schools and kindergartens are increasing. The numbers of children from varying cultural and ethnic groups have maintained similar increases, as have the numbers of three-, four-, and five-year-old children who are enrolled. There has been an increase in the enrollment of children whose mothers work outside of the home.

The figures on licensed child care facilities in the Midwest are as diverse as other statistics pertaining to the area. As of 1986, for example, North Dakota and South Dakota each had fewer than 100 licensed child care centers, whereas Michigan had almost 2,500 licensed centers (*Directory of Child Day Care Centers*, 1986).

References

Directory of Child Day Care Centers. (1986). (Volume 2: North Central) Phoenix: Oryx Press.

United States Bureau of the Census. (1989). *Statistical abstract of the United States*. Washington, DC: U.S. Government Printing Office.

World Almanac, The. (1990). New York: Scripps Howard Co.

L. Todd

Northeast

The Northeast region of the United States, the smallest region in terms of land area in the United States, is the most heavily populated. It is estimated that nearly one out of four people in the United States lives in the Northeast.

With the Atlantic Ocean its eastern border and the Appalachian Mountains as its western border, the Northeast region includes 13 states and the District of Columbia. The New England states of Maine, New Hampshire, Vermont, Massachusetts, Connecticut, and Rhode Island, the Mid-Atlantic states of New York, New Jersey and Pennsylvania, the South-Atlantic states of Delaware, Maryland, Virginia and West Virginia, as well as the District of Columbia comprise the Northeast.

The population of the Northeast continues to increase with the exception of that of the District of Columbia. The following chart indicates the total population by state and the total population of children under five years of age in each state.

	Total Population (Number in 1,000s)	Children Under Five (Number in 1,000s)
New York	17,772	1,230
Pennsylvania	11,888	776
New Jersey	7,619	499
Massachusetts	5,832	381
Virgina	5,787	408
Maryland	4,463	323
Connecticut	3,189	209
West Virginia	1,918	122
Maine	1,173	82
New Hampshire	1,027	73
Rhode Island	975	61
Delaware	633	45
Dist. of Columbia	626	46
Vermont	541	73

Source: U.S. Bureau of the Census, 1989.

With the majority of the population of the Northeast living in cities, the region is considered an urban area. In the District of Columbia, 100 percent of the population is urban. In New Jersey, New York, Rhode Island, Massachusetts, and Maryland over 80 percent of the population lives in urban areas of the states. Over 50 percent of the population in New Hampshire, Delaware, and Virginia lives in urban settings. In contrast are Maine and West Virginia with under 50 percent of the population residing in urban areas.

Attracting people from all over the world, the cities of the Northeast are cosmopolitan. Ethnic populations that include African-Americans, people from the English-speaking Caribbean, Asian-Americans, Hispanics, Greek-Americans, Italian-Americans, and others reside in the cities as well as in the rural areas. In one school system alone, there are children representing 26 different nationalities and ethnic groups. Nearly 25 percent of the population of Maryland, 73 percent of the District of Columbia, and 20 percent of the populations of New York, New Jersey, and Delaware are people of color.

Economic Diversity

Economic diversity exists in the Northeast. Although a location of great wealth, the region also contains great poverty. The Children's Defense Fund (1988) states that nearly 22 percent of children under the age of six living in the cities of the Northeast are living in poverty. In New York, Maine, Vermont, Massachusetts, Rhode Island, New Jersey, Pennsylvania, Delaware, Virginia, West Virginia, and the District of Columbia, over 20 percent of the children under the age of five live in poverty.

The incidence of poverty will increase in the future. It has been estimated that in the future over 30 percent of the children in New York City will live in poverty, partly because they will be living in single-parent households. In 50 percent of these homes, the parent will not have graduated from high school and will be unemployable.

At this writing, the District of Columbia has the highest number of children in the region living in female-headed households (37.3 percent). This is followed by New York (19.6 percent), and Connecticut, Massachusetts, Rhode Island, New Jersey, Delaware, and Maryland, each with over 15 percent of the children living in female-headed households. In the remaining states within the region—Maine, New Hampshire, Vermont, Pennsylvania, Virginia and West Virginia—under 15 percent of the children live in female-headed households (U.S. Bureau of the Census, 1989).

Living in poverty has been related to higher infant mortality rates and higher fertility rates among the young. In the Northeast, the District of Columbia has the highest infant mortality rate, with over 20 infants per 1,000 dying before their first birthday. In Connecticut, New York, New Jersey, Pennsylvania, Delaware, Maryland, Virginia, and West Virginia, over 10 infants per 1,000 die within the first year.

More than 17 percent of the infants in the District of Columbia and West Virginia are born to teenaged mothers. Over 10 percent of infants in New Hampshire, Rhode Island, New York, Pennsylvania, Delaware, Maryland, and Virginia are born to teenaged mothers, and under 10 percent in Maine, Vermont, Massachusetts, Connecticut, and New Jersey.

Education

Educational opportunities vary within the Northeast. In the states of New Hampshire, Vermont, Massachusetts, and Connecticut, over 70 percent of the parents 25 years old and older have completed at least 12 years of education, and 60 percent of the parents in the remaining states have completed high school. The estimated public school expenditures by pupil vary from a low of $1,800 in West Virginia to upwards of $7,000 per pupil in some New York State school districts.

References

Center for Educational Statistics: Public Elementary and Secondary Education in the United States, 1982–83 and 1983–84. A Statistical Compendium. Washington, DC: U.S. Department of Education.

Children's Defense Fund. (1988). *A call for action to make our nation safe for children: A briefing book on the status of American children in 1988.* Washington, DC: Children's Defense Fund.

National Center for Education Statistics. (1988). *Digest of education statistics.* Washington, DC: U.S. Department of Education.

United States Bureau of the Census. (1989). Statistical Abstract of the United States. Washington, DC: U.S. Government Printing Office.

C. Seefeldt, with K. McClennahan

South and Southeast

In the South and southeastern United States there were 6,403,000 children under the age of five years in 1988. That figure represents an increase of 15.5 percent between 1980 and 1988.

According to figures reported in 1988, southern women between the ages of 16 and 34 years each had an average of 1.409 children. Black women had an average of 1.804 children; Hispanic women, 1.536 children; and white women, 1.356 children.

The average family income in the South in 1988 was $28,951. The 1987 median educational attainment for adults 25 years and older in the South was 12.6 years of schooling (12.6 for whites, 12.3 for blacks, and 12.0 for Hispanics). For males, it was 12.6 and for females, 12.5.

In 1987 there was a large discrepancy between whites and people of color in both low birth weight babies, and babies born to teenaged mothers (under 20 years of age) in the South. Almost twice as many children of color (10.6 percent to 15.4 percent) were born with low birth weights than were white children (5.0 percent to 8.6 percent).

White teenaged mothers gave birth to 13.1 percent of the babies born in 1987. Teenaged mothers of color gave birth to 23 percent of the babies born during the same period.

Infant mortality in the South in 1987 was relatively high, with a median of 17.7 percent for infants of color and 9.3 percent for white infants when neonatal and postnatal mortality rates were combined.

In one typical southern/southeastern state, there were 39,101 instances of child abuse reported in 1987. Of those instances, 56 percent consisted of neglect, 25 percent were physical abuse, 12 percent were sexual abuse, and 7 percent were classified under the category of "other."

References

Georgia Council on Child Abuse, Inc. (Personal communication, June 14, 1988).

Southern Regional Project on Infant Mortality in cooperation with Southern Governors' Association and Southern Legislative Conference. (1989). *A bold step: The South acts to reduce infant mortality.* Washington, DC: Southern Regional Project on Infant Mortality.

United States Bureau of the Census. (1988). *Educational attainment in the United States: March 1987 and 1988.* Current Population Reports, Series P-20, No. 426. Washington, DC: U.S. Government Printing Office.

United States Bureau of the Census. (1989). *Fertility of American women, June 1988.* Current Population Reports, Series P-20, No. 436. Washington, DC: U.S. Government Printing Office.

United States Bureau of the Census. (1989). *Household and family characteristics: March 1988.* Current Population Reports, Series P-20, No. 437. Washington, DC: U.S. Government Printing Office.

J. Nurss

Southwest

The Southwest region, composed of Arizona, Arkansas, New Mexico, Oklahoma, and Texas, had a population of 23,562,025 in 1980, comprising 10 percent of the population of the United States (U.S. Bureau of the Census, 1986). In the Southwest, 11.9 percent of the population was nine years of age and under, while the United States census recorded 14.6 percent of the population in this age group. The median age in the region was 29, as opposed to 30 years for the country as a whole, because of the disproportionate numbers of young adults.

All the states in the region experienced population growth in both rural and urban areas from 1970 to 1980, with Arizona showing the greatest population increase, and Oklahoma the smallest increase. Arizona also had the highest ratio of urban to rural population, 83.8 percent to 16.2 percent. Of the region's population, 71 percent was urban and 29 percent was rural, in comparison to 76 percent urban and 24 percent rural for the country as a whole.

The median income for states in this region in 1980 ranged from $12,214 (Arkansas) to $16,708 (Texas), with the average being $14,954. All states were well below the national median income of $21,023.

Ethnically, the population of this region with some duplicated count (black of Hispanic origin, for example) is as follows:

	White	Black	Hispanic	Asian	Indian
Arizona	82%	3%	16%	.8%	5.6%
Arkansas	83%	16%	1%	.3%	.4%
New Mexico	75%	2%	37%	.5%	11.2%
Oklahoma	86%	7%	2%	.6%	5.9%
Texas	79%	12%	21%	.8%	.3%
S.W. Region (Average)	81%	8.0%	15.0%	.6%	4.7%
U.S.	83%	11.7%	6.4%	1.6%	.6%

Source: U.S. Bureau of the Census, 1986.

Enrollment in programs for children from age three to kindergarten age varies. Arizona reports 27,851 out of 122,898 children, or 23 percent enrolled in programs under public,

church-related, or private auspices. Arkansas reports 103,668, or 17 percent, enrolled. New Mexico's census of 64,851 children indicated 18 percent enrollment, Oklahoma's census of 135,584 children indicated 25 percent enrollment, and Texas' census of 676,882 children also indicated 25 percent enrollment. Of these programs, the proportion of public enrollment versus private (church-related or otherwise) ranges from 28 percent in Texas, to 36 percent in Arkansas, to 39 percent in Arizona, to 41 percent in Oklahoma, and 42 percent in New Mexico. Nationally, publicly sponsored programs provide 37 percent of the total services for children three to six years of age (U.S Bureau of the Census, 1980).

Private schools serving children through the elementary grades report enrollments of less than 5 percent of the child population in Oklahoma and Arkansas, and between 5 percent and 9.9 percent in Arizona, New Mexico, and Texas. This figure includes religiously affiliated schools.

References

United States Bureau of the Census. (1980). Census of Population PO80–1–B1. Washington, DC: U.S. Government Printing Office.

United States Bureau of the Census. (1986). State Population and Household Estimates, With Age, Sex, and Components of Change: 1981–1987 Series, p. 25. Washington, DC: U.S. Government Printing Office.

C. Brownstein

West (California)

Summarized below are the available data on the increase in population, changes in racial and ethnic composition, status of families, and the health of California's children. The data on children in California reveal the following:

- a continued increase in the child population into the twenty-first century, with culturally diverse groups and people of color reflecting a larger proportion of the child population;
- half of the children being Hispanic, Asian, or Asian-American by the year 2000;

- a significant increase in single-parent families where the mother is the head of household;
- the number of babies born to single mothers doubling since 1975;
- decreasing size of the average California family;
- significant increases in the number of children living under the poverty level or just above it since 1981 (children of families in the wealthiest 20 percent are significantly better off, while children of families in the bottom 20 percent are significantly worse off);
- a rising infant mortality rate;
- new immigrant and poor children being least likely to be immunized; and
- significant increases in child abuse.

Population Trends

The number of children from birth to nine years of age has increased steadily in the 1980s and is expected to continue to increase into the twenty-first century. Fertility patterns, the number of women of childbearing age, and levels of immigration contribute to the growth of the child population. Immigration into California has increased the numbers of women of childbearing age and the child population. There appears to be a lower rate of fertility among women born in California and a higher rate of fertility among the recent immigration population (Kirst, 1989, p. 14). It is projected that half the children in California by the year 2000 will be Asian or Asian-American or Hispanic, and that people of color will be in the majority in California by the year 2010.

The urban areas of California currently house 91 percent of its children. More than half of all California children live in the area around Los Angeles, and over 70 percent live in the ten largest counties. Shifts in population are expected with significant growth occurring in suburban and rural counties. California had the largest number of children in the range from birth to five years of age in 1988 (Children's Defense Fund, 1990, p. 154).

Family Life Profile

California's family profile has changed dramatically. It is estimated that approximately 60 percent to 65 percent of children live in families with both biological parents present, and 10 percent are estimated to be living in two-parent families with one biological parent. These figures represent a decrease since 1970 of 14,500 households in which children are living with two biological parents. During this same time period, the number of children living in households with only the mother present has increased by approximately 6,000 (Kirst, 1989, p. 34). It is predicted that half of today's children will live with a single parent at some point in their lives.

These changes in family profile are attributed to two major factors. The first factor is that divorces have doubled in the last 20 years, with the largest number occurring among black families. The fewest number of divorces occur in Asian or Asian-American families. It is estimated that approximately 30 percent of the children presently living in California will experience divorce in their families before they reach the age of 16.

The second factor affecting the California family profile is an increase in births to unmarried mothers. One baby in four was born

1970 Total Population 0–9 by Race/Ethnic Group

Year	White	Black	Hispanic	Asian & Other	Total
1970	2,484,603	309,942	597,217	117,814	3,509,576
1980	1,780,186	301,498	1,036,858	255,882	3,374,424
1990	2,088,875	412,093	1,639,455	522,281	4,662,704
2000	1,410,131	383,554	1,836,443	540,852	4,561,147
2010	1,609,245	416,302	2,217,647	616,028	4,859,182

Source: California Department of Finance, Population Research Unit. *Projected Total Population for California by Race/Ethnicity*. February, 1988.

to a single mother in California in 1986, as compared to one in five in 1975, and one in ten in 1966. Available data show variations among ethnic and racial groups. Twenty-five percent of white children, 35 percent of Hispanic children, and 52 percent of black children were born to single mothers in 1986. There has been an increase in rate of births among unmarried white women and a decline in births to married white couples. Most unmarried mothers are over 20 years of age.

Teenaged Parenting

There has been a substantial decrease in the overall birthrate to teenaged mothers over the last 20 years. The data show that the birthrate for teens was approximately 69,000 in 1970 and approximately 53,000 in 1986. There has been an increase, however, in births to mothers under 15 years of age (from 800 in 1970 to 1,100 in 1986). More than one-fourth of the fathers are teenagers, and half of the fathers are between the ages of 20 and 24. A smaller percentage of teenaged mothers are married than in the past—32 percent in 1986 as opposed to 62 percent in 1970. Blacks and Hispanics have higher birthrates than whites and Asians or Asian-Americans (Kirst, 1989, p. 39).

Size of Family

Family size had decreased in 1980. Seventy-seven percent of all California families with children under 18 had one or two children, while 23 percent had three or more. In 1970, 66 percent of the families had one or two children, and 33 percent had three or more. Black and Southeast Asian families tend to have 1.8 children. In comparison, Hispanic families tend to have 2.7 children, and white families tend to have 1.4 children (The Achievement Council, 1988, p. 6).

Income Level

An overview of the economic well-being of California's children indicates that many more children from birth to 17 years of age are living just above or below the poverty line. In 1980 about one in six children grew up in poverty. By 1986 the poverty rate had increased

to one in four children. The rates are higher among people of color. White families fared best with approximately 7,000 fewer families in the lowest 20 percent of earners by 1985, while 6,000 more white families found themselves among the top 20 percent. In contrast, the number of Hispanic families in the lowest 20 percent of earners increased dramatically from 217,069 to 366,375. Although there were slightly fewer black families in the lowest earning group, the income of those in the bottom 60 percent declined by about 5 percent.

Infant Mortality

California ranked fourteenth in the country in infant mortality, a figure that represents a continued rise from 1984 (Children's Defense Fund, 1990, p. 159). Prematurity (a birth weight of less than 5 pounds 5 ounces) is cited as the primary cause of infant deaths. Low infant birth weight and infant mortality are higher for women who obtain no prenatal care. Statistics also show that black babies are twice as likely as white babies to experience low birth weight or death within the first year of life. California ranked thirty-fourth in the United States with women who had late or no prenatal care (Children's Defense Fund, 1990, p. 158).

Immunizations

California law requires that children under the age of seven be immunized for pertussis and mumps. Rigorous enforcement by the school districts have helped in controlling these diseases. Sixty percent of toddlers, however, have not received the recommended immunization schedule of DTP, polio, measles, mumps, and rubella by their second birthday. Children from low-income families and children of color are more likely not to have received these immunizations. These populations do not have easy access to immunization services. Language and cultural barriers, particularly among new immigrants, also place children at greater risk for being immunized. The rise in vaccine costs has exacerbated the problem. Although millions of children have been immunized through the California Immunization Program, this program does not serve a large proportion of children younger than school age, who are new immigrants, and/or come from low-income families (Kirst, 1989, p. 156).

Child Abuse

The available data indicate that the numbers of child abuse cases reported and investigated between 1987 and 1988 have increased (see table, below).

Child Abuse Reports Filed

Type of Abuse	1987	1988	% increase
Sexual	64,338	83,098	29.1
Physical	108,974	139,122	27.7
Severe Neglect	38,162	46,177	21.0
General Neglect	109,876	145,217	32.2
Emotional	10,847	15,586	43.7
Exploitation	1,255	2,416	92.5
Caretaker Absence	37,182	45,470	22.3
Total	370,634	477,086	28.8

Source: State Department of Social Services, Data Processing and Statistical Services Bureau, 1990.

Some of the increase may be attributable to a change in the reporting system that went into effect in 1988. An unknown percentage of the increase, however, may be accounted for by a higher incidence of drug/alcohol related cases (70 percent to 80 percent of all child abuse cases in some California counties), massive increases in the incidence of drug babies, and increasing skill at detecting abuse.

Summary

The data presented reflect
- California's increasing child population from predominantly white to predominantly people of color;
- the changing family structure;
- the growing disparity between the wealthiest and the poorest families, mainly along racial/ethnic lines; and
- the concentration of poverty in the big cities.

The health and well-being of California's children require new policies. The data bases available in the areas of income level, size of family, and child abuse provide no breakdown by age and gender. Data on children from birth to eight years of age are limited, and the developmental needs of children are qualitatively different from older children. Intelligent policies must be formulated on the basis of data that reflect the needs of specific age groups.

References

Achievement Council, The. (1988). *Unfinished business: Fulfilling our children's promise.* Los Angeles: Author.

Assembly Office of Research. (1986). *California 2000: A people in transition.* Sacramento: Author.

California Department of Finance, Population Research Unit. (1988). *Projected total population for California by race/ethnicity, July 1, 1970–2000 with age/sex detail.*

Children's Defense Fund. (1990). *S.O.S. America! A children's defense budget.* Washington, DC: National Association for the Education of Young Children.

Joint Select Task Force on the Changing Family. (1989). *Planning a family policy for California: First year report of the joint select task force on the changing family.* Sacramento: Author.

Kirst, M. W. (1989). *Conditions of children in California.* Berkeley: Policy Analysis for California Education.

H. C. Neal

West/Northwest

The West/Northwest region of the United States includes the states of Alaska, Colorado, Hawaii, Idaho, Montana, Nevada, Oregon, Utah, Washington, and Wyoming. Regional data and projections for population increase, age structure, linguistic, age-specific mortality, and reported child abuse/neglect are summarized below.
- Overall population growth is consistent at moderate to rapid rates;
- Crude birth rates and positive net migration exceed national norms;
- The regional age structure is youthful;
- The 0–9 age group averages more than 15 percent of the population;

- Twenty percent of the population aged 5–14 is from a non-English-language-background (NELB);
- The number of children (5–14) with limited-English-proficiency (LEP) is growing;
- Minorities include indigenous and recent immigrant residents;
- Despite a more youthful age structure, infant and age-specific (0–19) mortality rates are comparable to national averages;
- Reported child abuse/neglect rates are comparatively high and rising;
- There is significant intrastate demographic disparity within this extensive geographic region.

velopments cause intraregional movement, but few people are leaving the region itself.

Children in the 0–9 age group constitute a significant proportion of the West/Northwest population. Four states (Alaska, Idaho, Wyoming, and Utah) have markedly young populations. The pronatalist influence of the Church of Latter Day Saints (Mormons) is evident in the latter. Between 1980 and 1990, the percentage of 0–9-year-olds increased in every state. Projections to the year 2000 indicate cohort declines in keeping with the aging of the United States population, though the region will remain more youthful than the nation as a whole.

Fig. 2: Children Under Ten
Percent of Total

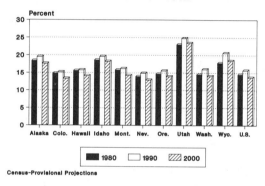

Census-Provisional Projections

Fig. 1: Population Change
Projected to 2000

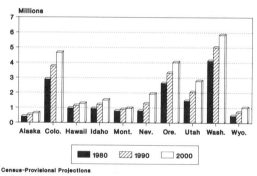

Census-Provisional Projections

Population Trends

The West/Northwest is a region of growth, with considerable variation from state to state. Positive net immigration creates a youthful age structure and comparatively high fertility for most states (average Crude Birth Rate, 16.9/1000). Much intranational immigration arises from positive environmental perceptions, energy resource employment, and recreational opportunities. International immigration includes both Hispanic and Pacific Rim origins, especially in coastal states. However, between 1980 and 1988, Idaho, Utah, Oregon, Montana, and Wyoming experienced school enrollment declines. "Boom-bust" energy de-

Ethnic Diversity

The West/Northwest population is becoming increasingly ethnically diverse. On average, 20 percent of public school students are people of color. The percentage is even higher in Alaska (34 percent) and Hawaii (76 percent), which contain significant indigeneous non-Caucasian populations. The growing number of people of color in Nevada (23 percent), however, is a recent occurrence. Asian, Pacific Islander, American Indian, and Alaskan Native populations are expanding most rapidly and contribute disproportionately to the school-age population. In contrast, the interior states of Idaho, Wyoming, and Montana have few minority residents.

The population of 5- to 14-year-olds of non-English-language-background (NELB) increased in every state between 1980 and 1990, and will continue to grow until at least the year 2,000. Linguistic diversity is primarily the product of recent immigration and, to a lesser extent, rapid growth of indigenous groups (e.g., American Indian, American Eskimo, and Aleut).

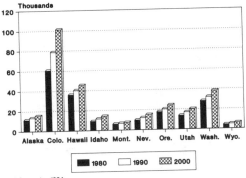

Fig. 3: Non-English-Language-Background Children 5-14

Oxford-Carpenter-1984

Rapid growth of NELB youth in Colorado stems from both long-term resident Hispanics and recent immigration. Hawaii, Oregon, and Washington are part of the Pacific Rim region, and a growing Asian population reflects this reality. Utah and Nevada also accommodate Asian immigration into their small base populations.

Child Well-Being

An array of indirect social indicators suggest positive child well-being in the West/Northwest region. Every state was below the national average for children living below the poverty level (1980), and for the rate of births to unwed mothers (1987). All states save one (Nevada) were below the national average for children living in single-parent households (1980), and every state fell short of the national norm for female households (1980).

Direct demographic indicators, however, point to a less positive nurturing environment. Although the region's Crude Death Rate (6.7/1000) was nearly 30 percent below the national average, reflecting a younger age structure, age-specific mortality rates suggest a less desirable situation. Infant Mortality Rates (IMR) in three of the states (Alaska, Idaho, and Oregon) exceed the national rate, with the regional IMR only 26 percent below the national level.

Mortality rates for children 0 through 5 are just 8 percent less than the nation's average, and for the 5 through 19 cohort, death rates are actually 2 percent higher than for the United States as a whole. In light of the positive social indicators cited above, the region's recorded levels of youth mortality are unexpectedly high.

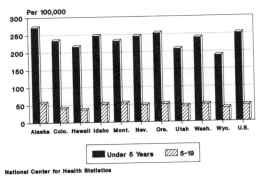

Fig. 4: Age Specific Mortality 1987

National Center for Health Statistics

Reported cases of child abuse and neglect are comparatively high in the region and appear to be growing. In more than one-half of the states, the reported rates are significantly higher than the national average. Likewise, rates in eight states show growth tendencies between 1984 and 1986.

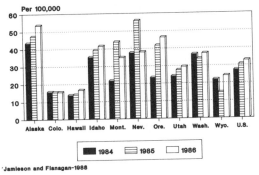

Fig. 5: Child Abuse and Neglect Reported Cases: (0-17)

Jamieson and Flanagan-1988

Summary

The data presented indicate the following:

• a region of youthful age structure with growth potential;

• increasing ethnic and linguistic diversity;

- an apparently stable social environment;
- unexpected levels of child mortality and reported abuse or neglect.

Generalization concerning a topic as dynamic as population, especially when related to a geographic region as large and diverse as the West/Northwest, should be applied with caution. The region straddles three distinct societies, that is, Pacific Rim, Anglo traditional, and Polar/sub-Polar. Internal and international migration strongly impact child populations, especially when the resident state population base is small. Children in traditional cultural groups and new minorities are beset by the struggle between their society and the dominant group's norms. Group-specific studies and data are needed as the basis for effective educational planning throughout the region.

References

Griffith, J. E., et al. (1989). American education: The challenge of change. *Population Bulletin*. Washington, DC: The Population Reference Bureau, Inc.

Jamieson, K. M., & Flanagan, T. J. (eds). (1988). *Sourcebook of criminal justice statistics—1988*. U. S. Department of Justice, Bureau of Justice Statistics. Washington, DC: United States Government Printing Office.

National Center for Health Statistics. (1989). *Vital statistics of the United States. 1989*. Vol. II, Mortality, Part B. Public Health Service. Washington, DC: United States Government Printing Office.

Oxford-Carpenter, R., et al. (1984). *Demographic projections of non-English-language-background and limited-English-proficient persons in the United States to the year 2000*. National Clearinghouse for Bilingual Education. Rosslyn, VA: InterAmerica Research Associates, Inc.

United States Bureau of the Census. (1983). *Provisional projections of the population of states, by age and sex: 1980 to 2000*. Washington, DC: United States Government Printing Office.

United States Bureau of the Census. (1986). *State and metropolitan area date book, 1986*. Washington, DC: United States Government Printing Office.

United States Department of Education. (1988). *Digest of educational statistics, 1988*. Office of Educational Research and Improvement. Washington, DC: United States Government Printing Office.

C. O. Collins

3.2 Sponsorships and Interest Groups

When early childhood education was first established in the United States, it was supported largely by private sponsors and interest groups. This circumstance meant that settings and programs tended to reflect the agendas of individuals or groups that saw early education as an avenue to achieving their particular and sometimes idiosyncratic goals. In more recent years, public funding for early education has increased, with the result that purposes have been more publicly defined, and programs in their various settings have more frequently become conduits of federal, state, or local policy on the care and education of young children. Private sponsorship is still an important source of support for the care and education of young children in the United States, however. This section traces past courses of program sponsorship and unfolds the complexities of present-day funding.

L. R. Williams

History of Sponsorships and Interest Groups

Funding sources and interest groups have strongly influenced the development of early childhood education in the United States. Reflection on the assumptions and circumstances that led to their involvement can inform early childhood advocates and policy planners about some of the longstanding issues in early education and help them to appraise future directions in early education (Takanishi, 1977).

Several cyclical themes seem to underlie the involvement of sponsors and interest groups in early childhood education, including (1) early education as a means of social reform, a means of family support, a protection against poverty, and a provision for equality of opportunity; (2) quality control of early care, socialization, and education outside the home; and (3) the shifting roles of women in balancing work and family responsibilities. The following discussion describes how these themes have emerged and been interpreted by different sponsors and interest groups in different historical periods.

Overview of Historical Themes in Early Education

Parent fees have usually covered the largest portion of early childhood education costs over the past 160 years. Philanthropies began to support child care as a means of social reform for immigrants and the poor in the late 1800s. Government funding for social welfare and emerging professionalization of early childhood education and child care developed during the early 1900s.

Most state governments established regulations for licensing and monitoring day care after World War II, following the federal government's involvement in providing day care for large numbers of mothers in the wartime work force. When questions of economic equity were raised in the 1960s, the federal government funded only regulated early childhood education for targeted low-income populations. The numbers of working women had been increasing steadily since the 1950s, and by the 1970s, women were making progress toward economic equity.

As concerns shifted toward universal funding of child care, the federal government moved its emphasis from direct funding of child care services for low-income families to indirect funding through tax credits to parents. This new emphasis encouraged greater privatization of early childhood education and broadened consumer choice for parents in middle- and upper-income brackets.

Early Interest in Preprimary Children

Widespread interest in the education of preprimary children in the United States first emerged in the 1830s. When many parents began to send their three- and four-year-old children to a local common school, officials and educators not only questioned the additional expense involved and the disruptions to discipline but also suggested that early schooling would have "hothouse" effects on children. Eventually, rules were established excluding children under the age of five or six (Strickland, 1982).

Another form of early education, the infant school, briefly surfaced at about the same time. Designed to provide activity and nurturance, the infant school, as envisioned by British social reformer Robert Owen, was part of a dream to improve social conditions for workers and to build utopian communities through education. Bronson Alcott, an American educational visionary who was drawn to Owen's ideas about the nature and needs of young children, started several infant schools in the United States, depending on funding from parent fees or patron charity. Infant schools spread to various cities along the eastern seaboard during the early 1830s. The movement lacked adequate financial resources, however, and did not survive (Strickland, 1982).

The fireside education movement was another influence on the development of early childhood education. The Industrial Revolution, which had moved work outside the home and into factories, was perceived by many as eroding the strength and influence of the family. Women and clergy began to write articles and books of domestic advice that placed mothers on a moral pedestal and made a cult of their domestic responsibilities. These responsibilities were understood to include the education and moral protection of the young, for which mothers were deemed to be uniquely qualified. A form of parent education, this domestic advice was aimed at women of some means who might have had servants, rather than at low-income families. The advice flooded the newly emerging popular press and convinced many women that a young child's needs could be met only within the family and not by extrafamilial care and education (Strickland, 1982).

Early Education as Social Reform and Family Support

Civic-minded women and reformist charity workers focused national attention on the plight of children from low-income families, particularly those in urban areas, and initiated many "child saving" programs and reforms during the last quarter of the 1800s (Cahan, 1989). These reformists were concerned about the well-being of toddlers left unsupervised while mothers worked. "Child savers" established day nurseries, therefore, as a way to help keep families together. Most of these early day nurseries were funded by philanthropists or public charities and often were located in settlement houses; numbers grew from 175 in 1897 to 695 in 1916. Perhaps because their purpose was chiefly custodial, day nurseries, unlike kindergartens, became tied to the social welfare system.

Championed by Elizabeth Peabody in the late nineteenth century, many early kindergartens sought to socialize and assimilate immigrant children and their parents into the mainstream of the United States (Cahan, 1989). These kindergartens were funded by missions, churches, and philanthropic organizations that saw the kindergarten as a way to provide children with moral benefits and thus to improve society, as well as a vehicle for aiding young children in distress. The Women's Christian Temperance Union, for example, established kindergartens in at least 20 cities and believed that this early training would develop adults free from alcoholic temptation (Weber, 1969).

The National Education Association (NEA) passed a resolution in 1885 recommending the incorporation of kindergartens into public schools. Thereafter, when philanthropic organizations ran into financial difficulties, they asked public schools for use of their vacant rooms as kindergarten sites. School boards later were persuaded to assume all financial and administrative responsibilities for kindergartens (Braun & Edwards, 1972). The International Kindergarten Union (IKU), the first early childhood professional organization, also promoted the acceptance of the kindergarten into public schools. Established in 1892 at an NEA meeting, the IKU later became the Association for Childhood Education International (Wortham, 1985).

Quality Control of Early Care and Socialization Outside the Home

Reports of undesirable conditions in day nurseries, following similar findings about orphanages and foster homes, focused attention by 1916 on the role of day nurseries in promoting child welfare and family cohesiveness. In response to such queries, the U.S. Children's Bureau, established in 1912, developed standards for various types of out-of-home child care. The Child Welfare League of America, organized in 1920, also helped to improve standards through publications and collaboration with various agencies. Over the next few years, child advocates began to campaign for enforcement of standards by state regulation—a slow process (Bremner, 1974).

The nursery school movement emerged during the 1920s to serve primarily middle- and upper-income families. Most programs emphasized guidance of children's social and emotional development and parent education. The Laura Spelman Rockefeller Foundation funded nursery schools and supported the establishment of child study institutes at universities and colleges in almost every region of the Unites States (Senn, 1975). Seventy-four institutions of higher education sponsored nursery schools by 1931 as sites for child development research and teacher training. The nursery school movement contributed to the increasing professionalism of early childhood education. Patty Smith Hill, a well-known kindergarten advocate, organized the first meeting of the National Committee on Nursery Schools in 1926. This group became the National Association for Nursery Educators and later, the current National Association for the Education of Young Children (NAEYC) (Braun & Edwards, 1972). The nursery school movement, however, remained mainly in the private sector, with fewer than 500 nursery schools in the United States by 1932 (Cahan, 1989).

Under the Federal Emergency Relief Fund Administration of the 1930s, federal monies were allocated directly to emergency nursery schools administered through local public school systems. These New Deal programs provided jobs primarily for unemployed teachers, nurses, and dietitians, to relieve some of the misery experienced by children of low-income families during the Great Depression and were aimed at safeguarding the health and welfare of children from such families. More than 1,900 of these nursery schools existed by 1935. Most teachers employed by the New Deal nursery schools had neither nursery school preparation nor experience and were required to attend institutes that trained them in early childhood education (Bremner, 1974).

Support for Working Mothers and Quality Control

During World War II, marking the end of the Great Depression, more than 50 percent of the work force consisted of women, and prompted the United States House Committee on Public Buildings and Grounds to include child care centers in war-impact areas among the allocations for defense and public works. The Lanham Act, enacted in 1942, provided federal assistance for more than 3,000 emergency day care centers by 1944 (Cahan, 1989). Inasmuch as 13 states received two-thirds of the funds, day care centers became more common in heavily populated states with the biggest defense factories. State officials objected to federal aid being given directly to communities, rather than to the states. Funding for Lanham Act day care centers continued, however, until 1946, when the federal government regarded the centers to be state and local responsibilities. Only four states in some way extended funding to these day care centers after 1946 (Bremner, 1974).

In other ways, state governments were gradually assuming more responsibility for day care. Thirty-six states had established licensing regulations for day nurseries and day care centers by 1953. These regulations sometimes offered little protection, particularly as short-ages of well-qualified day care personnel existed (Bremner, 1974; Phillips, Lande & Goldberg, 1990). Although sociologists and popular parenting experts during the 1950s were urging mothers to resume domestic responsibilities for the good of their children's mental health, the percentage of married working mothers increased by 80 percent between 1940 and 1958. Nearly all of these working mothers relied on informal child care arrangements in family settings, with only 4 percent using group care in 1958 (Cahan, 1989).

Return to Early Education as Social Reform

Media documentaries, child development researchers, and civil rights activists focused public attention on the detrimental and cyclical effects of poverty during the 1960s. The federal government responded to this crisis with social reform legislation, including the Economic Opportunity Act of 1964. The centerpiece of this legislation was Project Head Start, a preschool program for children from low-income families. To plan the program, the federal government drew on advice from child development experts. Head Start built on ideas about the importance of early intervention that had been recognized earlier by infant school advocates. Head Start was designed to be community based, involve parents, promote children's social competence, and provide a comprehensive child development program. Initiated in 1965 as a summer-only program for 550,000 children, it was popular with participating communities and soon became a year-long, half-day program at most sites despite disappointing initial evaluations (Bremner, 1974). The Carnegie Corporation of New York and the Ford Foundation of New York became involved in funding subsequent Head Start evaluation and research, as well as developing a popular children's television program, "Sesame Street," presented as an alternative form of early education (Carnegie Corporation of New York, 1982).

Licensed day care, in general, continued to be in short supply, although the Social Security Act of 1962 provided modest funding for licensed day care services to assist welfare families. Despite efforts of groups such as the Child Welfare League, the public still tended to associate day care use with troubled families.

Return to Working Mothers, Quality Control, and Family Support

Day care emerged on many fronts as a critical issue during the 1970s. White House conferences in the early 1970s recommended federal support for comprehensive, quality child care, staff training, child development research, and a publicity campaign to broaden public understanding and support for child care (Grubb, 1987). As an extension of the 1964 Economic Opportunity Act, Congress passed legislation for universal child care that President Richard Nixon vetoed. He objected to the child care provisions as fiscally irresponsible, administratively unworkable, and family weakening because they morally committed the government to communal child rearing approaches as opposed to family centered approaches (Bremner, 1974).

During the same decade, agonized debates on national standards for child care programs occurred among early childhood professionals and policy makers. Eventually, some minimal standards were established but never implemented (Kahn & Kamerman, 1987; Phillips, Lande, & Goldberg, 1990). Modest increases in federal child care funds during this period as well as expanded Head Start funds were available for low-income families. The use of day care by middle-income working parents also was growing rapidly. Employers, with the aid of federal tax incentives, were beginning to assist employees in finding child care and setting up day care centers (Friedman, 1984), while private day care franchises also were expanding (Kagan, 1989b).

The Children's Defense Fund (CDF) was established in 1973 as a nonprofit organization to gather and disseminate information about the needs of children in the United States and to educate the public and policy makers about policy options for meeting those

needs. Funded by foundations, corporate grants, and individual contributions, CDF, with a staff at this writing of about 90 individuals, has become a strong advocate for policies affecting children, especially children from low-income families (Tomkins, 1989).

The Ronald Reagan administration cutbacks during the 1980s affected all programs for low-income families, including child care programs. The public again became concerned about growing poverty and homelessness. Policy papers on early childhood education began to emerge not only from child advocates and professional groups but from state and city governments and from corporate groups as well (Born, 1989; Gnezda & Sonnier, 1988; Grubb, 1987; Reisman, Moore, & Fitzgerald, 1988; Sale, 1989). Funding for early childhood education, especially prekindergarten programs, expanded in many states (Kagan, 1989a).

Employers, recognizing more than ever before the relationship of child care to work absenteeism, stress, productivity, and to the quality of the future work force, began to coordinate support for employee child care needs, such as information and referral services (Friedman, 1984; Galinsky, 1989 [see Friedman, 1984]; Secretary's Task Force, 1988). Longitudinal studies of programs such as the Perry Preschool Project provided convincing and frequently cited evidence of the investment value of quality early childhood programs and influenced the Ford Foundation to make substantial increases in support for early childhood education (Ford Foundation, 1989). Child care quality, at the same time, has become a key legislative issue (U.S. General Accounting Office, 1990).

Changes in tax policy have allowed more Americans to take a deduction for child care on their own tax forms and have tended to give middle- and upper-income families child care options. Maximizing parental choice through funding for publicity campaigns on child care options has become another key legislative issue (Reisman, Moore, & Fitzgerald, 1988). Family day care homes and before and after school-age child care are now recognized child care options in government legislation.

More than 100 child care bills were introduced in Congress during the late 1980s. These included comprehensive child care legislation supported by over 150 different organizations. In legislative debates, the funding of church-based day care and the issue of separation of church and state have emerged. Churches today, as in the past, are primary providers of child care, providing about a third of all centers (Freeman, 1986; Tomkins, 1989). Another issue has been the respective roles of federal and state governments in child care regulation and the inclusion of federal standards to guide states in the improvement of their regulations.

Summary

As early childhood education developed in the United States, interest groups and sponsors became involved in response to major concerns about social reform, quality control, and changing roles of women relative to work and family. The emphasis of these concerns has shifted at different times. Conflict, compromise, and struggle for control of the directions that early education would take followed the shifting perspectives. In the past, government and philanthropic funding was a significant and often singular impetus to developing the field. More recently, early childhood education has become highly diversified, involving both public and private interest groups and sponsors. Collaboration among these various sponsors and interest groups seems essential to the future development of high quality programs in order to support working families and the nation's future (Kagan, 1989a; Reisman, Moore, & Fitzgerald, 1988).

References

Born, C. E. (1989). *Our future and our only hope: A survey of city halls regarding children and families.* Washington, DC: National League of Cities.

Braun, S. J., & Edwards, E. P. (1972). *History and theory of early childhood education.* Belmont, CA: Wadsworth.

Bremner, R.H. (1974). *Children and youth in America: A documentary history.* Cambridge: Harvard University Press.

Cahan, E. D. (1989). *Past caring: A history of U.S. preschool care and education for the poor, 1820–1965.* New York: National Center for Children in Poverty.

Carnegie Corporation of New York. (1982). *Annual report 1981 for the fiscal year ended September 30.* New York: Author.

Ford Foundation. (1989). *Early childhood services: A national challenge.* New York: Author.

Freeman, M. (1986). *Called to act: Stories of child advocacy in our churches.* New York: National Council of Churches.

Friedman, D. E. (1984). The challenges of employer-supported child care: Meeting parent needs. In Galinsky, E. (1989). Update on employer-supported child care. *Young Children, 44* (6), 75–77.

Gnezda, T., & Sonnier, C. (1988). *Early childhood education: The status of state involvement.* Denver: National Council of State Legislatures.

Grubb, W. N. (1987). *Young children face the states: Issues and options for early childhood programs.* Washington, DC: Center for Policy Research in Education.

Kagan, S. L. (1989a). Early care and education: Tackling the tough issues. *Phi Delta Kappan, 70* (5), 433–439.

Kagan, S. L. (1989b). For-profit and non-profit child care: Similarities and differences. *Young Children, 45* (1), 4–10.

Kahn, A. J., & Kamerman, S. B. (1987). *Child care: Facing the hard choices.* Dover, MA: Auburn House.

Phillips, D., Lande, J., & Goldberg, M. (1990). The state of child care regulations. *Early Childhood Research Quarterly, 5* (2) 151–179.

Katz, L. G. (ed.). *Current topics in early childhood education,* (pp. 165–188), Vol. 5. Norwood, NJ: Ablex.

Reisman, B., Moore, A. J., & Fitzgerald K. (1988). *Child care: The bottom line. An economic and child care policy paper.* New York: Child Care Action Campaign.

Sale, J. S. (April, 1989). *The impact on child care providers of the Report of the Committee on Child Development Research and Public Policy, Panel on Child Care Policy of the National Academy of Sciences National Research Council.* Paper presented at the Biennial Meeting of the Society for Research in Child Development, Kansas City (ERIC Document Reproduction No. ED 306 104).

Secretary's Task Force. (April 1988). *Child Care: A workforce issue* (Report of the Secretary's Task Force, Executive Summary). Washington, DC: U.S. Department of Labor.

Senn, M. J. E. (1975). *Insights on the child development movement in the United States. Monographs of the Society for Research in Child Development, 40* (3–4, Serial No. 161).

Strickland, C. E. (1982). Paths not taken: Seminal models of early childhood education in Jacksonian America. In B. Spodek (ed.), *Handbook of research in early childhood education* (pp. 321–340). New York: Free Press.

Takanishi, R. (1977). Federal involvement in early education (1933–1973): The need for historical perspectives. In L. G. Katz (ed.), *Current topics in early childhood education*, Vol 1. (pp. 139–163). Norwood, NJ: Ablex.

Tomkins, C. (March 27, 1989). Profiles: A sense of urgency. *New Yorker*, pp. 48–50, 54, 56, 60–64, 66–74.

U.S. General Accounting Office. (1990). *Early childhood education: What are the costs of high quality programs?* (Briefing Report to the Chairman, Committee on Labor and Human Resources, U.S. Senate: GAO/HRD-90–43BR). Washington, DC: Author.

Weber, E. (1969). *The kindergarten: Its encounter with educational thought in America.* New York: Teachers College Press.

Wortham, S. C. (1985). Frontiers of challenge: Association for Childhood Education International. *Childhood Education, 62* (2), 74–79.

M. A. Jensen

Sources of Funding for Early Childhood Programs

Early childhood programs come in a variety of forms in the United States. A basic definition of an early childhood program is any planned set of interactions among adults and children, organized by adults and designed to promote healthy growth and development of children between birth and eight years of age. Early childhood programs include what are commonly referred to as infant-toddler centers, family day care homes, nursery schools, preschools, child care centers, day care centers, Head Start, prekindergartens, kindergartens, the primary grades, and nanny services, among others. Two distinct systems operate in the United States, one for children under five, and one for children five years of age and older. The second is primarily the public school system.

Funding Sources for Children Younger than Five Years Old

In practice, there is less distinction today than in the past between the care and education of young children. The majority of mothers of young children work outside their homes, and early education is widely recognized as a valuable experience. Many nursery schools offer programs longer than the once traditional three hours, and it would be difficult to find any providers of child care who do not believe that they are educating young children.

There is an especially wide variety of funding sources for early education programs for these younger children. Some sources of funds are allocations to support only one kind of program, such as Head Start (which provides education for low-income, preschool-aged children), or to buy a particular service for a certain group of families, such as child care (supported by various public subsidies) for low-income working parents. These are called categorical funding sources. Other available funds are allocated for a particular purpose, such as care for children so that their parents can work (the Dependent Care Tax Credit), but can be used to support many different kinds of early childhood programs. No matter what the purposes or other restrictions, the underlying premise of all sources of such funding for younger children is that payment is made for a particular child.

By far the largest source of funding for early childhood programs for children under five years of age is parents. Public sources from federal, state, and local taxes are the next largest source. Charitable or philanthropic funds (donated by foundations and corporations) provide the smallest share of funding for these programs. The following table illustrates the major sources of funds, who receives the funding, what kinds of early childhood programs the funds can be used for, and an estimate of the total annual amount of funding from each source.

Public Sources of Funds. There are seven main ways that the federal government funds early childhood programs—indirectly through the Internal Revenue Code in the form of the Dependent Care Tax Credits and Dependent Care Assistance Plans for parents and tax credits for employers; and directly through the Social Services Block Grant (SSBG) (used by states to purchase child care for low-income families and sometimes called Title XX), Head Start (comprehensive education for low-income preschoolers), the Child Care Food Program (nutrition), Chapter I of the Education Consolidation and Improvement Act (compensatory education), and the Education of the Handicapped Act (special education). There are actually 46 different federal programs that provide some funds for early childhood programs (U.S. General Accounting Office, 1989). Nearly 90 percent of the total $6.6 billion, however, comes from only four programs (the Dependent Care Tax Credit, Title XX, Head Start, and the Child Care Food Program).

Similarly, there are at least seven ways that states fund early childhood programs—indirectly through state dependent care tax cred-

Major Sources and Annual Amounts of Funding for Early Childhood Programs for Children Below Kindergarten Age

Source of Funds	Recipient of Funds	Allowable Use of Funds	Total Annual Expenditure
Parents	local community agencies, schools, centers, family day care homes, & individuals	education and care as determined by parent	$20–30 billion
Federal agencies			
Dept. of Health & Human Services			
Head Start	local nonprofit agencies and some public schools children 0–5	comprehensive education for disadvantaged	$1.5 billion, federal & local combined
Social Services Block Grant	states for purchase of care in local centers & family day care homes	care for children of low-income working parent(s)	$1.2 billion, federal and state combined
Dept. of Agriculture			
Child Care Food Program	state for use by schools, centers, & family day care homes	food served to children	$586 million, federal
Dept. of Treasury			
Dependent Care Tax Credit	parent for any legal form of program or individual	care required so parent(s) can work or attend school	$3.4 billion, federal
Dept. of Education			
Chapter I (pre-k only)	local public school districts	compensatory education	$60 million, federal
Preschool Handicapped	state education agencies for public and private schools	special education	$2 billion, federal, state, & local combined

its for parents and child care tax credits for employers, and directly through state child care subsidy programs (in all 50 states and the District of Columbia), state-funded prekindergarten programs (in about 30 states and the District of Columbia), state-funded parent education programs (in about 6 states), and through contributions to Head Start (in 11 states and the District of Columbia) and to preschool special education (in most states).

On the local level, some cities and counties appropriate local tax monies for child care and other forms of early childhood education. Some municipalities also operate child care programs directly. A municipality can simultaneously receive federal and state funds, appropriate other local funds, and operate early childhood programs. In most communities, a multitude of local public and private agencies are the ultimate recipients of the parents' and/ or public funding sources (federal, state, and/ or local), and these agencies and individuals are the direct operators of early childhood programs.

Proportion of Total Funding from Different Sources. The best estimate for the nation as a whole is that parents are spending between $20 and $30 billion a year for child care and early education programs for their own children. The total tax expenditure for the federal Dependent Care Tax Credit exceeded $3 billion in Fiscal Year 1988 for services provided under various auspices to an unknown number of children. By contrast, total federal funding for Head Start is just over $1 billion and serves roughly 450,000 children, mainly four-year-olds, nationwide. Since Head Start funds must be matched at the rate of 25 percent local to 75 percent federal, funds from the local match increase the Head Start total by about $300 million. Federal SSBG/Title XX expenditures are about $700 million. While it is close to impossible to estimate service levels, subsidized child care probably serves roughly the same number of children as Head Start, that is, close to 500,000 children under the age of five.

By comparison, in 1987, about $300 million in state funds were being spent annually on part-day prekindergarten programs (including state-funded prekindergarten programs, state contributions to Head Start, and state-funded parent education programs) for roughly 250,000 children between the ages of three and five, with the majority being four-year-olds (Mitchell, Seligson, & Marx, 1989). Taking all sources into account, a good estimate of the total national expenditure on early childhood programs of all sorts for children under the age of five from all public and private sources would be from $30 billion to $35 billion annually.

Funding Sources for Children Five Years of Age and Older

In the system for children under five, public and private sources of funds can be combined to support a program. By contrast, public and private funds are kept quite separate in the system for children five years of age and older. Public funds support the public school system, while the private school system relies on nonpublic funds, primarily parent tuition for independent schools, or on religious organizations' support for parochial and other religiously affiliated schools. The public school system is by far the larger. While the proportion varies from community to community, across the nation more than 90% of children five years of age and older attend public school.

Sources of Support for the Public School System. The public school system is financed by tax revenues collected from all taxpayers, not only those who have children enrolled in the school system. The underlying premise is that the system of public schooling is being paid for, not each individual child. All children are eligible once they reach the entry age deemed appropriate by their local system. Their parents are not charged directly for their participation in this system of early childhood education.

Tax support for public schools comes from local property taxes, state taxes, and federal tax revenues. The proportionate share from these sources has varied over time. In 1920 the local contribution was 68 percent, the state was 30 percent, and the federal share a mere 2 percent. Federal support of education grew slowly to around 8 percent in 1970, and to a high of nearly 10 percent in 1981, and then declined to about 6 percent in 1985, where it has stayed to the present (Stern, 1988). State support for education has grown over the years and, in 1979, exceeded the local share. The relative proportion of funding derived from these three sources varies from state to state and within each state. In 1989–1990, a total of $198.6 billion was spent on public education K–12 nationwide; 50 percent of this total was from state sources, 44 percent, from local, and 6 percent from federal sources (Stern 1988). The amount of philanthropic funds that support the public school system, while large compared to the amount in the preschool sector, is a very modest proportion of the total, less than a fraction of 1 percent.

The Flow of Tax Dollars to School Districts. Local tax dollars flow directly to public school districts in two basic ways. In school districts that operate as agencies within a local governmental unit such as a city or county, the district's budget goes through an approval process. These are called fiscally dependent school districts. Other school districts, called fiscally independent school districts, are authorized to levy taxes directly. State tax dollars are distributed to school districts through aid formulas that are usually based on actual attendance figures and may take into account other factors such as the relative wealth of the district and the proportion of educationally needy (e.g., handicapped, non-English speaking) students. Federal tax dollars are mainly categorical. The major components of federal categorical support and the expenditures for 1989–90 were Chapter I ($4.6 billion) (U.S. Department of Education, Office of Compensatory Programs, Chapter I), and the School Food Program ($4 billion) (U.S. Department of Agriculture, 1988–89).

Inequity in Financing. The tax base supporting the public schools is relatively stable and generous compared to the very modest tax support for younger children. The capacity of the tax base, however, varies widely from community to community, that is, those areas with large amounts of valuable property can raise more money for their schools than areas with less valuable property can raise. Furthermore, tax capacity varies from state to state. For example, if every state taxed all potential tax bases, such as personal income, sales, property and corporate income, at the present average U.S. rate, Alaska would be able to raise nearly four times the revenues that Mississippi could (Council of Chief State School Officers, 1989). School financing is being challenged in many states on the basis of inequity among local districts. Texas, Kentucky, and New Jersey, among other states, have recently instituted major reforms of their education finance systems.

References

Council of Chief State School Officers. (1989). *State education indicators, 1988.* Washington, DC: Author.

Mitchell, A. W., Seligson, M., & Marx, F. (1989). *Early childhood programs and the public school: Between promise and practice.* Dover, MA: Auburn House.

Stern, J. D. (ed.). (1988). *1988 education indicators (CS 88–624).* Washington, DC: National Center for Education Statistics, Office of Educational Research and Improvement, U.S. Department of Education.

U.S. Department of Agriculture, Child Nutrition Division. (1988–89). *Expenditures for the school lunch and breakfast programs, 1988–89.* Washington, DC: Author.

U.S. Department of Education. (1989). *12th annual report to Congress on the implementation of the education of the handicapped act.* Washington, DC: Author.

U.S. Department of Education, Office of Compensatory Programs, Chapter I. (no date).

U.S. General Accounting Office. (1989). *Child care: Government funding sources, coordination, and service availability.* (GAO/HRD-90–26BR). Washington, DC: Author.

A. W. Mitchell

Foundations, Potential Funding by

Those involved in advancing early childhood education frequently are engaged in developing new programs to meet current needs, or xpanding existing programs. For many, these oals may be accomplished only with funds from external sources. Sources of funding may be public, such as government support, or private, which includes foundations and corporations. In times of diminishing or insufficient government support, private sources of funding become more important to the grant seeker. Thus, private foundations and corporate foundations are being turned to increasingly by the nonprofit sector as government support has diminished.

The Foundation Directory (12th edition) defines a foundation as a nongovernmental nonprofit organization. Generally established by a philanthropic individual, family, or corporation, the foundation uses its funds to advance, maintain, or aid educational, religious, medical, or other charitable activities serving the common good, primarily by making grants to nonprofit organizations.

While foundation grants may seem to represent a relatively small sector of giving (5.9 percent), and foundations receive many more requests than they can possibly fund, foundation support is attainable through a well-written proposal that matches the interests of the specific foundation and adherence to its guidelines. Grant seekers should keep in mind that foundations and corporations are showing renewed interest in children, and increased concern regarding the impact of poverty and homelessness on their development. Consequently, more serious attention is being paid to programs that provide nurturing and enriching environments for children.

It is the charge of the grant seeker to understand the mission of a particular foundation, and express in a written proposal how the foundation's goals will be furthered by foundation support of the grant seeker's organization or program. Grant seekers are generally discouraged from applying to foundations that do not have an interest in the nonprofit group's area of activity. For example, it is unlikely that a foundation that solely funds cancer research would award a grant for an early childhood teacher education program.

The grant seeker must conduct research on the potential funding organization before submitting a written proposal. The Foundation Center, established by foundations to provide a resource library, information and assistance services, and publications to nonprofit organizations, has offices in New York, San Francisco, Washington, D.C., and Cleveland. A selection of the Foundation Center publications also are available at cooperating libraries and other organizations. Those interested in the location of the cooperating collection nearest to them, may wish to call the 800 number provided in the bibliography, or consult *The Foundation Directory. The Foundation Directory* is a useful volume to begin research to identify appropriate foundations for possible grants. The subject index references those foundations having made grants in the field of early childhood education. The grant seeker may find it useful to compile a list of foundations who have previously made grants in their field of interest. *The Directory* is available at the Foundation Center, cooperating collections, and the reference section of many public libraries.

Other volumes that are useful in identifying potential sources of funding include the *Foundation Grants Index* and *Grants for Children and Youth*. Both are published by the Foundation Center. The latter has a subject index and recipient index. It lists grants of $5,000 or more for infants, children, and youth (to age 18) programs and services. The Foundation Center's *Source Book Profiles* and the *Taft Corporate Giving Directory* are helpful directories for reference and research. The library collection of the Foundation Center includes *Grantmakers for Children and Youth: Membership Directory*. Foundations provide brief information on the specific areas within children/youth issues that are of interest, as well as the names of program officers or trustees, and sample grants made.

It is recommended that grant seekers narrow the list of potential grantors to the most promising prospects by continuing their research. Many foundations publish annual reports, guidelines for applicants, and in some cases, application forms. The grant seeker should request this information and review it carefully. Once it is ascertained that the project falls within the foundation's area of interest, the prospective applicant should determine whether the foundation has established any geographical restrictions or geographical priorities for its grantmaking activities. Careful analysis of the size and type of awards should be made to determine appropriateness of the applicant's project and amount of request.

Typically, a short proposal letter and various appendices or supporting documents are required by the Foundation. Instructional guides for composing proposals are available, such as *Writing Winning Proposals.*

Many nonprofit organizations identify any personal contacts on the foundation's board of directors or among program officials, prior to submitting a proposal. Some applicants have found it helpful to discuss their organization and projects with a foundation officer. While this is often difficult to arrange, the feedback provided can be very useful.

After grants are awarded, it is recommended that the nonprofit organization maintain regular contact with the foundation. This may be accomplished through periodic telephone calls, brief notes on the progress of the funded project, or newsletters from the organization. The foundation is kept abreast of the nonprofit organization's activities, and may well be a continuing source of support for future projects.

Considerable effort is often expended in seeking grants, and letters of declination from foundations are inevitable. It is important to bear in mind, however, that early childhood educators, professionals and concerned individuals, and foundation officials alike, are working toward the same goals. Both wish to promote the healthy development of children. When grants are awarded, all parties, young children, educators and the foundation, reap the benefits.

References

Finn, M. (1982). *Fundraising for early childhood programs: Getting started and getting results.* Washington, DC: National Association for the Education of Young Children.

Gooch, J. M. (1987). *Writing winning proposals.* Washington, DC: Council for Advancement and Support of Education.

Janowski, K. E. (ed). (1988). *Taft corporate giving directory.* Washington, DC: The Taft Group.

Jones, F. (ed). (1989). *Source book profiles.* New York: The Foundation Center.

Kovacs, R. (ed). (1989). *Foundation grants index.* (17th ed.) New York: The Foundation Center.

Kovacs, R. (ed). (1989). *Comsearch: Grants for children and youth.* New York: The Foundation Center.

Leonard, M. (ed). (1989). *Grantmakers for children and youth: Membership directory.* Washington, DC: Grantmakers for Children and Youth.

Olson, S. (ed). (1989). *The foundation directory* (12th ed.). New York: The Foundation Center.

Weber, N. (ed). (1989). *Giving USA: The annual report on philanthropy for the year 1988.* New York: AAFRC Trust for Philanthropy.

E. S. Berkowitz

3.3 Early Childhood Settings in the Public Sector

The public sector encompasses programs supported by federal, state, or municipal funds, for children from birth through the age of eight. Some of the programs, such as Title XX Day Care and Head Start, serve children from low-income families and operate under strict guidelines to determine financial eligibility for enrollment. Other programs, such as public school kindergarten and first through third grades (the primary grades) in public schools are open to all children living within specified districts who qualify by age. Still others, like some public school prekindergarten programs, are targeted toward children who present some circumstance or condition that puts them "at risk" for subsequent achievement in school.

The largest number of public sector programs, and the greatest amount of public sector funds, serve children from five to eight years of age (in public school kindergarten through the third grade). As has been noted above, however, some publicly funded programs (Head Start, some forms of child care, and public school prekindergarten programs) are provided for children under the age of five who have been identified as needing early educational services to increase their chances of success in their later schooling.

The articles that follow describe the variety of early childhood settings and programs that can be found under public sponsorship. The articles are arranged alphabetically, except for those that elaborate information on an immediately preceding topic.

L. R. Williams

Child Care Support

Federal support of child care and early childhood programs appears to be characterized by ambivalence. On the one hand, there is a wish to meet the child care needs of families, and on the other, there is a desire to stay out of family life. Nevertheless, successive administrations have attempted to meet the needs of working parents for child care and early education.

Current funding and administrative procedures vary, but most programs operate as federal-state partnerships. Direct federal support for programs for young children comes mainly from Title XX of the Social Securities Act through block grant funds and through special legislative initiatives such as Title I of the Elementary and Secondary Education Act from 1965–1987 and Chapter I since 1981.

Additional federal support is provided through categorical grants made to state agencies for specific purposes. Agencies are required to meet strict eligibility criteria with respect to program components and community participation. Approximately $10 billion dollars was provided to states through categorical funding grants in Fiscal Year 1989 (Sugarman, 1989).

States also receive federal reimbursement under the Aid to Families with Dependent Children (AFDC) program (Title IV of the Social Security Act) for child care for working parents. The Family Support Act requires all states to make available Job Opportunities and Basic Skill Training Programs (JOBS Programs) that include education, training, and employment activities for AFDC recipients. Chief beneficiaries of this program have been families with children between one and three years of age (Blank, 1989).

Indirect federal support is provided in two ways. The first is the Dependent Tax Care Credit, which is the single largest source of federal funding for child care and allows all families to deduct 20 percent to 30 percent of their annual child care expenses from their income tax bill. The second is AFDC, through which recipients may deduct the costs of child care from the welfare benefits they receive. Since many AFDC families do not earn enough to pay for child care up front, they cannot claim this benefit (Martinez, 1986).

Major funding for new programs for four-year-olds has come mainly from state governments. Twenty-four states currently fund prekindergarten programs, and four others support existing programs. Generally, state funding for existing four-year-olds programs is minimal, and program costs vary from state to state. In 15 states, state education departments or community agencies operate prekindergarten programs, and others are moving in this direction.

Public sector programs funded by federal-state partnerships totaled approximately $30 billion in 1989. Major recipients of these funds were the Head Start programs for at-risk preschool children, child nutrition programs, the Social Services Block Grant Funds for child care, and allocations for early intervention for handicapped infants and toddlers (Sugarman, 1989). These programs are compensatory, and appropriations often fluctuate.

To ensure the intended disbursement of funds, public sector programs usually have strong mandates and detailed prescriptions for program implementation. Strict procedures exist for monitoring administrative practices and for involving parents. Concern often centers on the quality of programs, the kinds of cultural sensitivities shown by administrators and staff, and the degree of empowerment ascribed to parents and teachers (Ibid.).

References

Blank, H. (1989). Child Care and Welfare Reform: New Opportunities for Families. *Young Children, 44* (1), 28–30.

Martinez, S. (1986). Child Care and Public Policy. In N. Gunzenhauser & B. Caldwell (eds.), *Group Care for Young Children.* (pp. 71–77). Skillman N.J.: Johnson & Johnson.

Sugarman, J. M. (1989). Federal support revisited. In F. J. Macchiarola & A. Gartner (eds.), *Caring for America's Children.* (pp. 99–106). Proceedings of the Academy of Political Science, *37* (2). New York: Academy of Political Science.

L. C. Taharally

Child Care in the Military

Department of Defense (DoD) involvement in child care grew out of the changing demographics of the Armed Forces and the reflection of general societal trends affecting military personnel and their families. Approximately 48 percent of military personnel (representing both enlisted and officer personnel) are now married with children. The number of dual military couples further complicates child care needs. As in the civilian sector, increasing numbers of spouses are entering the labor force, and for the most part, these spouses work because of financial necessity.

In addition to the changing demographics, there are unique aspects of the military life style that call for a DoD child care program. One-fourth of military families live overseas, and depending on their location, off-base child care may not be available. Family separations are routine (for example, one-fifth or more of Navy wives are separated from their spouses for more than six months a year). Finally, military members are constantly on the move. One-half of the spouses of enlisted personnel report having moved at least six times in a fifteen-year period. For spouses of officers, there were an average of nine moves over the same period. As a result of this mobility, military families are not able to stay on waiting lists for off-base child care and usually do not have an extended family near the base to offer support and care in times of need.

In offering child care, the DoD does not seek to assume parental responsibilities. From its beginnings in the department, child care has been seen as a readiness issue for the military force, and it has evolved into a productivity issue for the civilian workers. Child care is not regarded as an entitlement, nor is it seen as a social welfare program. Rather, it is the DoD's response to the need to recruit, retain, and motivate the highest quality of both military and civilian personnel for the department.

Background

It is not known when the first child care was established at a military installation; however, there are individuals employed in the current program who began employment in child care over 30 years ago. Most child care centers serving the military prior to 1978 were operated as parent cooperatives, by military wives' clubs, or by private organizations. In most of the remaining cases, chaplains and military exchange managers offered drop-in care during chapel services or while parents were shopping.

As the number of employed spouses among military families increased, the type of child care needs changed from hourly or drop-in to part- and full-day care. The number of families needing child care services also increased. In response armed services began building facilities specifically for child care. The centers grew in size and complexity, and professional management was needed to ensure a smooth operation and quality care. The armed services began operating child care centers as part of their Morale, Welfare, and Recreation (MWR) programs in the 1970s, and requested appropriated funds for child development managers. Regulations reflecting the special requirements of the military were established based on a composite of federal guidelines and state regulations.

Center-Based Child Care

The DoD at this writing operates 690 child care centers at 424 installations around the world. Military child care centers are large in comparison to other federal agency and private sector facilities; the average center serves over 150 children. The capacity exceeds 69,000 children. The children served in DoD centers are between six weeks and twelve years of age. One distinctive feature of DoD centers is that over one-third of the children are younger than three years of age.

DoD child development centers are staffed by civilian employees paid from appropriated funds and nonappropriated funds (generated from parent fees and charges). Over half of these individuals are spouses or family members of military personnel. Most of the directors or managers of the centers are civil service employees. Most caregivers in military child development centers are nonappropriated fund employees. The DoD implemented a new pay plan for caregivers in June 1990 in an effort to reduce the turnover rates and to improve the quality of care provided. Raises and promotions are tied to completion of training and job performance.

The DoD has established minimum standards for military child development centers. These standards are based on state requirements and generally accepted child development theory and practice. Generally, DoD standards are at or near the median state standards in relationship to staff/child ratios, group size, and staff training.

On most military installations a child development center is operated that offers hourly, part-time, and full-time day care to children six weeks through twelve years of age. The center is usually open during a typical duty day for the installation, as well as during some evening and weekend hours. The objective of the center is to provide care for the children while their parents perform military or family responsibilities.

DoD policy is to promote the intellectual, social, emotional, and physical development of children. The individual service regulations and training programs are designed to ensure that the DoD programs provide experiences that enhance each child's development. Each program is required to offer a daily schedule of learning experiences to include dramatic play, music, games, reading, physical activi-

ties, nutrition and cooking activities, and field trips. In addition, each center must establish individual activity rooms and playgrounds equipped with appropriate play materials and equipment. Each service requires that the caregivers receive training, both before working with children and throughout their employment, on how to care for and facilitate the development of children. This training includes child development, child abuse prevention, cardiopulmonary resuscitation, and first aid training.

Non-Center–Based Child Care

The individual armed services branches offer non-center–based child care programs, including family day care programs that certify military spouses to provide care for a small number of children in their private quarters. These programs recruit, train, screen, and inspect the quarters of eligible individuals before granting them approval to operate a family day care home. Currently, there are over 11,000 certified family day care homes on DoD installations.

At some locations, the armed services offer before and after school care for families with school-aged children as part of the MWR Youth Activities program or the Child Development Program. These programs are designed to offer supervised recreation, nutritious snacks, and opportunities for leisure skill development to children before and after school and during school holidays, including the summer months. The military child development centers provide information on the child care services available on the installation, including a list of the certified family day care homes. In addition, the child development program and the family support facility on each installation may offer information on licensed child care services off the installation, if such are available.

Family day care and before and after school programs are cost effective ways of offering child care services because they make use of existing facilities. In addition, limited appropriated funds are required for staffing these programs because the care is provided by individuals who are paid from the fees provided by the parents. At this writing, over 59,000 children are cared for each day in certified military family day care homes.

Eligibility

Eligibility for use of DoD child development programs and other MWR programs is established by a DoD directive that at this writing is under revision. Under the present system, active duty military assigned to the installation have first priority. Active duty personnel from other installations are given second priority. DoD civilians may use the child care centers when space is available. Overseas, DoD civilians have a higher priority.

References

Department of Defense Instruction 6060.2 (March 3, 1989). Child development program.
Military Child Care Act of 1989, Public Law 101-189, November 29, 1989.

L. K. Smith

Head Start

Project Head Start was conceived in February 1965 and was launched across the country during that summer. The idea was generated by a panel of developmentally oriented scientists and policy makers who found in the research literature of the time a basis for early educational intervention as a means of averting subsequent educational failure in low-income children. Head Start, however, was never regarded as an exclusively educational venture, as health and social services always were considered vital components.

During its first summer, Head Start served only those children who would be starting school in the fall. As only about half the states had public kindergartens at that time, many of the children were already six years old, and none was younger than five. Subsequently, the program has been adjusted to cover those of three to six years of age and operates year round rather than only during the summer.

Head Start has sometimes been referred to as the first attack launched in the war on poverty during the administration of President Lyndon B. Johnson. The President's wife, Lady Bird Johnson, was the honorary chair of the program during its early years. Thus, Head Start represented a timely wedding of an empirical basis for social action and a political climate that allowed the action to occur.

Parent and community response to Head Start was overwhelming from the outset. In the first frenzied summer, thousands of early childhood and health professionals worked to get the program underway, assisted by thousands of volunteers who perceived its merits. Although all of the programs had a certain amount of local autonomy, a few national guidelines had to be observed. For instance, each grantee had to organize an Advisory Board, 51 percent of whose membership was to be comprised of parents. Many under-educated, low-income parents became skilled in serving as advocates for their children through participation in Head Start Advisory Board meetings. Also, many of the parents became interested in early childhood as a vocation and obtained the necessary training to secure jobs in the field. Parent involvement has always been a cornerstone of Head Start philosophy.

In spite of fiscal cutbacks that have threatened its existence over the years, Head Start's national popularity has ensured continuous funding. At this writing, approximately one-fourth of the eligible children are enrolled.

Immediately after the first summer program, a few evaluation studies were reported, most of which dealt with very small samples and inadequate controls (Zigler & Valentine, 1979). In contrast, the most widely publicized study reported on a national sample of over 4,000 children (Cicirelli, 1969). Results from that study were widely interpreted as showing that Head Start produced immediate gains in IQ and academic readiness that quickly diminished after the children reached elementary school. Program supporters offered immediate rebuttals, stressing the comprehensive nature of Head Start and offering reminders that program goals also included health, nutrition, parent, and community variables. Nevertheless, following this report, widespread criticism of Head Start became a popular pastime. This criticism had little impact, though, on either public acceptance or federal funding of the program.

More recently, an attempt was made to analyze and synthesize the results of an entire generation of Head Start research as a means of documenting program contributions. Generally referred to as the Head Start Synthesis Study, this work consisted of review of more than 200 reports of evaluations on some aspect of Head Start, as well as meta-analysis of 76 of those studies (McKey et al., 1985). Although the results of this analysis are so far-reaching and complex as to resist summarization, they showed that Head Start is associated with a spurt in cognitive development, higher self-esteem and achievement motivation, and improved health. Without additional support, academic advantages appear to weaken by the third or fourth grade. Even so, fewer Head Start than control children were found to fail a grade or be assigned to special education.

Head Start has touched the lives of millions of children and their families. Furthermore, public acceptance of the "head start" idea has helped produce a renaissance in the field of early childhood education as a whole. Much of the expansion of early intervention programs that has occurred during the past quarter of a century can be traced directly to the impact of Head Start.

References

Cicirelli, V. G. (1969). Project Head Start, a national evaluation: Summary of the study. In Hays, D.G. (ed.), *Britannica Review of American Education*, Vol 1, (pp. 235–243). Chicago: Encyclopedia Britannica.

McKey, R. H., Condelli, L., Ganson, H., Barrett, B., McConkey, C., & Plantz, M. (1985). *Final report on the impact of Head Start on children, families, and communities.* Washington, DC: CSR, Inc.

Zigler, E., & Valentine, J. (1979). *Project Head Start: A legacy of the war on poverty.* New York: The Free Press.

B. M. Caldwell

Head Start Program Evaluation
(See **Head Start.**)

Infant Intervention and Enrichment Programs

In the early 1960s and 1970s, federally funded pioneer programs were created for infants and toddlers, primarily to prevent the declines in cognitive scores consistently found for babies raised in poverty. During that time, a variety of models were designed for infant intervention and enrichment. Some of these programs were broadly developmental, while others were narrowly conceived.

Francis Palmer's Tutorial Model for toddlers promoted concept training (e.g., tall/short). The Home Visitation Model, pioneered by Ira Gordon, employed paraprofessionals to teach parents sequenced Piagetian sensorimotor activities that they could do with their infants. Phyllis Levenstein's Mother-Child Home Visit Program encouraged mother-toddler verbal interactions around carefully selected books and toys.

Home enrichment tutorial models, used extensively with isolated rural families and severely handicapped infants, seemed particularly appropriate when cultural/linguistic barriers made outreach imperative. The Bromwich Parent Interaction Program employed teams of two professionals to serve Hispanic families. Missouri's Parents as Teachers Project provided state-funded home visits for new parents.

Backyard centers, parents as classroom aides, drop-in centers as supports for stressed new parents (such as BEEP in Massachusetts) and parent-infant group meetings proliferated. Costly therapeutic-educational models pioneered by Selma Fraiberg attempted to modify abusive, rejecting, and inappropriate parenting. Stanley Greenspan and colleagues provided intensive individual and peer group therapy for each infant.

Other psychodynamic and ethological theorists expressed concern that early nonmaternal care might be detrimental to infants' development of basic trust and secure attachment with the primary caregiver. This concern led to careful consideration of infants' age at the time of entry into an infant care program and the daily duration of nonmaternal care. The Syracuse Children's Center, for example, enrolled babies at six months for a half-day program. When the baby reached 18 months, the program became full day.

Early group care programs sought to demonstrate that such care in itself (1) would not be detrimental to infant development, (2) could optimize development of at-risk babies, and (3) could serve as a support for employed parents without harming infant-parent attachment. Research results must be interpreted cautiously, since these programs were university based and offered a high quality of care. A study done at the Frank Porter Graham Center with fetally malnourished infants from low-income families, reported that quality care from three months onward led to near normal IQs at thirty-six months, compared to retarded IQs for control infants (Ramey & Gowan, 1986).

The first studies done at the Syracuse Children's Center reported that group care was not a factor in dilution of infant-mother attachment (Caldwell et al., 1970). For both program and control infants, however, lower levels of home stimulation were associated with poorer attachment. The Syracuse Family Development Research Program (FDRP), an omnibus model, trained paraprofessionals to work weekly with low-income families, beginning prior to the birth of an infant and providing group care for the infant from six to sixty months of age. FDRP goals included health, nutrition, early learning and language skills, positive problem solving, family cohesiveness, and use of community resources.

Two longitudinal studies provided insights into the pitfalls and successes of group care. In the Milwaukee Project, infants of low IQ, low-income mothers attended a high-quality care program with excellent infant-staff ratios. The children showed impressive IQ gains as preschoolers. Failing academic records and antisocial truancy characterized their teenage years, however. It seemed clear that infant enrichment without continued family and

child supports could not serve as an inoculation against effects of poverty and family disorganization. In contrast, the FDRP juvenile delinquency rates and costs were much lower for program youths at the age of 15 years, and school achievement of African-American program females (but not males) was significantly higher than for controls.

Some research suggests that full-time group care may increase the possibility of insecure-avoidant attachment with the mother by one year of age and higher aggression scores of preschoolers with peers. More extensive caregiver training and child development knowledge and higher caregiver stability are associated with rises in toddlers' cognitive scores. Quality infant enrichment programs may be critical to enhance the development of babies at risk (Honig, 1990). Programs also may need a strong parent-education component to support positive emotional development in infants, however.

References

Caldwell, B. M., Wright, C., Honig, A. S., & Tannenbaum, J. (1970). Infant day care and attachment. *American Journal of Orthopsychiatry*, *40* (3), 396–412.

Honig, A. S. (1990). Infant/toddler education: Principles, practices, and promises. In Seefeldt, C. (ed.), *Continuing issues in early childhood education*. (pp. 61–105). Columbus, OH: Charles Merrill.

Ramey, C. T., & Gowan, J. W. (1986). A general systems approach to modifying risk for retarded development. In Honig, A. S. (ed.), *Risk factors in infancy*. New York: Gordon & Breach.

A. S. Honig

Kindergarten

The term "Kindergarten" is usually used for programs for five-year-old children. Although kindergarten is not mandatory in most states, it is estimated that 97 percent of all eligible children attend kindergarten (National Association of Elementary School Principals, 1985).

The idea of kindergarten is not new in this country. In 1647 Massachusetts required that each community establish a school for young children (Spodek, 1985). Over time, the role that kindergarten has played in society has changed along with changing societal needs and changing philosophical and theoretical trends (Peck, McCaig, & Sapp, 1988).

Kindergarten has been viewed as a bridge between home and school, as preparation for academics, as remediation for the effects of poverty, as a way of socializing children, and as academic training itself. More recently, all-day kindergarten has been viewed as a means to ensure that children who would otherwise receive many disparate experiences during their day (such as day care, school, and after-school child care) would have a consistent experience in a single setting (Gullo, 1990).

Today there are many factors that are influencing kindergarten policies and practices (Freeman, 1990). They include the use of tests, age of entry policies, prior prekindergarten experiences, familial patterns, political issues, and the nature of the curriculum itself.

The issue currently facing kindergarten is the extent to which developmentally appropriate practice is being implemented. "It was over 100 years ago that the foundation for early childhood was laid. Such European pioneers as Froebel and Montessori envisioned an environment for young children that was nurturing, active, relevant to their needs and supportive of their development. . . . American kindergarten pioneers devoted their professional lives to implementing this same vision. We have come to a time in our history when it is imperative that we revisit our 'ancestors.' If we do, we can only come to the conclusion that, with regard to kindergarten, the standards of the past still apply" (Gullo, 1990, p. 39).

References

Freeman, E. B. (1990). Issues in kindergarten policy and practice. *Young Children, 45* (4), 29–34.

Gullo, D. F. (1990). The changing family context: Implications for the development of all-day kindergarten. *Young Children, 45* (4), 35–39.

National Association of Elementary School Principals. (1985). The statistical trends. *Principal, 64* (5), 16–17.

Peck, J. T., McCaig, G., & Sapp, M. E. (1988). *Kindergarten policies: What is best for children?* Washington, DC: National Association for the Education of Young Children.

Spodek, B. (1985). Early childhood education's past as prologue: Roots of contemporary concerns. *Young Children, 40* (5), 3–7.

D. F. Gullo

All-Day Kindergarten

All-day or full-day kindergarten is becoming commonplace in many school districts. In an all-day kindergarten, children usually follow the same schedule as children in the primary grades.

All-day kindergartens respond to an educational need. This scheduling format allows for more individualization of the curriculum than is possible in a half-day program. A teacher who has the same kindergarten children for the entire day will be able to know the children and their families better.

The all-day kindergarten also allows the teacher to accommodate individual differences better through horizontal expansion of the curriculum. This means that the teacher gives children many different experiences that are integrated across the various curriculum areas, rather than adding academic content that may be developmentally inappropriate (Gullo, 1990a).

In addition, the all-day kindergarten responds to a societal need. With the vast majority of children living in homes with dual-career families or single-parent working families, there is an increased need for an extended program for children. A high quality, developmentally appropriate program in a consistent environment must be viewed as better than multiple daily care arrangements, each with its different standards and policies.

Research on the all-day kindergarten has demonstrated many benefits. The research suggests that a full-day of kindergarten is not detrimental to five- and six-year-olds. The evidence shows that the children who participate in this type of kindergarten benefit academically (Gullo, Bersani, Clements, & Bayless, 1986), as well as socially and emotionally (Peck, McCaig, & Sapp, 1988). Besides benefits for children, research has demonstrated that there are benefits for teachers. Teachers tend to feel less rushed. In addition, when compared to teachers in half-day or alternate-day kindergarten programs, all-day kindergarten teachers were better able to predict their children's level of academic performance (Gullo, 1990b).

References

Gullo, D. F. (1990a). The changing family context: Implications for the development of all-day kindergartens. *Young Children*, *45* (4), 35–39.

Gullo, D. F. (1990b). Kindergarten schedules: Effects on teachers' ability to assess academic achievement. *Early Childhood Research Quarterly*, *5* (1), 43–52.

Gullo, D. F., Bersani, C., Clements, D., & Bayless, K. M. (1986). A comparative study of all-day, alternate-day, and half-day kindergarten schedules: Effects on achievement and classroom social behaviors. *Journal of Research in Childhood Education*, *1* (1), 87–94.

Peck, J. T., McCaig, G., & Sapp, M. E. (1988). *Kindergarten policies: What is best for children?* Washington, DC: National Association for the Education of Young Children.

D. F. Gullo

Alternate- and Extended-Day Kindergarten

Alternate-day kindergarten is a term that is used in reference to a particular scheduling format for kindergarten. Sometimes in this format, children come to school for a full school day, every other day. A school generally opts for this type of schedule in order to save money in busing children between the morning and afternoon kindergarten sessions.

There are many ways in which the alternate-day schedule is formatted. For example, children may come on a Monday and Thursday, or Tuesday and Friday, with Wednesday being a swing day, where one group comes during "A" week and the other group comes during "B" week. In other school systems, children come on Monday, Wednesday, and Friday or Tuesday and Thursday for one semester, then the groups switch for the second

semester. In still another format, children attend every morning, but part of the group remains either two or three afternoons each week for additional small group and individual activities.

The thinking behind alternate-day kindergarten is that children still get the requisite number of hours, and money is saved by eliminating a bus run. There have been some concerns expressed as well. A main concern is that there may be too much inconsistency for children who come to school only every other day or alternating afternoons. In conjunction with this concern, if a child misses a day of school in the alternating full-day format, depending on the day, it may be possible that it will be three or four days before the child is back in school again.

Most research is unclear as to the effectiveness of these types of programs on child performance. Most studies show that for middle-class children, there is no difference in achievement scores between groups of children attending kindergarten for half-days every day, or for a full day every other day (Gullo & Clements, 1984; Gullo, Bersani, Clements, & Bayless, 1986).

In response to societal need, some kindergarten programs have gone to an extended day format. In this format, children who are in need of child care before or after kindergarten, are able to remain in the same school building and participate in another program that is an extension of the kindergarten. Some districts have added an hour to their half-day program and have called that addition an extended day.

References

Gullo, D. F., & Clements, D. (1984). The effects of kindergarten schedule on achievement, classroom behavior and attendance. *Journal of Educational Research*, *78* (1), 51–56.

Gullo, D. F., Bersani, C., Clements, D., & Bayless, K. M. (1986). A comparative study of all-day, alternate-day, and half-day kindergarten schedules: Effects on achievement and classroom social behaviors. *Journal of Research in Childhood Education*, *1* (1), 87–94.

D. F. Gullo

Half-Day Kindergarten

Half-day kindergarten is the term used to refer to a particular scheduling format used in kindergarten. In this format, children attend school for a half day, usually for two and one-half to three hours. In most schools that use this scheduling format, there is both a morning and an afternoon session. A single teacher usually will teach both sessions.

In the research comparing the effectiveness of half-day kindergarten to other scheduling formats, a few studies found it to be superior. One study found that children who attended half-day kindergarten performed higher academically than children who attended alternate-day kindergarten (Pigge, 1979). It also was found that boys seemed to profit more from the half-day schedule. In another study, it was found that there was no difference in academic performance between children attending a half-day or alternate-day kindergarten (Gullo & Clements, 1984). In a study comparing teachers, however, it was found that teachers who teach in the half-day format were better able to predict academic performance of their children than teachers teaching in an alternate-day schedule (Gullo, 1990).

Although the half-day format is considered the "traditional" kindergarten schedule, it is interesting to note that when it began in the 1800s, kindergarten followed a full-day schedule. Today, many school districts are abandoning the half-day format in favor of the full-day or alternate-day kindergarten schedule.

References

Gullo, D. F. (1990). Kindergarten schedules: Effects on teachers' ability to assess academic achievement. *Early Childhood Research Quarterly, 5* (1), 43–52.

Gullo, D. F., & Clements, D. (1984). The effects of kindergarten schedule on achievement, classroom behavior and attendance. *Journal of Educational Research, 78* (1), 51–56.

Pigge, F. L. (1979). *A two-year comparative study of the possible effects of alternate day, full day and daily half-day kindergarten organization patterns.* Bowling Green, OH: Bowling Green State University.

D. F. Gullo

Prekindergarten: School-Based Programs

Throughout the United States, an increasing number of three- and four-year-old children are receiving services from the public schools. Whereas only 8 states had had legislation for prekindergarten programs before 1980, an additional 18 states had allocated such funds by 1987. Of these 26 states, 24 fund pilot or statewide prekindergarten programs, 9 contribute additional funds to Head Start, and 2 provide parent education. Approximately half of these programs are for four-year-olds only, with the rest serving three-year-olds as well. The 26 states served about 206,000 children in 1987. Although the nature, focus, length, and funding of these programs differ dramatically, important trends are emerging as the nation's schools expand and craft innovative services for young children.

First, the majority (two-thirds) of school-based early childhood programs are targeted to serve children with special needs, including those youngsters who are developmentally at risk, handicapped, non-English dominant, or economically disadvantaged. Because slots are limited, states and municipalities must make the difficult choice of serving first those most in need or allowing open enrollment. Second, until recently, the majority of programs used federal dollars (typically Chapter I of ECIA, 94–142, or Head Start) and some state appropriations. Third, as more women join the paid labor force, schools are considering expanding their programs or linking with non-school-based programs to provide full-day services.

Recent resurgence of interest in school-based programs is being driven not solely by the needs of working parents but also by research that documents the efficacy of early intervention. Impressive results have led to a focus on preventing problems before they begin. In addition, research has stressed the importance of parents and community, and many programs now incorporate parents through parenting education, family support, or volunteer and decision-making activities. Also documenting the need for programs to nourish young children's scholastic and social competence, research has spurred programs to meet children's health, nutritional, social, and psychological needs, whether through direct service or through referral to community agencies.

Research also has been useful in improving early childhood pedagogy. Early childhood specialists and developmental psychologists have coalesced to provide valuable guidance on developmentally appropriate services. Documented in the National Association for the Education of Young Children's publication, *Developmentally Appropriate Practice* (*DAP*), such practices are taking root. In spite of *DAP*'s positive and pervasive impact, however, some prekindergarten programs do pursue more academic and structured orientations than those recommended in *DAP*.

References

Bredekamp, S. (1986). *Developmentally appropriate practice*. Washington, DC: National Association for the Education of Young Children.

Kagan, S. L. (February 1989). Early care and education: Tackling the tough issues. *Phi Delta Kappan, 70* (6), 433–439.

Kagan, S. L., & Zigler, E. F. (eds.). (1987). *Early schooling: The national debate*. New Haven: Yale University Press.

Marx, F., & Seligson, M. (1988). *The public school early childhood study: The state survey*. New York: Bank Street College of Education.

S. L. Kagan & D. M Lonow

Primary Grades

The beginning of formal public schooling for young children is known as the primary grades or the primary grammar school. It usually begins when children are six years old and ends when children have completed the third grade. What should constitute the educational program for these three years has posed an ongoing dilemma for educators. Because these grades are sandwiched between educational programs for younger children and elementary/secondary programs, primary teachers often integrate each of these points of view into their curricula. Such integration may cause variability, heated battles, and radical changes in the primary grade programs.

Historically, the primary grades in the United States were modeled after the European schools but were funded by state and local governments as well as by religious groups. Those early schools, often called Latin grammar schools, were designed to give young boys religious instruction, along with instruction in reading, writing, and math. Such schools usually hired male teachers who used memorization and whippings as their teaching methods.

After the Revolutionary War, the citizens of the new United States realized the need for a state school system that would be free to all children. New subjects such as art, history, homemaking, music, and nature study were added to the curriculum. This broadening of scope allowed the children's needs to gain more attention. Educational leaders realized the need for active learning in the primary grades and were beginning to use such methods in their curriculum. Not only was the school curriculum changing, but the teacher's image also was shifting from the school master who often moved from town to town, to the school mistress who was beginning to see herself as a professional.

In the nineteenth century, primary schools won their place by identifying their role in the total educational experience of the learner (Forest, 1935). That victory proved to be a problem because upper grades then expected the primary grades to prepare children for later school work, rather than to help children meet their current social, emotional, physical, and intellectual needs. This view of preparation for later schooling dominated primary education for many years. It has been largely because of early childhood educators' influence that some primary schools have been able to break free of such domination.

Today the purpose of the primary grades is to socialize all children regardless of their cultural, ethnic, and linguistic backgrounds, and to help them to develop their intellectual, social, emotional, and physical abilities to their fullest potential. The children in the primary grades are expected to read, write, use numbers, and engage in art, music, science, history, geography, and other related subjects. In addition to this academic component of the primary grades, teachers of these grades are expected to teach character education to children. This component includes notions of responsibility, right and wrong, citizenship, and autonomy.

Primary grade teachers in public schools must hold at least an initial teaching certificate from the state department of education. Depending on the state, however, their preparation may be either in early childhood or elementary education. They are still faced with the dilemma of what constitutes appropriate pedagogy, though the dilemma may be lessening as knowledge of how young children learn becomes increasingly available to primary school teachers and administrators.

References

Bredekamp, S. (1987). NAEYC position statement on developmentally appropriate practice in the primary grades serving children 5–8 years old. In Bredekamp, S. (ed.), *Developmentally appropriate practice in early childhood programs serving children from birth through age eight.* Washington, DC: National Association for the Education of Young Children.

Forest, I. (1935). *The school for the child from two to eight.* New York: Ginn and Company.

National Association of Elementary School Principals. (1990). *Early childhood education and the elementary school principal: Standards for quality programs for young children.* Alexandria, VA: Author.

National Association of State Boards of Education. (1988). *Right from the start: The report of the National Association of State Boards of Education.* Alexandria, VA: Author.

J. B. Taylor

Primary School Follow Through Programs

Follow Through began in 1967 to "follow through" in the primary school on the gains made by disadvantaged children in Head Start. The program is unique in that early childhood program developers work with cooperating school districts as sponsors of an early childhood program model.

The sponsors developed their models by using a variety of theoretical and philosophical perspectives. The Bank Street College of Education, for example, sponsors a model that was developed on the basis of Bank Street's long history of child-centered education. Known as the "Developmental Interaction Model," the program emphasizes helping children to develop ego strength.

The model known as the "Behavior Analysis Classroom" was developed by the University of Kansas on the basis of its emphasis on principles of behavior analysis, and focuses on the development of academic skills. Similarly, the University of Oregon sponsors a model, called "Direct Instruction," that is based on an analysis of direct teaching and on application of laboratory learning principles to the reading, language, and mathematics curricula of the primary school. The High/Scope Educational Research Foundation sponsors still another model, "The Cognitively Oriented Curriculum," that has emerged by inferring educational implications from the cognitive developmental theory of Jean Piaget. The goal of this model is to help children construct their own knowledge and become fluent problem solvers.

These are only 4 examples of the 22 different models that were operating in the early 1970s in 173 local school districts, serving 84,000 children and over 4,000 teachers. The models embody varying beliefs about how children learn and about the process of education. They differ in their goals for children and on how they want teachers to teach. The models are similar, however, in that they all focus on individualizing instruction, involve parents in the schooling of their children, and demonstrate concern about the difficulties experienced in public schools by many children from low-income homes.

From 1968 through 1975, the Follow Through Program was subject to massive evaluation efforts in the Follow Through Planned Variation Experiments (Stebbins et al., 1977) supported by the United States Office of Education. In these studies, investigators used several instruments to gather scores achieved by children in Follow Through programs and by similar children who were not in such programs. Using these data, it was possible to compare the differences exhibited by children in different communities supported by the same sponsor, in different communities supported by different sponsors, and in all Follow Through programs regardless of community and sponsor. In addition, most of the sponsors and communities gathered data on their own programs (Hodges, et al., 1980).

After 1975 each community and sponsor had to provide evidence in order to gain approval from the Federal Joint Dissemination Review Panel (FJDRP). The Stanford Research Institute also studied Follow Through by visiting classrooms and gathering firsthand data (Stallings 1975). All of these studies provide insight into the education of children who were not succeeding in conventional schooling (Rhine, 1981).

The Follow Through data and the experiences of the sponsors and local school systems in trying to meet the needs of such children are unique. They are used infrequently in a time when there is still much difficulty in educating the hard to reach and often disengaged learners in our schools. If the current trend of parental choice of schools, as well as trends toward school-based management continue, then the models created through Follow Through can offer some viable alternatives.

References

Hodges, W., Branden, A., Feldman, R., Follins, J. Love, J., Sheehan, R., Lumbley, J., Osborn, J., Rentfrow, R., Houston, J., & Lee, C. (1980). *Follow Through: Forces for change in the primary schools.* Ypsilanti, MI: The High/Scope Press.

Rhine, W. R. (ed). (1981). *Making schools more effective: New directions for Follow Through.* New York: Academic Press.

Stallings, J. (1975). Implementation and child effects of teaching practices in Follow Through classrooms. *Monographs of the Society for Research in Child Development. 40*, Nos. 7–8.

Stebbins, L. B., St. Pierre, R. G., Proper, E. C., Anderson, R. B., & Cerva, T. R. (1977). *The Follow Through Planned Variation experiment, Volume IIA, national evaluation: An evaluation of Follow Through.* Washington, DC: U.S. Office of Education.

W. Hodges

School-Age Child Care

School-age child care describes programs that serve children before and after regular school hours as well as during the summer and holidays when schools are not in session. These programs are referred to by many names including "extended day programs," "latchkey programs," or "before and after school programs." They are designed to meet the physical, social-emotional, and intellectual needs of children within a nurturing, child-centered environment. The programs are sponsored by a range of organizations, including community centers, parks and recreation departments, elementary schools, churches and synagogues, and day care centers.

Recent social, economic, and cultural changes have created a need to serve the school-age child outside the formal hours of the school day. School-age child care is not a new phenomenon. Charities and day nurseries provided care for school-age children as early as 1894 (Seligson, 1986). The number of families needing such care, however, is growing rapidly.

School-age programs responsive to children have child growth and development principles as their core. Kindergarten-age children, primary-age children, and older children have different needs and interests. Characteristics of responsive school-age curricula include providing opportunities for initiative, supporting children's sense of competence, supporting children's peer associations, involving adults appropriately, complementing the school's curriculum emphasizing recreational activities, and involving children in the community (Neugebauer, 1980). A relaxed, informal environment offers children opportunities to make choices, develop relationships, or do homework.

Space for school-age child care varies. The ideal space reflects a homelike atmosphere suitable for small groups of children and is designated specifically for the program. Shared space such as the gymnasium, cafeteria, or classroom, however, is often the only option for school-age child care programs.

Materials for school-age child care programs should be plentiful and accessible and should be chosen to be in keeping with a child-centered approach. They should encourage children's creativity and foster experiences of success.

The single most significant component of any school-age program is the staff who works with the children. These adults should understand child development, possess good organizational skills, have the ability to create appropriate activities, and interact positively with parents.

The need and demand for school-age child care programs poses a myriad of challenges. The school's role as a child care provider, with its attendant legal, financial, administrative, and staffing issues, poses questions. Yet, the development and growth in quality of school-age child care programs are indicative of real progress by educators in responding to societal changes. Through coordinated, collaborative efforts of families, schools, and communities, children's need for support can be met.

References

Neugebauer, R. (1980). School age day care: Getting it off the ground. *Child Care Information Exchange*, No. 10, 9–15.

Seligson, M. (1986). Child care for the school-age child. *Phi Delta Kappan, 67* (9), 637–640.

S. W. Nall

3.4 Early Childhood Settings in the Private Sector

Programs for children from birth through eight years of age in the private sector are supported through parent fees, churches, synagogues, or other religious institutions, privately run community agencies, corporations, foundation grants, and proprietors. While the full age span of children is served, most private programs are designed for children under five years of age, where there is a dearth of publicly funded early childhood programs.

Private programs are not subject to federal, state, or local guidelines regarding which populations they may serve, but they must meet state or locally determined minimum standards in order to be licensed and registered. These standards focus most often on the health, well-being, and safety of children attending such programs, and occasionally on the components of the educational program.

The articles that follow describe the variety of early childhood settings and programs that can be found under private sponsorship. The articles are arranged alphabetically, except for those that elaborate on an immediately preceding topic.

L. R. Williams

At-Home Education

A small but growing minority of families (between 100,000 and 500,000 in number) in all parts of the United States choose to educate their children at home. Laws regarding home education vary from state to state. Some require parents to submit an affidavit simply notifying the school district or the department of education of their intent to teach their children at home. Others allow parents to register their homes as private schools. Requirements about how much additional material the parents must submit vary as well, possibly including lists of materials to be used, monthly or annual reports, standardized test scores, or portfolios of work.

Home educators live in urban centers, in suburban neighborhoods, on farms, and in rural communities. In many home-educating families, one or both parents work at home; but there is also a good number of single-parent homeschoolers and families in which both parents work outside the home.

Some parents are strongly motivated by religious beliefs. Others prefer home education's flexibility and its ability to conform to a particular child's needs and interests. Some parents turn to home education after their child has had difficulty in school. In general, homeschooling parents have in common the belief that they can help their children learn and that they enjoy doing so.

Some home educators follow the traditional school structure, adhering to a regular schedule and using school materials. Others follow an approach based on real-world activities and on the child's interests. A child in such a home may, for example, learn arithmetic from cooking and making change, and writing from publishing a neighborhood newsletter or writing letters.

Children taught at home tend to score as well or better than their peers in school on standardized tests when tests are required or when they choose to take those tests. Homeschoolers who choose to enter school generally do so successfully, and some have been accepted by colleges and universities.

Home-educated children do not generally suffer from social isolation, as many critics of the alternative suggest. They participate in many group activities such as scouts, 4-H clubs, after-school sports, music activities, and other activities and groups that draw on the neighborhood and community rather than on the school. Many participate in activities of their local homeschool support group, such as writing clubs, group games, field trips, and other workshops and events. In addition, homeschoolers often have access to a wider range of social opportunities than is usually available in school. It is common for homeschoolers to have adult friends and to consider their siblings close friends. It is also common for homeschoolers to be involved in apprenticeship or volunteer opportunities outside the home, such as working in a food co-op, volunteering at a nursing home, or being an intern at the local library.

References

Colfax, D., & Colfax, M. (1988). *Homeschooling for excellence*. New York: Warner Books.

Holt, J. (1981). *Teach your own*. New York: Delacorte Press.

Richman, H., & Richman, S. (1988). *The three R's at home*. Kittaning, PA: Pennsylvania Homeschoolers.

Wallace, N. (1983). *Better than school*. Burdett, NY: Larson Publications.

S. Sheffer

Centers for the Homeless

During the Ronald Reagan administration, the federal government cut virtually all support for low-income housing. This created a crisis of homelessness for tens of thousands of people. The lack of available, affordable housing, coupled with a job market that increasingly has moved workers downward into low-paying jobs, forced thousands of families into the streets.

Homeless and hungry, most of these families entered into a system that placed them in "transitional housing" either in hotels or shelters. While these accommodations were intended to be short term, many families found themselves spending months or even years in these facilities. The children, who are the most vulnerable within the homeless population, have been hit the hardest by this crisis.

In recent years, thousands of young children have been passing their infancy and preschool years in conditions certain to cause them tremendous stress and likely to mar their futures. The youngest children must spend most of their time in cribs, strollers, or the arms of their parents. Children of preschool age spend their time in small, airless rooms and dangerous hallways. There is little opportunity for the kind of explorative and interactive play that lays the foundation for healthy physical, emotional, and cognitive development.

Although children in these situations need early childhood programs, they have been even less likely to have access to them than has the general population. In some instances, private, nonprofit organizations such as the Children's Aid Society, The Association to Benefit Children, and Women In Need have set up preschool programs within shelters and hotels. Funding from government agencies often has been difficult to obtain. Where it has been available, it has fallen far short of meeting the need, with little or no funding provided for child care of the most vulnerable, infants and toddlers.

For those dedicated early childhood professionals who have set up programs within hotels and shelters, there have been a myriad of problems to confront. Finding qualified staff has been extremely difficult. Early childhood teachers, already overworked and underpaid, have been understandably reluctant to take jobs in settings that are physically and emotionally draining. Therefore, much of the staff within these programs are well intentioned but untrained in basic concepts of early childhood development and education. Even for those teachers with degrees in early childhood education, teaching within homeless programs confronts them with challenges that their studies did not cover. As the director of child care at the Prince George Hotel in New York City so aptly put it, "Every month is September, and every day is Monday." The constant changes within the group, and the level of trauma that individual children are living through make it virtually impossible to apply the basic teaching methods that one uses in the average preschool classroom. Even so, government guidelines expect the child care programs for the homeless to conform to the same basic format as other preschool programs in terms of group size and teacher/child ratios.

In some cases, child care programs for the homeless have been expected to manage with even fewer resources than other programs have. For example, in New York City there are strict licensing regulations governing staff/child ratios and teacher qualifications for early childhood programs. Yet the state in its *New York State Part 900 Regulations Governing Family Shelters* published a different and lower set of standards for child care programs in transitional shelters.

There is a great deal of attention now being paid to moving homeless families out of the hotels. Many, however, are not being relocated to permanent housing but are instead moving into shelters. It is essential that each of these shelters be able to provide a program for the young children in residence. For these programs to be effective, they require a higher staff/child ratio than the average preschool program, smaller groups of children, funding for staff training, and a system for involving parents in the day-to-day education of their children.

Cities must look forward in their planning. Presently, they are moving families back into permanent housing in communities in which child care facilities already are inadequate to meet the needs of the current population. If relocated families get priority placements in the day care programs that exist, other low-income families will lose their places. In either case, many families will be left without the necessary child care to allow them to work or pursue training and education. In order to escape the homeless system, families need to have jobs and the child care necessary to be able to work.

Reference

Berezin, J. (1988). *Promises to keep: Child care for New York City's homeless children.* New York: Child Care, Inc.

J. Berezin

Child Care Programs

The term "child care" is used to describe programs for infants, toddlers, preschoolers and primary-age children, which are either full or part time and which provide educational and nurturing services. Traditionally, most child care programs have been provided by the private sector rather than as part of the public school system.

Supply and demand have shaped the provision of child care services. There has been a growing need for child care in the United States. With more than 50 percent of mothers now working and large increases in the employment rates of mothers with very young children, the need for full-time child care programs has quickly exceeded the supply of programs. To meet the need for child care, many previously part-day programs have expanded either to full-day programs or to "wrap-around child care." Wrap-around child care programs provide care for children before and after the morning enrichment or preschool experience. In addition, many full-day programs have been initiated.

Private child care programs legally can be nonprofit or profit. If a program is nonprofit, all of the money in the budget goes to support the needs of the program, including rent, insurance, and teaching staff salaries. Many different agencies sponsor nonprofit child care. These agencies include churches and synagogues, parent cooperatives, private schools for older children, community agencies including the Y's, United Way, child guidance centers, universities and colleges, hospitals and businesses, as well as individuals who choose to run their child care center as a nonprofit entity. Churches provide the largest proportion of nonprofit care.

Most proprietary or for-profit child care programs have been small, independent centers owned by an individual person or family. The fastest growing form of child care in the United States, however, is for-profit chains. Chains are legal business arrangements. In a chain, the owner owns and operates at least two different child care centers. Some chains are relatively small and locally based. Other chains are national in scope and may include several thousand centers.

Initial research on full-day child care programs compared children who remained at home with their mothers, to children in full-day care. The first wave of studies concluded that there were no detrimental effects of full-day care on children's development (Belsky & Steinberg, 1978). These studies were done primarily in model programs. As child care expanded and researchers began to study community-based programs, it became clear that child care programs were extremely heterogeneous in quality (Ruopp et al., 1979; Whitebook, Howes & Phillips, 1989). Subsequent research identified the components of quality in child care programs and documented the detrimental effects of low-quality child care on children's concurrent and long-term

development (Phillips & Howes, 1987; Howes, 1988).

Most researchers and policy makers now agree that high-quality child care is defined by low child-to-adult ratios and highly educated and trained teachers. These conditions enable teachers to provide individualized and developmentally appropriate care for children. Recent evidence suggests that an additional component of quality in child care programs is the adult work environment, including the salaries and benefits paid to teachers and their working conditions (Whitebook et al., 1989).

Salaries in the child care professions traditionally have been very low. Despite recent increases in those salaries, child care teachers' wages actually have declined relative to inflation (Ibid.). Teachers unable to afford to stay in the field are leaving it at a rate of over 40 percent per year. This situation has created a crisis in child care, as programs are having difficulty in finding and retaining educated and trained teachers. The teacher crisis is also a crisis in the quality of care provided for children.

Nonprofit child care centers provide a better quality of care for children than do for-profit centers (Ibid., 1989). Investigators have found that they have better adult/child ratios, smaller groups of children, and higher scores on the Early Childhood Environmental Rating Scale (Harms & Clifford, 1980). Nonprofit child care centers also provide better adult work environments than do for-profit child care. In addition, nonprofit child care centers have lower turnover rates than for-profit child care centers (Whitebook, op. cit.; Child Care Employee Project, 1989).

References

Belsky, J., & Steinberg, L. (1978). The effects of day care. *Child Development, 49*, 929–949.

Child Care Employee Project. (1989). Personal communication.

Harms, T., & Clifford, R. (1980). *Early Childhood Environment Rating Scale*. New York: Teachers College Press.

Howes, C. (1988). Can the age of entry and the quality of infant child care predict behaviors in kindergarten? *Developmental Psychology, 24* (1), 53–57.

Phillips, D.A., & Howes, C. (1987). Indicators of quality in child care: Review of the research. In D. A. Phillips (ed.), *Quality in child care: What does research tell us?* Research Monograph. Washington, DC: National Association for the Education of Young Children.

Ruopp, R., Travers, J., Glantz, F. & Coelen, C. (1979). *Children at the center.* Cambridge, MA: Abt Books.

Whitebook, M., Howes, C., & Phillips, D., & Pemberton, C. (1989). Who cares? Child care teachers and the quality of care in America. *Young Children, 45* (1), 41–45.

C. Howes

Church/Synagogue and Community Agency Child Care

Churches, synagogues, and community agencies are a major source of child care and early childhood education in the United States. Church and synagogues alone are the largest providers of early childhood programs—part-time nursery schools and mother's- or parent's-day-out programs for enrichment and socialization purposes, and an increasing amount of full-day child care for working parents. The National Council of Churches of Christ estimates that as many as 50 percent of all preschool children in early childhood programs are enrolled in church- or synagogue-sponsored care settings (Linder, Mattis, & Rogers, 1983). While church-related programs are primarily center based, both the National Council of Churches of Christ and the National Council of Jewish Women have initiated projects to improve the supply and quality of family home care (National Council of Churches, 1989; National Council of Jewish Women, n.d.).

Most church- or synagogue-sponsored child care evolved as a ministry for members of the congregations or the broader community or as a social outreach mission to improve the lives of low-income children and their parents. Because of these roots, the church has contributed substantial subsidy to underwrite program costs. Traditionally, the church has provided low-cost, high-quality education and care, often by caregivers who are church members and who receive little compensation for their services. In recent years, however, more churches have expected their early childhood programs to operate on a balanced budget of parent fees and even to assist in paying church overhead costs. Some leaders in the field believe that this trend has severely reduced the quality of services provided or the outreach efforts to serve lower income children and their parents.

In addition to churches and synagogues, a variety of community agencies provide significant amounts of child care. Two large sources are the Young Men's and Women's Christian Associations (YMCA and YWCA), and the Young Men's and Women's Hebrew Associations (YMHA and YWHA), which are major providers of preschool and school-age child care in metropolitan communities. The YMCA of USA estimates that of its 1,775 Y's in 1988, 8 percent provided infant and toddler care; 26 percent, preschool care; and 54 percent, school-age care (YMCA, 1989). Although some Y child care services are located in Y facilities, the majority of the school-age care occurs in school buildings donated or leased by school boards. The rapid increase in this service has spawned generous criticism from for-profit operators in some areas of the country. Although it is unclear whether the Y child care is a business that generates revenue for the Y or a charitable service, in some communities the Y has provided substantial scholarships for children whose parents cannot pay any or all of the cost (Pekow, 1989).

There are a host of other nonprofit community agencies that are known to provide child care services including Boys' and Girls' Clubs, neighborhood and community centers, parent cooperatives, and even Senior Citizen Centers. Usually these agencies charge parents according to income, using a sliding scale fee. In addition to parent fees, these programs are subsidized by a variety of private funds from civic clubs, professional organizations, business and industry, consortia of churches, or United Way or United Givers Fund.

In some states, private nonprofit agencies contract with state or local governments for varying amounts of federal funds from Social Services Block Grant (SSBG), Community Services Block Grant (CSBG), Community Development Block Grant (CDBG), Carl Perkins Vocational Education Act, Job Training Partnership Act (JTPA), Family Support Act, or state and public local funds to serve eligible children. Others rely on private charities, foundations, and local fundraising projects. The majority of these programs receive food cost reimbursements from the USDA Child and Adult Care Food Program (CACFP). The infinite variety of community agency providers and the array of funding mechanisms illustrate the ingenuity of local community leaders in their struggle to provide needed child care services in the absence of a national child care system. (See also Section 3.2, **Religious Early Childhood Education** and **Sources of Funding for Early Childhood Programs.**)

References

Lindner, E., Mattis, M. C., & Rogers, J. R. (1983). *When churches mind the children: A study of day care in local parishes.* Ypsilanti, MI: High Scope Press.

National Council of Churches. (March/April 1989). *Ecumenical child care newsletter, 2* (2). New York: Author.

National Council of Jewish Women. (n.d.). *Highlights of the national family day care project.* New York: Author.

Pekow, C. (March 13, 1989). Battle in public schools: YMCAs and for-profit fight for latchkey kids, *Day Care Information Service Special Report, 18* (6).

Young Men's Christian Association. (1989). *1989 statistical summary.* Chicago: YMCA, USA.

J. Camp

Day Care
(See **Child Care Programs.**)

Drop-In Child Care Centers

A classroom or center that takes children on an hourly basis, usually for an hourly fee, is considered a drop-in child care facility. Drop-in care is designed to meet short-term and random child care needs. The center may require advance registration and notification of planned attendance to assure proper staffing. Drop-in child care has been, for the most part, designed for parents who are at home, and operates outside of the government subsidized systems.

Drop-in child care, like all other forms of child care, requires licensing. The number of children in attendance and the staff/child ratio depend upon local or state government licensing requirements. The youngest child cared for in the group will determine the required staff/child ratio for a given day.

Drop-in child care may serve a broad arena of parental and child needs. It also may have many different names and administrative support systems. Churches, hospitals, clinics, resorts, recreational centers, health clubs, community centers, shopping malls, airports, cruise ships, schools, children and youth agencies, and child day care facilities all may house and operate this type of child care. The labels or names may vary greatly from "Mother's Day Out," "Stay and Play," or "Drop-A-Tot" to a reference to "Nursery Care Available."

A high-quality program provides experienced and well-trained staff who has extra sensitivity to the constantly changing nature of group participants, and who recognizes the separation anxieties of children and parents. The staff must give special attention to licensing, first aid, emergency procedures, and a range of age-appropriate activities in order to carry out a safe and healthy program.

References

Hildebrand, V. (1986). *Introduction to early childhood education.* New York: Macmillan.

Maxim, G. W. (1989). *The very young.* Columbus, OH: Merrill.

A. E. Nelson

Family Day Care (Home-Based Child Care)

Family day care involves out-of-home care of a child by a nonrelative in her home. Typically, the total number of children is six or fewer, although this does vary by state and locale. Family day care is the most frequently used form of out-of-home care for preschool children, particularly for infants and toddlers. There are 2.6 million children in regulated family day care, and 2.7 million in unregulated family day care (Hofferth, 1989). According to the National Day Care Home Study (NDCHS), 94 percent of family day care homes are informal and independent, while 3 percent are regulated (licensed or registered) and independent (Divine-Hawkins, 1981). The remaining 3 percent are regulated and connected to a sponsoring agency, usually in order to access USDA Child Care Food Program funding and to receive training and/or supervision.

The typical family day care provider is a married woman in her thirties with children of her own, who earns approximately one dollar per hour per child to supplement the family's income. Formal training among family day care providers in child care or child development/early childhood education is rare, and job turnover is high (estimated to be 40 percent to 50 percent per year). Nonetheless, expressed job satisfaction also is high (Bollin, 1989; Kontos, 1990).

Since 1977 the number of licensed family day care homes has increased by one-third (Hofferth, 1989). Speculation regarding the reasons for this increase focus on the fact that family day care resembles home care more than center care does, is less expensive than center care, and is more elastic than center programs because start-up and recruitment of families can be quicker. Preference for family day care as measured by its use, however, is probably more a reflection of access and/or affordability. Few families using centers switch to family day care, although the reverse is quite common (Kahn & Kamerman, 1987). Preferences also may be a reflection of children's changing needs as they develop. Many see family day care as ideal for infants and toddlers but view more structured, center-based programs as better for preschoolers.

Numerous comparisons have been made between the physical settings and children's and adults' behaviors in family day care versus center care. Results vary with the measures used, but the relatively few differences are noteworthy. For instance, one study found that the only difference in caregiving behaviors between centers and family day care homes was the greater likelihood of home caregivers to ignore toddler requests, which was still a rare occurrence in either case (Howes, 1983). Another study found that children in day care homes were more likely to engage in cognitive, verbal, and exploratory activities, and in play, than children in centers (Cochran, 1977). The day care providers in this study engaged in more teaching and supervision/small talk than the center teachers. The New York Infant Day Care Study found few differences in the kinds of daily activities and interactions of babies in family day care versus center care (Golden et al., 1979). There were, however, large differences in the number of safety hazards and nutrition provided through meals and snacks that favored center care.

In general, the research comparing family day care with center care has shown that both environments can be nurturing environments for children. A recent study in Canada is one of the few to have measured the quality of family day care environments and their effects on children. This study found that family day care quality was related to level of cognitive stimulation provided in the home (Goelman, Shapiro, & Pence, 1990). When family characteristics are similar, the quality of children's play reflects the quality of the program (Howes & Stewart, 1987), and the father's education correlates with children's intellectual development and receptive language (Kontos, 1990). Other studies found that children in family day care demonstrated lower cognitive and social competence than children in center-based settings, partially as a function of family background characteristics (Clarke-Stewart, 1987).

Results of the Victoria Day Care Research Project found that single mothers with less education were more likely to place their children in family day care than center care and that their children's language development was poorer than the children of married mothers who had more education (Goelman & Pence, 1987). Family day care quality seems to range from poor to adequate (Kontos, 1989) and influences children's development in tandem with the family context.

References

Bollin, G. (March 1989). *Diversity in attitudes about family day care among sponsored family day care providers*. Paper presented at the American Educational Research Association annual meeting, San Francisco.

Clark-Stewart, K. A. (1987). Predicting child development from child care forms and features: The Chicago study. In D. Phillips (ed.). *Quality in child care: What does research tell us?* (pp. 21–41). Washington, DC: National Association for the Education of Young Children.

Cochran, M. (1977). A comparison of group day and family child-rearing patterns in Sweden. *Child Development, 48* (2), 702–707.

Divine-Hawkins, P. (1981). *Family day care in the United States: Executive summary*. Final Report of the National Day Care Home Study. Cambridge, MA: Abt Associates.

Goelman H, & Pence, A. (1987). Some aspects of the relationships between family structures and child language development in three types of day care. In D. Peters & S. Kontos (eds.), *Continuity and discontinuity of experience in child care* (pp. 129–146). Annual advances in applied developmental psychology, Vol. 2. Norwood, NJ: Ablex Publishing.

Goelman, H., Shapiro, E., & Pence, A. (1990). Family environment and family day care. *Family Relations, 39* (1), 14–19.

Golden, M., Rosenbluth, L., Grossi, M., Policare, H., Freeman, H., & Brownlee, M. (1979). *The New York Infant Day Care Study: A comparative study of licensed group and family infant day care programs and the effects of these programs on their families*. New York: Medical and Health Research Association of New York, Inc.

Hofferth, S. (1989). What is the demand for and supply of child care in the United States? *Young Children, 44*, 28–33.

Howes, C. (1983). Caregiver behavior in center and family day care. *Journal of Applied Developmental Psychology, 4*, 99–107.

Howes, C., & Stewart, P. (1987). Child's play with adults, toys, and peers: An examination of family and child-care influences. *Developmental Psychology, 23* (3), 423–430.

Kahn, A., & Kamerman, S. (1987). *Child care: Facing the hard choices*. Dover, MA: Auburn.

Kontos, S. (March 1989). *Predictors of job satisfaction and child care quality in family day care*. Paper presented at the American Educational Research Association annual meeting, San Francisco.

Kontos, S. (April 1990). *Child, families, and child care: The search for connections*. Paper presented at the American Educational Research Association annual meeting, Boston.

S. Kontos

Group Child Care Homes

Group homes also are called large family day care homes. Group homes have many characteristics of center care. They tend to be more structured than small family day care homes and reflect the need for more organization due to the number of children and adults present.

Each state establishes its own group home regulations that address issues such as the maximum number of children to be served (usually from 12 to 15), the number of adults who must be present (usually 2), the age of the caregivers (usually primary caregivers must be over 18 years of age and an aide/assistant must be at least 14 years of age), the ages and numbers of children served (usually no more than 4 of the children may be under the age of 2), and the experience of the caregiver (in some states a caregiver must have one year of prior experience in a small family day care home for 6 or fewer children before opening a group home).

Group homes often are governed by stricter local regulations dealing with fire, zoning, building and safety requirements than are the small family day care homes. In many urban areas where housing costs have increased, small family day care operators have turned to the larger group homes as a way of serving more children and increasing their income. In doing so, they become subject to the more extended guidelines described above.

References

Clarke-Stewart, K. A. (1982). *Daycare*. Cambridge: Harvard University Press.

Collins, A., & Watson, E. (1976). *Family day care: A practical guide for parents, caregivers and professionals*. Boston: Beacon Press.

Emlen, A. (1980). Family day care for children under three. *Home Day Care: A Perspective*. Chicago: Roosevelt University College of Education.

Sale, J. S. (1984). Family day care homes. In Greenman, J. T., & Fuqua, R. W. *Making day care better*. New York: Teachers College Press.

J. S. Sale

Industry-Based Child Care

In response to the changing composition of the family and the rising number of women in the work force, some private sector companies have recognized employees' need for child care. In 1986 the New York Conference Board reported that about 3,500 private sector companies have responded to the problem of child care in one of the following ways:

- by providing financial assistance (e.g., Proctor & Gamble, CIGNA, Polaroid, Zayre Corporation);
- by providing information (e.g., American Express and International Business Machines);
- by revising work schedules (e.g., Corning Glass); and
- by creating child care facilities (e.g., Merck & Company) (Friedman, 1986; 1987).

Financial assistance may come in the form of flexible benefit plans, where employees choose the benefits that best match their family situations, or in the provision of discounts or company-paid vouchers for use at local child care programs. Some companies satisfy employees' critical information needs by creating child care resource and referral services. Other employers provide for parental leaves, part-time work, flexible work schedules, and job sharing to make employees' child care needs more manageable. Across the United States, about 150 companies operate their own child care facilities. While such centers are the most expensive option, employers report that their costs are offset by improved worker morale and increased company attractiveness

to new recruits. As a variant of this model, a limited number of companies are collaborating to support "near-site child care centers" that reduce the costs for an individual employer.

The United States has 6 million private sector employers. Despite empirical evidence that parent workers experience personal stress and professional dysfunction from their dual roles (Fernandez, 1986), the 3,500 employers that provide some form of systematic child care are clearly a very small minority.

References

Fernandez, J. P. (1986). *Child care and corporate productivity*. Lexington, MA: D.C. Heath.

Friedman, D. E. (March–April 1986). Child care for employees' kids. *Harvard Business Review*, *64* (2), 28–34.

Friedman, D. E. (1987). *Corporate financial assistance for child care*. Research Bulletin No. 177. New York: The Conference Board.

R. Trachtman

Infant/Toddler Child Care

Privately funded child care centers for infants and toddlers are found in a number of settings, including hospitals, colleges, businesses, churches, and synagogues. They also may be independently owned and operated. Programs vary in their philosophy and practice depending on the needs of the institution and families involved. Children sometimes are enrolled as young as six weeks of age, if permitted by the regulations of the local authorities, and programs may be full time and/or part time. Infant and toddler groups often are part of day care centers where there are older children as well, but programs may be exclusively for children younger than two or three years of age. Children within a group may be close in age, or the group may be mixed aged.

Funding for private infant/toddler programs generally comes from a combination of sources, including tuition/fees, grants, subsidies, donations, fundraising, and federal/state aid for income-eligible families. Programs may be for-profit or not-for-profit. Some centers are administered by an individual, but in most cases there is a board of directors responsible for the finances and other aspects of the program. Educational and administrative directors are hired by the board of directors to manage day-to-day operations.

Typically, privately sponsored programs for very young children were established in the United States either to provide custodial care (feeding, diapering, provisions for sleeping) to children of low-income families where the mother worked, or to provide enrichment activities to children of well-off families. However, these patterns began to change in the 1980s, as many middle-class and upper middle-class women began working outside of the home. The current situation coupled with increased understanding about the nature and needs of very young children has led to programs for infants and toddlers that offer opportunities for enhanced growth, development, and learning, as well as provision for meeting basic physical needs.

Child care centers for infants and toddlers may adhere to a holistic approach intended to facilitate social, emotional, cognitive, language, fine motor, and gross motor development, or to an approach that emphasizes one aspect of development or behavior. A program also may be based on a particular theory or development or learning (e.g., Piagetian theory or learning theory), or on a particular approach to interaction with very young children (e.g., Axtmann's Extended Family Model or Gordon's Home Visitation Model). Infant/toddler programs frequently advertise that they are child centered in that the children's needs and communications largely determine adult/child interactions and curricular activities. Many infant/toddler programs also call themselves "developmental," meaning either that children are expected to acquire skills and abilities at their own pace, or that a universal sequence of development is expected to unfold. Most infant/toddler programs include parent participation by fostering communication between parents and staff, and encouraging parents to visit the program.

College-based infant and toddler centers usually function to provide child care to faculty and/or students, at the same time as they provide a setting for studying the development of very young children. Campus centers may be part of an academic department such as early childhood education or developmental psychology. Typically, students receive credit for work in the center, and the caregiving staff is at least partially comprised of such students.

Research on infant and toddler development often is carried out in such centers by professors and students, and settings may have special provisions for conducting research, such as two-way mirrors to facilitate observation, video cameras, or heart-rate monitors. These centers (which might also be known as laboratory schools or child study centers) tend to emphasize the integration of theory, research, and practice when providing child care.

Infant and toddler centers in hospitals have become more common with the increasing shortage of nurses. In hospital-based settings, the personnel or human resources department usually establishes on-site child care as a way of recruiting and retaining qualified staff. Long hours of operation are typical to accommodate the extended working hours of doctors and nurses. Parents working in the hospital have the option of visiting their children during the day, possibly to share lunch time, or to breast-feed. Enrollment usually is open to children in the larger community when space is available.

On-site infant/toddler care in corporations also enables parents to be near their children during the workday. Large business organizations, or sometimes a group of a few small businesses, may finance infant/toddler care programs for their employees in order to strengthen morale and increase productivity, and to decrease absenteeism and turnover.

Other privately funded specialized infant/toddler programs include those in nursing homes, courts, and prisons. In addition, early intervention programs for infants and toddlers exist in order to enhance growth and learning in high-risk and developmentally delayed children. (See also **Laboratory Schools (College and University)**, and Section 3.3, **Early**

Childhood Settings in the Public Sector, Infant Intervention and Enrichment Programs.)

References

Axtmann, A. (1986). Friendships among infants? Yes indeed!, In D. Wolf (ed.) *Connecting* (pp. 12–17). Redmond, WA: Exchange Press.

Cataldo, C. Z. (1983). *Infant and toddler programs: A guide to very early childhood education.* Reading, MA: Addison-Wesley.

Gonzalez-Mena, J., & Eyer, D. W. (1989). *Infants, toddlers, and caregivers.* Mountain View, CA: Mayfield Publishing Company.

Gordon, I. J. (1970). Reaching the young child through parent education. *Childhood Education, 46* (5), 101–106.

Willis, A., & Ricciutti, H. (1975). *A good beginning for babies.* Washington, DC: National Association for the Education of Young Children.

E. S. Flicker

Proprietary (For-Profit) Child Care (See Child Care Programs.)

Elementary Schools

Private elementary schools, usually classified as church affiliated or independent, continue to represent a significant proportion of American education. There are more than 20,000 private schools in the United States, employing 13 percent of all teachers and educating more than 2.5 million elementary students. Approximately three out of every four of these private schools are religiously affiliated, and more than half of the students attend Catholic schools (Snyder, 1988).

The goal of private education is to provide a familial, personalized education under the direction of a headmaster or principal. Typically, the governance of the private elementary school is through an autonomous board of trustees who delegates power and authority to the head.

Major differences between public and private education are that the private schools generally have smaller enrollments, are privately managed and financed, and have a special relationship to the students because parents have selected the school.

Although the nonpublic schools embrace a diverse group of institutions, individual private schools tend, by their very nature, to have a homogeneous student population. A recent trend is to recruit a more diversified population through the availability of scholarships.

Parents select private education for their elementary school students for many reasons. Among these are the schools' practice of discipline, the curriculum, the academic quality, and the reinforcement of religious beliefs, as well as greater opportunity to become involved in the formulation of school policy.

References

Johnson, J. A., Collins, H. W., Dupuis, V. L. & Johansen, J. H. (1991). F*oundations of American education.* Boston: Allyn and Bacon.

Snyder, T. D. (1988). *Digest of educational statistics.* Washington, DC: National Center for Educational Statistics.

F. T. Bond

Intergenerational Programs

Intergenerational programs in school and nonschool settings are designed to provide a way for children, adults, and elders to interact with one another. In our culture, it is often not easy for three generations to share one another's living presence. Because the "continuity of all cultures depends on the living presence of at least three generations" (Mead, 1970, p. 3), many look to intergenerational programs as a means of reestablishing the relationships of caring that once developed naturally between generations.

Today, an estimated 100,000 older persons are involved in preschools and other settings working with young children. Programs are in child care centers, nursery schools, grade schools and high schools. They may be a part of Head Start, library, park and recreation programs, in museums, or associated with 4-H Clubs, churches, or other community associations and agencies.

The programs are diverse. In some, older people work directly with children. Elders may hold children on their laps as they read a story to them, take part in a birthday party and show how many candles they would have on their cake, or talk with children about their own childhood. In other programs the elders may not have direct contact with children but may work with staff or parents or serve in some other capacity. Regardless of their diversity, all intergenerational programs share the common goal of bringing young and old together to ensure that children, adults, and elders develop a sense of the continuity of human life.

Intergenerational programs build on the love and affection the young and old in our country hold for one another. Children do have a feeling of affection for older persons and think they are friendly, good, right, and wonderful. At the same time, however, they view the old as sick, tired, sad, wrinkled, and ugly. Further, children deny that they will grow old themselves and say they will feel very bad when they are old. By being with older persons who are healthy, active, and fulfilled, children may find it more difficult to accept the stereotypical ideas they hold about the negative aspects of age and aging.

References

Mead, M. (1970). *Culture and commitment: A study of the generation gap.* New York: American Museum of Natural History.

Seefeldt, C., & Warman, B. (1990). *Young and Old Together.* Washington, DC: National Association for the Education of Young Children.

C. Seefeldt

Kindergarten

Private kindergartens serve five-year-olds in areas where public school kindergartens are not available, or where parents choose to use a private program rather than a public school offering. In recent times, some parents have chosen to enroll their children in private kindergartens in order to bypass the public school's entry-age requirement. A number of independent (private) early childhood centers have kindergartens for the oldest group of children that they serve, while private elementary schools often have kindergartens for the youngest of their incoming children. Parents pay a fee for their children's attendance. Fees vary according to location, with urban areas usually being more expensive than rural ones. Entry requirements are determined by the individual programs.

The same controversies regarding scheduling that recently have affected public school kindergartens are prominent in private kindergartens. Private kindergartens traditionally have been half-day programs. Today, however, many half-day programs are giving way to full-day or extended hours programs that provide service for from four to six hours, instead of for a two and one-half to three-hour session.

The change in scheduling has come about in response to both a societal need and a perceived educational need. Many of the families who use private kindergartens in areas where public kindergarten is available are dual career. With both parents working, a longer kindergarten day may avoid the need for a second or even a third child care arrangement to cover the afternoon hours. The same population tends to be concerned about the preparation of kindergarteners for the rigorous academic programs selected for the children's next school experience.

Many private school kindergarteners go on to private elementary schools. Entry into certain private schools is competitive, and early acquisition of formal, academic skills may be one of the criteria for selection. For that reason, many private kindergartens have focused their curriculum on formal skill acquisition, rather than on the broader preparation that characterizes programs designed around the developmental characteristics of five-year-olds. Use of workbooks and many paper and pencil tasks may be prominent features of such programs.

Some private kindergartens, however, have adopted the National Association for the Education of Young Children's guidelines for developmentally appropriate practice

(Bredekamp, 1987). Those programs have concentrated on providing expanded opportunities for the children to practice problem solving and other intellectual and social skills with many different types of materials, such as sand, clay, blocks, and "table toys," as well as some paper and pencil tasks. (See also Section 3.5, **Early Childhood Settings in the Public Sector, Kindergarten.**)

References

Bredekamp, S. (1987). *Developmentally appropriate practice in early childhood programs serving children from birth through age 8.* Washington, DC: National Association for the Education of Young Children.

Fromberg, D. P. (1987). *The full day kindergarten.* New York: Teachers College Press.

L. R. Williams

Laboratory Schools (College and University)

As public education burgeoned toward the end of the nineteenth century, normal schools were established to provide teachers for the expanding public schools. Practice schools, where teachers in training could "practice" their new pedagogical skills with guidance, developed as part of these normal schools. Master practitioners in the practice schools collaborated with university/college researchers to find answers to questions about the dynamics of the classroom and the nature of learners.

In most instances, the philosophical and pedagogical foundations of the early lab schools were derived from the works of European philosophers such as Locke, Rousseau, Pestalozzi, and Froebel, as well as the American philosophers and theorists, including Thorndike, Dewey, and Kilpatrick. Thus, the lab schools had a close affinity with the early nursery schools in this country, both sharing a multidisciplinary, whole child approach.

Today's lab schools most often are housed in departments of home economics, education, or psychology. The director is usually a faculty member in the department sponsoring the lab. While many of today's lab schools retain the original lab school emphasis on training and research, their focus has shifted from general education to early childhood education, and the range of services has expanded to include day care and a full range of family support programs. The major purpose of the lab school, however, continues to be the exemplary education of future teachers.

Many lab schools, for example, now provide full-day programs, parenting seminars, play therapy, or family counseling, and have expanded the enrollment from preschool to include infant/toddler programs and after school care. A few offer flexible hours so that nontraditional students may leave their children during late afternoon and early evening hours. Students preparing for early childhood careers obtain in these modern lab schools quality experiences that reflect the wide range of services required by parents of today's young children. Other lab schools, continuing the research/training model, concentrate on a particular area of interest such as dyslexia, attention-deficit syndrome, and/or special curricular areas (Nichols, 1989).

Today's lab schools are training grounds not only for prospective teachers but also for child development specialists, early childhood researchers, nutritionists, child psychologists, and divinity students. Thus, their designation within the college or university sometimes has changed from "laboratory school" to one that is in keeping with the type of service offered, such as infant center, early childhood center, child care center, or parent-child center.

Currently, in addition to fulfilling training and research mandates, the lab schools serve the needs of faculty, staff, and students who require child care while they work and/or study at the college or university. Student teachers may still complete a practicum in the lab school, but they are just as likely to have an assignment at other centers. Research continues as an aim in other lab schools. The lab school, by remaining dynamic and flexible in its response to societal needs, still guides practitioners in what the current state of the art says is best for children and families.

References

Clifford, G. J., & Guthrie, J. W. (1988). *A brief history of the professional education school*. Chicago: University of Chicago Press.

Nichols, K. (September 1989). Report on laboratory schools shows viability of controlled clinics. *American Association of Colleges for Teacher Education Briefs*.

J. S. Delano

Nursery School (Prekindergarten)

Early childhood programs for three- and four-year-old children traditionally have been provided in the United States through nursery schools. Nursery schools generally are privately run and may exist as independent programs or as part of a larger early childhood program that also contains an infant/toddler section and a kindergarten for older children. Parents pay a fee for their children's attendance; the fees tend to vary according to geographical location, with urban areas usually being more expensive than rural ones. The programs determine their own criteria for accepting applicants.

Many nursery schools were founded in this country as part of the child study movement at the turn of the century and were attached to departments of home economics or child development in colleges or universities. Their purpose was to provide a setting where young women could be prepared for motherhood or for careers as early childhood teachers through observation of the patterns of development revealed in children's play.

The programs were designed to promote the children's social and emotional growth. To that end, nursery school teachers provided unstructured materials such as water, sand, paints and other art materials, and blocks to encourage the children to interact with one another and to use their creative imaginations in their play.

Today's nursery schools tend to focus on the development of thinking skills as well as on socioemotional development and include a variety of manipulative materials, puzzles, storybooks, and games, as well as the traditional unstructured materials mentioned above.

Many private nursery schools still offer only a half-day schedule. Separate groups of children may come in the morning and in the afternoon sessions or on alternating days of the week. Some nursery schools are coordinated with other child care programs so that children of dual-career or single-parent families will have care provided during the portion of the day when they are not in the nursery school program. (See also Section 3.3, **Early Childhood Settings in the Public Sector, Prekindergarten: School-Based Programs.**)

References

Pitcher, E., & Ames, L. (1964). *The guidance nursery school*. New York: Harper & Row.

Read, K. H. (1968). *The nursery school: A human relationships laboratory*, 4th ed. Philadelphia: Saunders.

L. R. Williams

Parent Cooperatives

The Parent Participation Nursery School was originally called the "Parent Cooperative Nursery School" or simply the "co-op." The basic premise behind the co-op is that continuing growth and learning of parents underlies that of children.

The first co-op was established in Chicago in 1916. Four schools were listed with the word "cooperative" in the 1931 White House Conference Report. Following World War II, the parent cooperative became a new "folk movement" in the United States. By 1954 it was estimated that 500 parent cooperatives existed in one-third of the states (Taylor, 1954). Co-op Councils were organized to exchange knowledge, skills, and standards, and manuals on how to organize and conduct a parent nursery school were widely shared.

In a typical co-op, parents come together to provide a play group or nursery school for their own young children. They work with a trained teacher/director who is often a member of the parent group. Ten or twelve families might begin a group. Usually about 20 families are needed to support the cost of a school site and a teacher's salary. In many co-ops, parents work in the instructional program for children or help maintain the school site, equipment, and materials.

The governance structure of co-ops is unique. Parents comprise the governing body that establishes policies and employs the teacher. The teacher, while employed by the parents, administers the children's program, provides parent education formally and informally, adjudicates interpersonal disputes, and helps parents understand the impact of their behavior on children by explicating aspects of child development and principles of child rearing.

The educational approach of the co-op is holistic and integrated. In the early days, co-ops drew on emerging knowledge of group dynamics as they struggled with governance, new roles required to manage a school, and developing skills for learning through discussion and in groups. Parents' personal needs also were met as friendships formed among families, many of whom had been displaced and isolated during World War II.

Although today there are fewer co-ops as more mothers have entered the work force, the influence of co-ops continues to be widespread. Some of the earliest have continued. Others have been taken over by a community agency but continue the tradition of parent involvement. Most of all, their influence has been extended as co-op parents and teachers have become leaders in many areas of early childhood education, including Head Start, early childhood special education, professional organizations, teacher education, private and public nursery schools and child care.

Reference

Taylor, K. W. (1954). *Parent cooperative nursery schools.* New York: Teachers College Bureau of Publications.

E. Brady

Religious Early Childhood Education

Religious early childhood education takes place in a variety of settings and forms. Forms may include weekday programs, Sunday/Saturday classes, Mothers-Day-Out programs, parenting classes for families with young children, occasional programs centered around religious holidays, or full-day care with a religious education/nurture base.

Weekday programs may be held in churches and synagogues, often for two to five half-days weekly. These programs may be centered around a specific religious curriculum and materials published by the sponsoring religious body. Alternatively, the programs and materials may be developed locally, sometimes reflecting an atmosphere of nurture and caring that communicates the concern and support of the community of faith.

These programs in most states require licensing by the appropriate child welfare agency and also are subject to local regulations regarding health and safety. There is usually a fee for the enrolled families to cover the expenses of the program's personnel and use of facilities. Ideally, the program is staffed by persons trained in early childhood education and care, who also are adequately knowledgeable about the tenets of the sponsoring body so that the foundations of those tenets may be incorporated into a developmentally appropriate curriculum.

Programs of full-day child care may also include forms of religious education and nurture when located in a church or synagogue. These programs may be sponsored by the hosting church or congregation as an outreach to the community and support for families, and may be developed and supported (sometimes even financially) as a membership outreach option within the parish or congregation.

Such programs, like all weekday programs, are subject to licensure as child care programs and must meet state standards on indoor and outdoor facilities, health and safety, and minimal teacher qualifications in child development and education. Once again, they are staffed ideally by persons knowledgeable in developmentally appropriate curriculum and in the foundational tenets of the affiliated religious body.

They are scheduled, in most instances, for five days each week from early morning to early evening (most typically, 8 a.m. to 6 p.m.) to accommodate the work schedules of the parents. In many programs, parents select the number of days that their child will be enrolled to meet their own schedule needs. The number of part-time "slots" available may, however, be limited if the need for full-day child care is critical in the community.

Saturday/Sunday School classes may be another offering to young children and their families. These programs most often use a curriculum prepared by the sponsoring religious body and are usually a segment of a larger program offered to children of all ages as well as to adults. These programs are typically staffed by volunteers and are taught in improvised spaces. The regulations affecting weekday programs are usually not applicable, with the exception of health and safety standards applied to all organizations serving the public.

Mothers-Day-Out programs are typically scheduled on a regular basis and staffed by church or congregation volunteers as a service to mothers of young children. The curriculum may include all the options outlined above for weekday and full-day programs. Children may enroll on an ad hoc basis up to the enrollment limitations determined by the space and staff available. Licensure may be required in some states depending on regulations regarding the care of children whose parents are off the premises. Programs are most often limited to one or two days a week on a nominal fee basis.

Parenting classes and programs for families with young children may be as varied as the programs for their children. These may include classes in child development and child rearing, parent involvement activities for parents of children enrolled in church- or synagogue-sponsored classes for children, parent/child classes for parents of infants/toddlers/twos, and/or support classes for full-time mothers (MOPs, Mothers of Preschoolers, is a prominent example of this form). Options also may include religious and/or Bible study classes and groups for parents that meet on a regular basis and offer child care during the time of the class. Prepared materials from religious bodies or from publishers offering family support curricula may be used for these classes, or informal programs and materials may be developed locally.

Occasional programs centered around the celebration of religious holidays may take on aspects of any or most of the program options discussed above. These most typically will be programs for parents and children or for intergenerational families especially designed to capture and communicate the nature and spirit of the holiday being featured.

Early childhood religious education often will be as varied as the settings in which it is provided. Good or exemplary programs will, however, have some common characteristics. Planning for religious early childhood education will include local early childhood professionals, religious educators and leaders, and boards of religious education from the sponsoring body. The inclusion of parents in planning will help to make the programs appropriate for local needs. Above all, the personnel leading the program must be knowledgeable in child development and early education, in religious education, and in local needs. (See also **Church/Synagogue and Community Agency Child Care** in this section.)

References

Blazer, D. (ed). (1989). *Religious education in early childhood*. New Haven, CT: Religious Education Association.

Morgenthaler, S. K. (1989). *Right from the start: A new parents' guide to child faith development*. River Forest, IL:Concordia.

S. K. Morgenthaler

3.5 Child Advocacy and Public Policy

This section examines areas of early childhood education that extend from classrooms or programs to the important arenas of advocacy and policy for children and their families. Federal initiatives such as the Head Start program and compensatory programs for economically disadvantaged young children have a political as well as an educational history. Early special education for young children also has grown from federal legislative initiatives that included strong parent and community components. The challenge of racial desegregation, with its own long history of advocacy and political struggle has influenced public policy and educational programs for young children.

Enormous changes have taken place in the American family that have subsequently placed many young children in need of comprehensive services and interventions and have changed the ways young children's needs are met. Economic and social structures have made it imperative for many mothers of young children to enter the work force, and available child care has not met the overwhelming demand. In some regions of the country, the child care services that do exist are not of high quality, and there is a high turnover of underpaid caregivers.

Children are now the largest group of low-income Americans at the same time as they are a dwindling resource for our future work force and economy. One-third of young adults entering the work force in the year 2000 will be people of color, but racism and associated disadvantages still plague people of color in the United States. Health, safety, and family violence issues continue to limit the opportunity for significant numbers of children in this country to experience acceptable levels of comfort and developmental growth. Young children watch many hours of television programming that tends to be mediocre or violent in content, and efforts to reduce advertising in children's programs have not yet been successful.

Public interest groups working for children's rights focus on a vision of society where all children are protected and nurtured. They conceptualize equity as a goal that would enable each young child to receive an equal opportunity to reach his or her highest potential. Advocacy groups around the United States are focusing on social, political, educational, and legislative efforts to improve the care and education of young children, as well as the overall social climate affecting children and families in this country.

Those who advocate for more and better early childhood programs can point to significant supportive longitudinal studies. Parents as well as early childhood educators can advocate successfully for programs and services as well as policies and legislation that protect the rights of children to wholesome care, health services, protection from harm, and the quality of education that will enable them to grow into stable and productive adults.

With all of the above considerations in mind, the articles that follow are arranged into two major sections focusing on, respectively, child advocacy and early childhood policies. Within each section, the articles appear alphabetically, except for when an article elaborates on a topic that has immediately preceded it.

B. S. Fennimore & R. Hitz

Child Advocacy

Advocacy is a term used to describe many types of action by educators, parents, human service professionals, and other concerned individuals for the purpose of supporting the well-being of others. In the case of advocacy on behalf of young children, those actions may include various ways of persuading others to take action on behalf of children's rights and welfare, including working within local and national organizations to refine approaches to societal and familial situations that endanger young children.

L. R. Williams

Advocacy Strategies

Over the past two decades, there has been an explosion in the number of early childhood programs across the country. This dramatic growth has been the result of both the need for child care for working families and the growing recognition of the value of early intervention. At the same time, there is increased knowledge about developmentally appropriate practice for all young children and a growing sense of what constitutes high quality in early childhood programs (Willer, 1987).

As early childhood education continues to hold the public's attention, early childhood educators are challenged to speak out, to advocate for the improvements that they know are essential to the development of young children. Early childhood educators view advocacy as part of a professional responsibility that includes sharing their knowledge with those who affect young children in the classroom, the living room, the board room, the news room, and even the court hearing room.

Advocacy efforts begin in the classrooms and homes where children spend the largest part of their day. Promoting best practice means sharing the latest early childhood developments with others in a nonthreatening way, encouraging new ideas, and supporting each other in work with young children.

Early childhood educators can be partners with parents. It is important to encourage parents to speak out on their own behalf and on behalf of their children. As professionals share their expertise with parents, they can be supportive of the parenting role and enlist parents in efforts to improve and expand the quality of early childhood programs (Lombardi, 1990).

As early childhood programs are expanding, policy makers are making important decisions affecting the lives of children and families. Advocates can gather information and share their knowledge with policy makers to inform decisions made at the local, state, and federal levels. Such activities include responding to administrative decisions, writing letters to legislators, testifying at hearings, and inviting policy makers to visit early childhood programs.

In a world that increasingly depends on the media, it is critical that early childhood educators creatively share their message of promoting quality in early childhood programs. Advocates can use the media by talking with local reporters about their programs, initiating news stories or guest editorials about critical early childhood issues, writing letters to the editor, inviting local television stations to special events, and taking advantage of local cable access stations to develop programs on early childhood issues.

Members of the business community have become interested in early childhood as they respond to the child care needs of their employees or consider the future work force of the country (Committee for Economic Development, 1991). Early childhood advocates enlist the support of the business community through presentations before local business groups and by encouraging linkages with companies that wish to provide or are providing some form of child care for their employees.

Early childhood advocacy is most effective when advocacy groups join together and increase their numbers as they speak out for children and families. Active participation in local early childhood organizations, child care teacher groups, or advocacy organizations is an important way to stay informed about issues. Having accurate and current information is the first step in having an impact on policies (Goffin & Lombardi, 1988).

The early childhood field has come a long way in recent years, but there is still important work to do. Advocates need to continue to give attention to promoting appropriate practice and improving the status and working conditions of early childhood teachers. As advocates foster a belief in change, build confidence in their activity, and develop the skills needed for effective communication, they can make a difference in the lives of young children.

References

Committee for Economic Development. (1991). *The unfinished agenda: A new vision for child development and education.* New York: Author.

Goffin, S. G., & Lombardi, J. (1988). *Speaking out: Early childhood advocacy.* Washington, DC: National Association for the Education of Young Children.

Lombardi, J. (November/December 1991). Encouraging parents as advocates. *Pre-K Today, 6* (3), 32–34.

Willer, B. (1987). *The growing crisis in child care: Quality, compensation, and affordability in early childhood programs.* Washington, DC: National Association for the Education of Young Children.

J. Lombardi

Children's Rights

Children's rights are a fundamental and growing part of human rights. The United Nations General Assembly, on November 20, 1989, the tenth anniversary of the International Year of the Child, adopted the Convention on the Rights of the Child, a landmark in the century-long struggle to assure that children receive the care and protection to which they are entitled. Within the first six months, seventy-four nations signed the Convention, which addresses a wide range of issues, including the use of children in armed conflicts, the problems of refugee children, and the right of children from ethnic and religious minorities to profess and practice their religion. The Convention provides that all children have a right to a family, a name, adequate health care, and education. The treaty becomes effective international law when ratified by 20 countries, and then becomes effective for those nations. This Convention has become a basic human rights document, for it concerns almost half the world's population.

The treaty reflects the concerns of economically poor countries and the recognition that the situation of children, internationally, has deteriorated over the decade of the 1980s. Poor children have become poorer. In 1984 alone, five million children died in Africa from causes related to hunger, and one in five children went hungry. In Latin America, 35.5 million children lived in absolute poverty in 1980, and the projection for the year 2000 is 51 million children in dire poverty in Latin America.

Children's rights in the United States also have taken on a particular urgency as the actual situation of children has deteriorated. Children are by far the poorest Americans. The number of children living in poverty grew by one-third in the 1980s. One in five U.S. children (12 million) lived in poverty in 1987. (In comparison, one in nine adults lived in poverty.) If the economy remains stable, one in four children by the year 2000 will be poor, three million more than today. One in five children has no health insurance.

The United States ranks eighteenth in the world in infant mortality and twenty-sixth in the world in keeping African-American babies alive through their first year of life. One in four mothers gives birth with no early prenatal care, although the cost of prenatal care is $600, and care for premature or low birth weight babies is over $1,000 per day in neonatal nurseries. Immunization rates for children have declined, and the incidence of preventable childhood diseases has risen. The exploding numbers of reports of child abuse and neglect include some 2,000 child deaths annually.

Child abandonment has increased dramatically; street children, some 30 to 100 million of them, populate the world's cities. Youth unemployment, drug addiction, and delinquency are among the consequences of hunger and poverty. In almost every region of the world, children are being targeted as deliberate victims of detention-without-trial, torture, assassination, and political disappearance.

Under the provisions of the Convention, governments agree to respect the rights and responsibilities of the family, offer support to the family when it is unable to provide an adequate standard of living, and help with family reunification when a family is separated. Articles are devoted to children's rights to health care, day care, and education. Provisions are made concerning abuse, neglect, and exploitation, adoption and foster care, custody disputes, and the prevention and treatment of narcotics use. It prohibits the death penalty for minors (currently five nations, including the United States, execute children for crimes committed at the age of 16 or 17), and directs that rehabilitation take precedence over punishment in the disposition of a child convicted of a crime. It provides for the cultural protection of children of minority populations within a nation. One of the most controversial provisions makes 15 the minimal age for military recruitment (the original draft set the minimum age at 17 years), and recognizes the need for special protection for children in times of war and armed conflict.

Children's rights policies promote the basic needs of children as matters of fundamental human rights. They incorporate many rights traditionally accorded to adults, but include in addition a notion of protection and special consideration made necessary by the dependence of younger people, and by what has been called their "incomplete rationality."

Thus, in the United States for example, children have been accorded the right to counsel and, furthermore, special rights to privacy of records in juvenile court proceedings. On the other hand, children's right to freedom of speech has been restricted by court rulings that place greater weight on the disciplinary needs of school authorities than on students' freedom of expression. Every state has enacted legislation providing for the removal of a child from her/his family under circumstances of abuse or neglect, and has devised special child employment protections. Issues include what are the rights of due process to children who have been committed to mental institutions by parents or guardians; the right of teenagers to the privacy of making a decision to terminate a pregnancy; the rights of children to challenge their suspension from school or their classification in special education programs; and the rights of children to support emancipation and treatment.

These tensions between the rights of children themselves as human beings, the rights of parents to determine such areas as punishment, education, or religion for the children, and the rights of states to protect and provide for its young citizens, often collide in litigation involving children's issues. Each of these interests is given constitutional sanction, yet these three interests are thickly intertwined and often contradict each other. In areas of custody, visitation, and abortion decisions, adults frequently claim rights based on family and property in relation to their children. It remains unclear, however, whether children themselves have rights to contact and visit their brothers and sisters. Thus, children's rights is a complex ethical and policy matter as well as a legal one.

In recent years, the "best interest of the child" has come into use as a legal standard. This formulation attempts to give children an independent voice in decisions crucial to their lives and to evaluate their interests on a case-by-case basis. It is a standard necessarily interpreted by an adult claiming to represent the "best interests of the child," such as a judge, a guardian *ad litem*, an expert psychiatrist, a social worker, or a parent. In fact, courts and agencies try to find the least detrimental alternative for the child.

Current conditions, taken together, constitute an escalating though "silent" form of violence against children. These conditions require better representation of children, better placement plans, and greater inroads into enforcing child abuse and neglect laws. The needs and rights of children in distress and of all children to care and protection has given the Convention on the Rights of the Child grave importance in all countries.

References

Castelle, K. (1990). *In the child's best interest.* Defense for Children International-USA.

Mnootin, R. H. (1985). *In the interests of children.* New York: W. H. Freeman.

Nurkse, D., & Castelle, K. (eds.). (1990). *Children's rights: Crisis and challenge.* Defense for Children International-USA.

B. Dohrn

Organizations, National Advocacy*

Action for Children's Television (ACT)
20 University Rd.
Cambridge, MA 02138
617-876-6620

Advocates for improvement in children's television programming. Distributes a newsletter, books, pamphlets, films, and other material on children and television.

Administration for Children, Youth and Families (ACYF)
P.O. Box 1182
Washington, DC 20013
202-755-7762

The primary agency within the federal government with responsibility for serving children and families. The three major bureaus are The Children's Bureau, The Head Start Bureau, and the Family and Youth Services Bureau.

The Alliance for Better Child Care (ABC)
122 C St., N.W., Suite 400
Washington, DC 20001
202-628-8787

A broad alliance of more than 100 national organizations working to increase support for child care. The focal point of the Alliance activities is support of a national child care bill. The Act for Better Child Care Services was introduced in Congress in fall 1987.

American Academy of Pediatrics
141 Northern Point Blvd.
P.O. Box 927
Elk Grove, IL 60009
800-433-9016

Provides information on health issues related to child care and young children.

American Association of University Women
2401 Virginia Ave., N.W.
Washington, DC 20047
202-785-7715

A membership organization of college and university graduates with branches in communities across the country. Many branches have strong legislative focus and interest in children's issues.

American Bar Association
The National Legal Resource Center for Child Advocacy and Protection
1800 M St., N.W., Suite 200 South
Washington, DC 20036
202-331-2250

Provides training and technical assistance to the child welfare community and serves as a clearinghouse on child welfare issues.

American Federation of State, County and Municipal Employees—AFL-CIO
1625 L St., NW
Washington, DC 20036
202-429-1130

The largest AFL-CIO union, representing 1.4 million public employees. Materials include videotapes, booklets, and public opinion polls on child care.

American Public Welfare Association
1125 15th St., N.W., Suite 300
Washington, DC 20005
202-293-7550

The national organization representing state human service agencies and local welfare departments.

Association for Childhood Education International
11141 Georgia Ave., Suite 200
Wheaton, MD 20902
301-942-2443 or 800-423-3563

A membership organization whose purpose is to establish, promote, and maintain high standards and practice for childhood learning and growth. A wide range of publications available on education and child care issues. Journal published five times a year.

Association for Supervision and Curriculum Development (ASCD)
125 N. West St.
Alexandria, VA 22314-2798
703-549-9110

Membership organization focused on curriculum and supervision. Currently has a focus on early childhood education. Publication on public school early childhood programs available along with others on early childhood issues and journal.

Association of Child Advocates
P.O. Box 5873
Cleveland, OH 44101-0873
216-881-2225

A national association of state-based child advocacy organizations. Provides an information systems network and technical assistance. Sponsors an annual conference on advocacy for children.

Association of Junior Leagues, Inc.
660 First Avenue
New York, NY 10016
212-683-1515

A membership organization with a history of concern and action in dealing with quality child care.

Center for Law and Social Policy
1616 P St., N.W., Suite 350
Washington, DC 20036
202-328-5140

A public-interest law firm; takes an active role in welfare reform.

Center for Public Advocacy Research
12 W. 37th St.
New York, NY 10018
212-564-9220

Committed to identifying important policy concerns, conducting research, and advocating for sound policy on issues affecting women, children, and youth. Reports on child care studies available on topics such as salaries and parents' concerns about policy.

Child Care Action Campaign
99 Hudson St., #1233
New York, NY 10013
212-334-9595

A coalition of leaders from diverse organizations advocating for high-quality child care. Activities include education, information service, proposing possible solutions, and technical assistance to governmental offices. Publishes bimonthly newsletter.

The Child Care Employee Project
P.O. Box 5603
Berkeley, CA 94705
415-653-9889

A clearinghouse on child care employee issues including salaries, status, and working conditions. Will provide technical assistance on conducting salary surveys. Publications on such topics are comparable worth/job discrimination, personnel policies, salary surveys, and strategies to raise child care workers' salaries. Newsletter, by subscription.

The Child Law Center
22 Second St., Fifth Floor
San Francisco, CA 94105
415-495-5498

Extensive information and assistance in legal and business aspects of child care. Tracks and reports on such issues as religious exemptions to licensing, zoning family day care, the inclusion of child care in the land use development process, and several other topics.

The Child Welfare League of America
440 First St., N.W., Suite 310
Washington, DC 20001
202-638-2952

A membership organization composed of people serving children and their families. Devoted to helping deprived, neglected, and abused children and families. Publishes a wide variety of material on advocacy and child care.

The Children's Defense Fund
122 C St., N.W.
Washington, DC 20001
202-628-8787 or 800-424-9602

Education about and advocacy for the needs of children, especially low-income, minority, and handicapped children. Publications includes a monthly newsletter, an annual analysis of the federal budget, and annual report on child care facts in the states.

The Children's Foundation
815 15th St., N.W., #928
Washington, DC 20005
202-347-3300

Information and materials on home-based child care issues. Publishes the *Family Day*

Care Bulletin and *Directory of Family Day Care Associates.* Also sponsors the National Family Child Care Advocacy Project and a resource clearinghouse.

Coalition of Labor Union Women
15 Union Square
New York, NY 10003
212-242-0700

A membership organization of female and male trade unionists interested in promoting working women's rights. Advocates for child care and family issues. Publications include "Bargaining for Child Care: A Union Parent's Guide."

Committee for Economic Development
477 Madison Ave.
New York, NY 10022
212-688-2063

A public policy research group whose membership includes mostly corporate executives. Report on *Children in Need* available.

Concerned Educators Allied for a Safe Environment (CEASE)
17 Gerry St.
Cambridge, MA 02138
617-864-0999

A national network of parents, teachers, and other advocates for young children working on peace and environmental issues. Newsletter and other publications available.

Council for Early Childhood Professional Recognition
1718 Connecticut Ave., N.W.
Washington, DC 20009
202-265-9090 or 800-424-4310

Credentials home-based child care providers, preschool and infant-toddler center-based caregivers, and home visitors. Bilingual specialization available.

Council of State Governments
Inn Works Pike
P.O. Box 11910
Lexington, KY 40578
606-252-2291

Publishes a wide variety of reports and studies on important issues facing states and state legislative structures.

Education Commission of the States
1860 Lincoln St., Suite 300
Denver, CO 80295
303-830-3600

An interstate compact that helps states leaders improve the quality of education in their states. Conducts policy research, surveys, and special studies; has an information clearinghouse; gives technical assistance to states. Reports include "Family Involvement in the Schools."

ERIC Clearinghouse on Elementary and Early Childhood Education (ERIC/EECE)
University of Illinois
805 W. Pennsylvania Ave.
Urbana, IL 61801-4877
217–333–1386

Publishes free newsletter on materials, publications, and events. Computer searches on any early childhood topic (ask your local libraries for more information). Also publishes the *Early Childhood Research Quarterly* with NAEYC and Ablex.

Family Resource Coalition
230 N. Michigan Ave., Suite 1625
Chicago, IL 60601
312-726-4750

A national grassroots network of individuals and organizations promoting the development of prevention-oriented, community-based programs to strengthen families. Serves as a national clearinghouse; provides technical assistance, a wide variety of publications, and a newsletter three times a year.

Food Research Action Coalition (FRAC)
1319 F St., N.W., Suite 500
Washington, DC 20004
202–393–5060

Works on issues of hunger and poverty in America. Wide range of publications including guide to state legislation on the operation of federal food programs.

High/Scope Educational Research Foundation
600 N. River St.
Ypsilanti, MI 48198
313–485–2000

A research development and training center whose principal focus is early childhood education. Newsletter and a wide variety of publications.

Institute for Women's Policy Research
1400 20th St., N.W., Suite 104
Washington, DC 20036
202–785–5100
Conducts research that informs public policy debate on women's issues. Fact sheet and papers on child care wages.

League of Women Voters
1730 M St., N.W.
Washington, DC 20036
202-429-1965
A citizens' education and research organization with a wide variety of publications on becoming more politically effective.

National Association for the Education of Young Children (NAEYC)
1834 Connecticut Ave., N.W.
Washington, DC 20009-5786
202-232-8777 or 800–424–2460
The largest professional group of early childhood educators. Publishes the journal *Young Children*, brochures, posters, videotapes, and books. National, state, and local affiliate groups offer training opportunities. Other programs are the Information Service and the Week of the Young Child.

National Association for Family Day Care
1815 15th St., N.W., Suite 928
Washington, DC 20005
Membership organization representing the needs and concerns of family day care providers, young children, parents, and child advocates.

National Association of Child Care Resource and Referral Agencies (NACCRRA)
2116 Campus Dr., S.E.
Rochester, MN 55904
507-287-2020
Promotes the development, maintenance, and expansion of quality child care resources and referral. Newsletter, bulletins, and other publications.

National Association of Counties
440 First St., N.W.
Washington, DC 20001
202-393-6226
Tracks issues facing counties—wide range of publications.

National Association of Early Childhood Specialists in State Departments of Education (NAECS/SDE)
(Ask NAEYC for current address.)
A national association of early childhood specialists who work in state education agencies. Position statement available on kindergarten entry and placement.

National Association of Early Childhood Teacher Educators
338 Peik Hall
University of Minnesota
Minneapolis, MN 55455
612-625-4039
Membership organization focused on early childhood teacher education issues. Publishes a journal three times a year.

National Association of Elementary School Principals
1615 Duke St.
Alexandria, VA 22314
703-684-3345
Represents and reports on issues facing elementary school principals. Journal published five times a year with May issue focused on early childhood education.

National Association of State Boards of Education (NASBE)
1012 Cameron St.
Alexandria, VA 22314
703-684-4000
Tracks issues and publishes reports on early childhood education issues in the states.

National Black Child Development Institute
1463 Rhode Island Ave., N.W.
Washington, DC 20005
202-387-1281
A membership organization, publishes a newsletter and policy reports relevant to issues facing Black children. Publications in-

clude guidelines for establishing early childhood programs in public schools.

National Center for Clinical Infant Programs
733 15th St., N.W., Suite 912
Washington, DC 20006
202-347-0308
Publishes information and sponsors conferences on infant health and development. Newsletter published five times a year.

National Coalition for Campus Child Care, Inc.
P.O. Box 413
Milwaukee, WI 53201
A membership organization that focuses on campus child care issues. Newsletter and other publications available.

National Commission on Working Women/ Wider Opportunities for Women
1325 G St., N.W.—Lower Level
Washington, DC 20005
202-737-5764
Focuses on the needs and concerns of the approximately 80% of women in the work force concentrated in low-paying, low-status jobs. Publications on child care employee issues.

National Committee for the Prevention of Child Abuse
332 S. Michigan Ave., Suite 950
Chicago, IL 60604-4357
312-663-3520
Serves as a clearinghouse with a wide variety of publications on child abuse prevention.

National Conference of State Legislatures
444 N. Capitol St., N.W., Suite 500
Washington, DC 20001
202-624-5400
Serves the country's state lawmakers and their staffs. A wide variety of information on state legislatures and issues they face, including early childhood education.

National Council of Churches Ecumenical Child Care Network
475 Riverside Dr., Room 572
New York, NY 10115-0050
212-870-3342
Membership organization serves church-housed child care programs. Newsletter and a variety of publications on child care.

National Council of Jewish Women
53 W. 23rd St.
New York, NY 10010
212-645-4048
A membership organization with sections nationwide. Has child study center that focuses on child care and family issues.

National Governors' Association
444 N. Capitol St., N.W., Suite 250
Washington, DC 20001
202-624-5300
The association of state governors focuses on shaping and implementation of national policy and leadership on state issues. A variety of publications on state issues including child care.

National Head Start Association
1309 King St., Suite 200
Alexandria, VA 22314
703-739-0875
The association of directors, parents, friends, and staff of Head Start. Quarterly newsletter.

National League of Cities
1301 Pennsylvania Ave., N.W.
Washington, DC 20004
202-626-3000
Focuses on issues facing U.S. cities. Publication available on children and family issues.

National Organization for Women (NOW) Legal Defense and Education Fund
99 Hudson St., 12th Floor
New York, NY 10013
212-925-6635
Dedicated to achieving equal opportunities for women in the workplace, in schools, in the courts, and in the family. Publications on child care tax credit.

National PTA
700 N. Rush St.
Chicago, IL 60611-2571
312-787-0977

A membership organization representing parents in more than 26,000 schools including preschools. Child care publications available.

National Urban League
500 E. 62nd St.
New York, NY 10021
212-310-9238

Social services and civil rights organization with local affiliates in 34 states. Sponsors national forums on various child care issues.

National Women's Law Center
1616 P St., N.W., Suite 100
Washington, DC 20036
202-328-5160

National legal association working on issues that affect women, especially low-income women. Several child care publications, including child care tax credit.

9–5 National Association of Working Women
614 Superior Ave., N.W., Suite 852
Cleveland, OH 44113
216-566-9308

Membership group for office workers. Child Care, along with other working family policies, is a strong group focus.

Save the Children Child Care Support Center
1340 Spring St., N.W., Suite 200
Atlanta, GA 30309
404-885-1578

Sponsors yearly conference for home-based child care providers. Publications include a guide to home-based child care and audio-visual training resources.

School-Age Child Care Project
Wellesley College
Center for Research on Women
Wellesley, MA 02181
617-431-1453

Clearinghouse on school-age child care issues; publishes newsletter and policy reports.

Society for Research in Child Development
100 North Carolina Ave., S.E., Suite 1
Washington, DC 20003
202-543-9582

Focuses on child development research. Publishes newsletter, journal, and other information important to advocates.

Southern Association on Children Under Six (SACUS)
P.O. Box 5403, Brady Station
Little Rock, AR 72215

A membership organization with members in 13 southern states committed to the welfare of children and families and the professionals who serve them. Journals, books, and position statements available.

Work/Family Directions, Inc.
9 Galen St., Suite 230
Watertown, MA 02172
617-923-1535

Offers a broad range of options and services to assist companies in adapting to the changing labor force. Provides a national resource and referral network for companies. Publications include compilation of state child care regulations.

Work and Family Information Center
The Conference Board
845 Third Ave.
New York, NY 10022
212-759-0900

Clearinghouse for information concerning interrelationship between work and family, and employer-supported child care, including resource and referral services, family day care satellites, and parent fee subsidies.

U.S. Department of Commerce—Bureau of the Census
Washington, DC 20233
Public Information Office
301-763-4040
Data User Services Division
301-763-4100

U.S. Department of Labor—Bureau of Labor Statistics
441 G St., N.W.
Washington, DC 20212
202-523-1222

U.S. House of Representatives Select Committee on Children, Youth and Families
House of Representatives, Room H2-385
House Annex 2
Washington, DC 20515
202-226-7660

Studies and reports on a wide range of issues facing children and families.

J. Lombardi

*From Goffin, S., & Lombardi, J. (1989). *Child Advocacy*, pp. 111–117. Reprinted with permission of the National Association for the Education of Young Children.

Parent Action

Parent Action is an independent parent advocacy and public education organization located in Washington, D.C. The mission of Parent Action is to improve the well-being of families by helping parents harness their power to influence public policy, business practices, their personal lives, and the lives of their families. Parent Action's stated goals are to give parents a vehicle to effect changes beneficial to American families, to engender an enhanced respect and appreciation for the role of parent in American society, to move family issues to the top of the national political and economic agendas, and to stabilize and improve the overall well-being of families. Two-thirds of parents surveyed in the United States believe that family life is worse in general, and half of all parents surveyed indicated they were worse off now than they were ten years ago (Gallup Poll, 1989).

Parent Action emerged from an increasing awareness that parents across the country were deeply concerned about their children's future and were seeking representation in their role as parents in the public and private debates on issues that directly affect their lives. The founders of Parent Action, Dr. T. Berry Brazelton (internationally known pediatrician), Susan Deconcini (founder of the Senate Child Care Center) and Bernice Weissbourd (president of the Family Resource Coalition) came together to seek ways to channel the concerns of parents into positive action. Originally organized in 1988 as a division of the Family Resource Coalition, the initial success of the group led to its becoming an independent organization in late 1989. Parent Action's guiding principles are to improve the economic standing of families, improve child care choices for families, help parents find ways to balance their home and family lives through improved government and business policies, improve access to health care, improve educational opportunities, and expand community-based programs that build strong families.

Parent Action supports local, state, and national initiatives that implement those guiding principles, and thereby enhances opportunities for families of diverse economic, racial, and ethnic backgrounds. In doing so, it has supported such legislation as the Child Care Bill, Family and Medical Leave Act, and Family Resource Programs. It has developed strategies to assist the grass-roots advocacy of parents working toward better conditions in their own community, as well as toward influencing legislation in their states and in the nation.

Undergirding the public education effort is the development of Parent Action as a national resource center for disseminating information on parents' issues and priorities, as well as on the demographic, social, and economic standing of parents. By increasing an understanding of the factors contributing to the worries of parents and by creating a climate of opinion that recognizes the value of being a parent in shaping the next generation of citizens, Parent Action sets the stage for policies sensitive and responsive to families' needs.

Reference/Resource

Materials available from: Parent Action, P.O. Box 1719, Washington, DC 20012-1719.

B. Weissbourd

Early Childhood Policies

Early childhood policy encompasses the legislation and guidelines that give shape to particular legislative programs and provide protection and support to young children and their families. Program guidelines may determine who is eligible to participate in the program, the overall purpose of the program, the qualifications of the teachers, the amount and type of parent involvement expected, the kinds of assessment of children's progress needed for continued program funding, and the expectations for management of funds.

Child and family welfare policy may focus on identifying conditions that put children at risk or ensure the protection of young children. Some of the policies described below (particularly those referring to child welfare and safety) have legal implications, as their neglect could result in occurrences subject to legal action.

For publicly funded programs, policy may originate at the federal, the state, or the local level. Policy for private programs originates from each program's governing board, as well as from federal, state, or local legislation. The articles that follow identify legislation and policies focused on the well-being of young children across a wide variety of settings and programs.

L. R. Williams

Child Abuse Legislation

Every child has the right not to be abused physically, emotionally, or sexually. In the United States, each state has legislation protecting its children from abuse and neglect. With the unprecedented explosion in reporting of child abuse cases throughout the 1980s, the need to obtain children's testimony has become acute; a variety of measures has been legislated to provide alternatives or modifications to in-court testimony by children. In addition, the growing number of children adrift in the foster care system has spurred legislation requiring states to make efforts to keep families together before long-term separation becomes necessary.

States have followed three legislative approaches to protect child testimony: (1) creating a hearsay exception for statements made by victimized children; (2) permitting children to testify on closed circuit television; and (3) videotaping testimony for replay at trial. Uniform Rule of Evidence 807, approved by the

American Bar Association House of Delegates, incorporates all three methods.

Illinois, for example, adopted legislation in 1988 permitting videotaped testimony in a criminal trial. These provisions included measures for live, closed-circuit television testimony and hearsay exceptions in sexual abuse prosecutions involving children under 13 years of age when there is corroborating evidence of the crime. Further laws authorized the judge to determine the competency of a child witness and to exclude all persons from the courtroom while the victim is testifying except the media and persons with a direct interest in the case.

The Illinois law was modeled on a Texas statute permitting videotaped evidence. The Texas statute had been successful in achieving defendants' guilty pleas on the basis of taped direct testimony of child victims, eliminating the need for trial and cross-examination. The Illinois Supreme Court, however, held that the videotape provision in the Illinois law violated the defendant's constitutional right to confrontation. In a similar restriction in 1988, the United States Supreme Court overturned an Iowa statute that permitted a child to testify from behind a screen. In 1990, however, the United States Supreme Court upheld a Maryland law permitting child abuse victims to testify by closed-circuit television, if the judge determines that their presence in the courtroom would cause serious emotional distress and affect their ability to testify. There are currently some 24 states that permit closed-circuit television in child abuse cases.

Nearly 1.6 million children were reported abused or neglected in 1986, an increase of 160 percent since 1980. Each year, more than 440,000 children nationally spend some time in foster care. Increasingly, placement in foster care has become multiple placements, and more than 50 percent of these children stayed in foster care for over two years. Federal and state law requires that child welfare agencies make "reasonable efforts" to work with families to prevent the removal of a child. The law further requires that, where removal is necessary, agencies must identify and provide help to reunite the family safely. Acts such as the Family Preservation Act in Illinois provide for increased family preservation services to be made available to avoid inappropriate foster care, reunify families where possible, and assist families who adopt children to adjust to their new conditions. This program currently offers intensive home-based programs of placement prevention under the title "Family First" for a limited number of families in all counties. Many other states have developed laws patterned on the pioneer program in Tacoma, Washington, that offered intensive services to families in danger of losing their child or children. Ninety percent of the families in the Tacoma program remain together after nine years.

Reference

Harding, M. (ed.). (1983). *Foster children in the courts.* Boston: Butterworth Legal Publications.

B. Dohrn

Child Care Policy

Child care policy addresses a number of issues involving children and their families. It includes local, state, and national legislation, and the process of implementing legislation, as well as unwritten societal expectations. Child care policies vary considerably between regions and within the United States, reflecting differing perspectives about what is best for young children. Child care is a subject of constant debate in political, educational, and social realms, and the lack of a universal child care policy is part of this controversy.

Public policies typically develop around the values and mores of a given culture. In the United States, however, values and mores differ with the many cultures that exist. Some groups attempt to preserve their identity in this multicultural society by maintaining traditional rules about child rearing. Other groups modify their child-rearing practices with the changing social, political, and economic times. Religious fundamentalists, for example, have been known to lobby against policies that pro-

vide public funds for child care programs, arguing that day care is detrimental to the maintenance of families in the United States. Central to such lobbying efforts is the idea that young children (especially infants and toddlers) belong at home with their mothers. On the other side of the debate are those who claim that publicly funded child care is necessary in order to enable parents to seek and maintain employment, and thus support their families.

Child care policies are also the outcome of knowledge derived from psychological and social research. Prior to 1980, most of the research focusing on the effects of day care on young children indicated that day care had no harmful outcomes. In fact, early child care programs seemed to enhance cognitive and social development, particularly for low-income "disadvantaged" children. Moreover, child care programs with a parent education component were found to affect positively the functioning of the entire family. Several new studies during the 1980s, however, reported findings suggesting that day care children were more aggressive and less cooperative than those who were not placed in early out-of-home care (Belsky, 1986). In addition, attachment to the mother was sometimes found to be impaired when infants were placed into full-time day care. Those opposed to child care legislation often cite such findings, even though the research is not conclusive. The findings from day care research have not been consistent and need to be interpreted cautiously by policy makers, due to the breadth of the methodological problems inherent in the research.

Funding day care and after-school programs is a major focus for child care advocates. Although the federal government funds the Head Start program and provides some child care subsidies for income eligible families, there is a serious lack of space in publicly funded early childhood programs. In New York City, for example, only about 20 percent of the eligible children receive day care services. Politicians often look to private industry to provide the needed funding for day care.

Yet, only 1 percent of private companies offer on-site day care, and only 10 percent of businesses offer their employees any day care benefits (e.g., flexible hours, parental leave, or allocation of pre-taxed salary for day care). Privately funded day care programs are so expensive to operate that usually only high-income families can manage the fees. Many families must compromise regarding the quality of care in order to find affordable child care for their children.

Other important child care issues are the lack of federal regulations regarding the care of young children, and the lack of a national parental leave policy. The United States is the only industrialized nation not to have a parental leave policy or federal child care regulations. The only child care subsidy for middle-income families is a modest tax credit for child care. It has been suggested that the families in the United States are in crisis partly because of the need for social and governmental support for child care.

If implemented, effective child care policies would provide a vehicle for protecting young children and ultimately offering parents viable options regarding child care. Child care policies would acknowledge a role for both government and society in the care of young children and would ease the burden now carried by most contemporary families.

References

Belsky, J. (1986). Infant day care: A cause for concern? *Zero to Three. VI* (5), 1–7.

Miller, A. B. (1990). *The day care dilemma: Critical concerns for American families*. New York: Plenum Press.

Reisman, B., Moore, A. J., & Fitzgerald, K. (1988). *Child care: The bottom line—an economic and child care policy paper*. New York: Child Care Action Campaign.

Zigler, E. F., & Gordon, E. W. (1982). *Day care—Scientific and social policy issues*. Dover, MA: Auburn House.

Zigler, E. F., & Lang, M. E. (1991). *Child care choices—Balancing the needs of children, families and society*. New York: The Free Press.

E. S. Flicker

Child Welfare Policy

Policies currently exist in the United States that focus on the widespread needs of children and families. These policies address family income and employment, housing, health, and education. The Job Training Partnership Act, for example, helps families to move from poverty to self-sustenance through training. Many of the 1 million American teenagers who become pregnant each year, or their partners, are at risk for dropping out of school. The Job Corps assists these and other young high school drop-outs with poor employment prospects to find jobs (Children's Defense Fund, 1989). The JOBS program from the Family Support Act of 1988 serves families receiving Aid for Families with Dependent Children (AFDC).

Income supplements include Earned Income Credit for low-income working families, Food Stamps, and the Low-Income Home Energy Assistance Program. Families also receive potential financial assistance through federal and state Child Support Enforcement, and through provision of out-of-home care for children whose parents cannot provide adequate care and protection (Children's Defense Fund, 1990).

The increasing homelessness of families with young children, reflecting increased poverty within this group, has caused concerned citizens to urge the federal government to address the dwindling availability of low-income housing by reinvesting in the effective public housing and Section 8 programs that were heavily funded in the 1960s and 1970s (Children's Defense Fund, 1990).

The need for comprehensive health services for American children whose parents are unemployed or uninsured is met in part by the provision of the Early and Periodic Screening, Diagnosis, and Treatment Program available to Medicaid-eligible families. The supplemental food program for Women, Infants, and Children (WIC) provides necessary nourishment, while the Title IV Maternal and Child Health Services Block provides funds for medical intervention.

Federal support of educational services for children whose economic circumstances may create potential delay in achievement is provided by the Head Start program, and by the services of Chapter I (of the Elementary and Secondary Education Act) interventions in schools. Educational advocates concerned about the continuing achievement gap between white children and children of color in American public schools are urging federal and state attention to equity in funding and programming, partnership with business, and focus on developmentally appropriate and multicultural curricula. At the same time, they are recommending a decreased focus on early grouping, labeling, and achievement testing of children (Children's Defense Fund, 1990; Bredekamp, 1987).

A positive indication of national attention to the overall needs of children and families in the United States is the recent formation of the prestigious National Commission on Children. The Commission is charged with the responsibility to develop policy agendas for enhancing opportunities for all children to achieve their fullest potential (Hymes, 1990).

References

Bredekamp, S. (ed.). (1987). *Developmentally appropriate practice in early childhood programs serving children from birth through age 8.* Washington, DC: National Association for the Education of Young Children.

Children's Defense Fund. (1989). *A children's defense budget.* Washington, DC: Author.

Children's Defense Fund. (1990). *S.O.S. America! A children's defense budget.* Washington, DC: Author.

Hymes. J. L. (1990). *Early childhood education. The year in review. A look at 1989.* Washington, DC: National Association for the Education of Young Children.

B. S. Fennimore

Compensatory, Chapter 1, and Migratory Education Policy

Federal assistance to low-income youth in the United States began on April 11, 1965, with the enactment of Title I of the Elementary and Secondary Education Act (ESEA), currently known as Chapter 1 of Title 1 of the amended ESEA. Provision of assistance was based on the premise that inadequate educational programs were responsible for depressed student achievement, which in turn led to diminished adult earning capacity and poverty.

Members of the First Session of the Eighty-ninth Congress intended the funds to strengthen inadequate programs by allowing public schools to hire additional special staff, acquire equipment, and supplement instructional budgets. Since there was not enough funding to serve all students, the available funds were designated for public schools serving high concentrations of children from low-income families. In the minority report on the legislation, it was pointed out that early childhood education was virtually left out of the bill (Elementary and Secondary Education Act of 1965).

Opponents of the act believe that this law shifts power from the local and the state to the federal level, and that the act allows the federal government to take funds by taxation that might otherwise be spent on education by parents and local communities. For the past ten years, the act has had bipartisan support (Jennings, 1985). That support has been given by members of Congress representing areas with high percentages of low-income populations. The Children's Defense Fund and the Lawyers' Committee on Civil Rights also have been long-term supporters of the program.

The initial act had few restrictions on the use of funds and came close to representing the "general aid" envisioned by the act's opponents. The nine sets of amendments passed by subsequent sessions of Congress, however, have focused the use of funds through law, regulations, and policy.

The Chapter 1 programs across the nation today serve those children that are not learning at the same rate as others of their chronological age. They have increased the achievement levels of significant numbers of these students. Millions of these students have gone on to become productive adults, and programs funded though Chapter 1 received a significant part of the credit for their success.

Actions taken to focus on early childhood have included Follow Through, which was intended to strengthen the impact of the Head Start program, and now the Even Start program, which is a subpart of the 1988 Chapter 1 law (Public Law 100–297). Private school students also are served by Chapter 1 programs. The courts, however, have mandated that a division between state and religion must be maintained.

References

Elementary and Secondary Education Act of 1965, H.R. 2362. 89th Congress, 1st Session, Public Law 89–10. Reports, Bills, Debate, and Act.

Elementary and secondary education conference report to accompany H.R. 5. United States House of Representatives Report 100–567.

Jennings, J. (1985). The elementary and secondary education act: 1960's and 1970's. In *A compilation of papers on the twentieth anniversary of the elementary and secondary education act of 1965.* Washington, DC: The Subcommittee on Elementary and Secondary and Vocational Education of the Committee on Education and Labor, United States House of Representatives, Serial No. 99–D.

Halperin, S. (1985). ESEA twenty years later: A political retrospective. In *A compilation of papers on the twentieth anniversary of the elementary and secondary education act of 1965.* Washington, DC: The Subcommittee on Elementary and Secondary and Vocational Education and Labor, United States House of Representatives, Serial No. 99–D.

C. E. Eberhardt

Head Start Policy

Head Start originated from a congressional mandate in 1964 that established a new federal agency, the Office of Economic Opportunity (OEO) as part of the movement that became known as the War on Poverty. At that time, advisors to President Lyndon B. Johnson were launching a large number of programs, including Job Corps, VISTA Volunteers, and the Community Action Program. These programs were designed for people of all ages except for young children. The director of the Office of Economic Opportunity, R. Sargent Shriver, soon became convinced, however, that a high percentage of the poor in the United States were, in fact, children; and he felt that the War on Poverty should do something to give young children a boost before they began school. The result was a new program, soon named Head Start, that was not directly mandated by Congress.

As conceptualized by Shriver's senior OEO staff, Head Start was to be a massive summer program for children about to enter kindergarten or first grade. The program was to consist of health screenings, immunizations, and nutrition, with some social enrichment, play and kindergarten-type activities, and field trips. The OEO staff believed that better health and a variety of enrichment experiences would help ready children to meet the expectations (stemming from dominant, middle-class North American culture) that they would encounter in typical public school classrooms.

The administration of Head Start was located within that of the Community Action Program (CAP), one part of the Office of Economic Opportunity. The CAP staff was dedicated to the twin concepts of creating opportunities for low-income people, and the maximum feasible participation of those people at every level of program and service affecting them. For that reason, even the earliest documents describing Head Start mention parent participation in every phase of program implementation and encourage the creation of employment opportunities for low-income parents within the program.

Within the first few years of the establishment of Head Start, task forces were assigned to produce documents that would explicate program policy. One of the first of these was Issuance 70.2 (Office of Child Development, 1970), formulated between 1968 and 1970. That document outlined four functions for Head Start parents, namely, participation in the process of making decisions about the nature and operation of the program (through their local Parent Advisory Committee or PAC); participation in the classroom as paid employees, volunteers, or observers; becoming involved in activities that they themselves would develop to meet their own interests;

and working with their children (in their homes or other settings) in cooperation with the staff of the Head Start center. Exactly how the policy on parent involvement was to be implemented at the local level was determined by the local agencies responsible for the disbursement of Head Start funds.

From the late 1960s through the early 1970s, the administration of Head Start was the responsibility of the newly created Office of Child Development (OCD). OCD sponsored the formulation of a more comprehensive set of policy guidelines that are known as the Head Start Program Performance Standards (Office of Child Development, n.d.). The Performance Standards became generally available to Head Start programs in 1975 and were established as the basis for monitoring the work of existing Head Start programs around the country and for preparing proposals for new Head Start programs.

The Performance Standards are divided into four sections reflecting the four major components of the Head Start program, that is, Education, Health and Nutrition, Social Services, and Parent Involvement. Each section contains specific guidance on the elements that must appear in a local program in order for that program to be "validated" and therefore to continue to receive Head Start funds. Local programs are expected to be in compliance with the Standards or, at least, to demonstrate steady and substantial progress toward meeting the Standards.

This period also saw the creation of policy on the preparation of Head Start staff, particularly staff members hired from the populations served by the program, who generally had little formal preparation in early childhood education. At first Head Start, through its Regional Training Offices, contracted with local colleges and universities to provide such preparation and/or in-service support. This arrangement was known as the Head Start Supplementary Training Program (HSST). Head Start Regional Training Officers (RTOs) themselves also directed large- and small-scale in-service training for the Head Start staffs in their region. Later, the Child Development

Associate (CDA) Program was developed to credential Head Start staff through a set of experiences including study and on-site practice following the disseminated CDA guidelines (Office of Child Development, 1973). Today, the CDA credential is used not only in Head Start but in many other early childhood programs throughout the country as well.

In the mid-1970s, the Office of Child Development became the Administration for Children, Youth and Families (ACYF) within the Human Development Services branch of the Department of Health and Human Services. Policy formulation continued, with efforts toward refinement of the overall program. One of the initiatives that arose during this period was the Head Start Strategy for Spanish-Speaking Children. This was the first attempt of Head Start to move from a "cultural deficit" orientation in its program planning toward a "cultural difference" understanding of the depressed academic performance of many children from what were then considered to be minority populations. The original focus on the Spanish-speaking child soon broadened to include children and families across a wide variety of linguistic and cultural groups. The Strategy sponsored research on the development of culturally and linguistically diverse children, the establishment of multicultural resource centers across the various regions of the country, and the development of early childhood bilingual and multicultural curricula. Special funding for this effort existed until 1980, when a new federal administration sought cutbacks in the Head Start program.

Head Start was able to survive the political realities of the late 1970s and the 1980s because of the history of its founding and the unique features of its initial conceptualization. The federal government had founded Head Start and other War on Poverty programs in response to a groundswell of public opinion demanding that the society of the United States become more inclusive. Because it was part of a massive movement to bring greater economic opportunity and equality to low-income people and members of minority groups on the part of two Presidents and a multiracial, bipartisan progressive coalition over a 15-year period, by 1980, Head Start was too firmly planted and too popular to be easily uprooted by those who did not see the need for it.

Other factors that have contributed to Head Start's continuance include its focus on providing jobs and new careers for low-income populations, as well as growth in political sophistication for thousands of low-income people; its alliance with the media who became convinced of its efficacy through a concerted public relations effort; and its design as a comprehensive program, involving the major professional social work organizations and university faculties, public health services, dental and nutritional services, and early childhood advocacy organizations such as the National Association for the Education of Young Children. Many professionals had a deep interest in seeing Head Start continue because of their extended work with the program. As a result, Head Start policy formulation and subsequent program implementation continues to the present day.

References

Office of Child Development (OCD). (1970). *Issuance 70.2*. Washington, DC: United States Government Printing Office.

Office of Child Development (OCD). (1973). *The CDA program: The child development associate, a guide for training*. Washington, DC: United States Government Printing Office.

Office of Child Development (OCD). (n.d.). Head Start program performance standards. *OCD-HS Head Start Policy Manual*, OCD Notice N-30-364-4. Washington, DC: United States Government Printing Office.

P. Greenberg & L.R. Williams

Health Care Policies

Health care policies implemented in early childhood education programs are designed to promote and maintain children's health. Government agencies often require routine health visits and immunizations, and enforce infection control.

The American Academy of Pediatrics (AAP) has established guidelines for preventive pediatric health care. Health maintenance visits include a thorough physical examination, specific growth measurements, behavioral and developmental assessments, sensory screening, and anticipatory guidance for injury prevention. The AAP recommends that routine visits be scheduled at 1, 2, 4, 6, 9, 12, 15, 18, and 24 months, then annually until 6 years of age, and every other year thereafter. These visits stress continuity as well as appropriateness of medical care. Infants and children with special health or psychosocial problems need to be evaluated more frequently (Committee on Psychosocial Aspects of Child and Family Health, 1988).

The immunization schedule proposed by the AAP recently has been revised in response to emerging epidemics and availability of new vaccines. The current AAP schedule for active immunization of normal infants and children is as follows (Phillips, 1991, pp. 70–71):

- *Diptheria-Tetanus-Pertussis (DTP)*: 2, 4, 6, 15, or 18 months, between 4 and 6 years of age;
- *Diptheria-Tetanus (DT)*: between 14 and 16 years of age and then repeated every 10 years;
- *Trivalent Oral Polio Vaccine (TOPV)*: 2, 4, 15, and 18 months, between 4 and 6 years of age;
- *Measles-Mumps-Rubella (MMR)*: 15 months of age and 12 years of age;
- *Haemophilus Influenzae Type B Conjugate Vaccine (HIB)*: as of February 1991 (Committee on Infectious Diseases,1991), two H. Influenzae Type B vaccine regimens have been licensed by the Federal Drug Administration: HbOC and PRP-OMP. When using HbOC, the initial three doses are given at two-month intervals starting at two months of age. The fourth dose is given at 15 months. When using PRP-OMP, the initial two doses are given at two-month intervals starting at two months of age. A third dose is given at 12 months.

Medical experts recommend that each early childhood education facility follow specific state requirements as immunization mandates may vary in different states. Also, recommendations often change during epidemics.

As prevention is an integral part of health maintenance, infants and children need to be screened for potentially correctable health problems. Newborn screening for metabolic disorders is routinely performed in accordance with state law. Although iron deficiency is common in preschool children, there is no standardized schedule for hemoglobin or hematocrit determinations. The AAP suggests performing a hemoglobin or hematocrit at least once during early infancy, early childhood, late childhood, and adolescence (Committee on Psychosocial Aspects of Child and Family Health, 1988). Lead intoxication is also prevalent in children 1 to 6 years of age. Since most children are asymptomatic, screening programs are necessary to identify affected individuals as these children are at increased risk for future neurobehavioral and cognitive impairment (Behrman & Vaughan, 1987). The Centers for Disease Control recommend utilizing measurement of the free erythrocyte protoporphyrin (FEP) for lead screening. All children need to be screened at 9 to 12 months, and then annually through 6 years of age. Children in high-risk groups need to be screened more frequently (Centers for Disease Control, 1985).

The American Academy of Ophthalmology recommends annual vision screening for school-aged children (Newacheck & Halfon, 1988). Since much educational material is color coded, testing for color blindness should be done as soon as a child can count (Committee on School Health, 1987). Even mild hearing loss in a child may adversely affect language and learning. Therefore, hearing screening utilizing pure tone audiometry should be conducted in preschool, kindergarten, and first grade, and then every two to three years. Children with known hearing loss need to be tested annually (Committee on School Health, 1987).

Tuberculosis is a highly communicable disease that causes significant morbidity and mortality in children. From 1978 to 1988 case rates have nearly tripled for children less than 15 years of age (Inselman, 1990). Modern screening employs the Mantoux test (using 0.1 ml of 5TU-PPD). Use of the tine test is no longer recommended. Low-risk groups can have skin tests performed at 12 to 15 months of age. Medical experts recommend that this test be repeated before school entrance and again in adolescence. High-risk groups, especially children from neighborhoods where the case rate is higher than the national average, should be tested annually (Committee on Infectious Diseases, 1988).

In order to safeguard the health of children, early childhood education programs need to adhere to strict infection control measures. Infants and toddlers, in particular, spread infection through their close physical contacts and normal hand and object-mouthing behaviors. Basic sanitation standards should be established and implemented. The following guidelines may be helpful (Committee on Infectious Diseases, 1988; Committee on Early Childhood, Adoption and Dependent Care, 1987):

1. Younger children, especially those in diapers, should be separated from older children.
2. Teething rings, pacifiers, and bottles should not be interchanged among children and should be sanitized regularly (wash with dish-washing detergent and water, rinse in freshly prepared household bleach solution, and rinse again in water).
3. Children and staff should wash hands before and after toileting or diapering, before and after meal preparation or eating meals. Soap and running water should be used. The hands should be rubbed vigorously. All surfaces must be washed including back of hands, wrists, between fingers, and under fingernails. After thorough rinsing, paper towels should be used to dry hands.
4. Communal toys should be sanitized regularly.
5. Disposable towels should be used whenever possible. Washcloths, towels, and tissues should not be shared.

6. Food handling and diaper areas should be separated and sanitized daily.
7. Blood or other body fluids should be cleaned from surfaces with freshly diluted household bleach.

Although there are very few illnesses for which children should be excluded from childhood education programs, certain diseases, such as chicken pox, necessitate exclusion until a contagious period has elapsed. In writing exclusion policies, consideration should be given to state laws, local public health recommendations, and advice from medical consultants. Generally, children with fever, diarrhea, vomiting, irritability, excessive sleepiness, or who are unable to participate in normal play or learning activities should remain home (Committee on Early Childhood, Adoption and Dependent Care, 1987).

Staff should know about those children who have chronic illness, and particularly those who are immunodeficient, as these children may be at increased risk for acquiring numerous and potentially life-threatening infections. Children infected with the human immunodeficiency virus (HIV) should only be excluded from early childhood educational programs if they exhibit persistent biting behaviors or have exudative skin lesions (Brunell et al., 1987). Finally, children who become ill during school hours should be physically separated from other children in order to minimize infectious spread.

In summary, early childhood education programs have a responsibility for promoting the health and well-being of children. To achieve this goal these programs need to address certain health issues. Requirements for regular medical evaluations, adherence to recommended immunization schedules, endorsement of appropriate exclusion policies, and the encouragement of good hygienic practices are important measures to be followed. (See also **Immunization Policies**, next article.)

References

Behrman, R. E., & Vaughan, V. C. (1987). *Nelson textbook of pediatrics*. Philadelphia: W. B. Saunders Company.

Brunell, P. A., Daum, R. S., Giebink, G. S., Hall, C. B., McCracken, G. H., Nahmias, A. J., Phillips, C. F., Plotkin, S. A., & Wright, H. T. (1987). Health guidelines for the attendance in daycare and foster care settings of children infected with Human Immunodeficiency Virus. *Pediatrics, 79*, 466–471.

Centers for Disease Control (1985). *Preventing lead poisoning in young children*. Atlanta: U.S. Department of Health and Human Services.

Committee on Early Childhood, Adoption and Dependent Care. (1987). *Health in day care: A manual for health professionals*. Elk Grove Village, IL: American Academy of Pediatrics.

Committee on Infectious Diseases. (March 1991). *Haemophilus Influenzae Type B Conjugate Vaccines: Recommendations for immunization of infants and children at 2 months of age and older: Update*. American Academy of Pediatrics News.

Committee on Psychosocial Aspects of Child and Family Health. (1988). *Guidelines for health supervision II*. Elk Grove Village, IL: American Academy of Pediatrics.

Committee on School Health. (1987). *School health: A guide for health professionals*. Elk Grove Village, IL: American Academy of Pediatrics.

Inselman, L. S. (1990). Tuberculosis in children: An unsettling forecast. *Contemporary Pediatrics, 7*, 110–130.

Newacheck, P. W., & Halfon, N. (1988). Preventive care use by school-aged children: Differences by socioeconomic status. *Pediatrics, 82*, 402–468.

Phillips, C. F. (1991). Keeping up with the changing immunization schedule. *Contemporary Pediatrics, 8*, 20–46.

D. Ersenio-Jenssen & J. Fagin

Immunization Policies

The use of immunizations to control and prevent specific infectious diseases is an established component of comprehensive health care. Barring any preexisting medical condition that contraindicates administration of an immunization, the recommended age to begin the basic series is two months old, followed by the appropriate number of doses and/or boosters to complete the series, and establish optimum protection.

The Committee on Infectious Diseases of the American Academy of Pediatrics (AAP), and the Health and Human Services Advisory Committee on Immunization Practices (ACIP) issue immunization schedules for children, with periodic revisions as new knowledge emerges. These recommendations for immunizations, however, are general guidelines and may be subject to modification as individual state and/or community needs warrant.

All states have enacted legislation requiring proof of specific immunizations prior to school entry; however, minimum requirements for school attendance should be obtained from individual state boards of education and/or departments of public health to ensure compliance. In general, current established guidelines recommend that children between the ages of two months and six years be immunized against the following:

- Diptheria, Tetanus, Pertussis (DTP);
- Polio (OPV);
- Measles, Mumps, and Rubella (MMR); and
- Haemophilus Influenzae Type B (HIB).

Although not a vaccine, tuberculosis skin testing is also recommended in some areas prior to school entry.

Established procedures regarding immunization requirements in early childhood settings should include the following:

1. An exclusion policy for children who do not provide documented proof of immunity to required immunization mandates;
2. Accurate documentation of all immunization dates (basic series as well as boosters) received to date;
3. Protocol for reporting cases of suspected communicable disease outbreaks to local health departments;
4. Procedure for protecting those children who have no or incomplete protection against infectious disease, due to either medical contraindication or immunodeficiency.

(See also **Health Care Policies**, above.)

Reference

Committee on Early Childhood, Adoption and Dependent Care (1987). *Health in day care: A manual for health professionals.* Elk Grove Village, IL: American Academy of Pediatrics.

J. M. Gray

Kindergarten Policy
(See Section 3.3, **Early Childhood Settings in the Public Sector, Kindergarten.**)

Media (Television) Policies

Television has captured the attention of children and adults since the 1950s. On the average, children today watch from 20 to 30 hours of television a week. With the advent of cable television, more than half of the U.S. households have been introduced to new independent stations offering a variety of children's and/or adult programming. This expanded schedule gives children an introduction to the world. It also exposes them to music videos and R-rated movies.

The topic of children and television has long been subject to social, economic, political, and advocatory considerations. Three action groups that have figured prominently during the last three decades are the Council on Children, Media and Merchandizing (CCMM), the National Association for Better Broadcasting (NABB), and the Action for Children's Television (ACT). The CCMM concentrated on the need to review advertising for children during the 1960s and 1970s. The NABB has stressed responsibilities in broadcasting and awareness of the public's rights since 1950. ACT, active from 1968 to 1992, directs its efforts toward encouraging better age-specific children's programming, as well as reducing the number of commercials and commercial-based programs.

Throughout the 1970s and the 1980s other groups have become involved in the children's television issue. The American Academy of Pediatrics has raised concerns about the commercialization of children's television, while the Parent Teacher Association (PTA) has focused on media literacy.

In addition to the exploitation of children as consumers, prolonged inactivity and the effect of watching violence have been some other common concerns. The Surgeon General's study of television and social behavior, *Television and Growing Up: The Impact of Violence*, (1972) gave credibility and some stature to the application of child development theories related to the subject of children and television.

Television's commercial influence increased in the early 1980s with the deregulation of the Federal Communication Commission (FCC), which brought forth the opportunity for more commercial time during children's programming. Prior to this time, there were federally imposed limits on the number of commercial minutes that could be run per hour. Although ACT, NABB, and a limited number of legislators brought attention to reimplementing imposed guidelines on children's programming, the governmental and industrial supporters of the First Amendment have continued to block major changes.

Efforts to improve the content of children's television have been led by the Children's Television Workshop with programs such as "Sesame Street." The Public Broadcasting System and some cable stations have also worked at developing quality programs through applied communication techniques.

Video games and home video recorders are two phenomena related to television that hold the fascination of children and adults alike. Video games allow millions of children to interact with computer animated characters, while home video recorders give children access to films ranging from the most benign to the most violent.

The televison of tomorrow will assume a multitude of new forms and functions that will increase its influence over children's lives. Television's capacity to serve families is dependent on how selectively they use it. To help children become critical viewers, parents need to model positive television viewing habits, help children understand how television works, and encourage dialogue that allows children to express their interests and concerns about the shows that they watch. (See also Section 5.5 **Technology and Education**.)

References

Surgeon General's Scientific Advisor Committee on Television and Social Behavior. (1972). *Television and growing up: The impact of televised violence*. (DHEW Publication No. HSM 72-90). Washington, D.C.: U.S. Government Printing Office.

Pamela Tuchscherer

Prekindergarten Policy
(See Section 3.3, **Early Childhood Settings in the Public Sector, Prekindergarten**.)

Safety Policies
The National Association for the Education of Young Children (NAEYC) has expressed concern about the safety of children in child care facilities (NAEYC, 1989), and the National Survey of Preschool Playgrounds has revealed a wide array of existing hazards on playgrounds in the United States (Wortham & Frost, 1991). To meet these situations, NAEYC has prepared materials focusing on safety within early childhood facilities (Kendrick, Kaufman, & Messenger, 1988; NAEYC, 1989), and both the Consumer Product Safety Commission and the American Society for Testing of Materials have published guidelines and standards on playground safety. The guidelines and standards recognize the seriousness of current statistics on injuries to young children.

In 1984 the National Center for Health Statistics reported that injury was the leading cause of death for children one through four years of age in this country. Most of these deaths resulted from automobiles, followed by drownings, fires, suffocation, and falls. For injuries that are not fatal, studies of children treated in emergency rooms show that falls from furniture or nursery equipment are the major sources of injury for infants and young children (Gallagher et al., 1984; Rivara, 1982).

Examination of several recent studies allows some generalization about such injuries (Elardo, Solomons, & Snyder, 1987; Chang, Lugg, & Nebedum, 1989; Sacks, et al., 1989). The most dangerous time of day is approximately 11:00 a.m., and the colder months appear to be safer for young children. Injury rates are highest among toddlers, and boys have a higher injury rate than girls. A bump on the head is the most common injury. The injury rate in licensed day care centers indicates that children are safer in centers than at home. In one study, toddlers were nearly twice as safe in day care centers (Sacks et al., 1989).

The Centers for Disease Control (1988) reported that 82,108 preschool children were injured at day care centers during the period 1983–1987; of these injuries, approximately one-third were related to playground equipment. The U.S. Consumer Product Safety Commission reported that falls to the ground account for 60 percent of playground injuries (Rutherford, 1978). A four-foot fall onto packed earth can be fatal, yet approximately half of day care playground equipment is not installed over an impact-absorbing surface (Davis & McCarthy, 1988), and most of this equipment is not properly installed or maintained (Wortham & Frost, 1991).

Many child care workers have limited or no training in proper playground supervision. Child care center operators should develop safety education programs for all staff, and child "safety proofing" of all facilities should be given high priority.

References

Centers for Disease Control. (October 21, 1988). *Morbidity and mortality weekly report, 37* (41), 629–632.

Chang, A., Lugg, M. M., & Nebedum, A. (1989). Injuries among preschool children enrolled in day care centers. *Pediatrics, 82* (2), 272–277.

Davis, W. S., & McCarthy, P. L. (1988). Safety in day care centers [abstract]. *American Journal of Diseases of Children,* 142; 386.

Elardo, R., Solomons, H. C., & Snyder, B. C. (1987). An analysis of accidents at a day care center. *The American Journal of Orthopsychiatry, 57* (1), 60–65.

Gallagher, S. S., Finson, K., Guyer, B., & Goodenough, S. S. (1984). The incidence of injuries among 87,000 Massachusetts children and adolescents. *American Journal of Public Health,* 74 (8), 1340–1347.

Kendrick, A. S., Kaufman, R., & Messenger, K. P. (1988). *Healthy young children: A manual for programs.* Washington, DC: National Association for the Education of Young Children.

National Association for the Education of Young Children. (1989). *Facility design for early childhood programs.* Washington, DC: NAEYC.

National Center for Health Statistics. (1984). *Vital statistics of the United States, 1980.* [Vol. II, Part A]. Hyattsville, MD: U.S. Government Printing Office.

Rivara, F. P. (1982). Epidemiology of childhood injuries. In Bergman, A. B. (ed.), *Preventing childhood injuries: Report of the 12th Ross Roundtable on Critical Approaches to Common Pediatric Problems* (pp. 13–18). Columbus, OH: Ross Labs.

Rutherford, G. W., Jr. (1978). *Injuries associated with public playground equipment.* Washington, DC: U.S. Consumer Product Safety Commission.

Sacks, J. J., Smith, J. D., Kaplan, K. M., Lambert, D. A., & Sattin, R. W. (1989). The epidemiology of injuries in Atlanta day care centers. *Journal of the American Medical Association, 262* (12), 1641–1645.

Wortham, S. C., & Frost, J. L. (eds.). (1991). *Playgrounds for young children: American survey and perspectives.* Reston, VA: American Alliance for Health, Physical Education, Recreation and Dance.

R. Elardo & J. L. Frost

School Desegregation Policy

An examination of progress in desegregation over the past 30 years reveals a mixture of success and failure in achieving equality in educational opportunity (Miller & Repa, 1986). The impact of litigation and legislation on desegregation at the federal, state, and local levels can be seen in key court cases that provided the legal framework within which schools were to be desegregated.

Brown vs. Board of Education of Topeka (1954) addressed the constitutionality of separate but equal educational facilities in relation to the equal protection clause of the Fourteenth Amendment. In *Green vs. County School Board of New Kent County* (1968), the issue addressed the legality of a freedom-of-choice plan in a rural and residentially integrated Virginia town with only two schools—one for African-Americans and one for whites. In *Swann vs. Charlotte-Mecklenberg County Board of Education* (1971), the Supreme Court was forced to deal directly with the issue of the precise racial balance in each school, which highlighted the issue of busing.

By the mid-1970s, it became increasingly evident that systemwide busing alone would not achieve integrated schools in many of the nation's largest cities. *Milliken vs. Bradley* (1977) was the first case that went beyond pupil assignment. The Supreme Court endorsed mandatory support for remedial programs. *Lau vs. Nichols* (1974) was the major legal decision that impacted on the meaning of equal educational opportunities for linguistic minorities. Later cases, such as *Jose P. vs. Ambach* (1983), went one step further and ordered the New York City Board of Education to hire school personnel who were specially trained to work with limited-english-proficient (LEP) students in their first language.

Court decisions in *Liddel vs. Board of Education of the City of St. Louis* (1981) and in *United States vs. Yonkers Board of Education* (1986) brought together issues of school and housing desegregation. Several court cases also ruled on regional desegregation plans. In *Little Rock School District vs. Pulaski County* (1986) the court ordered three independent school systems to reduce racial segregation by developing a joint magnet school program. In another case concerning *Liddel vs. Board of Education of the City of St. Louis* (1986), the court tried to change the direction of the school district after eight years of an inter-district, one-way student transfer program.

In a recent decision in *Brown vs. Board of Education of Topeka* (1989), the Tenth Circuit Court of Appeals ruled that the school officials had not considered all possibilities for desegregating the school. The U.S. Supreme Court is presently reviewing *Jenkins vs. Missouri* (1989) to determine if local taxes can be raised to pay for a desegregation plan. In *Morgan v. Nucci* (1988), U.S. District Judge Garity allowed the Boston school system to deter-

mine their own controlled-choice assignment plan. The court's decision in *Riddik v. School Board of the City of Norfolk* (1984) to allow the Norfolk school district to return to the old school plan left large numbers of all–African-American schools, which was a setback for proponents of desegregation. In New York in 1988, the Yonkers public schools under a federal court order to desegregate its schools has sued the New York State Education Department to expand and improve the remedy in desegregating its schools, thus making the state a codefendant in the case. At this writing, this litigation is under review by the federal district judge.

The passage of time since the Supreme Court's landmark 1954 ruling in *Brown vs. Board of Education* has not diminished the need for vigilant oversight of the issues directly related to the desegregation of our public schools. Despite the public's focus on the judicial termination issues presently under review by the Supreme Court in *Dowell vs. Oklahoma City Board of Education*, the overwhelming number of school districts in this country with multiracial student populations are nowhere near the termination stages presently at issue before the Court. Quite to the contrary, many districts continue to grapple with the earliest stages of the desegregation process, from the development and initial implementation of remedial plans to the many now-familiar follow-through desegregation issues, such as classroom segregation; discriminatory assignments to specific special education programs; discriminatory disciplinary procedures; staff hiring, assignment and training; the myriad issues associated with multicultural and multilingual education; parent and community involvement; and conflict resolution and human relations training in general.

There also has been a growing interest in utilizing magnet schools and programs as the focal point for school desegregation. More and more districts have expressed an active interest in desegregation plans that rely for their driving impetus on educational improvements in the district. The proven successes of magnet schools and programs in select districts particularly in Buffalo and Yonkers, New York, where they form the hub of court-ordered systemwide desegregation plans, and in districts like Montclair, New Jersey, and New Rochelle, New York, where they form the hub of voluntary systemwide desegregation plans, have spurred expressions of interest from numerous other districts that are addressing desegregation problems.

To be sure, school desegregation does not represent the total solution to the separation of Americans within society. Employment, income, and housing are other important causes of stratification. Desegregation, however, dispels the ignorance and reduces the mistrust that keeps groups at arm's length. At the same time, it enhances aspirations and provides opportunities for those trapped at the bottom rungs of society.

We have, however, experienced a curious parallel, if not a dilemma in American education in regard to the twin movements of early childhood education and desegregation. In the second half of the twentieth century, education has been characterized by increases in the provision of educational programs for preschool-aged children. Clearly, Head Start can be shown to make a positive difference in the lives of children, particularly those from low-income families. Similarly, attendance in kindergarten has increased dramatically in recent years. While desegregation and early childhood education have occurred over the same period of time, these movements appear to have had very little overlap in their implementation. Obviously, early childhood education has not been a part of most desegregation plans because it has not been a required part of regular school programs. Hence, there are few examples of early childhood education programs that we can point to in desegregation plans. Yet, as far back as 1965 in the *Booker vs. Plainfield* ruling, the New Jersey State Supreme Court made the following observation:

> In society such as ours, it is not enough that the 3 Rs are being taught properly, for there are other vital considerations. The children must learn to respect and live with one another in multiracial,

multicultural communities—and the earlier foundations may be laid for good citizenship and broad participation in the mainstream of affairs.

The Buffalo desegregation plan is a notable exception in the chronicle of school desegregation. Phase 1 of the Buffalo remedy called for the development of magnet schools that became the centerpiece of Buffalo's desegregation efforts. But Phase 11 created early childhood centers—the first and only time early childhood programs have been used as integral to a desegregation remedy. These centers housed children beginning at age four through the second grade. Children are bused to the centers from all over the city. The program is nearly ten years old. All schools are integrated and the plan is highly successful. Some other school districts have since followed Buffalo's example.

If we believe, as the court did in the *Booker vs. Plainfield* ruling, that children must learn to respect and live with one another and the earlier they do so the better, then the Buffalo experience holds some valuable lessons for all schools and school districts. The issues at the heart of the Buffalo plan are today's concerns—race and education, excellence and equity, the locus of control in the educational process, and early and equal opportunity for learning for all children. The understanding of the relationship of these issues will enhance our ability as a nation to provide quality education to all of our citizens.

References

Brown vs. Board of Education of Topeka, 347 U.S. 483 (1954).

Brown vs. Board of Education of Topeka, 1989. unpublished.

Green vs. County School Board of New Kent County, 391, U.S. 430 (1968).

Jenkins vs. Missouri, 639 F Supp. (1985).

Jose P. vs. Ambach, 669 F2d 865 (1983).

Lau vs. Nichols, 414 U.S. 563 (1974).

Liddell vs. Board of Education of the City of St. Louis, 667 F. 2d 643 (8th Cir.1981).

Liddell vs. Board of Education of St. Louis, 640 SW 2nd. 121, (1986).

Miller, L. P., & Repa, T. (1986). Equity and excellence: An emerging trend in the desegregation of schools. In L. P. Miller (ed.), *Brown Plus Thirty*. (pp. 75–82). NY: Metropolitan Center for Educational Research, Development and Training.

Milliken vs. Bradley, 433 U.S. 282 (1977).

Morgan vs. Nucci, DC Mass 602 F. Supp. 806 (1988).

Riddick vs. School Board of the City of Norfolk, F. Supp. (1 VA. 1984) Civil Action Civil No. 84–1815 4th Circuit.

Swann vs. Charlotte-Mecklenberg County Board of Education, 402 U.S. 1 (1971).

United Stated vs. Yonkers Board of Education, 635 F. Supp. (1986).

L. P. Miller

Special Education Policy

Early childhood special education refers to specialized instruction and related services provided to children with, and at-risk for, disabilities who are between the ages of birth and six years. Its historical roots rest in the development of special education programs but were subject to the same social and political forces that affected early childhood generally.

The earliest special education programs for children younger than compulsory school age are traced to the 1930s, when "Sunshine Homes" were established for blind infants. For the next 30 years, funding for these homes and other early intervention programs came largely from philanthropic organizations and private agencies.

Federal efforts in special education of children with disabilities began in the early 1960s. In 1968 Congress passed the Handicapped Children's Early Education Assistance Act, designed to fund model programs across the United States that would demonstrate good practice in assessment and programming for young children with disabilities. By 1982 the Handicapped Children's Early Education Program (HCEEP) had funded 280 projects, 80 percent of which had been continued by state and local school programs.

In the 1990s, early childhood special education is implemented largely under the auspices of the Individuals with Disabilities Education Act (IDEA), a large multifunction bill first passed in the early 1970s. It was the 1975 amendment, however, that changed the face of special education in the United States. That amendment, popularly known as Public Law 94–142, provided for a free, appropriate, public education for every child with a disability. The federal government reimbursed state education agencies for the excess cost of special education for every child enrolled, requiring states to guarantee adherence to the law's provisions. P.L. 94–142 also established the right of the child's parents to participate in the decision-making process, including the development of an Individualized Education Program (IEP), at the same time as it mandated due process procedures and parental consent prior to evaluation and placement.

Free, appropriate public education in the least restrictive environment, individualized instruction, and parent involvement have been the hallmarks of special education ever since. From 1977 to 1993, however, the provisions of P.L. 94–142 applied to children younger than compulsory school age only if state law permitted. Nevertheless, during the 1987–1988 school year, 29,728 birth to two-year-olds and 336,984 three to five-year-olds received early childhood special education services under the auspices of this legislation (U.S. Department of Education, 1989).

Public Law 99–457, the 1986 amendments to IDEA, extended the provisions of P.L. 94–142 down to age three. Regardless of state law, if states want to receive the financial benefits of IDEA, they must, by 1993, provide special education and related services to children with disabilities beginning at age three years. These amendments also established a new Part H of IDEA, which encouraged states to provide early intervention services to handicapped and at-risk infants and toddlers, including the development of an Individualized Family Service Plan (IFSP). Many of the provisions of the early intervention program are still being defined.

While much of the impetus for this legislation came from political figures, most notably, Lowell Weicker (Connecticut), Tom

Harkin (Iowa), Thomas Safford (Vermont), and Pat Williams (Montana), its passage was due to the advocacy efforts of several key parent and professional organizations. The Council for Exceptional Children (CEC), the largest professional organization of special educators in the world, has been instrumental in improving services for children with disabilities. The Division for Early Childhood (DEC), one of CEC's several divisions, was heavily involved in the development and passage of P.L. 99–457.

The greatest advocacy work has, however, come from parents themselves. Working either as individuals attempting to obtain an education for their young children with disabilities, or as part of regional or national groups, such as the Association for Retarded Citizens (ARC), United Cerebral Palsy (UCP), or the National Association for Parents of the Visually Impaired (NAPVI), parents have been the mainstay of the special education advocacy movement. They remain today not only "the single most important resource a child has" (Robinson, 1982) but also the crucial partners in all early childhood special education programs.

References

Robinson, L. W. (1982). *Parents to the rescue.* Austin, TX: National Association for Parents of the Visually Impaired, Inc.

U.S. Department of Education. (1989). *Eleventh annual report to Congress on the implementation of the Education of the Handicapped Act.* Washington, DC: U.S. Government Printing Office.

K. A. Ferrell

Regional Policy Trends in Financing, Licensing, and Regulation

Federal early childhood policy is applied to all publicly and many privately funded programs across the country. There are, however, some dimensions of educational policy that vary from region to region of the United States. Most particularly, those relate to program licensing and monitoring, the availability of certain forms of early childhood programs (such as public school kindergarten or prekindergarten), and teacher preparation and certification.

The Northeast and Mid-Atlantic regions of the United States are the most densely populated areas of the country. Extremely dense population may be experienced as depersonalization; ecological and social damage can occur under such circumstances. Despite the concurrent presence of agricultural pockets within these regions, it may be particularly important to prepare early childhood educators who can balance urban pressures for young children.

The South and Southeast have added kindergartens to public schools relatively recently, a circumstance that may influence early childhood curriculum. Both the South and the Southeast have experienced the greatest recent growth in population. The rise in population suggests that there is a real and pressing issue of expanding services in order to care adequately for low-income, culturally diverse, rural and urban children. The West, reflecting major growth in a culturally diverse population and among people of color, similarly is faced with an expanding demand for early childhood services.

In contrast with these regions, the populations of the Midwest appear to be relatively homogeneous. Therefore, there are fewer pressures for bilingual and/or multicultural programs. The industrial sections of the Midwest are in decline, however, and families are experiencing the pressures of unemployment and the need for family services. Agricultural industries there are remaining comparatively steady.

In general, the costs of child care parallel housing costs. The smallest expenditures are made in the Southeast and the Southwest. The most expensive services exist in New York, Boston, San Francisco, and other large cities and affluent suburbs, while rural areas have the lowest expenditures.

As each state has its own system of data collection and its own set of priorities, there are some variations in the precise topics addressed from region to region in the articles below. There is enough similarity, however, to allow for comparison across regions and the correlation of trends with issues receiving either local or national attention.

D. P. Fromberg & L. R. Williams

Midwest

The Midwest region, also recognized as the North Central region, is comprised of 12 states. These states are Illinois, Indiana, Iowa, Kansas, Michigan, Minnesota, Missouri, Nebraska, North Dakota, Ohio, South Dakota, and Wisconsin, and they represent a wide cross section of the nation's population. In all 12 states, a licensing procedure for child care facilities has been established. In several states, the licensing program is under the jurisdiction of the Department of Human Services, whereas in others, the program is carried out by Departments of Social Services, Family Services, Health, or Child Welfare.

All of the states, with the exception of Wisconsin, utilize a renewable state level license. Wisconsin has employed a regional license level. Indiana, Iowa, Kansas, Minnesota, Missouri, North Dakota, Ohio, and South Dakota require an annual renewal procedure. Illinois, Michigan, Nebraska, and Wisconsin require renewal every two years.

All of the states in the Midwest region recognize and license both center-based child care programs and family- or home-based programs. The National Association for the Education of Young Children reported in 1985 that this region had over 12,900 licensed child care centers and over 39,600 licensed family- or home-based programs. Given all available data on the increase of women returning to the work force, this number is surely on the increase.

In each of the states, standards have been established to assist programs in providing appropriate care for children. These standards provide for the health and safety of the children. Included as a part of the standards in each state are the staff/child ratios and the minimum square footage of space available per child. For example, in Ohio, the necessary square footage per child indoors is 35 square feet. Outdoor available space must include 60 square feet per child. In Iowa, the indoor standard is the same (35 square feet per child), but the outdoor requirement is 75 square feet per child. The staff/child ratios are unique to each state's standards and are set according to the age of the child. For example, for infants up to eighteen months old, Illinois, Iowa, and Michigan have a ratio of one staff member for each four infants, while Ohio has a ratio of one to five. Michigan feels that one staff member for every four toddlers is appropriate. Illinois has one to eight, Iowa lists one to six, and Ohio has a ratio of one to seven (Rhodes & Real, 1985; Child Day Care Centers and Preschools, 1988). The ratios are set for each age group (infant, toddler, three-year-olds, four-year-olds, five-year-olds, and school-aged children). In several states, group sizes also are given. For instance, Ohio lists group size as twice the maximum number of the staff/child ratio.

In all areas of the Midwest, there are interesting and innovative programs to serve the needs of young children. In Minneapolis, Minnesota, for example, there is a program to send trained child care providers into the home of a sick child for one or several days. The service is available on a first-come, first-served basis. Evanston, Illinois, has Family Focus, which promotes effective parenting for children through the age of three by providing classes and support groups for parents and by helping parents to locate needed services. Businesses in the Minneapolis-St. Paul area of Minnesota have the opportunity to contribute to the 2% Club—2 percent of their pretax earnings are donated to a community service. These businesses do not have on-site child care, but they support a variety of services for young children.

The federally funded Head Start program exists in a variety of formats in each of the region's states. The program may include both center-based programs and Home Start, where teachers visit the child in the home and work with both child and parent. Some programs are full-day, but the majority of the programs use a half-day model. Head Start programs exist in both urban and rural areas. The programs include a strong parent-involvement component and are individually constructed to meet the needs of the children and families served while also meeting broad federal standards.

All of the states provide kindergarten for all who request it. Most of the state kindergarten consultants regard the purposes of kindergarten to be balanced between social and academic development. Many states in the region indicate that both half-day and full-day kindergartens are available in their districts. A child may spend as few as two or as many as six hours a day in kindergarten (Robinson, 1987). In most states in this region, a bachelor's degree is required for teaching in a kindergarten classroom.

References

Child Day Care Centers and Preschools: Licensing Standards and Procedures from the States of Iowa and Ohio. (1988).

Rhodes, G. L., & Real, M. (1985). *Day care: Investing in Ohio's children.* Columbus, OH: Children's Defense Fund.

Robinson, S. L. (1987). The state of kindergarten offerings in the United States. *Childhood Education, 64* (1), 23–28.

National Association for the Education of Young Children. (1985). *Child care boom.* Washington, DC: NAEYC, #761.

Washington, V., & Oyemade, U. J. (1987). *Project Head Start: Past, present, and future trends in the context of family needs.* New York: Garland.

L. Todd

Northeast

The Northeast region includes 13 states and the District of Columbia. The New England states of Maine, New Hampshire, Vermont, Massachusetts, Rhode Island, and Connecticut, the Mid-Atlantic states of New York, New Jersey, and Pennsylvania, the South-Atlantic states of Delaware, Maryland, Virginia and West Virginia, as well as the District of Columbia comprise the Northeast.

Provisions for child care differ by state within the region. All states within the region, with the exception of West Virginia, require that child care programs be either licensed or registered. The following table presents information on the regulation of child care centers under state law.

Greater numbers of children are enrolled in nursery schools, preschools, and kindergartens than ever before.

Child Care Regulation

State	Regulation	Training Required	Inspections per Year
Connecticut	License	No	1 per 2 years
Delaware	License	Yes	1
District of Columbia	License	No	1
Maine	License	No	1
Maryland	Registration	No	1
Massachusetts	Registration	Yes	Not Known
New Hampshire	Registration	Yes	3 per 2 years
New Jersey	License	No	1 per 3 years
New York	License	No	1
Pennsylvania	Registration	No	20% sample
Rhode Island	License	Yes	1 per 2 years
Vermont	License & Registration	No	2
Virginia	License	No	2
West Virginia	Reg. (Voluntary)	No	1

Source: National Center for Educational Statistics, 1988.

Children Enrolled in Nursery Schools and Kindergartens

State	Tot. Pop. 0–5	Nursery		Kindergarten	
		Public	Private	Public	Private
Connecticut	185,188	13,754	26,771	34,553	4,861
Delaware	41,151	2,086	5,012	6,465	1,575
District of Columbia	34,365	4,003	3,300	6,000	1,218
Maine	78,514	4,565	6,187	14,662	1,028
Maryland	272,274	16,623	31,960	45,410	8,999
Massachusetts	337,215	21,862	40,715	62,898	8,133
New Jersey	464,289	30,829	59,386	77,149	16,999
New York	1,135,982	64,426	111,774	175,640	43,256
Pennsylavnia	747,458	34,287	69,740	123,430	22,495
Rhode Island	56,692	3,022	6,116	9,095	6,116
Vermont	35,998	2,016	2,843	5,345	1,078
Virginia	360,686	13,404	39,336	64,140	11,276
West Virginia	145,583	4,411	5,394	27,210	1,701
U.S. Summary	16,348,254	894,313	1,535,338	2,697,067	513,031

Source: National Center for Educational Statistics, 1984.

With the current expansion of Head Start, the number of children enrolled in Head Start will increase in the coming decade. Recent Head Start enrollment is found in the following table.

State	Enrollment
New York	24,611
New Jersey	9,645
Massachusetts	8,147
Pennsylvania	7,062
Virginia	5,591
Maryland	5,305
Connecticut	4,220
West Virginia	4,008
Maine	2,385
District of Columbia	2,285
Rhode Island	1,858
Delaware	936
Vermont	871
New Hampshire	748

Source: Statistical Abstract of the United States, 1989.

References

Children's Defense Fund. (1988). *A call for action to make our nation safe for children: A briefing book on the status of American children in 1988*. Washington, DC: Children's Defense Fund.

National Center for Education Statistics. (1988). *Digest of education statistics*. Washington, DC: U.S. Department of Education.

National Center for Educational Statistics. (1982–83 & 1983–84). *Public Elementary and Secondary Education in the United States, A Statistical Compendium*. Washington, DC: U.S. Department of Education.

Statistical Abstract of the United States. (1989). Washington, DC: U.S. Department of Commerce, Bureau of the Census.

C. Seefeldt

South and Southeast

Approximately 2,112,990 children under five years of age are cared for outside the home in the South and Southeast. Of these, 464,858 are in family day care homes, 338,078 are in child care centers, and the rest are cared for by relatives in their own or the relative's home. The average cost of child care for children under three years of age in Atlanta was $77 a week in 1989. Costs for children over three years of age were somewhat lower. Costs for child care in rural areas of the South and Southeast also were somewhat lower than for urban areas.

The majority of the states do not regulate class size. Those states that do, regulate according to the age of the children. The range for infants is 6 to 14 children per class (with a median of 9), for toddlers, 6 to 24 children (with a median of 12), for 3-year-olds, 10 to 25 children (with a median of 18), and for 4-year-olds, 20 to 25 children per class (with a median of 20).

All of the states have maximum allowable staff/child ratios. For infants, the range is from 1 to 4 to 1 to 8 with a median of 1 to 6. For toddlers, the range is from 1 to 4 to 1 to 12 with a median of 1 to 6; and for 3-year-olds, the range is from 1 to 8 to 1 to 15 with a median of 1 to 12. For 4-year-olds, the range is from 1 to 8 to 1 to 20 with a median of 1 to 16.

Kindergarten provision in the South and Southeast in 1987 was mixed, having both half-day and full-day programs. The trend was toward full-day programs. By the beginning of the 1990s all of the states in the South and Southeast provided state-funded kindergarten for all children. According to a 1989 survey, the most common date by which children must be five years old to begin kindergarten in the South and Southeast was September 1 The entrance birth dates ranged from September 1 to December 31, with a median of September 30.

Qualifications for staff in child care centers in the South and Southeast were minimal. For directors, 40 percent of the states required no training at all, 40 percent had an education and an experience requirement, and the remainder had either an education or an experience requirement. For teachers, 77 percent of the states had no minimum qualification. The remaining had a qualification of education and/or experience.

References

Lunn, S. E. (1988). Georgia day care standards weak. *Outlook*. Winter, 30.

National Association for the Education of Young Children. (1989). Testing, tracking & timing: Challenging policies that deny equity and access to young children, *The Early Childhood Advocate*, *1* (1), 5.

Robinson, S. L. (1987). Kindergarten in America: Five major trends. *Phi Delta Kappan*, *68* (7), 529–530.

Save the Children, Atlanta (Personal communication, November 1989).

Wilkes, D. L. (Personal communication, November 1989).

J. Nurss

Southwest

The Southwest region is comprised of five states, including Arizona, Arkansas, New Mexico, Oklahoma, and Texas. All the states in the region require licensure for early childhood programs. Licensing or registration requirements vary as indicated below(Morgan, 1986). Staff/child ratios are regulated throughout the region but vary greatly in relation to the ages of the children and the standards for each state. Detailed requirements can be obtained from state departments of licensing.

The Center Accreditation Project of the National Association for the Education of Young Children (NAEYC) reported that 126 programs in the Southwest region had been evaluated and received accreditation. Ninety-six were in Texas, comprising 76 percent of the regional accredited programs, 13.3 percent of the national total, and 1.8 percent of the total centers in Texas (NAEYC, 1989). Arizona had 17 accredited centers, 2 percent of

Licensing Regulations for Early Childhood Programs

	**Sq Ft. per Child	Group Size Requirement	Staff/Child Ratio	Program Requirement	Health/Safety Requirement	Staff Training/ Yearly	*Director Training /Yearly	Licensing Visits Ppr year
Arizona	25/75		X	X	X	12		2
Arkansas	35/75		X	X	X	10	10	3–4
New Mexico	35/60	X	X	X	X	12	12	2
Oklahoma	35/75		X		X	4	4	4
Texas	30/80	X	X	X	X	15	20	2

*number of hours
**inside/outside

Source: Morgan (1986). National State of Child Care Regulations.

the state total. New Mexico with five had 1.4 percent of its centers accredited, Oklahoma, with six centers, had 0.4 percent, and Arkansas, with two centers, had 0.1 percent of its centers accredited. All of the states had large numbers of centers that were awaiting site visits for validation. Across the United States, 720 centers are accredited (NAEYC, 1989).

Public early childhood programs are not universally available to all children in the Southwest. Segments of the community have early childhood programs available to them if they are low-income or of kindergarten age.

Head Start programs exist in all of the southwestern states, but not all the children who are eligible can attend because of limited funding. Head Start is currently serving one out of six eligible low-income children, and 90 percent of the children served are at or below the poverty level. Head Start in the region also serves children with handicapping conditions, 80 percent of whom have a speech or health impairment. Ten percent of the children in the New Mexico Head Start program can be categorized as having a handicapping condition. The total number of children served by Head Start in the region is approximately 53,000. Texas alone serves nearly 25,000 (Head Start Bureau, 1986).

Kindergarten programs also are available in the Southwest region. As is true of other parts of the United States, 90 percent of the eligible children attend kindergarten. Public school prekindergarten programs are available in Texas (Gnezda & Robison, 1986). Children in Texas prekindergarten programs are four-year-olds from low-income families or of limited-English proficiency. If 15 or more such children live in a district, the district must offer a prekindergarten program. At this writing, approximately 34,500 children are served in 405 half-day programs. The Texas prekindergarten curriculum stresses language development and developmentally appropriate activities and is under the jurisdiction of the Texas Education Agency.

High Scope programs, both public and private, are found in the region. Strongly influenced by Piagetian theory, High Scope programs include active learning, hands-on experiences, and a balance between teacher- and child-initiated learning. Other independent, private programs in the region include church-related programs and Montessori programs. A unique early childhood public school program exemplifying a continuous program for children from infancy to school age is located in Arkansas. Originally known as the Kramer project, the program provides a combination of custodial care and an educational curriculum (Caldwell, 1989).

Child care programs that are licensed by State Departments of Human Services exist in each state of the region. These include infant and toddler programs, nursery programs, and general child care programs in both profit and nonprofit contexts. Each state has its own specific requirements for licensing such programs (Blank & Wilkins, 1986).

Education and training for directors, teachers, and child care staff is available throughout the region. The range of programs encompasses introductory child development information offered in high schools to doctoral degrees within universities, as well as workshops and seminars under the auspices of various professional groups and private consultants. All states in the region offer courses in vocational training centers, community or junior colleges, and universities. All states have institutions that offer bachelor's degrees in early childhood education. All but Arkansas offer master's degrees, and Arizona and Texas offer doctoral degrees in early childhood education.

There were 27,161 persons nationwide who had received their Child Development Associate (CDA) certification from the Child Development Associate Consortium as of February 28, 1989. Of these, 765 (2.8 percent) were in Arizona, 617 (2.4 percent) were in Oklahoma, and 2,138 (7.9 percent) were in Texas (Council for Early Childhood Professional Recognition, 1989).

References

Blank, H., & Wilkins, A. (1986). *Child care: Whose priority? A state child care fact book*. Washington, DC: Children's Defense Fund.

Caldwell, B. J. (1989). A comprehensive model for integrating child care and early childhood education. *Teachers College Record, 90* (3), 404–414.

Council for Early Childhood Professional Recognition. (1989). Washington, DC: CDA Consortium.

Department of Health and Human Services. (1987). *Project Head Start: Statistical fact sheet.* Washington, DC: Administration for Children, Youth and Families, Office of Human Development Services, Department of Health and Human Services.

Head Start Bureau. (1986). *The status of handicapped children in Head Start programs. The thirteenth annual report of the U.S. Department of Health and Human Services of services provided to handicapped children in Project Head Start.* Washington, DC: U.S. Department of Health and Human Services, Office of Human Development Services, Administration of Children, Youth and Families, Head Start Bureau.

Gnezda, T., & Robison, S. (1986). *State approaches to early childhood education.* Denver, CO: National Conference of State Legislatures.

Morgan, G. (ed.). (1986). *National state of child care regulations.* Watertown, MA: Work/Family Directions.

National Association for the Education of Young Children. (1989). *Center accreditation project.* Washington, DC: NAEYC.

Porzell, M. (ed.). (1991). *National directory of early childhood training programs in post secondary institutions.* Washington, DC: Council for Early Childhood Professional Recognition.

C. Brownstein & M. Waldon

3.6 Sociocultural Studies of the Effectiveness of Early Childhood Education

In the 1960s, people became interested in early childhood education as a way to help prevent problems faced by young children living in poverty—problems that include school failure and dropout, delinquency and crime, and continuing poverty into adulthood. Some educational psychologists initiated early childhood education programs for young children living in poverty and employed scientific designs to study the effects of these programs over the years.

In their first few years, these studies found evidence of improvements in children's intellectual performance that lasted several years after program completion—a finding that has since been replicated in another 50 studies reviewed by the Head Start Synthesis project (McKey et al., 1985). The eventual fade-out of effects on children's intellectual performance led some to believe that all effects of these programs would fade away, but consistent evidence of fade-out has been found only for children's intellectual performance. It appears that the subsequent educational programs of these children did not provide the extra intellectual stimulation that the early childhood education programs had provided.

At least seven long-term studies have found evidence that good programs for young children living in poverty produce important long-term benefits. Four of these studies followed participants to ages 18–21: (a) the Perry Preschool study (Berrueta-Clement et al., 1984); (b) the Early Training Project study (Gray, Ramsey, & Klaus, 1982); (c) the Project HOPE study (Gotts, 1989); and (d) the Head Start study in Rome, Georgia (cited by Berrueta-Clement et al., 1984). The remaining three studies followed participants to ages 9–13: (e) the Syracuse study (Lally, Mangione, & Honig, 1988); (f) the Harlem study (Palmer, 1983); and (g) the New York public school prekindergarten study (cited by Berrueta-Clement et al., 1984). Long-term findings reported by the Consortium for Longitudinal Studies (Lazar et al., 1982) included the findings from three of these studies (Perry, Early Training, and Harlem).

These studies found that the young children who participated in the programs outperformed their peers with similar backgrounds who did not participate in the programs in the following socially important ways (each with a possibility of chance occurrence of less than 0.05):

1. Six of the seven studies with relevant data reported fewer students placed in special education or retained in grade.
2. The four studies with relevant data reported more youths graduating from high school.

3. Two of the three studies with relevant data reported that their students averaged higher on achievement tests over the years.
4. Two of the three studies with relevant data reported fewer youths arrested.
5. One of the two studies with relevant data reported fewer teenage pregnancies.
6. The one study with relevant data reported more teenagers employed and fewer receiving general welfare assistance.
7. The one study with relevant data found that taxpayers profited substantially from the effects of their investment in the program.

This last finding, from the Perry Preschool study, deserves elaboration. In 1989 constant dollars discounted at 3 percent, the two-school-year program cost taxpayers $13,423 per participant—$6,713 per year. Costs were relatively high because the program maintained a staff/child ratio of one to six, paid all the teachers public school salaries, and included weekly home visits to each child. In the long run, however, the program saved taxpayers a total of $40,219 per participant—three times the original investment, a net return of $26,796 per participant. These financial benefits came from savings in special education, crime, and welfare assistance, and higher tax revenues due to projected increases in lifetime earnings.

All the programs examined in these studies served young children living in poverty who were at special risk of school failure. They all operated for at least one school year, and most operated for at least two. All the children began the programs at some time between infancy and age five years. Although not precise replications of each other, the programs did have substantial similarities that merit their characterization as "high quality." Most of their teachers were trained in early childhood education to carry out explicitly stated, developmentally appropriate curricula.

These teachers received curriculum support and in-service training from their supervisors. Most of the programs maintained classes of fewer than 20 children for every pair of teaching adults. Most of them provided home visits or regularly involved parents in other ways.

These findings suggest two public policy developments. First, good programs should be available at public expense for all young children living in poverty. Second, policy makers and early childhood program providers should join together to provide, ensure, and verify that all early childhood programs develop and maintain a high level of program quality.

References

Berrueta-Clement, J. R., Schweinhart, L. J., Barnett, W. S., Epstein, A. S., & Weikart, D. P. (1984). *Changed lives: The effects of the Perry Preschool Program on youths through age 19.* High/Scope Press.

Gotts, E. E. (1989). *Hope, preschool to graduation: Contributions to parenting and school-family relations theory and practice.* Appalachia Educational Laboratory.

Gray, S. W., Ramsey, B. K., & Klaus, R. A. (1982). *From 3 to 20—The Early Training project.* University Park Press.

Lally, J. R., Mangione, P. L., & Honig, A. S. (1988). The Syracuse University Family Development Research Program, Long-range impact of an early intervention with low-income children and their families. In D. R. Powell (ed.), *Parent education as early childhood intervention: Emerging directions is theory, research, and practice* (pp. 79–104). Norwood, NJ: Ablex.

Lazer, I., Darlington, R., Murray, H., Royce, J., & Snipper, A. (1982). Lasting effects of early education. *Monographs of the Society for Research in Child Development, 47* (1–2, Serial No. 194).

McKey, R. H., Condelli, L., Ganson, H., Barrett, B. J., McConkey, C., & Plantz, M. C. (1985). *The impact of Head Start on children, families and communities* (Final report of the Head Start Evaluation, Synthesis, and Utilization project). CSR.

Palmer, F. H. (1983). The Harlem study: Effects by type of training, age of training, and social class. In Consortium for Longitudinal Studies, *As the twig is bent . . . Lasting effects of preschool programs* (pp. 201–236). Hillsdale, NJ: Erlbaum.

L. Schweinhart

Chapter 4

PERSPECTIVES ON CHILDREN

Chapter *4*

PERSPECTIVES ON CHILDREN

Introduction

This chapter specifically addresses concerns that are, in great degree, represented throughout this volume. By separately highlighting children's development, the sources of present beliefs and understandings about how development takes place are more readily understood.

It is apparent, in viewing various theories, perspectives, and approaches to studying children, that there are distinctly different conclusions that educators and other students of child development have drawn about how children develop and what these views imply for their education. Arguments concerning whether children are formed primarily through external shaping, inevitable inherited maturational clocks, or varied external-internal combinations, have strongly influenced the field. The outcomes of this dialogue are reflected in the ways in which educators study, assess, and evaluate young children, as well as how the teaching-learning process takes place.

The early childhood education profession has a history of incorporating developmental theory into its practices. While there are curriculum models primarily based on a single theory [e.g., Distar (behavioral); Montessori (maturational); High Scope (cognitive)], the vast majority of early childhood practices are based on a combination of theories. No single theory can respond to all of the educational needs of young children in today's society. It is important, however, to note that the manner in which one views a child's development has a profound impact on the kind of curriculum and environment that one will plan for and provide. The theories discussed fall into the following four groups: (a) behavioral, (b) cognitive-transactional, (c) psychoanalytic, and (d) normative-maturational.

Behavioral Theory

The view of the child from a behavioral viewpoint can best be exemplified by the work of

B. F. Skinner (1968). In this view, learning is understood to occur as the environment shapes the child's behavior. The child is born with the necessary psychological equipment and with a basic set of responses. When the outside forces of the environment impinge on these responses, new responses are developed and new combinations of responses emerge.

Psychological constructs that are associated with this viewpoint are reinforcement, punishment, shaping, operant conditioning, modeling, and imitation. Behaviors are sustained or increased through reinforcement and extinguished through total lack of attention to the behavior. Children learn more complex behaviors through the process of shaping. That is, they are reinforced for successive approximations of the "goal" behavior.

The behavioral view of learning contributes to educational programs in early childhood education that depend on external rewards and punishments to elicit and control behaviors. A major emphasis of these types of programs is to define narrowly the behaviors that are to be achieved in the curricular objectives. Some educators believe that when it is used as the only curricular implementation strategy the behavioral view is, at times, too rigid and the curriculum too inflexible. Included in the practices emanating from this view would be a regular schedule of pupil assessment. The purpose of these assessments would be to measure the child's overt behavioral changes in direct response to the curriculum.

Cognitive-Transactional Theory

The chief proponent of this point of view for early childhood education is Jean Piaget (Piaget & Inhelder, 1969). In this theory, the child is viewed as naturally active. Development occurs through the process of adaptation, in which the person seeks experiences in the environment. Development proceeds through the interaction of the processes of biological maturation, physical experiences, and social experiences.

Development takes place on a continuum of four stages. In the sensorimotor stage—birth to two years—the physical environment is acted upon directly by the child. The child comes to know the world through these physical experiences. In the preoperational stage— two to seven years—children's thinking becomes representational, but their actions and thoughts are limited by intuitive thinking that is constrained by the cognitive structures of egocentricity and centration. Because of these cognitive structures children's thinking is limited by their ability to focus perceptually on only a limited number of variables at a time. In the concrete operational stage—seven to eleven years—the child's thinking becomes characterized by using logical reasoning. In formal operations— 11 plus years—thinking is characterized by hypothetical-deductive reasoning.

Lev S. Vygotsky (1986) emphasized the social role of the adult as the child's teacher, in influencing the child's development. The effective teacher recognizes what tasks the child can accomplish alone and what tasks the child can accomplish with the assistance of an adult or a more competent peer.

Early childhood programs based on this theoretical perspective emphasize planning environments that respond to the child and that match the child's level of development. The child is expected to make choices, and the curriculum is flexible so that it can accommodate the needs of children at various levels within a stage of development.

Psychodynamic Theory

Psychodynamic theorists believe that there is a connection between children's capacity to handle emotion and their ability to think. With its roots in the work of Sigmund Freud, the psychodynamic theory of personality development is best exemplified in early childhood education by the writings of Erik Erikson (1963). According to psychodynamic theory, a child is born with basic drives, and these drives must be channeled. How these drives are channeled in childhood ultimately lead to the determination of what kind of adult the child will become.

Erikson viewed these drives as being channeled through a series of stages or crises. In each of these crises there is a focal developmental issue at stake. In childhood, the crises are "trust versus mistrust" (infancy); "autonomy versus shame and doubt" (toddler); "initiative versus guilt" (preschool); and "industry versus inferiority" (school age). There are three mechanisms involved in facilitating the child's passage from crisis to crisis. They include biological readiness, psychological readiness, and social interaction. These mechanisms interact and determine when and how the crisis will be resolved.

The educational implications of this theory include facilitating children's abilities to cope with their feelings, their environment, and themselves within that environment. This can be accomplished by providing a physical and social environment that is emotionally supportive, physically appropriate for the child's level of development, and socially responsive and consistent.

Normative-Maturational Theory

The normative-maturational viewpoint is represented best by the work of Arnold Gesell (1940) and his associates. According to this view a child is primarily a product of his or her genetic potential, though the influence of the environment is acknowledged. Although children are born with a full set of genes to guide their development, the environment may affect the ease with which they progress from developmental stage to developmental stage, the relative quality or fullness of development in each stage, and the general patterns that development takes. The specific role of the environment is to provide a proper physical and emotionally supportive setting in which development is to take place.

Educational practices in early childhood education that reflect this viewpoint are focused around the concept of "readiness." According to normative-maturational theory, the term "readiness" means matching the child's developmental stage to the curricular demands made upon him or her. The primary focus is on evaluating the child's level of development

in order to determine whether the child is ready for a particular predetermined curriculum.

Play as an Integrating Factor

The degree to which children play that is present in early childhood settings is perhaps one of the most prominent issues and representations of a teacher's developmental perspective. External shapers would be expected to provide less opportunity for play than would those who hold other positions. John Dewey (1933), on the other hand, proposes that play be part of a continuum of focus that ranges between fooling, play, work, and drudgery. He contends that the interplay of work and play is the legitimate realm of education.

A large body of research indicates that play makes a difference in the development of language, social competence, creativity and imagination, and thinking skills. Play is both a condition of learning and an activity that is worthwhile for its own sake. Sociodramatic play in particular—as contrasted with playing games, playing with objects, or playing alone—has been found to integrate many aspects of development.

When young children play with another or others, they are able to move into and out of the play, take turns, plan, negotiate, and try out many alternatives. In these ways, they extend their ability to understand others' views and rights and grow in their awareness of the play process itself. Through universal play signals and gestures of "becoming" another being or object, speaking and behaving differently, children become more adept at setting and using the rules of the pretend play. All of these processes build children's cognitive development through shared language, social negotiations, and imagery. In these ways, play serves as "an ultimate integrator of human experience (Fromberg, 1990, p. 223)." The developmental theories described in this chapter infer varied, relative emphases on play.

The chapter begins with an overview of the theories historically and presently in use, followed by a brief consideration of key contributors to these theories. It includes a description of the various characteristics of young children's development. In addition, the discussion focuses on sequences of development and domains within the whole child's experience as well as on the general characteristics of children, beginning in infancy and continuing through the primary school years. There is also an integrated discussion of special learning needs of young children.

A major theme throughout this volume is recognition of the potency of sociocultural context in children's development. For that reason, this chapter discusses selected aspects of social influences on development. The chapter ends with two sections on how educators and other early childhood professionals have studied, assessed, and evaluated the interactions between young children's developmental characteristics and the sociocultural influences that affect their lives.

References

Dewey, J. (1933). *How we think*. Lexington, MA: D.C. Heath.

Erikson, E. (1963). *Childhood and society*. New York: Norton.

Fromberg, D. P. (1990). Play issues in early childhood education. In C. Seefeldt (ed.), *Continuing issues in early childhood education*, (pp. 223–243). Columbus, OH: Merrill.

Gesell, A. (1940). *The first five years of life: A guide to the study of the preschool child*. New York: Harper & Row.

Piaget, J., & Inhelder, B. (1969). *The psychology of the child*. New York: Basic Books.

Skinner, B. F. (1968). *Science and human behavior*. New York: Free Press.

Vygotsky, L. S. (1986). *Thought and language*. Cambridge: MIT Press.

D. P. Fromberg & D. F. Gullo

4.1 History of Child Development and Learning Theory

Early childhood educators hold child development theory in high regard as a primary consideration in providing developmentally appropriate education for young children. The acceptance of a particular theoretical position influences how educators attempt to understand and interpret the behavior of a preliterate or preverbal human being. In turn, interpreting behavior from a particular theoretical perspective leads to a defined range of possible provisions for children. This section discusses the history of child development theory, beginning in the nineteenth century, and traces some of the major influences on current thinking.

Humans have long understood that children are not miniature adults and that childhood is a period of life with its own unique characteristics and processes (Hiner & Hawes, 1991). This basic understanding of children and childhood, however, was refined and systematized only after the study of children began to emerge as a professional field in the late nineteenth century. Among the precursors who created the intellectual foundations for modern child development studies were John Locke, Jean-Jacques Rousseau, Charles Darwin, Wilhelm Preyer, Sigmund Freud, and James Baldwin (Borstelmann, 1983; Cairns, 1983; Cleverley & Phillips, 1986; Kessen, 1965; Sears, 1975; Senn, 1975).

John Locke (1632–1704), the famous English physician, philosopher, and political theorist, profoundly challenged traditional assumptions about children (Locke, 1690). Locke argued that the newborn child is essentially a *tabula rasa*, or blank sheet, on which experience inscribes its lessons. Although Locke was convinced that the environment is the primary factor shaping individual development, he did not deny that children are, to some degree, born with special temperaments, abilities, and predispositions. Children, he believed, learn through association, repetition, imitation, rewards, and punishments. He said that parents and other adults should mold the character of children by controlling their environment to encourage self-control (Borstelmann, 1983; Crain, 1980; Cleverly & Phillips, 1986). The roots of contemporary behaviorist theory and practice are present in Locke's views.

The French philosopher Jean-Jacques Rousseau (1712–1778) agreed with Locke that the environment is very important in human development, but he was much less inclined than Locke to intervene directly in children's lives because he believed that they are born with a natural capacity for healthy growth and development. Rousseau urged adults to make certain that their interactions with children were consistent with the different capacities and needs they exhibited during the four basic stages in their development, which include infancy (birth to two years), childhood (ages two to twelve years), late childhood (twelve to fifteen years), and adolescence (fifteen to twenty five years). Rousseau (1761; 1762) explained his ideas about human development in his eighteenth century publications (Borstelmann, 1983; Crain, 1980; Kessen, 1965; Mitzenheim, 1985). Rousseau's contentions form part of the foundations for contemporary constructivist, as well as humanist, outlooks.

Charles Darwin (1809–1882) shared Rousseau's respect, if not his romantic admiration, for the efficacy of natural processes. While Rousseau, however, focused his attention on children and political theory, Darwin sought to understand and describe the biological mechanisms and processes that control and regulate all living things. His nineteenth-century books revolutionized biology and also profoundly affected the study of children (Darwin, 1859; 1871). To some extent Darwin confirmed and reinforced both Locke's environmentalism and Rousseau's naturalistic developmentalism. After Darwin, scholars found it more difficult to think of children abstractly, apart from nature, and free from the influence of their changing environment (Borstelmann, 1983; Kessen, 1965). The influence of Darwin's theories is reflected in contemporary maturationist perspectives on children's development.

Wilhelm Thierry Preyer (1841–1897), a prominent German Darwinian and physiology professor, was one of the first scholars to make a systematic effort to place the study of children in an evolutionary framework. His influential work combined data from a baby diary he kept during his son's first three years with information gleaned from animal studies (1882). Preyer emphasized the importance of individual differences among children and challenged the Lockean assumption that experience is the most important factor in individual development. He asserted that humans do not develop their minds or psyches by experience alone, but must through their experience "fill out and animate" their "inherited endowments, the remains of the experiences of [their] ancestors" (cited in Tobach, 1982, p. 215; see also Kessen, 1965).

Sigmund Freud (1856–1939) did not think that the newborn child was a *tabula rasa*, nor did he agree with Rousseau that the child was innately good, at least by nineteenth-century standards, but he did share with Darwin and Preyer a belief in the importance of biological processes in the psychological development of children. Freud, trained as a neurobiologist in Vienna, eventually entered clinical work, where he became particularly interested in the possible relationship between physical and mental illnesses. As early as 1895, he and his colleague, Joseph Breuer, were convinced that many of his adult patients' problems were deeply rooted in their sexual experiences as children (Breuer & Freud, 1893–1895/1957). By 1909, when G. Stanley Hall (1844–1924) invited Freud to present a series of lectures at Clark University, he had begun to fashion a comprehensive theory of children's emotional development. He made his first major presentation of these ideas in his *Three Essays on the Theory of Sexuality* (1905) (Kessen, 1965). Freud's influence is apparent in contemporary psychodynamic theory and practices in early education.

James Mark Baldwin (1861–1934), philosopher and psychologist, was one of the first American scholars to make a sustained commitment to integrating the biological theory of organic adaptation with the doctrine of infant development (1895, cited in Cairns, 1983, p. 54). After systematically observing his two infant daughters for four years, Baldwin in 1895 published his evolutionary perspective on the mental development of children. For Baldwin, reason was "an evolving capacity of the mind" that depends heavily on imitation for its development (Wozniak, 1982, pp. 30–31). Then in 1897 he explored the implications of evolutionary theory for the social development of children. Later (1906–1911; 1915), he concentrated his energy increasingly on the construction of an evolutionary or genetic epistemology for psychology.

By 1910 the basic framework for modern developmental psychology had been identified. Contemporary behaviorism, social learning theories, cognitive developmental psychology, ethological and organismic theories, post-Freudian depth psychology, ecological psychology, maturational theories, and humanistic psychology all have their philosophical roots if not their experimental base in the work of Locke, Rousseau, Darwin, Preyer, Freud, Baldwin, and other nineteenth-century scholars who believed that children were worthy of serious academic study (Cleverley & Phillips, 1986; Horowitz & O'Brien, 1989; Kessen, 1965; Salkind, 1985; Vasta, 1989).

References

Baldwin, J. M. (1895). *Mental development in the child and the race*. New York: Macmillan.

Baldwin, J. M. (1897). *Social and ethical interpretation of mental development: A study in social psychology*. New York: Macmillan.

Breuer, J., & Freud, S. (1893–1895/1957). *Studies on hysteria*. New York: Basic Books.

Borstelmann, L. J. (1983). Children before psychology: Ideas about children from antiquity to the late 1800's. In N. R. H. Mussen (ed.), *Handbook of child psychology*, 4th ed. (pp. 1–40). New York: Wiley.

Cairns, R. B. (1983). The emergence of developmental psychology. *Handbook of child psychology*. 4th ed. (pp. 41–102). New York: Wiley.

Cleverley, J., & Phillips, D. C. (1986). *Visions of childhood* (rev. ed.). New York: Teachers College Press.

Crain, W. C. (1980). *Theories of development: Concepts and applications*. Englewood Cliffs, NJ: Prentice-Hall.

Darwin, C. (1859/1969). *The origin of the species*. New York: Penguin Books.

Darwin, C. (1871/1969). *The descent of man*. Portsmouth, NH: J. Murray.

Freud, S. (1905/1983). Three essays on the theory of sexuality. In the Standard Edition of *The complete psychological works of Freud*. (J. Strachey, ed. and trans.), Vol. 7. London: Hogarth.

Holt, R. R. (1989). *Freud reappraised: A fresh look at psychoanalytic theory*. New York: Guilford.

Holt, R. R. (1989). *Freud reappraised: A fresh look at psychoanalytic theory*. New York: Guilford.

Horowitz, F. D., & O'Brien, M. (1989). Children and their development: Knowledge base, research agenda, and social policy application. Special issue of *American Psychologist, 44*, 2: 97–145.

Hiner, N. R., & Hawes, J. M. (1991). *Children in comparative perspective: An international handbook and research guide*. Westport: Greenwood Press.

Kessen, W. (1965). *The child*. New York: Wiley.

Locke, J. (1690/1959). *An essay concerning human understanding* (R. Wilburn, ed.). London: Everyman's Library.

Mitzenheim, P. (1985). The importance of Rousseau's developmental thinking for child psychology. In Eckardt, G., Bringman, W.G., & Sprung, L. (eds.). *Contributions to a history of developmental psychology* (pp. 55–61). Berlin: Mouton.

Preyer, W. (1882/1888–1889). *The mind of the child* (2 vols.). New York: Appleton.

Rousseau, J.-J. (1762/1970) *The Emile of Jean-Jaques Rousseau: Selections*. (W. Boyd, trans.). New York: Teachers College Press.

Salkind, N. J. (1985). *Theories of human development* (2nd ed.). New York: Wiley.

Sears, R. (1975). Your ancients revisited: A history of child development. In E. M. Hetherington (ed.). *Review of child development research* (5th ed.) (pp. 1–71). New York: Wiley.

Senn, M. J. E. (1975). Insights on the child development movement in the United States. *Monographs of the Society for Research in Child Development, 40* (3–41, Serial No. 161).

Tobach, E. (1982). The relationships between Preyer's concept of psychogenesis and his views of Darwin's theory of evolution. In G. Eckhardt, L. Sprung, & W. Bringmann (eds.), *Contributions to a history of developmental psychology* (pp. 210–230). Mouton.

Vasta, R. (ed.) (1989). Six theories of child development: revised formulations and current issues. *Annals of Child Development, 6*, ix–285.

Wozniak, R.H. (1982). Metaphysics and science, reason and reality: The intellectual origins of genetic epistemology. In Broughton, J. M., & Freeman, Moir, D. J. (eds.). *The cognitive-developmental psychology of James Mark Baldwin* (pp. 9–45). Norwood, NJ: Ablex.

N. Ray Hiner

4.2 Key Figures in Child Development and Learning Theory

Within the section that follows, there are sketches of individuals who have made significant contributions to the fields of child development and learning theory. Their theoretical and research works represent the broad perspectives within the field of early childhood education as well as a varied range of positions. If any three of them were to find themselves able to engage in discussion, the contents of that discourse would be liable to resemble a heated debate more than a session of basic agreement, although mutual admiration and respect for the power of different positions might prevail. The section of sketches is organized alphabetically for convenient access.

D. P. Fromberg

Ainsworth, Mary B.

Mary B. Ainsworth (1913–) has enhanced our understanding of emotional development in the earliest years through research grounded in the attachment theory of John Bowlby. She studies "maternal sensitivity," "attachment behaviors," and the "Strange Situation," a research paradigm. Her longitudinal study found that maternal promptness and consistency of response to infant crying reduces the amount of crying and contributes to the development of noncrying modes of communication (Bell & Ainsworth, 1972). This study discredited the popular belief of "Spare the rod and spoil the child," and has led parents, teachers, and therapists to accept that warm, sensitive care is basic to the growth and competence of young children.

Researchers have used Ainsworth's Strange Situation research (Ainsworth & Wittig, 1969) paradigm to assess infants' social and emotional development as well as to identify and measure attachment behaviors. The Strange Situation provides a precise method for studying the organizational power of attachment (Sroufe & Waters, 1977). There is, however, controversy concerning interpretation of the findings obtained through the Strange Situation in relation to subsequent formulation of social policy. Some policy makers have understood the findings to be a caution against infant day care, seeing such care as posing a risk to infants' social and emotional development. Other policy makers have felt that the Strange Situation is too specialized in its purpose to warrant such an interpretation.

References

Ainsworth, M., & Wittig, B. (1969). Attachment and exploratory behavior of one year-olds in a strange situation. In B. Foss (ed.), *Determinants of infant behavior*, Vol. IV, (pp. 113–136). Methuen.

Bell, S., & Ainsworth, M. (1972). Infant crying and maternal responsiveness. *Child Development, 43* (4), 1171–1190.

Sroufe, A., and Waters, E. (1977). Attachment as an organizational construct. *Child Development,48* (4), 1184–1199.

A. Axtmann

Baldwin, James Mark

(See Section 4.1, **History of Child Development and Learning Theory**, above.)

Brazelton, T. Berry

T. Berry Brazelton (1918–) developed and published the Brazelton Neonatal Behavioral Assessment Scale (1984), which includes parent participation. As a research tool, the Scale is used increasingly for the assessment of infants born disabled and at risk from drug exposure and for other handicapping conditions (see Section 4.5, **Special Learning Needs, Prenatal Drug Abuse**, below). In addition, Brazelton has conducted research concerning early mother-infant interaction, attachment, and problems of infant colic. He has championed developmental pediatrics in the United States, provided leadership in such organizations as the National Center for Clinical Infant Programs and the Society for Research in Child Development, and supported the needs of young families through popular media.

References

Brazelton, T. B. (1984). *Neonatal Behavioral Assessment Scale*. London, England: Spastics International Medial Publications.

Brazelton, T. B. (1984). *To listen to a child: Understanding the normal problems of growing up*. Reading, MA: Addison-Wesley.

Brazelton, T. B., & Cramer, B. (1989). *The earliest relationship: Parents, infants and the drama of early attachment*. Reading, MA: Addison-Wesley.

A. Axtmann

Bruner, Jerome S.

In contrast to prevailing theories of the 1950s that stressed drives or responsiveness to rewards or punishments, Jerome S. Bruner (1915–) viewed human beings as rational and concerned with the discovery and creation of order in their world. His position has been extended by his research.

He has influenced United States psychology and education in many varied and profound ways. One major theme that has threaded through his work in perception, cognition, psycholinguistics, and education is his opposition to behaviorism and reductionism in general.

He formulated a "hypothesis theory" of perception that stated that the perception of external stimuli is influenced by internal events such as attitudes, values, expectancies, and psychodynamic defenses. This paradigm, that people generate hypotheses about their world, led Bruner to a theory of thinking. He and his associates studied the hypotheses and strategies by which people solve problems.

He next became interested in the development of cognition and studied the theories of Jean Piaget and Lev S. Vygotsky. Based upon this work, he formulated a description of modes of representation of knowledge, including enactive (storing information through habits of action); iconic (storing through images); and symbolic (storing through more abstact systems such as language forms).

Later, he studied children's cognitive development from a cross-cultural perspective in an effort to uncover the effects of particular cultures on thinking. Eventually, this interest led him to study infant development, particularly the acquisition of language within the infant-mother relationship. He developed the concept of "format," a task in which mother and child share an intention to get something done with words. Before the child can perform the action, the mother does it for the child. Once the child is able, the mother thereafter expects the child to do it. The mother is the child's "scaffold" as she guides her child's attention and questions, provides answering labels if needed, and confirms his or her offer of whatever it might be. As the child gains competence, the mother raises her criterion. The potential transfer of the notion of format to early childhood education is obvious. In regard to pedagogy, Bruner found gifted teachers to shape and try out what he and his group were producing.

References

Bruner, J. S. (1960). *The process of education.*Cambridge: Harvard University Press.

Bruner, J. S. (1966). *Toward a theory of instruction*. Cambridge: Harvard University Press.

Bruner, J. S. (1983). *Child's talk: Learning to use language*. New York: Norton.

Bruner, J. S., Goodnow, J. J., & Austin, G. A. (1956). *A study in thinking*. New York: Wiley.

Bruner, J. S., Olver, R.R., Greenfield, P. M., et al. (1966). *Studies in cognitive growth*. New York: Wiley.

R. Formanek

Erikson, Erik

Beginning with his now classic *Childhood and Society (1950/1963)*, Erik Erikson (1902–) has become one of the most widely read and influential writers in the psychodynamic movement. The importance of his work derives from the lucidity of his psychodynamic analysis of developmental processes and his elaboration of a psychosocial perspective of psychoanalytic theory that places great emphasis on ego functioning. He is especially well known for his psychosocial portrayal of the stages of development originally formulated in Sigmund Freud's theory of psychosexual development, and for his extension of this mode of analysis of psychological functioning to stages beyond childhood. In so doing, Erikson both anticipated and contributed substantively to the new interest in adult development.

His theoretical constructs that pertain to the role of "a sense of trust" and "ego identity" as influencing human development, have gained unusually wide acceptance. His analysis of the role of play in early development focuses on the interplay of culturally determined symbols and values with the young child's psychic economy. He also emphasized the role of "developmental needs" as a way to understand developmental stages in terms of the principal developmental tasks that they pose, and the alternative pathways that are typically chosen by children in light of both their cultural milieu and their characterological trends.

Erikson has devoted much of his later work to the psycho-historical analysis of biography, wherein he has attempted to account for the accomplishments of such figures as Martin Luther and Mohandas K. Gandhi.

References

Erikson, E. H. (1950). *Childhood and society*. New York: Norton.

Erikson, E. H. (1959). *Young man Luther*. Winchester, MA: Faber & Faber.

Erikson, E. H. (1970). *Gandhi's truth: On the origins of militant non-violence*. New York: Norton.

Erikson, E. H. (1980). *Identity and the life cycle*. New York: Norton.

H. Zimiles

Freud, Anna

The youngest of Sigmund Freud's children, Anna Freud (1925–1982) extended psychoanalytic theory, practice, and application in ways that have had a major impact on how practitioners in a wide range of international educational therapeutic, and legal settings perceive and treat children. She elaborated psychoanalytic theory by directly observing children in both school and clinical settings, in conjunction with reconstruction from the analysis of child patients.

She studied the impact on young children of severe deprivation imposed by World War II, particularly separation from the mother. She and her associate, Dorothy Burlingham, found that those children in residential nurseries who remained with their mothers showed little distress by the chaos of war if their mothers were relatively calm, while those who had been separated from their mothers showed regressive patterns. This finding led to their reorganizing the nurseries into small units with a "substitute mother." Especially in the early days, psychoanalytic theory focused on the role of the mother in child rearing. The father, although powerful, was a somewhat shadowy figure whose functions often were seen as more symbolic than actual. The fathers of children whom they studied usually were in military service or had been killed.

In another study, she and Sophie Dann studied orphaned three-year-olds who had survived concentration camps without any family life. The children's attachment to each other was more intense than with the caretaking adults, and they were able to adapt successfully in their new environment.

After the war, Anna Freud set up the Hampstead Clinic in London that offered analytic therapy to children, counseling to parents, and training for analytic child therapists. It became recognized internationally for child therapy groups.

Her development of "ego psychology," shifted the analytic focus away from drives (id) to focus on normal development. In the 1950 the Hampstead Clinic instituted a nursery school for normal children. An important concept that she talked about to groups of teachers and parents of young children was the significance to normal and aberrant behavior of "developmental lines," sequences of aspects of personality development, such as dependency to self-reliance or egocentricity to empathy and mutuality. She stressed that the "disequilibrium between developmental lines" is to be expected in normal development.

References

Freud, A. (1967–1982). *The Writings of Anna Freud.* (8 vols.) Madison, CT: International University Press.

Freud, A. (1946). *The psycho-analytical treatment of children.* New York: International Universities Press.

E. K. Shapiro

Freud, Sigmund (1856–1939)

(See Section 4.1, Child Development and Learning Theory, above.)

Gesell, Arnold

Arnold Gesell (1880–1961) became internationally known as the first developmentalist to provide substantial, systematic descriptions of the ways in which human behavior develops. He maintained that although each infant and child is a unique individual, human behavior develops in a patterned, predictable way that is very similar from one human being to another. Much of his early work was carried out at a time when many insisted that there was no basic shape or pattern to either individuality or behavior but that children were shaped by environmental influences.

Arnold Gesell contended that environmental factors modulate and inflect but do not determine the progressions of development and that, since interaction between maturation and environment is the heart of the matter, neither should be emphasized at the expense of the other. The majority of his publications were devoted to a description of the ways in which many aspects of infant and child behavior develop. In addition to observation and other research tools, he used film and produced many films.

Among his contributions to the field of child development are his descriptions of the patterned changes of behavior that occur at various stages, his norms of human behavior, and his belief that much school failure could be prevented if all children began school on the basis of their behavioral rather than chronological age.

Reference

Ames, L. B. (1989). *Arnold Gesell: Themes of his work.* Human Sciences Press.

L. B. Ames

Greenspan, Stanley

Child psychoanalyst Stanley Greenspan (1941–) and his colleagues have created a structuralist approach to understanding emotional development in the early years. Their classification system identifies behaviors in infants and young children as related to descriptions of caregiver behaviors. This system is helping practitioners provide support and remedial intervention for very young children.

References

Greenspan, S. (1990). Comprehensive clinical approaches to infants and their families: Psychodynamic and developmental perspectives. In S. Meisels & J. Shonkoff (eds.), *Handbook of early childhood intervention* (pp. 150–171). New York: Cambridge University Press.

Greenspan, S., & Greenspan, M. (1985). *First feelings.* New York: Viking.

A. Axtmann

Hall, G. Stanley

Influenced by the work of Charles Darwin and Ernst Haeckel, G. Stanley Hall (1844–1924) stated that the stages of the individual's mental development reenacted the steps of evolution, in effect, that ontogeny recapitulates phylogeny. His importance to the field of early childhood consists primarily in his then novel emphasis on empirical investigations.

Hall and his students constructed 194 questionnaires on such topics as anger, doll play, toys, the sense of self, children's fears, animism, and pity. He also studied and reported on children's curiosity, collecting, the contents of children's minds, and he applied his findings to education. This work extended by that of his followers initiated the child study movement in the United States.

Consistent with the views of his contemporaries in the medical profession and society in general (with the exclusion of feminists), G. Stanley Hall advocated that girls receive an education different from boys. He voiced the then current view that higher education would interfere with the woman's ability and/ or desire to be a mother.

G. Stanley Hall founded the first United States psychology laboratory in 1883 at The Johns Hopkins University and the first psychological periodical in this country, the *American Journal of Psychology*, in 1887. He promoted the founding of the American Psychological Association in 1892 and served as its first president. While at Clark University in 1905, he sponsored Sigmund Freud's lecture tour in the United States. Hall is considered to be the first United States child psychologist, and also contributed to the early study of adolescence.

References

Haeckel, E. (1874). *Anthropogenie* (2nd. ed). Leipzig: Engelmann.

Hall, G. S. (1904). *Adolescence: Its psychology, and its relations to physiology, anthropology, sociology, sex, crime, religion and education*. New York: Appleton.

Hall, G. S. (1907). *Aspects of child life and education*. Boston: Ginn.

Hall, G. S. (1923). *Life and confessions of a psychologist*. New York: Appleton.

R. Formanek

Isaacs, Susan Sutherland (Fairhurst)

Susan Isaacs' (1885–1948) writings about education and child development were based largely on her experience as director of the Malting House School for Young Children in Cambridge, England. She and the school's educational staff made written observations of children in the school setting. They produced a detailed body of descriptive data that illuminated adult and child interactions as well as the interplay of cognitive, social, and emotional aspects of development. Susan Isaacs highlighted the importance of play both for children's development and as a vehicle for enriching adults' understanding of children's ideas and fantasies.

Isaacs was a psychoanalytically oriented educator, influenced by both Melanie Klein and John Dewey, although she denied that Malting House was a "psychoanalytic school." She was knowledgeable about the controversial psychological issues of the time, many of which continue into the present. She argued for the value of qualitative records as opposed to developmental and rating scales that were associated with the work of Arnold Gesell. She questioned Jean Piaget's use of clinical interviews as a way to study children's reasoning and moral development, preferring to study children in the context of everyday life.

References

Isaacs, S. S. (1930/1960). *Intellectual growth of children*. London: Routledge & Kegan Paul.

Isaacs, S. S. (1933/1972). *Social development in young children*. New York: Schocken.

E. K. Shapiro

Mahler, Margaret

Margaret Mahler (1897–1985), a psychoanalyst, presented a theory of separation and individuation applying to the first three years of life that is based on a longitudinal observational study. Mahler's theory of developing individuality and beginning emotional object constancy is divided into the subphases of Differentiation and the Development of Body Image, Practicing, Rapprochement, and Consolidation.

Mahler's theory has been challenged by Daniel Stern's position that the infant possesses a sense of emergent self from birth and is able to self-organize from birth (Stern, 1985). Mahler's views, nevertheless, continue to influence practitioners' thinking about the toddler years.

References

Mahler, M., Pine, F., & Bergman, A. (1975). *The psychoanalytic birth of the human infant: Symbiosis and individuation*. New York: Basic Books.

Stern, D. (1985). *The interpersonal world of the infant: A view from psychoanalysis and developmental psychology*. New York: Basic Books.

A. Axtmann

Piaget, Jean

Jean Piaget (1896–1980), a Swiss epistemologist, studied children as a means of investigating the nature, sources, and development of human knowledge. His theory of constructivism describes stages of development in the child's process of constructing knowledge. Constructivism states that human beings acquire knowledge by building it from the inside, rather than by internalizing it directly from the outside. For example, for infants at birth, objects do not exist unless they are in sight. As babies construct spatial relationships, based on their experiences, they create the idea for themselves that objects continue to exist in space even when they are not visible. Constructivists oppose empiricism, the theory stating that knowledge has its sources in the environment and that the child acquires it by internalizing it directly through the senses.

The educational implication of constructivism is that teachers must encourage children's mental actions, their process of making sense of things and events by going through many levels of trial and error. This principle is in contrast with traditional education that tries to transmit knowledge and moral values in ready-made forms.

References

Piaget, J. (1951/1946). *Play, dreams, and imitation in childhood*. New York: Norton.

Piaget, Jean. (1965/1932). *The moral judgment of the child*. New York: Free Press.

Piaget, Jean. (1973/1948). *To understand is to invent*. New York: Grossman.

Piaget, J., & Inhelder, B. (1969/1966). *The psychology of the child*. New York: Basic Books.

C. Kamii

Preyer, Wilhelm Thierry

(See Section 4.1, History of Child Development and Learning Theory, above)

Skinner, Burrhus Frederic

B. F. Skinner (1904–1989) transformed John B. Watson's classical behaviorism into contemporary behavior analysis, superseding a mechanistic stimulus-response psychology with one that emphasized the selection of behavior based upon its consequences. Behavior is presumed to be lawful and orderly, as well as understandable to the extent that it can be predicted and controlled by the variables of which it is a function.

Beginning with animal psychology, he studied the distinction between respondent (reflex) and operant behavior and analyzed operant behavior as activity that was strengthened or repeated as a consequence of rewards or punishments. His unit of analysis comprised a three-term contingency, including an antecedent stimulus leading to a response and then to a consequent stimulus. He delineated principles that described the functional interdependencies among the contingency events as well as methods and apparatus for the experimental analysis of the behavior of individual organisms, such as the operant chamber known as the Skinner Box.

In his later studies he analyzed the complex contingencies of reinforcement, interpreted language in terms of established principles of behavior, made distinctions between contingency-shaped behavior—activity shaped and maintained by its consequences, such as catching a ball—and rule-governed behavior—activity governed by verbal rules such as following directions. He applied his analysis to education in such forms as programmed instruction, as well as to cultural practices such as economic, social, and political systems.

Currently, the experimental analysis of behavior is integral to an ongoing strand of research on learning and motivation. The applications of behavior analysis are prominent in the form of some classroom management and peer tutoring systems, as well as in clinical psychology practices that train persons with developmental disabilities to improve their language and social skills. They also can be found in the fields of rehabilitation, such as for head injuries. B. F. Skinner's philosophy of the science of behavior remains an alternative philosophy of the mind.

References

Skinner, B. F. (1968). *Science and human behavior.* New York: Free Press.

E. K. Morris & J. T. Todd

Vygotsky, Lev Semenovich

L. S. Vygotsky (1896–1934) generally is regarded as the seminal figure in twentieth century Soviet psychology. Raised in the small provincial city of Gomel, he studied law, philosophy, and psychology in Moscow just prior to the Russian Revolution. After his studies he served for several years on the Teachers College faculty in Gomel (1917–1924), and then returned to Moscow, where he quickly rose to a position of eminence in psychological circles, largely through his ability to join psychological theorizing and inquiry to Marxist principles.

Vygotsky periodically was afflicted with tuberculosis during the last 15 years of his life. Despite this, he was a man of enormous energy and genius whose value as a psychological and educational thinker is only now receiving recognition in the West. Because of his illness his prodigious accomplishments were a race against time. Shortly after his death in 1934 at the age of 37, his works were suppressed by Stalin's regime and were not resuscitated until the mid-1950s. Although, strictly speaking, Vygotsky is a historical figure, his ideas continue to have a timeliness and freshness, particularly in the West. His theory draws society, thinking, language, development, and learning into a systematic synthesis that transcends its early twentieth-century Marxist origins.

The basic claim of Vygotsky's theory is that all higher mental functions have their origin in social relations and practice. The structure and import of significant social practice is deposited by society into sign systems, particularly spoken language. Speech, in turn, is actively internalized by the developing child and serves to transform biologically given mental functions, such as memory, perception, and attention, into historically and socioculturally conditioned functions.

Perhaps Vygotsky's greatest contribution was the recognition that meaning is a necessary component of both collective social life and individual mental life. Consequently, the mechanism that mediates between society and the child's mind necessarily must be simultaneously social, mental, and meaningful. He proposed spoken language as the most obvious and ubiquitous instance of such a mediating process. As the verbally encoded terms of social practice are internalized, they increasingly become the terms of the child's mental life and, conversely, the terms in which the child externalizes his or her contributions to society. Thus, to paraphrase the title of one of Vygotsky's books, *Mind in Society,* the theory construes human development as the bidirectional process of getting society into the mind and the mind into society.

References

Rieber, R. W., & Carton, A. S. (eds.). (1987). *The collected works of L. S. Vygotsky.* (trans., Minick). New York: Plenum.
Vygotsky, L. S. (1978). *Mind in society.* Cambridge: Harvard University Press.

P. C. Lee

Watson, John Broadus

John B. Watson (1878–1958), founded and actively promoted classical behaviorism, and was instrumental in transforming the study of the mind into the study of behavior. He also extended his study of child development and popularized his views in advice to parents.

His early experimental and ethological research on nonhumans included studies in maze learning, perception, homing, and the relationships between brain physiology and behavior. These studies focused on the learning ability of young animals.

Later, he studied human children's development of emotions and such skills as handedness, emphasizing that learning was a lifelong process. In his often cited article, "Conditioned Emotional Reactions" (1920), known as the "Little Albert" case study, he and Rosalie Rayner examined how a child could acquire fears through classical (Pavlovian) conditioning. They associated a fear-eliciting noise (unconditioned aversive stimulus) with a rat (a neutral stimulus), and conditioned Albert to fear the rodent (now a conditioned aversive stimulus).

His later work included child behavior therapy through systematic desensitization and modeling and wrote and lectured actively on behaviorism and child rearing. Some of his later views, regarded as extreme by some, included strict behaviorism and the recommendation that children should be rotated among caregivers.

References

Buckley, K. W. (1989). *Mechanical man: J.B. Watson and the beginnings of behaviorism.* New York: Guilford.

Watson, J. B. (1930). *Behaviorism* (2nd ed). New York: Norton.

Watson, J. B., & Watson, R. R. (1928). *The psychological care of infant and child.* New York: Norton.

E. K. Morris & J. T. Todd

Whiting, Beatrice, and Whiting, John

Beatrice Whiting (1914–) and John Whiting (1908–) have worked as anthropologists who studied the interaction of culture and human development. They have attempted to integrate psychoanalytic and learning theory concepts to explain personality development.

Their studies began with climate, ecology, and modes of subsistence—factors that shape cultural patterns of daily life, which in turn influence customs of child rearing. They also studied the relative influences of cultural and biological influences on development and behavior.

Their methods set new standards for cross-cultural research. John Whiting showed how to use extant files of anthropological data to test systematically hypotheses about socialization patterns and child and adult behaviors. Beatrice Whiting collected precise new observational data to compare child life around the world.

The Six Culture Study, and its outgrowths, provide the most complete accounts available of the learning environments experienced by human infants and children in relation to the goals and expectations of the culture in which they live.

References

Whiting, B. B. (ed.). (1963). *Six cultures: Studies of Child Rearing.* Cambridge: Harvard University Press.

Whiting, B. B., & Edwards, C. P. (1988). *Children of different worlds: The formation of social behavior.* Cambridge: Harvard University Press.

Whiting, J. W. M., & Child, I. L. (1953). *Child training and personality.* New Haven, CT: Yale University Press

C. P. Edwards

4.3 Theories of Child Development and Learning

The articles that follow contain descriptions of five major theories of child development and learning that have been influential in the United States. These articles extend some of the preceding biographical sketches and overviews. With rare exceptions, it is unlikely to find any one of these theoretical positions practiced in a consistently pure form. It is more likely that observations of early childhood programs would indicate a stronger orientation toward one or more of these positions than toward another.

At the present time, there is a strong research trend that is building from constructivist theory toward educational practices. Most professional observers of early childhood education settings can identify the predominating theories in a particular setting, as well as the possible alternative, sometimes contradictory practices that reflect the varied training and beliefs of the administrators and teachers. Parents who are considering which of several possible local child care centers or nursery schools to select might review these theories and weigh the values that they imply in relation to their own.

D. P. Fromberg

Behaviorist

The first behavioral accounts of development emerged around 1920 with John B. Watson's classical behaviorism, and formal theories emerged in the 1940s when research on learning began to influence experimental child psychology. With the passing of that tradition into the 1970s, Sidney W. Bijou and Donald M. Baer's behavior analysis of child development became, and remain, the dominant behavioral perspective. John B. Watson is known best for extending classical (Pavlovian) conditioning to the acquisition and elimination of emotions. He advised Mary Cover Jones as she systematically desensitized a child's fear of rabbits by bringing the child and rabbit into progressively closer contact while in the presence of child-preferred food and peers.

Classical behaviorism envisioned development as a lifelong process that could be studied objectively. Some commentators see a possible limitation in John B. Watson's seeming denial of biological and mental contributions to development. Critics view his theory as mechanistic, empty-organism psychology.

The first behavioral theories of development were stimulus-response learning theory accounts of psychoanalytic concepts concerning social and personality development. These social learning theories (SLTs) were based on Clark Hull's drive-reduction model, which proposes that behavior is set in motion by stimuli that arouse internal conditioned and unconditioned drives. Thus, when a response produced conditions that were seen as reducing the drives, that response was learned. This (psycho)dynamic SLT was developed and expanded mainly between the 1940s and 1960s by John Dollard, Neal Miller, and Robert Sears. It was used to explain the development of early parent-child relations, including dependency, identification, and sex-typing. Jacob L. Gewirtz also contributed to this

tradition, offering behavior-analytic accounts of social development in terms of attachment and dependency.

The next generation of social learning theorists, during the period between 1960 and 1980, began to account for development in terms of mediating cognitive, rather than drive reduction, processes. According to this theory, represented by the work of Albert Bandura, there were additional cognitive control processes taking place between stimulus and response such as attributions, representations, and feelings of efficacy.

Research in this tradition contributed to the literatures on aggression, imitation, and observational learning. By the mid-1970s, cognitive SLT was eclipsed by Jean Piaget's cognitive-developmental theory and subsequently became more a theory of social cognition that considered how children's knowledge affected their behavior.

The current behavior analysis of development differs significantly from the older traditions by encompassing both public and private activity, such as covert self-instruction, as its subject matter; by incorporating both Pavlovian/respondent and reinforcement/operant behavioral processes; and by viewing biology as part of all behavior. Unlike SLT, behavior analysis does not invoke intervening hypothetical constructs to explain relationships between behavior and the environment, but rather takes those constructs, such as drives and cognition, as references to behavioral relations that require explanation.

From the outset, Sidney W. Bijou, Donald M. Baer, and their colleagues have applied the behavior analysis of development in early childhood and special education as well as in clinical child psychology. More recently, the behavior analysis approach to development has begun to (a) analyze the contexts in which the behavioral processes such as reinforcement are embedded, including such setting events as the effects of aversive social encounters on the functions of other social stimuli; and (b) view development as a continuously evolving historical process in which both the child and the environment actively and interdependently engage. Thus, the movement appears to be toward less implicitly mechanistic and more explicitly contextual views.

References

Bandura, A. (1977). *Social learning theory*. Englewood Cliffs, NJ: Prentice-Hall.

Bijou, S. W. (1989). Behavior analysis. In R. Vasta (ed.), *Annals of child development Vol. 6, Six theories of child development: Revised formulations and current issues* (pp. 61–83). Greenwich, CT: JAI Press.

Bijou, S. W., & Baer, D. M. (1978). *The behavior analysis of child development*. Englewood Cliffs, NJ: Prentice-Hall.

Gewirtz, J. L. (ed.). (1972). *Attachment and dependency*. New York: Wiley.

Miller, N. E., & Dollard, J. (1941). *Social learning and imitation*. New Haven, CT: Yale University Press.

Sears, R. R., Maccoby, E., & Levin, H. (1957). *Patterns of child rearing*. New York: Harper.

Watson, J. B., & Watson, R. R. (1928). *The psychoanalytic care of infant and child*. New York: Norton.

E. K. Morris & B. D. Midgley

Constructivist

Constructivism is a general approach to epistemology, that is, to theorizing about the nature of human knowledge. This approach takes the position that knowledge is neither a copy of the external world nor a reflection of pre-formed structures in the mind. Rather it is built up over time as the result of *constructive action* by the knower. The developing child constructs its knowledge and its mind step by step (or stage by stage) from less to more mature forms. In constructivist accounts the term knowledge refers primarily to the structure and dynamic process of knowing and thinking and only secondarily to content.

All versions of constructivism would tend to agree on these general points but would divide sharply in most other respects, depending on where they stand on two issues—knowledge as an individual versus social construction and the role of the real world in the formation of knowledge.

With regard to the first issue, some kinds of constructivism view the formation of knowledge and mind as primarily (or even exclusively) an individual activity. Jean Piaget's theory (see Section 4.2, **Piaget, Jean** above), for example, is a markedly individualist constructivism. The Piagetian infant is an autonomous, self-regulating "physicist" who, first, acts upon the world of objects; second, feeds back into its mind the more general features of its actions; third, builds up its structures of knowledge and mind through this feedback; and fourth, uses these built-up structures to guide its further action upon the world. Through this process the Piagetian infant constructs its knowledge and mind in essential isolation from the input of other people. The most that can be said for social influence in this account is that it has a blocking or restraining function. It does not positively facilitate or amplify the child's constructive actions.

In contrast to the individualist approach, there is also a social development theory type of constructivism (Berger & Luckmann, 1966; Vygotsky, 1962/1986). Social constructivism posits that knowledge exists primarily in the collectively held words, grammars, gestures, and rituals people use to articulate and display meaning to each other. It is out of these basic materials that the child constructs its mind in interaction with others. In Vygotsky's theory, for example, the child grows up in a continuing "conversation" with the other, such as parent, peer, teacher, and internalizes the terms of this conversation as the terms of its own thought. The Vygotskian child collaborates with the other in the *co-construction* of the higher structures of its own mind. In this sense social constructivism construes knowledge and mind as deeply social and presents a strong contrast to individual constructivism.

The various types of constructivism also diverge on the importance assigned to the real world in the construction of knowledge. The Piagetian infant described above is in intimate contact with the actual world of objects. This infant's knowing actions, that is, its knowledge, are jointly constructed by its mind and the objects acted upon. In contrast, the Piagetian adolescent is a formal logician whose thinking is distant from the actual world. Since the mental actions in this "formal operational" stage are guided by the rules internal to logic, their rightness does not require empirical checks with the real world. If, for example, A is greater than B and B is greater than C, then it logically follows that A is greater than C, and no empirical check against reality is necessary. Such rationalist constructions of knowledge assign no importance to the real world. In Piaget's theory, then, we find two types of constructivism—an infant realism and an adolescent rational idealism, the former connected to the real world of objects, and the latter disengaged from it.

The same contrasting treatments of external reality can be found in social constructivism. In some radical social accounts, for example, a "fact" is not something the mind carves out and tests against nature. Rather it is whatever people agree to view as a fact; that is, it is an outcome of social negotiation and may or may not bear any correspondence to external reality. In other kinds of social constructivism, however, the external realities of nature, culture, and history have a significant constructive role, along with the knowing person, in the formation of knowledge. In this more objective type, knowledge is more than a social collusion; it is also tempered and facilitated by an independent and preexisting reality. Vygotsky's theory is a good example of the latter type. In Vygotsky's account, the child co-constructs its own mind with other people and out of the materials provided by culture, society, and nature. Thus, the Vygotskian child is both a social negotiator and a realist.

It should be noted that the differences among the several types of constructivism are more a matter of emphasis than of sharp delineation on every point. All types agree that knowledge is constructed, not pre-formed or copied. They disagree on how it is constructed, that is, on the relative weights they assign to the constructive power of the knowing child, the real world, and other people.

References

Berger, P., & Luckmann, T. (1966). *The social construction of reality*. New York: Doubleday.

Gergen, K. J. (1985). The social constructionist movement in modern psychology. *American Psychologist, 40* (3), 266–275.

Kitchener, R. F. (1986). *Piaget's theory of knowledge*. New Haven, CT: Yale University Press.

Vygotsky, L. S. (1962; sec. ed. 1986). *Thought and language*. Cambridge: MIT Press.

P. C. Lee

Maturationist

Maturation has been defined as the process of bringing, or coming, to full development or maturity. As commonly used in developmental theories of child development, this term contrasts with behavior theory and the processes of conditioning. Maturationists contend, rather, that the nervous system grows according to its own intrinsic pattern and thereby establishes the primary forms of behavior, regardless of outside stimulation.

Maturationists admit to a reciprocal relationship between heredity and environment. Although these forces can be discussed separately in theory, human life depends upon their interaction.

Maturation theory applies equally to mental and physical phenomena. It is possible to consider a maturational kind of mechanism, represented by language, in the sphere of symbolic thinking. At the same time that mental and physical spheres are influenced and elaborated by social and environmental factors, they require a substratum of maturation similar to that which underlies the simpler sensorimotor functions of behavior such as creeping, walking, and prehension.

The affective life of the infant also matures in a way that is similar to mental and physical development. Fear, for instance, may be an original tendency, but it is subject to the genetic alterations of maturation as well as to organization by environmental conditions. In an attempt to understand better the respective influences of heredity and environment, Arnold Gesell studied one of a pair of identical twins as a control, without intervention, while he made substantial efforts to train the other twin in such behaviors as stair climbing, block building, and language. The series of twin studies demonstrated that even when one twin had been trained successfully to perform a behavior, the performance of the untrained twin after a short time was equivalent, without intervening training. He concluded that, although outside intervention can in some instances temporarily speed up or improve some behaviors, it has no substantial or lasting results. The studies concluded that maturational forces appear primarily to determine when any behavior can come to fruition.

Reference

Ames, L. B. (1989). *Arnold Gesell: Themes of his work.* New York: Human Sciences Press.

L. B. Ames

Psychodynamic

Psychodynamic theory, derived from or strongly influenced by the psychoanalytic theory developed by Sigmund Freud, generally refers to theories of human behavior that focus on intrapsychic forces within the individual. Psychoanalytic theory focuses on the early years of life, marking infancy and early childhood as crucial for the later development of personality, thereby highlighting the importance of early experiences.

The image of the infant and young child as a sensual being, besieged by impulse, torn by conflict, and desirous of instant gratification, supplanted a romantic notion of childhood innocence. Sigmund Freud's theory of human sexuality referred to all bodily pleasures as well as adult sexual experience. Although initially controversial, his views have influenced contemporary views about children and sexuality itself.

Perhaps his most significant concept is that of the unconscious, that behavior is determined by impulses, motives, and feelings of which humans are unaware. Thus, observable behavior may have an underlying, latent sig-

nificance as well as a literal, manifest content. In this view, behavior has symbolic as well as obvious significance. This concept led to an interest in children's play and artwork as representations of their feelings, conflicts, fears, fantasies, and understandings.

Freud (1933/1965) hypothesized that psychic life consisted of three powerful interacting forces including the id, the seat of drive and impulse; the ego, the organized reality-centered aspect of the self that emerges from the id as the individual interacts with others and the environment; and the superego, the moral self or conscience, which develops from internalizing parental and societal prohibitions and sanctions. He described a sequence of psychosexual stages that focus on the locus of pleasure and conflict, including the oral, anal, phallic, latent, and genital. Within this framework, he specified the markers of normal as well as pathological development.

He proposed that all young children develop an intense love for the parent of the opposite sex and want to eliminate the same sex parent whom they see as a rival. The Oedipus complex for boys and the Electra, for girls, label this conflict. Inasmuch as these desires are unacceptable to society as well as the child, they normally are repressed. In learning to cope with "instinctual drives" and adapting to social demands, children develop various defenses such as repression, projection, and sublimation.

Psychoanalytic theory emphasized the role of the parents, especially mothers, in children's development. Inasmuch as parents have enormous control over their children's lives, they may use their authority well or abuse it. These observations have implications for the potential role of the teacher.

There were attempts, in the early days, to construct a model of child rearing or education that was free of conflict. This goal was found to be impossible because social constraints and some frustration are inevitable conditions of human life. A more realistic role for adults, however, included mediating child conflict and thwarting irrational needs while clarifying confusion, explaining prohibitions, and limiting threats. Several educational enterprises that were inspired by the goal of creating environments to minimize conflict were A. S. Neill's Summerhill school in England, Margaret Naumberg's Walden School in New York City, Bruno Bettelheim's Orthogenic School in Chicago, and numerous preschools.

Erik Erikson (1950/1963) reinterpreted the psychosexual stages in ways that accentuated the interactive nature of development while reducing the stress on biological factors. His polarized stages define healthy versus unhealthy adaptation, including trust versus mistrust in infancy, autonomy versus shame and doubt in toddlerhood, initiative versus guilt in the preschool age, and industry versus inferiority in school age children. For adolescents, the core issue is the search for identity versus role diffusion, for young adults, intimacy versus isolation, and for older adults, generativity versus stagnation and ego integrity versus despair. Generativity is an invented term that denotes concern for the next generation in such work as being a teacher, parent, or other worker for child advocacy.

There have been revisions to the basic Freudian theory that include Harry Stack Sullivan's focus on the importance of interpersonal relationships in development, Margaret Mahler's analysis of separation-individuation, and John Bowlby's work on attachment that represents a blend of psychodynamic theory and ethology. In general, psychodynamic theory contrasts with behaviorism, which emphasizes the primacy of external rewards and punishments and other theories that highlight the role of situational factors. Revisions have considered, however, the importance of environmental and interpersonal forces.

References

Erikson, E. (1950/1963). *Childhood and society.* New York: Norton.

Freud, S. (1933/1965). *New introductory lectures on psychoanalysis.* New York: Norton.

E. K. Shapiro

Socialization

Within the field of psychology, a number of theories have attempted to explain socialization, with psychoanalytic and behavioral theories dominating the field during this century. Currently, however, there is an attempt to build an integrated theory of socialization that considers biological and cognitive factors in addition to social and cultural transmission.

Socialization theory is a way to understand and describe how infants and children become partners in social interaction, family members, and citizens. Studies in this field have had a fundamental impact on professional practice in schools, clinical, and medical settings as well as on general child rearing practices.

A major research focus has been on how behaviors, values, motives, and attitudes are transmitted from one generation to the next. Studies of the complex process of socialization have been rooted in the academic disciplines of psychology, sociology, and anthropology. Consequently, complementary research has emerged that deals with individuals, societal roles and institutions, and the surrounding cultural system. The agents of socialization are the persons and institutions that control how and what children learn. In more technical societies, the most powerful agents have been parents, peers, teachers, and the mass media. In more kin-centered cultures, members of the extended family and community such as sibling caretakers, grandparents, and religious elders, may predominate.

The process of socialization denotes direct reinforcements such as rewards and punishments as one important method of influence. Observation, imitation, and identification are the other main ways that children learn from people, especially from their attachment and authority figures. The socialization process also can be described by considering stages of socialization, that is, the qualitatively different agendas held by people at different life stages.

In addition, a theory of socialization accounts for contexts of socialization that are available to children such as home, child care center, school, and neighborhood. Societal and cultural values determine what kinds of work, play, and learning activities are possible in these settings as well as who might be the child's social partners. The age, gender, and kinship relations of other people to the child strongly influence what kinds of social interaction each child will observe, find useful, and practice.

Children participate in shaping their own socialization. They select their own preferred models for imitation and identification as well as their own favorite settings and activities, thereby influencing the direction in which their personalities develop.

References

Damon, W. (1983). *Social and personality development: Infancy through adolescence.* New York: Norton.

Handel, G. (ed.). (1988). *Childhood socialization.* Hawthorne, NY: Aldine de Gruyter.

Whiting, B., & Edwards, C. P. (1988). *Children of different worlds: The formation of social behavior.* Cambridge: Harvard University Press.

C. P. Edwards

4.4 Domains of Development

Different theories of child development imply different directions for pursuing research that might confirm or deny the assertions of the theory. Investigators have engaged in studies that attempt to describe the directions and stages of children's development from particular perspectives. They also have attempted to understand how growth takes place by looking at behaviors that characterize young children. Although these characteristics are integrated within a unique mix of personal, social, and other contextual factors for each child, the articles attempt to focus on them in turn as a way to highlight their combined importance. There is a discussion of some of the investigators' findings in the section that follows. It is organized alphabetically, except where logic suggests otherwise, into various domains of development that define the char-

acteristics of young children from a variety of points of view.

D. P. Fromberg

Aesthetic Development

People engage in aesthetic and art experiences whenever they attend to the appearances of things and find them interesting. Aesthetic experiences begin at birth and gradually are shaped by culture (Parsons, 1987). Most researchers agree that the early stages of aesthetic development are universal in that they exist in all cultures (Feldman, 1980).

In the scribbling and early symbolic stages, the child has little grasp of the idea of pictorial representation. Part of the development of aesthetic experience is the advent of "romancing," the ability to invent or read one's own meaning into subject matter (Gardner, 1980).

Mildred J. Parsons (1987) has proposed a stage theory of aesthetic development that begins in the preschool years. At this stage, children experience "intuitive delight" in most paintings, a compelling interest in color, and an imaginative associative response to subject matter. Paintings, along with other pleasurable experiences such as hearing a story read or singing a song, engender strong reactions from children who enjoy experiences for their own sake. Inasmuch as young children are egocentric, adults would not expect them to analyze the relevance of elements to a specific artwork or to appreciate others' perspectives. One view holds that children at this age are "a-dualistic" in that they cannot be expected to distinguish between self and other, thought and action, and internal and external influences (Baldwin, 1911).

When children are at the stage of beginning elementary school, they deal primarily with representation and emulation of subject matter that is marked by realism and conventional beauty. They are able to derive meaning and organize responses about the subject matter. Adults do not expect them to be aware that the experiences of others differ from their own. Although children now can separate themselves from the object world, they do not yet possess reflective ability. Preferring realistic and conventional beauty, reflected by societal influences, they interpret expressions of works of art as simply sad, happy, or weird, with concrete emotions attributed to the subject that is portrayed. The capacity to be reflective about art and aesthetic experience changes with age and appears in different forms at each developmental stage. Understanding the work of art for its beauty, expressiveness, and other significant qualities is a goal that is common to artistic development.

References

Baldwin, J. M. (1911). *Thought and action*. George Allen.

Feldman, D. H. (1980). *Beyond universals in cognitive development*. Norwood, NJ: Ablex.

Gardner, H. (1980). *Artful scribbles*. New York: Basic Books.

Parsons, M. J. (1987). *How we understand art*. New York: Cambridge University Press.

A. C. Swann

Cognitive-Intellectual Development

Young children think differently from adults. The ancients recognized this truism (Lao-tse, 604–531 B.C.; Plato, 428–348 B.C.), as have many others since then. An important innovation, beginning in the last century (starting with Preyer, 1881/1889), has been the use of more-or-less standard observational categories to describe children's thinking. The research literature of developmental psychology has collected observational categories to create a kind of observational catalog of the multifarious ways in which growing children's intellects change (e.g., Cohen & Gross, 1979; Flavell & Markman, 1983). Out of this catalog, investigators have constructed innumerable chronologies showing what the changes are, when they typically occur, and in what order they typically occur. Any such chronology must first define what to include, at each age, under the term "cognitive-intellectual."

The discussion that follows describes four prevalent approaches to defining "cognitive-intellectual." Cognitive developmental works cited below are sources for their respective chronologies of cognitive-intellectual.

Development in Epistemological Concepts

A philosophical analysis of fundamental assumptions and concepts on which humans build knowledge and understanding is one approach to defining "cognitive-intellectual." The eighteenth-century philosophers David Hume and Immanuel Kant, for example, wrote about such *epistemologies*. Others subsequently have used their categories for analyzing human understanding as a framework to observe children's psychological development. Bühler (1930) and Stern (1924, 391–397) took this approach in their studies of when and how young children develop *causal inference*, as Hume conceived of it. Piaget (1928, 1929, 1930, 1954) took this approach when he examined development in terms of quantity, substance, number, part-whole relations, causality, and other Kantian categories (Elkind & Flavell, 1969; Sigel & Hooper, 1968). A weakness of this approach is that it begs the question of whether the philosophical framework was a good one to choose. A strength is that the emergence of such philosophical categories has proven to be observable in children.

Development Relative to Age Norms

An approach that has complementary strengths and weaknesses is the approach taken by Binet and Simon (1916), in whose laboratory Piaget once worked. The Binet-Simon approach heavily influenced the work of Gesell (1926) and his successors (e.g., Ames et al., 1979). Extending the empirical tradition of the child study movement (Kirkpatrick, 1917; Preyer, 1881/1889), Binet and Simon cataloged a diverse array of tasks in terms of observed *task mental age*—the age at which 65 percent to 75 percent of children can successfully perform the task (Terman, 1916, pp. 36–37). *Child mental age* describes the upper level of task difficulty (as gauged by task mental age) that a child can successfully perform at a given point in time—irrespective of the child's chronological age.

A weakness of the Binet-Simon approach, noted by Wohlwill (1973), is that its definition of development is inherently age calibrated, thereby preordaining age differences. A corollary criticism is that its definition of development inherently is tied to the group in which norms for task mental age are observed, thereby preordaining a culture-loaded definition of development. In a sense, this approach also begs the question of what counts as "cognitive-intellectual": Although Binet's theory of intelligence emphasized a person's ability to judge, comprehend, and reason, the tasks that Binet and Simon actually catalogued were so varied as to defy rational juxtaposition. A strength of this approach is that the resulting descriptions of development are applicable simultaneously to *between-age differences* and *within-age differences* (in individual precocity or intelligence). And there is a contention among developmentalists (Fischer, 1980) that any theory of cognitive development should address both kinds of differences.

Development in Working Memory
Adults' limited capacity to process information (Miller, 1956) is a kind of ceiling toward which children expand. A third approach to defining "cognitive-intellectual" focuses on this capacity, which has been termed "attention span" (Baldwin, 1895), "mental grasp" (Kirkpatrick, 1917, 279–280), "M-power" or "M-space" (Case, 1974, 1985; Pascual-Leone, 1980), and (by most information-processing psychologists) *working memory*. Investigators within this framework study such questions as, How many things can a child keep simultaneously in mind? How much disruption of thought processes is caused when more items to juggle mentally are added? The increase in working memory as children grow older plausibly can account for some important developmental phenomena that Piaget described (Case, 1985; Pascual-Leone, 1980). And individual differences in working memory plausibly can account for some within-age intellectual differences that Binet and his successors have described (Jensen, 1982). Thus, a strength of this approach is that it addresses both *within-age differences* and *between-age differences*. A weakness is that its definition of what counts as cognitive-intellectual is too restrictive. In terms of Sternberg's (1988) three components of human intelligence, this approach emphasizes *performance components* of human intelligence and disregards *metacomponents* and *knowledge-acquisition components*.

Development in Representation
A fourth approach to defining "cognitive-intellectual" focuses on the mental representations that children use. This approach, generally classified as *cognitive science* (Posner, 1989), has roots in Gestalt psychology (Koffka, 1925) and the work of others (Bruner, 1966a, 1966b; Craik, 1943; Vygotsky 1934/1962, 1978). The theorists and researchers connected with cognitive science mainly attribute qualitative shifts in children's performance to changes in the mental representations that children use. Children, in this view, shift their representational capacities partly by internalizing aspects of their cultural environment and partly by personal constructions.

"Figurative schemes," in the neo-Piagetian parlance of Case (1974), develop that represent ideas, facts, and perceivable patterns. "Production systems" (Klahr, 1989), "problem-solving rules" (Siegler, 1981), or "operative schemes" (Case, 1974) reflect a second type of development that represents rules for mental and physical actions that children can take.

In a third type of development, children employ master plans by which they orchestrate other types of representation that developmentalists refer to as "metacomponents" (Sternberg, 1988) or "executive schemes" (Case, 1974). As Gardner (1985, pp. 383–384) has bemoaned, "Any number of vocabularies and frameworks have been constructed in an effort to characterize the representational level—scripts, schemas, symbols, frames, images, mental models, to name just a few. And any number of terms describe the operations carried out upon these mental entities—transformations, conjunctions, deletions, reversals, and so on." A strength of this approach is its generality: It can embrace all types of intellectual activity, and it has proven to be a powerful tool for analyzing children's performance. A weakness is that one cannot say whether developmental changes stem from newly learned symbols, per se, or from underlying changes in cognitive architectures, which thereby made the new form of symbol processing learnable (Newell, Rosenbloom, & Laird, 1989).

Nature-Nurture in Development

There are alternative explanations about what gives rise to development, regardless of any description of it. In this matter, development has its own nature-nurture debate. Those whose explanations are at the nature end of the spectrum emphasize the influence of maturation and neural architecture (biological processes thought to be primarily under genetic control). Those at the nurture end emphasize the social and physical environment as sources of change. How to apportion credit between nature and nurture for within-age differences is a debate that has raged for more than half a century; apportioning credit for between-age differences is no simpler.

We may one day conclude that the nature-nurture debate was a historical dead end into which we led ourselves by asking the wrong question. As studies of the individual appropriateness of instruction have shown, neural architecture sometimes dictates not whether an intellectual function can be performed, but how best to perform it (Brown & Campione, 1982; Feuerstein, 1980). The neural architecture of our brains, far from being fixed by genes, can itself change in response to the environment we experience (Diamond, 1991). Successes of genetic engineering suggest that, as our knowledge grows, even the genes themselves will be subject to environment-wrought change. Lastly, as studies of cultural context have shown, the question is sometimes a matter neither of "can do" nor of "how to do," but of "whether to do" (Au & Mason, 1983; Heath, 1983).

References

Ames , L. B., Gillespie, C., Haines, J., & Ilg, F. L. (1979). *The Gesell Institute's child from one to six: Evaluating the behavior of the preschool child.* New York: Harper & Row.

Au, K. H., & Mason, J. M. (1983). Cultural congruence in classroom participation structures: Achieving a balance of rights. *Discourse Processes, 6* (2), 145–167.

Baldwin, J. M. (1895). *Mental development in the child and the race: Methods and processes.* New York: Macmillan.

Binet, A., & Simon, T. (1916). *The development of intelligence in children.* Trans. by E. S. Kite. Baltimore: Williams & Wilkins. (Originally published in 1908 in *Année Psychologique.*)

Brown, A. L., & Campione, J. C. (1982). Modifying intelligence or modifying cognitive skills: More than a semantic quibble? In D. K. Detterman & R. J. Sternberg (eds.), *How and how much can intelligence be increased* (pp. 215–230). Norwood, NJ: Ablex.

Bruner, J. (1966a). On cognitive growth. In J. S. Bruner, R. R. Oliver, & P. M. Greenfield (eds.), *Studies in cognitive growth* (pp. 1–29). New York: Wiley.

Bruner, J. (1966b). On cognitive growth II. In J. S. Bruner, R. R. Olver, & P. M. Greenfield (eds.), *Studies in cognitive growth* (pp. 30–67). New York: Wiley.

Bühler, K. (1930). *Die geistige Entwicklung des Kindes* (5 ed.). (O. A. Oeser, trans.). *The mental development of the child: A summary of modern psychology theory.* New York: Harcourt, Brace.

Case, R. (1974). Structures and strictures: Some functional limitations on the course of cognitive growth. *Cognitive Psychology, 6* (4), 544–574.

Case, R. (1985). *Intellectual development from birth to adulthood.* New York: Academic Press.

Cohen, M. A., & Gross, P. J. (1979). *The developmental resource: Behavioral sequences for assessment and program planning* (Vols. 1 & 2). New York: Grune & Stratton.

Craik, K. (1943). *The nature of explanation.* Cambridge, England: Cambridge University Press.

Diamond, M. C. (1991). *Enriching heredity: The impact of the environment on the anatomy of the brain.* New York: The Free Press.

Elkind, D., & Flavell, J. H. (eds.). (1969). *Studies in cognitive development: Essays in honor of Jean Piaget.* New York: Oxford University Press.

Feuerstein, R. (1980). *Instrumental enrichment: An intervention program for cognitive modifiability.* Baltimore: University Park Press.

Fischer, K. (1980). A theory of cognitive development: The control and construction of hierarchies of skills. *Psychological Review, 87* (6), 477–531.

Flavell, J. H., & Markman, E. M. (eds.). (1983). *Handbook of child psychology: Vol. 3. Cognitive development.* (P. H. Mussen, series ed.). New York: Wiley.

Gardner, H. (1985). *The mind's new science: A history of the cognitive revolution.* New York: Basic Books.

Gesell, A. (1926). *The mental growth of the pre-school child.* New York: Macmillan.

Heath, S. B. (1983). *Ways with words: Language. life, and work in communities and classrooms.* New York: Cambridge University Press.

Jensen, A. R. (1982). The chronometry of intelligence. In R. J. Sternberg (ed.), *Advances in the psychology of human intelligence* (Vol. 1). Hillsdale, NJ: Erlbaum.

Kirkpatrick, E. A. (1917). *Fundamentals of child study* (3rd ed.). New York: Macmillan.

Klahr, D. (1989). Information processing approaches to cognitive development. In R. Vasta (ed.), *Annals of child development* (pp. 131–183). Greenwich, CT: JAI Press.

Koffka, K. (1925). *The growth of the mind.* New York: Harcourt, Brace.

Miller, G. A. (1956). The magical number seven, plus or minus two: Some limits on our capacity for processing information. *Psychological Review, 63* (2), 81–97.

Newell, A., Rosenbloom, P. S., & Laird, J. E. (1989). In M. I. Posner (ed.), *Foundations of cognitive science* (pp. 93–131). Cambridge, MA: MIT Press.

Pascual-Leone, J. (1980). Constructive problems for constructive theories: The current relevance of Piaget's work and a critique of information-processing simulation psychology. In R. H. Kluwe & H. Spada (eds.), *Developmental models of thinking* (pp. 263–296). New York: Academic Press.

Piaget, J. (1928). *Judgment and reasoning in the child.* (M. Worden, trans.). New York: Harcourt, Brace. (Originally published in French in 1924.)

Piaget, J. (1929). *The child's conception of the world.* (J. Tomlinson & A. Tomlinson, trans.). New York: Harcourt, Brace. (Originally published in French in 1926.)

Piaget, J. (1930). *The child's conception of physical causality.* (M. Worden, trans.). New York: Harcourt, Brace. (Originally published in French in 1927.)

Piaget, J. (1954). *The construction of reality in the child.* (M. Cook, trans.). New York: Basic Books. (Originally published in French in 1937.)

Posner, M. I. (ed.). (1989). *Foundations of cognitive science.* Cambridge, MA: MIT Press.

Preyer, W. (1889/1881). *The mind of the child, Part II: The development of the intellect.* (H. W. Brown, trans.). New York: Appleton.

Siegler, R. S. (1981). Developmental sequences within and between concepts. *Monographs of the Society for Research in Child Development, 46* (2), Whole No.

Sigel, I. E., & Hooper, F. H. (eds.). (1968). *Logical thinking in children: Research based on Piaget's theory.* New York: Holt, Rinehart and Winston.

Stern, W. (1924). *Psychology of early childhood: Up to the sixth year of age* (3rd ed.). (A. Barwell, trans.). New York: Henry Holt and Company.

Sternberg, R. J. (1988). *The triarchic mind: A new theory of human intelligence.* New York: Penguin Books.

Sternberg, R. J. (1990). Wisdom and its relations to intelligence and creativity. In R. J. Sternberg (ed.), *Wisdom: Its nature, origins, and development* (pp. 142–159). New York: Cambridge University Press.

Terman, L. M. (1916). *The measurement of intelligence.* Boston: Houghton Mifflin.

Vygotsky, L. S. (1934/1962). *Thought and language* (E. Hanfmann & G. Vakar, trans.). Cambridge, MA: MIT Press.

Vygotsky, L. S. (1978). *Mind in society: The development of higher psychological processes* (M. Cole, V. John-Steiner, S. Scribner, & E. Souberman, eds. and trans.). Cambridge: Harvard University Press.

Wohlwill, J. F. (1973). *The study of behavioral development.* New York: Academic Press.

G. G. Price

Emotional and Social Development

There is a strong interaction between emotional, social, and cognitive development in early childhood, which depends upon environment and opportunity.

Observations of the earliest experiences between the infant and primary caregiver can reveal the young child's repertoire of emotions. By three months of age, infants may feel emotions such as joy, interest, surprise, fear, anger, disgust, and sadness. Elation and affection develop by the end of the first year, and jealousy, by eighteen months of age (Fallon & McGovern, 1978).

Erik Erikson (1950/1963) presented three psychosocial stages that define the early years of life. In infancy, a reliable caregiver can promote a sense of trust, whereas inconsistent handling can lead to feelings of anxiety, upset, and a sense of mistrust. Early childhood, corresponding in this framework to the child's second year of life, is a time when children increasingly attempt to control their own behavior and establish feelings of autonomy. When children reach the play age, constructive activities begin and the conscience develops. In this stage, they become aware of their abilities to initiate activities and control their environment and themselves.

Children can develop social/emotional competence through both planned and unplanned interactions with adults and peers. Infants tend to engage in solitary play, exploring toys and objects in their environment rather than interacting with peers. As children grow older, their dependence on peers increases. During the second year of life, opportunities for parallel play can support the evolution of taking turns and interactive social play. Research has found that experience with peers, rather than chronological age in itself, affects the type of play that takes place (Howes, 1980). Through pretend play, children practice and develop an understanding of social roles and interactions. Developmentally appropriate play opportunities can enhance the social competence of young children.

Emotional understanding is necessary to the development of a sense of self and to relationships with others. Children begin with a recognition of feelings, such as happiness, sadness, and anger, until, around the age of five years, they begin to understand how others may feel about them. Teachers who provide opportunities for appropriate play experiences can support healthy emotional development.

Activities that enhance the acquisition of emotional competence would include talking about the incidents that arouse feelings and the ways in which children express their feelings. For example, preschoolers can discuss the things that make them sad or happy. They can learn that it is all right to become angry, but the feeling should be expressed by words rather than by hitting, fighting, or destruction of materials. They also can learn to interpret facial expressions and tones of voice that signify specific feelings. Interpreting others' feelings can help children to develop positive social interactions. Teachers have effectively used photographs, stories, and songs in order to help children explore their feelings and behaviors. Modeling, role playing, and the use of puppets also help young children to practice alternative behaviors in a risk-free setting.

References

Erikson, E. H. (1950/1963). *Childhood and society.* (2nd ed). New York: Norton.

Fallon, N. H., & McGovern, J. E. (1978). *Young children with special needs.* Columbus, OH: Merrill.

Howes, C. (1980). Peer play scale as an index of complexity of peer interaction. *Developmental Psychology, 16* (4), 371–372.

R. Gold

Infant Emotional Development

Infant emotional capacities are, in fact, quite organized, as investigators have shown by using new theoretical perspectives along with recent methodological advances that include objective coding schemes for facial expression, gestural behavior, and vocalizing; and videotape recordings of infant behavior.

Infants display affective configurations of facial expressions, gestures, and vocalizations that are appropriate to the meaning of events and their context. For example, infants as young as two months of age smile, make open palm gestures, and display positive vocalizations when a familiar person greets them. They make angry facial expressions, fussy vocalizations, and look away, however, when a person acts in an unusual way. These affective configurations develop sequentially, becoming more differentiated with age so that, by the end of the first year, the infant displays organized configurations of joy, fear, sadness, anger, interest, and possibly shame.

The infant also appreciates and responds to the affective configurations of others, responding to smiles with positive affect configurations, and to expressions of sadness and anger with negative affect behaviors. This exchange of emotional information between infants and their caretakers allows them to engage in and regulate complicated social interactions that are the context for the child's development of personality.

These findings have replaced the view that infant emotions are disorganizing forces that disrupt directed behavior and require cognitive regulation. Sigmund Freud argued, for example, that the ego must develop in order to control the id (libidinal forces). Current research methods, however, reveal that infants can focus emotional behavior and behave in socially responsive ways.

References

Tronick, E. Z. (1989). Emotions and emotional communication in infants. *American Psychologist, 44*, (2), 112–19.

Mussen, P. H. (ed.). (1983). *Handbook of child psychology, Vol. 2., Infancy and developmental psychology*. New York: Wiley.

E. Z. Tronick

Childhood Emotional Development
(See **Self-Identity**, below.)

Motivation

Most motivation theorists would agree that young children possess, "a fundamental human urge to be effective, competent and independent, to understand the world and to act with skill" (Donaldson, 1979, p. 118). Children who continue to exhibit these characteristics as they mature possess what is known as intrinsic motivation. Children who are intrinsically motivated prefer challenging tasks over easy ones; tend to be motivated by curiosity and the desire to learn, rather than solely by a desire to please the teacher; prefer to work independently rather than to be dependent on their teachers; and tend to be more concerned with doing the best they can rather than performing primarily to gain teacher approval or grades (Stipek, 1986). Because of their sense of autonomy, curiosity, and pride in their accomplishments, such children have positive self-esteem and a strong sense of efficacy.

Many children, however, lose both the desire to learn and the sense of competence that accompanies success shortly after entering formal schooling (Covington & Beery, 1976; Donaldson, 1979; Nicholls, 1989). Although there would appear to be some developmental factors involved in this process, such as the transition from the physical exploration of early childhood to the strictly academic work often required in school, and the increasing ability of children to compare their performance with that of their peers (Dweck & Elliot, 1983; Stipek, 1984), the primary cause is probably the nature of the intellectual and emotional climate of classrooms.

There is agreement among the aforecited authors as well as John Goodlad (1984) that many schools fail to nurture either the competence or curiosity needed for self-motivation. When many of the tasks are set by adults, when the means of performing the tasks are dictated by adults, and when adults often judge the outcomes, children begin to feel powerless and to perceive school as meaningless.

Another common problem is that the messages that adults give students undermine intrinsic motivation. This happens, for example, when teachers give extrinsic rewards such as candy, stickers, or stars for academic performance and provide predominantly evaluative feedback, such as grades and scores, rather than encourage children to view errors as productive learning opportunities. In addition, the competitive ethos of many schools, in which success for one student often comes at the expense of another, easily leads to a decline in self-esteem and a suppression of effort by students who feel less than fully successful or competitive.

The message from the literature is clear. Children gain efficacy from challenge. They gain a sense of autonomy from choice. They become meaningfully involved when the curriculum and teaching approach give primacy to student voice, relevance, and involvement. They learn to focus on learning rather than on performance when they receive informative instead of evaluative feedback. They learn to become competent, independent learners when teachers emphasize learning for learning's sake and create cooperative learning environments.

References

Covington, M. V. O., & Beery, R. G. (1976). *Self-worth and school learning.* New York: Holt, Rinehart & Winston.

Donaldson, M. (1979). *Children's minds.* New York: Norton.

Dweck, C. S., & Elliot, E. S. (1983). Achievement motivation. In E. M. Hetherington (ed.), *Handbook of child psychology: Vol. 4, Socialization, personality, and social development,* (pp. 643–691). New York: Wiley.

Goodlad, J. (1984). *A place called school.* New York: McGraw-Hill.

Nicholls, J. G. (1989). *The competitive ethos and democratic education.* Cambridge: Harvard University Press.

Stipek, D. J. (1984). Developmental aspects of motivation in children. In R. Ames & C. Ames (eds.), *Research on motivation in education: Vol 1. Student motivation,* (pp. 145–174). New York: Academic.

Stipek, D. J. (1986). *Motivation to learn: From theory to practice.* Englewood Cliffs, NJ: Prentice-Hall.

M. O'Loughlin

Self-Esteem

Self-esteem is a person's sense of competence and efficacy resulting in positive feelings of self. The origins of self-esteem begin early in life. Infants whose needs are attended to when they indicate discomfort begin to develop a sense of self. At first an infant's sense of self is physical, but soon the child develops an awareness of self as separate from others in the affective and social domains as well. This sense of self is obtained from the responses and messages of those around the child. These responses and messages shape the concept of self that the child begins to develop. The child who is responded to with consistent care and unconditional love begins to develop self-esteem. Conversely, the child who receives inconsistent care and conditional love receives different messages regarding self and worth (Erikson, 1963/1950).

As young children grow, how they resolve the problems associated with their various social and emotional stages of development affect their feelings toward themselves (Ibid.). When they are successful in resembling the models around them, they achieve self-esteem (Ibid.). As children begin to try out tasks such as walking or talking, their attempts and eventual mastery signal to them how competent they are. The importance given to the tasks are determined by what those around them value. Thus, a critical factor in the development of self-esteem is the culture of the group and what its members value. Children quickly learn the values and rules of the culture into which they are born and by the time they enter school, they already have developed feelings about their self-worth.

In every culture there are demands for achievement. In North American culture, one of the institutionalized areas for achievement is the school. How children experience a sense of competence and achievement in school is related to how their self, family, ethnicity, race, and social class are viewed. Children who experience more than one cultural system can continue to develop self-esteem if the cultural systems are valued. If the home cultural system is not valued, the child experiences conflict and may develop a low self-esteem. How the school reacts to the child, therefore, is also critical to the development of self-esteem.

Children who have learned never to look directly at the person who reprimands them may be confused when the school message is that what has been taught at home is wrong. Similarly, children from cooperative cultures may behave in ways that are antithetical to what is valued in competitive cultures. How children see their efforts appreciated by those significant to them affects how they view themselves as individuals and as part of a group. The simple act of putting a child's picture on display in school or at home may be the source of pride for one child. For another child, to take the picture home will be the accomplishment. Although these examples may be demonstrations of preferences, they also may be learned cultural expectations. Teachers, therefore, must be aware not only of the individual developmental levels of the child but of the expectations of the child's culture as well.

The school can help children to develop self-esteem by responding to their individuality and by including in positive ways their cultures and experiences in the content of teaching, and as an integral part of the teaching process. How people around them react and feel about them deeply affects how children feel about themselves. Children whose backgrounds and experiences are valued gain in confidence and self-esteem. Teachers and adults who work from the strengths children bring to a situation will help children enhance their feelings of worth and self-esteem. Self-esteem has a direct impact on children's motivation and achievement levels in the learning process.

References

Erikson, E. (1963/1950). *Childhood and society* (rev. ed.). New York: Norton.

Erikson, E. (1968). *Identity, youth and crisis.* New York: Norton.

Ramsey, P. G. (1987). *Teaching and learning in a diverse world.* New York: Teachers College Press.

Williams, L. R., De Gaetano, Y., Harrington, C. C., & Sutherland, I. R. (1985). *ALERTA: A multicultural bilingual approach to teaching young children.* Reading, MA: Addison-Wesley.

Y. De Gaetano

Self-Identity

The development of self-identity in children is part of a quest for mastery within the world. The process begins in the security of the child's first attachment, a bond that, if properly formed, gives the child the necessary support to begin the process of separating from the primary caregivers. This bond is necessary in order for the child to establish a trusting relationship with others and to act upon the world.

The child first manifests a desire for independence and mastery in toddlerhood, a period of intense physical exploration of the world, and continues in early childhood with the growth of intellectual curiosity. Healthy progress of this early process of identity formation culminates in middle childhood with the child's development of feelings of competence, efficacy, and perseverance. These characteristics indicate that the child has developed a stable, positive sense of self-identity that will form the basis for positive relationships and productive work experiences throughout the life span.

The process just described is at the heart of Erik Erikson's psychosocial theory of identity development. Although identity development is continuous, he suggests that there are predictable events throughout the life span that trigger crises, the resolution of which can have lasting positive or negative effects on identity formation. He identifies the first and most fundamental crisis that children encounter as the crisis of basic trust versus mistrust. Children who are cared for in a warm and nurturing environment develop a deep sense of basic trust. This sense of trust, absent in neglected children, lays an essential foundation for the development of a healthy personality.

In toddlerhood, children face the crisis between expressions of autonomy and experiences of shame and doubt. Children who have had reasonable opportunities to express themselves and to explore their world develop a healthy sense of themselves as beings who can act upon the world in their own right. Toddlers who are subject to undue restrictions and criticism suffer damage to self-esteem and have difficulty gaining the sense of agency that is critical to healthy development.

In the early childhood period, about four to six years of age, children experience the crisis of initiative versus guilt. Children now have the capacity to use their imaginations and to ask deep and searching questions. Children who have positive experiences with teachers and parents emerge from this stage with the belief that active questioning, intellectual curiosity, and initiative are virtues. Children whose ideas are discouraged by others, or who are made to feel guilty for asking, become inhibited and depend upon adults to provide direction and answers.

Later, in middle childhood, about six to twelve years of age, children's experiences can lead them either to tend toward a sense of industry or feelings of inferiority. Home and school experiences that emphasize what a child can do foster a sense of competence and efficacy, while excessive emphasis on performing to please adults, or to do better than other peers, can foster a sense of inferiority. Thus, in order to foster a healthy sense of identity in children, parents, caregivers, and teachers need to create a climate that fosters trust, autonomy, initiative, and a sense of competence in children of all ages (Elkind, 1987; Erikson, 1950, 1968; Newman & Newman, 1987).

References

Elkind, D. (1987). *Miseducation: Preschoolers at risk.* New York: Knopf.

Erikson, E. (1950/1963). *Childhood and society* (rev. ed.). New York: Norton.

Erikson, E. (1968). *Identity, youth and crisis.* New York: Norton.

Newman, B. M., & Newman, P. R. (1987). *Development through life. A psychosocial approach* (4th ed.). Belmont, CA: Dorsey.

M. O'Loughlin

Imagination and Symbolic Thinking

Symbolic thinking or semiotics is the general ability to use and interpret signs. A sign is something that represents something else. Imagination is mental imagery that takes a "what if" stance. Fantasy is the ultimate in nonliteral thinking because it moves beyond reality and direct experience to products of the imagination.

Symbolic thinking, imagination, and fantasy are interrelated because each is a form of nonliteral thinking. When a young child wraps a block in a receiving blanket and says, "This is my baby," the child is using symbolic thinking; the block stands for something else. If the child has formed a mental picture of the baby, imagination is at work. When the child elaborates on that image to create an imagi-

nary character and responds to it, then he or she is engaging in fantasy play.

Jean Piaget explains how the line of demarcation between fantasy and reality in young children wavers and blurs (1951). This phenomenon explains why young children can be as frightened by a picture (picture realism), attribute thought and intentions to inanimate objects (animism), are terrified by nightmares (night terrors), and why imaginary creatures (such as ghosts, vampires, and monsters) are among the preschool child's worst fears.

Other more friendly manifestations of the child's imagination at work also are common. Children may use a favorite blanket as a sign for needing comfort, closeness, and reassurance (a nonsocial attachment object). They may invent an imaginary companion, a purely invisible playmate(s), or treat a toy as if it were alive. Because young children often speak their thoughts out loud (private speech), adults sometimes can overhear the imaginative process in action during a child's play.

Adults may regard such behaviors as strange simply because they are unusual behaviors in adults. For young children, however, an active imagination is a normal and desirable characteristic. Most experts in the fields of education and psychology consider a rich fantasy life during childhood to be associated with a well-adjusted personality and creativity. Ironically, many adults find themselves struggling to recapture that active imagination that may have been unappreciated and misunderstood during the early years.

References

Cobb, E. (1977). *The ecology of imagination in childhood.* New York: Columbia University Press.

Egan, K., & Nadaner, D. (eds.). (1988). *Imagination and education.* New York: Teachers College Press.

Fraiberg, S. (1968). *The magic years.* New York: Scribner.

Jalongo, M. R. (1984). Children's fantasy: Childhood is the time to live splendidly as a child. *PTA Today, 10* (4), 7–10.

Jalongo, M. R. (1987). Do "security" blankets belong in preschool." *Young Children, 42* (3), 3–8.

Jalongo, M. R. (1984). Imaginary companions in children's lives and literature. *Childhood Education, 60* (3), 166–171.

Johnson, M. (1987). *The body in the mind: The bodily basis of meaning, imagination, and reason.* Chicago: University of Chicago Press.

Piaget, J. (1951). *Play, dreams, and imitation in childhood.* New York: Norton.

Singer, J. (Ed.). (1973). *The child's world of make-believe.* New York: Academic.

Warnock, M. (1976). *Imagination.* Berkeley: University of California.

M. R. Jalongo

Humor

Humor has diverse interpretations and many definitions. There are about 30 synonyms for the words "humor" and "humorous" (Keith-Spiegel, 1972). Some (Freud, 1960; Grotchean, 1957) have viewed humor as a liberating, enabling, and creative force, while others like Plato and Hobbes have pointed out the ugly and destructive aspect of humor (Levine, 1953). Theories of humor, similarly, focus on a range of humor from being a relief mechanism that enables people to cope with anxiety and adversity to being an expression of aggression and revenge against people or society (Ibid.).

Components of humor that have helped shape current theoretical syntheses include the stimulus, or "joke"; the responder, or appreciator of the joke; and the context (Goodchilds, 1972). Major theories and research about humor (Kaya & Carton, 1978) have been synthesized into the following three important implications for education:

- First, investigators found that, on the basis of studying two cultures (the United States and Turkey) youngsters' comprehension, interpretation, and production of humorous materials follow the Piagetian stages of development.
- Second, if younger children expect the stimulus to be funny, they respond to humorous materials with laughter, whether or not they comprehend the element of humor represented. Children, however, are much more likely to appreciate nonsensical humor than adults do. United States youngsters and adults perceive that

moral stimuli are least funny. Adults prefer materials that represent aggressive put-down or have an element of cognitive twist, although young children prefer these in slapstick format rather than in joke format. Film makers have used children's responsiveness to absurdities effectively, especially in cartoons.

- Third, contexts play an important role in humor. Situations that children perceive as trite and familiar do not arouse a humorous response. Nor do situations that are extremely threatening. Humorous responses are most likely to occur in contexts that are unexpected but within the experimental range, and may be anxiety provoking, but not seriously threatening. Within these ranges, some children have learned to use humor very effectively in coping with adversity. On the other hand, in extreme and adverse conditions, psychoanalysts have observed psychotic children to respond by undifferentiating and inappropriate laughter (Wolfenstein, 1954). Although instruction through humorous materials seems to be an effective method, research evidence in this area is sparse and inconclusive. (See also Section 5.7, **Strategies of Teaching**, below.)

References

Freud, S. (1960). *Jokes and their relation to the unconscious.* New York: Norton.

Goodchilds, J. D. (1972). On being witty: Causes, correlates, and consequences. In J.H. Goldstein & P. E. McGhee (eds.), *The psychology of humor: Theoretical perspectives and empirical issues* (pp. 173–193). New York: Academic Press.

Grotchean, M. (1957). *Beyond laughter: A psychoanalytic approach to humor.* New York: McGraw-Hill.

Kaya, E., & Carton, A. S. (1978). *A cross cultural study of humor preference and humor production.* Paper presented at the American Educational Research Association Annual Meeting.

Keith-Spiegel, P. (1972). Early conceptions of humor: Variations and issues. In J. H. Goldstein & P. E. McGhee (eds.), *The psychology of humor: Theoretical perspectives and empirical issues* (pp. 1–39). New York: Academic Press.

Levine, J. (ed.). (1953). *Motivation in humor.* Atherton.

McGhee, P. E., & Goldstein, J. H. (1983). *Handbook of humor research, Vol II, Applied studies.* New York: Springer-Verlag.

Piaget, J. (1951). *Play, dreams, and imitation in childhood.* New York: Norton.

Wolfenstein, M. (1954). *Children's humor: A psychological analysis.* New York: Free Press.

E. Kaya-Carton

Language Acquisition

Children acquire language as a means of communicating with the people important to them. While language and communication patterns within families may vary, the process of acquiring language is the same for all children. Though different theories do exist, there is convincing evidence that humans are born with an innate propensity to acquire language.

From birth, children listen to the language spoken around and to them. They inductively extract the regularities or rules of language and use these to create their own utterances. Thus, a two-year-old who says, "No go home," is demonstrating an understanding of English word order and negation as well as expressing a desire. The child's use of "foots" indicates that she understands the plural rule but has overgeneralized it. With experience, children's rule system or syntax will become more complex as they master more mature forms and the exceptions to the rules.

There also are different theories about the role that adults and their language play in the language acquisition process. Most research suggests that children do not need direct instruction to learn to speak. While imitation of adult language may play a role in some situations, it is not the primary source of children's language. What is needed is a meaningful context in which adults engage children in increasingly complex ways. In these situations, children acquire syntax, or grammar; the semantic, or meaning system; and pragmatics, or ways of using language appropriately.

The prerequisites and sequence of language acquisition also are the same for all children. Laying the groundwork for language, the central nervous system and vocal and auditory mechanisms mature. Cognitive, social, and language abilities become increasingly complex, each stimulating the other.

Shortly after birth, infants attend to the sounds of human speech. Prelinguistic communication develops as they learn that crying brings an immediate response. At approximately three months of age, infants begin to coo, using vowel sounds to vocalize. At about the same time, pseudo-conversations develop as infants learn to take turns with an adult in a cooperative exchange.

At about six months of age, infants begin to babble as they play with consonants and vowels. Starting with sounds that are easiest to produce and progressing to more difficult ones, they eventually focus on the sounds of the language they hear. Intonation patterns are mastered so that by about nine to twelve months of age, infants' babbling resembles "real talk." Notably, infants can comprehend some of what is said to them, even though they cannot produce words themselves.

The linguistic stage typically begins between ten and eighteen months of age. Though infants continue to babble, they can now produce their first word, usually the name of an important person, object, or action such as "up." These words are "holophrases," since an entire phrase is embedded in each. Adults in such interactions must rely on the context and the child's gestures to interpret their utterances. The meanings of first words are often over- or under-extended. Children may refer to all furry animals as "kitty" or only one's own pet.

Between eighteen and thirty months of age, children often begin to produce two words together as their cognitive ability to combine two ideas such as "milk" and "allgone" develops. Next, three words, then more, are produced. This "telegraphic speech" packs a lot of meaning into simple word combinations.

Between approximately three and six years of age, as cognitive and social abilities grow, children's vocabulary also expands, sentences become longer, and conversations improve. As their comprehension of the connections between events develops, children begin to connect sentences with conjunctions and use relative clauses. As egocentrism declines, they are able to accommodate better what they say to their listener's perspective. Broader experiences influence vocabulary and conceptual development.

At the same time, language is becoming less embedded in concrete situations. Language for pretend play develops, and around six years of age, metalinguistic awareness is growing.

By the time children have entered the first grade, they have mastered most of the grammatical system of their language and the basic conversational conventions. The most complex aspects of the grammar, such as passive forms, are acquired by 12 years of age. The phonetic or sound system of the language is mastered at about eight years of age. The lexicon, or word system, continues to develop throughout life. In sum, while the major work of language acquisition is accomplished in early childhood, it is an ongoing process that is rooted in the children's meaningful experiences as they communicate with others.

References

de Villiers, P. A., & de Villiers, J. G. (1979). *Early language.* Cambridge: Harvard University Press. (See also "Out of the mouths of babes: The acquisition of language," 16mm film developed by the authors. Canadian Broadcasting Corporation.)

Genishi, C. (1988). Children's language: Learning words from experience. *Young Children, 44* (4), 16–23.

Menyuk, P. (1985). Early communicative and language behavior. In J. Rosenblith & J. E. Sims-Knight, *In the beginning: Development in the first two years* (pp. 449–477). Monterey, CA: Brooks/Cole.

Pflaum, S. W. (1986). *The development of language and literacy in young children.* Columbus, OH: Merrill.

D. Volk

Bilingual Language Development

When the development of two languages—bilingual language development—occurs before the age of five years, the processes involved in first and second language acquisition are similar (Garcia, 1983). This implies that all the complexities inherent in first language acquisition also are being developed in a second language. Included are the development of systems of phonology, morphology, syntax, and semantics. Bilingual language development in the early years also occurs at the same time that children are developing other capabilities. Children's developmental levels, both physical and psychological, their individual linguistic ability, and their social interactions all affect the development of two languages. These factors are interactive and to some extent interdependent.

As with the acquisition and development of one language, the acquisition of two languages in early childhood can occur without formal instruction. Young children can be exposed to one language in the home and another outside the home, two languages each used consistently by particular persons (one person–one language) within the home, or the mixed usage of two languages in the home. Although studies show that bilingualism results in all cases, researchers have not determined which approach best enables a young child to become bilingual. Outcomes of case studies done on individual children seem to indicate that one person–one language provide the least mixing of the two languages in the children's minds (McLaughlin, 1984).

When communication takes place in two languages, young children begin to understand and eventually produce utterances from both languages. Initially, however, they use the two linguistic systems as one without distinction (Hakuta, 1986). By the time children are approximately two or three years of age, they can differentiate between the two languages in usage, and they also are able to translate. Thus, young children who are exposed to more than one language seem to have an early awareness of languages as symbol systems.

In addition to the process of language acquisition, there are social rules that are culturally related to each language. Some of the social rules governing interaction concern how certain people are to be addressed, what is considered appropriate tone and timbre in different settings, and the meaning of nonverbal communication messages associated with the language. Children learn these rules from those around them and from the social interactions that become associated with each language. Thus the function of language and the social domains associated with each language are important factors in bilingual language development.

By the time children are ready for school, they have learned not just how to communicate in two languages, but they also know with whom to use each language and the appropriate communication rules for the context in which they find themselves. Young bilingual children demonstrate age-appropriate bilingual communication competence (Volk, 1991).

Children who continue to be exposed to two languages in a systematic way will continue to develop the two languages and become proficient bilinguals, that is, their two languages will develop at a level appropriate to their age and developmental levels. When dual language development is discontinued, as often happens when children begin school, partial bilingualism may be the result for some children and still other groups of children may only obtain limited bilingualism. In these situations one language begins to replace the other.

The dominant language utilized as the medium of instruction by the school and the language considered as that of power and prestige by society as a whole affects the continued development of the two languages. How society values each language and the concomitant prevailing attitudes toward the nondominant language will affect bilingual language development. People in many parts of the world associate individual bilingualism with the socioeconomic class to which a person belongs. Those languages associated with low income and minority groups have a low status value and tend to be replaced by the more prestigious power language (Cummins, 1986).

Researchers have characterized "semilingualism" as the displacement of the native language with a second language before children master the first one at an age-appropriate level. In such situations, it is very likely that children also will develop insufficiently the second language. Thus, children are said to lack proficiency in both languages, which results in negative cognitive and emotional consequences (Paulston, 1975, in Diaz, 1983).

Investigators have studied the advantages and disadvantages of bilingualism. Early studies found that bilingualism had negative cognitive effects on children. These studies have been disputed on the basis of faulty methodological approaches. The most recent studies all point to the advantages of proficient bilingualism, especially with regard to cognition. Researchers argue that proficient bilinguals have greater "cognitive flexibility" (a term that includes diverse cognitive tasks), than monolinguals (Diaz, 1983). Other studies indicate that bilingual children develop earlier metalinguistic skills than do monolingual children (Bialystok, 1986). Although more research needs to be done on the effects of bilingual language development in the early childhood years, a significant body of research indicates that the important factor in obtaining positive cognitive effects from dual language development seems to be the development of proficient bilinguals.

References

Bialystok, E. (1986). Factors in the growth of linguistic awareness. *Child Development, 57* (2), 498–510.

Cummins, J. (1986). Empowering minority students: A framework for intervention. *Harvard Educational Review, 56* (1), 18–36.

Diaz, R. (1983). Thought and two languages: The impact of bilingualism in cognitive development. *Review of Research in Education, 10,* 23–54.

Garcia, E. E. (1983). *Early childhood bilingualism.* Albuquerque, NM: University of New Mexico Press.

Hakuta, K. (1986). *Mirror of language.* New York: Basic Books.

McLaughlin, B. (1984). *Second language acquisition in childhood, Vol. 1, Preschool children* (sec. ed.). Hillsdale, NJ: Erlbaum.

Volk, D. (1991). Communication competence in a bilingual early childhood classroom. In Saravia Shore, M., & Arvizu, W. (eds.), *Communicative* and cross-cultural competencies: Ethnographies of educational programs for language minority students in community contexts. New York: Garland.

Y. De Gaetano

Metalinguistic Ability, Development of

Two qualitatively different, related achievements in language development are primary linguistic skills that include the automatic understanding and production of language in an interactive social context and the emergence of metalinguistic skills. Metalinguistic skill is the ability to reflect consciously upon the nature and properties of language and to manipulate and make judgments about the linguistic code.

The importance of understanding children's metalinguistic development is manifold. At the most general level, Jean Piaget proposes that awareness of any practical skills allows a child to choose behavior deliberately that is most effective in a particular situation rather than to proceed by trial and error (Piaget, 1976; 1978). Some researchers believe that language awareness is crucial to the development of literacy (Yaden & Templeton, 1986). Others suggest that such awareness is tied to the child's developing ability gradually to disembed language from its context of immediate, concrete, and personal experience in which it is initially learned and used (Wells, 1981). Metalinguistic skill also has been suggested as an important means through which individuals learn additional language skills (Karmiloff-Smith, 1979).

Pinpointing when metalinguistic skills first emerge is complicated by the lack of consensus among researchers regarding what types of behaviors qualify as being metalinguistic, and what methodologies to use in studying these skills. In general, by the age of six or seven years, children are able to demonstrate skill on a wide variety of experimental tasks designed to tap their awareness of language. Some examples include segmenting words into sounds, a skill that is correlated with learning to read; making judgments about syntactic and morphologic errors in sentences; and making judgments about ambiguity and synonymy.

Younger preschool children also have been successful at segmenting sentences into words and words into syllables but, unlike somewhat older children, are unable to segment words into their component sounds. Preschoolers can successfully judge semantic anomalies in sentences but seem unaware of syntactic and morphologic errors.

Some researchers, using naturalistic data, found that very young children display skills that reflect rudimentary metalinguistic ability (van Kleeck, 1982). For example, they are able to correct semantic, syntactic, morphologic, and lexical errors in their own and others' speech. They often will demonstrate an awareness of the sound system in their spontaneously produced rhyming and alliteration. While these general developmental trends have been documented, metalinguistic skill development shows marked individual variation, far more so than the development of primary linguistic abilities.

References

Karmiloff-Smith, A. (1979). *A functional approach to child language.* New York: Cambridge University Press.

Piaget, J. (1976). *The grasp of consciousness.* Cambridge: Harvard University Press.

Piaget, J. (1978). *Success and understanding.* Cambridge: Harvard University Press.

van Kleeck, A. (1982). The emergence of linguistic awareness: A cognitive framework. *Merrill-Palmer Quarterly, 28* (2), 237–266.

Wells, G. (1981). *Learning through interaction: The study of language development.* New York: Cambridge University Press.

Yaden, D., & Templeton, W. (eds). (1986). *Metalinguistic awareness and beginning literacy.* Portsmouth, NH: Heinemann.

A. van Kleeck

Moral Development

Young children construct knowledge of good and bad, right and wrong, that is qualitatively different from that of older children or adults. For example, young children might define a lie as a "naughty word" and say that it is wrong to lie because punishment will follow (Piaget, 1932/1965). This finding indicates that children cannot judge intention. Moreover, they learn to understand rules according to their stage of cognitive development, that is, the ways in which they make sense of their own experiences, rather than simply by adopting or internalizing adult standards by direct transmission.

Jean Piaget described a morality of obedience, or heteronomy, and a morality of autonomy. Heteronomous morality means being regulated by others and conforming to rules that are accepted and followed without question. Autonomous morality means being self-regulated by principles based on internal feelings of necessity for relating to others in moral ways.

Lawrence Kohlberg, inspired by Jean Piaget's work, found that children have their own morality that develops through an invariant sequence of six universal stages, including preconventional, conventional, and postconventional levels. Preconventional individuals, including most children under nine years of age, as well as some adolescents, delinquents, and criminals, have no personal commitment to rules that they perceive as external.

Conventional morality means conforming to and upholding the rules, expectations, and conventions of society because they exist. Individuals at the postconventional level accept rules that are based on underlying moral principles.

Kohlberg's work describes moral type A (heteronomous) and B (autonomous) behaviors at each stage. He and his colleagues found evidence that development generally moves from heteronomous to autonomous type, and once accomplished, the individual does not go through a heteronomous phase at the next stage. Moral action appears to follow autonomous moral judgments.

In heteronomous relationships, Jean Piaget perceives that children's reasons for behavior are external to their own reasoning and systems of personal interests. Adults prescribe what children should do by providing ready-made rules, instructions for behavior, and constraints or coercion. Heteronomous teaching practices range along a continuum from hostile and punitive methods to sugar-coated coercion such as cajoling or bribery.

In order to help children to survive, parents and teachers must regulate children externally in many ways. Adults oblige children to eat certain foods at certain times, bathe before bed, avoid touching dangerous, delicate, or important objects, and so forth. The child thus is forced to comply with often incomprehensible rules. When governed continually by the values, beliefs, and ideas of others, however, children practice a submission that can lead to mindless conformity in both moral and intellectual spheres.

This kind of morality of obedience or duty may socialize only the surface behavior and reinforce the child's tendency to rely on external regulation. Such children are unlikely to have the motivation to question, analyze, or examine their own convictions and construct their own reasons for following rules.

An autonomous or cooperative adult-child relationship differs from the morality of obedience because it is characterized by mutual respect. By providing the possibilities for children to regulate their own behavior voluntarily and to elaborate, at least in part, their own rules, values, and guidelines for action, adults open the way for children to develop the capacity to think independently and creatively, to construct a decentered personality, and to develop moral feelings of reciprocity in all kinds of social relations.

Essentially, the difference between the two types of adult-child relationships is a difference in the exercise of power. Autonomous relationships develop the capacity to be cooperative, coordinating one's own feelings and perspective with a consciousness of another's feelings and viewpoint. The motive for such decentering and reciprocity begins in a feeling of mutual affection and trust that becomes elaborated into feelings of sympathy and consciousness of the intentions of others. Cooperation is a social relation in which an adult is able to respect children as people with rights to exercise their wills according to their capacities. The adult increasingly favors and supports the children's regulation of their own behavior.

The teacher who cultivates this type of relation with children is a companion and guide who expresses respect for children and practices cooperation rather than coercion. Teacher interventions promote the constructive process. These include such activities as dilemma discussions, group decisionmaking through dialogue and voting, coming to terms with different points of view in many types of situations, and providing legitimate choices. In particular, when teachers encourage children to listen to each other's point of view, propose solutions, and come to mutual agreement, they are providing opportunities for children to construct moral development in the context of interpersonal conflicts.

Moral development occurs in the context of intellectual and emotional development. Decentering, autonomy, and cooperation are processes that are simultaneously cognitive and emotional. Thus, adult cooperation liberates children's possibilities for construction of their intelligence, their personalities, and their moral and social feelings.

Special Learning Needs and Equity

Children who are normal or advanced in their intellectual development tend to suffer less from the effects of heteronomy than at-risk children. This is because children who are slower learners or delayed intellectually are less able to take the point of view of the adult and understand some of the reasons behind adult coercion. They also suffer less to the degree that they have confidence in themselves and simply discount the adult view. While perhaps placating adult wishes, children can sometimes retain their autonomy despite adult controls. In contrast, children who have special learning needs suffer more when they are unable to understand coercion except as completely arbitrary. Coercive environments for these at-risk children increase inequities in education.

Often, education for children in low-income communities also is based on strict, even harsh, discipline. Some emotional aspects of pervasive coercion are submissiveness, feelings of inferiority that accompany acceptance of another person's superiority, lack of confidence, and low motivation to consider reasons for rules. Some cognitive aspects of coercion are orientation to the ideas of others, an unquestioning, uncritical attitude, and an intellect that does not think beyond what is superficially observable. Both at-risk and economically poor children are most vulnerable, and thus the most likely to manifest the effects of heteronomy, which might include rebellion, conformity at the price of loss of will, and calculation. Calculation in this sense means following adult rules when the adult is watching but doing what one likes when the adult is not watching.

A moral curriculum (often called the "hidden curriculum") is inherent in school although it has been recognized only recently. Whether or not teachers are aware of its existence, children certainly know very well what the moral messages are.

References

DeVries, R., & Kohlberg, L. (1990). *Constructivist early education: Overview and comparison with other programs.* Washington, DC: National Association for the Education of Young Children.

Kohlberg, L. (1987). *Child psychology and childhood education: The cognitive-developmental view.* New York: Longman.

Piaget, J., with Baechler, N., Feldweg, A. M., Lambercier, M., Martinez-Mont, L., Maso, N., Piaget, V., & Rombert, M. (1932/1965). *The moral judgment of the child.* New York: Viking.

R. DeVries

Justice Reasoning and Social Cognition

Jean Piaget (1932/1965) outlined a theory of moral development in which he proposed that children develop concepts about morality through an interactive, constructive process. In his interviews with, and observations of, children, Piaget demonstrated that children reason about fairness and justice in their daily encounters with peers. Following his work, Lawrence Kohlberg (1969) expanded Piaget's theory into a six-stage system that characterized how individuals make moral judgments throughout the life span. Kohlberg proposed that the moral reasoning of young children was punishment oriented.

A body of research has extended from their work. One researcher, for instance, found that children of primary school age, when evaluating problems about how to divide resources in a fair way, based their judgments on equality and reciprocity rather than solely in terms of punishment and retribution (Damon, 1988). Other researchers have found that children of preschool age made moral judgments about their own prosocial behavior (Eisenberg-Berg, & Hand, 1979).

Three social-cognitive domains were identified in an investigation of how individuals develop concepts about authority, customs, interpersonal relations and the self, as distinct from concepts about justice (Turiel, 1983). They include the moral domain that refers to concepts of justice, welfare, and rights; the societal domain that refers to concepts of social conventions and group customs; and the psychological domain that pertains to concepts of the self and psychological judgments.

Using this social-cognitive model, investigators have studied the conceptual distinctions that children of preschool age make between rules that are based on moral concerns, such as hitting and not sharing, and those that stem from social-conventional issues, such as school rules and social customs (Nucci & Turiel, 1978; Smetana, 1985). They found that children evaluate moral transgressions as wrong on the basis of intrinsic aspects of the act, such as, "Hitting is wrong because it hurts someone," rather than solely on what an authority says is right or wrong. When asked if it would be all right to hit someone if the teachers said it was alright, children said that it still would be wrong. Another study of parent-child and sibling exchanges in the home prior to the preschool period identified categories of morality and social convention (Dunn, 1988).

Thus, research from a social-cognitive perspective has shown that the development of justice concepts emerges during the preschool period and that young children are capable of recognizing the necessity of fairness in their familiar everyday problems. Investigations about social-cognitive judgments in early childhood support Piaget's contention that children develop social and moral understanding through a reflective and interactive process.

References

Damon, W. (1988). *The moral child.* New York: Free Press.

Dunn, J. (1988). *The beginning of social understanding.* Cambridge: Harvard University Press.

Eisenberg-Berg, N., & Hand, M. (1979). The relationship of preschoolers' reasoning about prosocial moral conflicts to prosocial behavior. *Child Development, 50* (2), 356–363.

Kohlberg, L. (1969). Stage and sequence: The cognitive-developmental approach to socialization. In D. A. Goslin (ed.), *Handbook of socialization theory and research* (pp. 347–480). Chicago: Rand McNally.

Nucci, L. P., & Turiel, E. (1978). Social interactions and the development of social concepts in preschool children. *Child Development, 49* (2), 400–407.

Piaget, J., with Baechler, N., Feldweg, A. M., Lambercier, M., Martinez-Mont, L., Mason, N., Piaget, V., & Rambert, M. (1932/1965). *The moral judgment of the child.* New York: Viking.

Smetana, J. G. (1985). Preschool children's conceptions of transgressions: The effects of varying moral and conventional domain-related attributes. *Developmental Psychology 21* (1), 18–29.

Turiel, E. (1983). *The development of social knowledge: Morality and convention.* New York: Cambridge University Press.

M. Killen

Religious Concepts

The development of religious concepts begins through the cognitive, social, and emotional development of the child. This spiritual, or faith, development is the growth of a relationship with spiritual concepts that are identified by the individual faith community.

The religious or spiritual concepts of a particular faith community represent the shared values of that community or group. These shared values are codified into a shared vocabulary in order to communicate and elaborate those values. They, in fact, are the labels for shared understandings of experiences and relationships.

While religious values may vary from one religious group to another, and may have different labels from group to group, there appears to be a core of identifiable concepts and/or values that transcend the differences between groups. While some may be controversial, these concepts are a representative sample of religious values. They range from faith and faithfulness, trust and trustworthiness, hope and optimism, love and valuing of self as special, to forgiveness and unconditional love. Each of these concepts is based upon the young child's experiences with the ideas embodied in these concepts and values.

The young child acquires religious concepts from the real experiences that form the basis for all learning in early childhood. In the realm of religious experiences, the experiences themselves are not as different as the motivation and valuing of the experiences, as well as their religious labeling.

The child's interaction with adults who represent the faith community also is key to the development of religious concepts. These persons provide real, everyday, and ordinary experiences representative of adult religious concepts and provide opportunities for children to add each experience to their pool of experiences for later sorting and building of relationships among concepts and ideas.

The adults who provide experiences for later identification as religious concepts also must provide the shared vocabulary and labels for those experiences in ways that signal that the experience represents a shared value and religious concept of the faith community. It is the child's repeated experiences in the faith community that lead to the labeling of events as faith related, and to labeling of feelings within themselves as valued and validated by their faith community.

Two of James Fowler's (1981, 1989) seven stages in the development of faith occur in early childhood. The first stage, preconscious faith, develops from birth to age three. In this stage, the child is developing a sense of self as separate from the self of others. This development depends upon a sense of dependability and responsibility in the young child's immediate environment and the adults in that environment.

The second stage, intuitive-projective faith, develops from three to eight years of age. This stage is a fantasy-filled imitative phase in which the child is influenced by the moods, actions, emotions, and stories of observable adults who practice the faith of the child's faith community. The young child sorts these experiences into concepts by using prelogical thought processes that develop later into faith concepts. In these ways, the development of religious understanding, within a particular community context, integrates conceptual, social, and emotional development.

References

Blazer, D. (ed.). (1989). *Religious education in early childhood*. New Haven, CT: Religious Education Association.

Fowler, J. W. (1981). *Stages of faith: The psychology of human development and the quests for meaning*. New York: Harper & Row.

Fowler, J. W. (1989). Strength for the journey: Early childhood development of selfhood and faith. In D. Blazer, (ed.), *Religious education in early childhood*, (pp. 1–36). New Haven, CT: Religious Education Association.

Morgenthaler, S .K. (1989). *Right from the start: A new parents' guide to child faith development*. St. Louis: Concordia.

S. K. Morgenthaler

Physical and Motor Development

Movement is a barometer of growth as well as a means of expression during early childhood. Dramatic gains in control over movement proceed in an invariant and predictable direction, from the head to the feet, and from the center of the body out toward the extremities. As motor abilities evolve, they facilitate perceptual and cognitive abilities. Extensive data have been organized about specific to general developmental activities (Bayley, 1935; Gesell & Amatruda, 1941).

Several factors facilitate motor development, including the integration of reflex patterns, myelinization of nerve fibers, and physical growth. Volitional movements emerge as higher centers in the brain begin to function and inhibit reflexes. In particular, the asymmetrical tonic neck reflex (ATNR) initially reinforces the relation between the eye and the hand. This reflex is apparent when turning the head to one side causes the arm on the same side to extend in the classic fencing pose. After this reflex is inhibited, voluntary grasping can occur.

The myelin sheath, which insulates nerve fibers, increases the conduction velocity of nerve impulses to the musculature. As motor responses are initiated more quickly, improved coordination results.

Physical growth also makes a significant contribution to motor abilities. Children triple their weight during the first year of life. In subsequent years, body proportions change markedly. During the second to fifth year of life, height gains are twice that of weight gains. The head, which initially dominates one-fourth of the child's body length, approaches the adult ratio of about one to eight. The trunk grows more slowly than the arms and legs. Longer limbs offer the mechanical advantage of greater leverage, allowing for increased speed.

Rapid bone growth accounts for much of the child's weight gain in the first five years of life. Muscle tissue develops at a slower, more constant rate, equal to about one-fourth the weight gain per year. By age five, however, the increase in muscle tissue accounts for three-quarters of the weight gain. Strength, a function of additional muscle tissue, increases by 65 percent from ages three to six. Movement repertoires expand with enhanced muscular energy for power and speed.

The movement patterns of walking, running, jumping, throwing, striking, and catching, and the progression of their development from immature to mature forms have been identified (Wickstrom, 1977). Mature movement patterns also form the basis for later sports skills. In various ways, inasmuch as motor skills contribute to a child's self-esteem, independence, and competence, parents and teachers must continue to nurture development in the motor domain.

References

Bayley, N. (1935). The development of motor abilities during the first three years. *Monographs of the Society for Research in Child development, 1,* Serial No. 1.

Curtis, S. R. (1982). *The joy of movement in early childhood.* New York: Teachers College Press.

Espenscade, A. S., & Eckert, H. M. (1980). *Motor development* (2nd ed). Columbus, OH: Merrill.

Gesell, A., & Amatruda, C. S. (1941). *Developmental diagnosis.* New York: Harper.

Keogh, J. F., & Sugden, D. (1985). *Movement skill development.* New York: Macmillan.

Ridenour, M. V. (ed.). (1978). *Motor development Issues and applications.* Pennington, NJ: Princeton Book Co.

Wickstrom, R. (1977). *Fundamental motor patterns* (2nd ed). Lea & Febiger.

S. R. Curtis

Play, the Role of, in Development

Theorists have considered play from the perspectives of social and anthropological concerns as well as child development. The psychodynamic theorists were the first to write about the value of play in development. Sigmund Freud's theory viewed play as the child's way of expressing aggression, sexuality, and anxiety. His views also formed the basis for play therapy as a medium in which to resolve emotional problems.

There is also an interpretation of his view that has affected teaching practice that includes play as a way in which children might work out emotional conflict (Isaacs, 1933/1972). Erik Erikson also has appreciated play as a way to create a sense of mastery over both immediate and imaginary situations (Erikson, 1950; 1977). His view, which includes broad play stages, contends that a healthy ego and sense of purpose in life builds from the child's freedom to play out life's conflicts, frustrations, and fears, through such content as the enactment of a heroic role. Thus, early "autocosmic" play centers on the child's body in the form of vocalization and sensory perception. Later play enters the "microsphere," or realm of toys and objects. Thereafter, the young child's play enters into the "macrosphere," or the social world of shared play with others.

Jean Piaget considered the personal as well as the biological roots of play (1945/1962). He focused on the role of play within the stages of cognitive development, particularly egocentric, personal thought. For him, play is a self-focused activity in which children impose their own organization on experience (assimilation), and consolidate their past experience and behavior.

Stage I in his theory is sensorimotor, functional, or practice play. Beginning in infancy, this stage consists of the pleasurable repetition of activity. Stage II, symbolic play, begins at 12 to 18 months. It is marked by pretense and the symbolic transformation of objects and actions. Within symbolic play, children begin by practicing their own behavior outside its usual contexts and extending to dramatic role play that is coordinated with peers while containing complex plots and themes. Stage III consists of games with rules, characterized by competition and mutually negotiated or formal rule structure. Rules also exist in dramatic play and in ritualized cooperative games such as ring-around-the-rosy. Until about the age of seven years, these games are not marked by consideration of the perspectives of others and consistent adherence to rules (Kamii & DeVries, 1980). Games with rules predominate in the play of human beings in middle childhood through adulthood, although both functional play and dramatic play appear as motor activity and fantasy from the early years and continue throughout life (Bergen, 1987).

Among the social theorists, Lev S. Vygotsky emphasized the social nature of thought and language as they develop through symbolic play (1976). He proposed that thought develops as meaning increasingly becomes removed from its anchor in real objects that are used symbolically in play. The ties to concrete objects become loosened as mental representation of meaning increasingly predominates.

For example, the child who begins to pretend with a toy replica of a telephone progresses to a telephone represented by a building block. The unstructured building block keeps meaning from evaporating. Thereafter, the child plays with an imaginary telephone where gestures and words convey the child's intended meaning. He also saw play as a medium in which children develop a sense of rules. Similar to the psychodynamic theorists, he also saw play as a way of accommodating to unrealizable desires in life. Another socially oriented theorist, George Herbert Mead, used play as a way to describe the development of the self. An initial Play Stage begins as children take the roles of others, for example, by alternating roles of parent and baby.

These role transformations take place with little cohesiveness or coordination of roles but represent the stages of differentiating the "I" as self from the "me" as social object. In the Game Stage, the child tries out the perspectives of other players and begins to understand the relationships of roles to one another and to the real selves of the role players. Children coordinate the perspectives of others with regard to their own role and negotiate the structure of role play with others. For example, a four-year-old may play simultaneously the roles of wife, banker, and mother. In the Generalized Other Stage, the final stage, children are able to coordinate perspectives of self and others while adhering to a generally accepted set of shared meanings.

Within the social theorists' tradition, James Mark Baldwin (1906) stressed the importance of imitation and role play in the organization of a coherent sense of self. He saw the ability to pretend as a foundation for later creative thinking and scientific hypothesizing, a view that is compatible with Vygotsky's work. Baldwin, in a view that also is compatible with George Herbert Mead's contentions, also saw play as a means of differentiating parts of the self, in this case the mental self from the physical self, as children use their bodies to represent pretend realities created in their minds.

In another viewpoint based upon stages, Mary Parten identified six levels of social participation in preschool-age play, ranging from unoccupied and onlooker behavior, to solitary play, to several forms of group play, including parallel, associative, and cooperative play. The hierarchical nature of solitary and parallel play in Parten's model recently has been questioned.

Solitary play often is found to be cognitively complex in nature and, therefore, may not always represent the immature level she suggested. Solitary play is currently thought to function both as an option for the more sophisticated player to obtain privacy and/or a limitation for the less sophisticated player who lacks the skills necessary to enter into group play. Parallel play also may change in function as the child develops, representing a limitation on the child's social functioning, or alternatively, a "treading water" strategy for children who play adjacent to others before attempting to enter group play (Johnson, Christie, & Yawkey, 1987; Monighan-Nourot, Scales, Van Hoorn, with Almy, 1987).

These issues, the concern for studying the complexity of play within a combined social and cognitive play episode (Pepler & Rubin, 1982), and the rapidly growing research literature about play, help to highlight its importance for early childhood education.

References

Baldwin, J. M. (1906). *Social and ethical interpretations in mental development* (4th ed.). New York: Macmillan.

Bergen, D. (ed.). (1987). *Play as a medium for learning.* Portsmouth, NH: Heinemann.

Erikson, E. H. (1950/1963). *Childhood and society.* New York: Norton.

Erikson, E. H. (1977). *Toys and reasons.* New York: Norton.

Isaacs, S. (1933/1972). *Social development in young children.* London: Routledge & Kegan Paul.

Johnson, J., Christie, J., & Yawkey, T. (1987). *Play and early childhood development.* Glenview, IL: Scott, Foresman.

Kamii, C., & DeVries, R. (1980). *Group games in early childhood education: Implications of Piaget's theory.* Washington, DC: National Association for the Education of Young Children.

Mead, G. H. (1934). *Mind, self, and society.* Chicago: University of Chicago Press.

Monighan-Nourot, P., Scales, B., Van Hoorn, J., with Almy, M. (1987). *Looking at children's play: A bridge between theory and practice.* New York: Teachers College Press.

Parten, M. B. (1932). Social participation among preschool children. *Journal of Abnormal Psychology, 27* (3), 243–269.

Pepler, P. J., & Rubin, K. H. (eds.). (1982). *The play of children: Current theory and research.* New York: Karger.

Piaget, J. (1945/1962). *Play, dreams, and imitation in childhood.* New York: Norton.

Vygotsky, L. S. (1976). Play and its role in the mental development of the child. In J. S. Bruner, A. Jolly, and K. Sylva (eds.) *Play—Its role in development and evolution* (pp. 537–554). New York: Basic Books.

P. Monighan-Nourot

Social Development and Development of Relationships

The psychological study of children's social development has had a long and rich history. As early as the 1920s and 1930s, researchers examined the roots of sharing, helping, and caring behaviors; hostile, aggressive behaviors; and social participatory behaviors. A classic study, for example, noted that children became less solitary and more cooperative and sociable in their play from the toddler through the kindergarten years (Parten, 1932). At the same time, researchers found that from early through middle childhood, the frequency and complexity of children's prosocial behaviors increased and the frequency of their aggressive behaviors declined, becoming less physical and more varied (see Parke & Slaby, 1983; Radke-Yarrow, Zahn-Waxler, & Chapman, 1983 for relevant reviews).

The earliest studies of children's social development were conducted at approximately the same time that Jean Piaget was suggesting possible cognitive underpinnings to the developmental courses of social behaviors. Piaget (1926) indicated that young children's thoughts about their social worlds (their social cognition) could best be described as egocentric in nature; that is, until the end of the preoperational period (by six or seven years of age), children had neither the will nor the skill to judge and understand the thoughts, emotions, and intentions of others. Furthermore, being immersed in here and now thinking and in their own perspectives on the world, young children could not understand the consequences of their social actions either for themselves or for others. Despite the fact that researchers have observed in the past two decades that young children are nearly as egocentric as Piaget suggested (Rubin & Howe, 1986), there appear to be stages of social cognitive understanding that progress from the early childhood years through early adolescence (Selman, 1980). Moreover, these stages of social understanding appear to be reliably associated with social development. Thus, children of the same age who differ with regard to their ability to understand the thoughts, emotions, and intentions of others are also different in the degree to which they demonstrate prosocial and antisocial behaviors as well as socially competent behaviors. Those children who are less cognitively advanced are less prosocial, less sociable, and less socially skilled; they are also more likely to demonstrate aggressive behaviors in the peer group (Shantz, 1983).

One interesting question that has emerged in the literature on children's social development concerns what the "costs" are for children who remain egocentric or who continue to behave aggressively or in a withdrawn fashion once they reach primary school age. Recent research has demonstrated that both aggression and withdrawal are relatively stable from the early years of childhood. Furthermore, both phenomena are predictive of peer rejection in the middle years of childhood. The significance of these findings lies in reports that peer rejection and aggression in middle childhood forecasts delinquency, aggression, and adolescent school dropouts, whereas rejection and anxious-withdrawal behavior predicts internalized difficulties such as loneliness and depression in early adolescence (Parker & Asher, 1987; Rubin, Hymel, & Mills, 1989).

It is also important to note that sociable young children who are popular with their peers generally are socially skilled. Like rejection, aggression, and withdrawal, sociability and popularity are relatively stable phenomena and both are predictive of later socioemotional adjustment.

Given the significance of children's social skills or social deficits for both their concurrent peer relationships as well as for their later socioemotional well-being, researchers have examined those factors that contribute to their development in the first place. Recent studies have found that under some circumstances, maternal insensitivity and unresponsiveness to infants predicts the development of insecure infant-mother attachment relationships. In turn, these insecure relationships provide the infant and toddler with an internal working model, or cognitive representation, of what comprises relationships in general. It is not surprising, therefore, that insecurely attached infants appear to be at risk for social developmental difficulties when they enter preschool (Sroufe, 1983). Some insecure, anxious-avoidant babies appear particualrly at risk for aggression, and those who are anxious-resistant appear at greater risk for withdrawal. On the other hand, securely attached infants who have adaptive cognitive representations of relationships, appear to be well-adjusted preschoolers. They are less egocentric, more socially competent, and more popular among their peers than their insecure counterparts.

In summary, there appear to be logical continuities between the quality of babies' relationships with their mothers and the quality of subsequent relationships with preschool age and older peers. Furthermore, researchers have identified a predictive relation between the quality of early parental child care and the development of socially competent or incompetent behaviors in children. Finally, links can be drawn between the quality of infant-parent relationships, the quality of child-peer relationships and social competence in early and middle childhood, and subsequent socioemotional adjustment in adolescence. These links are important for those working with infants and young children. If practitioners can identify an insecure infant- or toddler-mother relationship, then perhaps some form of parent training program may be developed. In subsequent years, given that both aggression and anxious withdrawal are stable developmental phenomena and predictive of later socioemotional difficulties, their frequent demonstration in preschool should signal the early childhood caregiver or educator to seek some form of intervention from providers of social skills training services.

References

Parke, R. D., & Slaby, R. G. (1983). The development of aggression. In P. H. Mussen (ed.), *Handbook of child psychology, Vol. 4. Socialization, personality and social development* (pp. 547–621). New York: Wiley.

Parker, J., & Asher, S. (1987). Peer relations and later personal adjustment: Are low-accepted children at risk? *Psychological Bulletin, 102* (3), 357–389.

Parten, M. (1932). Social participation among preschool children. *Journal of Abnormal and Social Psychology, 27,* 247–269.

Piaget, J. (1926). *The language and thought of the child.* London: Routledge & Kegan Paul.

Radke-Yarrow, M., Zahn-Waxler, C., & Chapman, M. (1983). Children's prosocial dispositions and behavior. In P. H. Mussen (ed.), *Handbook of child psychology, Vol. 4. Socialization, personality and social development* (pp. 469–545). New York: Wiley.

Rubin, K. H., & Howe, J. N. (1986). Play and social cognition. In G. Fein & M. Rivken (eds.), *The young child at play,* (pp. 113–125). Washington, DC: National Association for the Education of Young Children.

Rubin, K.H., Hymel, S., & Mills, R. S. L. (1989). Sociability and social withdrawal in childhood: Stability and outcomes. *Journal of Personality, 57* (2), 237–255.

Selman, R. (1980). *The development of interpersonal understanding.* San Diego, CA: Academic Press.

Shantz, C. U. (1983). Social cognition. In P. H. Mussen (ed.), In J. Flavell & E. Markman (eds.) *Handbook of child psychology, Vol. 3. Socialization, personality and social development* (pp. 495–555). New York: Wiley.

Sroufe, L. A. (1983). Infant-caregiver attachment and patterns of adaptation in preschool: Roots of maladaptation and competence. In M. Perlmutter (ed.), *The Minnesota symposia on child psychology, Vol. 16* (pp. 41–76). Hillsdale, NJ: Erlbaum.

K. H. Rubin

Social Cognition

Social cognition is concerned generally with interrelations between social behavior and cognition. A basic assumption in this area of study is that children's conceptualizations of others affect the ways in which they interact with them (Shantz, 1983) and that social behavior and cognition are interconnected. The thoughts that preschool-age children have about others are based upon concrete, typically behavioral dimensions. With age, they develop the ability to attend to more abstract, psychological dimensions. Significant dimensions of social cognition include the ways children think about individuals and the relationships between and among individuals (Ibid.).

As they conceptualize individuals, preschool-age children seem to be able to infer intentions for others' actions and to consider why events happened. They have difficulty, however, differentiating accidental from intentional acts, and assume that all acts are intentional. This confusion probably is due to the fact that children's early conceptualizations are based on others' overt behaviors. Children's conceptualization of individuals may be related to aggressive and/or prosocial behavior, but the evidence is mixed. Preschoolers' abilities to empathize with others are not related to aggression. Aggression, however, is related to their inabilities to differentiate among ambiguous social provocation situations, such as play fighting rather than real fighting. Training programs for older children have successfully reduced aggressive behavior by helping them to understand the way other individuals think about events. Children's ability to attend to individuals' psychological characteristics is related to such prosocial behavior as cooperation and kindness.

At a more advanced level, social cognition involves conceptualizations of relations between individuals, such as friendships and conflicts. Similar to their concepts of individuals, preschoolers' concepts of friends are concrete. Friends are peers with whom to share toys and have fun. Only in middle childhood, after eight years of age, do mutual trust and psychological dispositions become important. Therefore, preschoolers' friends tend to be similar in terms of age, sex, and race. Resolution of conflicts involve children in solving social problems, such as how to get a turn to play with a particular toy by exchanging toys with one another. Children who have such a varied and positive repertoire of strategies are the most effective problem solvers. They also are popular with their peers.

At a more mature level of social cognition, children focus on concepts of relations among individuals, particularly relations that involve dominance and affiliation. Dominance, in this context, involves power relations within a group. Although preschool age children tend to overestimate their own power or toughness, compared to other children, dominance hierarchies do exist. For example, some children consistently get their way when interacting in groups. These dominance relations, which are stable throughout childhood, tend to reduce group conflict because children recognize the hierarchy in a group and tend not to initiate conflicts with their more powerful peers. Social affiliation involves peers with whom children spend their time. Young children's conceptualizations of friendship, like their social cognitions, initially are based on concrete, behavioral criteria. They later develop in middle childhood into increasingly abstract and psychological criteria.

Reference

Shantz, C. (1983). Social cognition. In J. Flavell & E. Markman (eds.), *Handbook of child psychology, Vol. 3: Cognitive development* (pp. 495–555). New York: Wiley.

A. D. Pellegrini

4.5 Sequences of Development and Child Characteristics

Students of child development tend to agree on the sequence of development that children experience but have differences regarding the ages at which particular characteristics occur. It is important to consider that children at a particular age may manifest some of the behaviors that investigators generally attribute to a different age. At the same time, investigators and educators expect that a range of development, because of individual differences in the rate of growth, is natural. With these considerations in mind, the following section is organized according to ages of children.

D. P. Fromberg

Prenatal Development and Characteristics

Prenatal development lasts between 37 and 42 weeks, beginning at conception and ending at birth. When an ovum and sperm unite, the result is a single-celled zygote that immediately starts to grow and transform into a newborn infant. The zygote contains 23 chromosomes from the ovum and 23 chromosomes from the sperm, each with thousands of genes carrying the genetic blueprints for all further development (e.g., gender; eye, hair, and skin color; body type; predispositions to certain diseases; and temperament). Within the first 12 hours of conception, the zygote divides and becomes two-celled through the process of mitosis, and starts to travel down the fallopian tube toward the mother's uterus. During this first phase of prenatal development known as the germinal period, the blastocyst, as it is now referred to, continues to increase in number of cells, appearing like a spherical pack of bubbles with a hollowed center.

Within 48 hours the blastocyst has 8 cells. The cells are not as large, and the entire blastocyst is about the same size as the original fertilized egg, that is, smaller than a pinhead. The blastocyst propels itself with the help of hairlike cilia. It will be three to five days before the blastocyst reaches the uterus and another four to five days before it implants itself in the uterine lining where it will stay for the remainder of the pregnancy.

Once attached to the uterus, the blastocyst is an embryo, and the six- to nine-week embryonic period begins. By now there are at least 100 cells, differentiated for various functions. The outer layer of cells (ectoderm) will develop into skin, hair, sensory organs, and the nervous system. The inner layer of cells (endoderm) will become the digestive tract and respiratory system. A middle layer of cells (mesoderm) later develops into the skeleton, circulatory, and muscular systems. Other cells create the amniotic sac, a protective fluid environment for the embryo. There also are specialized cells that form the umbilical cord and placenta.

The placenta and umbilical cord connect to link the embryo to the mother. This connection will be the source of all nutrients and disposal of waste products when the embryonic period ends. Until then, sustenance is received via hairlike projections from the embryo, called villa, that absorb maternal blood present in the uterine lining.

Four weeks after conception, the embryo is about 1/4 inch long, 10,000 times its original size. The heart, though only partially developed, pulsates and pumps blood. The glandular systems of the body also begin to function. A brain, backbone, and spinal canal are developing, as is the digestive system, liver, and kidneys. Small buds are now present that later become arms and legs, and the skeleton and muscles have developed sufficiently to give form to the embryo. At this time, the embryo seems to have a tail, often explained with the theory of recapitulation, that is, repeating the evolutionary stages of humankind during embryonic development.

At around eight weeks (the beginning of the fetal period), the growing organism is about 1 1/2 inches long and weighs 1/8 ounce. The fetus clearly looks human with a disproportionately large head, and arms, legs, hands, and feet. There is a nose, mouth, tongue, eyes, and ears, though they are not yet fully developed or functional. The tail-like feature has disappeared.

After three months, in the second of three trimesters of prenatal development, the fetus is on average three inches long and weighs an ounce. Limbs and digits are fully formed, and fingernails and toenails are growing. The heart beats strongly and rapidly. The fetus can open its mouth and swallow, and moves about in the embryonic sac. By the end of the fourth month, the fetus has grown to more than six inches long, weighing roughly five ounces.

During the fifth month, hair on the head and eyebrows grow. The body is covered with a waxy substance called vernix, and a fine, silky hair called lanugo, most of which will fall off before birth. The eyes open and close, and the ears are capable of detecting sounds. The fetus utilizes reflexes such as sucking, grasping, kicking, and hiccuping. At the end of the month, the fetus will be 10 to 12 inches long and will weigh 1/2 to one pound. Its lungs are now able to function outside the uterus, and the fetus is considered viable, able to survive if born. The fetus can breathe and cry.

In the sixth month, the fetus will grow to about 14 inches and 1 1/2 pounds. The fetus is thin and has wrinkled skin. The skin is less transparent than earlier, but blood vessels can still be seen. Fat will now begin to accumulate under the skin. The fat will serve to protect the infant from varying temperatures after birth.

The third trimester begins in the seventh month. During this last phase, development will be primarily growth of existing tissues and organs. The fetus will gain most of its prebirth weight and continue to increase in length. More than five pounds will be gained in the seventh and eighth months. By the end of the eighth month the fetus weighs 4 1/2 to 6 pounds and is 17 to 18 inches long. All of the sensory systems and vital organs of the body are functional. The fetus also has acquired immunities against many diseases. The immunities build up from the mother's antibodies passed to the infant through the amniotic fluid and the exchange of blood from mother to child.

Large movements are less possible for the fetus in the last stage of development because of a lack of space, although arms and legs still can be extended. In most instances the fetus rotates so that its head is pointing down. In the ninth month the head of the fetus moves closer to the mother's pelvis in preparation for birth. The fetus will be on average 20 inches in length, and will weigh 7 pounds at full term, with about 6,000 billion cells. Labor begins when the fetus starts to exit the uterus, and ends when the fetus has passed through the vaginal canal and opening. A baby is born. (See also Section 4.6, **Special Learning Needs/Individual Needs, Prenatal Substance Abuse**, below.)

References

Hales, D. (1989). *Pregnancy and birth*. New York: Chelsea House.

Nilsson, L., Ingelman-Sunberg, A., & Wirsen, C. (1966/1984). *A child is born*. New York: Dell.

Nilsson, L. (August, 1990). The first days of creation. *Life, 30* (10), 26–46.

E. S. Flicker

Infant and Toddler Development and Characteristics

Infants learn to represent the world mentally, to communicate with language, and to form affectionate relationships by their second birthday. They begin to acquire knowledge about their cultural community and their role in that community within a social context.

Child development specialists have described the period of infancy as three sub-periods, in which distinctively new forms of behavior emerge (Cole & Cole, 1989). The first sub-period begins at birth with all sensory systems working at a rudimentary level. The organization of the sensory systems at birth or early in life help infants to form relationships with caregivers and to orient themselves to their social world. Newborns are able to discriminate between the human voice and other sounds, and favor their mother's voice, in comparison to the voices of other women, by four to five weeks of age. They choose to look at their mother's face rather than the face of strangers within the first two days of life.

Infants must depend upon their caregivers for survival and interact with the social and physical world with these responses and reflexes. Infants and caregivers spend considerable time, during the first ten weeks of life, mutually adjusting to and influencing each others' behavioral patterns in order to fit the tempo of life in their household and community.

The social smile signals the emergence of the second sub-period at about ten weeks of age. During this sub-period, infants' involvement with the object world becomes increasingly purposeful throughout the first year. Eight-month-olds, for example, begin to understand that objects continue to exist even when they are not visible, a process termed object permanence. Object permanence, however, may not develop fully until two years of age. Infants are also able to recall events that occurred during the second half-year of life, and can associate features such as voice and face with a single object, such as their mother. Motor abilities also change markedly. Most nine-month-olds can move about on their own, usually by crawling. These burgeoning abilities are linked to social and emotional developments in the infant's life.

Most seven- to nine-month-olds show signs of wariness around strangers, a phenomenon known as stranger anxiety. This development is related to their skill in remembering and comparing events, part of the infant's ability to anticipate events and to recognize familiar objects and situations. Fear develops around the time when infants begin to move about on their own, which also marks the emergence of new forms of distal communication. For example, infants begin to rely on the emotional cues of others in ambiguous situations in order to regulate their own behavior, a process termed social referencing. Toward the end of the first year of life, infants form special and lasting emotional ties to their primary caregivers, called attachment. The type of attachment they develop depends upon the nature of care that they receive.

The major achievement of the third sub-period is the emancipation of toddlers, during the second year of life, from the here and now. Their developing ability to represent the world mentally allows them to consider the consequences of their actions without directly experiencing them. Language skills are another important achievement in this period. Toddlers are able to use words to represent objects, people, or events, and are able to follow relatively complicated directions. Two-year-olds are able to engage in symbolic play, and younger toddlers are able to imitate an activity in its absence, termed deferred imitation.

Toward the end of infancy, in the third year of life, toddlers begin to develop a sense of self and a sense of societal standards. They become increasingly autonomous as they develop. Thus, the events that mark this sub-period of infancy have an important influence on the nature of toddlers' relationships with caregivers and other community members.

Reference

Cole, M., & Cole, S. (1989). *The development of children*. New York: Scientific American Books.

G. A. Morelli

Preschooler Development and Characteristics

The period from three to five years of age is a time of growth, transition, and consolidation (Bee, 1985). Growth and change, although following a universal sequence, can vary quantitatively and qualitatively among children and within the individual child. Every child is unique as a result of interrelated internal/maturational and external/environmental forces.

During this period, muscular development contributes to growth of gross motor abilities including jumping, climbing, pedaling, hopping, throwing, and catching. Children have a high energy level and establish hand dominance. Fine motor abilities and eye-hand coordination lead to proficiency with tools, such as markers and paint brushes, and care of self, such as dressing, undressing, and brushing teeth. They are able to manipulate small objects such as beads, puzzles, and blocks.

Preschool-age children actively explore their environment. Problem solving by trial and error at three years of age evolves into beginning planning skills and the ability to predict outcomes by five years of age. During this period, children continue to develop the ability to represent ideas and events through symbolic play (Johnson, Christie, & Yawkey, 1987). Theoreticians and researchers have characterized the thinking of preschool-age children as egocentric because these children have difficulty perceiving others' views, assign animate qualities to nonliving objects, and engage in magical thinking (Harris, 1986).

Children increasingly develop the ability to attend to more than one attribute of an object or situation, and to classify and order objects on the basis of one or more dimensions (Peters & Willis, 1978). They generally can reason from one specific situation to another specific situation. Their reasoning is based upon how things appear rather than upon an understanding of reversible thinking or transformations that occur, for example, when quantity is conserved (Bjorklund, 1989; Harris, 1986). Children's continuing difficulty in distinguishing real from pretend often leads them to feel fearful.

During these years, children's vocabulary expands rapidly, and they acquire the rules of language use as well as listening skills. They ask questions, engage in conversation, create oral texts for sociodramatic play, and play with the sound structures of language, such as rhyming. Children at this age, however, find it difficult to respond to how, why, and when questions. They begin to understand that written language conveys ideas and meanings. By the end of this period, many children are able to read a few words in context and to recognize and, often, to write their own names.

Children engage in increasingly elaborate social pretend play episodes with themes that evolve from familiar into fantasy content. Roles in play increasingly become collaborative, flexible, and sustained over time, as children also develop an understanding of friendship (Bee, 1985). Children are more likely to choose same-sex play groups as they establish their gender identity. Children's abilities to see others' perspectives is evident in their developing empathy, taking turns, and generosity (Smith, 1981).

The concept of self evolves as the preschool-age child displays initiative and growing independence. The ability to express a range of emotions verbally and to assert a point of view enhances these developments. The years between three and five are important for the development of a sense of competence that can serve as a foundation for later development.

References

Bee, H. (1985). *The developing child*. New York: Harper & Row.

Bjorklund, D. F. (1989). *Children's thinking: Developmental function and individual differences*. Pacific Grove, CA: Brooks/Cole.

Harris, A. D. (1986). *Child development*. West.

Johnson, J., Christie, J., & Yawkey, T. (1987). *Play and early childhood development*. Glenview, IL: Scott, Foresman.

Peters, D. L. , & Willis, S. L. (1978). *Early childhood*. Belmont, CA: Wadsworth.

Seefeldt, C., & Barbour, N. (1990). *Early childhood education* (2nd ed). Bell & Howell.

Smith, C. (1981). *Promoting social development in young children*. Mountain View, CA: Mayfield.

C. Bersani

Kindergarten-Age Children, Development and Characteristics of

Children in kindergarten are five or six years of age. During this age, according to Jean Piaget, children's thinking can be characterized as intuitive in nature. That is, they rely more on their visual and auditory perception for knowledge than they do on logical thought processes. The results of this are that these children can focus only on one or two variables of a situation at a time, and the variables they focus on are usually some perceptual characteristic of the situation. Children of this age rely on their own point of view of things for information, and they seldom are able to take another person's perspective.

Kindergarten children also can be characterized by the wide variability found in their rates of development. Because of this wide variability, not all five- or six-year-olds are doing or can be expected to be doing the same thing at the same time. The variability in developmental rates affects all areas including cognitive, language, social-emotional, and physical. The differences in rates of development are due to the differences in maturation found among children at this age and the differences in the types and quality of experiences that these children have had in their lives.

Children at this age are curious about the physical and social worlds around them and deeply involved with their peers. Their language ability is expansive, and they rely on this as a primary means for social interaction and exploration. They constantly are asking questions and are striving to make more sense out of their environment by interacting with it.

Because of these characteristics, exemplary teachers strive to do the following:

- Use concrete props and visual aids whenever possible to illustrate ideas and help children understand what adults are talking about;
- Make instruction relatively short, using actions as well as words;
- Make sure that the activities are relevant to the life experiences of the children;
- Give children a great deal of physical practice with the facts and skills that will serve as building blocks for later development;
- Encourage manipulation of physical objects during instructional activities; and
- Encourage language and social interaction among children when they are engaged in instructional activities.

D. F. Gullo

Primary School Children, Development and Characteristics of

Primary-age children, five- to eight-year-olds, enter into radically new relationships with adults, peers, and the physical environment. New societal expectations and rights reflect developmental changes and also open up the possibilities for further growth.

The cognitive stage of concrete operations emerges between the ages of five and seven years. Children now can construct mental reversibility, enabling them to organize logical-mathematical, spatial-temporal, and causal relationships, and to begin the systematic learning of reading, writing, and mathematics. They learn best by actively manipulating and transforming real materials. They then discover and symbolically represent the patterns that exist in language, mathematics, social relationships, and the physical world. An integrated curriculum that is grounded in children's interests is a conducive environment for this kind of learning.

The psycho-social stage in which children develop a sense of industry, contrasted with inferiority, brings new social-emotional capacities. Children move from egocentrism to an awareness of themselves both as autonomous individuals and as members of a peer group. Consequently, they increasingly become cognizant of other viewpoints, extend their capacity for empathy, and learn how to coordinate different needs and ideas for solving problems.

The peer group plays a key role in cognitive growth and in the development of a morality based on mutual respect and reciprocity rather than reliance only on adult reinforcement. Dispositions toward learning that include a sense of curiosity, wonder, persistence, and belief in one's competence, that sprouted during the preschool years, now bloom more fully or wither, depending on the kind of support that children receive at home and school. For children of this age, cooperative learning is a significant method for promoting growth in all developmental domains.

Children explore the multifaceted aspects of their own and others' identity as individuals and as members of different societal groups, including groups of gender, race, ethnicity, class, age, and disabilities. Prevailing social prejudices and discriminatory practices directed at different groups influence their attitudes toward themselves and others. Although biased feelings and behavior may crystallize, children of this age, with their passionate concern about fairness for themselves and their peers, also respond to anti-bias curriculum for individual and social justice.

Physical growth remains important, although it occurs at a slower pace than the extremely rapid development of the first five years of life. Daily physical activity is necessary in order to build small and large motor skills, self-esteem through expression of newly acquired physical power and control, and to support cognitive development. Long periods of inactivity, such as doing paper and pencil desk work, not only are cognitively inappropriate, but fatigue primary-age children more than do strenuous physical activities such as running or bicycling.

Each child has an individual pattern of growth within the universal and predictable sequences of human development. There is enormous individual variation within the normal range of pacing and development. Cultural patterns of child rearing also affect the ways in which children gain and demonstrate developmental competence. Development in one dimension influences and is influenced by development in the other dimensions. Socialization and school problems often result from a failure to attend to these integrated principles of development.

Hurrying children to acquire skills more quickly than is developmentally appropriate, overemphasizing competition and comparison among children, and stressing the mastery of narrowly defined academic skills, also sabotage healthy growth. Such adult expectations can produce fragmented development, lessen children's optimism about their own abilities and about school, stifle their motivation to learn, and threaten their motivation to use acquired skills. Sensitive attention to the developmental needs of the primary-age child enables adults to foster healthy, optimum development that builds on the foundation of the preschool years and prepares the way for the next stage in children's journey toward maturity.

References

Bredekamp, S. (ed.) (1987). *Developmentally appropriate practice in early childhood programs serving children from birth through age 8.* Washington, DC: National Association for the Education of Young Children.

Derman-Sparks, L., & ABC Task Force (1989). *Anti-bias curriculum: Tools for empowering young children*. Washington, DC: National Association for the Education of Young Children.

Elkind, D. (1981). *The hurried child*. Reading, MA: Addison-Wesley.

Erikson, E. H. (1950/1963). *Childhood and society* (2nd.ed.). New Workers.

Oakes, J. (1985). *How schools structure inequality*. New Haven, CT: Yale University Press.

Piaget, J., & Inhelder, B. (1969). *The psychology of the child*. New York: Basic Books.

L. Derman-Sparks

4.6 Special Learning Needs/ Individual Needs

Particular learning needs are generic to all children. Those individuals who develop in unusual ways, including faster- as well as slower-developing children, might require special educational provisions.

Early labeling of children, often based upon minimal forms of standardized assessment, can contribute to the devaluing of human worth and dignity. This section opens with articles that discuss the issues and implications of labeling young children and the positive alternative of teacher and parental influences in mediating young children's learning experiences. It continues with discussions of problems that may arise in emotional and social development, perceptual development, and physical development. Later articles address the contemporary issue of the physical results of prenatal substance abuse and subsequent developmental problems.

These circumstances lead to a consideration of provisions for the growing numbers of medically fragile/technology dependent children. Substance abuse and medical technologies have an impact upon classrooms, as affected children present unique behavioral profiles that require adaptive teaching. Children with these conditions also add unique responsibilities to their family members' lives.

Children's special learning needs reflect part of the continuum of development that is described in this section. Children with special needs are not viewed here as persons who should be targets of assessment and classification.

D. P. Fromberg

Labeling Young Children, Issues and Implications of

The practice of labeling the special learning needs of young children in early childhood education may be one step in the process of providing appropriate educational services. It is also a reason for caution and concern on the part of educators, parents, and children.

Early childhood educators are concerned particularly about the inappropriate use of labels, such as Learning Disabilities (LD), Attention Deficit Disorder (ADD), and Developmental Delay; the mislabeling of children, especially culturally diverse children, by means of inappropriate use of standardized tests for placement, promotion, or retention decisions; and the use of noncategorical labels, such as "children at risk," as mandated by Public Law 99-457.

The definition of learning disabilities has changed markedly over the past 30 years (Lerner, 1985). The two characteristics of learning disabilities that have remained salient throughout that time, however, include academic difficulties that appear as a discrepancy between the person's estimated ability and actual performance and the persistence of identifying behaviors over time.

These criteria for labeling may not be appropriate for young children inasmuch as academic learning problems may not arise until children begin formal instruction in the first grade. Labeling before this time may not be justified (Karnes & Stoneburner, 1983). Inasmuch as instruction in many kindergarten and first grade classrooms may not be developmentally appropriate for all children (Bredekamp, 1987), learning difficulties that develop as a function of the curriculum may be confused with, or mask, a learning disability or attention deficit disorder. Therefore, screening for learning disabilities must take into account the widely varied individual rates of development that occur during the preschool years.

Another issue concerning labeling is the use of standardized tests in the placement, promotion, or retention decisions of young children (Hilliard, 1984; Perrone, 1990). The misuse of readiness tests for placement or retention in kindergarten results in the labeling of some children as "unready" or as "failures" if they are retained (see Section 4.9, **Child Assessment and Evaluation**). These practices have special significance for the culturally diverse children who may be mislabeled (Hilliard, 1984).

Yet another issue concerns the use of noncategorical labeling. Public Law 99-457 mandates services to all children of three to five years of age who demonstrate a developmental delay and provides incentives to states for services to children from birth to two years of age who are considered "at risk" for future problems. Children may be labeled "at risk" when the following conditions are present: biological risk that may influence later development, such as fetal alcohol syndrome or prematurity; established risk such as Down's syndrome, which affects development; and environmental risk, such as an adolescent mother or birth into a family with a known history of abuse or mental retardation (Peterson, 1987). Under the federal law, each state may establish its own criteria for the at-risk category. This is a concern because some states' definitions may be too broad, thereby allowing services for more children than can be served, whereas other states' definitions may be too narrow, thereby omitting children who need services. It is apparent, therefore, that those who make decisions concerning the labeling of young children need to consider an array of factors, based upon a variety of valid sources.

References

Bredekamp, S. (ed.). (1987). *Developmentally appropriate practice in early childhood programs serving children from birth through age 8*. Washington, DC: National Association for the Education of Young Children.

Hilliard, A. (1984). IQ testing as the emperor's new clothes: A critique of Jensen's *Bias in mental testing*. In C. R. Reynolds & R. T. Brown (eds.), *Perspectives on bias in mental testing* (pp. 139–170). New York: Plenum.

Karnes, M. B., & Stoneburner, R. L. (1983). Prevention of learning disabilities: Preschool assessment and intervention. In J. D. McKinney & L. Feagans (eds.), *Current topics in learning disabilities* (pp. 149-178). Norwood, NJ: Ablex.

Lerner, J. (1985). *Learning disabilities: Theories, diagnosis, and teaching strategies*. Boston: Houghton Mifflin.

Perrone, V. (1990). How did we get here? In C. Kamii (ed.), *Achievement testing in the early grades: The games grown-ups play* (pp. 1–13). Washington, DC: National Association for the Education of Young Children.

Peterson, N. L. (1987). *Early intervention for handicapped and at-risk children: An introduction to early childhood–special education*. Denver, CO: Love.

C. A. Buzzelli

Mediated Learning Experiences and At-Risk Children

The More Intelligent and Sensitive Child Program (MISC) is the first empirical attempt to define, assess, and modify those parent behavior variables that constitute the necessary and sufficient conditions for a quality early parent-child interaction. This program studies specific behaviors that affect a young child's capacity to learn from new experiences. The MISC program is designed to affect children's "appetites" for such experiences as precise and clear perceptions, finding links and associations between things, planning, evaluating, and reality testing.

Children who have not developed these needs through mediational interactions with a caring adult tend to live in an impoverished, emotionally flat, meaningless world that feels "fragmented" from moment to moment. The child who has not developed the self-direction that generates a search for meaning and focus may not be able to benefit even from a rich and supposedly "stimulating" environment. Children also need to develop the capacity to compare and inquire about things that are not perceived directly by the senses at any particular moment.

Parents and other caregivers, within the framework of the MISC program, learn to (1) improve their perceptions of the child, of his or her chances to develop, and of their own role as caregivers; (2) raise their awareness of the possibilities for establishing sensitive, emotionally communicative interaction with the child, while focusing on interpreting and responding with approval to the child's expressive signals and initiatives; and (3) improve the quality of mediation by identifying and intensifying behaviors that provide quality mediation to the child.

The criteria for these behaviors are based upon Reuven Feuerstein's theory of cognitive modifiability and are observable during parent-child interaction. Parents learn to use these behaviors and to praise in a way that invites generalization and transfer to other caregiving situations. The three most basic components of a quality mediation include focusing, affecting, and expanding.

Focusing includes all attempts by an adult to assure that the child focuses on something she or he wishes to share. These behaviors include attempts by adults to match environmental stimuli with the child's interests and capacities at a particular moment.

Affecting relates to the emotional energy invested by the adult partner during interaction with the young child, and in attempts to excite the child and convey the significance of objects, people, relations, and environmental events.

Expanding includes all adult behavior that is meant to expand the child's awareness of relationships between different environmental phenomena, such as cause and effect; past, present, and future relations; explanations; and social and cultural transmissions.

Any cultural context and the content of any specific situation lend themselves to meeting the basic objectives of the MISC program to improve adult-child mediational patterns. The program is designed to enhance indigenous child-rearing practices and has been adapted for use in countries that include the United States, Norway, Israel, Sri Lanka, Indonesia, Portugal, and Ethiopia. This program also can be used with a variety of populations including high-risk babies, such as those born at very low birth weight; Down's syndrome babies with other neonatal risk factors; and normal children from low-income homes, as well as with gifted young children.

Abundant research indicates that most basic factors affecting cognitive and emotional development either are amplified or circumvented by the kind and amount of human interaction to which a young child is exposed. In order to examine the immediate and sustained effects of the MISC program, a series of research studies were conducted prior to the start of the program, as well as a five-year longitudinal study. Findings indicated that the quality of parent mediations with their children could be modified significantly. Once modified, changes persisted over years. In addition, enhancing the quality of mediation with young children affected their cognitive performance, social, and emotional behavior. Those children whose parents participated in the program had better language and abstract reasoning skills, willingly offered their ideas about associations and relationships between things, and were able to praise and appreciate other people's success. Thus, children who receive quality mediation from caring adults tend to provide quality mediation to others.

References

Feuerstein, R. (1980). *Instrumental Enrichment.* Baltimore: University Park Press.

P. S. Klein & K. Hundeide

Emotional and Social Needs

Since 1986, under Public Law 99-457 all states are required to provide services for children with handicapping conditions from three to five years. Unlike Public Law 94-142, however, the Individuals with Disabilities Education Act, funding is not linked to specific diagnostic labels. Rather, the identification of a developmental delay or at risk for a developmental delay is sufficient.

Ecological assessment of home, preschool, and community are included in the evaluation. Many of the early childhood assessments include the area of social/emotional development. Observation of the child in different settings, parent/teacher questionnaires, and interviews are used to understand social/emotional development.

It is particularly difficult to diagnose emotional disturbance in young children. Many of the behaviors upon which evaluators focus can be present in most young children (Lidz, 1983; Claridge, 1985). Therefore, many factors are taken into account, including general activity level and/or temperament as well as the environment or situation in which and for which the preschooler is being assessed (Bailey & Rouse, 1989). The behavioral differences between young children who are considered to be seriously emotionally disturbed and normal children "are often differences in the frequency, intensity and duration of the undesirable behavior" (Claridge, 1985, p. 133). In addition, these perceived differences may be related to the reactions of others in the child's environment based upon their own temperamental, socioeconomic, and cultural backgrounds and legal constraints (Ibid.). If a child is predisposed to a specific temperament, the environmental interactions can react upon it and/or cause it to emerge. These environmental factors include, but are not limited to, eating habits, educational setting, cultural patterns, family supports, and parenting (Ibid.; Thomas, Chess, & Birch, 1969).

Many social/emotional problems appear to be an outgrowth of disturbance in other areas. Social interactions, for example, can be affected when children have problems in communication skills. Poor motor performance and/or communication and language disorders can hamper the ability for interactive play, in which case some children withdraw while others may become aggressive.

Extremes in temperament, such as withdrawl, anxiety, fear of new situations, and aggressive tendencies, may isolate children from interactions with their age mates, thus contributing to social maladjustment through a lack of practice. (See also Chapter 5, Section 5.2, **Curriculum Approaches, Special Education Programs, Emotionally Disturbed.**)

References

Bailey, D. B., & Rouse, T. S. (1989). *Assessing infants and preschoolers with handicaps*. Columbus, OH: Merrill

Claridge, G. (1985). *Origins of mental illness*. Cambridge, MA: Basil Blackwell.

Lidz, C. S. (1983). Emotional disturbance of preschool children. *Exceptional Children, 15* (3), 164–167.

McLaughlin, J. A., & Lewis, R. B. *Assessing special children* (3rd ed.). Columbus, OH: Merrill.

Thomas, A., Chess, S., & Birch, H. (1969). *Temperamental behavior disorder in children*. San Francisco: University Press.

R. Gold

Intellectual Disabilities

Young children with mental handicaps lag behind their chronological age peers in all areas of development. While each child has a unique pattern of characteristics, children with mental retardation may demonstrate low achievement, inappropriate classroom performance, poor memory, and generalized delays in each of the developmental domains.

Generalized delay, combined with deficits in adaptive behavior, distinguishes children with mental retardation from those with learning disabilities. While children with mental retardation achieve developmental skills at an overall slower rate, children with learning disabilities appear to function at their chronological age but experience unexpected difficulty with certain types of skills.

Children with special learning needs often experience difficulties with discrimination, classification, mediation, imitation, speech and language, social interaction, and development of independence skills. Instructional strategies to address the learning needs of young children with mental retardation or learning disabilities are similar. These include systematic, detailed instruction presented in small sequential steps with concrete materials, where there are opportunities for overlearning and repeated practice. This procedure helps to build in mediation and rehearsal to address the problems in short-term memory, eliminates an over-reliance on imitation and incidental learning, and prevents the delay and frustration of cumulative failure.

Providing instruction in small learning groups also can increase practice, when teachers encourage each child in the group to repeat new information as it is presented. Because children with intellectual impairments are easily distracted by competing stimuli in the learning environment, they learn best when teachers use clear, simple language and minimize extraneous noise, movement, and materials during instruction. In addition, children with mental impairments may not find learning inherently pleasurable. Therefore, many teachers provide external motivation to reinforce positive behaviors. Oral language stimulation and practice can ameliorate children's communication development, which often is characterized by articulation errors, smaller vocabularies, and shorter sentences.

Problems in social development emanate from immaturity and consequent inappropriate interactions with peers and adults. A partially integrated setting that provides models for behavior without creating the fear and embarrassment often experienced in totally integrated settings, or the unrealistic expectations and confidence that frequently result from placement in segregated settings, may assist children with mental impairments to acquire social skills (Alberto, 1979).

Timing is critical to implementing any of these instructional strategies, because the incidence of mental disabilities increases as children approach school age, presumably because of better identification procedures (McLean, Burdg, & Hall, 1987). While children with severe and multiple disabilities are identified in infancy, especially if the disability is visible, mental impairments are not always apparent until the child is placed in a situation where comparisons can be made to peers. It appears likely that the changes in the availability of early child care will increase the earlier identification of children with mental impairments and provide the additional opportunities necessary for ameliorating learning problems. (See also Chapter 5, Section 5.2, Curriculum Approaches, Special Education, Developmentally Delayed.)

References

Alberto, P. A. (1979). The young mentally retarded child. In S. G. Garwood, *Educating young handicapped children. A developmental approach* (pp. 293–322).

McLean, M., Burdg, N. B., & Hall, E. G. (1987). Developmental differences in learning. In J. T. Neisworth & S. J. Bagnato (eds.), *The young exceptional child: Early development and education* (pp. 297–318). New York: Macmillan.

K. A. Ferrell

Perceptual Disabilities

Much of what is known about the special learning needs of young children with perceptual impairments is based on concepts of sensorimotor development (Piaget, 1954) and perceptual organization (Gibson, 1969). The quantity and quality of sensory information that young children acquire by vision, hearing, touch, taste, and smell establish the foundation for all learning in early childhood as they form the prerequisites to cognition. Individuals obtain information about the world through the five primary senses, which then interact internally to lead to a second level of sensory information—awareness of movement (kinesthetic), space (spatial), position (proprioceptive), and touch (haptic). When there is a disturbance in sensory input, either because a sensory system is impaired or because another disability interferes with input, there is no guarantee that children with disabilities perceive the world in the same manner as do children without disabilities.

Perceptual disabilities are not a category included under the Education of the Handicapped Act. In order to be eligible for special education and related services in early childhood, children must meet one of the following definitions (see 34 C.F.R. 300.5):

Deaf: "a hearing impairment . . . so severe that the child is impaired in processing linguistic information through hearing, with or without amplification," including about 0.1% of all preschoolers (Stedt & Moores, 1987);

Hard of hearing: "a hearing impairment, whether permanent or fluctuating, which adversely affects a child's educational performance," affecting about 6% of preschoolers (Ibid.);

Visually handicapped: "a visual impairment, which, even with correction, adversely affects a child's educational performance . . . , [including] both partially seeing and blind children," affecting about 0.1% of preschoolers (Scholl, 1986); and

Deaf-blind: "concomitant hearing and visual impairments, the combination of which causes such severe communication and other developmental and educational problems that they cannot be accommodated in special education programs solely for deaf or blind children" (Ibid.).

Other etiologies may cause perceptual learning problems because of their interference with the normal manner of obtaining information, such as:

Orthopedically impaired: "a severe orthopedic impairment which adversely affects a child's educational performance. The term includes impairments caused by congenital anomaly . . . , impairments caused by disease, and impairments from other causes," affecting an estimated 0.5% of children (Kasari, Larson, & Veltman, 1987);

Other health impaired: autism or "limited strength, vitality or alertness, due to chronic or acute health problems," affecting about 5% to 7% of the preschool population (McCarthy, 1987); and

Specific learning disability: "a disorder in one or more of the basic psychological processes involved in understanding or in using language," affecting an estimated 10% of preschoolers (McLean, Burdg, & Hall, 1987); and

Multihandicapped: "concomitant impairments . . . , the combination of which causes such severe educational problems that they cannot be accommodated in special education programs solely for one of the impairments" (34 C.F.R. 300.5).

Young children who do not have perceptual disabilities share at least one characteristic—without intervention, learning occurs by chance. Typical infants have a multitude of sensory information available at any one time, and they learn almost incidentally.

Adults cannot assume that incidental learning occurs for children with perceptual impairments, who require many adaptations and enhancements to the learning environment. These usually involve selecting toys and materials that possess multiple sensory attributes; utilizing a structured approach, with predictable times and events; accentuating sensory cues in the environment; integrating instruction into naturally occurring situations; focusing on the needs of the whole child in the context of the family, rather than focusing on the disability; and creating opportunities for learning, instead of waiting for them to happen.

Current issues in early childhood special education involve methods of improving social interactions (Strain & Kohler, 1988) of young children with disabilities, clarifying realistic expectations for family involvement (Dunst, Trivette, & Deal, 1989), and integration with normally developing children (Odom & McEvoy, 1988). While none of these is exclusively owned by children with perceptual disabilities, federal legislative initiatives (see Chapter 3, Section 3.5, **Child Advocacy and Public Policy**) have made these issues the focus of research and practice for the 1990s. (See also Chapter 5, Section 5.2, **Curriculum Approaches, Special Education Programs, Perceptual Impairments**.)

References

34 Code of Federal Regulations 300.5 (Assistance to States for Education of Handicapped Children).

Dunst, C. J., Trivette, C. M., & Deal, A. G. (1989). *Enabling and empowering families: Principles and guidelines for practice.* Cambridge, MA: Brookline Books.

Gibson, J. J. (1969). *The senses considered as perceptual systems.* Boston: Houghton Mifflin.

Kasari C., Larson, M. A., & Veltman, M. A. (1987). Differences in neuromotor development. In J. T. Neisworth & S. J. Bagnato (eds.), *The young exceptional child* (pp. 319–349). New York: Macmillan.

McCarthy, M. (1987). Chronic illness and hospitalization. In J. T. Neisworth & S. J. Bagnato (eds.), *The young exceptional child* (pp. 230–259). New York: Macmillan.

McLean, M., Burdg, N. B., & Hall, E. G. (1987). Developmental differences in learning. In J. T. Neisworth & S. J. Bagnato (eds.), *The young exceptional child* (pp. 297–318). New York: Macmillan.

Odom, S. L., & McEvoy, M. A. (1988). Integration of young children with handicaps and normally developing children. In S. L. Odom & M. B. Karnes (eds.), *Early intervention for infants and children with handicaps* (pp. 241–268). Baltimore, MD: Brookes.

Piaget, J. (1954). *The construction of reality in the child* (M. Cook, trans.). New York: Ballantine Books.

Scholl, G. T. (ed). (1986). *Foundations of education for blind and visually handicapped children and youth*. New York: American Foundation for the Blind.

Stedt, J. D., & Moores, D. F. (1987). Developmental differences in hearing. In J. T. Neisworth & S. J. Bagnato (eds.), *The young exceptional child* (pp. 414–442). New York: Macmillan.

Strain, P. S., & Kohler, F. W. (1988). Social skill intervention with young children with handicaps: Some new conceptualizations and directions. In S. L. Odom & M. B. Karnes (eds.), *Early intervention for infants and children with handicaps* (pp. 129–144). Baltimore, MD: Brookes.

K. A. Ferrell

Physical Disabilities

Physical and health impairments generally are organized into the three following categories: *neurological disorders*, involving the brain and spinal column; *musculoskeletal disorders*, involving the muscles and skeleton; and *chronic health impairments*, comprising a variety of conditions associated with metabolic, endocrine, and cardiac disorders. Young children with any of these impairments participate primarily in early childhood special education, although many are integrated into regular education programs. For many of the integrated children, the curriculum does not require adaptation; rather, their special health and physical needs often necessitate creative management, flexible scheduling, and involvement of a number of related services personnel.

Neurological impairments include (a) cerebral palsy, a brain lesion occurring either before or during birth, or during early childhood, a "nonprogressive condition [that] renders the child incapable of coordinating his [or her] muscle actions... [or]... maintain[ing] normal postures and balance in performing normal movements and motor skills" (Langley, 1979, p. 89); (b) epilepsy, a seizure disorder caused by too much electrical activity within the brain; (c) spina bifida, an opening in the spinal column where the vertebrae did not fuse in utero, resulting in paralysis of the body below the site of the lesion; and (d) hydrocephalus, excessive production of cerebrospinal fluid, which creates increased pressure on the brain and resulting paralysis.

The most common types of musculoskeletal conditions are (a) muscular dystrophy, a progressive weakening of skeletal muscles; (b) osteogenesis imperfecta, a disorder producing very weak and fragile bones; (c) juvenile rheumatoid arthritis, an inflammation of the joints that often results in irritability, loss of appetite, anemia, and chronic pain; and (d) spinal deformities, such as lordosis and scoliosis, caused by weak trunk muscles or congenital malformation of the vertebra.

Chronic health impairments include (a) cystic fibrosis, a dysfunction of the exocrine glands resulting in thick mucus secretions into the respiratory and intestinal tracts; (b) asthma, a difficulty in breathing resulting from narrowed bronchial tubes; (c) hemophilia, a dysfunction in blood clotting; (d) burns, which may result in joint contractures and decubiti (bedsores), besides the obvious problems from loss of body fluids and susceptibility to infection; (e) HIV infection, affecting the immunological system, which appears to be transmitted in utero and which manifests in early childhood as increased vulnerability to infection and progressive dysfunction of most body systems; and (f) substance abuse, a relatively recent concern for early childhood. Infants and young children who have been exposed to drugs and other toxic substances in utero experience a range of physical and health disorders, beginning with substance withdrawal shortly after birth and manifesting in early childhood as short attention span, memory loss, suspected cognitive delay, and social/emotional disturbance. Efforts to study these children are currently in progress (see Section **4.6, Special Learning Needs/Individual Needs, Prenatal Substance Abuse**).

Educational programs for young children with physical and health impairments almost always include a range of personnel, including physical and occupational therapists, speech therapists, nurses, and nutritionists. The teacher's role within this multidisciplinary team is to individualize instruction by adapting materials, curriculum, and the environment to meet the routine needs of the disability. A barrier-free classroom, which allows easy movement of wheelchairs, space for storing adaptive equipment (e.g., wedges, prone boards, standing tables, and special chairs), and child-sized furniture, is one way that the teacher can manage the environment to encourage child involvement and participation.

Curricular adaptations will depend on the severity of the disability. One approach is an "ongoing curriculum" that integrates skills into every activity, rather than working on individual skills in an isolated manner (Langley, 1979). Most activities in the curriculum can be accomplished by attaching handles, velcro, or magnets to puzzle pieces, crayons, and other utensils. Children with physical impairments sometimes experience difficulties in communication, both expressively and receptively. The motor or respiratory disability may make articulation difficult, and the poor articulation sometimes creates impatience in the listener. Children may become discouraged and talk as little as possible, or not at all; other children may talk excessively, although their language demonstrates conceptual gaps from an absence of direct experience. Other physical impairments prohibit speech, and in such cases a variety of communication boards and computer devices are commercially available.

Self-care skills are a large part of the early childhood curriculum. Self-sufficiency within physical limitations should be promoted; not only does this establish the basis for later adult independence, but it contributes to the formation of a healthy self-concept.

Physical education activities and exercises will usually need to be approved by the child's physician, as some physical and health impairments may prohibit participation even in adaptive physical education programs. In addition, children with physical and other health impairments fatigue easily, in part because of the sheer effort of movement but also because many children are under extensive medical regimens with numerous side effects.

Children with physical and health impairments are susceptible to infection and may have a poor attendance record. In addition, their days are filled with therapies, administration of medicine, and inordinate amounts of time devoted to activities of daily living, such as eating, dressing, toileting, and bathing. It is a challenge to develop an early childhood program that is both comprehensive and consistent when faced with such competing but equally important demands. (See also Chapter 5, Section 5.2, **Curriculum Approaches, Special Education Programs, Physical Impairments.**)

References

Langley, M. B. (1979). Working with young physically-impaired children: Part A—The nature of physical handicaps. In S. G. Garwood, *Educating young handicapped children: A developmental approach*, (pp. 73-107). Orem, UT: Aspen.

K. A. Ferrell

Prenatal Substance Abuse

The maternal use of illegal drugs during pregnancy affects approximately 11 percent of newborns annually in the United States. Different drugs have different effects, placing the child exposed in utero at risk for developmental, learning, behavioral, and psychosocial problems. There is no one-on-one relationship between the type of drug used, the frequency or chronicity of drug use, and subsequent developmental outcome. Rather, there is a continuum of the impact on the developing child, ranging from the child being significantly affected to being relatively unaffected.

The frequency and severity of the problem of prenatal substance abuse, however, continues to grow. Critical educational issues in relation to this problem include preparing for the impact of prematurity, congenital malformations, neurological deficits, and physical, psychosocial, and developmental delays on children affected prenatally by maternal substance abuse.

Fetal Alcohol Syndrome (FAS). Maternal alcohol abuse has been identified as a significant factor in perinatal morbidity and mortality. Between the early 1800s and 1970, literature alluded to the detrimental effects of alcohol on pregnancy. However, no specific set of adverse perinatal outcomes, however, were identified in association with alcohol use until 1968, when Lemoine and coworkers (1968) described the now well-accepted stigmata of Fetal Alcohol Syndrome (FAS).

Alcohol crosses the placenta freely and attains the same concentration in the fetus as in the mother. While the mechanism of alcohol's toxic effects on the fetus is not well understood, the most serious adverse effects associated with maternal alcohol consumption is FAS. FAS is a clinically observable entity with specific parameters for diagnosis that include prenatal and/or postnatal growth retardation (weight, length, and/or head circumference below the tenth percentile); central nervous system involvement, including signs of neurologic abnormality, developmental delay, or intellectual impairment; characteristic facial dysmorphology with at least two of the following clinical features: microcephaly, microopthalmia and/or palpebral fissures, and poorly developed philtrum, thin upper lip, or flattening of the maxillary area (Werner & Morse, 1988).

FAS has been reported in scientific literature worldwide and occurs in all ethnic groups and at all socioeconomic levels. Although FAS is a clinically recognizable syndrome, the diagnosis cannot be made on the basis of any single distinctive feature. Alcohol-related defects occur in approximately 40,000 births per year, and alcohol's effects on fetal development encompass a wide range, with FAS at the far end of the spectrum. Investigators note that some children exposed to alcohol in utero exhibit components of the syndrome in the absence of full FAS. When one or two clinical features occur, the terms "possible fetal alcohol effects (FAE)" or "alcohol-related birth defects" are used. The incidence rate of FAE is difficult to determine as the symptoms are not specific, but are estimated to occur about three times more frequently than FAS (Ibid). Disturbances to the central nervous system (CNS) are the most serious consequences of exposure to alcohol in utero. Symptoms consistent with CNS dysfunction are reported as delays in mental and motor development, hyperactivity, altered sleep patterns, feeding problems, language dysfunction, and perceptual problems. Some of these symptoms have been observed in the absence of facial dysmorphology or growth retardation.

Longitudinal studies of children with FAS report mild to moderate mental retardation. Mean IQ scores were reported between 70 and 89, with individual scores covering a broader range, from a low of 16 to a high of 130. Learning abilities improved when symptoms such as hyperactivity were reduced. In some cases the improvement was attributed to a specific intervention; in others improvement was linked to the passage of time (Ibid.).

Nevertheless, hyperactivity is consistently noted to be the most persistent behavioral disturbance, presenting a serious obstacle to learning and school performance. When hyperactivity is combined with attention deficits, perceptual problems, and language delays, the determination of cognitive ability is compromised.

While clinical and experimental literature provide a growing data base related to understanding the mechanisms of alcohol's adverse effect on fetal development, there remain major areas of controversy surrounding the precise assessment of the long-term impact on the developing child. Early identification and early educational intervention continue to provide the best opportunity for maximizing the development and educational potential of children with alcohol-related deficits and/or delays.

Effects of Cocaine Exposure in Utero. Since 1985 cocaine use by women in the United States has grown rapidly, posing a significant threat to a developing fetus. The National Association for Perinatal Addiction Research and Education (NAPARE) estimates that as many as 11 percent (375,000) of infants may be affected by prenatal maternal drug abuse; 25 percent in large cities (Schneider, 1989).

Studies of cocaine's effects on fetal development have shown that cocaine interferes with the supply of blood and oxygen to the fetus by causing constriction of the blood vessels (Chasnoff, 1988). Cocaine crosses the placental barrier and readily acts on the CNS as a stimulant, while peripherally causing vasoconstriction. Use of cocaine at any time during gestation places both the mother and fetus at risk for prenatal complications that include intrauterine growth retardation, in utero cerebrovascular accidents, spontaneous abortion, premature delivery, and abruptio placenta.

Variables affecting the extent of the effects on fetal development are determined by the amount of cocaine exposure and the stage of pregnancy at the time of exposure. Unlike infants exposed to alcohol in utero, the cocaine-exposed infant has no characteristic facial dysmorphology but may exhibit a range of serious health problems requiring medical intervention and follow-up, including congenital malformations of the skull, cardiovascular system, urinary tract, and extremities; cerebral infarction, seizures, cortical atrophy, and neurodevelopmental delay due to CNS abnormalities; respiratory problems with an increased risk for sudden infant death syndrome (SIDS); and failure to thrive.

Recognized clinical signs of prenatal cocaine exposure in infants are characterized by hyperirritability, poor feeding patterns, high respiratory and heart rates, increased startle responses, tremors, and irregular sleep patterns. Because some of these effects persist beyond the first few weeks of life, they may be indications of protracted CNS dysfunction.

Infants exposed to cocaine in utero display very low thresholds for overstimulation and require assistance from caretakers to maintain control of their hyperexcitable, immature nervous systems. Research data show these behavioral characteristics to be part of the cluster of characteristics that describe a large percentage of infants with established exposure to cocaine in utero (Griffith, 1988). These infants also generally display more immature movement patterns and more problems with extensor muscle tone, placing them at risk for motor delay or dysfunction.

Assessments of the behavior of infants exposed to cocaine in utero show atypical results. Studies using the Brazelton Neonatal Behavioral Assessment Scale report that cocaine exposed infants demonstrated poor state control and poor interactive capabilities, poorer consolability, and significant differences in reflexive and motoric responses (Ibid.). The infants showed impaired ability to interact with and respond to their caregivers, requiring intense intervention to establish orientation, motor control, and state regulation. These behavioral characteristics were more likely to inhibit mother-infant interaction and added substantial risk to the attachment process. Such factors suppress the optimal caregiving required of these infants, and in some cases, may predispose them to physical abuse and/or neglect.

United States educators, in pilot programs for preschool-aged children prenatally exposed to cocaine, report continued behavioral difficulties. Behaviors observed in the preschool-aged child include low frustration tolerance, poor impulse control, lack of ability to regulate behavior, extreme emotional lability, and difficulty with developing attachments. These children also demonstrate deficits in fine motor skills and speech/language development. They also exhibit distractibility, hyperactivity, lack of self-organization, and decreased response to verbal direction, requiring frequent one-to-one attention and highly structured educational environments (Cole, 1989).

Data on the school-aged child exposed to cocaine in utero is just now being gathered. The oldest children systematically being studied are five to six years old. Whether the effects of cocaine exposure will continue to impact beyond early childhood is still unclear. Experts in the field believe a small percentage of these children will be significantly developmentally disabled and will qualify for special education services already in place; others will have no behavioral, developmental, psychosocial, or learning difficulties requiring educational services beyond regular education; and yet, an unpredictable number of cocaine-exposed children will present atypical learning and behavioral patterns that will place them at continued risk for reaching maximum educational potential in the typical classroom.

Inasmuch as there is no absolute profile of developmental outcome for these at-risk children, interventions to date have focused on prevention, early assessment, and implementation of educational strategies that address all risk factors affecting development. Leaders in the field also emphasize collaboration between medical professionals, community service agencies, and education professionals, in order to comprehensively coordinate services for these children and their families.

References

Chasnoff, I. J. (ed.). (1988). *Drugs, alcohol, pregnancy, and parenting.* Norwell, MA: Kluwer Academic.

Cole, C. K. (1989, November 22). Preschool drug exposed children: Testimony to U.S. House of Representatives Select Committee on Children, Youth and Family. Chicago: National Association for Perinatal Addiction Research and Education.

Greer, J. V. (1990). The drug babies. *Exceptional children, 56* (5), 382–84.

Griffith, D. R. (1988). The effects of perinatal cocaine exposure on infant neurobehavior and early maternal-infant interactions. In I. J. Chasnoff (ed.), *Drug, alcohol, pregnancy, and parenting* (pp. 105–113). Norwell, MA: Kluwer Academic.

Howard, J., et al. (1989). The development of young children of substance-abusing parents: Insight from seven years of intervention and research. *Zero to Three, 9* (5), 8–12.

Lemoine, P., et al. (1968). Les enfants de parents alcooliques: Anomalies observées à propos de 27 cas. *Quest Med, 21,* 476–482.

Regan, D. O., Ehrlich, S. M., & Finnegan, L. P. (1987). Infants of drug addicts: At risk for child abuse, neglect, and placement in foster care. *Neurotoxicology and Teratology, 9,* 315–319.

Schneider, I. A. (1989). Infant exposure to cocaine: Implications for developmental assessment and intervention. *Infants and Young Children, 2* (1), 25–36.

Werner, L., & Morse, B. A. (1988). Clinical perspectives and prevention. In I. J. Chasnoff (ed.), *Drug, alcohol, pregnancy, and parenting* (pp. 127-148). Norwell, MA: Kluwer Academic.

Weston, D. R., et al. (1989). Drug exposed babies: Research and clinical issues. *Zero to Three, 9* (5), 1–7.

Model Projects/Natural Resources

Fetal Alcohol Education Program
Boston University School of Medicine
7 Kent Street
Brookline, MA 02146

FAS Network
P.O. Box 746
Pacific City, OR 97135

Intensive Care Project Development Center
747 52nd Street
Oakland, CA 94609

In Utero Cocaine Exposure: Effect on Fetal and Neonatal State Organization
Child Development Unit
Box 3364
Department of Pediatrics and Obstetrics
Duke University Medical Center
Durham, NC 22710
(919) 684-5513

March of Dimes Birth Defects Foundation
1275 Mamaronneck Avenue
White Plains, NY 10605
(914) 428-7100

National Association for Perinatal Addiction Research and Education (NAPARE)
11 E. Hubbard Street, Suite 200
Chicago, IL 60611
(312) 329-2512

National Clearing House for Alcohol and Drug Information (NCADI)
P.O. Box 2345
Rockville, MD 20852
(301) 468-2600

P.E.D. Program
Salvin
Special Education Center
Los Angeles Unified School District
1925 S. Budlong Avenue
Los Angeles, CA 90007
(213) 731-0703

Perinatal Center for Chemical Dependence
Northwestern Memorial Hospital
320 E. Huron Street
Chicago, IL 60611

Primary Diagnostic Services
Hillsborough County School District
Tampa, FL

UCLA Intervention Program
UCLA Department of Pediatrics
100 Veteran Avenue
Los Angeles, CA 90024-1797
(213) 825-4622

J. M. Gray

Medically Fragile/Technology-Dependent Children

Advances in medical technology have led to the survival of children who formerly would have succumbed to their physical impairment or chronic illness. These high-risk children often require intense, expensive, and complex types of specialized medical procedures to support life function and/or to maintain health.

Transitioning children with special health care needs from hospital environments to home settings implies transitioning from home to school. As parents seek educational placements for their medically fragile/technology dependent children, educators, who just ten years ago were challenged with meeting the needs of children requiring clean intermittent catheterization (CIC) in school, now are challenged with meeting the specialized needs of children who may require ventilator dependence, tracheostomy care, gastrostomy tube, and nasogastric tube feedings.

As many as 100,000 infants and children in the United States are estimated to be technology dependent, and the numbers are likely to increase. Factors associated with the expected increase are advances in the care and survival of extremely premature infants, and advances in medical treatment and equipment that extend the life expectancy of chronically ill children. Parallel with survival, however, is the probability of medical fragility and/or dependency on medical technology for maintenance of life.

An accepted definition of a "technology dependent child" developed by the United States Congress Task Force on Technology Dependent Children (1988) includes, persons from birth through 21 years of age; who have a chronic disability; require routine use of a medical device to compensate for the loss of a sustaining body function, for example, dependence on mechanical ventilators or other device-based respiratory or nutritional support, including tracheostomy tube care, oxygen support, and intravenous and internal tube feeding; and require daily, ongoing care and/or monitoring by trained personnel.

A growing body of case law clearly identifies relevant issues for concern to the education system. Concomitant issues being decided through litigation, both locally and nationally, include qualifications of school personnel who implement medical procedures that extend beyond the scope of their customary responsibilities and/or competence (*Irving v. Tatro*); and fiscal responsibility for specialized personnel and specialized equipment (*Bevin v. Wright* and *Detsel v. Board of Education*).

As interpretation of the scope of "related services" and "least restrictive environment" under P.L. 94-142 continues to be debated in the courts, educators of the 1990s must be ready to deal with both the educational needs and the environmental adaptations these children may require. The early childhood setting in all likelihood will be the first educational experience for the medically fragile/technology dependent child.

Providing the "most safe" environment, whether in the regular or special education setting, is a priority for children with complex medical needs. Informed school administrators consider the following general guidelines and principles when developing the individual education plan (IEP) for medically fragile/technology dependent children: delineation of staff roles and responsibilities with assignment of a case manager who is preferably a school nurse; determination of qualifications, training, and/or funding of individuals required to implement medical procedures (in some cases a private duty nurse may be needed); obtain parent and physician authorization to implement specific medical/health procedures during the school day; develop a health care plan as part of the IEP process, including necessary protocols for emergency procedures; determination of environmental adaptations required when assessing issues of life safety (classroom and transportation); determination of funding sources for equipment and medical supplies, with identification of additional resources as needed; communication, collaboration, and cooperation between parents, health care professionals, social service agencies, and educational personnel; and continuing education and inservice education specific to the child's health status and health care needs, as warranted by the child's changing medical/health status. Preparing for the complex needs of the medically fragile/technology dependent student is challenging and can be simplified by school personnel who are ready to address the issues.

References

Bevin H. v. Wright, 666 F. Supp. 71 (W.D. Pa. 1987).

Council for Exceptional Children. (1988). Final Report: CEC ad hoc committee on medically fragile.

Detsel v. Board of Education. Second Circuit Court of Appeals, 820 F2d 587 (1987). Cert. denied U.S. Supreme Court (1987).

Irving Independent School District v. Tatro. 481 F. Supp. 1724, (1979), 625 F2d. 557, (1980); 104 S.Ct. 3371, (1984).

Gray, Judith M. (1990, March). The Medically Fragile/Technology Dependent Student. Unpublished Master's Thesis. National College of Education.

Sirvis, B. (1988, Summer). Students with Special Health Care Needs. *Teaching Exceptional Children, 20* (4), 40–44.

U.S. Congress, Office of Technology Assessment. (1987). Technology-dependent children: Hospital v. Home care—A Technical Memorandum, OTA-TM-H-38. United States Government Printing Office.

U.S. Congress. (1988). Report to Congress and the Secretary by the Task Force on Technology Dependent Children. United States Government Printing Office.

Model Projects/National Resources

Several states have developed procedure manuals addressing issues related to implementing health care procedures in the school setting. The following resources may be helpful to education facilities when developing agency guidelines.

Children Assisted by Medical Technology in Educational Settings: Guidelines for Care, 1989.
Contact: Project School Care
  Childrens Hospital
  300 Longwood Avenue
  Boston, MA 02115

Management of Students with Health Impairments in the School Setting, in press.
Contact: Illinois State Board of Education
  100 North First Street
  Springfield, IL 62777

Managing the School Age Child with a Chronic Health Condition, 1988.
Contact: Pathfinder
  500 West 39th Street
  Minneapolis, MN 55411

Procedure Guidelines for Health Care of Special Needs Students in the School Setting, 1988.
Contact: Community Nursing Section
  Colorado Dept. of Health
  4210 East 11th Avenue
  Denver, CO 80220

School Health Nursing Services for Medically Complex Children, 1987.
Contact: State Health Office of Maternal Child and Special Health Programs
  1317 Winewood Boulevard
  Tallahassee, FL 32304

J. M. Gray

4.7 Contexts of Development

When young children find themselves in different places, with different people, of different ages, at different times, and under different conditions, they grow in varied ways. Their family structure, cultural practices and myths, physical and economic circumstances, status, and neighborhood, including peer group presence and opportunities, all contribute to the unique confluence of forces that affect how children develop.

The various contexts into which young children are born, and in which they grow, affect the nature of their learning experiences and expectancies. These environmental conditions provide varied opportunities for exposure to information and social feedback, as well as degrees of independence, security, and/or neglect. In order to develop a more accurate picture of how children grow, therefore, it is important to frame that process within the ecological, sociocultural, and geographic situations that they experience. The articles in this section consider these issues through the lenses of social, cultural, family, classroom, neighborhood, peer group, mythological, and physical health perspectives.

D. P. Fromberg

Ecological and Sociocultural Influences

Ecological descriptions provide an overall picture of people's niches in the world. With respect to children, they give us a sense of the whole child and the numerous social and cultural influences that might affect the child. Through these descriptions we can learn what predicaments loom largest in children's lives and how circumstances might be changed to foster their development.

A classic project seeking to determine the ecology of human development was conducted by Barker and Wright (1951). These researchers spent hundreds of hours discovering, observing, and describing the natural ecology of school children in various communities in the United States. Barker and Wright revealed many relationships among settings in which children found themselves and the characteristics of children's behavior in these settings.

Within child development, Bronfenbrenner (1979) more recently has advocated the study of development in context in terms of interacting concentric systems or ecological levels. As a result of considerable research in how the child's environment affects his or her growth and well-being, the conventional wisdom about how to promote early childhood and family development has shifted from a child-centered to a more ecological approach,

one that emphasizes the importance of interrelationships between the child and the family in neighborhoods and communities and the social supports available for them. Families, rather than just children, have become the appropriate unit of study.

Because we are a democratic society that values freedom of religion, freedom of speech, freedom of the press and of family values, we are also a society that reflects many cultural differences. Each culture within the society of the United States has unique language patterns and rituals, and each has its own perception of family structure, roles, and functioning. The work of anthropologists and sociolinguists (those who study the social aspects of language), has been fundamental to understanding the behavior and values of varied social groups (Cazden, John, & Hymes, 1972; Whiting & Edwards, 1988). In-depth studies of whole communities also are reminders of the complex interactions between school performance and societal factors, such as whether students are recent immigrants or native-born members of minorities in the United States (Ogbu, 1978).

In many ways the similarities among the various cultures of the United States are striking. Children are valued and respected, but outward manifestations of valuing are sometimes quite different. Attempts recently have been made to preserve much of the cultural heritage of minority groups, for one's cultural heritage affects one's life in many ways regardless of the efforts to assimilate or acculturate into mainstream society. In early childhood programs greater emphasis may need to be placed on the appreciation and preservation of unique language varieties, values, rituals, and ethnic traditions in our pluralistic society.

Curricula for Young Children in Context

There is an emerging consensus among educators that the quality of implementation (including staff training and supervision, parent involvement, and administrative leadership) matters as much as the curriculum of early child programs. Gray and Klaus (1970) and a host of other subsequent investigators (e.g., Berrueta-Clement et al., 1984) demonstrated that early childhood development programs worked best when mothers were actively involved in planning and carrying out learning projects. Moreover, we now can begin to generalize that participation by child, family, school, and community is essential to help children in trouble, whatever the cause of the difficulty. Programs that take their educational tasks seriously know now that they must extend their efforts beyond the child and to the earliest years of the child's life in order to enhance her or his chances for a bright school future.

We have learned since the 1960s that certain programs can produce significant "real world" gains for children. We still, however, seek to understand exactly *how* these programs bring about these effects. Is it, as Bronfenbrenner (1979) hypothesizes, because the parent-child system is reinforced with positive consequences for the amount and types of parent-child interactions? Or is it as Zigler and Berman (1983) have suggested that these programs have positive effects on parents and their sense of control over the child's future that are then translated directly and indirectly into effects on children? It is possible, too, that some of these indirect effects stem from events outside the family and the program and are thus difficult to specify.

An example of an "out-of-family influence" is the civil rights movement, which promoted a new liaison between families and schools (Hobbs, 1978). Until that period schools had unquestioned dominion over the life of a child while in school. The programs tended to be respectful of the wishes of middle-class parents with the competence and confidence to demand reasonable decisions about their children, but they have been much less sensitive to the wishes of parents lacking skills in managing their institutional worlds.

Today court orders, legislation, and consent of parents and administrative guidelines require the informal consent of parents and guardians for decisions substantially affecting the well-being of a child. They also require

provision of due process for decision making when caregivers and the programs are in conflict. No early childhood plan will work effectively without designing systems that include the family as the unit of primary responsibility for its members. This notion can be carried forward and constructed to involve families and schools in the context of caring communities and to provide an optimal array of resources for the rearing of our children.

In coming years more children from troubled homes will be in need of early education. The rise in stresses on the family, along with urbanization and increased mobility, and the sapping of family authority by the media and other influences all have widened the distance between home and school. That distance is greater still for children whose class, race, and family income differ most from those of the school staff. When intervention programs make special efforts to bridge cultural and social discontinuities and to enlist parents and other kin in educating the children, there can be far-reaching benefits. In particular, appreciating the strengths of nonnuclear families can promote links between schools and communities. Families in stressful circumstances may nonetheless contribute to children's development, for example, in becoming literate (Taylor & Dorsey-Gaines, 1988). As early childhood programs are further developed and refined, the challenge is to bring closer together families, communities, and other institutions that educate in the interest of enriched opportunities for all children.

References

Barker, R., & Wright, H. (1951). *One boy's day.* New York: Harper & Row.

Berrueta-Clement, J., Schweinhart, L., Barnett, W., Epstein, A., & Weikart, D. (1984). *Changed lives.* Ypsilanti, MI: High/Scope Press.

Bronfenbrenner, U. (1979). *The ecology of human development: Experiments by nature and design.* Cambridge: Harvard University Press.

Cazden, C. B., John, V. S., & Hymes, D. (eds.). (1972). *Functions of language in the classroom.* New York: Teachers College Press.

Gray, S. W., & Klaus, R. A. (1970). The Early Training Project: Seventh year report. *Child Development, 41* (4), 909–924.

Hobbs, N. (1978). Families, schools, and communities: An ecosystem for children. *Teachers College Record*, 79, 756–766.

Ogbu, J. U. (1978). *Minority education and caste: The American system in cross-cultural perspective.* New York: Academic.

Taylor, D., & Dorsey-Gaines, C. (1988). *Growing up literate: Learning from inner-city families.*

Whiting, B. B., & Edwards, C. P. (1988). *Children of different worlds: The formation of social behavior.* Cambridge: Harvard University Press.

Zigler, E., & Berman, W. (1983). Discerning the future of early childhood intervention. *American Psychologist*, 38 (8), 894–906.

M. Burke

Class and Caste Variations

Most child development research has focused on the universals of development and has explained differences in developmental outcomes as the effects of either genetic deficiencies or environmental hazards (Ogbu, 1983). These assumptions have led to compensatory programs such as Head Start, which seek to counteract some environmental deficiencies by providing experiences that replicate white middle-class childhoods. With his cultural-ecological model of development, John Ogbu rejects this deficit orientation and demonstrates how different developmental outcomes reflect competencies appropriate to a particular set of circumstances and future adult roles.

From a cultural-ecological perspective, child-rearing practices are developed by each group to teach their children the competencies that are most adaptive for their particular circumstances. These circumstances in turn are influenced by the broader environment, which includes the social, political, and economic system and the place of a particular group within that system. For example, a middle-class child who is likely to become a manager or other professional needs different skills than a child from a low-income family who may need to learn how to function successfully in a more menial job. From this perspective evaluative cross-social class comparisons of child-rearing practices are fallacious because the developmental goals are different.

According to John Ogbu (1978, 1983), many non-white racial groups in this country are viewed and treated as castelike minorities. Ogbu points out that members of groups that were conquered, enslaved, and/or dispossessed (in particular, Native Americans, Mexican-Americans, Puerto Rican–Americans, and African-Americans) have occupied the place of lower-caste groups and have been the targets of the most severe and intransigent discrimination. They have been stigmatized and excluded from higher status opportunities and roles, and their aspirations and their confidence in the educational and occupational systems have eroded from generations of disappointments and betrayed hopes. For families in these groups, survival is a challenge, and their children often feel alienated from the world of middle-class education and institutions.

The economic hardships in turn cause stress on families that may adversely affect children's socioemotional functioning (McLoyd, 1990). Aside from the material deprivations, constant stigmatization means that many families live in a state of "mundane extreme environmental stress" (Peters, 1985), the day-to-day tension of enduring racially related episodes that may vary from annoying to life threatening. For example, trips to restaurants and stores, which might be pleasurable family outings, are often ruined by overt or covert discriminatory actions on the part of waiters or salespeople (Peters, 1985).

According to Ogbu, members of these castelike minorities have developed alternative survival strategies that are appropriate to the marginal resources available to them. Ogbu (1983) uses the example of inner-city blacks to illustrate how different adult roles emerge in response to these circumstances and how specific child-rearing patterns teach children the instrumental competencies to fill these roles. Because conventional employment is limited to dead-end, peripheral, and unstable jobs, many adolescents and adults are skeptical about the benefits of education and mainstream jobs and turn to alternative economies, such as the street economy, which are more attractive and lucrative. As they grow up, children in these communities develop an admiration for those adults who are making it "outside of the conventional strategies of schooling and wage labor" (p. 57) and learn the appropriate skills and strategies. Some of these roles, such as hustling and pimping, require a high level of self-reliance, defiance, aggressiveness and manipulativeness. Ogbu shows how patterns of child rearing in the black community, often evaluated as deficient by middle-class standards, in fact, do help children develop these competencies. At the same time, these behaviors may be maladaptive for middle-class institutions such as schools. Moreover, Ogbu points out, members of castelike minorities often develop secondary cultural differences, behaviors, and values defined in opposition to the dominant culture that increase children's resistance to schooling.

Not all ethnic groups have suffered the same level of discrimination. According to Ogbu (1978) immigrants who came more or less voluntarily to this country expected hardships, but were generally optimistic about the possibilities for future generations. They often created communities that provided support, a connection with their former lives, and a buffer from the discrimination they experienced in this country. As a result, their members were able to take advantage of the opportunities that they found in this country and became successful in conventional schooling and jobs.

Ogbu's model and conclusions about child-rearing patterns has been criticized as potentially supporting the deficit model of differences because he uses research findings from studies of black families done from a deficit orientation to support his case that child-rearing patterns lead to particular competencies (Bronfenbrenner, 1986). Bronfenbrenner also raises questions about Ogbu's characterization of black culture and shows how it fails to consider the range of life styles of blacks and the effects of different economic circumstances and historical times. Spencer (1990) points out that a caste system is rigid and cannot account for the movement between statuses that oc-

curs and the diverse circumstances within groups.

Despite some potential limitations and overgeneralizations in his analysis, Ogbu's cultural-ecological model and his identification of castelike minorities offers a powerful tool for a more forthright analysis of the social class structure of our society and the effects of intransigent discrimination and exclusion. His model also has opened the way for a penetrating critique of Eurocentric research on minority children and a new wave of research in which children and their families are studied within their particular contexts.

References

Bronfenbrenner, U. (1986). Summary. In M. B. Spencer, G. K. Brookins, & W. R. Allen (eds.), *Beginnings: The social and affective development of black children* (pp. 67–73). Hillsdale, NJ: Erlbaum.

McLoyd, V. C. (1990). The impact of economic hardship on black families and children: Psychological distress, parenting, and socioemotional development. *Child Development, 61* (2), 311–346.

Ogbu, J. U. (1986). A cultural ecology of competence among inner-city blacks. In M. B. Spencer, G. K. Brookins, & W. R. Allen (eds.), *Beginnings: The social and affective development of black children* (pp. 45–66). Hillsdale, NJ: Erlbaum.

Ogbu, J. U. (1978). *Minority education and caste.* New York: Academic Press.

Ogbu, J. U. (1983). Socialization: A cultural ecological approach. In K. M. Borman (ed.), *The social life of children in a changing society*, pp. 253–267. Norwood, NJ: Ablex.

Peters, M. F. (1985). Racial socialization of young black children. In H. P. McAdoo & J. L. McAdoo (eds.), *Black children: Social, educational, and parental environments* (pp. 159–173). Newbury Park, CA: Sage.

Spencer, M. B. (1990). Development of minority children: An introduction. *Child Development, 61* (2), 267–269.

P. G. Ramsey

Cultural/Ethnicity Variations

Children are socialized as members of an ethnic group that shares certain behaviors, customs, attitudes, and language or language style. They quickly learn the acceptable form for greeting or taking leave of someone, such as shaking right hands or waving hello or goodbye with the correct hand and arm movements. Some of the socialization is direct, as when children are taught to eat with chopsticks. In other cases, children learn behaviors through more subtle and covert means like body language. In this way children as young as three and four years are able to identify with their own group; and by the age of eight years, they apparently have a relatively consistent view of ethnicity.

In developing this awareness of ethnic group membership, children must learn the accepted social roles in order to conform to the group. But considerable variation exists in the degree to which groups uphold their ethnicity. Thus, a Mexican-American child may choose to abandon Spanish in favor of English as the preferred language of communication. Still another child may learn that not speaking Spanish means not being Mexican-American and will strive to maintain the language in order to also maintain an ethnic identity. Researchers have shown that this growing sense of ethnicity has both a cognitive and an affective component. Children develop concepts about skin color or certain customs, such as eating with chopsticks or speaking a language other than English. They also demonstrate certain attitudes toward their own and others' ethnicity. Young children, for example, may display a negative attitude toward their own or another child's skin color. They may view eating with chopsticks as "funny."

These concepts and attitudes, however, are not influenced solely by membership in the ethnic group. The status of the group, in fact, plays a significant role in ethnic identification, as in the case of African-Americans and Hispanics (Latinos), two ethnic minority groups that occupy a position of low status in the United States. Relative to other groups, they exhibit major social and economic problems. Many Hispanics, moreover, are limited English or non-English speaking, further highlighting their differences from the dominant group. The perception that these characteristics are common to most or the entire group affects how children are socialized by agencies such as the school.

Some researchers claim that the educational problems faced by many ethnic and language minority groups may be explained by contrasting socialization patterns between the family or group and the school. Thus, while the family and the ethnic group are influencing the child in one manner, the larger society and the school may be influencing the child in a different manner. The result is a conflict in expectations that children are hard pressed to handle.

Ethnicity, then, plays a significant role in how children are socialized both within and outside the group. This interaction with others, together with maturation, affects the child's social and personal identity. Since ethnic groups are part of the larger society and society is not static, the influence of ethnicity on child development must also be viewed as dynamic.

References

Garcia, E. (1983). *Bilingualism in early childhood.* Albuquerque, NM: University of New Mexico Press.

Garcia, R.. (1990). *Teaching in a pluralistic society: Concepts, models, strategies.* (2nd ed.). New York: Hayden & Row.

Goodman, M. (1964). *Race awareness in young children.* New York: Collier Publishing Company.

Milner, D. (1983). *Children and race ten years on.* London: Ward Loch.

Simoes, Antonio Jr. (1976). *The bilingual child.* New York: Academic Press.

S. Cavazos Peña

Family Contexts

The family today is different than 100, 50, or even 20 years ago. A young child today is likely to have only one sibling, a mother who works, and a father more involved in child rearing. Almost half of all children will live with only one parent. Most will receive a considerable amount of daily care from a nonrelative. Although the family has changed in form, it is still the most stable component of this society and the most significant influence on a child. Parents are children's first nurturers, socializers, and educators. The parent-child relationship ensures the survival and shapes the future of the child.

The primary function of the family is socialization. In this process, parents help children develop a well-rounded, emotionally healthy personality by teaching them the knowledge, skills, and character traits that will enable them to become effective, fully functioning adults. Through socialization children acquire a concept of self as they learn to incorporate the attitudes and expectations of others into their personalities. The development of a positive self-concept supports children in their attempts to regulate their own behavior and become self-disciplined. Socialization also supplies the goals for later development, teaching the skills, social roles, and attitudes that will relate to schooling, adult roles, and occupations.

Until recently, a unidirectional model of socialization was the focus of research on the family. Now the focus is more on a concept of developmental interaction. Investigators no longer see the parent-child relationship as one sided or causal. They recognize that children have unique personalities and developmental needs that serve as stimuli for the psychosocial development of parents.

The current model of the family is not bidirectional, either, but part of a social system. The system includes all the interactions among people inside and outside the family unit, including grandparents, friends, and other social support groups. Thus, the family is a unit included within a web of other relationships; the child, adult, and environment intertwine in influencing child rearing and socialization. Therefore, the stress of income level, jobs, illness, and divorce can influence the effectiveness of the family. In turn, the positive influence of the family can meet children's basic needs for love and security when adults communicate to children that they love and enjoy them. Children who are securely attached to a parent are able to get along better with others.

Families also influence children through the kinds of new experiences that they provide. Tasks appropriate to each new stage of development help children develop positive attitudes toward learning. A safe physical environment that is full of interesting things to see and touch fosters curiosity and exploratory behavior. Parents who enjoy spending time with their children teach play and language skills through playful interactions, talking, reading, and listening to them, and by asking questions that encourage thinking.

Families can stimulate perseverance when adults have reasonable expectations, explain them clearly, and provide praise and recognition. Children can experience motivation to learn when they come to expect that mistakes and failure are part of learning.

Finally, parents can help to meet children's need to become increasingly independent by encouraging them to make choices, and help them learn to take responsibility for possessions and personal belongings. Parents help children assume an active role in organizing their environments. They are available to their children but do not do things for children that they can do for themselves.

It is apparent, however, that there are families in which parents feel overwhelmed by life, whose homes are chaotic, and who spend either too much or not enough time with their children. These families may not be meeting children's basic needs. Parent education, social support networks, and family counseling can make a positive difference. Thus, exemplary early childhood education programs have a parent component to better understand how each child's family is functioning and to offer the support that each family needs.

References

Belsky, J., Lerner, R., & Spanier, B. (1984). *The child in the family.* New York: Random House.

Berger, E. (1991). *Parents as partners in education.* New York: Macmillan.

Bigner, J. (1989). *Parent-child relations.* New York: Macmillan.

Cataldo, C. (1987). *Parent education for early childhood.* New York: Teachers College Press.

Jaffe, M. (1991). *Understanding parenting.* Dubuque, IA: William C. Brown.

Papalia, D., & Olds, S. W. (1990). *A child's world*. New York: McGraw-Hill.

M. K. Ross

Parents as First Teacher

The early years of development, beginning at birth, are formative years that lay the foundation for a child's success in school. Parents, during this time, are their child's first and most influential teachers. Research on parents who do an outstanding job during their child's first three years suggests that the more parents know about child development, the better they can foster their child's physical, social, emotional, and intellectual growth (White, 1985).

It is through the ongoing parent-child interactions that the young child develops concepts about self, attitudes, and values, as well as behavioral patterns (Chodorow, 1978; Erikson, 1963/1950; Freud, 1962). The foundation for the attachment bond between infant and parent is the parent's loving response, first to the infant's crying and later to the infant's exploration and/or attention seeking. This attachment during the first year of life contributes to the infant's development of a sense of trust in others and in self (Erikson, 1963/1950).

Through everyday experiences, young children develop the ability to understand language and then to speak. As parents talk to their children, beginning with the earliest moments of life, they are teaching them to speak by describing what the infant is paying attention to or what the parent is doing. In the child's second year, simple conversations with the child and reading simple, enjoyable stories, stimulate the child's understanding and speech. Conversations become increasingly complex as time passes. Inasmuch as language and thinking are intertwined, parents stimulate their child's thinking when they encourage conversation. For example, parents offer explanations and together with their child, plan and reflect upon shared experiences.

Young children are curious. Their observations and explorations are the foundations of their cognitive development. Learning comes easily to young children whose parents provide opportunities to explore and give them encouragement and assistance.

During the early years, children learn about people and objects through play. Parents can have multiple roles in their child's play by providing space and materials, giving praise and encouragement, suggesting ideas, and participating actively. Play initially involves exploration. By fourteen to eighteen months of age, children enjoy simple pretending and, by three years of age, engage in elaborate role play and constructions. By the time children are two years of age, parents can offer opportunities for their children to play with age mates, either informally, in play groups, or in early childhood centers.

As the child matures, parents set limits, a task that may be challenging as children in their second year begin to be aware of themselves as separate persons, and in this process, test both themselves and their parents. When parents also provide predictable routines, consistent rules, and age-appropriate explanations, their child experiences love and security, develops self-control, and learns how to get along with others.

References

Chodorow, N. (1978). *The reproduction of mothering: Psychoanalysis and the sociology of gender*. Berkeley: University of California Press.

Erikson, E. H. (1963/1950). *Childhood and society*. New York: Norton.

Freud, S. (1962). *Three essays on the theory of sexuality*. New York: Basic Books.

White, B. (1985). *The first three years of life*. Englewood Cliffs, NJ: Prentice-Hall.

C. S. Klass

Gender Identification

Well before the age of three years, children understand whether they are female or male and have begun to acquire culturally appropriate gender roles. As children learn their sexual identity, they simultaneously learn that this distinction has important meaning for themselves and others. Everyone is a gendered human being, and gender appears to be a primary distinction in all societies.

In the United States, appropriate gender membership is taught beginning at birth when the new arrival is heralded as either a girl or a boy. In hospital nurseries, the name tags and blankets often are color coded to accentuate this difference. Once the gender labeling has begun, family members and caregivers direct many societal expectations, attitudes, events, and objects about gender toward the baby. In the months directly following their birth, babies live in a world of clothes, toys, and rooms that reflect their gender. Ruffles and frills typically adorn the clothing of girls, who from birth are taught that decor and appearance are proper interests. Boys' clothing, in contrast, is tailored plainly, and allows boys to engage in activities that foreshadow their action-oriented future.

Family members and caregivers treat girls and boys differently. Although boys are more susceptible to disease and handicaps, they are more likely to be labeled strong and referred to as tough or brutish. Through words and gestures caregivers focus the male infant on his potential strength and power. A female baby of the same size often is perceived as delicate and tiny. She also may be compared to a doll, a decorative, passive, and malleable object. Parents and other caregivers insure that girls and boys engage in gender appropriate activities. This influence, however, is not equal for both sexes. Parents actively discourage boys from engaging in female-type activities because they fear that their sons will be seen as weak. On the other hand, parents often encourage girls to engage in male-type activities, and they may be proud of their tomboys. There is no similarly neutral male corollary term. This difference reflects the societal status of males and females and the expectation that men should be able to compete. Girls try out the male role more willingly since they have learned that role flexibility is more acceptable for females.

By three years of age, children have learned that they are either a boy or girl, will understand that the distinction is important, and will have both clear and muddied ideas about these distinctions. The notion that dogs are male and cats female is one of the more ludicrous muddied ideas.

Children's relationships with their parents further solidify gender roles. For most young children, the mother is the principal caregiver and the principal parent. Girls learn early that they will grow up to be like their mothers, and boys also learn that they will grow up to be unlike their mothers. Attachment and closeness to the mother is much more appropriate for the young girl, and intimacy and closeness remain a priority for many females. Males, however, learn to be independent of their mothers at a young age and strive toward independence and self-reliance. People in the United States often equate independence with adulthood. Feminist theorists have been challenging the tendency to posit male behavior as the human norm (de Beauvoir, 1959). These theorists point to early and continuing differences in patterns of gender role education as a way to understand the differing behavior profiles and personalities that females and males exhibit.

Thus, from the moment of birth and in every aspect of their lives, children are treated differentially by sex. They quickly learn their sexual identity, whether they are biologically male or female. Along with this identity, they also learn gender roles, the specific social expectations for males and females. As this process occurs, they increasingly spend more time in single-gender groups, which increases the polarity between males and females in this society.

References

de Beauvoir, S. (1959). *The second sex*. New York: Knopf.

Gilligan, A. (1989). *Making connections: The relational worlds of adolescent girls at the Emma Willard School*. Troy, NY: Emma Willard School.

Klein, S. S. (ed.). (1985). *Handbook for achieving sex equity through education*. Baltimore: Johns Hopkins University Press.

S. Greenberg

Gender and Play

Children are surrounded by environmental input about gender from family, peers, and the media. At the same time, they make their own attempts to understand the world and to form categories that help to organize the world. Gender provides one convenient way for them to accomplish this cognitive organization. In addition, society suffuses the gender distinction with affect, making gender perhaps the most salient parameter of social categorization.

One way to measure a very young child's knowledge about gender is to use a gender labeling task (Leinbach & Fagot, 1986). Children vary greatly in terms of the age when they acquire gender labels. There has been research concerning how parent practices affect the age at which children acquire gender labels. Observations of parents interacting at home with their 18-month-old children, prior to the acquisition of labels, found that differences in the parents' responses to the child's sex-typed play behaviors predicted whether the child would be early or late in acquiring the ability to label gender (Fagot & Leinbach, 1989).

The parents of children who labeled gender early gave more attention, both positive and negative, when their children were playing with either male- or female-sex–typed toys regardless of the sex of the child. These observations suggest that the amount of affective responses, rather than cognitive information alone, influences the sex-role education of boys and girls. Moreover, the affective responses of parents toward sex-typed behavior may serve to communicate to children the importance of gender. In this way, children who receive more affective responses are more likely to perceive gender as an important category and to work at understanding the system of role expectations.

Children who have acquired gender labels engage in more same-sex peer play (Fagot, Leinbach, & Hagan, 1986). Early labelers, who acquired labels prior to 28 months of age, exhibited more sex-typed choices of toys at that age than later labelers, even though the two groups had not differed when observed ten months earlier (Fagot & Leinbach, 1989). Thus, the child's construction of a gender schema reflects the behavioral, cognitive, and affective influences of the familial environment.

References

Fagot, B. I., & Leinbach, M. D. (1989). The young child's gender schema: Environmental input, internal organization. *Child Development, 60* (3), 663–672.

Fagot, B. I., Leinbach, M. D., & Hagan, R. (1986). Gender labeling and adoption of sex-typed behaviors. *Developmental Psychology, 22* (4), 440–443.

Leinbach, M. D., & Fagot, B. I. (1986). Acquisition of gender labeling: A test for toddlers. *Sex Roles, 15* (11/12), 655–666.

B. I. Fagot

Peer Culture

The activity of preschool-age children outside the family unit marks a major change in their worlds. An initial peer culture develops as young children engage in informal activities with siblings and playmates, participate in organized play groups, and attend nursery schools. According to ethnographic studies of United States and Italian preschool children, children attempt to produce and share social activities with other children as a way to gain control over their own lives (Corsaro, 1985; 1988).

Children demonstrate the basic themes of control and communal sharing through their creations, enactments, and enjoyment of a range of behavioral routines. They attempt to transform confusions and ambiguities about the adult world into the familiar and shared routines of the peer culture, by engaging in activities such as fantasy play. From this interpretive perspective, beyond their gradual attainment of adult skills and knowledge, they eventually reproduce the adult worlds in their active production and movement through a series of peer cultures across time.

Teacher interventions into peer activities can be important points of cultural contact for children. It is during such contacts and feedback by teachers that children feel encouraged to reflect upon the general social significance of their everyday activities. In this sense, early childhood teachers serve as partners in children's movement toward the eventual reproduction of the social order.

References

Corsaro, W. A. (1985). *Friendship and peer culture in the early years.* Norwood, NJ: Ablex.

Corsaro, W. A. (1988). Routines in the peer culture of American and Italian nursery school children. *Sociology of Education 61* (1), 1–14.

W. A. Corsaro

Classroom Peer Interaction

The classroom is a major context for children's peer interactions, social encounters with age mates, because schools tend to group children according to chronological age. Peer relationships during childhood not only are a source of immediate satisfaction or frustration to children but have life-long consequences for social adjustment (Segal & Yahares, 1979). Although young children's peer interactions tend to be transitory by adult standards, these interactions convey important messages about the self and offer children opportunities for social learning.

Robert Selman (1980) has proposed that the very young child's peer relationships follow a series of overlapping stages. These stages include Momentary Playmateship, between two and six years of age, during which children demonstrate brief gestures of friendship, such as offering a toy to a peer; One-way Assistance, between four and nine years of age, in which another child's compliance with requests determines the nature of the peer relationship; and Two-way Fairweather Cooperation, between seven and twelve years of age, when peer relationships exist by virtue of mutual interests and desirable personality traits.

The behaviors that cause children to be accepted, rejected, or neglected by peers remain rather consistent as children mature. Children who are accepted by their peers are perceived to be outgoing, cooperative, and friendly. Children who are sought by peers as companions blend in with ongoing activities rather than interrupt them. They express both positive and negative feedback in socially acceptable ways. Rejected children, on the other hand, are seen as restless, anxious, aggressive, disruptive, and demanding of teacher attention. Neglected children have been described as quiet and shy (Burton, 1987).

There have been efforts to help children who are at risk for peer rejection or neglect. Some attempts have involved "coaching" children in the skills of friendship, such as ways to gain entry into social groups; to express approval and support; to manage conflicts appropriately; and to exercise sensitivity and tact (Rubin, 1980).

Some studies have shown that social skills training can help to ameliorate disturbances in peer relationships (Asher & Gottman, 1981). When parents and teachers understand about the skills of friendships, they can exert a positive influence on children's peer interactions in classrooms.

Historically, programs for young children have emphasized peer relationships. Currently, there is considerable pressure to introduce formal, academic instruction in the preschool and kindergarten years. This practice has undermined the social skills training that is essential to the formation of satisfying peer relationships in the ecological context of the school.

References

Asher, S. R., & Gottman, J. M. (eds.). (1981). *The development of children's friendships.* New York: Cambridge University Press.

Burton, C. (1987). Problems in children's peer relations: A broadening perspective. In L. G. Katz (ed.), *Current topics in early childhood education, Vol. 7* (pp. 59–84). Norwood, NJ: Ablex.

Jalongo, M. R. (1992). Promoting peer acceptance of the newly immigrated child. In A. Eddowes & J. Quisenberry (eds.), *Readings from Childhood Education.* Association for Childhood Education International.

Rubin, K. H., & Ross, H. S. (1982). *Peer relationships and social skills in childhood.* New York: Springer-Verlag.

Rubin, Z. (1980). *Children's friendships*. Cambridge: Harvard University Press.

Segal, J., & Yahares, H. (1979). *A child's journey: Forces that shape the lives of our young.* New York: McGraw-Hill.

Selman, R.L. (1980). *The growth of interpersonal understanding.* San Diego, CA: Academic.

Smith, C. A. (1982). *Promoting the social development of young children.* Mountain View, CA: Mayfield.

M. R. Jalongo

Neighborhoods

Neighborhoods, along with the family, are important developmentally because they influence the kinds of physical, social, and affective opportunities and experiences children have and, thus, the competencies they develop.

Studies that analyze the influence of neighborhoods upon children's lives most often consider the child's everyday needs for experiences of autonomy from adults (Bryant, 1985; Parke, 1978; Tuan, 1978). Investigators have considered the study of neighborhood spaces, objects, activities, and persons that children encounter in ways that are structured and unstructured, planned and unplanned, formal and informal. (Bryant, 1985; Moore & Young, 1978). The varied roles that neighborhood participants assume, whether they are male or female, older or younger, family or friends, also define children's experiences (Bryant, 1985; Whiting & Edwards, 1988).

The direct effects of neighborhoods on children occur when peer or adult social support is readily available and through children's physical encounters during daily outings (Nagy & Baird, 1978). Indirect effects of neighborhoods usually influence the caretaking behavior of parents, inasmuch as social or physical influences are mediated by another person or object (Cochran & Brassard, 1979; Cotterell, 1986).

Some salient neighborhood characteristics most affect early childhood development. Safety, for example, is affected by pollution, traffic, and violent crimes (Moore & Young, 1978; Parke, 1978; Zill, in press). Parents and young children have concerns about actual as well as perceived safety matters. The accessibility of neighborhood opportunities for children also affects them as they walk, ride a bicycle, take a taxi or bus, with or without supervision (Bryant, 1985). Children who live in environments in which they can move around with greater independence, receive more support for their own autonomy. Elements of the physical environment that include natural resources such as the presence of water, sand, mud, trees for climbing (Tuan, 1978), and domestic and wild animals (Bryant, 1985; Tuan, 1978), also offer opportunities for observation, use, or restriction of children's behavior.

Population density (Tietjen, 1989) and the stability of residents (Cotterell, 1986), are other factors that may have an effect on children's social competence. For example, a highly mobile population may mean that children encounter a series of interrupted relationships (Tietjen, 1989), that may restrain the capacity of children to trust others. The age distribution in a community (Cotterell, 1986) might affect a child's experiences if, for example, there is limited access to other children or undue restrictions imposed by a preponderance of adults. Home hindrances to the use of a neighborhood, rules about leaving the home setting, or the extent of television use also contribute to children's experiencing of independence (Moore & Young, 1978; Parke, 1978).

Children also may be influenced by varied opportunities to adapt to the physical characteristics of their environments, as well as the willingness of others to assume multiple roles (Moore & Young, 1978; Tietjen, 1989). Different neighborhoods are more or less conducive to offering children opportunities for autonomy and privacy from adults and opportunities to recreate physical objects in the neighborhood (Bryant, 1985; Moore & Young, 1978; Tuan, 1978).

It is important to understand how the range of neighborhood factors influence children's educational experiences. For example, while providing opportunities for privacy in light of safety concerns can be problematic, especially for young children, focusing only on these needs is shortsighted. Inasmuch as children are the primary consumers of residential neighborhoods, their caretakers need to consider their perspectives in the best interests of their education.

References

Bryant, B. (1985). The neighborhood walk: Sources of support in middle childhood. *Monographs of the Society for Research in Child Development, 50* (Serial No. 210).

Cochran, M., & Brassard, J. A. (1979). Child development and personal social networks. *Child Development, 50* (3), 601–616.

Cotterell, J. L. (1986). Work and community influences on the quality of child rearing. *Child Development, 57* (2), 362–374.

Garbarino, J. (1982). *Children and families in the social environment.* Hawthorne, NY: Aldine.

Moore, R., & Young, D. (1978). Childhood outdoors: Toward a social ecology of the landscape. In I. Altman & J. F. Wohlwill (eds.), *Children and the environment* (pp. 83–130). New York: Plenum.

Nagy, J. N., & Baird, J. C. (1978). Children as environmental planners. In I. Altman & J. F. Wohlwill (eds.), *Children and the environment* (pp. 259–294). New York: Plenum.

Parke, R. (1978). Children's home environments. In I. Altman & J. F. Wohlwill (eds.), *Children and the environment* (pp. 33–81). New York: Plenum.

Tietjen, A. M. (1989). The ecology of children's social support networks. In D. Belle (ed.), *Children's social networks and social supports.* New York: Wiley.

Tuan, Y. (1978). Children and the natural environment. In I. Altman & J. F. Wohlwill (eds.), *Children and the environment,* (pp. 6-31). New York: Plenum.

Whiting, G., & Edwards, C. (1988). *Children of different worlds.* Cambridge: Harvard University Press.

Zill, N. (in press). *Learning to listen to children.* New York: Cambridge University Press.

B. Bryant

Nutrition, Health, and Safety

Nutrition, health, and safety concerns provide part of the context for the overall development of young children. There is a clear and demonstrated relationship between the physical well-being of individuals and their overall ability to perform well in other spheres of their lives. The articles that follow detail some of the parameters now profoundly affecting the quality of many children's lives.

L. R. Williams

Nutrition

Nutrition in early childhood consists of actual food intake as well as the feeding process itself. In early infancy, basic requirements are satisfied by breast milk or commercial infant formula. Appropriate supplemental foods are added as the infant matures. The process progresses from total dependency on a particular caregiver toward independent feeding.

Children need a variety of foods that supply adequate amounts of protein, fat, carbohydrates, vitamins, and minerals. The amount required depends on age, size, gender, genetic make-up, and physical activity (Pipes, 1989). Generally, young children require three meals plus two to three planned snacks daily. Once food is offered, parents should encourage children to respond to internal "hunger-satiety" stimuli, and to decide for themselves how much and when to eat (Satter, 1987). Successful mastery of feeding skills and the expansion of food selection contribute to a child's self-esteem, behavior, and performance.

Children in the United States, according to a 1986 National Food Consumption Survey, were consuming adequate levels of all nutrients except for iron and zinc (Nutrition Monitoring Division, 1987). Low-income children failed to meet the Recommended Daily Allowance (RDA) for vitamin E. African-American children did not appear to meet the RDA for vitamin B6, calcium, and magnesium.

Some investigators have concluded that undernutrition in early childhood may be associated with increased morbidity and mortality, growth failure, and possible long-term deficits in behavioral and cognitive performance (Dobbing, 1985; Galler, 1984). The impact of undernutrition is dependent upon the nutrient(s) involved and the duration, severity, and timing of the episode(s). If undernutrition occurs during the first two years of life, there may be decreased brain growth and development. Iron deficiency anemia in early childhood has been associated with slower mental and motor development as well as behavioral alterations such as decreased attention span (Lozoff, 1988). It is difficult, however, to sort out a strictly nutritional impact on intellectual, physical, social, and emotional development from environmental and social factors.

Results of numerous studies (Galler, 1984) suggest that although compensatory growth takes place when undernourished children receive adequate food, the impairment of intellectual performance (measured by standardized intelligence tests and Piagetian tests) and classroom behavior persist into adolescence. Even short-term food deprivation, such as skipping breakfast, may result in decreased attention and impaired learning performance (Pollitt, Garza, & Shulman, 1982–1983). The relationship between nutrition and hyperactivity (Pipes, 1989) is marked by different views. In general, nutrition is a significant factor in children's development and educational potential.

References

Dobbing, J. (1985). Infant nutrition and later achievement. *American Journal of Clinical Nutrition, 41* (2), 477.

Galler, J. R. (1984). The behavioral consequences of malnutrition in early life. In J. R. Galler (ed.), *Nutrition and Behavior* (p. 63). New York: Plenum.

Lozoff, B. (1988). Behavioral alterations in iron deficiency. *Advances in Pediatrics, 35,* 331.

Nutrition Monitoring Division .(1987). Nationwide food consumption survey: CSFII. *Nutrition Today, 22* (5), 36–39.

Pipes, P. (1989). *Nutrition in infancy and childhood.* St. Louis, MO: Mosby.

Pollitt, E., Lewis, N. L., Garza, C., & Shulman, R. J. (1982–1983). Fasting and cognitive function. *Journal of Psychiatric Research, 17* (2), 169–174.

Satter, E. (1987). *In child of mine.* Palo Alto, CA: Bull.

M. Sigman

Acquired Immune Deficiency Syndrome (AIDS)

Acquired Immune Deficiency Syndrome (AIDS) is a chronic illness that affects the body's immune and central nervous systems, making individuals susceptible to certain opportunistic infections and neurological impairments. Although the first isolated cases are thought to have appeared in the United States during the 1960s, and in Africa during the 1950s, AIDS was not recognized as a disease syndrome until 1981 when clusters of gay men in Los Angeles and New York were identified with rare forms of cancer (Kaposi's sarcoma) and pneumonia (Pneumocystis carinii pneumonia).

It is estimated that there are between 5 million and 10 million people worldwide infected with HIV (human immuno-deficiency virus), 1.5 million in the United States. As of November 30, 1991, there were 202,843 cases of AIDS in the United States, including 3,426 cases in children under the age of 13 years.

Adults who work with young children should be prepared to deal with a number of situations related to AIDS. Caring for a child with HIV infection can be undertaken with safety. Despite the epidemiological evidence to the contrary, many still worry incorrectly that AIDS can be transmitted easily through day-to-day interactions. AIDS is transmitted only through direct blood-to-blood or semen-to-blood contact, that is through sexual intercourse (vaginal, anal, oral), shared needles such as occurs in intravenous drug use, infected mothers passing the virus to a fetus, or transfusion of blood or a blood product. HIV also has been found in saliva, spinal fluid, tears, urine, and vaginal secretions. A few babies have contracted AIDS through breast milk. If regular contact with blood or bodily secretions containing blood, such as urine or feces, occurs, then universal infection control precautions should be used.

Most children with AIDS have contracted the disease from their mothers in utero or at birth, while the rest have come from blood transfusions or blood products. If a woman has HIV, there is a 30 percent to 40 percent chance that she will pass it on to the fetus. The profile of the disease in children is different than it is in adults because children are vulnerable to a broader range of bacterial infections. It is often difficult to make a definitive diagnosis in a newborn because of the variety of other illnesses and conditions that also can cause immune deficiency.

The life expectancy of children with AIDS is being extended through the use of new antiviral drugs and drugs to combat specific opportunistic infections. It appears, however, that those who have serious symptoms before the age of two years often die within a year of diagnosis, whereas those who are diagnosed later and do not become sick until they are five or six years of age have a much better prognosis.

Adults who work with young children also need to know how to help young children to understand AIDS. Increasing numbers of children are growing up in situations where a family member, friend, or neighbor has AIDS. Others become aware of the disease because of media exposure. Children need to be reassured that they are not directly at risk while they also are made aware of the serious impact of the disease on individuals and society at large.

Adults who work with young children also need to recognize prejudice. Increasingly, courts and legislative bodies are viewing AIDS as a disability, protected by antidiscrimination laws. Most policy guidelines for school provide for a case-by-case consideration of children with HIV infection who seek admission. Some adults, however, may continue to make unfavorable hidden judgments about people with AIDS because of how the disease is most frequently transmitted—sexual activity and needle sharing. These prejudices foster the climate of fear, isolation, and discrimination in which many people with AIDS are forced to live.

References

Hausherr, R. (1989). *Children and the AIDS virus: A book for children, parents, and teachers.* New York: Clarion.

Kirp, D. L. (1989). *Learning by heart: AIDS and schoolchildren in America's communities.* New Brunswick, NJ: Rutgers University Press.

Quackenbush, M., & Nelson, J. (1988). *The AIDS challenge: Prevention education for young people.* Santa Cruz, CA: Network Publications.

Quackenbush, M., & Villarreal, S. (1988). *"Does AIDS hurt": Educating young children about AIDS.* Santa Cruz, CA: Network Publications.

J. G. Silin

Child Abuse

Every year more than a million children in the United States are seriously abused by their parents or caretakers, and over 1,200 die from such abuse. Child maltreatment is a serious problem consisting of a range of underlying causes involving the individual, the family, the environment, and society. Despite the complexity of the problem, child maltreatment may be categorized into the four classifications of physical abuse, neglect, sexual abuse, and emotional maltreatment.

Physical abuse consists of nonaccidental injury, which may include severe beatings, burns, strangulation, or human bites. Neglect involves the failure to provide a child with the basic necessities of life, such as food, clothing, shelter, or medical care. Sexual abuse includes the exploitation of a child for the sexual gratification of an adult, as in rape, incest, fondling of the genitals, exhibitionism, or pornography. Emotional maltreatment is a pattern of behavior that attacks a child's emotional development and sense of self-worth. Examples include constant criticizing, belittling, insulting, rejecting, and providing no love, support, or guidance.

Since child abuse is not typically only one attack or one instance of a failure to meet a child's needs, the long-term effects are devastating. Child abuse usually involves a pattern of behavior that continues over a period of time. The longer the duration, the more difficult it is to stop and the more serious the consequences to the child become.

Abused and neglected children suffer from a range of developmental, emotional, and physical problems, both observable and hidden, as a result of their maltreatment. Although physical scars may heal, the psychological damage of maltreatment often persists into adulthood. It follows that victims of child maltreatment are at risk of growing up more troubled and more self-destructive than their nonabused peers and of developing personalities similar to those who abused them.

While much effort has been directed toward providing children with medical and protective services, evaluations of child abuse treatment programs over the past ten years have consistently underscored their limitations (Cohn & Daro, 1987; Daro, 1988). Because child welfare systems are designed to intervene after the fact, they are not set up to stop parents from becoming child abusers. Prevention programs targeted to parents before they become abusive or neglectful, however, do reduce the likelihood for further maltreatment. By providing parents with education on child development and family management along with emotional and financial support, these programs help them to cope successfully with the challenging demands of parenting.

Other key prevention services that could reduce child abuse include crisis and support services for parents under stress, preventive education for elementary school children, and therapeutic treatment for child survivors of abuse. Each of these services plays a significant role in breaking the cycle of abuse, and the goal of prevention is to have them in place for all.

References

Cohn, A., & Daro, D. (1987). Is treatment too late: What ten years of evaluative research tell us. *Child Abuse and Neglect, 11* (3), 433–442.

Daro, D. (1988). *Confronting child abuse.* New York: Free Press.

L. B. Mitchel

Substance Abuse
(See Section 4.6, **Special Learning Needs/ Individual Needs, Prenatal Substance Abuse.**)

4.8 Child Study and Observation

The aim of research in the fields of child study and education is, most essentially, to understand what constitutes meaningful experience for the child. To do this, researchers must find ways of paying attention so that they can describe the social, emotional, cognitive, and even the physical dynamics that engage children in different kinds of situations.

Research focusing on young children relies on observation as a central means of paying attention. By using various kinds of observational techniques, researchers explore the "lived-experience" of children (Suransky, 1982, p. 143) in order to examine focal issues of development, social interaction, and learning. Methods of observational research include experimental research either in laboratory settings or in the field, systematic case studies, as well as research in naturalistic settings. Other tools, such as interviews and questionnaires, also can be used to give researchers an eye into the child's universe as it exists, and as the child is constantly constructing it. Each method, however, examines a given problem in a different way and provides the researcher with a different kind of information (Irwin & Bushnell, 1980).

By using a combination of observation and other methods, researchers build a picture of the experience of focal individuals or groups of children. Moreover, the ways in which children approach learning, solve problems, seek out others—even patterns of language development and use—also are influenced by sociocultural practices and beliefs. This means that observations of child, family, and community are inseparable; in seeing one, we begin to see others. Patterns that characterize the child's activity within the family reflect not only developmental factors, but also family attitudes and routines evolving from the life of communities.

Research in education likewise focuses on a community, or family, of another sort—the classroom community created by both values and individual developmental issues that children bring from home, as well as new purposes and strategies that emerge as part of the school experience. One important aim of classroom research is to enhance the relationship between the theory and the practice of meeting the developmental needs of children in school. Because effective practice in the early childhood classroom rests upon the skilled observation of children, teachers themselves stand to make a unique contribution to this area as researchers of their own classrooms (Erickson, 1986; Genishi, this volume).

The articles in the following section explore some of the approaches that may be used to observe the activity of individual children, or groups of children, in the family, the community, or the classroom.

References

Erickson, F. (1986). Qualitative methods in research on teaching. In M. C. Wittrock (ed.), *Handbook of Research on Teaching* (pp. 119–161). New York: Macmillan.

Irwin, D. M., & Bushnell, M. M. (1980). *Observational strategies for child study*. New York: Holt, Reinhart, & Winston.

Suransky, V. P. (1982). *The erosion of childhood*. Chicago: University of Chicago Press.

S. Britsch

Individuals, Observation and Study of

Observation, taking notice through careful looking and listening, has been a "method of choice" for studying children since the late nineteenth century. It enables the study of processes that develop over time, as well as of young subjects who may resist interviews or experiments.

Like other research traditions, observational study reflects both the enduring goals and periodic shifts that mark the history of disciplines, in this case the overlapping fields of child study and education. One enduring goal, identified primarily with child study and developmental psychology, is to discover how universal developments such as cognition, language, perception, and play occur in all normal persons.

Another enduring goal, of interest to both psychologists and educators, is to discover how humans grow and change in the face of specific developmental situations such as toilet training, children's displays of dependence or independence in strange situations, and social development in child care settings. Researchers assume that the situations within which study takes place affect the processes of development under study. Researchers have pursued both goals through experiments and observation of groups and individuals (Sears, 1975).

Observing individuals usually provides much information about a small number of subjects. A researcher or teacher may study a single child, a number of children in an early childhood classroom, or all children in a group at different times. When the focus is on a small number of individuals, the goal is not to come to conclusions about groups of children or all children but to answer selected research questions, often through careful description of daily activities. Such questions might be, How does the child adapt in her/his first weeks of school? How do these children learn with particular art or mathematics materials?

Researchers' methods for observing individual children may be the same as those used for observing groups and range from handwritten notes to the use of videotape recordings (Center for Early Education and Development, 1988; Genishi, 1982). Notes may be anecdotes, what anthropologists call fieldnotes, or what ecological psychologists call specimen descriptions (Barker & Wright, 1951). How extensive these notes are depends on the researcher's purpose.

Other methods include time sampling—observing selected behaviors within uniform time intervals—and event sampling—observing all occurrences of a child's conflicts, questions, and crying. Such methods have advantages and disadvantages and, with the exception of note taking, are associated with numerical and statistical techniques for analysis when a large number of individuals is studied.

In contrast, some researchers have used primarily descriptive, qualitative, or interpretive methods to answer questions about universal processes in individuals, such as, How does a child develop intellectually (Piaget, 1937/ 1954)? Or, How does a child acquire a first language (Bloom, 1970)? Although these processes were thought to occur universally, researchers even have challenged Piaget's broad stages as they adapt his tasks to new cultures or situations (Bruner, Olver, & Greenfield, 1966; Donaldson, 1978). Research questions now are stated in terms of situations studied, for example, How does a child acquire language in her/his community (Schieffelin & Ochs, 1986)? What is seen as universal is the human ability to seek regularities, to construct theories about language or social situations; the theories that are constructed depend on the child's social and cultural situation (Vygotsky, 1978).

Teachers' interest in observing children in order to enhance each individual's learning is part of an ongoing tradition (Almy & Genishi, 1979; Paley, 1981; Pratt, 1948). The emphasis now is on the child's constructivism, particularly in the study of literacy development (Bussis et al., 1985; Dyson, 1989; Genishi & Dyson, 1984). This appreciation of children's own views and ways of learning has increased the use of methods associated with ethnography, the study of different aspects of a culture. The participant observer—one who at times participates in the situation she or he studies or observes—describes carefully, using a range of methods such as fieldnotes, interviews, and/or videotapes, in order to interpret and understand the meanings to participants of their experiences and activities.

The compatibility between the role of the participant observer with that of the child-oriented, observant teacher may account for the growing number of case studies that define individual teachers as researchers of themselves and their children (Monighan-Nourot, Scales, Van Hoorn, with Almy, 1987). In the enduring search for ways of understanding and fostering children's development and learning, the most significant recent shift has been toward viewing the teacher as a participant observer-researcher.

References

Almy, M., & Genishi, C. (1979). *Ways of studying children* (rev.ed). New York: Teachers College Press.

Barker, R. G., & Wright, H. F. (1951). *One boy's day*. New York: Harper & Row.

Bloom, L. (1970). *Language development: Form and function in emerging grammars*. Cambridge, MA: MIT Press.

Bruner, J. S., Olver, R., & Greenfield, P. (1966). *Studies in cognitive growth*. New York: Wiley.

Bussis, A. M., Chittenden, E. A., Amarel, M., & Klausner, E. (1985). *Inquiry into meaning: An investigation of learning to read*. Hillsdale, NJ: Erlbaum.

Center for Early Education and Development, University of Minnesota. (1988). *Looking at young children: Observing in early childhood settings* (videotape). New York: Teachers College Press.

Donaldson, M. (1978). *Children's minds*. New York: Norton.

Dyson, A. H. (1989). *Multiple worlds of child writers: Friends learning to write*. New York: Teachers College Press.

Genishi, C. (1982). Observational research methods for early childhood education. In B. Spodek (ed.), *Handbook of research in early childhood education* (pp. 564–591). New York: Free Press.

Genishi, C., & Dyson, A. H. (1984). *Language assessment in the early years*. Norwood, NJ: Ablex.

Monighan-Nourot, P., Scales, B., Van Hoorn, J., with Almy, M. (1987). *Looking at children's play: A bridge between theory and practice*. New York: Teachers College Press.

Piaget, J. (1937/1954). *The construction of reality in the child*. New York: Basic Books.

Paley, V. G. (1981). *Wally's stories*. Cambridge: Harvard University Press.

Pratt, C. (1948). *I learn from children: An adventure in progressive education*. New York: Simon & Schuster.

Schieffelin, B. B., & Ochs, E. (eds.). (1986). *Language socialization across cultures*. New York: Cambridge University Press.

Sears, R. R. (1975). Your ancients revisited: A history of child development. In E. M. Hetherington (ed.), *Review of child development research*, vol. 5 (pp. 1–73). Chicago: University of Chicago Press.

Vygotsky, L. S. (1978). *Mind in society: The development of higher psychological processes*. Cambridge, MA: MIT Press.

C. Genishi

Classrooms, Observation and Study of

Observation has been an integral part of research conducted in early childhood classrooms. Observational research shares some purposes in a cycle of discovery with those of child study. These include the identification and recording, either formally or informally, of children's actions and reactions, and the development and/or testing of ideas and theories about children's growth, development, and interactions with others (Irwin & Bushnell, 1980).

Researchers have employed a wide variety of models for observational research, reflecting the topics and approaches favored in psychology, anthropology, and sociology, and have used observation as a tool in descriptive, experimental, and training studies.

Implicit across this body of work is a recognition that classrooms are complex "streams of behavior" (Barker, 1968) that are difficult to grasp as a whole (Evertson & Grenn, 1986). Consequently, the diverse orientations and purposes of researchers vary in the portion of classroom "reality" they observe, how they observe it, and how they interpret it.

One early strand of observational research, begun in the 1930s, views the classroom as a setting to describe or assess some aspect of development. Much of this research observes naturally occurring or "naturalistic" behavior. Early pioneering work used then-new methods to gather normative information about children's social life and interactions in classrooms — time sampling to describe age-related changes in typical norms of social participation from solitary to cooperative behavior (Parten, 1932); and event sampling to illuminate the nature of children's quarrels (Dawes, 1934). In this continuing tradition, others have observed children's naturalistic behavior using social-cognitive categories derived from Mary Parten's research and Jean Piaget's theory (Rubin, Maioni, & Hornung, 1976).

Other researchers have treated classrooms as experimental laboratories in which they observe behavior following manipulation of either curricula, teaching practice, or physical environment. They have examined programs of early education, including Head Start, in this way, with observational data then related to developmental and academic outcomes (Beller, 1973; Miller & Dyer, 1975).

A second major strand of research tradition (Lewin, 1935; Barker, 1968; Bronfenbrenner, 1979) focuses on the presumably interdependent relationship between the content of classroom environment and participants' behavior. Generally, this research seeks to assess or to measure, rather than manipulate, these interacting elements as a strategy to inform our understanding of classroom life. Human ethologists, following a tradition in animal study, have developed rich descriptions of children's motor actions in the habitat of the classroom, including adaptive behavior such as children's rough-and-tumble play, their reactions to strangers, and their introduction to an ongoing group of peers (see Jones, 1972, for examples of such studies). Human ecologists have designed complex observational systems to describe and interrelate teachers' and children's actions, social interactions, and classroom setting features (Caldwell, 1969; Day, 1983).

A third strand of classroom study is qualitative and interpretive. Researchers recently have used ethnography with an emphasis on revealing "sociocultural laws" in classrooms. A traditional method used in anthropology and sociology, ethnography employs some combination of observation, participation, and interview to gain the perspectives of children and teachers on classroom life.

Some ethnographic studies have a fairly specific and circumscribed focus, for example, on particular classroom events such as circle time (Kantor, Elgas, & Fernie, 1989) or on the setting for free play and work (Corsaro, 1985); Mandell, 1986). Others have a broader concentration, such as how different aspects of classroom life relate to one another (Emihovich, 1982; Hatch, 1988), and to values and practices beyond the classroom (Lubeck, 1985). Observations often are conducted over time, recorded on audiotape, videotape, and/or in handwritten fieldnotes. Judgments and categories evolve inductively in the course of data collection and analysis. This growing body of work has provided a compelling view of how children first establish and maintain a "peer culture" in early childhood classrooms (Corsaro, 1985).

References

Barker, R. (1968). *Ecological psychology*. Palo Alto, CA: Stanford University Press.

Beller, K. (1973). Research on organized programs of early education. In R. Travers (ed.), *Second handbook of research on teaching*. Chicago: Rand McNally.

Bronfenbrenner, U. (1979). *The ecology of human development*. Cambridge: Harvard University Press.

Caldwell, B. (1969). A new approach to behavioral ecology. In J. Hill (ed.), *Minnesota symposia of child psychology, Vol. 2*. Minneapolis: University of Minnesota Press.

Corsaro, W. (1985). *Friendship and peer culture in the early years*. Norwood, NJ: Ablex.

Dawes, H. (1934). An analysis of two hundred quarrels of preschool children. *Child Development, 5*, 139–157.

Day, D. (1983). *Early childhood education: A human ecological approach*. Glenview, IL: Scott, Foresman.

Emihovich, C. (1982). Social interaction in two integrated kindergartens. *Integrated Education, 19* (3), 72–78.

Evertson, C., & Green, J. (1986). Observation as inquiry and method. In M. Wittrock (ed.), *Handbook of research on teaching, third edition*. New York: Macmillan.

Hatch, A. (1988). Learning to be an outsider: Peer stigmatization in kindergarten. *The Urban Review, 20* (1), 59–72.

Irwin, D., & Bushnell, M. (1980). *Observational strategies for child study*. New York; Holt, Rinehart, & Winston.

Jones, N. B. (1972). *Ethological studies of child behavior*. New York: Cambridge University Press.

Kantor, R., Elgas, P., & Fernie, D. (1989). First the look and then the sound: Creating conversations at circle time. *Early Childhood Research Quarterly, 4* (4), 433–448.

Lewin, K. (1935). *A dynamic theory of personality*. New York: McGraw-Hill.

Lubeck, S. (1985). *Sandbox society: Early education in black and white America—A comparative ethnography*. London: Falmer.

Mandell, N. (1986). Peer interaction in day care settings: Implications for social cognition. In P. A. Adler & P. Adler (eds.), *Sociological studies of child development. Vol. 1*. Greenwich, CT: JAI.

Miller, L., & Dyer, J. (1975). Four preschool programs: Their dimensions and effects. *Monographs of the Society for Research in Child Development, 40* (5–6), Serial #162.

Parten, M. (1932). Social participation among preschool children. *Journal of Abnormal and Social Psychology, 27* (3), 136–147.

Rubin, K., Maioni, T., & Hornung, M. (1976). Free play behaviors in middle and lower class preschoolers: Parten and Piaget revised. *Child Development, 47* (2), 414–419.

D. Fernie

Neighborhood/Community Child Study and Observation

Students of early childhood need extensive experience to comprehend interpersonal interaction styles, expressions of child curiosity and understanding, and family support of or interference with the growth of self-esteem, cooperation, prosocial interactions, and other vital skills for positive socioemotional growth. Traditionally, children are observed in schools, child care centers, or in their home environments. Some nontraditional child study sites permit repeatable observations, as in community laundromats, where children and parents come on a weekly basis. Other sites, such as fast food shops, permit one-shot glimpses of child-adult or child-sibling interactions.

The pediatric outpatient clinic provides opportunities to study the development of child fears and crying in response to actual medical procedures or in anticipation of them. One can also observe children's ability to engage their caregivers in positive interactions during long waits, their bodily expressions of restlessness, their habitual experiences of being sensitively responded to, tenderly comforted, or threatened with parent requests. In waiting rooms, some children receive empathic, tuned-in responses from caregivers and clinic staff, while others receive habitually insensitive management. The following observation was made in such a setting. In a pediatric outpatient clinic, a four-year-old boy sat several seats away from a young woman totally absorbed in her new baby. When the nurse called the mother to come into an examination cubicle, the boy turned out to be the older child of the woman. It was later determined that the mother, who had the new baby by a different father, had transferred her hostility toward the boy's father into neglect and rejection of the preschooler who was seated with no visible communication between him and his mother during the long clinic waiting period. Such parent-child patterns are rarely possible to observe in conventional child study sites.

Students in parenting and child development courses can practice using appropriate, positive, responsive interaction techniques while working with families in such untraditional child facilities as a pediatric outpatient clinic. Keeping a journal enhances the value of the experience. A student records puzzling, painful, or satisfying exchanges, and comments on how he or she would enhance such an interaction if given further opportunities in the nontraditional site. Journal entries help an instructor to monitor a student's growth toward more creativity in facilitative interactions with children and parents. The journal also provides a record, over time, of increasingly subtle observational skills in recognizing and understanding child developmental stages, norms, temperament styles, language skills, and parent-child communication patterns.

Shopping malls provide a myriad of opportunities for child study. Long waits on a line to see Santa Claus, the vision of an attractive open toy store display, or a child's fatigue as adults browse through items of no interest to a little one allow an observer to study children's responses outside of those normally found in a school or home setting. A crowded shopping mall, an elevator or a fast-moving escalator provide opportunities to watch the variety of coping mechanisms with which young children handle potentially stressful situations.

Fast food shops provide an unobtrusive vantage point for watching family dynamics, child skills at negotiating with parents for special treats or extra portions, and parental sensitivity or gross unresponsiveness to child attempts at conversation or requests for extra portions. In a fast food facility, for instance, a toddler tried over and over to gain her parents' attention. They ignored her overtures repeatedly. Finally, she knocked over her glass, spilling her soda. Angrily, they scolded her as they wiped up the mess. Her attempts to get attention only succeeded when she acted inappropriately, noncompliant with parental implicit and explicit rules (Honig, 1985). Fast food places allow students to learn firsthand how patterns of noncompliance, acting out, whining, angry interchanges, and other persistent, difficult-to-change behaviors, are actually rewarded or promoted by patterns of adult inattention or neglect until the forbidden actions occur.

Department stores provide many scenarios to observe children. A tired youngster paraded endlessly through departments of goods may balk at going further. The effects of power assertive techniques, such as threats or physical punishments, can be observed. A wider view of the relationship between parent discipline techniques and child cooperation or noncompliance may be observed. Some parents will try bribery, ignore child complaints, or use positive techniques such as induction (reasoning) or compliments for child patience. Proactive measures, such as providing an apple and crackers to ward off whining or negativism due to hunger and fatigue (Holden, 1983), can be observed in supermarkets. Food stores are excellent places for parents to teach young children categories of foods, qualities of produce, spatial locations of products, and other cognitive skills. Many children will exhibit executive competencies in supermarkets and show helpful actions that may not be readily evident in a child care center where the caregivers do much of the setting out of materials and cleanups for the children.

Standing behind a tree in a park or reading unobtrusively on a park bench permits observation of peer play. Preschoolers may show endless fascination, for example, with dog excreta, or talk about death, or boast about papa's prowess in frank interchanges that may not occur as easily in more conventional, more closely adult-monitored settings for child study. In particular, teasing, bargaining, group entry strategies, compromising, and fantasy play that incorporates natural elements in the surroundings can be observed in parks, playgrounds, or empty lots.

Tempo differences among children can be observed in restaurants and in parking lot sites. Children may want to dawdle with food, or finish far faster than adults. Adult strategies for handling child tempo styles in eating vary from calm acceptance to irritability. Not all adults are sensitive to the wide range of styles that children exhibit. Some children eat and move with alacrity; others are very poky. The impact of adult management styles on children's body grace, good humor, or feelings of alienation or support from their caregivers can be noted when adults are trying to move children into or out of cars in parking lots. Local airport waiting rooms furnish excellent case studies of differences in children's ability to modulate distress when forced to wait, or when hot and tired in strange surroundings.

Observing children during bus rides and observing their responses to getting off crowded trains or buses provides additional insights into children's responses to confinement, crowding, boredom, or worry about being crushed in a crowd, as well as the parental repertoire of responses to such stresses. Toy stores are especially helpful sites to watch children bargain with, wheedle, cajole, express delight, or act appreciative toward or angry at parents who do or do not purchase what the child wishes.

Variations in children's interests can be observed in a large toy store. Some children are fascinated by video and mechanical toys. Others gravitate more toward dolls or stuffed animals. Some spend time poring over puzzles or book selections. Children demonstrate a wide variety of life interests. Their toy preferences, when given opportunities to engage with a generous supply of play materials, may express pronounced gender differences de-

spite caregiver efforts to counteract sex bias in child rearing.

References

Holden, G. W. (1983). Avoiding conflict: Mothers as tacticians in the supermarket. *Child Development, 54* (1), 233–240.

Honig, A. S. (1985). Research in review: Compliance, control and discipline. *Young Children,* Part 1, *40* (2), 50–58; Part 2, *40* (3), 47–52.

A. S. Honig

Family Studies

The influence of families on young children has been a lively area of scientific inquiry within the child study movement. In recent years investigators have observed family processes in the home setting (Carew, 1980), largely because of the growing interest in the influence of the social context on individual behavior and because of criticisms of the traditional research laboratory as an artificial setting for studying children and their families. In general, there has been a resurgence of interest in the social contexts of family functioning (Bronfenbrenner, 1979), including ways in which a family's relations with the neighborhood, schools, extended family, and similar community resources influence the quality of family life and child development. Researchers have taken an active interest in rapid changes in family structures and life styles, with most attention focused on the effects on children of divorce, dual-worker families, nonfamilial child care arrangements, single parenthood, and adolescent parenting.

Studies have tended to consider more than one family dimension at a time, and have examined the two-way or bidirectional flow of influences in parent-child interactions (Clarke-Stewart, 1988; Parke, 1984). In response to evidence that children might influence their parents' behaviors (Bell, 1968), research procedures have considered the two-way flow of influences in parent-child exchanges, including the ways in which parent behaviors vary with children's age, gender, and temperament. This shift has been accompanied by a decrease in simple generalizations about one-way effects of parent characteristics on child socialization processes and an increased awareness of the complexities of understanding the family as a dynamic developmental context.

The mother-child relationship has been the most frequent area of investigation in studies of family influences. Investigators have given considerable attention to the effects on child development of maternal sensitivity, warmth, and responsiveness (Baumrind, 1967). Another relationship for recent study is the father-child relationship, with particular study of type or style of father-child interaction; however, there have been few studies of mother-father-child interaction. Investigators also have studied the effects of birth order, child spacing, sibling influences, and family size.

Many studies of the family collect information through parent questionnaires or interviews, or through rating scales that are completed by the parent or another person who knows the parent and child. There also is growing use of observational methods in studies of child-family interaction, especially in research aimed at understanding the process by which parents and children exert influence on one another. One of the most frequently used observational tools is the HOME measure, an observational rating scale that assesses a variety of home environment elements (Caldwell & Bradley, 1984). Researchers have been able to examine child and family behaviors at a fine-grained level with advances in videotape and other technologies for data collection. Also increasing are efforts to tap parents' beliefs and attitudes regarding their children and child development (Sigel, 1985).

In contrast with these contextual study emphases, early studies attempted to determine a causal linkage between dimensions of the family and child functioning. Typically, this involved examining one parental characteristic such as socioeconomic status or disciplinary technique in relation to a child characteristic such as academic achievement or social-emotional development.

Contemporary debates regarding methods for studying family influences include the advantages and limitations of measuring global family dimensions such as socioeconomic status versus fine-grained parent-child interaction factors such as facial expressions; using structured, semistructured, or unstructured situations for observing child-family interactions; and using diverse methods, including complex statistical techniques for determining the causes and effects of family-child interactions.

References

Baumrind, D. (1967). Child care practices anteceding three patterns of preschool behavior. *Genetic Psychology Monographs*, 75 (1st half), 43–88.

Bell, R .Q. (1968). A reinterpretation of the direction of effects in studies of socialization. *Psychological Review*, 75 (2), 81–95.

Bronfenbrenner, U. (1979). *The ecology of human development: Experiments by nature and design*. Cambridge: Harvard University Press.

Caldwell, B. M., & Bradley, R. H. (1984). *Home Observation for Measurement of the Environment, rev*. University of Arkansas at Little Rock.

Carew, J. (1980). Experience and the development of intelligence in young children. *Monographs of the Society for Research in Child Development*, 45 (1–2, Serial No. 183).

Clarke-Stewart, K. A. (1988). Parents' effects on children's development: A decade of progress? *Journal of Applied Developmental Psychology*, 9 (1), 41–84.

Parke, R. D. (ed.). (1984). *Review of Child Development Research, Vol. 6: The Family*. Chicago: University of Chicago Press.

Sigel, I. E. (ed.). (1985). *Parental belief systems*. Hillsdale, NJ: Erlbaum.

D. Powell

4.9 Child Assessment and Evaluation

Controversy stalks the practices of assessment and evaluation in early childhood education. The fact is that young children grow rapidly but not at a predictably steady pace. They respond differently in different settings and with familiar or less well known people. There is a gap between their competence and their capacity to communicate within limited time allotments. These characteristics suggest that valid assessment and evaluation require time, a commodity that is scarce in massive institutions and the practices associated with standardized tests. At the same time, there is a considerable body of evidence that teacher observations over time often are valid forms of evaluation. This evidence is important in planning policies as well as for curriculum development. Inasmuch as tests make assumptions about learning and worthwhile content, they also suggest implicit beliefs about curriculum.

The articles that follow discuss these kinds of issues and consider the observation, assessment, and evaluation trends, issues, and practices that are current in the United States. In addition, there is an alphabetized, annotated list of technical assessment terminology and, then, evaluation instruments that have been used with children from birth to eight years of age. The reader can find additional information in the sources listed below.

References

Kamii, C. (ed.). (1990). *Achievement testing in the early grades*. Washington, DC: National Association for the Education of Young Children.

Morrow, L. M., & Smith, J. K. (1990). *Assessment for instruction in early literacy*. Englewood Cliffs, NJ: Prentice-Hall.

Wortham, S. C. (1990). *Tests and measurement in early childhood education*. Columbus, OH: Merrill.

D. P. Fromberg

Child Assessment Trends, Concerns, and Issues

Teachers of young children constantly are observing the growth, development, and learning of young children in order to plan their activities, experiences, and future educational opportunities. These observations vary in the degree to which they are systematic, in the types of development and learning teachers observe, and in the ways in which they collect, report, and use data. In the 1980s there was a growing concern among early childhood educators in the United States about the types of information to collect and the manner in which to report and use data in planning for children's future education. A controversy developed over standardized readiness tests and developmental screening tests for young children, especially their use in retaining children in kindergarten or placing them in transition classes.

Problems arise when adults misuse assessment information. It is not the intention of informal teacher observation or formal tests of any type to be the sole criterion for grading the child, for making decisions about retention or promotion, or for evaluating the teacher or the school. Any such use of these data is inappropriate and can have disastrous results for children. (See **Retention and Redshirting**, below.) The controversy over misuse of assessment data includes using test results to label young children, particularly low-income, culturally diverse, and limited-English-proficient children (Bredekamp & Shepard, 1989), and to place young children in educational programs, particularly using test data to retain children in kindergarten or to place them in transition classes (Shepard & Smith, 1988; Charlesworth, 1989).

The difference in philosophy and approach between developmental screening and achievement instruments is an issue of concern for early childhood educators (Meisels, 1987). Critics of screening instruments note that maturation is only one aspect of development. Ignoring all other aspects of development and relying solely on these screening instruments to place the child in an educational setting may limit the child's opportunities for participation in those developmentally appropriate experiences in which the development would occur (Charlesworth, 1989). Readiness tests also are criticized for providing a total composite score that is subject to misuse by labeling a child and/or predicting future learning possibilities, incorrectly in some cases.

Another concern is when instruction and assessment do not match, that is, assessing with age-normed developmental screening tests and then teaching an academic curriculum to the whole class in a mastery fashion (Durkin, 1987). Similarly, school policies often require teachers to assess achievement of skills using a hierarchical code-emphasis approach to reading and writing, such as sound-letter correspondence, word recognition, and penmanship, but teach in a whole language, integrated manner. The latter approach requires observation and assessment of the child's concepts of print, understanding of the functions of reading and writing, attempts to use writing to communicate meaning, story retelling, and recognition of environmental print (Strickland & Morrow, 1989; Teale, 1988). Such measures are available (Clay, 1982; Nurss & McGauvran, 1986; Heald-Taylor, 1986) and will likely be used more widely in the 1990s.

Many programs for young children use a child-centered developmental curriculum designed to provide for individualized levels of participation depending on the child's developmental level. Teachers observe children's progress in order to plan activities for continuous development. Other programs for young children, however, especially primary level programs, are graded, with a set academic curriculum for children to master at each grade level. Assessment is supposed to determine if the child has mastered the objectives for that level. The shift from developmental to graded assessment often creates problems for young children.

Important principles to follow in appropriately using assessment data include the following:

- Use systematic, consistent instruments to collect and record information about young children so the results are reliable.
- Examine the instrument's content carefully to be certain it assesses the philosophy and content of the program presented, that is, that the results are valid.
- Make decisions regarding activities, curricula, materials, and placement based upon multiple sources of data.
- Use the assessment data for making instructional decisions about children, not to label or exclude them from appropriate educational opportunities or to judge teachers or programs.

References

Bredekamp, S., & Shepard, L. (1989). How best to protect children from inappropriate school expectations, practices, and policies. *Young Children, 44* (3), 14–24.

Charlesworth, R. (1989). "Behind" before they start? Deciding how to deal with the rest of kindergarten "failure." *Young Children, 44* (3), 5–13.

Clay, M. (1982). *Concepts about print. Sand and stones.* Portsmouth, NH: Heinemann.

Durkin, D. (1987). Testing in the kindergarten. *The Reading Teacher, 40* (8), 766–770.

Heald-Taylor, G. (1986). *Whole language strategies for ESL primary students.* Ontario Institute for Studies in Education Press.

Hiebert, E. H. (1988). The role of literacy experiences in early childhood programs. *The Elementary School Journal, 89* (2), 161–172.

Meisels, S. J. (1989). Uses and abuses of developmental screening and school readiness testing. *Young Children, 42* (2), 4–6, 68–73.

Nurss, J. R., & McGauvran, M. E. (1986). *Early School Inventory: Preliteracy.* San Diego, CA: The Psychological Corporation.

Shepard, L. A., & Smith, M. L. (1988). Escalating academic demand in kindergarten: Some nonsolutions. *Elementary School Journal, 89* (2), 135–146.

Strickland, D. S., & Morrow, L. M. (1989). Emerging readers and writers: Assessment and early literacy. *The Reading Teacher, 42* (8), 634–635.

Teale, W. H. (1988). Developmentally appropriate assessment of reading and writing in the early childhood classroom. *Elementary School Journal, 89* (2), 173–183.

J. R. Nurss

Observation Methods, Trends, Concerns, and Issues

Teachers' knowledge of child development and early childhood curriculum, as well as their philosophy of education, guides their informal observations of young children. Use of written instruments to record observations makes the data more systematic and useful for planning. Such instruments include systematic ways to record anecdotal notes, separating behaviors from evaluations; techniques to sample behavior over time or events; checklists of observed behaviors; and rating scales to evaluate behaviors on a scale related to children's development or mastery (Bentzen, 1985; Boehm & Weinberg, 1987; Cartwright & Cartwright, 1984; Cohen, Stern, and Balaban, 1983; and Irwin & Bushnell, 1980). Collections of data may include samples of the children's work, such as paintings, attempts to write their names, audio and/or videotapes of language and social interactions, as well as descriptions of the child's school, home, and community life. A team of professionals can make instructional recommendations after reviewing the complete behavioral record in a child study conference.

Formal tests that assess the child's development and learning may supplement these informal observations. They may be norm-referenced, standardized tests that compare the child's current level of achievement in specific areas to the achievement of other children of the same educational level throughout the country. Or the tests may be criterion referenced, standardized tests that compare the child's level of achievement to a set of objectives related to the curriculum and/or textbooks. These readiness tests, designed to assess the child's current level of learning in specified areas, provide teachers with information about what experiences the child is ready for next. Examples include the *Metropolitan Readiness Tests* (Nurss & McGauvran, 1986), the *California Achievement Tests* (1987), and the *Stanford Early School Achievement Test* (1989). Teachers can use the criterion-referenced information to plan instruction for children. Because they are group, paper-and-pencil tests, they can assess only limited areas of development. To supplement readiness tests in these other areas of development, teachers often use published national and state criterion-referenced observation instruments.

There also are developmental screening tests that compare the child's development to other children of the same chronological age (Meisels, 1987). Developmental screening tests provide the opportunity for teachers to obtain systematic information about various aspects of development by eliciting certain behavior from the children, for example, building a block tower, describing a recent birthday party, or walking along a line. Examples of developmental screening tests in use in the late 1980s include the *Gesell School Readiness Test: Complete Battery* (Ilg & Ames, 1972), *DIAL-R* (Mardell & Goldenberg, 1983), *Minnesota Preschool Inventory* (Ireton & Thwing, 1979), and *Brigance Inventory of Basic Skills* (Brigance, 1981). These instruments yield a developmental age, comparing the child with other children of a comparable chronological age. Their purpose is primarily to identify at risk children, children in need of special developmental programs. They may disregard the child's sociocultural context, home background, and previous educational experiences while relying heavily on maturational factors.

Careful selection of observation techniques, use of multiple sources of data, and reporting of information in order to plan developmentally appropriate experiences for the young child are essential practices. Teachers and administrators seeking further guidance in planning and using observation and assessment techniques with young children might consult the National Association for the Education of Young Children's *Position Statement on Standardized Testing of Young Children 3 Through 8 Years of Age* (1988).

References

Bentzen, W. R. (1985). *Seeing young children: A guide to observing and recording behavior.* Albany, NY: Delmar.

Boehm, A. E., & Weinberg, R. A. (1987). *The classroom observer: A guide for developing observation skills.* (2nd ed.). New York: Teachers College Press.

Brigance, A. (1981). *Brigance inventory of basic skills.* Curriculum Associates.

California Achievement Tests (1987). New York: CTB/McGraw-Hill.

Cartwright, C. A., & Cartwright, G. P. (1984). *Developing observation skills* (2nd ed.). New York: McGraw-Hill.

Cohen, D. H., Stern, V., & Balaban, N. (1983). *Observing and recording the behavior of young children.* (3rd ed.). New York: Teachers College Press.

Ilg, F. L., & Ames, L. B. (1972). *School readiness test: Complete battery.* Rosemont, NJ: Programs for Education.

Ireton, H. R., & Thwing, E. J. (1979). *Minnesota preschool inventory*. Minneapolis, MN: Behavior Science Systems.

Irwin, D. M., & Bushnell, M. M. (1980). *Observation strategies for child study*. New York: Holt, Rinehart & Winston.

Mardell, C., & Goldenberg, D. (1983). *DIAL-R*. Childcraft Education Corporation.

Meisels, S. J. (1987). Use and abuses of developmental screening and school readiness testing. *Young Children, 42* (2), 4–6, 68–73.

National Association for the Education of Young Children. (1988). Position statement on testing of young children 3 through 8 years of age. *Young Children, 43* (3), 42–47.

Nurss, J. R., & McGauvran, M. E. (1986). *Metropolitan Readiness Tests Assessment Program*. The Psychological Corporation.

Stanford Early School Achievement Tests. (1989). The Psychological Corporation.

J. R. Nurss

Evaluation Trends

The purposes of evaluation are to plan educational programs, account for the expenditure of funds, plan for individual children, communicate with parents, and screen for and diagnose children who may need special assistance. Developmental screening and observation of all children is an initial step that may identify children with special needs.

Children generally are evaluated on their achievement of the classroom curriculum by standardized tests. These tests can assist teachers in individualizing instruction for young children. They may, however, be unfair or biased against some children, such as those who come from culturally diverse backgrounds, have limited English proficiency, or come from low-income families. Testing may lead to mislabeling children as "smart" or "not smart," or serve as the basis for inappropriate retention. Standardized testing may reduce the scope of the curriculum to preparation for testing with undue emphasis on memorization and other simple skills. Social, emotional, moral, and physical development, higher order thinking skills, problem solving, and creativity may be underemphasized as a result. Testing also may put undue stress on young children at a time when they already are adjusting to new people and unfamiliar surroundings.

States and/or local school districts generally establish requirements for the assessment and evaluation of children. In order to focus on developmentally appropriate evaluation, it is helpful when parents, teachers, and administrators develop, review, and modify policies and guidelines collaboratively.

Report cards provide ratings and/or narrative descriptions of children's efforts at specified times during the school year, using letter grades, a numerical scale, or descriptive comments, such as, "needs improvement." They should indicate whether the rating is based on improvement and effort or grade-level expectations. Grades usually are not appropriate below first grade.

Parent-teacher conferences conducted on a regular basis provide the best forum, nevertheless, in order to exchange information about children. The most effective teachers plan conferences carefully and focus on eliciting, as well as providing, information about children that is drawn from consistent records of their performance, work samples, test scores, and adult observations.

Information, including test scores, that is entered into cumulative record folders is confidential. Federal law requires that such information be released only to the child's parents or legal guardians. Parents must sign permission forms for any testing other than regular classroom achievement testing. Parents may request information about their local school's policies regarding testing and the release of test scores and other evaluation data. These various efforts by parents and teachers are significant ways to ensure that young children receive developmentally appropriate educational services.

E. W. Gee

Retention and Redshirting

Retention and redshirting, the practice of postponing children's entry into school, increased nationally in the 1980s as a means to remove unready children from dramatically escalating academic demands in kindergarten and first grade. The intended benefits of retention and redshirting have not been borne out by research, and both practices have unintended side effects.

Kindergarten retention is a generic term used to refer to several different extra-year programs that include transition classrooms before first grade, "developmental" kindergarten before kindergarten, and repeating of kindergarten. Unlike retention for academic failure, an extra year before first grade is intended to prevent subsequent failure.

Advocates for extra-year programs deny that "developmental" or transitional classes should be categorized as retentions, because they provide unique curricula tailored to the developmental level of participants. The claim of developmentally appropriate curriculum is sometimes true. In other cases, the intermediate grade is merely a slowed-down version of the skill-driven curriculum in the regular grades. Local districts also vary tremendously in the type of children selected to participate. In some localities retention is recommended for slow learners or for children deficient in academic readiness skills while in other districts, slow learners are sent directly on to first grade with the extra-year treatment reserved for able learners who are socially immature.

In a review of 16 controlled studies on the effects of extra-year programs, the predominant finding is one of no difference (Shepard, 1989). When researchers follow extra-year children to the end of first grade or as far as fifth grade, and compare their performance to that of equally at-risk children who went directly on to first grade, they find that transition children perform no better academically despite being a year older for their grade. The conclusion of no benefit is true even for studies where children were selected on the basis of immaturity rather than for academic risk.

Although the majority of teachers believe that retention in kindergarten does not carry a social stigma "if handled properly," extra-year children are more likely to have lower self-concepts and poorer attitudes toward school when compared to control group children.

Parent interviews reveal both short-term and long-term distress associated with the retention decision.

Redshirting is a strategy whereby young athletes sit out a year so that they will become bigger, stronger, and more competitive. By the same reasoning, kindergarten retention sometimes is referred to as academic redshirting. Redshirting also includes the practice of holding children out of school for an extra year to begin kindergarten at six years of age, thus garnering the advantage of being older without the potential stigma of retention.

Holding children out of school, especially if they are boys with birthdays within a few months of the entrance cutoff date, is fostered by widespread popular belief that the youngest children in a grade are at risk. This risk tends to be exaggerated compared to the tiny effect found in the research literature. Based on more than a dozen studies, the average advantage of the oldest first graders compared to the youngest is only about seven or eight percentile points and disappears by third grade (Shepard & Smith, 1986).

Retention and redshirting contribute to the escalation of curriculum, as teachers adjust their instruction to the attention span and learning needs of six-year-olds. As a side effect of these practices, more and more normal five-year-olds are judged to be unready. Anecdotal reports from early childhood coordinators in many states and preliminary empirical data from districts in Colorado suggest further that holding children out of school is a middle-class phenomenon. If this is true, individual differences in kindergarten classes will be widened by adding socioeconomic effects to the age differences, thus increasing the "disadvantage" of inexperienced five-year-olds from low-income families.

References

Shepard, L. A. (1989). A review of research on kindergarten retention. In L. A. Shepard & M. L. Smith (eds.), *Flunking grades: Research and policies on retention*. New York: Falmer.

Shepard, L. A., & Smith, M. L. (1986). Synthesis of research on school readiness and kindergarten retention. *Educational Leadership, 44* (3), 78–86.

L. A. Shepard

Assessment Issues and Principles

Assessment of young children is the gathering of information through all relevant procedures needed to make meaningful decisions about children's development. At the early childhood level, adults need to make decisions regarding whether or not children's development falls within normal expectations, whether they are ready for schooling, what particular skills they have mastered; and which skills they need to develop. Assessment information can influence teaching goals and strategies, as well as the need for specific interventions, including special education. Increasingly, the focus of assessment is on the learning environments of home and school, as well as on the strengths and limitations of children. Assessment should be considered a dynamic and an ongoing process to provide insight into how children think, interact, and behave developmentally (Almy & Genishi, 1979; Boehm & Sandberg, 1982).

A number of principles guide the practice of early childhood assessment. The following are some of those principles:

1. The purpose of assessment, including screening, will substantially affect the nature of one's assessment program, both in scope and outcome.
2. Each group of children presents needs which are both common to all young children and which may reflect considerable diversity.
3. Effective assessment is a process, not a particular test or measure.
4. A test never should be used (i.e., misused) in isolation of other supporting information.
5. Observation of children over time and in their natural environments is the key assessment technique.
6. It is both questionable as a practice and a waste of valuable resources to assess children if the results are not going to be used to improve services to children.

There is widespread agreement that the goal of early childhood assessment should be the improvement of educational experiences for all children. According to the National Association for the Education of Young Children (NAEYC) in their position statement on standardized testing (1988, p. 14), "the purpose of testing must be to improve services for children and ensure that children benefit from their educational experiences." The outcomes of assessment can be used to improve education by viewing assessment as a *process* that is multifaceted, using a variety of procedures; applicable to learning about a child's strengths, strategies, and emerging skills, as well as weaknesses and needs; integral to the development of appropriate instruction or intervention; carried out with the expectation that children will change; and focused not only on the child but also on the child's learning environments. Therefore, taking into account the above outcomes, it can be expected that assessment can play a major role both in decision making and in developing learning experiences to meet child needs.

Assessment procedures can fall along a continuum in the following two ways: (1) Procedures used can range from informal to formal, and (2) The scope of activities can range from brief screening to comprehensive diagnosis.

Screening for school readiness and the identification of possible developmental delay using brief, easily administered measures is a widespread assessment practice. The downward extension of the Right to Education for All Handicapped Children Act (P.L. 99-457) mandates that states identify and serve all eligible preschool three- to five-year-old children with handicapping conditions. The definition of what constitutes "handicap" or "delay" is left up to states, but specific labels are not required.

A common model is to evaluate the effectiveness of assessment in terms of its accuracy in identifying four- or five-year-old children as being "at risk" who later indeed may have problems in school, and in identifying those who are not expected to encounter difficulty. A number of major problems relate to this "hit-rate" model including the following:

1. Screening generally involves brief measures, usually administered by strangers in an unfamiliar setting.
2. Young children are notably inconsistent. Assessors may not have the opportunity to elicit a child's best behavior.
3. Children who just manage to pass the screening may indeed be those who need special attention each time a new area of learning is introduced.
4. The model that focuses on child deficits does not take into account environmental factors that need to be altered. This model does not focus on areas of child strength or emerging development, information that also can be translated into instruction. The model does not focus on the learner strategies or styles.

An alternate more dynamic model (Boehm, 1990), referred to as a "multiple step–multiple procedure" model, involves not only testing but observation of the child over time in the natural environment. In addition, formal testing is followed by a review of errors and interviewing children to understand their learning strategies and by brief "mini-teaching" activities to help refine instructional decisions. The use of converging procedures can lead to a more accurate and ecologically valid picture of the child.

References

Almy, A., & Genishi, C. (1979). *Ways of Studying Children* (rev. ed.) New York: Teachers College Press.

Boehm, A. E. (1990). Assessment of Children's Knowledge of Basic Concepts. In Reynolds, C. R., & Kamphaus, R. W. (eds.), *Handbook of Psychological and Educational Assessment of Children: Intelligence & Achievement.* New York: Guilford Press.

Boehm, A. E., & Sandberg, B. (1982). Assessment of the Preschool Child. In Reynolds, C. R., & Gutkin, T. B. (eds.), *The Handbook of School Psychology.* New York: Wiley.

National Association for the Education of Young Children. Position Statement on Standardized Testing of Young Children 3 through 8 Years of Age. *Young Children, 43* (3), 42–47.

A. E. Boehm

Glossary of Assessment Terms

Ability—Ability refers to one's talent in doing something.

Achievement Test—A test measure of what a child has learned to do or the information a child has mastered, usually based on past instruction in school subjects such as reading and mathematics. The prior experiences of young children based on parent interactions, play, shared storybook reading, TV watching, family activities, and the toys provided are among the sources of a child's instruction during the preschool years. These experiences may be deliberate or incidental. Many tests used to assess young children tap the children's understanding based on these experiences and in the final analysis could be considered as achievement tests.

Adaptive Behavior—Adaptive behavior concerns a young child's developing ability to look after his or her own practical needs independently, to meet expected levels of behavior, and to take responsibility in an age appropriate manner. Tests that measure adaptive behavior are developmental schedules based on the observation of everyday behaviors. This observation may be obtained indirectly from caregivers through interview or may be carried out directly with the child.

Adaptive behavior is defined as "the effectiveness of an individual in coping with the natural and social demands of his or her environment" (American Association on Mental Deficiency, 1974). Federal regulations require that a measure of adaptive behavior be included when making decisions for placing children in special classes for the mentally retarded.

Areas of adaptive behavior generally considered with young children include independent functioning in self-help areas such as eating, dressing, and use of the toilet; physical, sensory, and motor development such as crawling, sitting, and walking; assuming responsibility for oneself; and socialization.

Age Norms (age scores)—Norms that tell the *average* age of typical children getting the same number of items right on a test or developmental scale. These norms may be referred to as a child's *developmental* or *educational age*. The age equivalent score refers to the age equivalent of a particular raw score on a standardized test and corresponds to years and months, such as five years, one month (5-01) or five years, eleven months (5-11).

Assessment—A general term covering all procedures used to understand children's functioning and to make instructional decisions. Assessment addresses many issues, in addition to the identification of problems areas. There are many forms of assessment including observation, interviews, standardized tests, informal measures, work samples, and parent report. Assessment has at least eight purposes (Boehm & Sandberg, 1982; Thurman & Widerstrom, 1990; Bailey, 1989), including the following:

1. Gaining an understanding of a child's overall development, including (a) identifying areas in which help or teaching is needed, and (b) pinpointing skills possessed, emerging, or needing to be developed;
2. Predicting readiness for instruction;
3. Understanding children's strategies and styles used when approaching tasks;
4. Initial identification of children at risk for later problems, in need of special education, or who are gifted;
5. In-depth evaluation or diagnosis;
6. Evaluating environmental factors that impact on learning and development;
7. Evaluating growth, progress, program effectiveness, and intervention effectiveness; and
8. Identifying appropriate forms and levels of instruction.

Assessment is not equivalent to testing and should be considered as an ongoing, dynamic process.

"At Risk"—A term used to describe a child who, on the basis of screening, may possibly encounter difficulty in future school learning. "At risk" is a prediction that may or may not come to pass. There is frequent confusion of prediction of "at risk" (a future problem) with identification of "high risk" (a current problem) (Adelman, 1982).

Basal—The first or lowest age level on a test at which all items are past or tasks are performed correctly forming the *base* of a child's performance.

Ceiling—The highest age level on which a child performs the criterion number of tasks on a test. Beyond this point, all items are failed. The child has reached the ceiling of his or her performance usually under unaided circumstances. With aid, however, some children might answer additional items.

Child Find—All procedures used to locate preschool children who might need special services to prevent later problems in school learning, including advertising, contacting health care personnel, day-care facilities, and other agencies serving young children. Comprehensive child find is essential to a school or districtwide screening program and involves not only efforts to contact all caretakers of children born in a given year, but also alerting them to the availability and desirability of screening and early intervention.

Cognitive Measures—Assessment procedures that assess the child's development of thinking and problem-solving skills and concepts such as comprehending word meanings, seeing relationships, dealing with abstractions, and following directions. Tests of intelligence, Piagetian tasks, and problem-solving tasks are examples of cognitive measures.

Correlation—A standard statistical method of expressing degree of relationship that exists between two measures. The *correlation coefficient* (r) is the numerical index used to express the relationship between these measures.

Correlations may take any value from +1.00 (perfect positive agreement), when a child scores perfectly on two tests, to –1.00 when a child receives the lowest score on one test and the highest on another.

Criterion-Referenced Testing (CRT)—Testing that determines whether or not a child has attained a specified standard of performance—often presented as a behavioral objective. Objectives may occur in any well-defined domain, such as cognitive, language, sensory, motor, social, or emotional. The advantage of CRT is that results focus on the child's mastery of an instructional or behavioral objective or of specified tasks, rather than on comparing a child's performance to that of others in the standardization (reference) group. A second outcome of CRT is that the results can be directly translated into instruction, instructional objectives, or individualized instructional plans (IEPs). An example of an objective tested is, "the child can identify colors by pointing to 6 of 8 objects presented."

Through research, a number of critical features of criterion-referenced tests have been identified as being most effective (Gronlund, 1973). These include the following:

- a carefully defined and specified set of tasks should be used;
- demonstrated competencies should be specified in behavioral terms (expected behavioral responses);
- detailed task analyses should be ordered in sequence;
- a well-formed statement of behavioral objectives (target behaviors) should be provided;
- standards of successful performance and the conditions that will prevail should be specified;
- the skill area should be adequately sampled;
- results should be scored and reported so that they clearly describe the child's performance; and
- criterion levels (standards) (i.e., the percentage correct or the number of items

that need to be answered correctly) should be stated specifically.

The criterion-referenced measurement refers only to the *method of interpreting* test results and can be applied to any standardized test (Ibid.). The test can be analyzed item by item or in terms of some stated expected level of performance for each area of the test.

Curriculum-Based Tests (CBT)—Tests that are closely related to criterion-referenced tests. Here, however, the test covers child mastery of the objectives specified by the particular curriculum used. CBT's are commonly used in preschool settings, with missed items becoming instructional objectives.

Developmental Assessment—Observation of children's development over time as they participate in a variety of activities.

Developmental Tests or Scales—The child's performance on a series of different tasks, the level of his or her skill or behavior, is observed and compared to the development of children of the same age. These tests or scales result in norm-referenced comparisons. The skills and behaviors are ordered from less difficult to more difficult. The ability to perform them depends on the physical, emotional-social, and mental development of the child. Examples include developmental checklists and adaptive behavior scales, which are widely used at early childhood levels.

Diagnosis—Comprehensive, in-depth procedures used to determine the source, nature, and extent of a child's special needs. Diagnosis aims at obtaining a deep, reliable, and practical understanding of a particular individual at a particular moment in time through research in miniature (Ginsburg, 1986).

Comprehensive testing is usually done by one or more trained specialists. Thus, diagnosis may be carried out by one individual (as in reading diagnosis) or by a multidisciplinary team including such individuals as physicians, school nurses, social workers, school psychologists, teachers, and early childhood specialists. Public Law 99-142 and its downward extension P.L. 99-457 mandate the use of a multidisciplinary team.

Diagnosis involves a broad range of procedures including observation, parent and teacher interviews, and formal and informal testing. Areas covered in diagnosis at early childhood levels include cognitive, social/emotional, physical/motor, speech and language, and self-help. Diagnosis leads not only to specific labeling, where necessary for children to receive special services, but to the development of recommendations and remedial plans that can either be carried out in the regular class or that lead to special education services. Diagnosis also helps determine the appropriateness of special programming to meet child needs. The term "diagnosis" is sometimes used synonymously with *comprehensive evaluation*.

Diagnosis involves the use of comprehensive procedures that generally include standardized tests, leading to the identification of problems, their causes, and their remediation.

Diagnostic Tests—Tests that are developed to help understand children's functioning in specific areas of learning. The focus is on areas such as reading, language, and fine motor skills, with the goal of understanding errors and acquiring specific information relative to planning instruction/intervention. Increasingly, diagnostic tests focus on the children's strategies and styles as they approach tasks.

It it important to note that diagnostic tests can be either criterion-referenced, norm-referenced, or a combination of both. The essential outcome is for the task/skill areas covered by tests to be analyzed in great detail.

Developmental Delay (Lag)—The degree to which children fall behind age expectations in major areas of development. Children with measurable developmental delays often are defined as being "at risk" for later learning problems. There is much variability by state and district in how the term "developmental delay" is defined. Generally, however, delay

refers to falling two standard deviations (S.D.) below the mean in one developmental area; falling one S.D. below the mean in two developmental areas; or scoring in the lowest quartile in areas not expressed in standard deviation units.

Dynamic Assessment—An assessment situation in which the examiner actively modifies the interaction in order to estimate what a child is capable of learning under appropriate conditions of learning. The learner is prodded and reinforced into a role of active seeker and organizer of information (Lidz, 1987). An interaction takes place in which the assessor seeks to estimate the degree of modifiability of the learner and the means by which positive changes in cognitive functioning can be induced and maintained. Assessors need to focus on what teaching conditions, including prompts, support, and reinforcers, will foster new learning. The product of assessment is change in the cognitive functioning of the learner, which is sometimes referred to as the "zone of proximal development" (Vygotsky, 1976). Dynamic assessment takes place through a test-teach-test format and, to date, largely has been conducted with nonverbal tasks.

Ecological Assessment—Assessment that focuses on environmental conditions provided in home and school settings that influence a child's learning.

Educational Age—Scores expressed in terms of the average chronological age of the child obtaining each score on a test of scale.

Educational Quotient—The relationship of the child's educational age to his or her chronological age. The age level score attained on an assessment device is divided by the child's chronological age.

Evaluation—Evaluation provides (a) assessment (or research) that determines how effectively an instructional program or behavioral intervention is working; (b) a determination on how well children are learning; and (c) a determination on whether or not a school placement or other specific program is appropriate for a given child. This final outcome includes evaluation for school admission. Evaluation provides essential data concerning the effectiveness of an instructional program, changes that are needed, and aids in the prediction of academic readiness (Boehm & Sandberg, 1982). Evaluation is sometimes used synonymously with comprehensive testing.

False Negatives—Assessment (usually screening) that misses children who either do or will have a learning problem. These children pass a screening test and therefore do not receive special attention. In the long run, it is probably better for a measure to err in the direction of some false negatives, than to miss children who might profit from early intervention.

False Positives—Assessment procedures that identify a child as having a current problem that does not exist or a future problem that does not materialize. Frequent reassessment should be conducted so that these children can be "declassified" or labeled and encouraged to realize their full potential in mainstream educational settings.

Formative & Summative Evaluation—Terms developed for use in curriculum evaluation. *Formative* tests are used early in the teaching process to guide instruction, using instructional screening tests. They also are used to appraise the effectiveness of ongoing instruction. *Summative* tests are used at the end of a unit or course of instruction to determine what children have learned or appraise how well a program is working.

Grade Equivalent Scores (GES or GS)—A child's score on a test is converted into grades and months of the school year. These scores conform to the grade organization of school where the school year is divided into ten units representing the September–June school calendar.

Thus, a grade score of 1-8 would correspond to the typical performance of grade 1 children during April. The child's score then is compared to the score of the typical child at that grade and month receiving each score on the test. Grade scores are one type of *developmental score* where a child's performance is compared to others in the same grade.

While appealing, grade scores are easily misinterpreted. A kindergarten child who receives a grade score of 2.0 on a reading readiness test administered at the end of kindergarten does *not* read like a child at the beginning of second grade. But this child does perform much better than most children at the end of kindergarten. Therefore, grade scores should be converted to percentile ranks so that scores from one test can be compared to another and common misinterpretations avoided.

Grade Norms—The average score on a standardized test obtained by an average child each month in school. (See *Grade Equivalent Scores*.)

Intelligence—In general, a child's overall ability to reason, think, and solve problems.

Intelligence Tests—Tests of a child's brightness or quickness to learn. These tests include a series of tasks that sample behaviors (verbal, nonverbal, and numerical) and result in a score indicative of cognitive functioning. They are one type of norm-referenced test that helps to predict a child's ability to learn school work.

Depending on the test, scores can be expressed in a number of ways, including the following:

- *General Cognitive Index (GCI)*—Form of intelligence quotient (IQ) score used on the McCarthy Scales.
- *Full Scale IQ (FSIQ)*—An IQ score based on both the verbal and performance portions of the Wechsler Intelligence Scales. The verbal scales require verbal response and result in a verbal IQ score (VIQ). The performance scales present items that do not require a verbal response, such as pointing to a detail missing from an ob-

ject. These result in a Performance IQ (PIQ).

- *Mental Age (MA)*—The number of items answered on a test of ability divided by the child's chronological age. A mental age of 100 corresponds to the average performance of a child of any chronological age.
- *Intelligence Quotient (IQ)*—The average IQ is 100. While it is widely understood that IQ = MA/CA x 100 (to get rid of the decimal points), most ability tests such as the Stanford-Binet (Form L M) relate this to different standard deviations at each age level and report ratio IQ's.

Item Analysis—Many manuals report the percentage of children who pass each item on standardized tests. This information represents the difficulty level of items. Thus, those passed by few children are difficult, and those passed by most children are easy. Criterion-referenced tests will maintain items that represent instructional goals even if the items are very difficult or very easy. The most difficult items missed and very easiest items passed by all or nearly all children are eliminated from norm-referenced tests.

Another concern is the degree to which items discriminate between children who, as a whole, score well or poorly on a test. Thus, if children who perform well on a test miss items that children who do not perform as well on the test pass, then these items are said to have poor discrimination. The goal is to revise or replace such items during test development.

Language development—Language development tests help determine a child's skill in understanding and using language. Language tests take a number of forms including those that tap *expressive* language and *receptive* language.

Expressive language (Productive Language) is a child's ability to *express* thoughts and to respond through the use of words and sentences. The child's use of productive language can be assessed through informal samples of speech as well as standardized tests. If the child's productions are recorded and compared to developmental and normative information, they can yield age equivalents that satisfy eligibility requirements in some states.

Receptive Language is a child's ability to understand spoken language including words, phrases, and grammatical structure. This understanding may be demonstrated by following commands, pointing to objects or situations depicted in pictures, or engaging in requested actions. Thus, there is a strong relationship between language and cognitive ability for the young child. Problem solving often depends on comprehension of spoken requests.

Mastery Tests—Tests that measures a child's mastery of curricular or behavioral objectives for a unit of instruction, usually organized by difficulty level.

Mean (M or X)—Mathematical average of all scores on a test. The scores of all children taking the test are added up and then divided by the total number of children taking the test.

Mastery Testing—Testing that measures levels of mastery that are set in learning areas. Children may learn the material at different rates. Mastery learning is used particularly in the area of basic skills.

Motor Test—A test that assesses a child's ability to move and coordinate his or her body and manipulate objects. The motor area is usually divided into several areas including gross motor, fine motor, and visual-motor (sometimes called perceptual-motor).

Normal Curve—A graphic and mathematical way of showing the normal distribution of scores of people taking a test. There are a number of terms and characteristics used to describe a child's functioning in relationship to the normal curve. These include

Mean—average (middle) point of all scores.

Median—The middle score of a group of scores.

Normal Curve Equivalents (NCE)—Transformation of normal standard scores so that each NCE corresponds to percentiles of the same value. NCEs are used mostly for research purposes.

Norms—Norms provide the basis for interpreting individual scores. They involve the translation of raw scores into some comparative measure (age scores, grade equivalent scores, percentile ranks, stanines or standard scores) that allow a child's test score to be compared to that of a comparable group. Test manuals provide information regarding the procedures used to construct norms. National norms describe how they represent the national population. Characteristics, such as age, sex, geographic region, race/cultural representation and district size, of the sample on which a test was standardized are detailed. Norms allow potential test users to determine whether the sample represents the group with which it will be used. Summary statistics are then presented relative to these groups. Tests must have acceptable levels of reliability and validity for scores to be interpreted meaningfully.

Local norms may need to be developed if the norms reported in the test manual do not represent the local population. After local norms are collected, it is possible to interpret test scores based on how other children in the same community perform. They also may be developed to arrive at local levels of expectancy.

Norm-Referenced Tests (NRT)—Tests that permit the comparison of an individual child's performance with that of a representative group of children of the same age or grade, usually defined as the standardization group. Scores from norm-referenced tests translate in a number of ways including means and standard deviation, age and grade scores, percentiles and standard scores such as stanines of "T" scores. The results indicate a child's relative position in the group. Norm-referenced scores are the most commonly used scores used to make major educational decisions for

purposes of selection and classification. Most states require that early childhood screening tests provide norm-referenced information.

Observational Assessment—Assessment of children's behavior and skills through observation. This is a key procedure at early childhood levels since children can be observed in the natural setting of the home, playground, or classroom. Observation can be carried out on an informal basis, such as writing down observations of a child's play behaviors, or on a structured basis, such as counting all occurrences and types of child language during a ten-minute period.

Indirect forms of observation depend on a person's *past* observations of a child. Questionnaires, checklists, rating scales, and interviews are usually based on past observations. In contrast, direct forms of observations focus on *ongoing* behaviors. Diaries, anecdotal records, running records, and observational schedules are direct observation procedures commonly used with young children.

Systematic observation of child behavior in the natural setting over time is the most powerful of all assessment approaches and also serves as a validity check with regard to information obtained from tests. Observation can capture emerging behaviors and the achievement of developmental milestones along with a child's natural variability across times of day and activity areas. With all its strengths, the adequacy of observational information depends on the training of observers, freedom of bias, adequate sampling, and observer agreement.

Important terms used relative to observation systems include the following:

Exhaustive—Systems that include all behaviors defining an area of concern. Clear definitions are essential.

Exclusive—Non-overlapping categories that are independent and distinguishable from other categories.

Time Sampling—Recording whether or not specified behaviors are observed during predetermined and fixed time periods such as every thirty seconds or every minute.

Time sampling procedures provide data relative to the frequency of occurrence of behaviors of concern over time.

Event Sampling—Recording every time during an observation period a specified target behavior occurs such as "child speaks to another child."

Category System—A system where behaviors of concern have been listed ahead of time.

Sign System—A system that can be used every time the child engages in a particular behavior of interest (the sign or event) such as "crying."

Observer Agreement—Two issues are of concern to users of observational procedures. These include (a) *intrarater agreement,* or the extent to which an observer is consistent (agrees with self) over time and (b) *interrater agreement,* or the extent to which different observers of the same situation agree.

Percentile Rank (PR)—A percentile indicates a child's relative position in a group. The percentile rank is a score that tells how a child ranks on a test in relationship to the distribution of raw scores of others in the group taking the test. It tells the percentage of children who score below the score obtained by a particular child. A child whose score receives a percentile rank of 34 means that the child scored at a level at or above 34 percent of children taking the test. The mean score of a test falls at the 50th percentile. The higher the percentile, the better the performance of the child.

While percentiles are relatively easy to understand, two areas of confusion often occur when interpreting assessment results in terms of percentiles to parents. First, a percentile does *not* refer to the percentage of items correct. Second, differences between scores at the high and low extremes of a distribution mean more than at the center of the distribution. Small changes in scores result in quite different percentiles at the extremes whereas large differences in scores result in small changes in percentile near the center of a distribution.

Quartile—One-quarter of the scores on a test, such as the highest 25 percent of scores or the lowest 25 percent of scores. Children who fall in each of these quartiles during screening often are further assessed for special talent or developmental delays, respectively. For example, the top 25 percent of scores in a distribution is referred to as Q1, or the top quartile. The lowest 25 percent of scores in a distribution is referred to as Q4, or the lowest quartile. Children scoring in the lowest quartile on screening are often seen as being "at risk" and are referred for diagnostic evaluation.

Deciles, dividing the performance of the group in ten units are used to further refine this process. As a particular measure, the tenth, or top, decile includes the top 10 percent of children's scores, and the first or bottom decile includes the bottom 10 percent of children's scores.

Range—The number of score points between the highest and lowest scores on a test.

Rating Scales (Forms)—A method of rating the quality of child behavior or skill, such as "persists with tasks," on a numerical scale or series of adjectives. Most rating scales are completed based on past observations of the child. They, however, may be completed during actual observation.

Raw Score—The number of items correct on a test.

Readiness Tests—Tests designed to assess a child's ability to benefit from past instruction and/or their preparedness to enter an academic program successfully. Kindergarten readiness and reading readiness tests are two major examples of tests that attempt to measure whether or not a child has developed (mastered) the skills thought to be necessary for success in kindergarten or beginning reading, usually at grade one. Appropriate levels of development across areas such as sensory motor, cognitive, language, and social-emotional are all essential for a child to be successful in kindergarten or grade one.

The selection of a particular readiness measure should be congruent with the instructional goals of individual school systems. Most readiness tests, however, place an emphasis on skills related to learning to read. Since the purpose of readiness tests is prediction, test manuals must provide documentation of their accuracy over time in identifying which children are successful or which children encounter difficulty.

Reliability—The consistency with which a test measures a child's understanding or behavior. The greater the consistency (reflected by a reliability coefficient that approaches +1.0), the greater the confidence test users have that test scores reflect differences in individuals rather than errors in measurement. Young children, whose skills are emerging, are not particularly consistent from one day to another, which affects their performance during testing. Answers may be available on one day or with particular examples and not available at another time. These child characteristics will influence and lower reliability coefficients.

Agreement between observers in an essential form of reliability required when observational procedures are used. Agreement between testers in administering and scoring tests is also essential.

A number of forms of reliability are reported in test manuals. These include the following

Test-retest reliability. This form of reliability requires two administrations of the test to all children over a brief period of time, usually no more than about a two-week interval between testing periods. Children's scores at both testing periods are then compared through use of a correlation coefficient. Test-retest coefficients of young children are never 100 percent perfect (r = 1.0 in statistical terms). Most evaluators, therefore, seek tests with test-retest correlations of 0.80 and above. While practice and recall can affect children's performance, these issues are less pressing at the early childhood level. Test-retest reliability is essential for early childhood measures.

Parallel Form (Alternate form) reliability. Two parallel (equal) versions of the same test, using the same procedures, are administered on two occasions to the same child. Like test-retest procedures, the two testings should occur over a brief interval. The goal is that the performance of a child on one form will be very similar to that on the second form. Correlations below +0.80 are problematic. The use of parallel forms resolves the problems of memory and practice and thus provides the most rigorous reliability test. Parallel forms, however, are not available for most early childhood measures.

Internal Approaches to Reliability. The question addressed here is whether items on a test measure the same thing. Naturally, many preschool tests cover multiple areas and do not necessarily measure the same thing. This question is more appropriate for tests covering more restricted areas. Two major procedures are used:

Split-half reliability takes place when the test is divided into two subtests having equal numbers of items. While this can be done in a number of ways, a common way is to correlate a child's performance on odd and even items in much the same way as an alternate form reliability. The Spearman-Brown prophecy formula is used to take into account the underestimates of reliability that result from the use of only half a test. Inasmuch as many preschool measures are brief to begin with, the use of split-half reliability coefficients is questionable.

The Coefficient Alpha takes place when each test item is viewed as it correlates with every other item and the total score. If all of the items are measuring the same thing or are related to the same attributes, they would have a perfect (100%) relationship with each other. Most early childhood tests measure different competency areas. Therefore, the relationship among items is less than perfect. Yet, this form of reliability is widely preferred as a measure of internal consistency. (The Kuder-Richardson formula is a frequently used procedure.)

Screening—Brief measures used with large numbers of children to serve at least two major purposes. The first purpose, often referred to as *developmental screening*, is to serve at the initial step to identify children who *may* need special services, including the gifted, the handicapped, and those at risk for developmental delay or later learning problems. The second purpose, referred to as *instructional* or *educational screening* is to identify specific areas of pupil knowledge and those needing development in relationship to preschool learning activities and primary grade curricula.

Screening generally involves brief measures administered to a large number of children. Children identified as being "at risk" through screening must next be seen for comprehensive diagnosis (or in-depth evaluation). Screening does not involve in-depth or diagnostic testing.

Screening may also serve as an initial procedure to identify a child's level of performance at the beginning of instruction in order to identify children who have skills, where skills are emerging and where skills are lacking, and to help teachers plan instruction. Screening, however, cannot tell us about the kind of problem a child has, nor can it tell us the kind of instructional program a child needs. At the preschool level, in order to help prevent failure, screening usually has the goal of the early identification of children who, because of problems of development and/or experience, may be least able to meet the typical expectations of school.

A screening measure is said to be "sensitive" if it correctly identifies children as being at risk who later turn out to have learning difficulties. A screening measure is said to be "specific" to the extent that it correctly identifies children who do not need further assessment and who progress normally in school (Meisels, 1989). Through screening, children are identified who need comprehensive assessment, often referred to as diagnosis.

Developmental Screening—Screening that attempts to identify those children who are at risk for later academic failure. The goal is to identify children with potentially handicapping conditions who will benefit from special education services. Developmental screening should be followed by comprehensive evaluation (birth to two years of age) or diagnosis of specific handicaps (age three and above).

Standard Score—A type of derived score that is based on the mean and standard deviation of a distribution that allows comparison of a child's performance from one test to another. Standard scores take into account that the average performance and distribution of scores of the same children are likely to vary when different tests are used. Thus the simple formula of

$$\frac{\text{child's test score} - \text{test mean}}{\text{standard deviation (SD)}} = \text{standard score}$$

allows users to compare scores across tests.

Standardized Test/Systematic Observation—A carefully designed set of tasks (or behaviors that are observed) that are administered and scored using uniform, specific procedures. Tasks are presented to all children using the same materials (in the cases of tests), procedures, and ground rules with assessors making only those modifications spelled out in the test manual. The purpose is to provide all children with the same opportunity to respond and to reduce sources of examiner bias and variability.

Tests enable users to quantify child performance in each area the test covers using consistent scoring criteria. Test manuals should include detailed information regarding the empirical basis for selecting items, the sample on whom the test was normed or field tested, data on reliability and validity, methods for interpreting scores, and the use of scores.

Systematic observation schedules need to provide detailed information supporting content, detailed procedures for carrying out observation, representative studies in which the schedule or procedure was used, methods for interpreting findings and documentation of validity and reliability. Observation procedures also allow users to quantify information relative to a child's performance.

Standard Error of Measurement (SEM)—If we had the opportunity to test a child over and over, and then average that performance (without giving the child the advantage of practice), the child's daily fluctuations and random errors would cancel each other out. This is exactly what the statistical procedure "standard error of measurement" aims to achieve.

An individual's functioning can change on a day-to-day basis (it can be better or worse) due to health, attention, interest, distractions, test characteristics, and examiner variables. These factors need to be taken into account when interpreting test scores. The mean and standard deviations of errors are calculated and expressed in standard deviation units. We would therefore expect the child's score to fall within the band between standard deviation (S.D.) units in the following way:

–3 S.D. –2 S.D. –1 S.D. child's score +1 S.D. +2 S.D. +3 S.D.

Score ± 1 S.D.: The child's score can be expected to be the true score about 68 percent of the time. In about one-third of the cases, however, there is an error.

Score ± 2 S.D.: The child's score can be expected to be the true score about 95 percent of the time. There is only a 5 percent chance of error.

Score ± 3 S.D.: The child's score can be expected to be the true score about 99 percent of the time. There is only a 1 percent chance of error.

Thus the SEM is extremely important for interpretation of tests and should be reported in test manuals. Increasingly, assessors are finding it useful to report the band of scores (range) in which a particular child's score falls. This practice helps users understand that a score is not a fixed point and can change. In general, preschool assessors have been slow to adopt this procedure.

Stanine—One form of reporting test scores achieved by dividing all the test scores represented on the normal curve into nine equal parts. Stanines range from a low of one to a high of nine, with the average being five. Each stanine represents one-half a standard deviation and makes it possible to compare different tests.

Strategy Oriented Assessment—Assessment that uses interview procedures to address questions related to the strategies a child uses to solve problems. From a clinical interview based on the procedures suggested by Jean Piaget (1929), assessors can learn about a child's related knowledge and problem-solving skills. Even very young children can produce this information (Boehm, 1990; Ginsberg, 1986).

Assessors using these procedures can understand strategies and styles that are encouraged by a child's culture; children's understanding that can be built upon in instruction; the meaning of errors; and the scope of the child's understanding related to the area assessed.

Test Floor—The lowest levels of a test or measure. It is essential that a sufficient number of items be included at the floor in order to gain a reasonable picture of child functioning. A small number of items at the lowest (and highest) levels is a problem for tests that span multiple age levels.

Validity—The degree to which a test, observational device, or any other assessment procedure measures what it claims to measure in a way that is free from systematic error. The question is whether a true picture of what we want to measure is being achieved. A test or observational procedure must be valid to have value for purposes of assessment. Therefore, validity studies must be reported. There are four major forms of validity that are of concern to early childhood assessors:

"An investigation of content validity required that the test developer or test user specify his [her] objectives and carefully define the performance domain in light of those objectives." (American Educational Research Association, et al., 1985, p.28.)

Content validity reflects the extent to which a test of observational measure represents the domain to be assessed. Content validity requires both a thorough task analysis of the area of concern and a review of related developmental research. Assessors should examine the rationale for inclusion of items on tests or observation systems and to determine whether they (a) include major areas of concern and (b) whether or not the items included match their assessment purposes.

Criterion-related validity includes both *congruent* (or *concurrent*) validity and *predictive* validity. *Congruent* validity refers to the extent to which the outcomes from one assessment measure relate to the outcomes of a second measure or outcome criteria, for example, the extent to which an observation of peer interactions relates to teacher ratings of peer interaction. A second measure of congruent (concurrent) validity is obtained by correlating the outcomes of one procedure with other similar procedures that have been administered during the same time period.

Criterion-related validity is usually present in the form of a validity coefficient (which is a correlation coefficient). Researchers want to see assessment measures that have a positive relationship between the two measures. If good performance of an individual is demonstrated on two measures that are perfectly related, we obtain a coefficient of 1.0. If the performance on two measures is equally poor, the correlation is −1.0. While a perfect relationship is rarely possible, the closer the correlations between two measures, the better. It is useful to look for a correlation of 0.70 or better between individually administered tests and 0.60 between group administered tests.

Predictive validity is another form of criterion validity that considers whether a score on a test (or observational measure) is related to performance at some later date on measures such as achievement tests, teacher ratings, or student grades. Another example of predictive validity is the extent to which a preschool screening test correctly identifies as "at risk" and "not at risk" those children who demonstrate learning problems at the end of grade one. Tests that miss many children who later have problems have questionable utility. Prediction of validity is essential for preschool assessors and is among the major criteria for considering use of a particular test. However, predictive validity fails to account for successful early interventions.

Construct validity is an assessment procedure that addresses such phenomena as self-concept, basic concept understanding, or creative thinking and is supported through the accumulation of research results regarding those who have high or low scores on an assessment measure. Some tests measure one major construct while others measure more than one construct, supported by factor analysis studies.

References

Adelman, H. (1982). Identify learning problems at an early age: A critical appraisal. *Journal of Clinical Child Psychology*, 11 (8), 255–261.

Anastasi, A. (1982). *Psychological Testing* (5th ed.). New York: Macmillan.

American Educational Research Association, American Psychological Association, and National Council on Measurement in Education. (1985). *Standards for educational and psychological testing.* Washington, DC: American Psychological Association.

Bailey, D. B., & Wolery, M. (1989). *Assessing Infants and Preschoolers with Handicaps.* Columbus, OH: Merrill.

Boehm, A.E., & Sandberg, B. (1982). Assessment of the preschool child. In Reynolds, C.R., & Gutkin, T.B. (eds.), *The Handbook of School Psychology*. New York: Wiley.

Ginsburg, H. P. (1986). Academic Diagnosis. In J. Valsiner (ed.), *The individual subject and scientific psychology* (pp. 235–260). New York: Plenum Press.

Gronlund, N. E. (1973). *Preparing Criterion-referenced Test for Classroom Instruction*. New York: Macmillan.

Lidz, C. (ed). (1987). *Dynamic Assessment.* New York: The Guilford Press.

Meisels, S. J. (1989). *Developmental screening in early childhood: A guide* (3rd ed.). Washington, DC: National Association for the Education of Young Children.

Nurss, J. R. (1987). *Readiness for Kindergarten*. ERIC Clearinghouse on Elementary and Early Childhood Education. Urbana, IL: University of Illinois.

Piaget, J. (1929). *The child's conception of the world*. New York: Harcourt, Brace and World.

Taylor, R. L. (1989). *Assessment of exceptional children: Educational and psychological procedures* (2nd ed.). Englewood Cliffs, NJ: Prentice-Hall.

Thurman, S. K., and Widerstrom, A. H. (1990). *Infants and Young Children with Special Needs: A Developmental and Ecological Approach* (2nd ed.). Baltimore: Brookes.

A. E. Boehm

Glossary of Assessment Instruments

Battelle Development Inventory—Normal and criterion-referenced tests that assess motoric, adaption, communication, cognition, and personal-social development of children from birth to eight years. The personal-social domain centers on the child's ability to engage in meaningful social interactions; the adaptive domain stresses behaviors that will enable the child to become independent; the motor scale assesses both gross and fine motor development; the communication domain examines receptive and expressive communication skills; and the cognitive domain focuses on conceptual skills and includes perceptual discrimination, memory, reasoning, and academic skills. Three procedures for administration can be used—structured administration, individual interviews of parent or guardian, or observation (Newbork et al., 1984).

The test must be administered by trained teachers or paraprofessionals. It is quite suitable for special education purposes, and provisions can be made for testing physically handicapped children.

Bayley Scales of Infant Development—Individually administered assessment that provides adequate measures of the developmental progress of infants (birth to two and a half years) and takes into account the geographic and socioeconomic studies of all children.

The Mental Scale is designed to assess the sensory-perceptual acuities and discriminations, early acquisition of object constancy and memory, vocalizations, and early evidence of generalization and classification. From these assessments a Mental Developmental Index is determined. The Motor Scale is designed to provide a measure of the degree of control of the body and coordination of large and small muscles. Scoring for the Motor Scale produces a Psychomotor Development Index (Bayley, 1969).

Training for administering the test includes practice training with one or more babies at each month of the first twelve months of age, and at each three-month age level from fifteen to thirty months.

Boehm Test of Basic Concepts (Preschool Version)— A norm-referenced, individually administered test that is designed to assess young children's (aged three to five years) mastery of basic concepts. This information is intended for use by the preschool teacher as an indicator of school readiness and as a guide for planning instruction. It also can be used to assess possible developmental delays in language acquisition. The test covers relational concepts of size, direction, position in space, and quantity. The content validity of this test is based on review of preschool curriculum and of the conceptual terms used by preschool teachers from which the test items were developed (Boehm, 1986).

The Boehm Test can be administered by teachers, paraprofessionals, psychoeducational specialists, speech educators, and speech and language therapists. One or two practice administrations are suggested as preparation for people experienced in test administration. Formal testing supervisors are advised for those with little experience in educational assessment. For special education purposes, the test is appropriate for use with children with movement limitations because only a pointing response is required of the child.

Brigance Diagnostic Inventory of Early Development—A criterion-referenced, individually administered test that is intended for use on children birth to seven years as an assessment instrument that serves to determine the developmental and performance level of the child, to identify areas of strengths and weaknesses, and to identify instructional objectives. It is further intended to serve as a guide for instruction and to develop individualized educational programs for children. The test covers preambulatory motor sequences, gross motor sequences, fine motor skills, self-help skills, language, general knowledge, reading readiness, and basic reading, math, and writing skills (Brigance, 1978).

Administering the test does not require specialized training in testing. The majority of the assessment procedures can be done by a paraprofessional with professional supervision. The test is also intended for special education populations. Specific information is provided for using the Inventory with Public Law 94-142 populations.

Cattell Infant Intelligence Scales—An untimed, norm-referenced, individually administered test for children aged two to thirty months, this downward extension of the Stanford-Binet Intelligence Scale assesses sensorimotor behaviors, the score of which produces a developmental age level in months. The scale has five items and one or two alternates for each age level, in case one is spoiled during administration (Cattell, 1960).

A strong background in child psychology and study of intelligence testing and training in the Scales is necessary for administering the test.

Circus—A group-administered (maximum 10 children) test designed to diagnose the instructional needs of individual children and to monitor and evaluate early education programs. The test can be administered to children aged three and a half to seven years on one of the following three levels: preschool and kindergarten (Level A), preschool, kindergarten, and beginning first graders (Level A and B), or ending kindergarten and beginning first grade (Level B) (Anderson & Bogat, 1976).

The test covers language and reading, perception, mathematics, information processing and experience, divergent production, attitudes and interests, and includes a teacher-program measure (a questionnaire about the educational environment). Subtests for each area differ by level of test. Settings are encouraged to choose the subtests that will best address the purpose of the assessment. A manual is provided for administering the test, and is designed for use by teachers and aids.

Cognitive Skills Assessment Battery—A standardized, criterion-referenced test designed for use with prekindergarten and kindergarten students. Orientation is toward the child's environment, discrimination of similarities and differences, comprehension and concept formation, coordination, and immediate and delayed memory. The CSAB can be administered at the beginning of the school year to assist teachers in planning instruction and at the end of the school year to provide objective evaluation in goal areas.

A total score is not obtained. Data by goal area for comparing children to the norming sample is available for both lower- and middle-income children. Investigation into the types of errors and the level of the response for making appropriate decisions is recommended. Designed to be administered by the teacher, the CSAB manual gives clear directions for following standardized procedures. Acceptable responses are clearly outlined in the manual (Boehm & Slater, 1981).

Denver Developmental Screening Inventory—Individually administered, norm-referenced testing for early identification of children (birth to six years) with developmental and behavioral problems. The DDSI is designed to assess four general developmental areas, including personal-social, fine motor, gross motor, and language (Frankenburg, et al., 1975).

Score outcomes include Delay (item passed by 90 percent of children who are younger),

Abnormal (two delays in two test sections), Untestable, and Normal.

No special training is required for administering the test, and forms and materials are available in Spanish.

Developmental Indicators for Assessment of Learning (Revised) (DIAL-R)—An individual screening instrument designed for use with children aged two to six years, DIAL-R assesses motor, conceptual, and language skills. (Vision and hearing screening is encouraged prior to administration of the tests.)

There are scaled scores for each subtest (each area and for the total score). These scaled scores can then be compared to the cut-off points by age listed in the manual (Mandel-Czudnowski & Goldenberg, 1983).

Special training is required for administering the test. For special education purposes. DIAL-R is useful only for identification of children in need of further evaluation for *potentially* at risk for later school difficulties or *potentially* advanced.

Developmental Profile II—An interview by someone well acquainted with the child (parent and teacher, depending on child's age) and/or a direct test, the Profile provides for assessment of children from birth to nine and a half years in five areas: (1) to determine eligibility for receiving special education and/or related services; (2) as a planning tool to develop a program consistent with the child's strengths and deficits; (3) to measure the child's progress; (4) to evaluate an entire educational program or service; and (5) as a component in periodic developmental screening programs (e.g., Child Find).

The 186 items in this inventory are designed to cover the following areas:

Physical Age: Including large- and small-muscle coordination, strength, stamina, flexibility, and sequential motor skills.
Self-Help Age: Coping independently with the environment, eating, dressing, and working.

Social Age: Interpersonal relationships, emotional needs for people, relating to friends, relatives, and other adults.
Academic Age: Intellectual abilities through evaluation of prerequisite school skills or actual academic achievement.
Communication Age: Expressive and receptive communication skills with both verbal and nonverbal language.

Scoring results in a developmental age and a profile of the difference between chronological and developmental age for each area. An IQ equivalence can be obtained from the academic scale if the child reaches a ceiling within the subtest. These scores should not be compared across ages.

Special training is required for administering the Profile. For purchase, the publisher, Western Psychological Services (Alpern, Boll, & Shearer, 1989), requires that if the test is being used for placement decisions, the user must show proof of advanced training in psychological testing and evaluation of children with handicapping conditions.

Early Screening Inventory—An individually administered, norm-referenced test, the Inventory is a developmental screening instrument for identifying the presence of possible school difficulties in children four to six years of age.

The Inventory covers expressive language, receptive language, reasoning, auditory reception, gross and fine motor skills, perceptual-motor, and behavior. A parent questionnaire covers health and medical history as well as behaviors in the home. A total score is then converted into an "OK," "rescreen," or "refer decision." Norms are provided according to age.

The Inventory is designed to be administered by teachers, other educators, and trained and monitored paraprofessionals. The test is also available in Spanish.

Gesell Development Schedules—An individual, norm-referenced performance scale for young children (four weeks to six years of age), often used for screening and for following up on infants who have difficulty at birth. Postural behavior, prehensory behavior, perceptual behavior, adaptive behavior, and language-social behavior is covered (Gesell, et al., 1940). The score outcome is designed to provide a developmental age to compare with the child's chronological age. Special training specific to the test is necessary.

Goodenough-Harris Draw-A-Man—A brief nonverbal test designed to measure intellectual maturity in children aged three to fifteen in their ability to perceive, abstract, and generalize as measured by drawing.

The test is administered either individually or in a group. The child is asked to draw first a man, then a woman, and then him- or herself. The test results in two IQ scores—(1) a point scale based on credit for specific details included in the drawings and (2) a quality scale based upon a comparison of the drawing to model drawings. No special training is required for administration, but administrators should practice scoring. For special education purposes, a measure is provided for information about a child's ability to perceive, abstract, and generalize, but the information is not recommended at this time for a basis for any placement decisions.

Metropolitan Readiness Test (MRT)—Administered to children preschool to kindergarten aged (Level I) and to kindergarten aged to first grade (Level II), the MRT assesses the underlying skills important for early school learning. Provides content-referenced information for planning instruction.

The areas covered in Level I (preschoolers and children in the first half-year of kindergarten) are auditory memory, rhyming, beginning consonants, letter recognition, visual matching, school language/listening, and quantitative language, with an optional copying test. Scores in this test level produce stanines and percentile ranks for the three skill area scores (auditory, visual, and language) and for the prereading composite score. Additionally, there are five quality levels for the optional copying test.

In Level 2 (second half-year of kindergarten and in the first grade), beginning consonants understanding, auditory memory, letter recognition, visual matching, finding patterns, school language and listening, quantitative concepts, and quantitative operations are covered, again with an optional copying test. Scoring produces percentile ranks and stanine scores for each skill area, the prereading composite scores, and the battery composite score. Again, there are five quality levels for the copying test. Means and standard deviations are provided for part scores.

The tests are norm referenced and provide content-referenced information as well, and are designed for small-group or individual administration. Two equivalent forms are available at each level. No special training is required, but the tests are intended for teacher administration. Clear directions are provided in the manual (Nurss & McGauvran, 1976).

Minnesota Child Development Inventory—A 320-item parent questionnaire requiring only yes and no answers (machine or hand scored), the Inventory is an assessment tool designed to discover a child's (aged three months to six years) performance in comparison to expectation according to age and sex. It is a supplement to an interview with the parent. The areas covered are general development, gross motor, fine motor, expressive language, comprehension-conceptual, situation comprehension, self-help, and personal social. In each area, children are scored according to their percentage below age expectation (Ireton & Thwing, 1974).

Ordinal Scales of Psychological Development—Assesses an infant's (birth to 26 months) level of sensorimotor development with the theory that if development in any of the areas is compromised, it will affect the emergence of general intelligence. The test follows the developmental stages of Piaget.

The test is made up of individually administered tasks that are set in specific situations. These tests aim to guage an infant's visual pursuit and permanence of object, means for obtaining desired environmental events, development of vocal imitation, development of gestural imitation, development of operational causality, construciton of object relations in space, and development of schemas for relating to objects (play).

The scales are ordinal in their design so that each successive item constitutes a hierarchical sequence. Although testing can be completed in one session, testing over two to three days for the best sample of behavior is recommended. A profile of a child's strengths and weaknesses across the areas is achieved in concrete and specific terms making them useful for educational programming. The Estimated Developmental Age (EDA) scores and the deviation from the norming sample achieved from each subscale are averaged to obtain overall EDA and deviation scales (Uzgiris & Hunt, 1975).

Use of these scales requires extensive knowledge of the items in order to adequately administer the scale. Interpreting the findings requires knowledge of child development in a Piagetian framework.

Peabody Picture Vocabulary Test (Revised)—An individually administered test designed primarily to measure an individual's (aged two and a half to four years) receptive vocabulary in Standard American English; two equivalent forms are available.

Vocabulary words are checked with age- and grade-level referenced lists; standard scores, percentiles, age equivalents, and stanine scores are provided (Dunn & Dunn, 1981).

For special education purposes, since the range of difficulty of items is broad, out-of-level testing is possible. The test is not recommended for visually impaired populations, and is not recommended as a screening device for cognitive functioning with special education students.

Portage Guide to Early Education (Revised) (PGEE-R)—Informal, criterion-referenced testing that is administered through direct observation or through interviewing the par-

ent or someone who knows the child well. Designed to assess behaviors typically developed in children from birth to six years of age, the PGEE-R is a package based on the view that "development is cumulative; what a child learns today is based on the skills he/she already exhibits." The Guide comes in three parts—(1) a checklist of behaviors on which to record an individual child's developmental progress, (2) a card file listing possible methods of teaching these behaviors, and (3) a manual of directions for use of the checklist and card file as well as methods for implementing activities. The areas covered by the test include infant stimulation, self-help, motor, socialization, language, and cognitive skills (Bluma et al., 1976).

The PGEE-R is intended for use by teachers and other educators. The manual is clear, and no additional training is necessary. For special education purposes, since the Guide was developed specifically for evaluating a child's current behavior and planning curriculum based on it, it is a useful tool for working with all children.

Preschool Inventory (Revised)—An individually administered, standardized battery of 64 items, designed for use with children three to six years of age, the Inventory is a brief assessment and screening procedure developed to give a measure of achievement in areas regarded as necessary for success in school. Another goal of the test is to identify deficits of disadvantaged children when they enter school so that those deficits may be reduced or eliminated. The test also serves to identify changes due to educational intervention (Caldwell, 1970).

Basic information and vocabulary; number concepts and ordination; concepts of size, shape, motion, and color; visual-motor performance; following instructions; and independence and self-help are the areas assessed by the test. Raw scores are converted to percentiles according to the child's age. The Inventory is designed to be administered by a trained paraprofessional or teacher.

Preschool Language Assessment, Experimental Edition—An individually administered, norm-referenced test designed to assess children's skills in coping with the language demands of the teaching situation. The test is designed for use with children from three years to five years, eleven months. Each item is scored numerically using a four-level criterion system and qualitatively using a seven-level criterion system. Norms consist of means and score ranges for children according to age and socioeconomic background (Blank, Rose, & Berlin, 1978; Haynes & Shipley, 1985).

Preschool Screening System (Field Trial Edition)—An individually administered screening system combined with a parent questionnaire designed to provide a quick survey of the learning skills of large numbers of entering kindergarten or nursery school children (aged four years, four months to five years, four months) so that the curriculum may be better oriented toward their needs.

The areas covered by the test include information processing skills in language, visual-motor, and gross motor areas. The parent questionnaire covers behavioral characteristics of the skills and behavior of the child at home, plus a short medical and developmental history (Hainsworth & Hainsworth, 1974).

The test can be administered by a trained teacher or paraprofessional. For special education purposes, the Screening System may be useful as a first step toward recognizing special training needs of preschool or kindergarten children.

Slosson Intelligence Test—An individually administered, untimed test that evaluates a person's (aged two to eighteen years) mental ability in a short period of time. Scores on this test produce intelligence quotients with a mean of 100 and a standard deviation of 15, percentile ranks, normal curve equivalents, and stanine categories (Slosson, 1984).

The Slosson Intelligence Test can be used by teachers, other educators, social workers, psychologists, and "other responsible persons who . . . need to evaluate an individual's men-

tal ability." Clear directions are contained in the manual.

Stanford-Binet Intelligence Scale (Fourth Edition) (SB:FE)—An individually administered, norm-referenced test that assesses the overall level of cognitive development in individuals aged two years to adult. The SB:FE helps to identify gifted students, and to differentiate between students who are mentally retarded and those who have specific learning difficulties. The four general areas covered by the test are verbal reasoning, abstract/visual reasoning, quantitative reasoning, and short-term memory. Sattler (1988) reports limited support for these areas and describes a different division of subtests based on factor analysis. For ages two to six, verbal comprehension and nonverbal reasoning/visualization best characterize the test. At 7 to 23 years of age, verbal comprehension, nonverbal reasoning/visualization and memory are the most appropriate.

There are 15 subtests total, each containing items of a similar type. Eight to thirteen of the subtests are administered, depending on the age of the subject. Standard age scores can be generated for each subtest and each area in addition to the overall IQ score (Thorndike, Hagen, & Sattler, 1986).

For appropriate administration and interpretation, the SB:FE requires extensive background in psychometric assessment, the effects of culture on performance and issues surrounding work with handicapped children. Additionally, training specific to the test should be undertaken. For special education purposes, the memory subtests may be especially helpful in the assessment of learning disabled children.

Stanford Early School Achievement Test: Level 1—A group-administered test designed to measure cognitive abilities upon entrance into kindergarten (Level 1), during and at the end of the kindergarten year, and at the beginning of the first grade (Level 2). According to the authors, this is not a readiness test. Rather, it purports to measure cognitive development to establish a base line where instructional experience may best begin (Madden, Gardner, & Collins, 1984).

The areas covered by the test include sounds and letters, word reading, listening to words and stories, math, and the environment. The test also includes a classroom planning guide to assist teachers with applying the test results in their classrooms.

Score outcomes produce percentile ranks, stanines, grade equivalents, and scaled scores. Different percentiles and stanines are given for private school students.

For administration, directions are clearly outlined in the teacher's manual, and no additional training is necessary. Directions for hand scoring, norms, and technical data are contained in the norms manual, separate from the directions for administration. The test is difficult for children with physical and other handicaps affecting writing.

Vineland Social Maturity Scale—A criterion-referenced test that assesses the level of an individual's (birth to adulthood) capacity for self-care and for independent living. The test covers self-help, self-direction, occupation, communication, locomotion, and socialization. Information is gathered by an interview of a person who knows the subject (parent, guardian, case manager). Three forms of the test are available—survey (297 items), expanded (577 items), and classroom (teacher is interviewed).

Standard scores are available based on the national standardization sample for the adaptive behavior domains (communication, daily living skills, socialization, and motor skills) and for the adaptive behavior composite score. Percentile ranks, stanine scores, and age equivalents are also available for the domains and the composite. There are descriptive categories for the maladaptive behavior domain (Sparrow, Balla, & Cicchetti, 1984).

In addition to familiarity with child development and handicapping conditions, the examiner needs to be trained in the use of the instrument and its scoring. For special education purposes, the norms for children with handicapping conditions in addition to regular norms make this a useful tool for understanding the social and self-help skills of all children. Interviewers need to be aware of the environmental conditions of the children being evaluated.

Wechsler Preschool and Primary Scale of Intelligence (Revised) (WPPSI-R)—A norm-referenced, individually administered test that "serves as an estimate of the individual's [aged three years to seven years, three months] capacity to understand and cope with the surrounding world." The Scale also serves as a measure of intelligence that is used in assisting in the diagnosis of mentally impaired and gifted children.

The verbal scale subtests of the Scale include information, comprehension, arithmetic, vocabulary, similarities, and sentences (optional). The performance scale includes object assembly, geometric design, block design, mazes, picture completion, and animal pegs (optional). The Full Scale includes both the verbal and performance scales. All questions are designed to allow the child to demonstrate knowledge of events or objects in the environment. Early items require a child to point to a picture, and later items require brief oral responses.

Of twelve subtests, ten are included in the calculations. There are three area scores—a Verbal IQ (VIQ), a Performance IQ (PIQ), and a Full Scale IQ (FSIQ), all with a mean of one hundred and a standard deviation of fifteen. Subtest scale scores with a mean of ten and a standard deviation of three are also computed to create a profile of a child's strengths and weaknesses (Wechsler, 1989).

For appropriate administration and interpretation, the WPPSI-R requires extensive background in psychometric assessment, the effects of culture on performance, and issues surrounding work with handicapped children. Additionally, training specific to the test should be undertaken.

References

Alpern, G., Boll, T., & Shearer, M. (1989). *Developmental Profile II*. Western Psychological Services.

Anderson, S., & Bogatz, G. A. (1976). *Circus*. Educational Testing Service.

Bayley, N. (1969). *Bayley Scales of Infant Development*. Psychological Corporation.

Blank, M., Rose, S. A., & Berlin, L. J. (1978). *Preschool Language Assessment Instrument, Experimental Edition*. Grune & Stratton.

Bluma, S., Shearer, M., Frohman, A., & Hilliard, J. (1976). *Portage Guide to Early Education-Revised* (PGEE-R). Cooperative Educational Service Agency.

Boehm, A. (1986). *Boehm Test of Basic Concepts—Preschool Version*. Psychological Corporation.

Boehm, A. E., & Slater, B. (1981). *Cognitive Skills Assessment Battery*. New York: Teachers College Press.

Brigance, A. (1978). *Brigance Diagnostic Inventory of Early Development*. Curriculum Associate Inc.

Caldwell, B. M. (1970). *Preschool Inventory—Revised*. Reading, MA: Addison-Wesley.

Cattell, P. (1960). *Cattell Infant Intelligence Scales*. Psychological Corporation.

Dunn, L., & Dunn, L. (1981). *Peabody Picture Vocabulary Test—Revised*. American Guidance Services.

Frankenburg, Dodds, Fandal, Kazuk, Cohrs. (1975). *Denver Developmental Screening Inventory*. Denver Developmental Materials.

Gesell, A., et al. (1940). *Gesell Development Schedules*. Psychological Corporation.

Hainsworth, P. K., & Hainsworth, M. L. (1974). *Preschool Screening System (Field Trial Edition)*. Available from the authors at P.S.S., Box 1635, Pawtucket, RI 02862.

Harris, D. (1963). *Goodenough-Harris Draw-A-Man*.

Haynes, W. O., & Shipley, K. G. (1985). "Review: Preschool language assessment instrument experimental edition." In Buros (ed.), *Mental measurement yearbook, 9th ed.*

Ireton, H., & Thwing, E. (1974). *Minnesota Child Development Inventory*. Minneapolis, MN: Behavior Science Systems.

Madden, Gardner, & Collins. (1984). *Stanford Early School Achievement Test: Level 1*. Psychological Corporation.

Mardell-Czudnowski, C. D., Goldenberg, D. S. (1983). *Developmental Indicators for the Assessment of Learning—Revised (DIAL-R)*. Childcraft Education Corp.

Meisels, S. J., & Wiske, M. S. (n.d.). *Early Screening Inventory*. New York: Teachers College Press.

Newborg, J., Stock, J., Wnek, L., Guidubaldi, J., & Sninicki, J. (1984). *Battelle Developmental Inventory*. DLM Teaching Resources.

Nurss, J., & McGauvran, M. (1976). *Metropolitan Readiness Test (MRT)*. Psychological Corporation.

Slosson, R. L. (1984). *Slosson Intelligence Test*. Slosson Educational Publications, Inc.

Sparrow, S., Balla, D., & Cicchetti, D. (1984). *Vineland Social Maturity Scale*. American Guidance Services.

Thorndike, R. L., Hagen, E. P., & Sattler, J. M. (1986). *Stanford-Binet Intelligence Scale—Fourth Edition (SB:FE)*. Riverside Publishing.

Uzgiris, I., & Hunt, J. M. (1975). *Assessment in Infancy: Ordinal Scales of Psychological Development*. Urbana, IL: University of Illinois Press.

Wechsler, D. (1989). *Wechsler Preschool and Primary Scale of Intelligence—Revised*. Psychological Corporation.

A. E. Boehm

Infant Assessment: Issues and Glossary

The assessment of infants and toddlers is an urgent issue for early childhood educators, as well as for health professionals and other specialists who work with children from birth to three years of age. Many children who are born organically handicapped and/or at risk for normal development due to prenatal drug exposure, premature birth, AIDS, and environmental deprivation are not identified in the first three years of life. Problems become apparent in kindergarten and the primary grades, when teachers are puzzled by disturbed behavior patterns with hidden etiology and little remedy within the regular classroom.

Part H of Public Law 99-457 (1985), which sets standards for programs designed to intervene before these children enter school, requires a multidisciplinary assessment of each child and comprehensive services, with periodic rescreening and reassessment that involves the family at all levels.

The predictability of assessment instruments designed for use with infants and toddlers remains an issue, as does the paucity of comprehensive instruments designed to meet the intervention needs of infants, toddlers, and their families.

Glossary

At this writing, the only assessment instrument comprehensive enough to fulfill the requirements summarized above is the *Connecticut Infant-Toddler Developmental Assessment* (IDA) (Provence, Erikson, Vater, & Palmeri, 1985). Designed for infants and toddlers from birth to three years of age, this instrument is used for intervention purposes. An interdisciplinary team assesses health and family/social issues, as well as the child's emotional development, interpersonal relationships, and the traditional skill areas. With parental involvement the information is integrated to produce and Individualized Family Service Plan (IFSP). It has been noted that "the developmental component is not a standardized test, and it does not stand alone outside the full IDA process" (Meisels & Provence, 1989).

A brief, alphabetized list of other assessment instruments designed for use in research, clinical, or educational settings with infants, toddlers, and their families follows.

Battelle Developmental Inventory (Newborg, Stock, Wnek, Guidubaldi, & Svinicki, 1984). Designed for research on the mental development of children from birth to eight years of age, this instrument yields scores in five domains. The domains include personal-social, adaptive, motor, communication, and cognition. The test manual includes instructions for modifying the test for handicapped children.

Bayley Scales of Infant Development (Bayley, 1969). Designed for research on the neuromotor and mental development of infants from two to thirty months of age, this scale consists of three components. They are the Mental Scale, Motor Scale, and Infant Behavior Record. Items on the Mental Scale assess sensory discrimination, eye-hand coordination, object permanence, vocal ability, and elementary problem solving. The Motor Scale assesses motor coordination, balance, and fine motor prehension. The Infant Behavior Record assesses general emotional tone, social responsiveness, and goal directedness. A norm-referenced test, these scales rank the child in comparison to a same-age reference group. The scale does not include instructions for use with handicapped infants.

Carolina Curriculum for Handicapped Infants and Infants at Risk (Johnson-Martin, Jens, & Attermeier, 1986). Designed for educational and therapeutic work with infants and toddlers ranging from 4 to 36 months of age, this inventory assesses the child's ability to manage the opportunities, challenges, and frustrations encountered in daily life. The inventory consists of 48 items categorized as sensorimotor organization, reactive behavior, and self-initiated behavior. These categories are grouped through systematic observation that yields a Coping Profile representing an integrated description of the child.

Gesell Developmental Schedules—Revised (Knobloch, Stevens, & Malone, 1987). Designed for diagnosis of the mental development of infants and toddlers from 4 to 36 months of age, this instrument assesses developmental progress in 5 domains. The domains are adaptive, gross motor, fine motor, language, and personal-social. The instrument is norm referenced on a highly homogeneous sample and includes no adaptation for handicapped infants.

Home Inventory (Caldwell, 1972). Designed for research with children of unspecified ages, this inventory assesses the quality of the home environment through systematic observation of emotional and verbal responsivity of mother, organization of the physical and temporal environment, and stimulation through toys, games, and reading materials. At this writing, the inventory is in a process of re-evaluation.

Infant Temperament Questionnaire, Revised (Carey & McDevitt, 1978). Designed for intervention with infants from four to eight months of age, this questionnaire assesses temperament as reflected in the child's individual behavioral style. It employs a parent questionnaire rather than direct observation to categorize behaviors for an individual profile of the child.

Neonatal Behavioral Assessment Scale (Brazelton, 1984). Designed for research and clinical work with families of newborn infants, this is an interactive instrument that assesses optimal performance. It measures the integration and separate functioning of the interactive, motoric, and autonomic systems, as well as states in healthy, full-term newborns, and in high-risk infants, with their families.

Parent Behavior Progression (Bromwich, 1983). Designed for research with children of unspecified ages, this instrument assesses maternal behaviors through two or three home observations of the mother with her child. The scoring is somewhat unclear.

Peabody Developmental Motor Scales (Folio & Fewell, 1983). Designed for program planning for individuals and groups of children from birth to 6.9 years of age, this set of scales evaluates gross motor and fine motor development. It categorizes items into skill areas such as balance or grasping.

Scales of Infant Psychological Development (Uzgiris & Hunt, 1975). Designed for research on the sensorimotor development of infants from birth to two years of age, this is an example of a criterion-referenced scale. The instrument focuses on how the child performs on a series of Piagetian-based items without comparison to a normative group. It measures emerging sensorimotor competencies as they progress both within and among seven domains, including visual pursuit and object permanence, means for obtaining desired environmental events, development of vocal imitation, development of gestural imitation, development of operational causality, construction of object relations in space, and de-velopment of schemes for relating object (play). It provides qualitative as well as quantitative information about the individual child.

Strange Situation (Ainsworth, Blehar, Waters, & Wall, 1978). Designed for research about the attachment of infants and toddlers ranging from 10 to 24 months of age, this instrument focuses on patterns of behavior exhibited by the child vis-à-vis the primary caregiver (mother) and an unfamiliar person within an unfamiliar environment, "the strange situation." The child's behavior is rated and grouped into three major patterns of attachment that include securely attached (Type B), avoidant (Type A), and resistant (Type C). (See Gibbs & Teti, 1990, pp. 191–214, for theoretical backgrounds and issues.)

Toddler Temperament Scale (Carey & McDevitt, 1978). This instrument assesses the coping skills and temperament development of toddlers from 12 months to 3 years of age. It is similar to the Infant Temperament Questionnaire, Revised (Carey & McDevitt), cited above.

References

Gibbs, E., & Teti, D. (1990). *Interdisciplinary assessment of infants: A guide for early intervention professionals.* Baltimore: Brookes Publishers.

Meisels, S., & Provence, S. (1989). *Screening and assessment: Guidelines for identifying young disabled and developmentally vulnerable children and their families.* Washington, DC: National Center for Clinical Infant Programs.

A. Axtmann

Chapter 5

EARLY CHILDHOOD CURRICULA AND PROGRAMS: VARIATIONS IN FORM AND CONTENT

Chapter *5*

EARLY CHILDHOOD CURRICULA AND PROGRAMS: VARIATIONS IN FORM AND CONTENT

Introduction

In the more than 150 years since early childhood education was introduced, and especially from 1960 onward, early childhood curricula and programs in the United States have assumed a wide variety in form and content. Variation in form and content has influenced the types of materials used, as well as the ways the classroom or early childhood center is furnished and arranged, the ways the day is scheduled, and the ways the world outside of the classroom is used to extend children's experience and learning.

Much of the variation is expressive of debates rooted in ancient questions of philosophy—what is the nature of knowledge, what knowledge is valuable and for whom, how does one understand "the good" for individuals in relation to "the good" for society, how do people create meaning in their lives, what constitutes beauty, and how might justice be actualized? While individual program designers, curriculum developers, researchers, policy makers, teachers, and parents may not always

have been consciously aware of these questions as they planned for and worked with young children, as members of a particular society and culture they have frequently played out such concerns in the multitude of their day-to-day decisions around children's care and education.

Most prominent have been decisions regarding what was to be taught, and how it was to be taught to young children. What was to be taught has been influenced by the identification of varying sources of knowledge, while the debate around how young children might best be taught has revolved around the definition of "developmentally appropriate" practice. (See Chapter 4 for a discussion of that definition.)

The sources of the knowledge bases in early childhood curricula and programs have differed depending upon how educators and parents interpret, value, and integrate several influences—what they believe society sanctions, what they perceive is worth knowing, what they understand about the nature of children and how they learn, and what strategies they have for teaching children within these contexts.

In the United States, there has been an emphasis on achievement of technical proficiency and literacy for the development of citizenship. The arts and humanities, and appreciation of present-time aesthetic concerns, have received less emphasis. The futurist cast of the technical world has tended toward a narrow, vertical educational outlook, rather than toward a broad, horizontal enrichment approach. Children in general have been expected to progress in a uniform fashion toward the mastery of skills. Competitive achievement is valued. Teachers who have themselves been educated in these vertical approaches tend to perpetuate them.

A particular concern of early childhood education is how young children might experience a developmentally appropriate curriculum. The proponents of varied perspectives each suggest that their interpretation is appropriate. Among the major positions assumed are the maturationist/socialization, the constructivist/intellectual, and the academic/determinist.

The maturationist/socialization group takes a largely laissez faire outlook in its belief that curriculum will emerge from children's interests and from their prior knowledge. In this view, the child's franchise predominates, and the teacher's position is to attempt to identify the directions that particular children wish to follow. Generally oriented toward present-time concerns of young children's personal and social development, some teachers in this framework sometimes provide unconnected activities and information based upon traditional, unexamined practice.

In the constructivist/intellectual position, the franchise for decisions is shared between teacher and child. This perspective is based upon the belief that worthwhile knowledge is an internal, inductive process through which young children build meanings as they interact with others and the physical world. Teachers are proactive by providing materials and activities that match children's developmental capacities. The constructivist position contends that schools need to adapt to children and that young children are capable of making connections among ideas.

The academicians take a largely determinist position in their belief that children should acquire a set body of skills and facts within certain time frames. Often teachers use materials and practices such as workbooks and recitations that require single, correct, teacher-determined and directed responses. In this view, the teacher's franchise predominates, and children are expected to conform.

In contrast to a focus on the development of the individual child represented by the positions articulated above is emphasis on the kind of society one hopes to produce through the care and education of young children. Educators make implicit decisions regarding whether existing societal structures will be maintained or in some way changed when they emphasize preparing children to function effectively within a democracy, a socialist system, or some other political system, or address issues of ecology in a global community, social justice in interaction with other people, humane treatment of animals, or world peace. The value systems inherent in the choices made will necessarily influence both content and teaching strategies.

Choice of value systems may revolve at its deepest level around conceptions of both the sources and the exercise of power. Power is a central issue in education. Inasmuch as young children are relatively vulnerable and powerless, this issue is particularly relevant in early childhood education. When children feel capable and have the sense that they are involved in legitimate choices among learning activities, they are more likely to be motivated to work in a focused way than when they feel obligated to do so. Maria Montessori's notion that the child should learn not for the sake of love of the teacher or fear of the teacher but for the sake of learning itself, reflects this issue of power. The teacher's important contribution is to offer a match between the child's possibilities and the need to achieve and extend learning.

A difference has been drawn between the academic/determinist and the constructivist/intellectual approaches to early childhood education in relation to defining the content of curriculum (see Section 5.2). There are also differences between the two perspectives in terms of understanding the distribution of power. In particular, academic approaches tend to expect children to follow teacher initiation of activities, whereas constructivist approaches tend to adapt to children's varied developmental stages and to seek shared control in the initiation of activities.

Power also may be understood to be a social, rather than an individual construction. Notions of what groups within a society should exercise power, how they should do so, and to what ends, lead back again to visions of the development or reconstruction of society as a whole. The issue remains of whose values are to be served by such visions.

The questions that guide research on early childhood curricula and programs necessarily follow the considerations articulated above. During the 1960s and 1970s, much of the research was focused on determining which programs were most effective in enabling children to succeed in their later school experience. Designs tended toward the experimental or quasi-experimental, with some groups of children receiving the treatment of a particular curriculum or program, while other children matched with the treatment group on certain variables acted as controls or comparison groups. A number of early childhood researchers were interested in ways that theory could be transformed into practice. The theories investigated generally followed one of the three perspectives described above, with a great deal of attention being given to the academic/determinist point of view.

More recently, however, the focus has changed from a question of which program is the best, to one of which curricula or programs work well for which children under what circumstances. More observational, descriptive, and ethnographic research methods are being employed. While interest in how theory might be translated into practice is still evident, now an equally potent question is how recognition of the intricacies of practice might influence the development of theory. The constructivist/intellectual perspective has enjoyed renewed attention in these investigations.

It seems reasonable to expect that the evaluation of curriculum and program effects would reflect the nature of the curriculum or program in question. That is, a technical, skills-oriented approach to curriculum would lead to a normative, standardized evaluation, based on discrete measurements of short-term accomplishments. A more constructively oriented curriculum in which children engage in projects designed to help them integrate skills by exploring issues and solving genuine problems would use a variety of complementary evaluation modes, such as observation, review of products, and interviews, as well as other written formats.

Assessment of the progress of individuals or groups of children also has reflected variation in theoretical perspective. Most schools today use examinations that test the isolated skills and informational accretions of academic programs. Constructivist forms of assessment, on the other hand, are multifaceted and are at a relatively early stage of development. In general, researchers have found that teachers' observations of young children are a valid form of assessment, along with documentation of children's performance of tasks and interviews of children done in a socially secure environment.

As an integral part of the varied forms of assessment and evaluation, the teacher may or may not be viewed as a curriculum developer, rather than as a consumer of packaged kits or textbooks. In using direct study and assessment of children's learning, a teacher who is seen as a curriculum developer engages in action research. This kind of teacher raises questions concerning how to help children learn most effectively, engages in likely means of influencing positive learning, and considers and documents what happens as a basis for future planning. In this way, the practitioner who is a curriculum developer also is a curriculum researcher who selects activities and experiences with deliberation.

The chapter that follows is divided into eight major sections covering the history of curriculum trends in early childhood education, description of a range of curricular and programmatic approaches, definition of early childhood curriculum domains, description of usual and technological learning materials for young children, discussion of the physical environments of early childhood education, identification of teaching strategies, and examination of broader settings in the form of field trips to extend experience and learning. Within each section, articles are generally arranged alphabetically, except when a topic is so related to one that precedes it that it must logically follow as an amplification.

In each of the eight sections, the philosophical debates and theoretical perspectives summarized above are represented. Thus, it can be seen that the forms and content of practice are parts of larger conceptions that need to be recognized in making knowledgeable choices.

D. P. Fromberg & L. R. Williams

5.1 Early Childhood Curriculum Trends and Issues in the United States

Early childhood curriculum trends in the United States trace their roots to European traditions that have been tempered by societal concerns about transforming society through the educational system. While access to universal education has been the hallmark of this nation, early childhood curriculum has been available in different ways across the nation for children on the basis of region, degree of affluence, and historical period.

The economic forces in this country have contributed directly to the provisions for early childhood education. The political and ideological fuel for curriculum trends also has been connected to the recognition of the economy's need for educated citizenry along with the willingness to fund early education in comparison with other priorities. Depending upon such forces, curriculum trends have been more or less instrumental or child centered, formal or informal, playful or worklike, hierarchical or collegial, uniform or diverse, and segmented or holistic. Control of curriculum policy has fluctuated between more or less federal or local involvement, although local control typically has predominated with the resulting variability based upon local priorities. The opening article in this section traces some of these trends. The other two articles focus on contemporary concerns for curriculum that demonstrate developmentally appropriate practice and consideration for children's long-term needs and possible perceptions of themselves in the educational process.

D. P. Fromberg

History of Early Childhood Curriculum Trends in the United States

Early childhood programs began in the United States with the introduction of the Infant School in the 1820s. The Infant School was created by Robert Owen who saw it as an instrument to reform industrialized society. The goal of Owen's Infant School was to educate students in good practical habits as well as to develop academic and reasoning skills. Owen built on the educational practices of contemporaries, such as Johann Pestalozzi. Children were taught to derive truth from their natural surroundings and learn right and wrong from the natural consequences of their actions. This short-lived approach to educating young children was followed by the introduction of Friedrich Froebel's kindergarten in 1856.

Kindergarten education, which was pioneered by Froebel in Germany, took root slowly and then expanded throughout the United States. Froebel's kindergarten program was based upon a set of assumptions about the unity of man, God, and nature. This unity could be found in the reconciliation of opposites, such that diversity could be found within this unity. Adults presented these concepts to children through symbolic activities consisting of manipulative materials called "gifts." Along with craft activities, or "occupations," songs, games, and nature study, the gifts comprised Froebel's kindergarten curriculum.

Froebel used the metaphor of the garden to characterize early childhood education. The kindergarten was to provide those elements needed to foster growth. To this end, the kindergarten teacher must follow the nature of the children. Froebel contended that play was an important part of early learning. His interpretation of play was highly teacher directed.

Around the turn of the century, early childhood curriculum in the United States took a number of different directions. Progressive educators reconstructed the kindergarten curriculum in response to the development of scientific knowledge about child development as well as to changes in society. At about this time, the nursery school was created in England, and the Montessori school, in Italy. All of these movements influenced early childhood curriculum in this country.

Building on the philosophy of John Dewey and the research of the child study movement, progressive kindergarten educators rejected Froebel's formal, symbolic approach to education. They saw the kindergarten as a place in which to introduce children into the social life of the community, which would be reflected in a miniature community constructed within the school. Children were expected to gather information from their surrounding world through direct experience with materials and activities. The program was to allow children to reconstruct that experience in the kindergarten in order to create their own knowledge. Children also were expected to use dramatic play as a powerful conceptual tool with which to represent the world around them symbolically. The goal of the progressive kindergarten was to move the children to higher levels of development through their interactions with the teacher and the experiences provided.

Montessori education was based on a philosophy of empiricism. Maria Montessori believed that children gained information through the senses. She developed a range of activities with specific materials that would help children become more sensitive to their environments, as well as learn how to bring order into their experiences. Montessori valued children's liberty and provided exercises in practical life as part of the curriculum in order to enable them to function more autonomously. The academic skills of reading, writing, and arithmetic, beginning with sensory experiences, also were a part of the curriculum.

Much like Owen's Infant School, Margaret Mcmillan's nursery school also was conceived as an instrument to reform industrialized society. The program dealt with all aspects of development, and children's imagination was nurtured as a way of helping them to become complex thinkers and problem solvers. These last three approaches to early childhood curriculum represented the range of early childhood practices until the mid-1960s when alternative models were created.

Some of the more modern programs represent a maturational approach to development, with programs following the lead of children, matching experiences to children's native ability without adults actively intervening to promote the extension of that ability. Other programs employ a cultural transmission approach, with children being told, in as efficient a way as possible, what they are expected to know. These programs often are based upon principles of applied behavioral analysis. Still other programs practice a progressive approach to education, sometimes building upon the theories of Jean Piaget. These programs provide a range of experiences and help children to reconstruct their experiences as a way of moving them toward more advanced stages of development. These curriculum alternatives are available in early childhood education today. (See also Chapter 2, Section 2.6, **Pioneers in Child Care and Early Childhood Education**.)

References

Spodek, B. (1973). *Early childhood education.* Englewood Cliffs, NJ: Prentice-Hall.

Spodek, B. (ed.). (1982). *Handbook of research in early childhood education.* New York: Free Press.

Weber, E. (1984). *Ideas influencing early childhood education.* New York: Teachers College Press.

B. Spodek

Advocacy for Developmentally Appropriate Practice

Developmentally appropriate practices (DAP) in early childhood education settings are both age and individually appropriate. There are two basic assumptions underlying DAP. First, young children have somewhat different physical, social, emotional, and learning needs than older children and adults. For example, young children are less able to understand abstract concepts and, therefore, they must be actively engaged with concrete manipulative materials in order to learn. Second, there are individual differences that should impact teaching practices. Same-age children vary widely in their rate of development, interests, aptitudes, temperament, and experiences.

In a sense, advocacy for DAP is as old as recognition of childhood as a special period of life different from all others. As early as the sixteenth century the Moravian bishop John Amos Comenius became an advocate for early education and practices that meet the unique learning needs of young children. From that time to the present the world-wide early childhood education movement has been led by people dedicated to providing developmentally appropriate experiences for young children.

Consensus on terminology and nature of developmentally appropriate practices was reached by early childhood education professionals in 1986, when the Governing Board of the National Association for the Education of Young Children approved a policy statement and published it in a book entitled *Developmentally Appropriate Practice in Early Childhood Programs Serving Children from Birth through Age 8*.

Traditional education has a different history from early childhood education and typically involves a subject matter orientation rather than a developmental orientation. Since traditional education dominates elementary and secondary programming, early childhood educators often find it necessary to advocate for practices based on a developmental perspective.

Advocacy for DAP can take place at various levels: individual, classroom, administrative and legislative. Early childhood educators frequently advocate for individual children whose needs are unique and are not being met by services offered to most other children. A physically disabled child, for example, may need special equipment to help him or her draw or write. To require the child to use the same writing materials that other children use would be developmentally inappropriate. At the classroom level teachers frequently adjust curriculum and practices to accommodate individual needs. In some cases, adopted curricula must be altered to meet the needs of the majority of children in a class. Teachers who make these changes must be prepared to explain and defend such changes to parents and administrators.

Many early childhood educators are becoming involved in advocacy at the administrative level where program regulations and guidelines are developed. When early childhood program curricula are adopted and policies developed, well-trained early childhood educators must be involved in order to present a developmental view. Increasingly, early childhood educators are also advocating for DAP at the legislative level. They do this by becoming involved in the legislative process to ensure that policies and laws best serve the interests of all children. Because of strong advocacy efforts, a growing number of state and local school boards are mandating DAP in early childhood programs. Some early childhood education legislative initiatives at the state and federal levels also refer to DAP.

Our understanding of child development is improving, but incomplete, and therefore, so is our understanding of what practices are most appropriate. The consensus regarding developmentally appropriate practices is, then, not so much advocacy for a specific set of methods as it is for the perspective that practices should be in harmony with children's needs.

References

Bredekamp, S. (ed.). (1987). *Developmentally appropriate practice in early childhood programs serving children from birth through age 8*. Washington DC: National Association for the Education of Young Children.

Comenius, J. A. (1967). *The great didactic of John Amos Comenius*, trans. and ed. M. W. Keatinge (1896, 1910). New York: Russell and Russell.

Fennimore, B. S. (1989). *Child advocacy for early childhood educators*. New York: Teachers College Press.

R. Hitz

Public School Entrance Age

School entrance age refers to the age when children are legally old enough to enter school. For example, many states require that children be five years of age by September 1st in order to enter kindergarten, or six years of age by September 1st in order to begin first grade. There has been a trend during the past 30 years to mandate entrance to kindergarten at increasingly older ages. An early survey found that most school districts require students to be five years old either by December or January 1st (Educational Research Service, 1958). In a later survey, December 1st was the most prevalent cutoff date, but there was a 12 percent rise in the number of districts that required children to be five years of age by September 1st (Ibid., 1975). A more recent survey showed that more than two-thirds of the states have an entrance date on or before October 1st (Education Commission of the States, 1985). A number of states and school districts recently have adopted summer entrance dates (Pavuk, 1987), thereby extending this trend toward raising the age of admission to school.

Those who support this trend believe that older children will be better able to handle the demands of the kindergarten curriculum. This belief suggests that readiness for school is based on finite accomplishments that might develop in those children who wait. The argument ignores, however, the fact that raising the entrance age in the past has not solved the problem of disadvantage to younger students because the youngness problem is relative, not absolute. The youngest children in the class might fare less well than their older peers, whether they are admitted to school in one district at the age of 4.9 years or fully 5 years in another district, or even age 7 in Finland (Gredler, 1975; Shepard & Smith, 1985). Raising the entrance age has the appearance of providing a temporary solution to the perceived problem of universal, uniform achievement. In time, however, teachers continue to need to adjust the curriculum to a new range of the now older age group. Thus, children whose birthdays fall close to any cutoff date might be at risk unless teachers create multiple, rather than uniform, curricular activities (Shepard & Smith, 1988). (See also Chapter 4, Section 4.9, **Retention and Redshirting.**)

References

Education Commission of the States. (November, 1985). State characteristics: Kindergartens. Denver, CO: Author.

Educational Research Service. (1958). *Administration policies for kindergarten and first grade, circular no. 3*. Arlington, VA: Author.

Educational Research Service. (1975). *Kindergarten and first grade minimum entrance age policies, circular no. 5*. Arlington, VA: Author.

Educational Research Service. (1986). Kindergarten programs and practices in public schools. *Principal, 65*, 22–23.

Gredler, G. (1975). Ethical and legal dilemmas in the assessment of readiness of children for school. In G. R. Gredler (ed.), *Ethical and legal factors in the practice of school psychology* (pp. 196–221). Pennsylvania State Department of Education.

Pavuk, A. (June 24, 1987). Legislatures, districts move to raise age for kindergarten. *Education Week, 6* (1), 17.

Shepard, L. A., & Smith, M. L. (March, 1985). *Boulder Valley kindergarten study: Retention practices and retention effects*. Boulder Valley Public Schools.

Shepard, L. A., & Smith, M. L. (1988). Escalating academic demand in kindergarten: Counterproductive policies. *The Elementary School Journal, 89* (2), 135–145.

M. E. Graue & L. A. Shepard

5.2 Curriculum Approaches

In visiting classrooms, it is rare to find in an exclusive form an instance of any one of the curriculum approaches presented below. In a sense, the supporters of each of the approaches feel correct in perceiving the need for a curriculum in their own image. Each is built upon some truths that are more and less evident, depending upon a particular philosophical stance, belief system, and personal values and priorities. Each model can point to roots in a dignified intellectual tradition and research that supports its position. Each can introduce you to satisfied teachers, parents, and children.

Current programs tend to emphasize curriculum positions that complement one another. For example, it is likely to find a combination of academic and unit curriculum or a combination of intellectual/constructivist, interdisciplinary, and project curriculum. Proportions, in such combinations, predictably vary from site to site. Each position in its own way can affect how children perceive their possibilities for influencing the world inside and outside of school.

The section that follows consists of two parts, each of which is presented in alphabetical order. The opening part discusses curriculum approaches for all children and the closing part presents curriculum emphases in use with children who have special learning needs.

D. P. Fromberg

Academics/Direct Instruction

A problem facing early childhood educators is how to teach reading, mathematics, and language concepts to young students in a sensitive, developmentally appropriate fashion (Warger, 1988). Fifty years ago, many believed that formal reading instruction should not begin until students were "ready" and that academics should not be taught until first grade. A good deal of research, however, demonstrates that four- and five-year-olds can benefit from systematic reading, language, and mathematics instruction (Anderson et al.,

1985). Recent evidence suggests that this type of instruction can lead to long-term benefits for low-income students.

Both formal and informal approaches can complement one another, although some academic classrooms tend toward largely formal approaches. Research on formal reading instruction indicates that students should be taught how to "break the code" through systematic phonics instruction (Adams, 1990), rather than a sight word approach. Students spend small amounts of time learning sounds in isolation and then learn how to read words, sentences, and brief stories. In mathematics, the emphasis is on basic number concepts and operations. This instruction is sequenced and organized carefully so that students experience high rates of daily success. Students rarely should be sitting at their desks filling out sheets. They should spend the major portion of instructional time engaged in substantive verbal interactions with a teacher.

In addition, children should participate in a more informal approach, often called emergent literacy or whole language. Students learn about the functions that written language can serve (Anderson et al., 1985). Teachers read stories to children, ask questions about stories, and encourage students to engage in projects related to the stories. Students also write stories, typically using invented spelling. They also use manipulatives in mathematics.

Many programs emphasize one approach and pay lip service to the other. It is becoming clear, however, that a combination of both formal and informal approaches is optimal for the cognitive development of young students.

References

Adams, M. J. (1990). *Beginning to read: Thinking and learning about print.* Center for the Study of Reading, University of Illinois.

Anderson, R. C., Hiebert, E. H., Scott, J. A., & Wilkinson, I. A. *Becoming a nation of readers: The report of the commission on reading.* Center for the Study of Reading, University of Illinois.

Warger, C. (ed.). (1988). *Public school early childhood programs.* Washington, DC: Association for Supervision and Curriculum Development.

Gersten, R., Darch, C., & Gleason, M. (1988). Effectiveness of a direct-instruction academic kindergarten for low income students. *Elementary School Journal*, 89 (2), 227–240.

R. Gersten

Constructivist/Intellectual Curriculum

Constructivist/Intellectual education in early childhood contrasts with and subsumes academic and socialization education. Ideas, concepts, and understandings that are meaningful to children make up the content focus of this approach. These ideas, concepts, and understandings may be rooted in the teacher's understanding of the disciplines of knowledge, but in early childhood education, children often learn through interdisciplinary means. The study of any experience, therefore, can take place when children use any tools for knowing, the ways of studying in multiple disciplines. In these ways, the study of the physical world might include multicultural social concerns; children learn skills as they integrate the skills of language literacy, mathematics, the arts, and problem solving into their studies. For example, primary-age children might study how people in different regions view the weather by looking at the effects of climate and terrain on jobs (geography and economics). They might survey local weather conditions (mathematics and science), record the findings (writing), read quality nonfiction trade books concerning different cultures, terrains, work, habitat, and other forms of human adaptation (language literacy), draw about or look at fine art productions concerning related areas of climate, culture, work around the world and at different times in history, and so forth.

The comparisons and contrasts that children perceive serve as important conditions of their learning. As children engage in actively making connections and comparisons, attempt to find out about questions that arise, and consider alternatives for solving problems or resolving contradictions, they construct their own perspectives. At the same time, they develop their own motives for learning and using integrated skills.

Thus, learning "content" within an intellectual approach is different from acquiring skills in isolation. Instead, children learn skills such as reading, writing, mathematics, and general problem solving within the context of meanings, thereby enriching their learning of both skills and content. Children can acquire attitudes and predispositions to learn and to be civilized social beings when they learn in an active context that is rich in subject matter that is important to them.

Teachers who employ an intellectual approach, therefore, adapt to young children's ways of learning. They plan activities for which there may be more than a single acceptable interpretation. They are interested in how children think and arrive at solutions to problems, even if those results would not be acceptable universally. Indeed, they accept alternative solutions to problems and can use them as part of the content that children study.

Teachers in constructivist/intellectual classrooms plan for young children to be active, mainly self-directed, question raisers. They provide activities that most often are concrete and physical, and adapt to children's natural ways of learning in order for children to experience a sense of competence and success.

Teachers recognize that effective learning takes place when children can interact with one another. Collaborative small group and individual activities predominate, although there are some whole group activities. In these various ways, young children have opportunities to construct their own understandings and concepts while learning to use skills as they develop and extend personally meaningful content.

In the past, many of these intellectual approaches were the restricted territory of children in gifted programs. Often, young school children from culturally diverse groups or low-income families experienced isolated instruction in skills or teacher requests for rote learnings. Cross-cultural research, however, has found that all children come to school with a wealth of rich personal experience that lends itself to constructive, intellectual study (Heath, 1983). The issue for young children involves the need for teachers to adapt curriculum to the distinct intellectual content that children bring to school and to use it as an axis around which to integrate skills learning.

References

Heath, S. B. (1983). *Ways with words: Language, life, and work in communities and classrooms.* New York: Cambridge University Press.

Fromberg, D. P. (1989). Kindergarten: Current circumstances affecting curriculum. *Teachers College Record*, 90 (3), 392–403.

D. P. Fromberg

Interdisciplinary Learning/ Integrated Curriculum

Interdisciplinary or integrative learning is "a knowledge view and curriculum approach that consciously applies methodology and language from more than one discipline to examine a central theme, issue, problem, topic, or experience (Jacobs, 1989, p. 8)." Through in-depth exploration of a particular area, young children learn relevant skills, gain content area and process knowledge, and become aware of relationships.

The integrated curriculum gained recognition through Susan Isaacs, a British practitioner who put John Dewey's theories into practice in the 1920s. Believing that children's cognitive learning depends upon their feelings, she used children's interests and social interactions to promote cognitive, language, psychomotor, and aesthetic growth (Isaacs, 1966). Isaacs' approach provided the basis for the British Primary Schools' "integrated day," which in turn gave rise to the open education movement of the 1960s and 1970s in the United States. An integrated curriculum is part of the contemporary guidelines for developmentally appropriate early childhood practice published by the National Association for the Education of Young Children (Bredekamp, 1987).

Interdisciplinary learning is both child centered and child empowering. Its philosophical underpinnings include trust in children's ability to make decisions and engage in higher order thinking; acknowledgment that learning extends beyond the classroom; and a recognition that children learn from peers, as well as from adults. "Family grouping," a cross-age or "vertical" grouping pattern common in British Primary Schools and some early childhood programs in the United States, capitalizes on the value of peer learning.

In practice, the integrated curriculum may appear "informal" due to children's heightened engagement with thematic materials and with each other. Successful interdisciplinary programs, however, have a well-planned underlying structure and cohesiveness. The role of early childhood teachers in integrated programs includes ongoing observation to determine children's interests and needs, design of intellectually worthwhile thematic activities, procurement of materials and resources, and management of the overall learning environment. In addition, teachers must guide children's pacing and help determine appropriate culminations for long-term learning experiences. Many of the tenets of the integrated day are exemplified in programs such as the Reggio Emilia (Italy) programs for young children (New, 1990).

Scheduling in interdisciplinary programs is flexible, providing large blocks of time for in-depth exploration, rather than being dictated by discrete subject matter time allotments. Often, small groups will work with problems or issues based on common interests, while some experiences or themes may be investigated by the whole class. Areas selected for long-term study should offer cross-disciplinary possibilities for classifying, connecting, and generalizing knowledge.

Skills acquisition in integrated curricula is functional, and students learn skills as they need to use them in meaningful contexts. As children experiment with temperature change, for example, they might conduct a cooking activity to see the impact of heat or cold. Formulating a shopping list, dealing with money and change, following printed directions, and measuring are a few task-related skills.

Integrated curricula also emphasize the functional aspects of literacy, and there are many parallels between the whole language approach (Goodman, 1986) and interdisciplinary learning. Aesthetic development also is part of cross-disciplinary study. Classrooms using an integrative approach abound with child-created products such as murals, writing, illustrations, pictorial graphs, and three-dimensional constructions.

Assessment in interdisciplinary programs tends to be individualized, with teachers viewing children's progress over time. Often, schools systematically maintain portfolios of children's products in order to assess development holistically and individually monitor discrete skills. Involving students in evaluation, through criteria that they establish cooperatively with the teachers, allows evaluation to become a tool for self-growth (Clark, 1986). Such involvement, like other child-centered aspects of the integrated curriculum, increases motivation and promotes shared responsibility for learning. (See also **Constructivist/Intellectual Curriculum**, above.)

References

Bredekamp, S. (ed.). (1987). *Developmentally appropriate practice in early childhood programs serving children from birth through age 8.* Washington, DC: National Association for the Education of Young Children.

Clark, B. (1986). *Optimizing learning: The integrative education model in the classroom.* Columbus, OH: Merrill.

Goodman, K. (1986). *What's whole in whole language?* Portsmouth, NH: Heinemann.

Isaacs, S. (1966). *Intellectual growth in young children.* New York: Schocken Books.

Jacobs, H. H. (ed.). (1989). *Interdisciplinary curriculum: Design and implementation.* Washington, DC: Association for Supervision and Curriculum Development.

Krogh, S. (1990). *The integrated early childhood curriculum.* New York: McGraw-Hill.

New, R. (1990). Excellent early education: A city in Italy has it. *Young Children, 45* (6), 4–10.

S. B. Cruikshank

Multicultural Education

The concept of multicultural education has evolved over the past 20 years. From the desegregation and ethnic studies movements of the 1960s and 1970s emerged a recognition that all children must learn to live in a diverse world. In the middle 1970s, the term "multicultural education" began to appear in the educational literature. The National Council for Accreditation of Teacher Education in 1977 mandated the inclusion of multicultural education in both the general education and professional studies components of teacher education.

Multicultural education represents a shift away from the emphasis on assimilating all cultures into an amalgamated "melting pot" to a recognition of the value of cultural pluralism. Inherent in this perspective is a respect for all ethnic, religious, and social class backgrounds, and a rejection of the deficit-oriented programs that sought to remediate young children who did not come from white, middle-class families. It is closely tied to bilingual education in both philosophy and in practice, although not all multicultural programs are bilingual, nor are all bilingual programs multicultural.

There are five different approaches to multicultural education that Christine Sleeter and Carl A. Grant (1988) describe. They include education of the culturally different, which often embodies a deficit-orientation toward diverse groups; single group studies, which are similar to ethnic studies programs of the 1970s in their focus on the history, traditions and life styles of separate groups; human relations courses and programs that focus on intergroup communication and cooperation; multicultural education, which emphasizes the positive and adaptive value of familiarity with many cultures for all children; and education that is multicultural and social reconstructionist, programs oriented toward changing the basic structures of society that allow and foster unequal relations among groups. They critique existing programs and curricula and advocate the fifth approach as the only one that authentically strives toward permanent social change.

The implementation of multicultural education has varied widely. Some programs use an "add-on" approach in which specific activities or units are added to the existing curriculum. For example, a school might have an "international" day in which children get a brief exposure to foods and customs from different cultures. Most advocates of multicultural early childhood education, however, view it as a process-oriented perspective that can be infused throughout the curriculum and program. They urge teachers and administrators to incorporate this perspective in all decisions about activities, materials, teaching practices, parent-school relations, and administrative structures.

One of the challenges for early childhood educators is to find and create developmentally appropriate activities that convey the complex issues inherent in multicultural education. The early development of attitudes and social relationships is an important curricular perspective that is supported by research (Ramsey, 1987).

Most authors in the field encourage teachers to use hands-on activities to integrate cultural, racial, and class differences into the curriculum in concrete and meaningful ways. Most multicultural early childhood education includes goals such as the acquisition of skills to form satisfying interpersonal relationships, growth in understanding and appreciating diverse ways of life, and in the ability to empathize with individuals from different groups. Family traditions and the local community also are incorporated into most multicultural programs. In keeping with social reconstructionists, some early childhood educators also stress the development of autonomy, critical thinking, and social responsibility so that young children will later be more prepared to challenge the inequities of the system and to work for social change.

Inasmuch as multicultural education challenges the assimilation policies that were traditionally a tenet of United States education, and inasmuch as it takes a firm stand against the inequities in society, it has created a considerable amount of controversy. Some schools either have not implemented it at all or have limited the implementation to isolated, surface types of activities. Many other early childhood educators, however, have successfully adopted a multicultural perspective and found that it has contributed a great deal to the goals and practices of early childhood education.

References

Derman-Sparks, L., and the A.B.C. Task Force. (1990). *Anti-bias curriculum*. Washington, DC: National Association for the Education of Young Children.

Kendall, F. E. (1983). *Diversity in the classroom*. New York: Teachers College Press.

Ramsey, P. G. (1987). *Teaching and learning in a diverse world: Multicultural education for young children*. New York: Teachers College Press.

Ramsey, P. G., Vold, E. B., & Williams, L. R. (1989). *Multicultural education: A source book*. New York: Garland.

Sleeter, C., & Grant, C. A. (1988). *Making choices for multicultural education: Five approaches to race, class, and gender*. Columbus, OH: Merrill.

Williams, L. R., De Gaetano, Y., Harrington, C. C., & Sutherland, I. R. (1985). *ALERTA: A multicultural, bilingual approach to teaching young children*. Reading, MA: Addison-Wesley.

P. G. Ramsey

Peace Education

The primary goal of peace education is to help young children develop the foundation of attitudes, values, and skills for their active participation in the adult political world. Because of how young children think, a peace education curriculum grows out of firsthand experience and involves almost every aspect of the teaching/learning process (Carlsson-Paige & Levin, 1985). Its specific content and how it is implemented depend on the particular teacher; the individual children, their developmental levels and prior experience; and the immediate circumstances that arise in a group setting. At the same time, several basic principles guide the development of a peace education curriculum.

First, teachers need to understand what the children know about the political and social world, about such things as interpersonal relations and power relationships, cooperation and conflict, right and wrong, how to affect their environment, and war, peace, and violence (Coles, 1986). Teachers can obtain the knowledge they need to guide practice through ongoing observation and discussion in an environment where children can use open-ended materials to express and expand their ideas and have many opportunities to become deeply involved in play.

Second, teachers use this knowledge to promote the children's sense of competence and personal efficacy, essential ingredients for active participation in the classroom community, and later for citizenship. Young children have a hard time making logical causal connections of thinking about how to create a desired effect. Therefore, classroom structures and practices that involve children in actively solving problems, making decisions, and taking responsibility in developmentally appropriate ways, help children learn how to use their ideas and actions to make a difference in the world.

Third, teachers use events that arise in the course of daily classroom life to help children learn cooperation and skills for resolving conflicts nonviolently. Cooperation is a difficult concept for young children to learn. It is understood gradually, as they learn to see how the part they play relates to the parts that others play, how what they do affects others, and how each player's actions connect to a whole experience. Because young children often do not think about the consequences of their actions, they can get into conflicts without premeditation. Teachers can acquire skills for negotiation and conflict resolution and help children when they look at a problem together, think about ways they might solve it, and find a solution that everyone can accept. In addition to using conflict situations that arise spontaneously, teachers can plan specific activities to help children develop a broader repertoire of conflict resolution skills (Kreidler, 1984).

Fourth, a peace education curriculum can help children appreciate and value diversity. Because young children tend to form broad categories that often are defined rigidly, however, they may stereotype cultural and racial groups. Classroom experiences that expose children to concrete and personal aspects of different cultures can expand their understanding of racial and cultural differences and help to break down stereotypes (Ramsey, 1987).

Lastly, information about violence and war permeates our environment. Violence is a major theme that young children experience through media and toys, and this has a powerful effect on their early political concepts. Teachers can do many things to affect the influence of media and toy violence on children (Carlsson-Paige & Levin, 1987). It is much more difficult, however, for young children to understand peace than war, because it is a more abstract, less observable concept in their lives. Nevertheless, young children can engage in meaningful activities that teach peace concepts (Educators for Social Responsibility, 1983; Reardon, 1988).

References

Carlsson-Paige, N., & Levin, D. E. (1985). *Helping young children understand peace, war and the nuclear threat*. Washington, DC: National Association for the Education of Young Children.

Carlsson-Paige, N., & Levin, D. E. (1987). *The war play dilemma: Balancing needs and values in the early childhood classroom*. New York: Teachers College Press.

Coles, R. (1986). *The political life of children*. New York: Atlantic Monthly Press.

Educators for Social Responsibility. (1983). *Perspectives: A teaching guide to concepts of peace*. Cambridge, MA: Author.

Kreidler, W. (1984). *Creative conflict resolution: More than 200 activities for keeping peace in the classroom*. Glenview, IL: Scott, Foresman.

Ramsey, P. G. (1987). *Teaching and learning in a diverse world: Multicultural education for young children*. New York: Teachers College Press.

Reardon, B. (ed.). (1988). *Education for social responsibility: Teacher-designed curricula for peace education, K–12*. New York: Teachers College Press.

N. Carlsson-Paige & D. E. Levin

Projects, Topics, and Themes

A thematic approach to curriculum planning consists of organizing activities around a central topic or idea, such as the food chain from farm to table, or variations in family composition and celebrations. The thematic approach can promote and reflect the cohesiveness of the curriculum, curricular integration across subject matter and/or developmental domains. Sometimes groups select themes that are based on the interests of the children. The teacher selects materials, books, and games, and develops activities.

In practice, there is a wide range of thematic approaches to curriculum organization, varying immensely in the extent to which they promote integration and cohesiveness. Some themes are little more than topics, such as "dinosaurs," or "pets." Other themes incorporate concepts that children can learn throughout curriculum areas, such as "friends," or "transportation."

Projects might include extended activities that generate varied participation for children such as building a playhouse or considering such a question as "How can you make it move?" These types of projects can help children to connect their experiences through a meaningful curriculum organization.

Teachers have found varied types of themes to be useful tools to plan the curriculum, to focus on ways to generate additional ideas, and to select activities from other sources. Themes also are useful to communicate to others the value of what is happening in an early childhood educational setting. (See also **Interdisciplinary Learning/Integrated Curriculum**, above.)

C. Chaillé

Unit Curriculum

Curriculum development within a framework of units emphasizes the "what" of learning. For example, teachers might offer a science unit on seeds, a social studies unit on transportation, or a mathematics unit on measurement. Within this framework, the primary, substantive work of curriculum development takes place prior to implementation. Teachers decide in advance planning what content they believe to be most important for young children to learn or acquire, and adults set goals and objectives accordingly.

Thus, the knowledge that teachers consider of most worth is predetermined and fixed, often dictated by subject matter specialists, or derived from adults' perceptions about what society or the community needs. Learning experiences then support the predetermined goals. Evaluation of children's achievements also reflects the unit goals and objectives, often with a focus on the mastery of specific content or finite skills. Since learning in the unit curriculum means that teachers transmit information to learners, teachers treat the curriculum as a product and teaching as a prescription for what occurs in classrooms. In turn, the role of the teacher mainly is that of a technical implementor. In the United States, the unit model of curriculum development predominates in primary classrooms as well as in many other early childhood settings.

References

Bruner, J. S. (1960). *The process of education.* Cambridge: Harvard University Press.
Tyler, R. (1949). *Basic principles of curriculum and instruction.* Chicago: University of Chicago Press.

A. L. Goodwin

Special Education Programs

Early childhood special education (ECSE) programs for children with disabilities may be (a) home based, where teachers and therapists make regularly scheduled visits; (b) center based, where the child and family travel to a facility; or (c) a combination of the two, where a center-based program provides home visits as a supplementary service. Early intervention services for infants and toddlers generally occur either exclusively in the home or in a combination home/center-based programs, while three- to five-year-olds usually attend self-contained or integrated classroom settings. The actual placement of a child will depend on the type and severity of the disability and the child's needs. Opportunities for integration with nonhandicapped peers are always a part of ECSE programs and range in scope from daily intervals of structured interaction to completely integrated classrooms of children with and without disabilities.

A multidisciplinary team, including parents, develops an individualized program in these settings for infants through five-year-olds. The plans consider the child's strengths, weaknesses, and learning needs, as well as cognitive, motor, behavior, communication, self-care, social/emotional development, and health status.

Federal regulations require parental permission prior to preliminary assessment of children, professional assessors who have specific training in the child's disability, and instruments and procedures that are valid. The regulations also require that the assessment be conducted in the child's and family's primary language.

An individual educational plan (IEP) is developed in a meeting with parents and professionals. It contains statements of the child's current level of performance; the extent and type of special education and related services needed; annual goals and short-term objectives; the amount of time the child will participate in regular education programs; the projected date for initiation and the anticipated duration of services; and evaluation criteria for determining the child's progress, at least annually. Infants and toddlers also must have an individualized family service plan (IFSP). It contains the same statements as the IEP, with the addition of family strengths and needs. The IFSP also requires the designation of a case manager and a statement of how transition will occur from early intervention to preschool services. The IFSP is reviewed every six months.

ECSE programs follow several models: medical, rehabilitation, developmental, Montessori, cognitive, applied behavioral analysis, cognitive-behavioral, or ecological-functional (Hanson & Lynch, 1989). The model determines the professionals who are employed, but most ECSE programs utilize individuals trained in special education, social work, speech/language pathology, occupational therapy, and physical therapy. All programs encourage parent involvement in a variety of ways that recognize and respond to individual cultures and communication styles.

Reference

Hanson, M. J., & Lynch, E. W. (1989). *Early intervention*. Austin, TX: Pro-Ed.

K. A. Ferrell

Developmentally Delayed

"Developmental delay" is a term that, when used about children under five years of age, indicates a comparative delay in mental, physical, or social-emotional development. The term also is used to denote a child who has been identified through preschool screening as "at risk," that is, at a lower level of school readiness than his or her peers.

Longitudinal studies have shown that early intervention has improved the growth and maintenance of progress for both nonhandicapped and developmentally delayed children. With an appropriate curriculum, they may never need special education. This is true especially for children with developmental learning disabilities that involve attention, memory, perceptual-motor function, thinking, and language (Lerner et al., 1987).

The philosophy of a particular early childhood education setting affects its curriculum emphasis. Today's programs appear to focus primarily on one of four major approaches. Rarely does a classroom adhere exclusively to a "pure" implementation of one curriculum approach. These alternative approaches are relevant currently because of recent concerns for special populations of children who are at risk for school success. Children often come from other cultures, from environments that limit their educational advantages in relation to schools, or have a variety of handicapping conditions. The strong influences of developmental, cognitive, and behavioral psychology affect contemporary curriculum options that Ruth E. Cook, Annette Tessler, and Virginia

B. Armbruster (1987) describe, including maturationist, behaviorist, psychosocial/psychoanalytic, and cognitive-interactionist approaches.

A child development, maturationist, or normal development approach focuses on enrichment. Proponents of this view assume that children are active learners who explore and learn through play. Many Head Start programs employ this approach, especially for compensatory experiences that teachers assume to be lacking in many of today's homes. An example would be the teacher's narrating the activities of a language-delayed child as she or he works in the sociodramatic play area.

The behaviorist approach concentrates on direct teaching of prerequisites for later academic skills. This model views the child as a passive learner who needs a high degree of structure and reinforcement in order to be activated. *Distar* is an example of such a curriculum.

The psychosocial/psychoanalytic approach is a model that centers upon the emotional/affective side of child development and stresses the development of positive social interaction and attitudes. The traditional socialization nursery school is an example of this approach.

The cognitive-interactionist approach focuses on the thinking and active problem solving of learners. This approach draws mainly upon the work of Jean Piaget and somewhat upon the work of Maria Montessori. An example of a cognitively oriented curriculum is the Perry Preschool Project, associated with the work of David Weikart and others. A strong influence on early childhood instruction today is discovery learning in a cognitive curriculum.

These same approaches are present in special education settings for developmentally delayed young children. There are some marked differences, however, in implementing such programs for children at risk, as discussed below. In fact, there is a second, parallel curriculum for such children, namely, written Individual Education Plans (IEP) specific to each child's learning profile of functional levels in major developmental domains. The IEP includes strengths, weaknesses, target objectives, specific approaches, adaptations, and forms of evaluation.

Early intervention for seriously delayed children often begins with infants at home, in order to reduce current problems and to prevent future difficulties. In a home-based curriculum, the parent receives training to work as a team member with supervision from an infant educator and/or therapist in a highly individualized diagnostic-prescriptive curriculum. The major curriculum emphases for children under three years of age are sensory-motor, gross motor, fine-motor, and self-help.

Intervention may need to continue through special center-based toddler and preschool programs, though many children with less severe developmental delays are integrated with children in regular nursery, day care, prekindergarten, and kindergarten programs. For the three- to five-year-old groups, the curriculum for developmentally delayed children is more involved with perceptual, cognitive, and language areas. Delays in development can persist for a long time. For these children, special curriculum approaches are offered in the primary grades through special classes or through regular classes that have resource room support. There are some highly specialized curricula developed for children who have hearing, visual, motor, and multiple impairments (Cook, Tessler, & Armbruster, 1987).

The degree of individualization in early childhood special education is more extensive than in regular classes. Teachers adapt instruction to the children's special needs. A great deal more observation, planning, evaluation, and team work is involved. Parents often learn to continue procedures at home. Many developmentally delayed children are not naturally curious and cannot direct themselves in approaches that depend on active exploration and discovery. Teachers may help by structuring activity selection, or adapting materials and tasks. Teachers may need to teach directly what other children learn incidentally, to teach many prerequisite skills, and to emphasize tangible instructional materials and hands-on experiences in concept development.

Minor curriculum modifications often are matters of common sense. In regular preschools and the early grades, some children are mildly mentally retarded. Early childhood teachers know that slower learners need more directed teaching, more demonstration, more repetition, and more structure; that breaking each instructional task into little steps and teaching them a bit at a time helps delayed children to achieve success; and that interaction with peers is a powerful tool in terms of learning social and language skills (Fromberg & Driscoll, 1985).

Children with unique developmental delays often need additional specialized support services such as speech/language therapy, physical therapy, and occupational therapy. Teachers and therapists as a team work together with parents to coordinate methods and curriculum objectives. (See also Chapter 4, Section 4.6, **Intellectual Disabilities and Mediated Learning Experiences and At-Risk Children.**)

References

Cook, R. E., Tessler, A., & Armbruster, V. B. (1987). *Adapting early childhood curricula for children with special needs.* Columbus, OH: Merrill.

Fromberg, D. P., & Driscoll, M. (1985). *The successful classroom: Management strategies for regular and special education teachers.* New York: Teachers College Press.

Lazarus, P. W. (1988). Creating educational advantages for the mainstreamed young exceptional child. *Special Education Monograph No. 1.* Hofstra University.

Lerner, J., Mardell-Czudnowski, C., & Goldenberg, D. (1987). *Special education for the early childhood years.* Englewood Cliffs, NJ: Prentice-Hall.

Neisworth, J. T., & Bagnato, S. J. (1987). *The young exceptional child: Early development and education.* New York: Macmillan.

P. W. Lazarus

Emotionally Disturbed

Children who are classified as emotionally disturbed have difficulties in peer and adult relationships, exhibit inappropriate behaviors, and evidence pervasive moods of unhappiness or depression. These problems are seen "over a long period of time and to a marked degree [which] adversely affects educational performance" (Federal Register, 1977). Children classified as schizophrenic also are included in this category of exceptionality.

Although the definition describes specific characteristics to be found in emotionally disturbed children, it is difficult to apply. Behavior disorder or emotional disturbance does not exist outside of a social context and therefore becomes subjective, based on "whatever behavior the chosen authority figures in a culture designate as intolerable (Kauffman, 1985, p. 16)." Young children who are considered to be emotionally disturbed or behavior disordered evidence problems in one or more of the following areas: activity levels, peer-to-peer and child/adult relationships, language, and emotional expression. Several types of behavior are characteristic of children who have been identified as emotionally disturbed. These include emotional lability; lack of affect, aggression; tantrums; and self-stimulation. Deviant speech patterns are common in children with childhood schizophrenia. An inability to express oneself verbally may cause extremes in behavior such as temper outbursts, physical aggression toward peers and adults, and destruction of materials. Motor problems may be the result of the disturbed behavior rather than part of the cause of emotional disturbance.

Identification includes the use of standardized tests, interviews with parents, teachers, and, when appropriate, the child, as well as making observations and/or ratings of behaviors in several settings. Physical examinations together with neurological and auditory evaluations also help to determine if there is a physical problem that is causing inappropriate behavior. Assessment attempts to provide information about the settings in which children manifest the disordered behaviors, their frequency, duration, and magnitude, and their effect on the child's relationships with others.

There are many approaches to educating young children with emotional disorders. Most programs incorporate a developmental curriculum and provide training in daily living skills together with opportunities to learn social skills through modeling and direct instruction. A prosocial skills curriculum for older children who have emotional and behavior disorders (Muscott, 1988) has been an integral part of most early childhood special education (ECSE) programs. Integration of youngsters with nonhandicapped peers for varying amounts of time (including full-time) is a priority in many programs. These peers may serve as models of appropriate behavior and increase the possibility of natural occasions during which children can practice newly learned skills.

Play activities are an integral part of all programs, providing opportunities for social interaction. Neighborhood visits and field trips expand opportunities to practice and generalize behaviors in other settings.

The instructional program includes the use of routines, reinforcement based upon shared criteria, recognition of feelings, and how to use words to express feelings. Children and teachers discuss alternate ways to behave and practice role-playing activities. Teacher modeling of appropriate behaviors and behavioral interventions also takes place. The educational goal is to replace inappropriate behaviors with more acceptable ones. Some teachers use "time out" with children who have difficulty controlling their behavior. The children leave the group setting for a brief, specified period of time, returning to the class or activity when the behavior is under control and the child is able to participate. Though programs for young children with emotional disorders stress the emotional/social domains, they also provide activities for cognitive, language, and motor development. (See also Chapter 4, Section 4.6, **Emotional and Social Needs.**)

References

Federal Register (Part IV). (1977). United States Government Printing Office, 42, 163.

Kauffman, J. M. (1985). *Characteristics of children's behavior disorders* (3rd ed.). Columbus, OH: Merrill.

Muscott, H. S. (1989). Facilitating the integration of children and youth with emotional disturbances and behavioral disorders through prosocial skills training. *Perceptions, 24* (1), 14–15.

R. Gold

Gifted

Special programs for young gifted children are designed to serve children from approximately two to eight years of age. Although two-year-olds may begin to manifest unique learning needs (Roedell, Jackson, & Robinson, 1980), young gifted children are among the last to be served. Several guidelines exist that recommend program considerations. The most effective program for a given child is one that fits that child's particular needs.

When the child enters the educational program, program personnel often conduct an assessment in order to identify strengths and weaknesses, interests, talents, and abilities, as well as socioemotional maturity and prior educational achievements. The match between the program goals and the child's talents and abilities is important for the continued development of young gifted children (Kitano, 1986).

Effective programs for young gifted children reflect a well-balanced environment that nurtures the cognitive, socioemotional, and physical development of the child. Such programs include a wide variety of independent as well as teacher-directed activities. A balance of life skills, socialization opportunities, and creative activities complements academic instruction. In addition, the programs are flexible enough to provide for the spontaneous exploration and acquisition of knowledge (Saunders & Espeland, 1986). They reflect a developmentally appropriate philosophy that provides for acceleration and enrichment of the content that is based on the unique learning needs of young gifted children. Grouping provisions are incorporated that consider individuals' abilities. Curriculum experiences integrate ideas, issues, and themes (Feldhusen, Van Tassel-Baska, & Seeley, 1989). Content focuses on the unique abilities and interests of the children and is sufficiently complex and challenging while not pressurizing.

Basic skills development includes critical thinking, creative thinking, problem solving, decision making, and exploratory research. Exemplary programs include the Astor Program (Erlich, 1978), the New Mexico State University Preschool for Gifted Children (Kitano, 1986), RAPHYT (Karnes, 1983), and the Child Development Preschool for Gifted Children (Roedell, Jackson, & Robinson, 1980). Continued research with regard to appropriate program designs as well as curriculum development currently is underway.

References

Erlich, V. (1978). *The Astor program for gifted children.* New York: Columbia University Press.

Feldhusen, J., Van-Tassel-Baska, J., & Seeley, K. (1989). *Excellence in educating the gifted.* Denver, CO: Love.

Karnes, M. B. (ed.). (1983). *The underserved: Our young gifted children.* Reston, VA: Council for Exceptional Children.

Kitano, K. (1986). Evaluating program options for young gifted children. In J. R. Whitmore (ed.), *Intellectual giftedness in young children: recognition and development.* Binghamton, NY: Haworth.

Kitano, M. K., & Kirby, D. F. (1987). *Gifted education: A comprehensive view.* Boston: Little, Brown.

Saunders, J., & Espeland, P. (1986). *Bringing out the best: A resource guide for parents of young gifted children.* Minneapolis, MN: Free Spirit.

Roedell, W., Jackson, N., & Robinson, H. (1980). *Gifted young children.* New York: Teachers College Press.

Van Tassel-Baska, J., Feldhusen, J., Seeley, K., Wheatley, G., Silverman, & Foster, W. (1988). *Comprehensive curriculum for gifted learners.* Boston: Allyn and Bacon.

Whitmore, J. R. (ed.). (1986). *Intellectual giftedness in young children: recognition and development.* Binghamton, NY: Haworth.

B. Shaklee

Learning Disabilities

Special educators face the problem of identifying young children who have specific learning disabilities (SLD). As set forth in Section 121.5 of the rules and regulations for Public Law 94-142, SLD is a processing disorder that affects performance in listening, thinking, speaking, reading, writing, spelling, and mathematics (Federal Register, 1977).

Though the federal definition has an academic orientation, certain aspects apply to the language and communication performance of young children, such as listening, thinking, and speaking. However, the lack of precision in the definition and a recognition of differential developmental patterns add to the problem of identification in early childhood (Mercer, Algozzine, & Trifellitti, 1979). Signs of learning disabilities can appear at different developmental stages. Many youngsters do not exhibit problems until they face academic demands. The disability label has been applied to preschoolers who have the kind of uneven patterns of development that may be precursors of academic learning problems.

Among the observable characteristics of children who have been identified as having learning disabilities are hyperactivity, perceptual-motor deficits, language deficits, memory and attention disorders, motor problems, incoordination and general disorientation, impulsivity, perseveration, emotional instability, and poor body image and self-concept (Cruickshank, 1972; Weber, 1974). These traits rarely appear in isolation but tend to appear as a cluster of behaviors (Siegel & Gold, 1982).

The identification of specific learning disabilities is determined by observation of behavioral characteristics in varied settings, in addition to an examination of language, fine and gross motor, cognitive, and social/emotional performance. If the resulting profile shows unevenness of performance, it may predict future problems. Early identification involves an interdisciplinary approach, including the special education teacher, psychologist, and language specialist. Depending upon the initial data, other professionals may be called upon, including a pediatrician, pediatric neurologist, nurse, social worker, or audiologist. Diagnosis takes place by observing children in varied settings and using several assessment devices as well as structured observation scales.

Young students with learning disabilities may be placed in early childhood special education center-based programs or in early childhood settings with nonhandicapped peers. The programs provide experiences to foster the development of fine and gross motor skills, cognitive performance, social/emotional and language functions. Special education teachers, speech/language clinicians, and occupational and physical therapists, provide structured individual and group instruction.

Programming for young children with learning disabilities may differ according to the philosophies of the service providers. Four specific types have been identified, including developmental, functional, longitudinal, or cognitive-developmental (Esterly & Griffin, 1987). The developmental approach uses a wide variety of activities and materials in order to enrich motor, language, cognitive, and social/emotional development.

Functional programs examine the children's behaviors, reinforcing appropriate behaviors while working toward the decrease of maladaptive ones. Eventually inappropriate behaviors are replaced with skills that will lead to higher levels of performance and independence.

In a longitudinal approach, the teacher or team determines the future skills the child will need in varied environments, such as school, home, and community. Priority skills needs form the basis of the curriculum.

The cognitive-developmental approach focuses on language, motor, social, and self-help skills. Children learn skills in a structured environment that helps them to apply their skills to real-life situations.

Regardless of orientation, most early childhood special education (ECSE) programs for children with learning disabilities stress language/communication skills. The speech/language therapist often provides instruction in a clinic setting and/or within the early childhood classroom, developing children's skills that are reinforced further by the special education teacher and parents.

Parent involvement, mandated by federal legislation (P.L. 94-142 and P.L. 99-457), is an integral part of special education preschool programs. Parent programs are individualized, depending upon the specific needs of the child and the family. Parents, often prepared in parent education programs, participate in developing the Individual Education Plan, extending school and center work at home, and engaging in child advocacy activities. (See also Chapter 4, Section 4.6, **Intellectual Disabilities**.)

References

Cartwright, C. A. (1981). Effective programs for parents of young handicapped children. *Topics in early childhood special education, 1* (3), 1–9.

Cruickshank, W. M. (1972). Some issues facing the field of learning disabilities. *Journal of Learning Disabilities, 20* (9), 380–388.

Esterly, D. L., & Griffin, H. C. (1987). Preschool programs for children with learning disabilities. *Journal of Learning Disabilities, 20* (9), 571–573.

Federal Register (Part IV). (1977). *42,* 163. United States Government Printing Office.

Mercer, G. D., Algozzine, B., & Trifellitti, J. (1979). Early identification—an analysis of research. *Learning Disabilities Quarterly, 2* (2), 12–24.

Siegel, E., & Gold, R. (1982). *Educating the learning disabled.* New York: Macmillan.

Weber, R. (ed.). (1974). *Handbook on learning disabilities: A prognosis for the child, the adolescent, the adult.* Englewood Cliffs, NJ: Prentice-Hall.

R. Gold

Mainstreaming

Mainstreaming, as a social policy, is the process of providing handicapped individuals with opportunities to participate in all of the social, recreational, and educational activities available to nonhandicapped members of society. In early childhood education, mainstreaming focuses on handicapped and nonhandicapped children working and playing together in the same classroom. The primary goal of mainstreaming young handicapped children is to insure them a curriculum based on appropriate developmental experiences and interactions with normally developing children. Nonhandicapped children become models as handicapped children learn the developmental skills that will enable them to function more productively and independently (Allen, 1990). At the same time, nonhandicapped children learn to accept, value, and be comfortable with a range of individual differences.

The terms "mainstreamed" and "integrated" are used interchangeably, although program distinctions have been proposed that are based on the ratio of handicapped to nonhandicapped children. Classes may be described as mainstreamed if 50 percent or more of the children are normally developing, and as integrated, if less then 50 percent are (Odom & McEvoy, 1988). Another variation is reverse mainstreaming, in which special education programs enroll normally developing children as the minority (Peterson, 1987).

The term "mainstreaming" gained popularity with the passage of the Education for All Handicapped Children Act, now called the Individuals with Disabilities Education Act (Public Law 94-142, 1975). Educating children in the least restrictive environment is the legal terminology for mainstreaming. The intent is that handicapped children should be educated, to the maximum extent possible, in programs serving normally developing children. In all programs receiving federal funds, including preschools and child care programs, special class placement and segregated schooling is prohibited unless "the nature and severity of the handicap is such that education in the regular classroom with the use of supplementary aids and services cannot be achieved satisfactorily" (Ibid.).

The intent of the least restrictive mandate is to educate handicapped and nonhandicapped children together to the maximum extent appropriate, while still meeting the special needs of each handicapped child. Decisions as to what is appropriate and least restrictive are made on an individual basis. The majority of young handicapped children benefit from a full-time program where most of the children are developing normally. Others require a dual placement, part of the time in the regular classroom, the rest in a special services setting. The least restrictive environment is determined individually for a particular child, at a particular time, and reassessed on a regular basis (Kendrick, Kaufmann, & Messenger, 1988).

To insure appropriate placement and program activities, the law requires that each handicapped child be provided an Individual Education Plan (IEP), planned by an interdisciplinary child study team in collaboration with the child's teachers and parents. The plan must specify the supplemental aids and services that will be provided to insure the handicapped child an appropriate education in the mainstream classroom.

References

Allen, K. E. (1990). *Mainstreaming in early childhood education*. Delmar.

Kendrick, A. S., Kaufmann, R., & Messenger, K. P. (eds.). (1988). *Healthy young children*. Washington, DC: National Association for the Education of Young Children.

Odom, S. L., & McEvoy, M. A. (1988). Integration of young children with handicaps and normally developing children. In S. L. Odom & M. B. Karnes (eds.), *Early intervention for infants and children with handicaps*. Baltimore, MD: Paul H. Brookes.

Peterson, N. L. (1987). *Early intervention for handicapped and at-risk children*. Denver, CO: Love.

K. E. Allen

Perceptual Impairments

Young children with sensory or perceptual impairments are defined in the Individuals with Disabilities Education Act (34 JC.F.R. Part 300) as deaf, hard of hearing, deaf-blind, and visually handicapped. To the extent that orthopedic impairments interfere with sensory processing, they, too, would fall into this category.

Programs for young children with perceptual impairments follow the same general provisions discussed above in "Special Education Programs" (Ferrell, 1986). Since perceptual impairments comprise a low prevalence disability, some aspects of service delivery are different.

The predominant mode of service delivery in early childhood special education (ECSE) programs for sensory impaired children is a self-contained, center-based program, with teachers specially trained in the specific disability. These programs address, in a structured and intense way, the unique learning needs of the children, relying on extensive tactual and environmental adaptations (Ferrell, 1986) and expressive and receptive communication (Stedt & Moores, 1987). Early childhood integration appears to be secondary to the development of a foundation of skills that will make later integration with typical peers more successful.

Teachers of the blind and visually impaired emphasize concrete experiences for children, since symbolization is difficult without a visual reference. Teachers and therapists also recognize that, in contrast to children with normal vision, the child with a visual disability learns from parts to wholes, somewhat like putting a jigsaw puzzle together without having seen the finished product. Orientation and mobility is also an important part of the ECSE curriculum, and children with visual disabilities receive specialized training in body awareness and traveling around the environment from an orientation and mobility specialist. Although there is no evidence that young children with visual disabilities follow the same developmental pattern as other children (Warren, 1984), current practice is to follow a developmental model of instruction, with strong emphasis on the functionality of the behavior and encouragement of independence.

The curriculum for young children who are deaf or hard of hearing emphasizes communication. Most programs utilize a total communication approach, employing speech, manual signs, auditory training, speech reading, and finger spelling. The most effective ECSE programs appear to be ones where a coordinated, total communication approach is utilized within a cognitive model (Stedt & Moores, 1987). (See also Chapter 4, Section 4.6, **Perceptual Disabilities**.)

References

Ferrell, K. A. (1986). Infancy and early childhood. In G. T. Scholl (ed.), *Foundations of education of blind and visually handicapped children and youth: Theory and practice*. New York: American Foundation for the Blind.

Stedt, J. D., & Moores, D. F. (1987). Developmental differences in hearing. In J. T. Neisworth, & S. J. Bagnato (eds.), *The young exceptional child* (pp. 414–442). New York: Macmillan.

Warren, D. L. (1984). *Blindness and early childhood development* (2nd ed.). New York: American Foundation for the Blind.

K. A. Ferrell

Physical Impairments

The capabilities of children with physical disabilities vary. Some children are very similar to normally developing children while others may have significant inabilities that challenge teachers to find ways of incorporating these children into developmentally appropriate activities. Teachers may feel inadequate in interacting with, teaching, and fully addressing these children's needs, as well as fearful about whether or not children's safety can be managed appropriately in early childhood programs. Simple questions, such as how much encouragement or help a child with physical disability needs may become difficult issues in regular early childhood settings.

Even children with significant physical limitations are more like than different from normally developing children. These children need to learn to make friends, follow rules, demonstrate creativity and problem solving, or work cooperatively with others, just as do normally developing children. Physical limitations of various types and degrees can hinder the abilities of children to learn in the same ways as normally developing children. Early childhood teachers are effective when they understand the impact of the disability on performance, have the resources to help facilitate learning, and value creative adaptations as a way of assisting a child to perform a task by using unconventional means.

More important than knowing that a child has a specific diagnosis is understanding the ways in which the unique problems associated with that diagnosis impact on performance. One child with cerebral palsy, for example, may learn to walk with practice and adult support, whereas the extent of the disability present may prevent another child from walking no matter how much therapy, encouragement, or support the child receives. Understanding how the disability influences a child's ability to perform is a first step both in establishing realistic expectations for a child and in beginning to use strategies that will promote a child's total development.

The greatest difference in working with children who have physical disabilities comes from the task and materials adaptations that may be beneficial for their learning. Teachers, parents, or specialists, such as occupational or physical therapists, may create adaptations for a particular child. They may purchase some adaptations from commercial special education and rehabilitation companies. Early childhood teachers first must identify a specific problem, for example, that a child has difficulty using a scissors. Special scissors that will help a child to cut (materials adaptation), or deciding that a child's job will be to paste rather than cut (task adaptation), both facilitate a child's participation and promote important skill learning. Children who have opportunities to perform activities in unconventional ways receive help at the same time in developing self-esteem, social abilities, and a variety of other essential skills that are critical to learning during the early childhood years.

References

Bigge, J. L., & O'Donnell, P. (1982). *Teaching individuals with physical and multiple disabilities* (2nd. ed). Columbus, OH: Merrill.

Safford, P. L. (1989). *Integrated teaching in early childhood*. New York: Longman.

Umbreit, J. (1983). *Physical disabilities and health impairments*. Columbus, OH: Merrill.

P. Campbell

5.3 Curriculum Domains

Although it is accurate to say that the practice of early childhood curriculum in the United States typically is interdisciplinary, this section highlights the various perspectives and ways by which young children learn. Whether an adult identifies an activity as more or less social studies or science, young children will perceive it in the context of their existing understandings. For communication purposes, however, this section presents curriculum domains separately, cautioning the reader to keep in mind the integrated educational uses that are reasonable and the integrated perceptions that children develop that are real.

Young children use perspectives and ways of knowing both to learn more and then to represent their learning. They learn more about how others perceive the world by viewing the art products of others, for example, and also create artistic representations of their own perceptions. They learn about quantitative relationships and how to represent them graphically and symbolically, and also set problems and raise mathematical questions for others to consider. In such ways, young children engage in a recursive relationship between acquiring knowledge and content as well as representing their findings in a variety of symbolic forms. These symbolic forms include language, sociodramatic play scripts, mathematical representations, art forms, constructions, and lived experiences, among others. The contrasts that children perceive as they use these various tools from varied perspectives provide opportunities for them to build up the content that they learn, connect, and integrate in their own ways.

This section is organized alphabetically, with related articles such as blocks and woodworking appearing after construction. The section closes with articles that deal with support for curriculum development in the form of community resource use.

D. P. Fromberg

Arts: Visual-Graphic and Spatial

Visual arts are prominent in early childhood programs. As children draw, paint, model or construct, they give expression to their thoughts, ideas, and experiences and feel the pleasure and deep personal satisfaction of accomplishment. Children's experiences with the graphic arts introduce them to the content of art and to the intrinsic value of art.

The goals of the visual arts in early childhood education are that children will be able to see and feel visual relationships, make art, learn about works of art, and talk about their art, as well as the art works of others.

Children's expression in the graphic arts follows developmental stages. Their first attempts at drawing, painting, modeling, or constructing are exploratory. They scribble freely without restraint with drawing tools and paints, and explore clay, pushing, pulling, and pounding it. By the age of four or five, children attempt to represent people, things, or objects as they draw, model, or build. A typical schema is an oval shape to represent a person. By the time children are in the primary grades they are able to refine, elaborate, and represent schemata for houses, animals, people, and other things in their environment.

Because the ability to represent things, objects, feelings, or experiences involves the use of symbols, children's drawing and painting are believed essential for learning to read and for mathematical readiness. Research supports the idea that art, as an early form of symbolic representation, is related to the development of early literacy and mathematical concepts.

A variety of media is used in early childhood for children's expression through the graphic arts. Children may draw with crayons, chalk, and markers on every type of paper—textured, colored, or smooth. They paint with tempera paints at easels or on paper spread on the floor or tables. When drawing and painting, children must think about some experience, idea, or feeling, find some way to represent this, and then transcribe these images on paper. Finger paints, either purchased or made from mixtures of corn starch, water, and washable tempera paints, can also be used. In finger-painting, children find greater freedom of movement and expression than when drawing.

Clay and all types of dough materials are used for modeling. By the end of kindergarten or in early primary grades children can be taught to slip pieces of clay together to create objects that can be fired and preserved. Other graphic arts methods that children use are cut and paste, collage, and construction. These methods, as well as modeling, permit children to create three-dimensional objects. Additional graphic arts activities are sewing with large plastic needles on open-weaved cloth, and weaving with any number of materials.

Children are introduced to the concept of artist as they talk about their own art and that of their classmates. Teachers share the art works of others with children and tell them about the artist who created the work, how the artist created it, and discuss its meaning with children. (See also Section 5.4, **Malleable Materials, Clay.**)

References

Herberholz, B., & Hanson, L. (1985). *Early childhood art* (3rd ed.). Dubuque, IA: Wm. C. Brown Publishers.

Seefeldt, C. (1987). The visual arts. In C. Seefeldt (ed.), *The early childhood curriculum: A review of current research* (pp. 183–210). New York: Teachers College Press.

C. Seefeldt

Construction

Constructive play, considered the most common form of play, is characterized by the manipulation of blocks and blocklike toys into constructions such as towers, cities, and forts. Jean Piaget (1962) places constructive play halfway between work and play due to the imitative nature predominating in dramatic play. This simulative type of constructive play includes skills in stacking, problem solving, and engineering feats. Narrowly defined, these activities are merely cognitive and physical routines, yet in the area of creativity, meaningful learning takes place because play alternates with these skills.

Symbolic configuration is another type of construction in which one thing stands for another, as children combine various types of materials. Art materials such as paint, play dough, and collage, for example, are layered and juxtaposed with building and play objects in ways that represent the child's reality. The object-rich environment of modern society provides many opportunities for this type of object manipulation and exploration.

In yet another use, objects function as props in various levels of symbolic play (Fein & Rivkin, 1986). Possibilities range from the use of single blocks to represent cars and trucks, complex constructions to represent adventure themes, or dress-up costume props to simulate characters or fully developed episodes in sociodramatic play. Sometimes objects suggest to children the various play themes that ensue (Garvey, 1977). When available in play settings, props such as clothing and furniture influence and support the scripts and roles of children's play.

As children mature, they move away from using realistic props and substitute more abstract props arising from the invented uses of objects. This development parallels the growth of children's symbolic expressions in three-dimensional materials such as clay, where they can demonstrate a meaningful articulation of spatial relationships.

Ideal educational experiences provide a balance of exploration and play (Forman & Hill, 1980), since research indicates that when children play with an object before it has been fully explored, their potential discovery of its specific properties may be limited (Hutt, 1971). Young children can feel competent when they have engaged in constructive play (Forman & Hill, 1980, p. 2), as each new creative act challenges them toward a higher level of mastery. Schools can implement these recommendations from researchers by offering a broad range of experiences in imaginative representation with three-dimensional media, coupled with ample opportunities for the expansion of object play into dramatic sequences.

References

Fein, G., & Rivkin, M. (eds.). (1986). *The young child at play: Reviews of research*, Vol. 4. Washington, DC: National Association for the Education of Young Children.

Forman, G., & Hill, F. (1980). *Constructive Play*. Belmont, CA: Wadsworth.

Garvey, C. (1977). *Play*. Cambridge, MA: Harvard University Press.

Golomb, C. (1974). *Young children's sculpture and drawing*. Cambridge, MA: Harvard University Press.

Hutt, C. (1971). Exploration and play in children. In R.E. Herron & B. Sutton-Smith (eds.), *Child's play*. (231–251). New York: Wiley.

Piaget, J. (1962). *Play, dreams, and imagination in childhood*. New York: Norton.

A. C. Swann

Blocks

(See Chapter 2, Section 2.3 **The Evolution of Unique Early Childhood Materials**, above and Section 5.4, **Curriculum Materials, Blocks**, below.).

Woodworking

Woodworking can be introduced at any time after age two and can provide lifelong learning and pleasure. Young children's cognitive, physical, social/emotional, and aesthetic development are all fostered through appropriate woodworking experiences. Additionally, woodworking offers a high-interest vehicle for incorporating other curricular areas such as math, the language arts, science, social studies, the arts, and ecology.

Children's woodworking interests and abilities vary widely. There is, however, a series of stages through which preschoolers typically pass as they engage in woodworking activities. In the first stage, children are *interested in process*. They use their senses to explore and manipulate the wood, rather than setting out to make a product, although they might name their finished creation. Two-year-olds, for example, might stack wood pieces, while three-year-olds may want to nail and saw. In the second stage, which is common for four-year-olds experienced in woodworking, *combining pieces* by nailing and gluing is typical. Experienced five-year-olds gradually enter the *product stage*, stage three, in which they want to make a product, although their interest in process remains important. In providing experiences appropriate for these stages, teachers and parents allow for, and encourage, individual differences.

Effective woodworking experiences are carefully planned and supervised, taking safety into account. It is important, for example, that appropriate wood and equipment are provided. Real adult tools, rather than toy tools, should be used, with the introduction of specific tools being determined by individual children's skills. Supportive adults can maximize children's participation and creativity within a safe environment by providing guidance and models, as opposed to assuming a directive role in woodworking activities.

Reference

Skeen, P., Garner, A. P., & Cartwright, S. (1984). *Woodworking for young children.* Washington, DC: National Association for the Education of Young Children.

P. Skeen

Creative Drama and Children's Theater

Early childhood educators interested in and appreciative of the value of informal play for young children can build toward more structured creative drama experiences. In creative drama, teachers encourage children to use their bodies and voices to interpret or enact part or all of a story or poem, moving from the author's words into their own movement and language (National Theatre Project, 1987). For example, children might "become" the witch and Hansel and Gretel, enacting the scene where the witch opens the door and invites the children into her house. In this case, children might interpret a small scene from a longer story and receive the full benefits from the participation-oriented experience, without the need to try to present the entire story for an audience. Children also might be involved in using their bodies to interpret the many movements described in a poem (Stewig, 1983).

Teachers interested in doing drama with children can use professional methods books and curriculum guides in order to learn more about how to do drama. Professional methods books describe the array of body and voice participation experiences in which children should be involved and suggest various approaches to introducing, leading, and evaluating drama sessions (Heinig, 1988). Curriculum guides issued by departments of education (Blazuk, 1985; Last, 1990) also are available. Typically, these provide organizational structures that identify outcomes, as well as teaching strategies for children at different developmental stages.

Advocates of drama in classrooms believe that it should be a regular, recurring part of children's education. They describe drama as an art form, recommending it as an aesthetic experience important for children's total growth (McCaslin, 1987).

Based upon research findings, others advocate drama because of its effect on children's self-concepts, abilities in language and reading skills, and their creativity (Stewig, in press). After only six hours of informal drama experiences, for example, twenty deprived urban seven-year-olds were significantly better able to describe themselves verbally and nonverbally, and were more self-aware (Noble, Egan, & McDowell, 1977).

Several studies investigated drama's effect on oral language. Following work with first- and second-graders who had auditory discrimination and articulation problems, investigators found that the creative drama group showed significant improvement over the control group (Woolf & Myers, 1968). In a correlational study, kindergarten children who did well in unstructured dramatics also had superior syntactic maturity, fluency, and language organization (Lewis, 1973). After 20 weeks of drama with 14 experimental groups of kindergarten and first-grade classes and their matched control groups, the experimental groups improved significantly in several language areas (Niedermeyer, 1972).

Another finding is that role taking affected greater syntactic complexity in kindergarten students (Schmidt, 1975). After four months of using thematic-fantasy play (similar to creative drama) with low socioeconomic preschoolers, experimental children were significantly better at remembering stories, at seeing causal relations between pictures, and at making inferences (Saltz & Johnson, 1974). Total verbal output of the experimental children also was significantly superior. In another study, the kindergarten drama group scored significantly higher on listening skills when compared with a group who had engaged in traditional reading readiness experiences (Tucker, 1971).

Some studies have focused on the effects of creative drama on reading. The effect of an individualized reading program approach, incorporating creative drama with disadvantaged students in grades one through four, was studied (Carlton & Moore, 1966). After treatment, students in the experimental group attained significantly higher reading scores. More recently, researchers investigated the reading comprehension of black, low-socioeconomic second graders who represented three reading levels (Henderson & Shanker, 1978). Two of three groups received basal reading instruction along with drama. Then the groups were reversed. Teacher-made comprehension tests following each lesson showed significantly greater gains when children participated in drama. Another study found that 108 children in kindergarten through second grade, after engaging in dramatics, developed better story comprehension than did those who engaged in discussion or drawing (Pellegrini & Galda, 1982).

Experts also report the effects of drama on creativity and problem solving. After a series of creative drama sessions, kindergarten children made significant gains on a creativity test (Hensel, 1974). Following drama experiences, second- and third-graders responded significantly better to problem-solving questions that were drawn from two standardized intelligence tests (Hartshorn & Brantley, 1973).

Drama experts have advocated for some time that informal creative drama, done in classrooms without an audience, is of value to children of all abilities. There is a wide variety of material for teachers, showing how to do drama with children, though much of this is oriented to kindergarten and older children, rather than to preschoolers (Brown, 1989).

Teachers of younger children, however, can adapt many ideas from primary-oriented materials. The research base now available indicates that doing drama regularly with all children improves their self-concept, language skills, reading skill, and creativity.

References

Blazuk, J. (Chair). (1985). *Elementary drama curriculum guide.* Edmonton, Alberta: Elementary Drama Ad Hoc Curriculum Committee.

Brown, V. (1989). Expanding horizons. *Youth Theatre Journal, 3* (3), 8–9.

Carlton, L., & Moore, R. H. (1966). The effects of self-directive dramatization on reading achievement and self-concept of culturally disadvantaged children. *Reading Teacher, 20* (3), 125–130.

Hartshorn, E., & Brantley, J. (1973). Effects of dramatic play on classroom problem-solving ability. *Journal of Educational Research, 66* (6), 243–246.

Heinig, R. B. (1988). *Creative drama for the classroom teacher.* Englewood Cliffs, NJ: Prentice-Hall.

Henderson, L. C., & Shanker, J. L. (1978). The use of interpretive dramatics versus basal reader workbooks for developing comprehension skills. *Reading World, 17* (3), 239–243.

Hensel, N. H. (1974). The development, implementation, and evaluation of a creative dramatics program (doctoral dissertation, University of Georgia, 1973). *Dissertation Abstracts International, 34,* 4562A. University Microfilms No. 74-4816.

Last, E. (Chair). (1990). *A guide to curriculum planning in drama.* Madison, WI: Department of Public Instruction.

Lewis, P. H. (1973). The relationship of sociodramatic play to various cognitive abilities in kindergarten children (doctoral dissertation, Ohio State University, 1972). *Dissertation Abstracts International, 33,* 6169A. University Microfilms No. 73-11, 525.

McCaslin, N. (1987). *Creative drama in the primary grades.* New York: Longman.

National Theatre Project. (1987). *A model drama theatre curriculum: Philosophy, goals, and objectives.* New Orleans: Anchorage Press.

Neidermeyer, F. (1972). The development of young children's drama and public speaking skills. *Elementary School Journal, 73* (2), 95–100.

Noble, G., Egan, P., & McDowell, S. (1977). Changing the self-concepts of seven-year-old deprived urban children by creative drama or videofeedback. *Social Behavior and Personality,* *5* (1), 55–64.

Pellegrini, A. D., & Galda, L. (1982). The effects of thematic-fantasy play training on the development of children's story comprehension. *American Educational Research Journal, 19* (3), 443–452.

Saltz, E., & Johnson, J. (1974). Training for thematic-fantasy play in culturally disadvantaged children. *Journal of Educational Psychology, 66* (4), 623–630.

Schmidt, E. (1975). Syntactic and semantic structures used by children in response to six modes of story presentation (doctoral dissertation, University of Washington, 1974). *Dissertation Abstracts International, 35,* 4879A. University Microfilms No. 79-4046.

Stewig, J. W. (1983). *Informal drama in the language arts program.* New York: Teachers College Press.

Stewig, J. W. (in press). Dramatic arts education. In H. E. Mitzel, J. H. Best, and W. Rabinowitz (eds.), *Encyclopedia of Educational Research* (6th edition). McMillan.

Tucker, J. K. (1971). The use of creative dramatics as an aid in developing reading readiness with kindergarten children (doctoral dissertation, University of Wisconsin, 1971). *Dissertation Abstracts International, 32,* 3471-3472A. University Microfilms No. 71-25, 508.

Woolf, G., & Myers, M. J. (1968). The effect of two ear-training procedures. *Exceptional Children, 4* (9), 659–665.

J. W. Stewig

Health, Nutrition, and Safety

The population of the United States lives a longer, healthier life today because of the conquest of infectious disease, changes in public health policy, and pharmacologic discoveries. Half of the premature illness and death in the United States, however, is a result of individuals' unhealthy life-style behaviors (U.S. Department of Health, Education, and Welfare, 1979). Consequently, a proactive educational approach would shift from a medical or disease approach to a health promotion model.

Practicing health promotion can be critical for parents and caregivers of early childhood populations. There is growing evidence that habits develop during childhood that are most closely related to various health problems. As many as 40 percent of children in this country exhibit one or more of the risk factors commonly associated with heart disease, including being overweight, high blood pressure, high cholesterol level, and lack of exercise (Ibid., p. 36).

Further, there is a strong and positive relationship between the health status of children and their ability to learn. Factors such as dietary patterns influence short-term memory, attention span, analytical abilities, and social and emotional functioning (Kolbe & Green, 1986). Project Head Start has recognized the importance of children's health and nutrition since its inception. Another effective federal program, WIC (Supplemental Food Program for Women, Infants and Children), insures high protein and iron-fortified foods to low-income infants, children up to the age of five years, and pregnant women. Nutrition education and medical evaluations also are provided.

In response to social, economic, and political forces, more children today are involved in formal early childhood programs, starting at younger ages, for longer periods of time (Bredekamp, 1987). Those who make decisions about appropriate programming for young children need to pay careful attention to both formal and informal health promotion efforts.

The National Association for the Education of Young Children (Bredekamp, 1987) suggests appropriate health, nutrition, and safety practices for caregivers of infants and toddlers that include health precautions to limit the spread of infectious disease, such as keeping records, assuring immunizations, maintaining adults in good health, modeling and reinforcing hand washing, keeping adults updated about common illnesses, and providing diaper changing areas that are sanitary. Provisions to insure a safe environment for children include the removal of physical hazards, provision of adequate supervision, having emergency information available, and providing appropriate dress for activities. Enhanced nutritional practices include serving healthy foods and supervising the settings in which children eat. In these ways, health and safety promotion is emphasized through activities, policies, and practices in the context of young children's daily lives.

References

Bredekamp, S. (ed.). (1987). *Developmentally appropriate practice in early childhood programs serving children from birth through age eight.* Washington, DC: National Association for the Education of Young Children.

Kolbe, L., & Green, L. (1986). Appropriate functions of health education in schools: Improving health and cognitive performance. In N. Kraisuegor (ed.), *Child health behavior: A behavioral pediatrics perspective* (pp. 178–184). New York: Wiley.

United States Department of Health, Education, and Welfare. (1979). *Healthy people: The surgeon general's report on health promotion and disease prevention.* (DHEW Publication No. 79-55071). United States Government Printing Office.

C. W. Symons & R. Scott Olds

Language Arts

The traditional definition of the language arts in early childhood education is that portion of the curriculum that involves the teaching of the communication processes, including listening, reading, and writing (Anderson & Lapp, 1979). In the past, these processes have been treated as separate components when taught to preservice teachers and to children in school. There were separate courses for teaching reading and for the language arts. Within early childhood classrooms as well, the language arts traditionally have been taught as separate skills.

Recent research in language, reading, and writing has made educators aware of the interrelationships among these communication skills and the necessity to view them not as separate entities, but rather as related sources for creating and understanding meanings.

"Early literacy development" now refers to the language arts in early childhood education because of this new awareness concerning the interrelated nature of the communication skills. Those who have studied both the development of reading and oral language in young children realized that language learn-ing is an integral part of learning to read. Reading has been defined in a variety of ways, including the use of one's language ability to decode and comprehend (Ruddell, 1971) and the interaction between the reader and written language (Goodman, 1967). Investigators have found strong relationships between reading and spoken language, and early readers come from homes where a great deal of oral language is present (Snow, 1983). Parents of early readers revealed in interviews that their children used sophisticated language structures.

Research indicates that young children make early attempts to try to communicate in writing (Clay, 1975). Analysis of writing samples indicates that they have imitated adult writing behaviors and that their scribbles, drawings, random letters, and invented spellings are early forms of writing (Sulzby, 1986).

Researchers and educators are referring increasingly to the separate aspects of the language arts as virtually one process. They view reading, writing, oral language, and listening as skills that build upon each other. Each adds to the proficiency in the other when they are cultivated concurrently, showing a dynamic relationship among them.

It has become apparent that the language arts must be taught together in a meaningful and functional interdisciplinary context, integrated throughout the school day, instead of being taught as separate skills (Morrow, 1989). For example, when learning about animals, teachers can develop children's oral language through discussion, enhance their listening with children's literature that focuses on animals, provide materials for independent reading that deal with animals, and encourage writing narrative and expository pieces about animals. Visiting a veterinarian's office provides a real reason for writing a thank you note as well as other related content. Such child-centered themes make the language arts meaningful and interesting.

Children's literature is one of the most important instructional materials used for the development of the language arts. As children listen to book language, they increase their vocabulary and expand their syntax (Chomsky, 1972; Cohen, 1968). Children's literature is also a source for independent reading and provides a model or guide for composing. Learning of the language arts in early childhood must be an active process for the child in a social context with adults and peers, a process based on meaningful experiences that children can view as having a function and a purpose.

References

Anderson, P., & Lapp, D. (1979). *Language skills in elementary education*. New York: Macmillan.

Chomsky, C. (1972). Stages in language development and reading. *Harvard Educational Review*, *42* (1), 1–33.

Clay, M. (1975). *What did I write?* Portsmouth, NH: Heinemann.

Cohen, D. (1968). The effects of literature on vocabulary and reading achievement. *Elementary English*, *45* (2) 209–213, 217.

Goodman, K. S. (1967). Reading: A psycholinguistic guessing game. *Journal of the Reading Specialist*, *6* (4), 126–135.

Morrow, L. M. (1989). *Literacy development in the early years: Helping children read and write*. Englewood Cliffs, NJ: Prentice-Hall.

Ruddell, R. (1971). *Oral language development and development of other language skills: Listening and speaking*. New York: Macmillan.

Snow, C. E. (1983). Literacy and language: Relationships during the preschool years. *Harvard Educational Review*, *53* (2), 165–189.

Sulzby, E. (1986). Kindergartners as writers and readers. In M. Farr (Ed.), *Advances in writing research: Vol. I, Children's early writing* (pp. 127–199). Norwood, NJ: Ablex.

L. M. Morrow

Language Experience

The Language Experience Approach involves writing children's ideas for them as they observe the writing process. Language Experience dictation always utilizes children's exact wording, and the resulting written materials are used by the child for reading.

A more formally planned Language Experience lesson is the group story, which revolves around a common experience or theme. The teacher uses an enlarged format to write children's contributions so that all can see, and after reading the finished product, it is generally posted for future reference and re-reading.

Individualized Language Experience dictation allows children full ownership of their own written products. As the adult writes down the child's dictation on regular sized paper, the child observes the writing. The teacher encourages the child to attempt reading the finished product from memory and to share it with others. Dictated materials often are bound into books, which children can use in the classroom library.

Spontaneous dictation can occur at children's requests or the teacher's suggestion. A teacher might suggest that children tell about their dramatic play so that events can be written down, or a child might ask an adult to label a finished art product.

The Language Experience Approach helps children to realize that what they say can be written down, and what is written down can be read. Through observing the writing process, children learn about writing, and through reading dictated stories from memory, they begin to recognize commonly used words and to formulate ideas about letter-sound relationships.

References

Ashton-Warner, S. (1963). *Teacher*. New York: Teachers College Press.

Fields, M. V., Spangler, K. L., & Lee, D. M. (1991). *Let's begin reading right: Developmentally appropriate beginning literacy* (2nd ed.). Columbus, OH: Merrill.

M. V. Fields

Literature

Literature for children reflects the values and lessons that each generation wants to foster in its young. All stories lean on the stories that preceded them by repeating patterns of characters, episodes, plots, or structures. The oldest literature comes from folklore, told around hearthstones long before stories were written down. A body of literature written expressly for children grew until there exists today a wealth of good books for the very young. Beatrix Potter's *The Tale of Peter Rabbit*, published in 1902, is a landmark in the history of children's books because it contains high quality art, interesting language, and strong characterization. The extent to which today's many wonderful books play a significant role in the lives of children depends upon how adults share this literary heritage with children.

Children who learn to read before kindergarten have been called "paper and pencil kids," and are the ones who have been read to regularly at home (Durkin, 1966). Research has found that children with more advanced linguistic development were exposed to more literature (Chomsky, 1972), and that reading comprehension at ages seven and eleven was directly related to literacy knowledge at five years of age (Wells, 1986). Study of a severely physically handicapped child found that books became a chief source of delight, a means of learning, and a calming influence during long hospital stays and sleepless nights (Butler, 1980). Other studies support and extend these dramatic findings (Clay, 1979; Doake, 1985; Ferreiro & Teberosky, 1982; Heath, 1982; Taylor & Strickland, 1986).

Children build a storehouse of language possibilities from the language they hear around them and develop their concept of story from the stories they hear. They use these stories as models upon which to base their own writing and storytelling (Blackburn, 1985; Harste, Woodward, & Burke, 1984; King & Rentel, 1983; Taylor & Strickland, 1986).

Criteria for selecting books include sturdy construction, rhythmic language and interesting vocabulary, appropriateness for the child's conceptual level, and mutual adult enjoyment of the story. Young children need books with sturdy and durable pages because they are developing coordination skills. Books for toddlers are constructed from cardboard, cloth, or plastic fabrics that withstand chewing, dribbles, and rough handling.

Good books for young children have interesting language worthy of emulation; and young children readily adopt words that they hear into their own vocabulary, eliminating adult concerns about word difficulty. The contexts and illustrations make the meanings clear. A study found that many excellent picture books use only 30 to 40 different words but are far richer than most of the controlled vocabulary books (Moe, 1989)

Books for young children should present experiences that are connected to their lives. Children draw parallels between books and the events and characters in their lives. This does not mean that books only should deal with familiar experiences since books are experiences in themselves from which children can learn. The goal in reading books to young children is to elicit their enjoyment. Therefore, adults should select books with which they can project their own feelings of enjoyment. Adults should share the wealth in books with children to enrich their minds, enchant their imaginations, and engage their hearts.

References

Blackburn, E. (1985). Stories never end. In J. Hansen, T. Newkirk, & D. Graves (eds.), *Breaking ground: Teachers relate reading and writing in the elementary school*. (pp. 3–13). Portsmouth, NH: Heinemann.

Butler, D. (1980). *Cushla and her books*. Portsmouth, NH: Heinemann.

Chomsky, C. (1972). Stages in language development and reading exposure. *Harvard Educational Review, 42* (1), 1–33.

Clay, M. (1979). *Reading: The patterning of complex behavior*. Portsmouth, NH: Heinemann.

Cullinan, B. (1989). *Literature and the child*. New York: Harcourt Brace Jovanovich.

Doake, D. B. (1985). Learning to read: It starts in the home. In D. R. Tovey & J. E. Kerber (eds.), *Roles in literacy learning: A new perspective* (pp. 2–9). Newark, DE: International Reading Association.

Durkin, D. (1966). *Children who read early*. New York; Teachers College Press.

Ferreiro, E., & Teberosky, A. (1982). *Literacy before schooling*. Portsmouth, NH: Heinemann.

Harste, J., Woodward, V., & Burke, C. (1984). *Language stories and literacy lessons*. Portsmouth, NH: Heinemann.

Heath, S. B. (1982). What no bedtime story means: Narrative skills at home and at school. *Language in Society, 11* (1), 49–76.

King, M., & Rentel, V. (1982). *Transition to writing*. ERIC 240603. NIE-G-79-0039.

Moe, A. (1989). Using picture books for reading vocabulary development. In J. W. Stewig & S. L. Sebesta (eds.), *Using literature in the elementary classroom* (pp. 23–34). Urbana, IL: National Council of Teachers of English.

Taylor, D., & Strickland, D. S. (1986). *Family storybook reading.* Portsmouth, NH: Heinemann.

Wells, G. (1986). *The meaning makers: Children learning language and using language to learn.* Portsmouth, NH: Heinemann.

B. E. Cullinan

Reading

Reading is the process by which a reader gains meaning from print. Current research in reading development suggests that reading and writing develop concurrently rather than sequentially (Teale & Sulzby, 1986). Children acquire writing and reading in generalized stages in a variety of ways (Chall, 1984; Mason, 1980). Children who have more reading and writing activities are more cognitively involved in literacy from birth.

The answer to the question of when and how reading should be taught to young children is complex. Researchers have examined the relationships between reading achievement and intelligence, age, perception, letter name knowledge, word consciousness, and metacognitive strategies. They have debated whether the reading program should concentrate on code (Chall, 1967), meaning (Goodman & Goodman, 1979), or the interaction of both (Adams, 1990). Studies have found that teacher effectiveness was the most important factor in learning to read and that no one approach was best (Bond & Dykstra, 1967).

Reading develops when children have opportunities to interact with varied forms of print, such as stories, poems, informational books, fairy tales, letters, charts, lunch lists, menus, labels, notes, and journals. When children listen to stories and learn about the functions of print, they develop an understanding of the links between oral and written language (Clay, 1977). There is no evidence to support the use of workbooks, worksheets, or homogeneous grouping in early childhood classes.

Study of those children who do read prior to formal schooling indicates that they come from homes in which they have been read to frequently by family members (Durkin, 1966). There is a strong relationship between children's oral language development and their exposure to literature (Chomsky, 1972). Children benefit from hearing storytelling at home and when teachers read aloud on a daily basis from a variety of literature in regular or enlarged books at school (Holdaway, 1979). These types of shared book experiences combine reading and writing and include opportunities for children to hear their favorite stories repeated. A rich classroom language environment also provides learning centers in which children interact with print and with each other. The classroom should have a listening center, an attractive library corner, and a program in which adult caregivers (teachers, aides, volunteers) regularly read aloud to children.

References

Adams, M. J. (1990). *Beginning to read: Thinking and learning about print.* Cambridge, MA: MIT Press.

Bond, G., & Dykstra, R. (1967). The cooperative research program in first grade reading instruction. *Reading Research Quarterly, 2* (4), 5–142.

Chall, J. (1984). *Stages of reading.* New York: McGraw-Hill.

Chall, J. (1967). *Learning to read: The great debate.* New York: McGraw-Hill.

Chomsky, C. (1972). Stages in language development and reading. *Harvard Educational Review, 42* (1), 1–33.

Clay, M. (1977). *Reading: The patterning of complex behavior.* Portsmouth, NH: Heinemann.

Durkin, D. (1966). *Children who read early.* New York: Teachers College Press.

Goodman, K., & Goodman, Y. (1979). Learning to read is natural. In L. B. Resnick & P. Weaver (eds.), *Theory and practice of early reading,* Vol. 2, (pp. 137–154). Hillsdale, NJ: Erlbaum.

Harste, J. C., Woodward, V., & Burke, C. (1984). *Language stories and literacy lessons.* Portsmouth, NH: Heinemann.

Holdaway, D. (1979). *The foundations of literacy.* Portsmouth, NH: Heinemann.

Mason, J. (1980). When do children begin to read: An exploration of four year old children's letter and work reading competencies. *Reading Research Quarterly*, *15* (2), 203–227.

Rumelhart, D. (1984). Understanding understanding. In T. Flood (ed.), *Understanding reading* (pp. 1–20). Hillsdale, NJ: Erlbaum.

Teale, W. H., & Sulzby, E. (1986). *Emergent literacy*. Norwood, NJ: Ablex.

A. Robb-Fund

Writing

Children's writing development begins prior to the primary grades, through playful and practical experiences occurring during the preschool years. Home activities such as making shopping lists, writing notes, and jotting down telephone messages provide observational evidence of the ways young children, through observing and helping others, are initiated into the use and functions of writing. Since such literacy activities vary in families and communities, children acquire different initial understandings of the functions of writing.

Young children do not simply imitate others' writing, but actively construct their own knowledge of how the writing system works. Toddlers as young as 18 months often handle writing instruments and scribble, a form of writing that may continue for several years. Children's earliest conventional writing generally consists of letters of their own and family members' names. However, children also explore the written medium by forming and arranging cursivelike script, letters, and letterlike forms (Clay, 1975). Through experimentation, print conventions such as directionality and the use of space become evident. Pictures are often an integral part of young children's communication and can initiate, accompany, and/or clarify writing.

Even for very young children, writing varies with purpose. For example, they may use cursivelike lines when producing longer discourselike stories, but attempt particular letters when producing shorter units like their names.

Researchers have examined children's construction of the spelling system, tracing early efforts like a three-year-old's string of circles and curvy lines, to more sophisticated forms like a six-year-old's invented spelling, for example, *ILVBS* (I love babies) (Ferreiro & Teberosky, 1982; Read, 1986). Initially, children may use letterlike forms or letters for each idea they represent. Later, they use initial and final consonants (CR = care), add vowels (CAR), employ letter patterns (CAER), then demonstrate conventional spelling (CARE). As children begin to represent the entire sound structure of words, they also attend to visual and morphological patterns such as *-ed*.

Children's early stories and reports may consist of labels or brief statements that are the seeds of more complex structures (Newkirk, 1989). Five- to eight-year-olds weave written words together with talking and drawing to create extended texts and gradually differentiate the distinctive functional properties of speech, pictures, and writing (Dyson, 1989). Conferences with teachers, and playful and critical talk with peers is important in this development (Graves, 1983). One developmental progression may be from preschoolers' using writing in social play to older children's engaging in social play through the written stories themselves, such as by including friends as characters in their texts (Dyson, 1989).

Early childhood educators should consider writing as part of an integrated language and literacy program. The role of the early childhood teacher includes providing many real opportunities for using writing across the curriculum and assessing children's efforts to support their writing growth (Genishi & Dyson, 1984). In these ways, children can learn to write in a meaningful, social environment.

References

Clay, M. (1975). *What did I write?* Portsmouth, NH: Heinemann.

Dyson, A. H. (1989). *Multiple worlds of child writers: Friends learn to write*. New York: Teachers College Press.

Ferreiro, E., & Teberosky, A. (1982). *Literacy before schooling*. Portsmouth, NH: Heinemann.

Genishi, C., & Dyson, A.H. (1984). *Language assessment in the early years*. Norwood, NJ: Ablex.

Graves, D. (1983). *Writing: Teachers and children at work*. Portsmouth, NH: Heinemann.

Newkirk, T. (1989). *More than stories: The range of children's writing*. Portsmouth, NH: Heinemann.

Read, C. (1986). *Children's creative spelling*. London: Routledge & Kegan Paul.

A. H. Dyson

Literacy Issues

Literacy issues in early childhood are essentially issues of power. Power is a central concern in education. As young children are relatively vulnerable and powerless, this issue is particularly relevant in early education. When children feel capable and have the sense that they are involved in choices from among legitimate learning activities, they are more likely to feel motivated to work in a focused way than when they feel obliged to do so. Maria Montessori's notion that the child should learn not for love or fear of the teacher, but for the sake of the learning itself, reflects this issue of power. The teacher's important contribution is to offer a match between the child's possibilities for learning and the need to achieve and extend learning.

In the introduction to this chapter, a difference was drawn between the academic and the intellectual/constructivist approaches to early childhood education in relation to defining the content of curriculum. (See **Academic/Direct Instruction** and **Constructivist /Intellectual Curriculum** articles in Section 5.2, above.) In particular, it was suggested that academic approaches tend to expect children to adapt to the instruction of preset, skills-based material, whereas intellectual/constructivist approaches tend to adapt to children's varied developmental stages, with children applying skills as they pursue varied concepts through direct experiences.

Articles in the section that follows present views about children's literacy learning that contrast with academic approaches. Academic approaches to learning literacy rely on the use of textbooks, teaching of discrete skills, and deductive means. Intellectually oriented, constructivist approaches to emergent literacy emphasize children's literature, oral language, and inductive means of learning.

Exemplary intellectual/constructivist teachers focus on conversations and discussions with individuals and small groups of children. As teachers talk with young children about science activities, interpersonal issues, critical writing and other arts projects, and children's experiences, teachers help children to extend their emerging literacy skills as well as other conceptual concerns. In order to extend children's inductive language learnings, teachers reflect upon their own practice and adapt their questioning in ways that help children to make their own connections. (See Section 5.7, **Strategies of Teaching,** for articles about reflective teaching, discussions, and questioning strategies.)

D. P. Fromberg

Language Differences

More than ever before, teachers of young children in the United States are likely to be faced with a wide diversity of language speakers in the classroom. Increasing numbers of children come from homes whose language or dialect differs from Standard English. Educators have adapted curricula to focus on bilingual education, programs in English as a Second Language (ESL), and methods designed to address the needs of speakers of nonstandard English dialects.

In school settings, children generally are considered to be bilingual learners if they function in dual-language environments, regardless of their proficiency in either language. Limited-English proficiency (LEP) is a term used to describe those linguistically unique students who have not yet achieved a full understanding of English. Along with bilingual learners, children who are LEP require programs that include concept acquisition and development in their native language, maintenance of their native language, second language acquisition (for example, English as a Second Language as needed), and experiences related to their own culture and the cultures of others.

Regional and socioeconomic factors influence the dialect of English that a child speaks. Much of the research on dialectal differences has focused on children who speak a dialect known as Black English and the possibility that their dialect may be a factor in their ability to learn. Nonstandard dialect speakers need a school environment that accepts their language and culture and uses it to facilitate a wide variety of language experiences. School experiences need to help them develop confidence and competence in all language use as they expand their language to include Standard English.

Many educators of young children are aware that during the very earliest years, a child's home language represents his or her primary mode of communication. By the age of five or six years, no matter what their home language, dialect, or ethnic background, young children already have gained remarkable control of their language systems. For children whose home language is not English, and for those who speak a dialect of English other than that of the school environment, the school is responsible for accepting and building on the children's natural language and for expanding it to include the language of the general culture. Thus, the bilingual learner is helped to retain and, ideally, strengthen his or her home language while acquiring English. Young dialectal speakers find support for their efforts to use whatever dialect feels most comfortable, while others in school model Standard English as a medium for meeting new needs. The following principles of language acquisition provide a theoretical framework for these ideas:

- Child language is learned in very much the same way, regardless of the language being learned or the learner's culture. The stages of development are regular and predictable.
- No matter what the child's natural language may be, it is still possible for the child to express feelings and to share information and experiences.
- It is quite common to find several variations or dialects of a language within a given language system. Dialectal speak-

ers, as with all children, have learned well the language to which they have been exposed.
- Speakers of any language or dialect vary in their ability to use language effectively. The limitations of an individual speaker are distinct from the language or dialect itself.

References

Brooks, C. K. (ed). (1985). *Tapping potential: English and language arts for the Black learner*. Urbana, IL: National Council of Teachers of English.

Rigg, P., & Enright, D. S. (eds.) (1986). *Children and ESL*. Urbana, IL: National Council of Teachers of English.

D. S. Strickland

Literacy, Emergent

Recent research studies have offered new insight into young children's reading and writing development (Clay, 1982). Results of studies provide important understandings about the nature of children's literacy learning and the kind of educational environment that best supports it. The unique dimensions of early literacy arise from studies that occur in both home and school environments and from the point of view of children who are 14 months of age and younger; from recognition that it is a complex activity with social, linguistic, and psychological aspects rather than simply a cognitive skill; and from recognition that it is multidimensional and tied to the child's natural surroundings. (Teale & Sulzby, 1989).

Literacy learning begins early in life and is ongoing. It is evident when children begin to distinguish between their favorite books and records and demonstrate their recognition of environmental print. These demonstrations of print awareness go well beyond mere imitation. Children construct their own knowledge through experimentation and exploration. As children search for patterns and make connections between events, they bring what they know to each situation and apply their own childlike logic to make sense of it.

Literacy develops concurrently with oral language. Fluency in oral language is no longer seen as a precursor to literacy, but as an ongoing goal to be accomplished with and through literacy, since each language process informs and supports all the others.

Learning to read and write are both social and cognitive endeavors. Children are active participants in the process. They are not merely interested in learning about literacy, but want to engage in it. A strong desire to communicate stimulates their experimentation with letters, words, signs, and other symbols. As children experiment, they not only become literate but learn about ideas through language as they also learn about language itself.

Researchers refer to this body of information as an emergent literacy perspective and make a point of distinguishing it from a reading readiness approach. While emergent literacy emphasizes children's ongoing development of skill in reading and writing, a readiness approach sets apart the period before formal instruction as a time for systematic teaching of skills meant to get children ready for real literacy experiences. Adults play major but differing roles in these two approaches. Those subscribing to an emergent literacy perspective focus on providing an environment that insures that certain literacy experiences occur. They encourage children to explore and experiment with print, intervening only to help children confirm their understandings and move from one level of understanding to another. Adults in a readiness program are more likely to act as transmitters of information about reading and writing, such as letter names and letter-sound relationships. Classrooms operating from an emergent literacy base provide children with easy access to reading and writing materials, incentives to draw/write stories and messages, time to read and reread favorite books, and time to share their literacy experiences with others.

References

Clay, M. (1982). *Observing young readers*. Portsmouth, NH: Heinemann.

Teale, W., & Sulzby, E. (1989). Emergent literacy. In D. S. Strickland & L. M. Morrow (eds.), *Emerging literacy: Young children learn to read and write* (pp. 1–15). Newark, DE: International Reading Association.

D. S. Strickland

Literacy, Oral

Oral literacy is the ability to use oral language (speaking and listening) in order to communicate effectively with others in a range of formal to informal situations. Effective oral language includes conversation, group discussion, telling and listening to stories, debate, and persuasion.

Some educators believe that oral language is essential for socialization and merits nurture in the early childhood curriculum (Egan, 1989). Lay persons often believe that, since the child already has learned to talk, there is little left to be done, except to correct improper usage and identify abnormalities for the speech therapist to correct. In the development of civilization, however, oral literacy has served as the bridge between ignorance and culture. The oral tales of Homer suggest that he traveled, entertained, and taught people with his stories. Jesus used the oral tradition as he shaped parables to teach about moral and ethical issues of the day. During medieval times, the primarily illiterate masses of people listened as church and government leaders read documents and stories to them. In each of these historical periods, the people valued the story and the story maker who brought meaning to their lives and recorded and validated their experiences.

For young children, oral literacy bridges the gap between chaos and order, lore and reason, and isolation and socialization. It is the way social life occurs. As children begin to order events, they attempt to report those events to others. Some of their early reporting relates to their own needs, labeling objects and events, and is egocentric and episodic in nature. This reporting is a beginning step in interacting with others as well as an early step in symbolically representing objects, events, experiences, and their own thoughts.

The story is one of the most basic forms of oral literacy in that stories help people to organize and remember events (Smith, 1989).

Children are surrounded by stories and gossip at home. Early in life they learn to order these events in time (Ferreiro & Sinclair, 1971). From this early exposure to personal stories, children grow into the use of narrative structure. Children also become more aware of stories as their parents read to them. As they listen to stories, children extend their ability to symbolize by constructing mental images of things and actions that they may not have actually experienced.

Children increasingly begin to use the story form to tell others about their own experiences. Early attempts often imitate adult stories or variations of the adult report form which has some story elements in it. Eager to make meaning out of their experiences and to talk about them, daily happenings provide children with a repertory of stories to share with peers or adults.

Young children use dramatic presentations or act out the experiences in order to help listeners better understand their messages. This action also allows children to sustain their mental imagery for longer periods of time.

Classrooms that support and enhance young children's story making provide an opportunity for children to continue and extend their out-of-school practices. Various activities such as daily news time and shared journals afford a forum for elaborating experiences. Center and play times also provide opportunities to talk.

It is through such classroom interaction that children will construct a need to make their experiences more permanent. Writing becomes a natural means to meet this need. When children construct the notion that writing is a tool for making their talk more permanent and accessible to a more distant audience, they have bridged the gap between oral and written literacy.

References

Egan, K. (1988). Education and the mental life of young children. In L. R. Williams & D. P. Fromberg (eds.), *Defining the field of early childhood education: An invitational symposium*. Charlottesville, VA: W. Alton Jones Foundation.

Ferreiro, E., & Sinclair, H. (1971). Temporal relationships in language. *International Journal of Psychology, 6* (1), 39–47.

Smith, F. (1989, June). What the brain does well. Paper presented at the Gulf Coast Writing Conference, Point Clear, Alabama.

J. B. Taylor

Literacy, Oral: Principles of Practice

A caregiver can set the stage for language development when she or he actively communicates with children and provides opportunities and support for children to understand, acquire, and use verbal and nonverbal means of communicating thoughts and feelings.

Young infants need adults who are attentive to their individual signals. Sensitive responsiveness to vocal messages encourages communication. Infants' early babblings and cooings are important practice for later verbal expression. Their speech development is facilitated by an encouraging partner who responds to their beginning communications, repeats their sounds, offers sounds for them to imitate, and explains events while they are taking place.

Mobile infants begin to jabber expressively, name familiar objects and people, and understand many new words and phrases. Adults can build on this communication by showing active interest in children's expressions, interpreting their first attempts at words, repeating and expanding on what they say, talking to them clearly, and telling them simple stories.

Older children daily increase their vocabularies and use of sentences. There is a wide range of normal language development during this time. Adults can communicate actively with all infants, toddlers, and young children by modeling good speech, listening to them carefully, expanding and using what they say, and helping them with new words and phrases. Language can be used in a variety of pleasurable ways each day—through songs, stories, directions, comfort, conversations, information, and play.

A vital part of promoting language development in children in child care situations comes from appreciating cultures, languages, and child-rearing practices different from one's own. The following are specific examples of how the caregiver working in a center or family day care home might act to support these visions of oral language development.

Some principles of listening and talking with children include:

- Talk often with individual children and stimulate conversation among them and with adults in the center or home;
- Be aware of the caregiver's role as a language model for children, and use affectionate and playful tones, clear speech, and responsive conversation;
- Listen attentively to children, try to understand what they want to communicate, and help them express themselves;
- Talk with children about special experiences and relationships in their families and home lives;
- Support non-English-speaking and bilingual children's attempts to develop and use both languages; and
- Recognize possible impairments or delays that affect hearing and speech, help families find resources, cooperate with treatment plans, and find ways to communicate positively with those children.

Some appropriate activities include the following:

- Provide activities that encourage children to develop listening and comprehension skills;
- Help children connect word meaning(s) to experience and real objects;
- Use a variety of songs, stories, books, and games (including those from the children's cultures) for language development.

Some principles of evaluation include the following:

- Have realistic expectations for each child's understanding and use of speech based on knowledge of language development and the individual child; and
- Recognize, understand, and respect local speech patterns and idioms.

Some effective practices in communicating with parents include the following:

- Share children's communication/language achievements with parents on a daily basis;
- Seek information from parents about their child's language and communication development in the home environment; and
- Respect the language of non-English-speaking families, encourage them to communicate freely with their children in the language the parents prefer, and help them find opportunities to learn English.

References

Bates, E., Benigni, L., Bretherton, I., Camaioni, L., & Volterra, V. (1979). *The emergence of symbols.* New York: Academic Press.

Bates, E., Bretherton, I., & Snyder, L. (1988). *From first words to grammar: Individual differences and dissociable mechanisms.* New York: Cambridge University Press.

Hakuta, K., & Garcia, E. (1989). Bilingualism and education. *American Psychologist, 44* (2), 374–379.

Moerk, E. (1977). *Pragmatic and semantic aspects of early language development.* Baltimore: University Park Press.

Stern, D. (1985). *The interpersonal world of the infant: A view from psychoanalysis and developmental psychology.* New York: Basic Books.

E. Garcia

Mathematics Literacy

Mathematics literacy has been defined in different ways as society has changed. The back-to-basics movement exemplifies a skills approach, which views literacy as a set of socially useful skills, and emphasizes memorizing facts such as 7 minus 2, and procedures such as how to add 3 and 5. Literacy also can be defined as a set of mathematical concepts necessary to understand mathematical skills. Research, however, indicates that children frequently memorize mathematical skills by rote and do not know how to apply them (Davis, 1984).

Another way of defining mathematical literacy is the capacity to use thinking skills necessary to solve problems. Problem solving entails understanding the problem (defining the unknown and deciding what information is relevant), devising a plan by choosing an appropriate strategy, carrying out the plan, and checking the solution.

The essential competencies for an information-based, technologically oriented society are different from those required just 20 years ago. With the advent of computers and calculators, understanding and problem solving are more important than memorizing computational facts and procedures.

Research on mathematical literacy shows the importance of children's informal (personal and largely counting-based) mathematical concepts and skills (Baroody, 1989; Ginsburg, 1989). This informal knowledge provides the foundation for meaningful learning of school mathematics. Rote memorization or learning difficulties can occur when teachers do not link primary-grade instruction to children's informal knowledge.

Informal knowledge develops throughout the preschool years. Without prompting, young children practice the number sequence and count collections of objects. They even begin to develop fundamental mathematics ideas, such as the fact that adding makes a collection larger or taking away one can be undone by adding one.

Informal knowledge can be fostered by playing math games and answering children's questions or tapping everyday activities such as setting the table. Effective early childhood programs provide many real opportunities to develop informal knowledge in a hands-on way, with the focus on encouraging children to construct their own concepts and invent solution procedures, rather than on memorizing information.

For kindergarten through grade four, the National Council of Teachers of Mathematics suggests fostering the ability to communicate mathematical ideas clearly; to reason logically; to analyze patterns and relationships; and to find connections between personal experience and school-taught mathematics, between concepts and procedures, and between various concrete and symbolic representations of concepts or procedures (Commission on Standards for School Mathematics, 1989). In the elementary grades, curricula should emphasize estimation of quantities, measurement, and computations; geometry and spatial sense; statistics and probability, such as collecting and graphing data that will be used to answer genuine questions; and fractions. Elementary children also should become familiar with computers and calculators. (See also **Physical Knowledge, Logico-mathematical Knowledge, and Social-arbitrary Knowledge,** below.)

References

Baroody, A. J. (1987). *Children's mathematical thinking: A developmental framework for preschool, primary, and special education teachers.* New York: Teachers College Press.

Baroody, A. J. (1989). *A guide to teaching mathematics in the primary grades.* Boston: Allyn and Bacon.

Commission on Standards for School Mathematics. (1989). *Curriculum and evaluation standards in school mathematics education.* Reston, VA: National Council of Teachers of Mathematics.

Davis, R. M. (1984). *Learning mathematics: The cognitive science approach to mathematics education.* Norwood, NJ: Ablex.

Ginsburg, H. P. (1989). *Children's arithmetic* (2nd ed.). Austin, TX: Pro-Ed.

A. J. Baroody

Mathematics

The study of mathematics is the study of relationships. As children observe relationships they learn to quantify their world and begin to develop logical and spatial awareness. When mathematical experiences are integrated with other domains of knowledge, children practice thinking skills applicable to all disciplines.

Play serves as the basis for early learning, and children's mathematical learning is an extension of play. First, children have many quantitative and spatial experiences, including varying duration of sound, embrace/enclosure and separation, sequence of events, and similarity and differences.

Early childhood mathematics content strands encompass patterns, structure and relationships, counting, number, number operations, fractions, geometry and visualization, measurement, probability and graphing, the use of calculators and computers, and problem solving. Language development that relates to mathematics and reasoning is integral to understanding content.

Processes related to early mathematical thinking are observing and inferring, comparing, classifying, and sequencing. These processes do not require the use of numbers and provide early problem-solving experiences. Manipulatives used to develop content and process strands include attribute blocks, pattern blocks, colored cubes, and natural objects such as pebbles.

Early number ideas are affected by conservation, one-to-one correspondence, classification, comparison patterns, sequences, and grouping. Number conservation means that the number of objects in a collection is unchanged even if the objects are rearranged. Children begin to conserve number between four and seven years of age. Conservation cannot be taught, as it is a result of the interaction between maturation and environment.

Commonly, young children count without attaching meaning to their words. This rote counting contrasts with rational counting when children count in order to determine the number in a collection and realize that the last number recited tells how many objects there are.

Grouping initially involves making collections of objects by two's, three's, and four's— all the way to ten's, followed by making exchanges at some grouping point. These experiences provide a foundation for understanding the concept of place value.

Understanding number operations relies on physically manipulating sets and discovering properties of set operations. It also depends on grasping concepts of number, counting, and grouping. Work with addition, subtraction, multiplication, and division should be based on concrete manipulation, such as joining groups of objects and removing objects from a group. Manipulative materials typically include counters such as beans, Unifix cubes, dominoes, Cuisenaire rods, and multibase blocks.

Fractional concepts begin to develop in the preschool years with children's sharing a cracker or orange with a friend. In kindergarten, the introduction of fractions should focus on children's experiences and utilize manipulative materials.

Young children are introduced to geometry and visualization when they learn about common environmental objects, then about shapes through a topological perspective, and finally, about Euclidean shapes typically taught in school. Their early perceptions are topological, since shapes are not seen as rigid but may be readily changed as they are moved about. Relationships such as "close to," "inside of," and "on" illustrate topological thinking. The first Euclidean stage through which children pass involves recognizing various shapes by repeatedly seeing them. Manipulative materials used to develop geometric ideas include blocks, common shapes, and geoboards.

Children's early measurement experiences initially focus on direct comparison and indirect comparison, both non-numeric measuring techniques. Direct comparison occurs when two objects are placed side by side to be compared, eliminating the need for any intermediate object or measuring tool. Indirect comparison occurs when an intermediate device such as a string is used to compare two objects that are not in proximity with one another. Generally, after direct and indirect comparisons, children will experience discrete measurement (assigning a numeric value of so many units to the property of an object, with arbitrary and standard units). The typical learning sequence is length, area, volume and capacity, weight and mass, time, and temperature. Manipulatives in this area include string, Cuisenaire rods, Unifix cubes, clay, balances, clocks, and thermometers.

Probability and graphing concepts generally are encountered when children enter school. Words such as "impossible," "always," and "sometimes" stimulate beginning probability study. The notion of the likelihood of an event's occurring can be developed through activities like drawing cubes from a bag, checker spinning, and predicting. Graphing occurs as children compare and record events from their experience, such as comparing collections of fruit. "Picture graphs" use pictorial representations of objects, while "symbolic graphs" use symbols to represent objects being compared. Early probability and graphing experiences should involve activities with concrete objects. Manipulatives typically include Unifix cubes, spinners, checkers, and pictures of objects.

Calculators and computers are the tools of mathematics, as is the process of problem solving. Skills involved in using calculators and computers sometimes are introduced at home. Problem solving involves skills that can be discussed and practiced. Young children are quite capable of problem solving and problem creating. Apart from some specific instruction and practice in problem solving, much of the problem-solving activity, like calculator and computer use, should be integrated into the child's total learning experience. (See also **Physical Knowledge, Logico-mathematical Knowledge, and Social-arbitrary Knowledge,** below.)

References

Copeland, R. W. (1984). *How children learn mathematics*. New York: Macmillan.

Cruikshank, D. E., & Sheffield, L. J. (1988). *Teaching mathematics to elementary children: A foundation for the future*. Columbus, OH: Merrill.

Cruikshank, D. E., Fitzgerald, D. L., & Jensen, L. R. (1980). *Young children learn mathematics*. Boston: Allyn and Bacon.

Ginsburg, H. P. (ed.). (1983). *The development of mathematical thinking*. New York: Academic Press.

Piaget, J. (1965). *The child's concept of number*. New York: Norton.

Piaget, J., & Inhelder, B. (1967). *The child's conception of space*. New York: Norton.

Skemp, R. (1971). *The psychology of learning mathematics*. New York: Penguin Books.

D. E. Cruikshank

Music

Left to their own natural inclinations, young children will integrate music throughout the course of their day. They will chant rhythmically with the rise and fall of the seesaw or joyfully sing a song in unison as they skip and dance along a sidewalk together. Music, likewise, can be purposely integrated throughout each day of a planned early childhood program. In focusing upon music, effective early childhood educators follow the lead of the children themselves, providing musical experiences that allow first and foremost for spontaneity, enjoyment, and individual self-expression.

Music can contribute to establishing the rhythms and routines of the day. For infants and toddlers, songs and lullabies can provide familiar rituals that bring a sense of security and calmness to tired or distressed children (Bayless & Ramsey, 1987). For older preschool children, songs can smooth transitions in the daily schedule. They can help children playfully shift from one activity to another; to alter the tone of activities, such as from noisy to quiet; and to tune children's interest into selected topics or themes. The challenge for adults is to acquire a wide repertoire of songs and musical games appropriate for varying ages, in order to retrieve them on a moment's notice.

Musical experiences also can provide a vehicle to facilitate other aspects of learning and development. For example, music can facilitate language development (Gullo, 1988). Singing gives children enjoyable practice with the rhythms and sounds of language. Teachers support children's language development by encouraging them to improvise familiar songs. By introducing songs and finger plays with accompanying motions, teachers create opportunities for children to connect words and actions or objects.

Musical experiences also affect children's cognitive and social development. Experiences with musical instruments, for example, can give children opportunities to construct knowledge of basic concepts and relationships. Something as simple as exploring a xylophone, for example, can impart new understandings of such concepts as high and low, loud and soft, up and down. Using rhythm instruments could yield insights into the physical properties of different materials and shapes.

Children's prosocial behavior also can be nurtured through musical activities that encourage cooperation and turn taking, while their cultural sensitivity can be expanded by exposure to the unique songs and dances of various cultural groups. Self-concept can be nourished by helping all children to feel competent as they engage in music-making activities.

The early childhood curriculum also includes music for music's sake. Teachers encourage children to create, perform, and listen to music for the pure pleasure of it. A music-rich early childhood setting would include listening centers with phonograph records and audiotapes, sound centers with different materials and instruments for experimenting with musical sounds, and group times featuring music-making adventures throughout the day. The central goal is to lead children to value and enjoy music, paving the way for a lifetime of musical appreciation and participation.

References

Bayless, K. M., & Ramsey, M. E. (1987). *Music: A way of life for the young child.* Columbus, OH: Merrill.

Gullo, D. F. (1988). Guidelines for facilitating language development. *Day Care and Early Education, 16* (2), 10–14.

C. B. Burton

Philosophy

Philosophy deals with ethical, aesthetic, logical and epistemological aspects of life. While philosophy generally is not taught as a discrete discipline in early childhood programs, children deal with philosophical issues such as good, right, fair, true, and beautiful, in terms of their social interactions, responses to children's literature, and products that they and others create.

As young children acquire linguistic skills, they also acquire logical skills. This cognitive growth allows them to draw inferences, make assumptions, give reasons, classify objects, and make judgments—skills similar to those used by adult philosophers. Terms such as good and true that puzzle adults, likewise intrigue children. In discussing such notions, children, like adults, discover that ideas such as these tend to remain contestable.

Because some educators accept the prevalent idea that all early childhood activities should be concrete, young children often are conceptually undernourished and abstraction deprived. Integrating philosophy into the curriculum restores a balance among affective, perceptual, and cognitive factors in education. Philosophy also is recommended for early elementary grades because it provides enrichment, as well as thinking skills that enhance academic achievement. Even more significant is the fact that philosophy improves children's abilities to formulate questions with regard to the ethical, aesthetic, logical, and epistemological aspects of what they study.

Young children learn best when they actively engage in philosophy, rather than simply hear about it. This entails converting the classroom into a "community of inquiry" in which children discuss with teachers, and each other, matters of philosophical interest, using their logical abilities. Children's literature provides an appropriate vehicle, particularly if teachers use a specially prepared curriculum that makes philosophical issues in stories more available. These issues originate in traditional academic philosophy, but teachers use them without their historical connections.

Since curriculum materials that help teachers use appropriate open-ended questions as discussion leads now are available in many languages, teachers in many countries teach primary-grade philosophy. Some United States educators recognize the importance of philosophy's ethical component and have advocated the inclusion of moral education into the elementary school curriculum. Increasingly, art and music educators are incorporating philosophical aesthetics into their offerings. Educators continue to consider whether the overall field of philosophy should be made part of the early elementary curriculum.

References

Lipman, M., Sharp, A. M., & Oscanyan. (1980). *Philosophy in the classroom* (2nd. ed.). Philadelphia, PA: Temple University Press.

Lipman, M. (1980). *Philosophy goes to school.* Philadelphia, PA: Temple University Press.

Matthews, G. (1980). *Philosophy and the young child.* Cambridge: Harvard University Press.

M. Lipman

Physical Education

Physical education involves simply learning how to move by moving. For a young child to learn to move, that child needs a variety of movement experiences and instruction. Too often, the total educational emphasis of an early childhood program is on the cognitive and affective domains. For today's children to be totally educated, however, they also must have psychomotor experiences.

The benefits derived from being physically fit include reaching optimal growth and development, possessing sufficient energy to function in today's world, and maintaining proper weight. There are six aspects (with related objectives) of early childhood physical education. First, optimal physical growth and development depend upon diet and exercise, such as running and jumping, as well as on heredity. Second, physical fitness includes having an acceptable amount of flexibility, strength, muscular endurance, and aerobic endurance. Flexibility is the ability to move through the full range of motion. Strength is the ability of a muscle to develop enough tension to move objects. Muscular endurance is the ability of a muscle to move objects repeatedly over time. Aerobic endurance is the ability of the circulatory and respiratory systems to provide the necessary oxygen and nutrients to the working muscle and to remove the byproducts. Third, the enhancement of thinking can take place when children participate in active games that require them to think, analyze, and decide on what movements to make. Fourth, easy performance of locomotor skills such as running, jumping, and skipping; and games skills such as throwing, catching, and kicking can occur with instruction. Fifth, social development, including such behaviors as self-restraint and cooperation through a variety of individual, partner, and group activities develop in opportune environments. Sixth, creative expression and appreciation of one's own physical accomplishments also take place in exemplary settings.

Activities appropriate for young children can include fitness activities, movement exploration, manipulative activities, perceptual motor activities, and rhythmic activities. Fitness activities include bending, stretching, jumping, squatting, balancing, extending, and running through focused activities and games. Movement exploration activities include the children's moving imaginatively as if they were in another form, such as an animal or object; or pretending to use a different medium, such as glue, water, ice, or an inclined plane. Manipulative activities include playing games with props, such as balloons, bean bags, or newspapers to define space for movement. Children might tap, toss, throw, catch, and balance materials. Perceptual motor activities encourage children to focus on isolated body parts or their combinations in movement activities. Rhythmic activities include games with directions, including singing games and chants. Additional details are available in the references.

References

Stillwell, J. (1987). *Making and using creative play equipment.* Champaign, IL: Human Kinetics.

Stillwell, J. (1988). *More fitness exercises for children.* Durham, NC: Great Activities.

J. Stillwell

Physical Knowledge, Logico-mathematical Knowledge, and Social-arbitrary Knowledge

Physical knowledge is knowledge that has its source mainly in objects. Physical knowledge, conceptualized by Jean Piaget, originates from the child's actions on, and observations of, the reactions of objects in the physical world. Actions on objects may stem from the child's desire to see what will happen (as when children push a pendulum for the first time); from the desire to verify an anticipation of what will happen (as when children try to hit a target that is out of range of the pendulum by aiming the bob); and from systematic experimentation that is a combination of these (as when a child pushes the pendulum harder, steps closer to the target, and lengthens the string). In the course of such actions, children have the possibility to construct relations of correspondence between actions and reactions, and these very gradually evolve over many years into causal, explanatory relations. As young children act on objects, and observe and think about their reactions, they construct not only knowledge of the object world but also of their own intelligence or logico-mathematical structure of reasoning.

Two types of physical knowledge activities are those that involve the *movement* of objects and those that involve *changes* in objects. Actions that children can perform on objects to make them move include pulling, pushing, rolling, kicking, jumping, blowing, sucking, throwing, swinging, twirling, balancing, and dropping. Changes in objects themselves occur when children cook apple sauce, mix paint powder and water, and freeze popsicles. Activities involving some aspects of both movement and changes in objects include finding out about whether an object sinks or floats, sifting, playing with mirrors, looking through a magnifying glass, touching objects with a magnet, and shadow play. Educational physical knowledge activities are observable and producible by the child, variable in reaction to varying actions, and immediate in reaction to the child's action.

Physical knowledge activities contrast with "science education" in which the objective often is to learn facts about the physical world. In such a content-oriented approach, the objectives often focus on children's becoming able to recognize, define, and describe. Children in the fact-oriented approach often spend much of their time listening to the teacher's explanations, looking at what the teacher shows, and doing what the teacher planned.

The physical knowledge approach, in contrast, is child centered. The teacher's objective is for children to pursue the problems and questions that the children develop. This approach emphasizes children's initiative, their actions on objects, their observations of the feedback from objects, and social interaction.

Physical knowledge activities differ conceptually and practically from "manipulative" activities. While physical knowledge activities involve the child's manipulation of objects, it is not the manipulation that is most important, but rather the child's reasoning through the construction of logico-mathematical relationships. Manipulative activities mainly involve children in sensory exercise and superficial actions, rather than focus on their construction of logico-mathematical relationships.

Logico-mathematical experience, in contrast, consists of actions on objects that introduce ideas about those characteristics that the objects do not have unless an individual can construct them personally. For example, number is not a property of any group of objects but consists of relationships created by an individual. That is, the "two-ness" of two objects does not exist in either object, but is a group of relationships coordinated by the individual who confers on them this characteristic of quantity. For example, noticing what happens when a ball is pushed is an isolated action, while recognizing a difference when a ball is pushed more forcefully requires coordinated actions—relating two or more actions and reactions.

Knowledge that has its source mainly in the knower is logico-mathematical knowledge.

Although Jean Piaget made these important distinctions, he then went on to point out that the different types of experience and knowledge are in reality inseparable. For example, when the child looks at six blue and two yellow blocks and thinks of them as blue ones and yellow ones, he or she is focusing on their specific properties on the one hand and also is activating a whole network of cognitive relationships on the other. That is, to think of the blocks as blocks, the child must distinguish their similarities and differences in relation to all other objects. In order to think of blueness, she or he must relate this property to all other colors. These networks of relationships constitute the general logico-mathematical framework that enables the child to recognize the blue and yellow blocks.

The two types of experiences actually exist in almost all actions as there can be no physical experience without a logico-mathematical framework, and at least for babies and young children, there can be no logico-mathematical experience without objects to put into relationship with one another. Thus, for Piaget, physical action on objects is crucial not only for the child's knowledge of objects themselves, but for the child's construction of intelligence as an instrument of knowing.

Social-arbitrary knowledge has people as its source. Social-arbitrary knowledge includes arbitrary information agreed upon by convention (such as, December 25th is Christmas Day) and rules agreed upon by coordination of points of view (such as, cars stay on the right side of the road). This type of knowledge is similar to physical knowledge in that it requires specific input from the external world. Some form of logico-mathematical framework, however, serves as the structure for this content. For example, the fact that there is no school on weekends can have meaning only in relation to weekdays, and thus fits into a structure that includes both school days and nonschool days.

Piaget's theory of physical and logico-mathematical knowledge provides a strong rationale for early childhood educational activities involving the children's actions on objects.

This theory enables teachers to go beyond the notion of external manipulative activities to think in terms of the child's internal construction of knowledge. (See also, **Mathematics Literacy** and **Mathematics,** above, and **Science, Natural,** and **Science, Physical,** below.)

References

DeVries, R., & Kohlberg, L. (1990). *Constructivist early childhood education.* Washington, DC: National Association for the Education of Young Children.

Kamii, C., & DeVries, R. (1978). *Physical knowledge in preschool education: Implications of Piaget's theory.* Englewood Cliffs, NJ: Prentice-Hall.

R. DeVries

Science, Natural

Long before they arrive in the classroom, infants use the tools of science to explore the natural world. They touch, taste, smell, look, and listen. In speech, "Whazzat?" and then "Why?" follow closely on "Mama" and "Daddy." Infants are a part of the natural world, and they are curious and interested in it. It is their exploration, their learning by experiencing that helps them to grow into healthy, thinking humans. By the same token, their inquisitive behavior can expose them to danger and can exhaust adults, who sometimes begin to discourage that behavior. As a result, natural curiosity often must be restimulated when children arrive in a classroom. The rewards are high, however, when adults join children in making discoveries.

Little children are intrigued with living things. A school year that starts with caterpillars feeding, pupating, and emerging as adult butterflies or moths can make arrival at school an exciting daily event. In the process much more than life cycle is learned; there are the needs of living things, the care and responsibility for another creature, the record keeping, the shared discovery, and the excitement of releasing the adult insects into their natural environment.

The variety of opportunity for exploration of the natural world is limitless. Topics might include the growth of plants, seasonal change, sun and shadow, animal habitat and behavior, children's own bodies, air, light, magnets, rocks and minerals, soil, water, temperature, and weather, as well as many other subjects the children themselves will introduce. Obviously, what is undertaken with children will be related to their age, their development, their attention span, and the frames of reference they bring from their cultures. A topic may be used several times during the early childhood years. Adopting a tree and making monthly observations may be a group activity for two- to four-year-olds. The same children at seven or eight years may each select a tree and write their own observational notes, with monthly drawings that incorporate comment on many of the other topics mentioned above.

Discovering shadows as no-sun spots and making them change is a learning activity for five-year-olds; but an ongoing study of hourly and/or monthly change in shadows can be exciting to eight-year-olds, when they begin to wonder about earth/sun relationships and begin to see the relevance of measuring, recording, predicting, and drawing conclusions about shadows.

Curriculum for early childhood should be an interwoven whole, and science has much to contribute to it. Exploration of the cultural knowledge that children bring with them to the classroom, for example, provides an opening for incorporation of natural science in study of animals or plants particular to regions where the children or their families have lived. Similarly, a tree-planting project in a city, or a project to check erosion in the country, may be a first experience in working with governmental agencies.

In providing an opportunity for children to make discoveries for themselves, science activities can enhance a feeling of self-worth, add excitement to learning basic skills, and contribute to an understanding of and appreciation for the environment. Children can develop skills used in decision making and, through these, an ability to function in an ever-changing world.

If parents and teachers feel inadequate in science, a good place to start is a children's library. An increasing number of quality trade books are being produced by authors who know both children and science. These books provide accurate, readable, exciting, activity-oriented information that can give adults security and enrich children's programs, supplementing discoveries the children have already made as they offer new challenges.

The Children's Book Council (New York City) and the National Teachers Association (Washington, D.C.) jointly publish an annual list of recommended books. The lists can be obtained by sending a stamped, self-addressed envelope to those societies. In addition, the American Nature Study Society (Homer, NY) annually gives the Eva L. Gordon award to an author whose books consistently are accurate, exciting, timely, and challenge children to involvement in hands-on science activities. (See also **Physical Knowledge, Logico-mathematical and Socio-arbitrary Knowledge**, above, and **Discussion, Conversation, and Questioning: Critical Thinking**, below.)

References

Heberman, E. (1989). *The city kid's field guide*. New York: Macmillan.

Russell, H. R. (1990). *Using the school ground to teach* (2nd ed.). Washington, DC: National Science Teachers Association.

H. R. Russell

Science, Physical

Physical science is the study of the nature and properties of energy and nonliving matter. Sometimes called physics, chemistry, astronomy, or geology, it comprises a huge body of knowledge that helps children understand the world around them. Physical science, like mathematics, language, and social studies, should be part of the early childhood curriculum. The inclusion of physical science activities increases young children's opportunities to develop visual-spatial, problem-solving, observation, creative thinking, and decision-making skills (Sprung, Froschl, & Campbell, 1985).

Concrete, child-centered activities can be incorporated into the daily curriculum. In the block area, for example, children explore the uses of inclined planes by building ramps of different heights and rolling objects down, predicting where they might stop. Water play can include small shaker containers filled with various powders, such as sugar, salt, baking powder, flour, and corn starch. By sprinkling different powders into water, children can discover which ones dissolve. Tossing games help children develop their spatial relationships as they toss bean bags into a basket or at other targets that children create.

As children engage in such activities, the teacher asks open-ended questions to spur children's observations. An open-ended question such as, "What do you think might happen if you make your ramp higher?" can help children develop their sense of inquiry. Teachers use words such as "scientist," "experiment," and "observe" when talking to children about their work.

Teachers also can encourage children to do simple research by looking in a book or asking someone else a question. Children can document the results of their experiments with minimal help by using age-appropriate methods such as experience charts, drawings, graphs, dictated stories, or journals.

Outside resources also can enhance the physical science program. Parents or community members who work in science have been invited to the classroom to discuss their work and do hands-on activities with children. A traditional field trip such as a visit to the bank or post office can include today's technology when the teacher arranges for workers to demonstrate how machines such as scanners, money machines, or electronic call boards work.

Equality of opportunity for all children is critical with regard to physical science since both female teachers and children tend to see science as the province of white males (Fort & Varney, 1989). This stereotype occurs because white girls, children of color of both sexes, low-income children, and children with disabilities are underrepresented in science

fields. Since the vast majority of early childhood teachers are females, many of whom have been minimally trained to teach science, physical science often is thought of as a subject that can be taught in the upper grades.

Early childhood is the time to begin to change science education. If programs create a "science is for everyone" attitude from the beginning of a child's education by providing age-appropriate activities that help all children explore the physical sciences, the pool of those participating in science will expand. This increase in human resources from underrepresented groups can benefit individuals as well as the larger society. (See also **Physical Knowledge, Logico-mathematical Knowledge, and Socio-arbitrary Knowledge,** above, and **Discussion, Conversation, and Questioning: Critical Thinking,** below.)

References

Althouse, R. (1988). *Investigating science with young children.* New York: Teachers College Press.

Fort, D. C., & Varney, H. L. (1989). How students see scientists: Mostly male, mostly white. *Science and Children, 26* (8), 8.

Kamii, C., & DeVries, R. (1978). *Physical knowledge in preschool education: Implications of Piaget's theory.* Englewood Cliffs, NJ: Prentice-Hall.

Sprung, B., Froschl, M., & Campbell, P. (1985). *What will happen if . . . : Young children and the scientific method.* New York: Educational Equity Concepts.

Stetten, M. (1979). *Let's play science: Projects for home and school.* New York: Harper & Row.

B. Sprung

Social Studies

Social studies is an enormous field. It includes everything related to humans and their interactions with each other and the environment. Embracing all of the disciplines from the social sciences, the social studies consist of many subject areas, including history, geography, economics, political science, multicultural education, ecology, current events, and other social science content areas. The social studies transmit the culture, or a way of life, to children. The knowledge, skills, attitudes, and values necessary to live in a democratic society are fostered throughout the social studies.

In early childhood education, social studies instruction is based on knowledge of how children grow, learn, and develop. The social studies are integrated and child centered. Children are introduced to the social studies through experiences that are fully integrated into daily activities and with each other. Rather than a separate subjects approach, content is integrated into a continuous whole.

For example, children may take a walk to the neighborhood grocery store. Their purpose may be to purchase vegetables to make "stone" soup (based upon a folk tale). On their way they will follow a map drawn by the teacher. At the store they will observe people carrying out a variety of jobs and as they select vegetables discuss where and how they grow. They may go to the back of the store and watch as boxes of other vegetables are unloaded. Finally, they select and pay for the vegetables.

Back in their school, a group may build houses and streets with blocks, experiencing concepts of mapping and at the same time practicing the skills of cooperating. Another group, while preparing vegetables, may talk about how their parents or grandparents prepare the same vegetables. Others may want to find out where the trucks were from and locate these places on a map.

Child centered, the social studies are taught through children's play and their actual encounters with real objects, people, and events in their environment. Knowledge of the culture of others is introduced in the same way, through actual experiences with people of other races, ethnic groups, and cultures. The developmental characteristics of each child, and each group of children, direct the selection of goals for the social studies.

In the 1930s, Lucy Sprague Mitchell challenged the traditional concept of the social studies as the memorization of a body of facts that were considered unchanging. She believed that the social studies curriculum should be based entirely on children's experiences.

Since that time, the predominant organizational pattern for social studies teaching in early childhood education has been that of an expanding, spiraling, concentric circles curriculum. Children first learn concepts of their home, family and neighborhood and, as they grow and their world expands, then learn concepts of things further away from them in time and space.

In more recent decades, there has been criticism of this concentric circles curriculum as insufficient in its middle-class orientation, as well as its lack of recognition of primary grade children's interests in events that are distant in time and space (Brophy, 1990). Other approaches to planning for the social studies include the structure of disciplines as a basis for content and/or ways of studying and generating knowledge about the social world; the emphasis on a cross-disciplinary preparation for citizenship through developing informed decision makers who could function within a global economy and outlook; and recent criticism of these process-oriented approaches that proposes major emphasis on history, with some geography and civics (Ibid.).

It is fair to say that a meaningful basis for young children's study of social experience characterizes the thinking of professional early childhood educators who propose that young children learn best when they are active in their own learning and have opportunities for direct experiences.

References

Brophy, J. (1990). Teaching social studies for understanding and higher-order applications. *Elementary School Journal, 90* (4), 351–417.

Mitchell, L. S. (1971/1934). *Young geographers*. New York: Bank Street College of Education.

Seefeldt, C. (1989). *Social studies for the preschool-primary child* (3rd. ed.). Columbus, OH: Merrill.

C. Seefeldt

Community Resource Use

All aspects of an integrated early childhood curriculum can be enriched by drawing upon community resources. Field trips to community sites relevant to curriculum content allow children to make concrete connections with material they are studying in school. For example, children might read a library book about hospitals in preparing for a visit to a local hospital. As a follow-up activity, community members who work in hospital care might come to class and share their vocations. Children's sociodramatic play can be extended through a local contribution of selected medical supplies, which might be used in a classroom hospital theme area.

Limited budgets for materials in early childhood education, particularly in the private sector, have been augmented by contributions from local businesses. Sawdust and wood scraps as well as wallpaper books or window decorations have been obtained from local stores.

Community members from various cultural backgrounds and expertise have come to classrooms to share foods, artifacts, expertise, and other experiences. Volunteers also help to create a lower child-adult ratio when they supervise activities such as woodworking or weaving. Head Start programs in particular have used parent and community volunteers. The Foster Grandparents programs also offer intergenerational experiences.

Decision makers in public and private policy making can act as advocates for quality early childhood education. By helping these community members to understand the need for and complexity of providing quality programming for young children, early childhood educators can expand community support and influence policy. (See also Chapter 3, Section 3.5, **Advocacy Strategies**; and **Field Trips**, below.)

Reference

Berger, E. (1987). *Parents as partners in education: The school and home working together* (2nd ed.). Columbus, OH: Merrill.

S. G. Goffin

Cooking

Cooking engages the imagination and curiosity of the young child and involves many aspects of the curriculum—mathematics, reading, language arts, science, and social studies. Children must decode the recipe, talk about it, estimate or measure, or count the ingredients. They see what happens to food when you apply heat or cold. They learn about where food comes from and how different people cook the same foods differently.

Cooking in the early childhood classroom involves the child physically and socially. Young children are delighted to mix, cut, crack, squeeze, chop, and pour the ingredients. Working together in a small group, children learn to wait their turn and perform the next step of the recipe. The purpose of the cooking experience suggested here integrates cooking with the ongoing daily activities of the classroom, rather than the more usual practice of special occasion or holiday cooking.

Through cooking, young children actively engage in the ideals of the social studies curriculum. The social studies curriculum is designed to develop responsible, self-directing individuals who can function and contribute as informed and caring members of family, community, and world groups. As they cook, children learn about the division of roles and responsibility involved in making food available. They begin to realize how milk gets from the cow to their tables in containers. They begin to follow the life of green beans from planting, harvesting, packaging, and selling to cooking. Young children and their teachers take trips into the community to shop for food. They share their cooking experiences or outcomes with community or parent volunteers. They discuss the value of food and its universal need, as well as diverse forms, in different cultures.

During the cooking process, young children touch, feel, observe changes in food, and then eat it. By using cooking tools, they extend their manual dexterity, and by discussing the activities, they extend their language skills and raise questions for the future. Food also is a nonverbal way of communicating caring and love.

Cooking can promote abstract thinking and language development by introducing children to new textures, colors, smells, tastes, and timing of events, while encouraging independence and interest in different foods.

References

Cooper, T. T., & Ratner, M. (1974). *Many hands cooking: An international cookbook for boys and girls.* New York: UNICEF.

Goodwin, M. T., & Pollen, G. (1974). *Creative food experiences for children.* Washington, DC: Center for Science in the Public Interest.

S. C. Carothers

Sociodrama

Sociodramatic play is both social and dramatic in that it involves two or more children in the joint creation of an imaginary situation. When playing firefighters, superheroes/heroines, family, store, or school, children enter into a shared world of pretense. Educators and researchers recognize sociodramatic play as the cornerstone of early childhood education programs (Paley, 1981; Smilansky, 1968).

Sociodramatic play reflects children's emotional, social, language and cognitive stages of development, as evident in their choice and enactment of themes. Pretending to fight a fire, for example, involves taking initiative and power in a life and death situation. Children often incorporate important features of their environmental settings and family life, such as the birth of a sibling, into play themes (Isaacs, 1933). Children's sociodramatic play has been observed in both traditional and industrial cultures throughout the world (Schwartzman, 1978), and play themes often reflect particular cultures.

In contrast to solitary play, sociodramatic play requires the mutual creation and coordination of situations and roles. With increased social development, sociodramatic play becomes more sustained and complex. Children become capable of assuming the multiple dimensions of a role, for example, the child who plays a banker, wife, and mother; of developing a theme that might continue for several days; and of participating with greater flexibility ("Now that we got the fire out, we gotta be builders and build the house."). With development, complexity also increases from simple and repetitive roles and situations, such as a pretend mother feeding the pretend baby, to more complex roles and situations, such as a pretend parent taking the pretend sick baby to the doctor. More mature children can use less realistic props, dramatize less familiar situations, and involve the perspective of more players in more complex roles. Researchers have found that intervention strategies can help children develop more complex and extended play (Smilansky, 1968).

Sociodramatic play involves not only the language demands of the pretend social situation (how firefighters or parents talk) but also the demands of entering an ongoing sociodrama ("And I'll be the dog, O.K.?"), and negotiating roles and rules ("You were the mother last time, so now you be the older sister.") (Monighan-Nourot, Scales, & Van Hoorn, with Almy, 1987). Through all of this activity children are creating, organizing, and expressing meaning. Sociodramatic play is a medium through which they practice ways of behaving in a complex world.

By observing children engaged in sociodramatic play, educators can informally assess children's development in many domains, while also learning about their culture. Teachers can best enhance children's growth through sociodramatic play by providing an environment rich in potential props and settings, unstructured time, and sensitive interventions.

References

Isaacs, S. (1933). *Social development in young children.* New York: Routledge & Kegan Paul.

Monighan-Nourot, P., Scales, B., & Van Hoorn, J., with Almy, M. (1987). *Looking at children's play: A bridge between theory and practice.* New York: Teachers College Press.

Paley, V. G. (1981). *Walley's stories.* Cambridge: Harvard University Press.

Schwartzman, H. B. (1978). *Transformations: The anthropology of children's play.* New York: Plenum.

Smilansky, S. (1968). *The effects of sociodramatic play on disadvantaged preschool children.* New York: Wiley.

J. Van Hoorn

Props

(See **Family Center and Alternatives**, below; **Creative Drama and Children's Theater**, above, and **Physical Education**, above.)

Family Center and Alternatives

The family center, sometimes called housekeeping or playhouse, has been a cornerstone of early childhood sociodramatic play. It frequently contains kitchen props, toy furniture such as a rocking chair and beds for dolls, and other props evocative of household themes. Dolls, doll clothes, and dress-up clothes for family roles also are usually included.

Most teachers view family center play as the natural extension of children's home lives into the sociodramatic play of the classroom. Early play "scripts" frequently portray family relations, and it is thought that most children find these scripts a familiar and safe basis for building their fantasy play (Garvey, 1977; Nelson & Seidman, 1984).

As children become comfortable with play peers and family themes, teachers may extend the family center by providing prop boxes and designating areas for community themes or the more thematically distanced adventure themes. Examples of community themes props include supermarket, post office, paint and construction workers, bakers, firefighters, hospital, laundromat, flower shop, shoe store, taxicab, service station, bus, and library. Themes that evoke adventurous roles outside the daily experience of children include astronaut, cowpoke, camping, airport, and sailboat (Singer & Singer, 1985). Additional themes may be based on characters and events in children's literature. Children can enact deeply felt themes and explore deep connections in their lives.

Many teachers report success when combining prop boxes with the block area and/or setting up theme areas adjacent to the family center as a means of integrating children who feel more "safe" with family play. Provision for more open-ended play themes reduces the possibility of family play becoming stereotyped and repetitive. In this way, teachers can meet the needs of children who find a family

script comforting and engaging, as well as those who choose to extend their dramatic play to thematically distanced themes.

Alternatives to family centers can be utilized as a means of encouraging cross-gender play. If most of the dramatic and costume play centers on housekeeping themes, girls tend to take over the area (Paley, 1984). Themes that encourage children to portray roles apart from their family experiences can alleviate gender stereotypes and are an important part of the early childhood curriculum.

Reference

Garvey, C. (1977). *Play*. New York: Cambridge University Press.

Nelson, K., & Seidman, S. (1984). Playing with scripts. In I. Bretherton (ed.), *Symbolic play: The development of social understanding* (pp. 45–71). New York: Academic Press.

Monighan-Nourot, P., Scales, B., & Van Hoorn, J., with Almy, M. (1987). *Looking at children's play: A bridge between theory and practice*. New York: Teachers College Press.

Paley, V. G. (1984). *Boys and girls: Superheroes in the doll corner*. Chicago: University of Chicago Press.

Singer, D., & Singer, J. (1985). *Make believe: Games and activities to foster imaginative play in young children*. Glenview, IL: Scott Foresman.

P. Monighan-Nourot

Puppetry

A primary contribution of puppetry to early childhood education is the facilitation of children's language development. Teachers can read, tell stories, or sing songs through the mouths of puppets, making those stories and songs come alive for children. Teachers' use of puppets in this way likewise models and stimulates the children's use of puppets for their own self-expression of ideas and feelings. Children can tell stories and talk to each other through puppets. One child working alone can dramatize a story or conversation by "assigning" each hand a different role and puppet.

Puppets used in early childhood education have included commercial hand and finger puppets, some of which portray children's favorite story characters. Teachers and children also make puppets out of such materials as socks, gloves in which each finger represents a different character, paper bags, paper plates, and sticks.

For preschool and kindergarten children, puppet-supported language activities are most effective when they are relatively informal. Reading and listening centers can be augmented by having puppets available to fit the theme of books and records or tapes that are on display. Similarly, puppets can be rotated into housekeeping and construction centers to provide props for different themes in children's sociodramatic play. Expectations for more formal, staged puppet performances are best reserved for older children, as young children's informal puppet play usually is episodic.

In addition to providing vehicles for enhancing children's language development, puppets can serve as important tools in teacher efforts to nurture children's social development. A central goal for all young children is to develop positive and healthy relationships with others. Toward this end, puppets are used to model positive social problem-solving skills for children. For example, teachers encourage young children to use verbal means rather than physically aggressive ways to resolve peer conflicts.

Another common concern is to help children acquire personal safety skills to use when potential problems arise, such as encounters with unfamiliar adults. Puppets can demonstrate relevant social skills in a concrete and meaningful manner. Puppets similarly can be used as a nonintimidating way to open up communication with children who are socially withdrawn or shy. The overall point here is that puppets can enable teachers to go beyond mere words to model and give young children developmentally appropriate opportunities to express social concerns and practice social skills.

Puppets also can help to nurture children's acceptance of diversity. Puppets that portray children from different cultural backgrounds or with different handicapping conditions can be casually integrated into children's play. The primary goal is to promote children's comfort with diversity, and to informally invite their questions and discussions regarding diversity. The potential applications of puppetry are vast, given the insights, imagination, and energy possessed by most early childhood teachers.

Reference

Batchelder, M., & Comer, V. L. (1956). *Puppets and plays: A creative approach*. New York: Harper.

C. B. Burton

5.4 Curriculum Materials

Concrete materials as well as direct personal experiences help young children to learn. This section presents descriptions of a selected array of curriculum materials that are used in early childhood education, as well as a discussion of issues concerning their selection and use. The virtue of most of these curriculum materials is that young children can use them in varied ways to fulfill varied purposes. They also can use most of them independently of adult intervention, after they have had instruction or minimal modeling of procedures.

The articles appear in alphabetical order, beginning with Blocks and closing with Writing Tools. In addition, there are articles about Outdoor Education Provisions and Outdoor Education Equipment. There also is discussion of such materials as commercial kits, textbooks, and workbooks, because they are used in some early childhood classrooms. The material focus of this section will continue in a separate section about Technology as Educative Material.

D. P. Fromberg

Blocks

The wooden blocks designed by Caroline Pratt are the most commonly used construction materials in early childhood classrooms. A rectangular block measuring 1 3/8" x 2 3/4" x 5 1/2" serves as the basic unit from which more than 18 different shapes are created by dividing or multiplying the basic unit. In addition, there are rounded shapes scaled to interface with the unit, such as pillars, circular and elliptical curves, right angles, and X switches. Young children use these maple wood blocks on the floor. The scaled accessories used in conjunction with blocks extend the dramatic play possibilities of block building. Accessories include such representations as rubber or wooden people and animals, transportation vehicles, and pulleys.

In addition to the Pratt blocks, there are sets of smaller scaled unit blocks in which the basic unit is 2" x 4" x 1". Children usually use these smaller blocks on tables. In addition to wood, there are hollow cardboard blocks often used in classrooms for toddlers, and a variety of plastic construction materials such as bristle blocks and the popular Lego sets.

For outdoor building, Caroline Pratt designed two block shapes, a 10" x 10" square and a long 10" x 20" rectangle. These hollow wooden blocks are enclosed on all sides and often are used with wooden ladders, sawhorses, boards, and large 30" x 40" packing boxes. Similar hollow outdoor wooden blocks open on two sides also are available. While these large blocks were designed for outdoor use, they are used also within the classroom. With either indoor or outdoor blocks, children construct structures large enough for them to enter directly as they engage in dramatic play. (See also Chapter 2, Section 2.5, **Blocks.**)

References

Cartwright, S. (1990). Learning with large blocks. *Young Children, 45* (3), 38–41.

Hirsch, E. S. (ed.). (1984). *The block book* (rev. ed.). Washington, DC: National Association for the Education of Young Children.

Provenzo, E. F., & Brett, A. (1983). *The complete block book.* Syracuse, NY: Syracuse University Press.

H. K. Cuffaro

Big Books, Shared Book Experiences

Enlarged texts, known as big books, are finding increasing use in early childhood class-rooms. Big books allow groups of children to see and react to the printed page as it is being read aloud, a factor believed to be of great importance when parents and children share books together. Shared book experiences (Holdaway, 1979) of this type encourage children to interact during the reading. They follow the print as it is tracked for them by the reader, and they attempt to read along with the predictable story lines and language. Repeated readings, supported by an adult as well as an independent activity, help children gain confidence with printed language. They re-enact the reading process as it has been demonstrated for them.

Shared book experiences allow teachers to engage children in a full range of literary activities, including making predictions about the story; participating in the reading of patterned and predictable language; noticing likenesses and differences in letters, words, and other print features; and discussing important elements of the story.

References

Holdaway, D. (1979). *The foundations of literacy.* Portsmouth, NH: Heinemann.

Lynch, P. (1986). *Using big books and predictable books.* New York: Scholastic.

Note also: The Wright Group, 10949 Technology Place, San Diego, CA 92127.

D. S. Strickland

Children's Literature

(See Section 5.3, **Literature,** above, and Chapter 2, Section 2.5, **Children's Literature in the United States, Evolution of.**)

Commercial Curriculum Kits

Today's market is inundated with commercially produced early childhood curriculum materials and kits promising exciting, successful, and easy ways to teach everything from language development to drug awareness to preschoolers through primary-aged children. These curriculum packages usually are conceptualized around a certain belief about how children learn, use research to back their claims, provide detailed teacher guides, and are organized around the use of certain materials that usually are provided for sale. They often are designed to be teacher-proof curriculum.

While many of these commercially prepared curriculum packages are found across the United States in preschool, kindergarten, and primary programs, there are some cautions to consider when selecting and using them. The quality of these materials varies in terms of what they purport to teach, how they suggest teaching it, and how much flexibility they allow the teacher. The cost of such materials in relation to the number of children who can benefit from its use is another consideration. The *Mathematics Their Way* as well as the *Peabody Language Development* kits are reviewed in order to illustrate the value and cautions to consider when selecting these kinds of materials.

Mathematics Their Way is a book that contains hands-on mathematics activities for children, kindergarten through second grade. There also is a newsletter designed as a supplement for teachers that they can use independently. Various publishers provide related concrete materials for sale such as manipulatives and containers that coincide with these activities, including geoboards, pattern blocks, Unifix cubes, pegs, place value boards, colored macaroni and wood, buttons, beads, tongs, souffle cups, and assorted letters. The program intends to make mathematical concepts meaningful for young children by providing opportunities for them to manipulate real and familiar materials.

The book contains chapters that include free exploration; patterns; sorting and classifying; counting; comparing; graphing; number at the conceptual, connective, and symbolic levels; advanced patterns; place value; and pattern book experiments. It provides a detailed appendix containing a glossary of materials coded within the text, suggestions for scheduling concept development, a management guide for integrating activities, and sample correspondence to parents with sug-

gestions for extending these concepts at home. Each chapter is organized for sequential use and contains suggestions about how to introduce new concepts to the total group and then for working with small groups.

Mathematics Their Way expects children to explore materials in playful and meaningful ways. The program designer intended that teachers would integrate math experiences with existing curriculum in language, science, and social studies. There is teacher flexibility in adapting activities to individual children's needs.

The *Peabody Language Development Kits* are designed for preschool through third grade use and contain four sequenced levels of language and cognitive activities. The goal of the program is to help children communicate ideas and think logically. The PLDK-R edition is designed for children who have delayed speech and language development, who speak a language other than English, have limited-English proficiency, or have mild to moderate learning disabilities.

Published materials include program rationale, related research and development, and detailed directions for teaching daily lessons. Each of four kits contains sequenced activities in 25 skill areas and 41 subject areas. Level P, for preschool and kindergarten children, focuses on syntax, language usage, and meaning, and incorporates tactile materials. Level 1, for first grade children, focuses on oral language and cognitive skills, along with more auditory and visual aids.

Level 2, for second grade children, focuses on divergent thinking, whereas Level 3, for third grade children, focuses on concept development. Each lesson plan lists materials provided in the kit and specifies exactly what the teacher has to say while working with small groups of children. Among the materials that accompany lesson manuals are color chips as well as picture cards and full color posters, magnetic geometric shapes, plastic fruits and vegetables, and sound books.

The *Peabody Language Development Kit—Revised* (PLDK-R) offers a structured speech and language program. If used daily as recommended, it can become repetitious and tedious. When adapted to the needs and interests of the children, it can be a source of speech and language development. Particularly with preschool and kindergarten children, teachers need to provide a variety of rich receptive and expressive language activities that supplement this kit. Although designed as a structured program, teachers can adapt and use this kit in a flexible manner.

References

Baratta-Lorton, M. (1976). *Mathematics their way: An activity centered mathematics program for early childhood education.* Reading, MA: Addison-Wesley.

Dunn, L. M., Smith, J., Dunn, L., Horton, K., & Smith, D. (1981). *Peabody language development kits* (rev. ed.) (PLDK-R). Circle Pines, MN: American Guidance Service.

Garland, C. (ed.). (1988). *Mathematics their way: Summary newsletter.* Center for Innovation in Education, 19225 Vineyard La., Saratoga, CA 95070.

J. P. Isenberg

Computer Software

(See Section 5.5, **Technology and Educative Materials,** below.)

Mathematically Oriented Materials

While many different manipulative materials can be used to promote mathematical concepts in young children, there are certain materials that have been specifically designed for that purpose. Two of the most popular, Cuisinaire Rods and Dienes Multibase Arithmetic Blocks are described in detail below. Other materials that foster mathematical concepts include parquetry blocks, Unifix cubes, unit blocks, geoboards, balance scales, and counting beads.

L. R. Williams

Cuisenaire Rods

Cuisenaire rods are plastic or wooden rods constructed in ten lengths that progress from one to ten centimeters. Each rod has a cross section of one square centimeter. Each rod of a different length has a specific identifying color. All rods of one centimeter are white, two-centimeter rods are red, three-centimeter rods are light green, four-centimeter rods are purple, five-centimeter rods are yellow, six-centimeter rods are dark green, seven-centimeter rods are black, eight-centimeter rods are brown, nine-centimeter rods are blue, and ten-centimeter rods are orange.

Cuisenaire rods are used in a variety of ways to promote prenumber and early number ideas. In using the rods, children have the opportunity to explore properties of concrete materials that are similar to the properties of number operations and relationships they will one day learn. Initially, children play with the rods, building and organizing the rods, and discovering the rods' visual and tactile properties. As teachers introduce more structured activities, children explore the properties of relationships, ordering by length, estimation, relationships among whole and fractional numbers, basic arithmetic operations, place value, and numeration.

References

Cuisenaire Company of America, 12 Church Street, New Rochelle, NY 11805.

D. E. Cruikshank

Dienes Multibase Arithmetic Blocks

Dienes Multibase Arithmetic Blocks (MAB) are designed to help children understand place value as well as addition and subtraction with regrouping. The basic set consists of a number of boxes, each of which contains four different pieces usually called units, longs, flats, and blocks. The units are all alike in particular boxes. The difference among the boxes resides in difference of scale among the longs, flats, and blocks. Figure 1 illustrates pieces in MAB 10. They are a physical embodiment of the numbers 1, 10, 100, and 1,000. The rate of exchange is ten units for one long, ten longs for one flat, ten flats for one block. As soon as ten pieces of one size are collected, they are exchanged for one of the next larger piece.

Thus, for example, the idea of 1,243 is represented by one block, two flats, four longs, and three units.

Figure 1

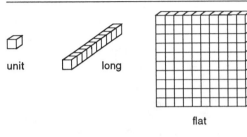

flat

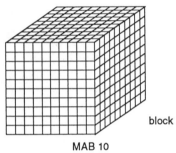

block

MAB 10

In MAB 2, the long contains two units; the flat, four units (two longs); and the block, eight units (two flats). Here the rate of exchange is two for the next larger piece. Consequently, the only numerals associated with MAB 2 are one and zero, because as soon as two of any piece are collected, they must be exchanged for one piece that is the next larger category. This is the binary numeration associated with computers. (See Figure 2.)

Figure 2

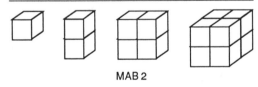

MAB 2

In MAB 3, 4, 5, and 6, the exchanges are respectively three for one, four for one, five for one, and six for one. When these materials are used skillfully and playfully by the teacher, they help children learn place value not merely at the associative level (to remember how the teacher did it), but at the conceptual level (to understand how our number system is put together and how it works).

References

Dienes, Z. P. (1966). *Modern mathematics for young children*. Boston: Herder & Herder.

ETA Daigger Co. *Multibase Arithmetic Blocks*. 150 West Kinzie St., Chicago, IL. 60610.

L. Goldberg

Malleable Materials

Malleable materials have the distinction of receiving their form from the direct action of the child upon them. For that reason, they hold a special appeal for young children, who enjoy shaping them to their purposes and according to their imagination. The Froebelian kindergartens used clay and paints as part of the "occupations" that made up a portion of their program. Early childhood programs strongly influenced by psychodynamic theory during the first half of this century included clay, sand, water, and fingerpaints as part of their curriculum to provide children with ways to express unconscious feelings about self and relationships with others. Today such materials are still seen as important for the child's sense of efficacy, creative expression, and concept development.

L. R. Williams

Clay

A most basic three-dimensional mathematical and art experience for young children comes from playing with nature's refined clay materials. Moist natural clay is found on river banks, in caves, or is sold by school supply companies. Clay is inexpensive but requires preparation before use. Malleable clay should be stored in plastic bags until needed. Used clay can be returned for reprocessing for future exploration.

Children poke, dent, twist, stretch, bend, separate, and join together clay. Simple tools for cutting and rolling are used, but the major tools are children's hands that provide tactile experiences.

As with any art form, adults should not stress the end results of what the young child is making but focus on the important process of exploring and playing with the clay. If a child is happy with a created form, it might be displayed for others to see or sent home for parents to see.

While young children are exploring the properties of this medium, and while they are attempting to solve the problems associated with creating products, they also have opportunities to develop their visual spatial skills. Visual spatial skills in turn support the development of mathematical concepts.

Natural clay can be fired in a kiln if it is properly wedged before the children work with it. That is, the clay is cut, thrown, and kneaded with adult help to remove air bubbles. A single firing produces clay with a bricklike texture, called bisque. Young children can paint bisque with a homemade glaze consisting of equal parts of tempera paint and Elmer's Glue-All, creating a satin finish. If the mixture is too thick, water can be used to dilute it for easy spreading with a brush. In warm weather, a substitute kiln could be an outdoor fireplace using sawdust for fuel, as described in Lendall Haskell's work (1979, p. 148).

Among modeling materials, natural clay has the most plasticity. Modeling clay is an alternative form, commercially available in most toy stores, that uses trade names such as, Newplast, Play-Doh, and Super Dough. It remains pliable when stored in a closed container, but will harden when left out in the air. Homemade dough is another alternative that children can help to create from flour (4 cups), salt (1 1/2 cups), water (1 3/4 cups), and cooking oil (2 tablespoons). It requires air tight storage when not in use and provides an inexpensive, non-toxic material for very young children. Although natural clay is uniquely malleable, all of these malleable materials are a source of pleasure and learning for young children. (See also Section 5.3, **Arts: Visual-Graphic and Spatial**, above.)

Reference

Haskell, L. L. (1979). *Art in the early childhood years.* Colombus, OH: Merrill.

L. L. Haskell

Paint and Other Media
(See **Arts: Visual-Graphic and Spatial**, above.)

Sand and Water

The early therapeutic and emotional rationale for sand and water play grew out of the child development movement led by G. Stanley Hall at the turn of this century and Sigmund Freud's psychoanalytic influence. John Dewey's emphasis on the child's purposes and the importance of problem solving also influenced early childhood educators who recognized the intellectual benefits of sand and water play. Social, symbolic, and language development also justify play with sand, water, mud, snow, and clay. Symbolic development occurs as children spontaneously pretend, for example, that they are making Kool-Aid or cakes, and use toy people and animals in conjunction with an infinite variety of representational efforts.

The more recent cognitive rationale for activities with sand and water has been conceptualized in terms of the developmental framework of constructivist education, informed by the research and theory of Jean Piaget. From this perspective, sand and water are materials for physical knowledge activities, fostering physical knowledge that leads to logico-mathematical knowledge. Young children who play with sand and water can experience possibilities for constructing knowledge about the properties of objects. This activity provides an excellent context for development of the very structure of reasoning and intelligence.

Constructivist education recognizes the preoperational nature of children's ideas about the physical world. This perspective recognizes that young children think in qualitatively different ways about the physical world, and their teachers need to provide experiences in which children test their own ideas. Young children's preoperational expectations lead to experiences of contradiction when their expectations are not confirmed, for example, when they expect certain materials to float or sink but observe a different outcome. According to Piaget, experiences of contradiction are essential to the development of logical reasoning.

From the constructivist perspective, the most cognitively useful sand and water activities are those that inspire children to act on objects in four ways: to see how they will react, to produce a desired effect, to become aware of how particular effects are produced, and to think about causes. Even at five and six years of age, children often do not know ahead of time what will happen and simply act to find out. At three years of age, children can have firm expectations (right or wrong) about what will happen, and can act to try to produce a particular effect. Children's anticipations about the working of the physical world reflect their logic, the logico-mathematical relations that they construct in the course of their specific experiences.

Teachers can foster the revision and construction of new relationships by encouraging children to try the same actions on different objects and different actions on the same object. For example, syringes respond differently to water and corn meal. After experiences with water, children are intrigued when they find that although they can pour corn meal like water, the corn meal does not go through the syringe. The actions of blowing ping pong balls or flour on water also produce different results.

Teachers can foster reasoning by asking children questions that correspond to the four ways of acting on objects: to test objects' reactions, "What do you think might happen if ... (you hold the styrofoam on the bottom)?"; to produce a particular effect, "How can you ... (move the ping pong ball across the water by blowing on it with a straw)?"; to heighten awareness of how to produce effects (suggest that one child show another how to create an effect); and to help children think about causes (consider asking children to wonder about "Why ... ?" mindful of its limitations for young children).

Sand and water play offer a variety of possibilities for children to confirm and disconfirm anticipations and to be active in the four ways

mentioned above. Young children can sift to make "soft sand," pour, dig, pack, brush and rake, sprinkle, and mark sand. In combination with water, children can mold and tunnel. They also can pour, squirt, spray, splash, sprinkle, and pump water, as well as combine it with other materials to produce changes in objects.

Young children find the movement of water especially intriguing and find fascinating possibilities in flexible and rigid tubes as well as containers with holes. Four-year-olds pour water into the short end of a J-shaped pipe and, with their preoperational expectations, expect the water to come out of the taller end. A fruitful problem for five-year-olds is how to get water through a tube from a bowl at one level to another bowl at a higher level. Children typically try to blow the water through the tube only to realize that when they remove the tube from the water, there is no water to blow. Kindergarten children have solved the problem by sucking instead of blowing, and follow-up activities with siphon bottles extended their experimentation and construction of knowledge.

Sand and water provide possibilities for educational activities for children of varied ages. Primary-age children can extend experimentation to consider causality of water flow, pressure, buoyancy, absorption, evaporation, freezing, reflection, wave motion, and other phenomena. Adult scientists are still studying the differences between flowing sand and flowing water. They are trying to understand the self-organized structures in flowing sand because these seem to mimic many natural systems and may provide the basis for understanding turbulence, avalanches, earthquakes, and sun spot activity.

References

Braun, S. J., & Edwards, E. P. (1972). *History and theory of early childhood education*. Belmont, CA: Charles A. Jones.

Hawkins, F. P. (1974). *The logic of action: Young children at work*. New York: Pantheon Books.

Hill, D. M. (1977). *Mud, sand, and water*. Washington, DC: National Association for the Education of Young Children.

Kamii, C., & DeVries, R. (1978). *Physical-knowledge activities in preschool education: Implications of Piaget's theory.* Englewood Cliffs, NJ: Prentice-Hall.

Zubrowskie, B. (1981). *Water, pumps and siphons.* Boston: Little, Brown.

R. DeVries, with A. Anderson, M. Arnold, C. Black, P. Fuller, R. P. Hines, C. Samuel, & M. Wilson

Outdoor Education Provisions

Playground equipment has evolved during the twentieth century from outdoor gymnasium equipment for older children and sand gardens for younger children to a wide array of equipment featuring safety, novelty, challenge, playability, and developmental appropriateness. The National Recreation Association (1928) guidelines for playground apparatus still influence playground development. Recent national surveys of playgrounds revealed a general state of poor design, limited play function and hazardous conditions (Bruya & Langendorfer, 1988).

In recent years the U.S. Consumer Product Safety Commission (1981) developed general guidelines for safety in surfacing, layout and design, equipment, and maintenance. These guidelines now are being revised. The American Society for Testing and Materials currently is developing national standards for playground surfacing, home playground equipment and playground equipment for public use. The potential for child injuries and fatalities on playground equipment that is poorly designed, improperly installed, poorly maintained or improperly supervised, coupled with the growing number of playground injury legal actions, make it essential that national guidelines and standards be applied in play equipment design.

Modern playground equipment is designed for maximum playability needs of children (Frost & Klein, 1989, 1983). Infant/toddler play equipment provides for perceptual/motor activities such as grasping, crawling, feeling, exploring and balancing, and for language, cognitive and social development, through interactive episodes with peers, and adults,

while using equipment. With increased maturity, modifications include materials and spaces for make believe and imaginative play, construction activities, and organized games, as well as equipment for a broad array of motor activities.

The best playground designers complement contemporary play equipment with gardens, animals, nature areas, water and sand, storage facilities, and arts and crafts materials. In addition, equipment and space are zoned to enhance children's movement from place to place, provide novelty and challenge, support solitary and group play, and enrich the various forms of play in which children engage (Frost & Sunderlin, 1985; Ebensen, 1986).

Professionals are redesigning play equipment to accommodate all children, including those with special needs. Since children learn and develop through play, those who have disabilities need special play opportunities (Moore, Goltsman, & Iacofano, 1987). The quality, diversity and accessibility of playground equipment affect the quality and diversity of children's play. Integration of disabled and able-bodied children requires accessibility (ramps, paths, conveyances), safety (protective surfaces, reasonable heights, close supervision), and playability (novelty, challenge, modifications for specific disabilities).

Playground equipment can be developed by selecting manufactured equipment, using a custom builder, or building it yourself. The build-it-yourself and custom builder patterns reduce costs but need professional supervision to reduce risks in equipment safety, liability, maintenance, durability, and playability. Manufactured playground equipment represents many levels of quality. The potential purchaser should secure assistance from literature and professionals in child development. (See also Chapter 3, Section 3.5, **Safety Policies.**)

References

Bruya, L. D., & Langendorfer, S. J. (1988). *Where our children play.* Reston, VA: American Alliance for Health, Physical Education, Recreation & Dance.

Ebensen, S. B. (1986). *An outdoor classroom.* Ypsilanti, MI: High/Scope Educational Research Foundation.

Frost, J. L., & Klein, B. (1989, 1983). *Children's play and playgrounds.* Playgrounds International, P.O. Box 33353, Austin, TX 78764.

Frost, J. L., & Sunderlin, S. (eds.). (1985). *When children play.* Wheaton, MD: Association for Childhood Education International.

Moore, R. G., Goltsman, S., & Iacofano, D. S. (1987). *Play for all guidelines.* Berkeley, CA: MIG Communications.

U.S. Consumer Product Safety Commission (1981). *A handbook for public playground safety. Vol. 1: General guidelines for new existing playgrounds.* Washington, DC: United States Government Printing Office.

J. L. Frost

Equipping an Outdoor Playground

The foremost consideration in equipping an outdoor playground is providing for a variety of movement possibilities. Manufacturers recently have combined the traditional swing, ladder, and climbing bar into one innovative design system to increase the number of movement choices as well as the number of children who can play in a limited space.

The most desirable of these contemporary designs includes several means by which children can ascend and descend on the apparatus. Children between two and four years of age are more likely to utilize gradual sloping ramps and inclines, whereas five-year-olds and older children find additional appeal in spiral platforms, wooden or rope ladders, cargo nets, and metal poles. The potential for movement is affected by accessibility features such as the angle of ramps or the height of a step rise.

Scaled to a child's size, cradle swings satisfy children between five months and two years of age, while tire swings supported from three points are more suitable for larger children. Slides with wide tracks can accommodate more than one individual and do not require heights greater than five feet in order to spark excitement. Preschool children can more easily grip horizontal ladders and modernized versions of jungle gyms when the rungs or bars are no more than one inch in diameter and the distance between rungs does not exceed 14 inches. Climbing frames that incorporate 1 1/2 inch rungs, and distances of 14 to 18 inches between crossbars, allow children over the age of five years to engage in numerous traveling movements. Children's ability to manipulate different pieces of equipment affects the extent to which they can crawl through, jump over, climb up, hang from, stretch beyond, and perform balance feats. All playground apparatus should coincide with children's physical maturation and should include a gradual series of challenges.

A second consideration in equipping an early childhood playground is to select equipment that can be easily altered and/or customized to match children's movement abilities. Highly functional structures provide the option of combining one freestanding trestle with another as part of a complete playset as well as an array of equipment accessories for expanded use. Seesaw extensions, horse swings, sling seats, miniature forts or playhouse packages, and metal-free slides, are typical optional devices that entice preschool children.

In order to foster creative play, a third consideration is to select natural or raw materials instead of commercially built equipment. Young children can carry, push, sit in or upon, or stack packing crates. They enjoy climbing on concrete that has been poured to resemble large insects or sea life as well as on tree stumps of varying heights and heavy spools. They also enjoy crawling through rubber tires embedded vertically in the ground, concrete ducts, and wooden barrels. When large structures illuminated in vivid primary colors are situated on surfaces of sand, sawdust, peat moss, fine gravel, and/or shredded tree bark, young children's exploratory nature can be aroused.

In addition to these equipment considerations, there are several planning procedures to assist in the development and design of effective playgrounds. The most crucial of these aids include creating site plans, surveying innovative structural designs, and seeking qualified help in making decisions. Planning procedures should emphasize the need for adequate space, land grading, drainage, and a variety of playground surfaces for the multitude of equipment items. Beyond the important technical features, a completed project should possess a special charm for young children.

Site plans are extremely important because available space and land conditions affect both the cost and function of the play space. Therefore, sketches or diagrams should reveal information about the location and size of the area; existing shade trees or shrubbery for hiding spaces; hills, moguls, or mounds for climbing, digging, hoeing, and raking; unobstructed flat surfaces for wheeled toys, tricycles, or scooters; asphalt areas for painted patterns such as hopscotch; spaces for anchored benches and tables for sedentary play; dwellings for fixed work benches; open landscapes of adventure play; fenced areas for toddler use; patches of greenery or raised flowerbeds for beautification; sprinklers or sprays for water play; and drinking fountains and paved walking paths. In the broadest sense, a detailed site plan identifies areas where various groups of young children can pursue their play activity simultaneously. It also reinforces earlier decisions regarding equipment selection.

Innovators also should investigate the feasibility and desirability of creative structural designs. Adventure playgrounds and playscapes are perhaps the two most frequently implemented designs. Popularized in England, Germany, Sweden, and Denmark, adventure playgrounds are characterized by the use of salvaged materials informally situated on plots of land that permit children to create their own adventurous play settings. Debarked trees, old toys, play huts, sheets of old canvas, wooden blocks, unbreakable containers, steel drums, railroad ties, and old boat frames are natural incentives for the preschool child's imaginative play. Likewise, slabs of lumber, pushcarts, wooden shacks, mock bridges, sawhorses, shovels, blunt tools, pulleys, disused vehicles, and other objects stimulate the primary-age child's physical prowess and eagerness to control the environment. Playscapes, like adventure playgrounds, use nontypical designs in order to sustain play and

problem-solving activity. The multipurpose function of sculptured figures with numerous hand and foot holes, modular units, geometric shapes, triangular domes, inverted shells, cave structures, interconnected platforms, tubular configurations, and other prefabricated or abstract equipment forms intrigue children at the same time that they are suited for use in limited spaces. Planners should consider lightweight synthetic materials, nonfixed foundations, concrete installation, and nonconventional arrangements made of wood or steel.

Private contractors usually are willing to answer questions related to a specific structure's safety features, durability, serviceability, and part replacement. Local city or town parks and recreation officials can sometimes provide information that simplifies plans, and can give advice about playground maintenance. Landscape designers and nurseries might suggest methods for lowering topographical costs, while school personnel often can provide a variety of catalogs containing graphic descriptions or photographs of innovative equipment for active and imaginative young children.

Resources

Helick, R. M., & Watkins, M. T. (1973). *Elements of preschool playgrounds*. Recent Graphic Services.

Rouard, M., & Simon, J. (1983). *Children's play spaces: From sandbox to adventure playground*. New York: Overlook Press.

Wilkinson, P. F. (ed.). (1980). *Innovation in play environments*. New York: St. Martin's Press.

R. Clements

Teacher-Made Materials

Teacher-made materials are utilized by effective early childhood educators as a means of individualizing instruction. Curriculum materials designed for a particular child or group of children enable teachers to address more appropriately developmental levels, specific skill needs, and child interests within the overall early childhood program.

Teacher-made materials can be used for free exploration, to promote social interaction, to expand a theme with an integrated program, to reinforce curriculum skills, or to change the focus of play within an area such as the housekeeping or block area. At times, teachers use these materials in conjunction with a specific lesson.

There are many different types of teacher-made materials that invite young children's active participation. Materials can be open-ended, promoting exploration and social interaction, or they can elicit more convergent responses. Some teacher-made materials are created for individual use, while others are meant for use in small group activities.

Self-correcting materials reflect the influence of Maria Montessori and often are designed to reinforce specific cognitive or psycho-motor skills. These offer children immediate feedback but generally result in convergent solutions or answers. Teacher-made materials designed to promote conceptual development in areas such as weighing or measuring might include the use of natural materials, thus putting into practice tenets of John Dewey. Such materials often are utilized in a social setting. Dewey's emphasis on connecting school and community also can be implemented through teacher-made materials. For example, using photographs of children in the class and community pictures in constructing materials personalizes instruction and makes school experiences relevant to young children.

Teacher-made materials are prominent in learning centers. Sorting activities, for example, are individualized through teacher-made materials in which children classify according to one, two, or three attributes, so that children can work at their own level and pace.

Quality teacher-made materials are sturdy, attractive, have child appeal, and address children's developmental levels. Laminating certain materials with clear plastic can prevent staining, thereby increasing the material's life span. Children use them most effectively when they understand the purpose of each material, as well as what to do when they finish with the material. When a series of materials is developed to reinforce a particular concept, materials are sequenced logically. Teacher-made materials serving as child-initiated activities are stored on low shelving for easy child access. When such materials will be introduced and how long they will remain available to children are decisions made by early childhood teachers as part of instructional planning.

Colleagues, professional books, and staff development offerings are valuable idea sources for teacher-made materials. Parents and older children can provide assistance in making those materials selected as worthwhile for the early childhood program.

References

Baratta-Lorton, M. (1972). *Workjobs*. Menlo Park, CA: Addison-Wesley.

Day, B. (1988). *Early childhood education: Creative learning activities*. New York: Macmillan.

Gilbert, L. B. (1984). *I can do it! I can do it!* Mt. Rainier, MD: Gryphon House.

S. B. Cruikshank

Textbooks and Workbooks

In recent times, a growing number of early childhood educators have turned to the use of workbooks and textbooks in an attempt to make instruction more uniform and systematic. These materials, with their accompanying teacher guidebooks, offer some teachers the sense of security that they have covered all the materials appropriate for the level they teach. Is is not uncommon for teachers to seek outside professional advice about curricular methods and materials. Producers of commercial materials may be one such resource.

Teachers should be wary, however, of any materials that run counter to what they know about child growth and development. They should avoid materials, for example, that reduce learning to a lockstep, narrowly defined set of discrete skills. Materials that require young children to sit quietly for extended periods of time or to respond in a manner better suited for older children are best avoided. Materials and activities should allow children to be active participants in their learning. They should broaden the range of possibilities for interaction and response, not narrow them. Teachers need to be very clear about the goals of their program and select only those materials that support their goals in a manner that is consistent with the way young children learn.

D. S. Strickland

Textbooks: Historical Context and Present Practice

Historically, the use of textbooks and workbooks in early childhood education has been a rarity. When these structured teaching materials were used, typically it was with children in the upper range of early childhood, the primary years. The earliest examples of illustrated texts were Comenius's *Orbus Pictus* (with several words accompanying each picture) and *Janua* (a Latin dictionary with definitions in the vernacular) in the seventeenth century. These texts were used with six- to twelve-year-olds. Since that time, texts and workbooks were not prominent in early childhood programs until the late 1960s in the United States, during the expanded federal support of such projects as the preschool Head Start Program. Concurrently, the primary grade Follow Through models were intended to provide Head Start graduates with enriched instructional programs through grade three.

Two of the Follow Through models that used texts and workbooks were the Engelmann-Becker model and the Behavior Analysis model. The Engelmann-Becker model, housed at the University of Oregon, is known for developing *DISTAR*, programmed instructional materials for language, reading, and mathematics. The Behavior Analysis model, housed at the University of Kansas, is known for the *Behavior Analysis Phonics Primer* and the *Behavior Analysis Handwriting Primer*. This model also has used the *Suppes Sets and Numbers* as well as the *Sullivan Programmed Reading* materials.

Another contemporary school that focuses on more formal education in reading, writing, mathematics, and second language acquisition for preschool children, including those from low-income homes, is Doman's Better Baby Institute in Philadelphia. In this program, staff trains parents to use flash cards to teach infants beginning at two to three months of age.

There has been a gradual trend to increase the use of texts and workbooks for preacademic tasks. Publishers are catering to this trend. For instance, the long-established *Weekly Reader*, an elementary school newspaper/worksheet, now offers a prekindergarten edition. The value of using these materials is considered controversial among early childhood educators. The issue dates from tensions that arose when St. Louis in 1873 became the first United States public school system to offer kindergarten education.

The few educators who currently use texts and workbooks for teaching mainly young, low-income children, believe that these materials will help the children to catch up with the achievement of middle-class children (Engelmann, Becker, Carnine, & Gersten, 1988). Presenting research findings to support their claim, they contend that no harmful side effects result from this teacher-centered education.

The early childhood profession generally believes that texts and workbooks are developmentally inappropriate for young children (Bredekamp, 1986). This perspective holds that appropriate practice is child centered, individualized, and supports all aspects of child development, including motor, social, language, creative, self-help, self-control, self-concept, and emotional development, as well as cognitive and preacademic skills. Developmentally Appropriate Practice (DAP) focuses attention on the interactive process of children with one another, adults, and concrete materials, not as a rote practice of isolated tasks. The proponents of DAP view texts and workbooks as teacher centered, group rather than individually oriented, nonsupportive of the whole child, and noninteractive.

References

Bredekamp, S. (ed.). (1986). Position statement on developmentally appropriate practice in early childhood programs serving children from birth through age 8. *Young Children*, *41* (6), 4–29.

Engelmann, S., Becker, W. C., Carnine, D., & Gersten, R. (1988). The direct instruction Follow Through model: Design and outcomes. *Education and Treatment of Children*, *11* (4), 303–317.

E. M. Goetz

Toys

(See Section 5.5, **Technology and Educative Materials, Toys.**)

Veri-Tech

Veri-Tech is a concrete material consisting of a box that contains tiles numbered 1 through 12. Children solve visual perceptual problems that are printed in booklets, using the tiles to designate their conclusions. Children can reverse the box of tiles at the end of the activity to check for a pattern. Matching patterns are printed in the series of small pamphlets that proceed rapidly from simple to increasingly difficult challenges.

Veri-Tech is a self-checking, concrete, manipulative material that young children use in the classroom to help them develop skills in visual discrimination, visual memory, relative quantity, directionality, sequencing, auditory and sound-symbol relationships, function, and an array of other categorical and thinking skills.

Kindergarten teachers find this material most effective when it is used independently by the children, self-chosen, self-paced, and self-sequenced, using a color-coded system that links the Veri-Tech components. Successful self-selection and self-direction is insured for individual children when they record their own progress on a card, developed by the teacher. The children find this a most satisfying activity. They engage in this activity with persistence, concentration, and determination.

Reference

Brault & Bouthillier. (1977). *Mini Veri-tech*. Montreal: Author.

J. McGinn

Writing Tools

A variety of writing tools should be available for children to dictate stories and messages or to write them independently. Young children like to select their own materials for writing; therefore, paper of varied colors, textures, and sizes should be included. Pencils, felt markers, chalk, and crayons appeal to young writers. Chalkboards, small writing slates, primary typewriters, and computers add interest and variety to the tools available. An alphabet chart and a chart with all the children's names should be displayed at eye level. Three dimensional letters of various sizes, colors, and textures, including magnetic letters and alphabet books also should be included.

D. S. Strickland

5.5 Technology and Educative Materials

Technology and related educative materials increasingly have become a part of the offerings of many early childhood programs since the early 1970s. Some early childhood educators have been strongly opposed to the use of such technologies, seeing them as running counter to an educational philosophy and practice focusing on the direct engagement of children with a wide variety of sensorial and manipulative, as well as print-based materials. Proponents of the new materials, on the other hand, have argued that technology is now a firm part of our larger culture, and that children's introduction to its various forms should be as routine as exposure to any other learning tool. These diverging points of view are explored in the articles below. The articles are arranged alphabetically.

L. R. Williams

Technology as a Learning Tool

Technologies can serve as tools of learning. They can be an essential aspect of a rich educational environment only if a human teacher embraces them into a humanistic and constructivist vision of early childhood education. To some, the notion of technology serving as educator evokes cold, mechanical images inconsistent with accepted approaches to early childhood education. Simple technologies such as books, however, always have been welcome aspects of the young child's classroom. Some educators fear that even these symbolic technologies are being used too much, too soon, and worry that more modern technologies might exacerbate the problem.

These opinions ignore the observation that much of the activity in which young children engage is symbolic. They communicate with gestures and language, and employ symbols in their play, song, and art. It appears, therefore, that young children might benefit from using appropriate technology.

There are other concerns, such as the limited capacities of certain technologies. Critics have written, for example, about the limited number of colors available in some computer programs. Such criticisms miss the important issues. Newer computers can show billions of colors, but this fact does not mean that they should replace 16-color crayon sets. Either old technologies, such as crayons and paint brushes, or new ones may be the most appropriate technology in a given situation. The most important question to answer concerns what would be the highest quality environment for a particular child or group of children at a particular time.

The new and old technologies discussed in this section offer opportunities for constructive, creative learning environments. Used wisely, they promise opportunities for children to control their own learning. They also present challenges. There is a need to understand the possibilities, advantages, and disadvantages of each technology, whether old or new.

The child of today will learn about, and from, these ubiquitous technologies, whether or not teachers use them. The challenge is for teachers to use them in ways that provide a human application.

D. H. Clements

Advocacy for Quality in Technology

As the most vulnerable members of the human community, children stand to gain or lose the most in a technocracy. We need to consider what tools they will need when they mature so that they will be able to harness technology for the greater human good. Perhaps the most important tool for the next generation is the skill to recognize and demand quality in the technologies and their products.

When federal funding in the 1970s, for example, produced curricula for teaching critical viewing skills, many educators assumed that the television medium needed no overt instruction. Had visual and "television" literacy been pursued with some intensity, there might be a generation of young people whose television consumption would reflect more thoughtfulness. The same also might be said about computer software at this time.

Young children can learn to recognize and expect quality in the aesthetics, engineering, or values of technology. In time, the demands of a more literate public might influence the quality of television programming. (See also Chapter 3, Section 3.5, **Advocacy Strategies;** and **Television Issues,** below.)

M. A. Cambré

Computers

Computers are being integrated increasingly into early childhood programs. More than 25 percent of licensed preschools had microcomputers as early as 1984 (Clements, 1985; 1987). By 1990 most of them had such access. There are still debates, however, about the wisdom of this trend. Questions arise concerning young children's physical and cognitive readiness to use computers and the impact of such use upon their social and educational development.

Research and practice have shown that young children can use computers with comfort and confidence. Preschoolers also can work cooperatively with minimal instruction and supervision, if they have preliminary help. Nevertheless, adults play a significant role in successful computer use. Children are more attentive, interested, and less frustrated when an adult is available (Clements, 1987).

Young children appear to spend approximately the same amount of time playing in a computer center as they do in drawing, talking, or playing in the block or arts centers. Play in these other centers, however, does not decrease when a computer is present. Thus, the computer can be an interesting, but not engrossing, activity for young children.

In retrospect, the early concern that computers would stifle playful social interaction appears to be overstated. Children prefer social use of computers and rarely work alone. Computer use actually can facilitate positive social interactions. Positive attitudes also increase, especially when children work in groups, write on the computer using a word processor, or write computer programs in Logo (Ibid.; Clements & Natasi, 1991). In contrast to recognition of these social and emotional benefits, most peoples' conception of a computer is as a "teaching machine." Research indicates, for example, that the most dramatic gains in the use of computer-assisted instruction (CAI) have been in mathematics, especially for young children and those young children who receive compensatory education. Usually this CAI has the form of drill and practice.

There is good reason to consider alternate forms of educational computing. First, children prefer programs that are animated, oriented toward problem solving, and interactive, that give them a feeling of control over the computer (Clements, 1987). Second, the full potential of computers in education may lie in such uses. Writing and programming with computers have notable potential.

Computers can help children explore writing through word processors. From the beginning, children can experiment with letters and words without being distracted by the fine motor aspects of handwriting. They write more in this medium, take increased pride in their writing, have fewer fine motor control problems, are more willing to take risks and revise, and build a sense of competence (Ibid.).

Many age appropriate word processors include speech synthesis, so that the computer can pronounce the letter names and words that children type. Such speech increases the interactivity of the computer as a writing tool. "Talking" word processors help children build links between conversation and composition. They develop an "inner voice" for constructing and editing their writing. Talking word processors also foster collaborative writing. Children tend to gather around and read a story aloud with the synthesizer (Clements & Nastasi, in press).

Programming in the computer language Logo is another example of an alternative richer application of computers. Jean Piaget's research demonstrated that young children learn about shapes not from their perception of the objects but from the actions they perform on these objects. They must internalize their actions and abstract the corresponding spatial and geometric ideas. Using Logo, young children can act by walking a path and then using the Logo turtle to draw it on the screen. The programming helps children link their intuitions about moving and drawing to more explicit mathematical ideas. In constructing a series of commands to draw a rectangle, for example, they analyze the visual components and make conclusions about its properties. Such activity helps them to develop a more sophisticated level of thinking (Ibid.).

Research has shown that work with Logo also can develop problem-solving and creative abilities in preschoolers and primary-grade children. The teacher was a critical element in each of these successful efforts by encouraging, questioning, prompting, modeling, and generally mediating children's interaction with the computer. Logo, like word processors, provides a rich environment for thinking, but it takes an active, knowledgeable teacher to facilitate and guide this thinking (Ibid.).

In sum, educators who use computer environments such as word processing and Logo can extend the quality of experiences for young children. "Teachers should be proactive in determining what could and should be. They know that the goal is to develop problem solvers, not programmers; communicators, not word processors; fulfilled children, not early achievers. The strength of quality computer applications is not that they replace the teacher, but that they allow the teacher to focus on the human parts of teaching" (Clements, 1987, p.42).

References

Clements, D. H. (1985). *Computers in early and primary education*. Englewood Cliffs, NJ: Prentice-Hall.

Clements, D. H. (1987). Computers and young children: A review of the research. *Young Children, 43* (1), 34–44.

Clements, D. H., & Nastasi, B. K. (1991). Computers and early childhood education. In T. Kratochwill, S. Elliott, & M. Gettinger (eds.), *Advances in school psychology: Preschool and early childhood treatment directions*. Hillsdale, NJ: Erlbaum.

D. H. Clements

Glossary, Computers

The following are some of the most commonly used terms related to computer use in the classroom.

Computer Assisted Instruction (CAI)—A method of teaching that uses a computer to present instructional materials. Students interact with the computer in such activities as drill and practice, tutorials, and simulations.

Computer—A device capable of accepting information, processing that information according to instructions, and producing the results of this processing.

Graphics—Any shapes, dots, lines, and colors that are drawn on a computer. They may include such representations as pictures, graphs, maps, diagrams.

Joystick—A small box with a movable stick and one or two buttons on the top that is attached to a computer and allows children to control movement of images on the computer screen. Moving the stick moves the screen images and pressing the buttons selects or "picks up" these images.

Logo—A computer language designed to be used by young and old learners. It includes "turtle graphics" and is said to encourage mathematical thinking and problem solving.

Mouse—A device attached to the computer that allows children to control movement of images (such as a cursor or pointer) on the computer screen. It is a box-shaped object with buttons on the top, a ball underneath, and a cord (giving it the appearance of a mouse). It is rolled gently to move the screen pointer and clicked (the buttons pushed) to select or "pick up" computer images.

Speech Synthesizer—A combination of electronic equipment and computer programs that enable a computer to produce humanlike speech.

Turtle—A "pointer" on the computer screen, or an actual robot that is directed by the child to create geometric shapes or pictures.

Word Processing—Computerized typing and composing. It can be used to rearrange words, sentences, paragraphs, and larger sections of text.

D. H. Clements

Video, Robots, and Other Technologies

Schools always have used some form of technology to help children represent their knowledge, beginning with the slate board and extending to the modern personal computer. This article discusses the educational value of video, robots, and alternative input/output devices for the computer.

With the advent of video cassettes and camcorders, video has made its way into most schools. The primary use of the video cassette player has been to show prerecorded educational video tapes. The use of the camcorder is new and worthy of our attention.

Researchers have found that immediate video replay was useful in helping seven-year-olds understand the "center of gravity" concept in balancing asymmetrical blocks (Fosnot, Forman, Edwards, & Goldhaber, 1988). The teacher would freeze frame the replay just as the child was about to place a block and then ask where the block will be placed on the fulcrum. This type of immediate questioning stimulated the children to reflect on their own thinking, which was immediately confirmed by releasing the pause button on the video player.

Other researchers have used video successfully to have children reflect on the posture sequence of cartwheels, headstands, and backward rolls (Forman & Lee, 1989). Through the use of video replay, freeze frame, and slow motion, children from five to seven years of age have begun to think more analytically and inferentially about the necessity of particular postures and the dynamics of body movement. Children used articulated paper dolls to represent and rethink the video sequence of their own bodies in motion.

Robot toys generally are considered an entertainment or a means to teach hand-eye coordination. Staging games with robots can offer great educational potential. Researchers asked two children to cooperatively knock over a block tower using a wheeled robot arm (Forman & Lee, 1988). One child pushed the control buttons but was shielded from viewing the robot. The other child could see the robot, could not control it, but instructed the operator on the whereabouts of the robot as it progressed. This game made it possible for children from four to seven years of age to practice communication skills such as when a message is ambiguous, differentiating an incomplete message from incomplete understanding of robot action, and considering ways to plan for problem solving in order to establish and enhance shared meanings.

Small battery operated robots can serve many other educational goals from planning skills, to cooperative play as well as symbolic play. The unique feature of robotic toys is the fact that robots have discrete actions through button presses that must be translated into an accurate and efficient sequence of component actions.

With reference to computers, the keyboard may be particularly unsuited as a communications channel to the computer for young children. The monitor screen, a two-dimensional display, may be unsuited as a feedback device for preschoolers. Thus, new work must be done to make both the input device and the display device more appropriate.

Graphic tablets, the mouse, thermometer, pressure gauge, and light sensor are now common input devices to help children see and create representations of events. The computer industry, however, has given much less attention to the display side of computer systems. There is a proposal that computers use three-dimensional displays, like robotic dolls, electric trains, and simulated machines that display the planning that young children use when programming the computer (Forman, 1988a; 1988b). This programming initially should be done as an automatic translation of the children's spontaneous manipulation of the display devices themselves (a combined input/output device). Thus, the intuitive knowledge common to young children can be re-presented by the computer both by making the input device move and by generating some elementary notation symbols on the computer screen. Advances along these lines are rumored concerning the future work of companies such as IBM (TM), Apple (TM), and Lego (TM).

References

Fosnot, C., Forman, G., Edwards, C., & Goldhaber, J. (1988). The development of understanding of balance and the effect of training via stop-action video. *Journal of Applied Developmental Psychology, 9* (1), 1–26.

Forman, G., & Lee, M. (1989). The use of video replay to enhance young children's representation of the body in motion. Technical report: Office of Research & Development, School of Education, University of Massachusetts, Amherst.

Forman, G. (1988a). Get a code of my act: The importance of automatic translation for the representational development of young children. *Genetic Epistemology, 16* (1), 5–10.

Forman, G. (1988b). Making intuitive knowledge explicit through future technology. In G. Forman & P. Pufall (eds.), *Constructivism in the computer age* (pp. 83–101). Hillsdale, NJ: Erlbaum.

Forman, G., & Lee, M. (1988). Cooperative problem solving of young children in referential communication tasks using robots in motion. Technical report: Office of R & D, School of Education, University of Massachusetts, Amherst.

G. Forman

Television Issues

Television in the United States has been broadly available since the 1950s. Children today watch television for an average of 20 to 30 hours a week. With the advent of cable television, more than half of the country's households have been introduced to new, independent stations offering additional programs. This expanded schedule introduces children to the world as well as to music videos and R-rated movies.

The issue of children and television has been subject to social, economic, political, and advocatory considerations. Three predominant action groups during the last three decades are the Council on Children, Media and Merchandising (CCMM), the National Association for Better Broadcasting (NABB), and the Action for Children's Television (ACT). The CCMM concentrated on the need to review advertising for children during the 1960s and 1970s. The NABB has stressed responsibilities in broadcasting and awareness of the public's rights since 1950. ACT, active from 1968 to 1992, worked toward encouraging age-specific children's programming, as well as reducing the number of commercials and commercial-based programs.

Throughout the 1970s and 1980s, other groups have become involved in the children's television issue. The American Academy of Pediatrics has raised concerns about the commercialization of children's television, while the National Parent Teachers Association has focused on media literacy.

In addition to the exploitation of children as consumers, other common concerns have been prolonged inactivity and the effect of watching violence. The Surgeon General's (1972) study of television and social behavior gave credibility and some stature to the application of child development theories related to the subject of children and television.

In the early 1980s television's commercial influence increased with the deregulation of the Federal Communications Commission (FCC), which brought forth the opportunity for more commercial time during children's programming. Prior to this time there were federally imposed limits on the number of commercial minutes that could be run per hour. Although ACT, NABB, and a limited number of legislators brought attention to imposing guidelines on children's programming, the governmental and industrial supporters of the First Amendment have continued to block major changes.

The Children's Television Workshop has led efforts to improve the content of children's television with programs such as "Sesame Street." The Public Broadcasting System and some cable stations also have worked at developing quality programs.

Video games and home video recorders are two phenomena related to television that absorb the fascination of children and adults alike. Video games allow millions of children to interact with computer-animated characters while home video recorders give children access to films ranging from the benign to the most violent. The television of tomorrow, including extended interactive video forms, is likely to assume many new forms and functions that can influence children's lives.

Television's capacity to serve families is dependent on how selectively they use it. In order to help children become critical viewers, parents need to model positive television viewing habits, provide for a balance with other activities, help young children understand how television works, and encourage dialogue that allows children to express their interests and concerns about the programs that they watch.

Reference

Surgeon General's Scientific Advisory Committee on Television and Social Behavior. (1972). *Television and growing up: The impact of televised violence*. (DHEW Publication No. HSM72-90). Washington D.C.: United States Government Printing Office.

G. Forman

Television, Influences

Television has influenced the consumption of food, toys, and clothing, as well as ways of speaking and behaving among children in the United States. National surveys indicate that the average preschooler watches about 28.5 hours of television per week (A. C. Nielsen Co., 1988). Much of this viewing time is devoted to programs geared for an older audience. Six-month-old infants already are "watching" more than an hour a day of television in homes where the television set is turned on between 4 and 6.5 hours daily (Hollenbeck & Slaby, 1979). During the time when babies watch TV, there is no one reacting to their smiles and noises or encouraging the interaction that provides a basis for later social and cognitive development. In general, households have their sets on about seven hours a day even if no one is watching (Liebert & Sprafkin, 1988).

In 1990 there were no regularly scheduled daily programs designed for preschoolers on the three major networks. When children outgrow the Public Television offerings, such as "Sesame Street" and "Mr. Rogers' Neighborhood," they often graduate to the situation comedies. Many young children also watch soap operas and other programs that contain episodes of violence, sexuality, and information that may be beyond their understandings, resulting in distortions of comprehension and sometimes fear, apprehension, and confusion.

Family life has been affected by television in that 78 percent of families use TV as a babysitter, 55 percent have altered meal times, and 60 percent have changed their sleeping patterns to accommodate program schedules. A study found that the involvement in social activities dropped after television was introduced to a small town that previously had no television reception because of its geographic location (Williams & Handford, 1986).

Children have been able to learn prosocial behaviors, such as task persistence and imaginative play, however, from segments of the Public Broadcasting programs, particularly when adults mediate or intervene during the watching (Singer & Singer, 1981). In addition, preschoolers who are light television viewers of an hour or less a day, also have more sophisticated language structure, due to the time spent in play where opportunities for socialized speech were ample (Ibid.)

Controlled television viewing at ages three and four years appeared to improve vocabulary and prereading skills, although heavy television viewing predicted lower scores (Rice, Huston, Truglio, & Wright, 1987). Fast paced programs such as "Sesame Street" may interfere, however, with some of the messages that the producers intended (Bryant, Zillman, & Brown, 1983). Slower paced programs have been designed to teach children simple cognitive tasks such as sorting, comparing size, and matching colors. Among these are the Australian "Humphrey the Bear" and the English "Playschool."

The picture of the world that young children receive from television viewing is that the desirable characters are male, youthful, white, and beautiful, while handicapped, old, female, dark-skinned, or non-English-speaking people are not as important (Liebert & Sprafkin, 1988). Researchers have found that there is a reliable causal effect of television on aggressive behavior (Huesmann & Eron, 1986; NIMH, 1982; Williams & Handford, 1986). On the positive side, both experimental and correlational evidence suggest that television can promote altruism and sympathy, as well as provide effective role models for learning such social behaviors as sharing, empathy, taking turns, and cooperating (Feshbach, 1988; Liebert & Sprafkin, 1988).

Preschoolers find it difficult to distinguish program materials from advertising, much as children before the age of eight years have general difficulty separating reality from fantasy. As a result, young children are particularly vulnerable to the appeal of TV advertising (Wirth, 1988). Children persuade their parents to buy products advertised on TV (Atkins, 1982), and the toy industry has used the program content itself to advertise its wares. The Federal Trade Commission (FTC) has the power to set industrywide standards in the form of trade regulation rules that specify deceptive practices in particular industries. Currently the FTC has been weakened because it can no longer rule on "unfair" advertising.

Preschoolers in particular are at some risk unless their parents assume the responsibility to limit and control television viewing. Certainly it makes little sense to expose children younger than three years of age to television. Beyond that age, a few minutes of programming specifically designed for children, such as the Public Broadcasting offerings, will not be harmful. Actually many programs can be useful if the parent mediates by explaining ideas and enhancing the program content with discussion. If a concept is presented, for example, the parent might use this in a real-life situation, such as taking a field trip to a place suggested such as a library, firehouse, post office; reading about an idea presented; storytelling; puppet making; drawing; listening to a record related to music on the program; or play acting a segment that was viewed. When parents are involved through control of hours, careful selection of programs, and explanation or discussion, television can be a useful tool in promoting children's intellectual and social growth.

References

Anderson, D. R., & Collins. P. A. (1988). *The impact on children's education: Television's influence on cognitive development*. Washington, DC: United States Government Printing Office.

A. C. Nielsen Co. (1988). *Report on television*. New York: Author.

Atkins, C. K. (1982). Television advertising and socialization to consumer roles. In D. Pearl, L. Bouthilet, & J. Lazar (eds.), *Television and behavior: Ten years of scientific progress and implications for the eighties*, Vol. 2, Technical Reviews (pp. 191–200). Washington, DC: United States Government Printing Office.

Bryant, J., Zillman, D., & Brown, D. (1983). Entertainment features in children's educational television: Effects on attention and information acquisition. In J. Bryant & D. R. Anderson (eds.), *Children's understanding of television* (pp. 221–240). New York: Academic Press.

Cook, T. D., Appleton, H., Conner, R. F., Shaffer, A., Tamkin, G., & Weber, S. J. (1975). *Sesame Street revisited*. New York: Russell Sage.

Feshbach, N. (1988). Television and the development of empathy. In S. O. Oskamp (ed.). *Television as a social issue. Applied social psychology annual*, #8 (pp. 261–269). Beverly Hills, CA: Sage.

Hollenbeck, A. R., & Slaby, R. G. (1979). Infant visual and vocal responses to television. *Child Development, 50* (1), 41–45.

Huesmann, L. R., & Eron, L. D. (eds.). (1986). *Television and the aggressive child: A cross-national comparison.* Hillsdale, NJ: Erlbaum.

Huston, A. C., Watkins, B., & Kunkel, D. (1984). Public policy and children's television. *American Psychologist, 44* (2), 424–433.

Johnson, N. (1967). *How to talk back to your television set.* Boston: Little, Brown.

Liebert, R. M., & Sprafkin, J. (1988). *The early window: Effects of television on children and youth* (3rd ed.). New York: Pergamon.

Pearl, D., Bouthilet, L., & Lazar, J. (eds.). (1982). *Television and behavior: Ten years of scientific progress and implications for the eighties.* DHHS Publication Nos. ADM82-1195, Vol. 1, and ADM82-1196, Vol. 2. Washington, DC: United States Government Printing Office.

Rice, M. L., Huston, A. C., Truglio, R., & Wright, J. C. (1987). Words from *Sesame Street:* Learning vocabulary while viewing. Unpublished manuscript. University of Kansas, Lawrence, KS.

Robinson, J. P. (1981). Television and leisure time: A new scenario. *Journal of Communication, 31* (1), 120–130.

Roper Organization. (1987). *America's watching: Public attitudes toward television.* Television Information Office, 745 Fifth Avenue, NY, NY 10151.

Schneider, C. (1987). *Children's television: The art, the business, and how it works.* Chicago: NTC Business Books.

Signorelli, N. (ed.). (1985). *Role portrayal and stereotyping on television: An annotated bibliography of studies related to women, minorities, aging, sexual behavior, health, and handicaps.* Westport, CT: Greenwood Press.

Singer, J. L., & Singer, D. G. (1981). *Television, imagination, and aggression: A study of preschoolers.* Hillsdale, NJ: Erlbaum.

Surgeon General's Scientific Advisory Committee on Television and Social Behavior. (1972). *Television and growing up: The impact of televised violence.* (DHEW Publication No. HSM72-90). Washington, DC: United States Government Printing Office.

Williams, T. M., & Handford, A. G. (1986). Television and other leisure activities. In T. M. Williams (ed.), *The impact of television: A natural experiment in three communities* (pp. 143–213). New York: Academic Press.

Wirth, T. (1988). The television environment: Cultivating the wasteland. In S. O. Oskamp (ed.), *Television as a social issue: Applied social psychology annual,* #8 (pp. 69–78). Beverly Hills, CA: Sage.

D. G. Singer & J. L. Singer

Glossary, Television

The following are terms, organizations, and practices commonly associated with television.

A. C. Nielsen & Co—A rating service that provides figures that are percentages (shares) of the total possible audience that a television program attracts. About 1,200 selected households representing a cross section of United States homes are paid a small sum so that patented audiometers can record television set activity.

Arbitron—A rating service using mail, telephone, and interview surveys as well as electronic meters that estimate the viewing audience for local TV stations.

Action for Children's Television (ACT)—A group of citizens based in Massachusetts, founded by Peggy Charren, that lobbied until 1992 for quality children's programming and for protection of children from exploitation by commercials.

Cable TV—Television service that provides households, for a fee, with a cable connection to a master antenna that picks up distant television signals.

Children's Advertising Review Unit (CARU)—Established in 1974 by the Better Business Bureau as a self-regulatory agency that promotes responsible advertising to children and responds to the public's concerns. CARU monitors broadcast and cable television, radio, and print media.

Corporation for Public Broadcasting—An autonomous board of 15 members appointed by the U.S. President on the advice and consent of the Senate. It is a means of channeling federal tax money into public television.

Federal Communications Commission (FCC)—Created in 1934 by an act of the U.S. Congress, this government agency has the power to grant a license to a broadcast based on the fact that public interest, convenience, and necessity would be served by such a grant. The FCC strictly adheres to the First Amendment. The FCC can limit an individual or group from operating more than one station in the same service (AM, FM, or TV), in the same geographic market, or more than 12 TV stations reaching more than 25 percent of United States television households.

Federal Trade Commission (FTC)—A government agency that regulates interstate commerce and in 1938 was given the power to protect consumers from false advertisements and unfair or deceptive acts or practices.

Public Broadcasting Service (PBS)—A service that develops and manages national programs serving the public interest. PBS was created by the Corporation for Public Broadcasting.

Satellite System—A device that receives and then retransmits TV signals over vast distances.

D. G. Singer & J. L. Singer

Textbooks

(See Section 5.4, Curriculum Materials, Textbooks and Workbooks, and Textbooks: Historical Context and Present Practice.)

Toys

Toys are objects that children play with, often miniature replicas of a familiar thing. They are ancient in origin. Evidence from archaeologists' digs suggest that in all societies, humans of every age have played with toys.

Until fairly recently, children's toys and playthings in the United States were homemade. The child either made toys out of rocks, sticks, seed pods, and other found objects, or used as toys things that adults discarded. Other toys were constructed by the child's parents or some other adults. Corn husks were twisted into dolls, wood whittled into wheeled pull toys or into a toy animal.

In the late 1800s, toy distributors imported and marketed European playthings. F.A.O. Schwarz is credited with being the first company to import and market toys in the United States (Schroeder, 1971). Currently, thousands of toys are manufactured and marketed in the United States, and the toy industry is big business.

Children play with toys to learn about their world rather than to pass the time. By playing with toys children develop fine and large motor skills, social concepts, intelligence, and creativity. Toys enable them to work off excess energy, express emotion, take initiative, and develop self-confidence. Because toys serve so many functions for children's growth, development, and learning, there is no one right set of toys for any one child (Oppenheim, 1987). Age is a factor that differentiates the suitability of toys.

Some toys are chosen for children to construct and create with, others for children to play together with peers. Toys may be used in "make believe" play, or outdoors for large muscle activity as children play ball, ride bikes, or fly kites. Toys such as stuffed animals also may be used passively, as a comfort for children, or for quiet, solitary play.

Open-ended toys can be used in any number of ways and do not lock the child into any one specific use. Children can use their imaginations with them and make their own decisions about their use. For example, blocks, clay, cardboard boxes, wooden farm animals, and construction blocks can be used for a number of purposes and in a variety of ways. The child must decide what to do with the toy, how to do it, and when she or he has fulfilled the goal. A detailed fire engine, on the other hand, can be used only one way, as a fire engine. The adult purchaser already has made the decisions for the child.

The major issue surrounding children's toys is commercialization. In order to sell toys, manufacturers advertise them as being educational, although toys often focus on the development of narrow, academic skills. Because they negate children's exploratory, active play, they may serve to limit their learning. Then too, toys are advertised as appropriate for the widest age range possible, although they may be dangerous for younger children or provide little challenge for the older ones.

A large issue is the licensing of toys. The Toy Manufacturers of America estimate that currently, nearly 50 percent of all toys are licensed products. These toys are not just advertised in between cartoons or television shows, they are the star of their own show (Ibid., p. 8). Licensed, the toy's likeness appears on greeting cards, records, books, diapers, lunch boxes, pencils, clothing, and hundreds of other items. This type of marketing "defines the kinds of toys produced, limits the kinds of toys we're buying, and ultimately constricts the quality of children's play itself" (Ibid., p. 7).

References

Oppenheim, J. (1987). *Buy me! Buy me!* New York: Pantheon Books.

Schroeder, J. J. (1971). *The wonderful world of toys, games, and dolls: 1860–1930.* Chicago: Follett.

C. Seefeldt

Toys and Equipment, Annotated List of*

The following list identifies toys and equipment commonly used in early childhood settings.

Infant to Twelve Months

Big Muscles:
    musical crib mobile, dangling toys for crib and carriage, bright plush balls

Little Muscles:
    rattles, teething rings, suction-base rattles, squeeze toys, busy box board, plastic bottles and toys for filling and dumping, bath toys, rubber blocks, simple cars for rolling

Make-Believe:
    Unbreakable mirror, dolls, and animals, toy phone

Art Materials:
    Variety of bright pictures

Furniture/Big Equipment:
    infant swing,

Books:
    cloth books

Toddlers (12–36 months)

Big Muscles:
    small wagon to fill and dump, low slide, infant swing with arms and back, ride toys to straddle (no pedals), small rocking horse, push-and-pull toys with noise

*Reprinted with permission of Oppenheim, J. (1989). *Buy me! Buy me!* New York: Pantheon.

Little Muscles:
    stacking and nesting toys, large peg-board toys, core with color rings, shape-sorting boxes and boards, hammer boards, large pop beads, drum, bath toys

Make-Believe:
    housekeeping toys such as mop, broom, vacuum, dishes and pots; rubber (tubbable) doll, doll's bed, small carriage, soft dolls; toy phone, teddy bear, dashboard and steering wheel toy, pocketbook, big ticking toy watch, toy cars

Construction:
    colored blocks, large hollow blocks (cardboard), oversized plastic snap blocks, sand toys: pail and shovel

Art Materials:
    paper, playdough, fat washable crayons

Furniture/Big Equipment:
    small table and chair, rocking chair

Preschoolers (3–6 years)

Big Muscles:
    animals on wheels, small trikes, straddle and pedal-type fire engine, car, tractor; full-size rocking horse, wagon, wheelbarrow, small sled, roller skates; jungle gym, medium-size slide, board for balancing, see-saw, punching bag, adjustable swing; sandbox toys such as tractor, snowplow, steam shovel, dump truck

Little Muscles:
    large beads for stringing, wind-up toys that make something happen, Jack-in-the-box, plastic tiles, parquetry blocks, lacing cards, pegboard, small garden tools, bubble pipe, rhythm instruments such as drum, cymbals, maracas

Make-Believe:
    housekeeping toys such as mop, broom, pots and pans, play dishes, vacuum cleaner, toy ironing board and iron, rubber (tubbable) doll with easy-on and -off clothes, doll carriage, doll dishes, doll bed and blankets; hand puppets, dress-up clothes and accessories such as pocketbooks, hats, shoes, jewelry, scarves, doctor and nurse kit; mini-world toys such as farms, airports, villages, trucks, cars, and people

Construction:
unpainted wooden unit blocks, non-electric trains and tracks, odd-shaped wooden blocks such as arches, ramps, y's, scaled-down people, animals, trucks and cars for block play, inter-locking blocks (Lego-type)

Art Materials:
watercolor markers, pregummed stickers, clay, large crayons, paper, pencils, playdough, poster paint, large brushes, fingerpaint, blackboard and chalk, paste, collage materials

Games & Puzzles:
screw-type toys, Colorform-type sticker toys, picture lotto, simple puzzles (start with whole-object pieces)

Furniture/Big Equipment:
sandbox, play stove, sink, oven, refrigerator, playhouse/fort (large box); workbench with vise, hammer, nails, saw, wood scraps; phonographs and records

*Early Middle Years** (6–8 years)*

Big Muscles:
jump rope, ice/roller skates, ring toss, skis, scooter, kites, horseshoes, small bike, croquet set, lightweight bat and ball, mitt, fishing gear

Little Muscles:
magnets, magnifying glass, pick-up sticks (wood are best), flashlight, harmonica, simple binoculars, tops, jacks, marbles, yo-yo

Make-Believe:
doll furniture, doll house, doll clothes and accessories; puppets and stage, toy sewing machine, toy register, miniature gas station, costumes for dress-up

Construction:
Tinkertoys, Lincoln Logs, simple Erector sets, Lego construction

Art Materials:
plasticine (nondrying clay), self-hardening clay, regular crayons, markers, simple cartridge-type camera

Games & Puzzles:
simple board games, card games, puzzles (20–100 pieces), dominoes,

anagrams letter games, checkers, Chinese Checkers, bingo

Furniture/Big Equipment:
tent, desk, bookshelf, phonograph, tape recorder

Crafts:
small wooden bead kit, knitting spool, simple sewing equipment (blunt needles), hand-operated drill, paper dolls, simple loom for weaving

Middle Years (8 years and up)

Big Muscles:
badminton set, basketball hoop and ball, magnetic darts, swimfins and goggles, medium-size bike, large sled, toboggan skates, skis, regular bat and ball, mitt

Little muscles:
remote-control cars, magic tricks, gyroscope, jewelry kits

Make-believe:
electric trains, preteen dolls with clothes and equipment, marionettes

Construction:
simple plastic models, erector sets with motors, models with engines,

Art Materials:
pastel crayons, color pencils, watercolor paints, papier mâché materials, clay, acrylic paints, oil paints, electronic drawing

Games & Puzzles:
board games that promote number, money, and word-building skills; card games, jigsaw puzzles (100 pieces and up), map puzzles, (United States and the world), calculator, electronic games, chess

Furniture/Big Equipment:
globe, bulletin board, simple microscope, telescope, typewriter, tape recorder with mike and blank tapes, walkie-talkie

Crafts:
printing set, paper model books of mini-worlds, lanyard lace, leathercraft material, wood-burning kit, plaster of paris kit, carving tools, nonpower woodworking materials, bead looms, ceramics

**Many toys from the preschool years will continue to be used by this age group.

J. Oppenheim

5.6 Physical Environments and Classroom Management

The most creative ideas for program plans and the most caring of teachers can fail to help young children learn unless teachers have provided for effective ways for communication to take place. Classroom situations at their best are somewhat artificial. Children in groups, therefore, need the security of routines, knowing what to expect, when to expect it, where to find, use, and store materials, and to whom they can turn for assistance and friendship.

Teachers can help children to have a more optimal learning experience by arranging physical environments in ways that help young children feel secure, independent, and competent; and organizing with children the management procedures that support these purposes. In these ways, teachers and children can produce civilized opportunities for communication.

The articles in this section appear in the two parts of physical environment and classroom management, respectively, although the content of these arrangements is interdependent. Within each part, the articles are in alphabetical order to facilitate retrieval.

D. P. Fromberg

Physical Environment

The physical environment in early childhood settings includes classroom arrangement and use of space, placement of curriculum materials and the display of child creations, and the use of outdoor space. How these elements are arranged and utilized reflects the teacher's philosophical view of how children develop and learn. In turn, the physical environment gives strong messages to young children regarding what learning is about and what their role should be in the educative process.

Many of the components of a child-centered physical environment can be traced to the work of early educators. John Dewey's views of interaction, constructive activity, and continuity led to providing natural materials such as wood and yarn to promote problem solving and a housekeeping area that builds on home and family life (Weber, 1984). Educators such as Jean-Jacques Rousseau, Friedrich Froebel, and Margaret and Rachel McMillan made use of the outdoor environment to support programmatic goals. The child-sized furniture evident today, as well as the notion of a "prepared environment," originated with Maria Montessori's work. Maintaining the child's perspective when organizing the physical environment continues to be an important guideline in contemporary developmentally appropriate practice.

Research indicates that spatial or social crowding affects children negatively, especially when space ratios are below 25 square feet per child (Ramsey & Reid, 1988). Recent concern for children's safety and well-being has resulted in state and local licensing and regulatory requirements. The Accreditation Criteria of the National Academy of Early Childhood Programs (Bredekamp, 1986) cites 35 square feet per child of usable activity space as a minimum, although between 40 and 50 square feet per child is preferred. A minimum of 75 square feet of outdoor play area per child also is suggested (Ibid.), and groups such as the Child Welfare League recommend 200 square feet.

An ongoing role of today's most thoughtful early childhood teachers is to structure existing physical environments to accommodate children's cognitive, language, social-emotional, physical, and aesthetic development. With physical arrangements, it is important to consider physical and safety needs, as well as instructional and socialization issues. Effective teachers make deliberate decisions that consider the question, "Does this physical arrangement reflect programmatic goals?"

They provide functional and aesthetically pleasing space for total group, small group, and individualized activities. The extent to which routines such as rest, toileting needs, feeding, and cleanup are easily managed largely depends upon physical arrangements. Cleanup of "messy" projects, for example, is expedited if activities are situated near a sink. Traffic patterns and safety issues also are important considerations as teachers plan for room arrangements and outdoor play provisions.

Individual needs also can influence space utilization. Due to the high activity level of child-centered programs, private spaces where children can seek solitude are important. Both children and adults need personal storage areas and ideally, facilities also include space for parent resources and home/school communication. Classrooms that have a comfortable homelike quality enhance home/school continuity.

Research suggests that schools can promote complex social interactions among children by including well-defined areas for groups of two to five children, protection from disruption and intrusion, enough small areas, and different seating pattern options, depending on the chosen task (Phyfe-Perkins & Shoemaker, 1986). Provisions for using space also can influence adult-child interactions. Diapering infants, for example, can provide for meaningful social development when caregiver and child interact in a quiet setting away from the classroom mainstream.

Children's developmental levels, ease of child access to spaces, and maintenance issues provide guides for the selection and display of materials. Research shows that the quality, number and accessibility of play materials, as well as the types of moveable objects provided in the environment, affect the types of play in which children engage (Ramsey & Reid, 1988). Open-ended materials such as sand or blocks have child appeal and foster multiple use, and areas such as housekeeping promote socialization and make-believe play. Child accessibility of materials increases their usage, along with expediting routines such as cleanup.

Recently, educators have considered the role of the classroom environment in stimulating literacy. They note that a literacy environment contains interesting things to read and write about, recording tools and materials, places to settle down, books everywhere, references, and display spaces and tools (Loughlin & Martin, 1987). Labeling equipment and materials, and providing functional print in the form of recipes, songs, charts, or sign-up sheets give children real reasons to read and write. Since child ownership is important in such environments, children's own work is prominently displayed at children's eye level.

Teachers use information gained from ongoing assessment, such as observation, to understand individual needs and interests, and then select related materials and activities. In addition, materials that reflect children and adults who are of color, who are "differently abled," and who are engaged in nonstereotypic gender activities should be provided (Derman-Sparks, 1989).

Providing for outdoor space should take into account developmental appropriateness, safety, complexity, challenge, creativity, durability, maintenance, and comfort (Vergeront, 1988). Evaluating outdoor play space in terms of variety and complexity can provide helpful guidelines for outdoor space design (Kritchevsky, Prescott, & Walling, 1977).

Special needs of children with handicaps should be considered in the design of both indoor and outdoor space. Ramps, wide doorways, and accessible materials contribute to the inclusiveness that should characterize school environments for young children.

References

Bredekamp, S. (ed.). (1986). *Accreditation criteria and procedures of the National Academy of Early Childhood Programs*. Washington, DC: National Association for the Education of Young Children.

Derman-Sparks, L., & the A.B.C. Task Force (1989). *Anti-bias curriculum: Tools for empowering young children*. Washington, DC: National Association for the Education of Young Children.

Kritchevsky, S., Prescott, E., & Walling, L. (1977). *Planning environments for young children: Physical space*. Washington, DC: National Association for the Education of Young Children

Loughlin, C., & Martin, M. (1987). *Supporting literacy: Developing effective learning environments*. New York: Teachers College Press.

Phyfe-Perkins, E., & Shoemaker, J. (1986). Indoor play environments: Research and design implications. In G. Fein & M. Rivkin (eds.), *The young children at play: Reviews of research, Vol. 4*. Washington, DC: National Association for the Education of Young Children.

Ramsey, P. G., & Reid, R. (1988). Designing play environments for preschool and kindergarten children. In D. Bergen (ed.), *Play as a medium for learning and development: A handbook for theory and practice*. Portsmouth, NH: Heinemann.

Vergeront, J. (1988). *Places and spaces for preschool and primary (Outdoors)*. Washington, DC: National Association for the Education of Young Children.

Weber, E. (1984). *Ideas influencing early childhood education: A theoretical analysis*. New York: Teachers College Press.

S. B. Cruikshank

Learning Centers

Learning centers are designated areas where young children learn to assume responsibility for their learning by interacting with their environment and with each other. Inherent in a learning centers approach is the belief that instructional experiences and materials should be planned carefully to meet children's interests, needs, learning styles, and developmental levels.

Historically, the use of learning centers evolved from the work of such educators as Johann Pestalozzi and John Dewey (Kimes Myers & Maurer, 1987). Susan Isaacs' work in England during the 1920s also reflects the hands-on approach evident in learning centers, as well as the notion that children's interests should be the organizing principle of early childhood curricula (Isaacs, 1966/1930).

Basic types of learning centers include "permanent" centers and "temporary" centers. Centers such as blockbuilding and the library corner generally remain in the classroom all year, although activities, themes, and materials will be varied over time. Other centers such as cooking or a dinosaur center may be "temporary" due to children's changing interests, space restraints, or the availability of adult supervision.

Space, safety, and management issues must be considered in establishing centers. Space should be clearly delineated by low dividers and/or tape on the floor if children are expected to use materials within a given area. Ideally, more quiet centers should be located adjacent to each other so active pastimes, such as woodworking, do not disturb others. Additionally, teachers should consider situating in close proximity those centers that offer cross-center possibilities. Blocks, for example, might be used to create structures within a housekeeping/store/ hospital area, thereby encouraging creativity and flexible use of materials.

Management issues to consider when planning centers include the number of children each center can accommodate; introduction, storage, and cleanup of materials; scheduling; and traffic flow. If centers are to be self-directing, children need to have a clear understanding (through pictorial and/or print directions or teacher introduction) of center guidelines. Safety issues such as fire exits and electrical outlets also must be taken into account as centers are established.

One of the many benefits of centers is that children can make meaningful decisions and can begin to monitor their own learning. Many teachers initiate learning centers with "free choice" but gradually move to using a Choice Chart accompanied by simple record keeping. During the course of a week, for example, children might check off on their individual center records those centers that they visited. In some settings, teachers and children attempt to choose each center at least once a week.

The role of the early childhood teacher with regard to learning centers includes ongoing planning, observation, circulation, and record keeping. To be responsive to children's changing needs and interests, centers should change over time. This entails planning each center on a weekly basis and linking center activities to current curriculum activities. Teachers can document anecdotally their observations of children working in centers, thus providing valuable knowledge about children's cognitive, social-emotional, and psychomotor growth. Then they can use this information for systematic planning of centers.

References

Isaacs, S. (1966/1930). *Intellectual growth of young children*. New York: Schocken.

Kimes Myers, B., & Maurer, K. (1987). Teaching with less talking: Learning centers in the kindergarten. *Young Children, 42* (5), 20–27.

S. B. Cruikshank

Space, Amount and Use of

Minimal legal standards for the amount and kind of space in early childhood physical environments grow out of a belief that the physical environment influences behavior. Most states specify the minimum number of square feet of space to be provided per child. The average is about 35 square feet, although the range is from 25 to 35 square feet. Along with other health, safety, and licensing requirements, there is variation across the states' human service department policies.

Current attention also has focused on the environment's impact on learning and curricula, as well as on the behaviors and interactions of both children and teachers. A well-planned learning environment considers the effect of physical space on programs and includes play units, boundaries, potential units, simple units, complex units, paths, and dead space (Prescott, Jones, & Kritchevsky, 1972). The quality of space can predict differences in both teachers' and children's behavior.

The arrangement of available space and materials influences children's actions, language, the making of choices, relationships with others, and the way materials are used. The environment influences cognitive development, as well as many social characteristics (Weinstein & Thomas, 1987). Some observers have found that four characteristics of the arranged learning environment may affect development, including spatial organization, provisioning for learning materials, arrangement, and organizing for special purposes (Loughlin & Suina, 1982). They have found that arrangements and usage tend to stabilize in classrooms, thus inhibiting adaptive changes.

Planned environmental utilization also has been found to promote literacy development (Loughlin & Martin, 1987). Optimum use of space potentials with varied print and nonprint materials can provide general information and opportunities for genuine communication.

When staff members have a clear picture of program purposes and goals, as well as a clear plan for using the environment to support specific curriculum needs and learning, analysis and prediction regarding space appear to be effective.

References

Loughlin, C., & Martin, M. (1987). *Supporting literacy.* New York: Teachers College Press.

Loughlin, C., & Suina, J. (1982). *The learning environment.* New York: Teachers College Press.

Prescott, E., Jones, E., with Kritchevsky, S. (1972). *Day-care as a child-rearing environment, Vol. 2.* Washington, DC: National Association for the Education of Young Children.

Weinstein, C., & Thomas, D. (1987). *Spaces for children: The built environment and child development.* New York: Plenum.

M. D. Martin

Special Education Provisions

Learning environments for children with disabilities are similar to those for all children. Educators stress the importance of "responsive, contingent environments . . . in which the infant's actions cause something predictable to happen" (Hanson & Lynch, 1989, p. 190), regardless of whether the setting is home or center based. Children with disabilities, according to these educators, are particularly vulnerable to developing "learned helplessness" (Seligman, 1975), in which they may learn skills but never seem to learn how to use them spontaneously.

Setting up the environment so that young children with disabilities learn that their actions can produce any number of results provides the motivation for continued learning. The contingencies can be either socially based, such as adults who recognize and respond to child cues, or physical in nature, such as positioning toys within easy (or even accidental) reach of the child, or selecting toys based on their action properties.

Young children with visual disabilities are particularly prone to the "fairy godmother syndrome" (Ferrell, 1985). This is actually a phenomenon that can be traced more to the adults in the environment than to the child, as it results from an overzealousness to assist and protect. Unfortunately, when people and objects appear out of nowhere and disappear back again, the learned helplessness that results also may lead to cognitive delay.

Another factor in creating learning environments involves the selection of age-appropriate toys. Toys should be selected for their ability to stimulate the acquisition of the next skill level, but should also reflect the child's chronological age. Nothing does more to stigmatize a child than to observe him or her playing with a toy normally reserved for play by much younger children. It immediately marks the child as developmentally delayed or mentally retarded. Choosing instructional materials for their critical function—what they might teach, rather than what they were presumed to teach—can assist in the integration of young children with disabilities by providing a common ground for all children in the classroom.

Many children with disabilities have specialized equipment needs. Children with orthopedic impairments may have such appliances as wheelchairs, walkers, standing tables, prone boards, scooters, modified chairs, wedges, and bolsters that assist them in independent movement, but that consume space in the classroom and may prevent social interaction. Classrooms should be arranged to promote child mobility without obstacles, including an area for storage. Additional aids and devices, ranging from adapted eating utensils for orthopedically impaired children, computers, and braille writers, to closed circuit televisions for children with visual disabilities, should be stored so that children can obtain them independently.

The physical design of the center-based program is modeled generally on research on early childhood environments. When the center-based program serves infants, however, some specialists advocate a homelike setting, with furniture and activities arranged much as they would be in the infant's home (Raynor, 1977). Because children with disabilities frequently have difficulty generalizing newly learned skills from the school environment to

home and vice versa, the homelike setting might foster learning by reducing the demands of the task.

Some early childhood special education classrooms also may include areas within them for the provision of related services. While related services traditionally have been offered on a pull-out basis (children are removed from the classroom and treated in another location), an emphasis on transdisciplinary teamwork has led to the provision of occupational and physical therapy within the classroom, with the active involvement of the teacher and paraprofessional. Research currently is underway to test the efficacy of both of these approaches.

References

Ferrell, K. A. (1985). *Reach out and teach*. New York: American Foundation for the Blind.

Hanson, M. J., & Lynch, E. W. (1989). *Early intervention*. Austin, TX: Pro-Ed.

Raynor, S. (1977). *The workbook: A manual for program development for visually impaired preschool children and their parents*. Ingham Intermediate School District, Mason, MI.

Seligman, M. (1975). *Helplessness: On depression, development and death*. San Francisco: Freeman.

K. A. Ferrell

Classroom Management

In its broad sense, classroom management focuses on maintaining an orderly classroom environment that promotes learning. Early childhood educators' managerial roles include the interdependent areas of classroom instruction, classroom climate, and adult interactions.

In managing classroom instruction, teachers plan appropriate learning experiences geared toward children's interests and cognitive/language, socioemotional, and psychomotor development. Program continuity can be enhanced when teachers plan across age/grade levels and coordinate with children's previous teachers. Effective teachers appear to choose activities with high levels of child involvement (Kauchak & Eggen, 1989). These activities are successful because they result in minimal amounts of student behaviors that interfere with the teacher's or other students' time.

In addition to planning learning experiences, teachers also must determine when and how activities should be implemented and culminated. This entails considering scheduling and pacing, the social interactions or grouping arrangements that will bring about desired outcomes, and the most appropriate materials to meet programmatic goals. Since child-centered programs utilize many concrete materials, classroom management involves creating or securing materials that may or may not be commercially available, sorting and retrieving materials, and determining how materials will be displayed for easy child access.

Part of teachers' managerial role includes the establishment of assessment and record-keeping procedures. Documented teacher observations, sociograms, interest inventories, and teacher checklists all produce information valuable for future instructional planning and for meeting individual needs. Such ongoing assessment also can guide decisions such as how long materials should remain in a given area or ways in which to modify learning centers.

The classroom climate is integrally related to instruction. Effective managers establish a climate with high expectations for all students (Kauchak & Eggen, 1989). How classroom space is organized communicates how independent and responsible the teacher wants the child to be (Fromberg, 1987). Classroom routines such as taking attendance or collecting milk money also can be undertaken in ways that promote independence, child ownership, and learning. For example, children entering the classroom can hang their printed name card under their photograph to indicate their presence that day.

Discipline is an important part of classroom management and should help young children develop self-control in appropriate ways (Spodek, Saracho, & Davis, 1987). Rules should be kept simple and to the minimum required for safe, smooth classroom operation and should be firmly, consistently enforced.

Primary-age children can benefit from involvement in establishing such guidelines. Adults can maintain a positive classroom climate when they indicate disapproval of a child's behavior, rather than disapproval of the child.

Change can be stressful for young children, and teacher preparation for transitions can ease anxiety (Bredekamp, 1986). Comments such as, "You can have one more turn on the slide, and then it's time to go in," often can relieve stress and prevent discipline problems.

Another area of classroom management involves adults such as paraprofessionals and volunteers. It is crucial that other adults know what teachers expect them to do on a given day and in what area they are to work in order to maximize their instructional contributions. In addition, classroom climate will be enhanced if these adults know classroom guidelines and the teacher's preferred method of discipline.

Management also entails the creation of structures for frequent home-school communication. Caregivers, for example, may write daily comments in a notebook that goes home with the child and returns the next day with parental information and comments. Along with frequent conferences, teachers also may keep checklists so that parents receive phone calls or visits at least once a month. When staff members, parents, and teachers interact frequently, children reap the benefits of well-designed and well-managed programs.

References

Bredekamp, S. (ed.). (1987). *Developmentally appropriate practice in early childhood programs serving children from birth through age 8.* Washington, DC: National Association for the Education of Young Children.

Fromberg, D. P. (1987). *The full-day kindergarten.* New York: Teachers College Press.

Kauchak, D., & Eggen, P. (1989). *Learning and teaching: Research-based methods.* Boston: Allyn and Bacon.

Spodek, B., Saracho, O., & Davis, M. (1987). *Foundations of early childhood education.* Englewood Cliffs, NJ: Prentice-Hall.

S. B. Cruikshank

Discipline

The word "discipline" connotes different meanings, such as guidance, punishment, behavior management, and others. Differences in attitude toward discipline have historical roots. As early as the seventeenth century, clerics offered contrasting opinions about childhood and the consequent nature of education and discipline. One view, that the child tended toward evil, suggested rigorous education with strict, even harsh, discipline. Another view, that the child was innocent and impressionable, suggested kindlier educational and disciplinary practices. With modern permutations, these conflicting interpretations still persist.

In an effective early childhood program, discipline is not just a matter of enforcing compliance to adult standards, but rather of guiding toward the development of socially responsive personal skills. Commonly discussed in the literature are the abilities to express strong feelings in acceptable ways, get along with others, and make responsible decisions.

Researchers have provided useful information about the nature of adult-child interactions that promote these abilities. Piaget's work has taught that children construct knowledge about social situations as a function of their experience over time, and that teachers must adapt expectations to what children, at their level of development, can understand. The theories of Erikson and Maslow, corroborated by research on attachment and self-esteem, indicate that warm adult-child relations are prerequisites for children's learning prosocial behaviors. *Unconditional positive regard* for the child, even while the adult addresses mistakes in behavior, is accepted early childhood practice.

The consensus in early childhood literature is that *positive discipline*, or child guidance, is the approach of choice. A firm but friendly guidance approach to discipline helps children learn from mistakes, but does not punish them for making mistakes. Recognizing that the young child gains most from success, the adult works to reduce frustrations that can lead to mistaken behavior. Most of all, the adult models communication skills that she or he would like the children to live by.

A first component of guidance discipline is prevention. The use of developmentally appropriate practice that allows for choices, physical activity, relaxation, and individual expression is important. A second component is the use of mediation skills. The teacher facilitates children's efforts at solving problems through encouragement, individual discussions, and group meetings. Third, the teacher intervenes without humiliating. She or he avoids public embarrassment, focuses on behavior rather than personalities, directs attention to alternatives, and uses "time out" as a last resort, a "cool down" time before individual discussion can occur. Fourth, the teacher problem-solves serious mistaken behavior. She or he collaborates with staff, parents, the child, and other professionals to understand the behavior, plan strategies, and evaluate results. (The teacher recognizes that serious mistaken behavior almost always is due to trouble in the child's life that cannot be handled by the the child alone.)

Fifth, the teacher practices reconciliation. Forgiveness helps children to come through conflicts with self-esteem intact, and thus better able to handle problems in the future. Reconciliation is also important because children depend on their caregivers and teachers, who can also make mistakes.

References

Hendrick, J. (1990). *The whole child: Developmental education for the early years.* Columbus, OH: Merrill.

Marlon, M. (1987). *Guidance of young children.* Columbus, OH: Merrill.

Minnesota Association for the Education of Young Children. (1987). *Developmentally appropriate guidance of young children.* St. Paul, MN: MnAYEC.

D. Gartrell

Pacing Instruction

Pacing refers to the teacher's process of organizing, and the frequency of implementing, learning experiences, while considering individual and group differences. Teachers must understand children's needs, abilities, and interests in order to decide what learning opportunities will be provided, when these will be scheduled, and the duration of learning experiences that "anticipate children's attention spans" (Fromberg, 1987, p. 67).

Effective pacing takes place when teachers provide children with many opportunities for choosing among varied activities, and children are able to examine in-depth projects that are intellectually, socially, and emotionally stimulating (Katz & Chard, 1989). Children also should be involved with establishing rules, procedures, and expectations for interacting within the learning environment; included in the planning of appropriate learning projects; and follow a flexible schedule.

Children become responsible for their own learning as they practice self-pacing. Teachers can empower children's decision making through deliberate planning and revision of the learning environment. A learning centers approach, for example, makes it possible for children to choose a center, complete a task, and clean up.

Pacing continuously involves the teacher's reflective decision making and sensitivity to young children who are involved in meaningful activities. Teachers who facilitate effective pacing understand child development, consider the child's perspective, and recognize each child's disposition to the learning environment (Marion, 1987).

References

Fromberg, D. P. (1987). *The full-day kindergarten.* New York: Teachers College Press.

Katz, L. G., & Chard, S. C. (1989). *Engaging children's minds: A project approach.* Norwood, NJ: Ablex.

Marion, M. (1987). *Guidance of young children.* Columbus, OH: Merrill.

R. P. Ambrose

Pacing Issues

Exemplary early childhood teachers provide a balanced schedule for children each day. They attempt to alternate active and sedentary pastimes for the entire group as well as for individuals. They create periods of rela-

tive rest. They consider balancing opportunities for exploration as well as engagement, or focused use of materials. For example, children would have time to explore how water pours, squirts, or fills before they would focus on particular problems to solve. Teachers support children's use of time for privacy and private activity, as well as for social participation, by providing opportunities in places such as nooks, crannies, and between dividers.

D. P. Fromberg

Record Keeping

Early childhood educators maintain a broad range of formal and informal records, including those required on children's attendance, health, special needs, and placement. The physical environment aspect of record keeping applies to the provision and use of space, materials, toys and equipment, and takes two forms. The first involves where things are, and how they are augmented, replaced, and modified, while the second applies to how children use the physical environment, including some records that the children themselves make.

Physical environment record keeping monitors the acquisition, storage, access, and retrieval of resources. Simple inventory systems and resupply schedules can be designed by teachers so materials and supplies are managed in an organized way. For example, color coding curriculum materials and numbering each to correspond to a curriculum goal can help teachers store and retrieve materials. Such an inventory system also alerts educators to gaps in existing resources, so appropriate decisions can be made when new materials are purchased. Records also must be kept on needed repairs, maintenance, or replacement to insure safe use of toys and equipment.

Documenting children's use of the physical environment is a second type of record keeping that supports developmentally appropriate goals. Simple checklists can be used to determine how often children use specific materials or learning centers. Such checklists also can record the progress of those children who have mastered curriculum skills or have particular interests, thereby providing a vehicle for forming flexible groups.

Equally important is the need to record the complexity and effective utilization of materials and play space by children (Kritchevsky, Prescott, & Walling, 1977). Periodic documentation in writing or by audio or videotape recording of language and play behaviors occurring at various play sites allows systematic comparison. Such practice can help insure that play sites are developmentally appropriate and well utilized by various groups, including both girls and boys. Teacher mediation in play events then becomes more effective because it is specifically relevant to children's interests and motivation, thus optimizing development through play (Monighan-Nourot, Scales, Van Hoorn, with Almy, 1987). Simplified sociograms can augment information about groups, showing friendship patterns, group stability and changes, and the ways in which individuals adjust to groups (Almy & Genishi, 1979).

Anecdotal records also can provide valuable insights into individuals' cognitive, language, physical, and socioemotional development that can help teachers determine which materials are appropriate at a given time. Systematically observing one-fifth of the class each day insures documentation of all children's progress during a week's time.

Record keeping can include children's products, such as periodic samples of drawing, writing, and storytelling. These testaments to children's advancing cognitive skills can be viewed along with social documentation, such as individual and group progress in thematic elaboration through peer play in such an area as the sociodramatic center.

Children also can learn to keep simple records. Child-made graphs and indices of change and progress can document important elements of sharing as well as the development of critical reflection and responsibility. Documentation of books children have read or written, and songs that they know, contribute powerfully to the construction of a sense of membership in a shared social world of learning. Kindergarten through third grade

children also can use simple individual checklists or contracts to monitor visits to specific learning centers during a week's time.

Wise and realistic decisions about what is necessary and valuable as record keeping undergirds the structure of developmentally appropriate practice. Teachers can learn much from exchanges with colleagues and need time to reflect on what these new records reveal about current holistic approaches to learning.

Accurate record keeping enhances home-school communication. Through well-interpreted documentation, teachers can give parents a clear picture of their child's progress, thereby increasing educational accountability. Such record keeping empowers teachers and parents because it is authentic and child centered, using classroom life as its source.

References

Almy, M., & Genishi, C. (1979). *Ways of studying children*. New York: Teachers College Press.

Kritchevsky, S., & Prescott, E., with Walling, L. (1977). *Physical space: Planning environments for young children*. Washington, DC: National Association for the Education of Young Children.

Monighan-Nourot, P., Scales, B., & Van Hoorn, J., with Almy, M. (1987). *Looking at children's play: A bridge between theory and practice*. New York: Teachers College Press.

B. Scales

Time Use

How teachers spend classroom time reflects the goals and priorities they have for their students (Kauchak & Eggen, 1989). Effective early childhood teachers must know programmatic goals, as well as individual children's developmental levels and interests, in order to make informed decisions about the use of time.

Both long-term and short-range instructional planning ultimately deal with time issues. Once the choice of a theme and/or lesson sequence has been made, for example, the teacher must decide when to initiate, develop, culminate, and evaluate the learning experience. Decisions that have an impact on children's learning include when to change the materials in a learning center or what children should do when they finish a group activity before the others.

The daily schedule should offer both stability and variety. Routines that involve all children, such as class meetings, snack, lunch, and rest time, can be scheduled for the same time each day, thereby providing security. Within this predictable framework, sedentary activities should alternate with more physically active experiences. Time allotments should reflect a balance of teacher-directed and child-initiated activities; individual, small group, and total group experiences; and activities in the cognitive/language, affective, social, psychomotor, and aesthetic domains. Transition times, which often prove difficult for children, can be made easier if children know clearly what will happen next, and if teachers try to make transitions an interesting time in themselves (Davidson, 1982).

Children need to engage in interesting activities that extend over days or weeks rather than in fragmented activities (Katz, 1988). Scheduling long time blocks in which children can choose among varied activities provides opportunities for children to pace themselves, thereby developing the stimulation sequence they need (Fromberg, 1987).

While the teacher ultimately is responsible for how time is used, child ownership also is important. Flexible scheduling provides time for spontaneous learning opportunities arising from children's interests or items they bring to class. When a learning centers approach is employed, children can make meaningful decisions about time. A sharing period following "centers time" can foster language development and emphasize the importance of children's work.

Cues from children are the best indicator of whether classroom time is being effectively utilized. Engagement with materials or eye contact, for example, can signal whether a child is on task. Nonengagement may indicate that a task is uninteresting or not developmentally appropriate. Observing children and talking with parents to determine individual rhythms can yield valuable information regarding the time of day when children learn best, "alone time" needs, and food intake requirements. Such information will enable responsive teachers to tailor the schedule to individual children rather than making children conform to a rigid adult-determined routine.

References

Bredekamp, S. (ed.). (1987). *Developmentally appropriate practice in early childhood programs serving children from birth through age 8*. Washington, DC: National Association for the Education of Young Children.

Davidson, J. (1982). Wasted time: ignored dilemma. In J. F. Brown (ed.), *Curriculum planning for young children*. Washington, DC: National Association for the Education of Young Children.

Fromberg, D. P. (1987). *The full-day kindergarten*. New York: Teachers College Press.

Katz, L. (1988). *Early childhood education: What research tells us*. Bloomington, IN: Phi Delta Kappa Educational Foundation.

Kauchak, D., & Eggen, P. (1989). *Learning and teaching: Research-based methods*. Boston: Allyn and Bacon.

S. B. Cruikshank

5.7 Strategies of Teaching

Strategies for teaching are a part of the ways in which teachers organize and manage instruction, and go to the heart of teaching, their interaction with children. The strategies that teachers select, no less than the curriculum plans that they favor, reflect their beliefs about how children develop and learn as well as what is valuable about what and how learning takes place. The articles in this section include some examples of strategies that arise from differing belief systems. Their presentation in alphabetical order is an attempt to provide easy reference rather than to obscure these differences. Briefly, these differences are variations on polar views of the child as a receiver of adult wisdom or the child as an active creator and connector of ideas; and of the rights of adults to decide about and actively control children's behavior or the rights of children to initiate activities and make choices that are developmentally possible and safe.

Articles such as those on Behavior Modification and Direct Instruction present more of the transmission view of education, whereas such articles as those dealing with Discussion, Humor, Inductive Model, Play, Pacing, and Team Teaching reflect a more constructivist viewpoint. Other articles tend to present a range of viewpoints in relation to the topics with which they deal.

D. P. Fromberg

Strategies of Teaching: Overview

The term "strategies of teaching" refers to various approaches teachers use interactively in the classroom to accomplish their objectives. Arenas of early childhood teaching strategies include alternatives for classroom management, teacher-child dialogues, and lesson presentations.

Effective classroom management consists of teaching strategies that early childhood teachers employ systematically, including modeling, rehearsing, and incentives to learn and maintain classroom procedures. Effective classroom managers give very specific feedback, both positive and negative, about children's performance. They spend a minimum amount of time on transitions. Directions are given only when children are attentive. They move around the classroom often and, when stationary, regularly scan the classroom.

Teacher-child dialogue is highly important in facilitating children's learning. This may be partly because young children more accurately take in information that is directed to them as individuals. Teachers also may personalize their message more when speaking to one of a few children rather than to a larger group.

Strategies of teaching through dialogue are used during children's play and nonplay activities. The following dialogue strategies are alternatives from which teachers may choose in maximizing the impact of their informal interaction with children:

- giving descriptive feedback to the child about what she or he is doing;

- reinforcing selected types of involvements or behaviors by distributing attention and approval;

- coaching, prompting, and giving suggestions to help children develop a more extensive repertoire;

- asking questions to stimulate children's expanded language use in order to represent their thoughts and prior experiences as well as to encourage them to attend to transformations, make predictions, observe effects, connect actions with events, and consider causality; and

- modeling desirable and/or more competent behavior.

There are several different lesson strategies that teachers can use when a teacher-directed activity is planned. These include direct instruction, deductive lessons with advance organizers, inductive lessons, modeling lessons, and open-ended group discussions. A teacher selects those lesson strategies most likely to accomplish particular objectives consistent with particular belief systems.

Direct instruction lessons, for example, follow specific steps in reaching teaching objectives. This approach became the basis for the commercially distributed DISTAR (Bereiter & Engelmann, 1966). Direct instruction lessons include the use of attention signals and response signals; the contrasting of instances and noninstances of a selected, very specific concept or discrimination; feedback and reinforcers; and rapid pacing with planned pauses, stimulus changes, surprises, and intentional mistakes. The strategy calls for lively, rhythmic interchanges and enthusiastic reinforcement.

Deductive lessons or advance organizer lessons progress from a presentation or discussion of already familiar general information and concepts to the gradual introduction of related material or concepts. The teacher emphasizes the relationships of new concepts or examples to the more general concepts. Hierarchical sequencing from general to specific is key to this strategy.

Inductive lessons begin with presenting an assortment of exemplars (particular actions, situations, objects, or pictures selected to represent a concept) and nonexamplars (actions, situations, objects, or pictures that do not represent the concept). Children are not told the teacher's criterion for inclusion or exclusion. They figure out or use the underlying concept that determines the categorization of some presentations as exemplars and others as not. Generalizations are constructed by learners rather than presented by teachers.

Modeling lessons are used to present a particular skill or procedure to a group of children or an individual. There are guidelines for procedures that systematically provide a model, followed by practice, mastery, and application of the skill or procedure (Charles, 1981, p. 156).

Repertoire-building lessons typically have a social problem as a focus but also may be used for building repertoire in other relevant, decision-making arenas. The actual or hypothetical problem or question to be addressed usually is presented through verbal description or simulated role playing. Once children understand the problem, the teacher asks for an individual to suggest a solution. This is recorded in writing, and other children add their ideas. Together, they generate a list of alternative solutions. This goal is not finding the "right" or "best" answer, but to build awareness of alternatives and viable possibilities.

Early childhood educators agree that the younger the child, the more likely it is that dialogue strategies will be more effective than lesson alternatives for furthering learning. When lessons are used, however, it is important to select strategies that match teaching objectives. Dialogue lesson strategies have many variations that teachers systematically incorporate into their repertoire as they continue to develop professional competence.

References

Anderson, L., Evertson, C., & Emmer, E. (1979). *Dimensions in classroom management derived from recent research*. Austin, TX: ERIC No. ED 175.

Bereiter, C., & Engelmann, S. (1966). *Teaching disadvantaged children in the preschool*. Englewood Cliffs, NJ: Prentice-Hall.

Charles, C. M. (1981). *Building classroom discipline: From model to practice*. New York: Longman.

Lay-Dopyera, M., & Dopyera, J. (1990). *Becoming a teacher of young children* (4th ed). New York: McGraw-Hill.

Spivack, G., Platt, J. J., & Sure, M. B. (1976). *The problem-solving approach to adjustment: A guide to research and intervention*. San Francisco: Jossey-Bass.

Tzelepis, A., Giblin, P. T., & Agronow, S. J. (1983). Effects of adult caregivers' behaviors on the activities, social interactions, and investments of nascent preschool day-care groups. *Journal of Applied Developmental Psychology, 4*(2), 201–216.

M. Lay-Dopyera

Behavior Modification

Behavior modification, the application of behavioral theory, operates on the underlying principle that behavior can be changed by altering the environment, both social and physical. Behavior is defined only by what is observable, for instance, actions and words, rather than by nonobservable factors such as motivation or feelings. Behavior is carefully defined, observed, and graphed by representing it in measurable units, such as the number of times a child hits or number of minutes a child cries within a specified time period.

One way behavior is learned is through the responses of others. When children get attention or reinforcement for a behavior, they are likely to repeat that behavior. Consistent reinforcement of, or attention to, desired behaviors will result in repetition of such behaviors, and consistent nonreinforcement or ignoring of undesirable behaviors will result in their reduction or extinction. "Time out" is one form of ignoring, when a child is removed for a few minutes from the reinforcement of the social situation. To change an undesirable behavior, it is important not only to ignore this behavior but also to reinforce competing positive behaviors. Reinforcement always should be contingent on the child's carrying out appropriate behavior. Children also learn behaviors by observing others.

Many early childhood settings use behavior modification principles. Those who use these principles believe that sensitive application of these techniques can provide a positive guidance system.

References

Essa, E.L. (1990). *Practical guide to solving preschool behavior problems*. Albany, NY: Delmar.

Marion, M. (1987). *Guidance of young children*. Columbus, OH: Merrill.

E. L. Essa

Cooperative Learning

Cooperative learning involves small heterogeneous groups of students working together to achieve a common goal. The teacher's role is that of guide or coach rather than direct instructor. The many benefits of cooperative learning include cognitive growth, the development of prosocial behavior, strengthening language and listening skills, and enhancing self-esteem.

Student-Team Learning (Slavin, 1981) is one approach to cooperative learning that consists of students working together in teams to master a set of worksheets on a lesson. Each member of a team then takes a quiz and contributes a score to his or her team based on individual performance. The individual student scores are based on how much the students have improved since the last performance rather than on how many answers are correct. This kind of scoring keeps the more academically able student from feeling resentful of a teammate who does not score perfectly on the quizzes. Group scores then are compared, and one group is named the winner.

Learning Together is another method described by Robert Slavin (1981), which he attributes to others (Johnson, Johnson, & Holubec, 1988). He describes a method in which "students work together in small groups to complete a single worksheet, for which the group receives praise and recognition" (Slavin, 1981, p. 656). Learning Together is more expansive than certain other cooperative strategies and explores classroom cooperation on a more general basis (Johnson, Johnson, & Holubec, 1988).

In Jigsaw (Aronson, 1978), each student in a five- or six-member group receives information on a topic the whole group is studying. Each becomes expert on his or her information segment through discussion with members from other groups who share the same segment. Each team member then returns to his or her original learning group, and together the group members teach each other the individual segments so that every member of the group ultimately has a thorough understanding of the broad topic.

The Group Investigation Method has students in small groups deciding "what they will learn, how they will organize themselves to learn it, and how they will communicate what they have learned to their classmates (Slavin, 1981, p. 656)."

Quintilian utilized cooperative learning strategies as early as the first century and Comenius, in the seventeenth century (Johnson, Johnson, & Holubec, 1988). In the United States, within the nineteenth century's Common School Movement, there also was a strong emphasis on cooperative learning.

Until recently, cooperative learning was used with older children, typically beginning in middle childhood, perhaps due to the belief in Jean Piaget's view that young children are egocentric. This view suggests that children who are unable to take one another's perspectives would be incapable of the give and take necessary for working cooperatively.

Research indicates, however, that young children are not necessarily egocentric (Donaldson, 1978) in this sense and that learning to decenter may well be a progressive process (Borke, 1971). Since young children collaborate spontaneously in informal settings (Strayer, 1980), cooperative learning may be particularly appropriate for early childhood.

In sociodramatic play, for example, two or more children might share mutual goals, ideas, and materials; make decisions; negotiate and bargain; coordinate actions to accomplish goals; and evaluate their own progress. While all of these cooperative behaviors rarely occur in a single situation, their frequency and duration indicate the richness of the cooperative experience (Goffin, 1987).

Early childhood teachers can promote co-operation by providing open-ended materials and activities such as water or sand play and block building. When children create a single art product or woodworking construction with limited resources, there is an opportunity to foster sharing and working together. In the primary grades, peer conferences can build cooperation within a "community of writers." Activities in other curriculum areas such as mathematics and social studies also lend themselves to cooperative interaction.

Systematic observation of children will aid the teacher in establishing pairs or small groups, in determining the duration of these groups, and in supporting students as they learn appropriate social interactions and cooperative behaviors. In addition, it is the teacher's modeling of the "we" versus "me" approach that instills in young children the value of cooperation in a competitive society.

References

Aronson, E. (1978). *The jigsaw classroom.* Beverly Hills, CA: Sage.

Borke, H. (1971). The development of empathy in Chinese and American children between three and six years of age: A cross-cultural study. *Developmental Psychology, 9* (1) 102–108.

Donaldson, M. (1978). *Children's minds.* New York: Norton.

Goffin, S. (1987). Cooperative behaviors: They need our support. *Young Children, 42* (2), 75–81.

Johnson, D., Johnson, R., & Holubec, E. (1988). *Cooperation in the classroom.* Edina, MN: Interaction.

Slavin, R. (1981). Synthesis of research on cooperative learning. *Educational Leadership, 38* (8), 655–60.

Strayer, F. F. (1980). Social ecology of the preschool peer group. In W. A. Collins (ed.), *The Minnesota symposium on child psychology,* Vol. 13 (pp. 165–196). Hillsdale, NJ: Erlbaum.

E. Kanas

Direct Instruction

Direct Instruction has two, interrelated meanings. It is the generic name for a pedagogy that is "academically focused, teacher-directed ... [with] sequenced and structured materials (Rosenshine, 1979, p. 38)." It is also a curriculum and pedagogy designed for low-income and culturally diverse children who may be at risk of school failure (Bereiter & Engelmann, 1966; Engelmann & Carnine, 1982).

The first definition was derived by analyzing research on effective teaching, primarily measures of achievement in mathematics and reading. The second definition was derived by analyzing the learning deficiencies of low-income young children, conventional classroom environments and curricula, and learning theory. Most early educators associate direct instruction with the second perspective, although the pedagogies are similar.

The second pedagogy is carefully scripted. Children in preschool through third grade are organized in instructional groups of five to eight children. Adults provide a fast paced 15 to 20 minute oral mode of instruction. The teacher typically presents the subject matter of the lesson and engages the children in group practice, with ample oral testing. A gamelike setting and praise are present. Teachers teach children to examine phenomena logically and to infer correct responses by applying logic.

Controversy has existed about the use of this method and the DISTAR curriculum, associated with the second perspective. Differences reflect the conception of the nature of development and learning as much as they do evidence of the effectiveness of direct instruction.

References

Bereiter, C., & Engelmann, S. (1966). *Teaching disadvantaged children in the preschool.* Englewood Cliffs, NJ: Prentice-Hall.

Engelmann, S., & Carnine, D. (1982). *Theory of instruction: Principles and applications.* New York: Irvington.

Rosenshine, B. V. (1979). Content, time, and direct instruction. In P. L. Peterson & H. J. Walberg (eds.), *Research on teaching: Concepts, findings and implications* (pp. 39–56). Berkeley, CA: McCutchan.

D. Day

Discussion, Conversation, and Questioning: Critical Thinking

Young children are capable of analyzing, synthesizing, and evaluating concrete and sensorimotor experiences, although they are at early developmental stages. The key variable in determining the level of thinking in the classroom is the teacher, rather than students' ages or abilities, or the teacher/child ratio.

The level of teacher questioning influences the level of children's answers, as well as their capacity to express authentic and discerning thought. If teachers pose only recall or reflex comprehension questions, children will respond on those levels. If, however, teachers provide linguistic cues that stimulate analysis or evaluative thinking, then children follow with an analysis or evaluation. Research overwhelmingly supports these principles, since it shows more than 80 percent of classroom questions are teacher initiated, and more than 80 percent of those questions require children to employ low levels of thinking (Bellack, 1966; Dillon, 1981).

The most direct method for obtaining information about the level of children's thinking is a linguistic analysis of transcripts of teacher-student conversations and discussions. The design of daily plans also can be analyzed in order to understand cognitive cues that teachers offer children. For example, use of verbs such as "name," "list," and "tell" request that students recall factual information. Retaining information is important, but unless children have opportunities to use this factual base to react and produce, it is likely that they will forget the information. In contrast, the linguistic cues such as "design," "construct," "compare," and "judge" encourage children to use higher order thinking, in which they have the opportunity to reflect upon and express their thinking. The cumulative effect of the teacher's daily exchanges and planned activities determine if, and how, children think critically.

Although observers expect science and mathematics to be disciplines that require problem-solving strategies, researchers have found that teachers usually present facts for retention, as opposed to encouraging children's active inquiry. An art project is one way in which children can give form to their feelings and perceptions. When teachers expect young children to follow a model or use a pattern, they have missed an opportunity for critical thinking to take place in the arts. Throughout the curriculum, therefore, teachers can help children think critically by sending the message, "You are capable of solving problems in creative ways."

Creative Problem Solving is a straightforward instructional model that can encourage critical thinking in early childhood classrooms (Osborne, 1970). Adults tell children that they are problem finders and solvers in all of the subjects they study as well as in their relationships with others. When reading a story, the teacher will ask children to find the problem, something that five-year-olds can do.

The role of the teacher is central in the process of fostering higher order thinking. The early childhood teacher committed to developing thinking skills needs grounding in models of cognitive processing and methods for translating these models into practice. Early childhood teachers have the dual functions of promoting critical and individual thinking at the same time that they are helping young children adjust to the school setting in socially competent ways. By using effective instructional models, early childhood teachers also can empower children to believe in themselves as thinkers.

References

Bellack, A. A., et al. (1966). *The language of the classroom*. Final report. New York: Teachers College Press.

Dillon, J. T. (1981). To Question or Not to Question During Discussion. *Journal of Teacher Education*, Part 1, *32* (5), 51–55.

Osborne, A. F. (1970). *Applied imagination*. New York: Scribner.

H. H. Jacobs

Grouping

One of the most controversial issues in primary education is the question of whether and how students should be grouped for instruction. Proponents of grouping students according to ability have argued that ability grouping lets high achievers move rapidly and gives low achievers attainable goals and extra help. Opponents have countered that ability grouping is unfair to low achievers, citing problems of poor peer models, low teacher expectations, concentration of culturally diverse students in low tracks, and slow instructional pace.

Ability grouping is not a single practice, but has many fundamentally different forms that have different educational as well as psychological effects. Various forms of ability grouping and their effects are discussed below.

Ability Grouped Class Assignment. In many elementary schools, students are assigned to self-contained classes on the basis of a general achievement or ability measure. At each grade level this might provide a high-achieving class, an average-achieving class, and a low-achieving class, with students assigned to classes according to some combination of a composite achievement measure, IQ scores, and/or teacher judgment. Students remain with the same ability-grouped classes for all academic subjects.

The achievement effects of ability-grouped class assignment, in comparison to heterogeneous grouping, are essentially zero (Slavin, 1987). There is some evidence that high achievers may gain from ability grouping at the expense of low achievers, but most studies find no such trend. Overall, the effects of ability grouping cluster closely around zero for students of all achievement levels.

Regrouping for Reading and/or Mathematics and Joplin Plan. One commonly used ability-grouping arrangement in elementary schools involves having students remain in heterogeneous classes most of the day but regrouping for selected subjects. For example, three second grade classes in a school might have reading scheduled at the same time. At reading time, students might leave their heterogeneous homerooms and go to a class organized according to reading level. In the Joplin Plan, this regrouping is done across grade lines, so

that a 2-1 reading class might contain first, second, and third graders.

Research on regrouping plans indicates that they can be instructionally effective if two conditions are fulfilled: Instructional level and pace must be completely adapted to student performance level, and the regrouping must be done for only one or two subjects so that students stay in heterogeneous placements most of the day (Slavin, 1987). The achievement effects of the Joplin Plan (which satisfies these criteria) have been particularly positive. On the other hand, when grouping has been done without adapting the pace or the level of instruction, or in more than two different subjects, no benefits for regrouping have been found.

Within-Class Ability Grouping. Within-class ability grouping is the practice of assigning students to homogeneous subgroups for instruction within the class. In general, each subgroup receives instruction at its own level and is allowed to progress at its own rate. Within-class ability grouping is virtually universal in elementary reading instruction and is common in elementary mathematics in the United States (Barr & Dreeben, 1983). Many teachers, however, are experimenting with ungrouped reading classes.

Methodologically adequate research on within-class ability grouping has been limited to the study of mathematics grouping. The research supports this practice. Effects of within-class grouping were somewhat higher for low achievers than for average and high achievers. There was some trend for effects to be more positive when the number of ability groups was two or three rather than four.

Cooperative Learning. Cooperative learning (Slavin, 1986; 1987) refers to various instructional methods in which students work in small, heterogeneous learning groups toward some sort of group goal. Cooperative learning methods often are used as alternatives to ability grouping. They differ from within-class ability grouping not only in that cooperative learning groups are small and heterogeneous but also in that these groups are expected to engage in a great deal of task-focused interaction, such as studying together, completing group assignments, or discussing a shared topic of interest.

Research on cooperative learning in elementary schools has found that the effects of this grouping strategy depend on how it is organized. Instructionally effective cooperative learning methods provide group rewards based on the individual learning of all group members. These include Student Teams-Achievement Divisions (Slavin, 1986), Teams-Games-Tournaments (DeVries & Slavin, 1978), Team Assisted Individualization (Slavin, 1987), Cooperative Integrated Reading and Composition (Stevens et al., 1987), and related methods.

Conclusions. Evidence from studies of various forms of ability grouping indicates that achievement effects depend on the types of programs evaluated. In general, ability-grouping plans are beneficial for student achievement only when they incorporate the following features (adapted from Slavin, 1987):

- Students who remain in heterogeneous classes most of the day are regrouped by performance level only in such subjects as reading and mathematics.
- The grouping plan reduces heterogeneity in the specific skill being taught.
- Group assignments are flexible and frequently reassessed.
- Teachers adapt their level and pace of instruction in regrouped classes to accommodate students' levels of readiness and learning rates.

The between-class grouping plan that most completely incorporates the four principles listed above is the Joplin Plan, in which students who remain in heterogeneous classes, except for reading, are grouped strictly according to reading level, are constantly reevaluated, and are accommodated for all achievement levels. Although there is controversy concerning the possibilities for integrating such skill instruction with ongoing classroom content, within-class ability grouping models in reading and mathematics also generally satisfy these criteria. In contrast, ability-grouped class assignment does not meet the four criteria because it segregates students all day, groups students on the basis of general ability or achievement rather than skill in a specific subject, and tends to be highly inflexible. Teachers may or may not adjust their level and pace of instruction to adapt to students' needs in this plan. Cooperative learning programs, particularly those that accommodate instruction to the needs of individual children, can serve as effective alternatives to ability grouping in the primary grades.

References

Barr, R., & Dreeben, R. (1983). *How schools work.* Chicago: University of Chicago Press.

DeVries, D. L., & Slavin, R. E. (1978). Teams-Games-Tournament (TGT): Review of ten classroom experiments. *Journal of Research and Development in Education, 12* (1), 28–38.

Slavin, R. E. (1986). *Using student team learning* (3rd ed.). Johns Hopkins Team Learning Project.

Slavin, R. E. (1987). Ability grouping and student achievement in elementary schools: A best evidence synthesis. *Review of Educational Research, 57* (6), 293–336.

Stevens, R. J., Madden, N. A., Slavin, R. E., & Farnish, A. M. (1987). Cooperative integrated reading and composition: Two field experiments. *Review of Educational Research, 22* (3), 433–454.

R. E. Slavin

Grouping in Programs for Children Under Six

Traditionally in the United States, young children are arranged in child care and education centers or in their school classes according to age levels. Thus, infants under the age of one are generally in one room, while toddlers are in another. There is a classroom for threes, or fours, or fives (kindergarten), and the majority of the children in the first grade are six years old.

Grouping within classrooms for children under the age of six has varied according to the philosophy and the understandings of the nature of child development and learning that underlie program designs. Programs that draw heavily on learning theory or on traditional schooling as determinants of practice have tended to group children according to initial assessments of ability and/or achievement. In some such programs, the children are regrouped periodically, according to their changing configurations of achievement. For example, a prekindergartener (four-year-old) might listen to stories with one group of children, while she works on problem-solving activities with another group of children chosen by the teacher. A first grader might be placed in a more advanced group for math activities, while remaining in a less advanced group for reading.

Another variation of this plan is a form of team teaching. One teacher or a specialist might take out groups of a congruent level of advancement from two or more classrooms for a science lesson, for instance, while the other children remain in their classrooms.

The rationale for these various forms of homogeneous grouping is that the teacher can more carefully observe and track children's progress under these circumstances, and that, as a result, curriculum planning can be more finely attuned to children's needs (Camp & Miller, 1972). Critics of homogeneous grouping plans point out that instruction within the groups often is not individualized, and that, when the groups are entirely subject centered, there are minimal opportunities for integrating one subject area with another.

On the other hand, young children with teachers who are strongly influenced by child development theory generally work in groups of their own choosing, according to their interest in a particular activity or their preference for companions. Teachers rotate around these self-constituted groups to ensure that all children have an opportunity to take part in planned activities (Hohmann, Banet, & Weikart, 1985).

The argument for mixed groupings within a class has been that children learn best when they can learn from each other as well as from adults, and that children who are more advanced in certain areas of development or in concept or skill acquisition are natural tutors of others. Critics of this approach note the complexity of record keeping under such circumstances and suggest that additional time is needed for teachers to do adequate planning.

Recently, the argument for heterogeneous grouping of young children across age levels has been extended to support of interage grouping for infants and toddlers (Axtmann, 1986), as well as for children from three to eight years of age (Katz, Evangelou, & Hartmann, 1990). This arrangement would mean, for example, that infants and toddlers or three-, four-, and five-year-olds would be in one classroom together, with one or more caregivers/teachers working on several levels at once. Interage groupings such as these have been used in England in the primary grades. Advocates point to positive social effects in broadening children's social perceptions, increasing instances of prosocial behavior, and encouraging more complex forms of play. They also draw on the work of Vygotsky (1978) to suggest "zone(s) of proximal development" created by having older children available as models to younger ones advances the skills and concept acquisition of both groups of children.

The essential question behind any decision regarding the grouping of young children, either in determining the age composition of classrooms, or learning groups within an age-level classroom, is how the decision reflects the program's underlying educational philosophy. Grouping choices should be made to be congruent with the overall intent of the program. (See also Chapter 4, Section 4.4, **Cognitive/Intellectual Development and Characteristics of Young Children, Social Development and Development of Relationships,** and Section 4.2, **Vygotsky, Lev Semenovich.**)

References

Axtmann, A. (1986). *Friendships among infants? Yes, indeed!* In D. Wolf (ed.), *Connecting* (pp. 12–17). Redmond, WA: Exchange Press.

Camp, J., & Miller, J. (1972). In R. K. Parker, *The preschool in action: Exploring early childhood programs* (pp. 382–409). Boston: Allyn and Bacon.

Hohmann, M., Banet, B., & Weikart, D. (1985). *Young children in action.* Ypsilanti, MI: High-Scope Educational Research Foundation.

Katz, L. G., Evangelou, D., & Hartmann, J. A. (1990). *The case for mixed-age grouping in early education*. Washington, DC: National Association for the Education of Young Children.

Vygotsky, L. (1978). *Mind in society: The development of higher psychological processes*. M. Cole, V. John-Steiner, S. Scribner, E. Souberman (eds.). Cambridge, MA: Harvard University Press.

L. R. Williams

Humor, Teaching with

Results of research on the use of humor in education show that critical thinking, literacy skills, and concept learning in content areas can improve when teachers use humor strategies (Bryant & Zillman, 1988; Korobkin, 1988; Warnock, 1989). There are also cultural differences in amount and type of humor use in classrooms (Okuda, 1990; Zadjman, 1990).

Young children's interest in learning, enthusiasm for exploring new activities, language play and creativity, and general zest for life are often positively influenced by a classroom climate in which teachers accept and encourage the expression of humor. Teachers of young children can use humor as a strategy to promote cognitive development, enhance social interaction, and strengthen emotional health.

In order to be used successfully, however, the humor must be appropriate for young children's stage of humor development and facilitate its further development. Therefore, humor strategies in the early childhood classroom are less centered on the performance and image enhancement of the teacher, as might be the case with older children and adults. Teachers may act as performers and models, but they also have important roles as initiators of humorous child-adult and child-child interactions; facilitators and context setters for children's spontaneous humor expression; and active responders, a good audience, to children's humor attempts. It is possible for teachers to inhibit humor expression by unsupportive responses to children's humor attempts, by conveying a "no-nonsense" and highly structured classroom standard, by discouraging humor because of fear of losing classroom control, or simply by lacking understanding of the types of language and actions that young children perceive to be funny.

Young children typically find humor in performing incongruous or fantasy actions; discovering surprising and incongruous objects, actions, and events; playing with sounds and meanings of language; engaging in exuberant mastery or movement play; and interacting with adults in teasing/joking play (Bergen, 1989; Bowes, 1981; Canzler, 1980; Krough, 1985; McGhee & Lloyd, 1982; Sherman, 1975). Infrequently, they may find potentially "shocking" materials to be funny, such as toileting or sexually explicit content and poorly disguised hostility to peers or adults. Their expressions may seem crude to adults because children have not yet learned the "joke facade" (Freud, 1960) with which adults cloak much of their sexual or hostile humor.

There is little research focusing on how teachers use their knowledge of young children's humor development to create a positive classroom climate. One study, however, in which teachers collected examples of young children's humor in their preschool and kindergarten classrooms, incidentally cited examples of teachers' humor strategies (Bergen, 1990).

Teacher performance as a humorous model was a strategy used in these classrooms, often occurring in large group time. The teacher told or read stories with incongruous characters, actions, and language; directed games in which exaggerated speech, facial emotions, or gestures were modeled; or asked the group to respond to riddles and jokes. When the early childhood teacher demonstrates humorous approaches and models the enjoyment of humor, it serves as a signal to children that it is appropriate for them to develop their own humor in the classroom.

Initiating, facilitating, and actively responding were early childhood teacher humor strategies that took place most often during small group activities, transitional times such as lunch, and free play times. The teacher might initiate a humorous interchange between children by soliciting a joke or riddle, facilitating humor by setting up a joke and encouraging children to be involved, or actively responding by appreciating the humor of children's capacity to "fool" the teacher by inverting reality. In turn, the teacher might engage in the strategy of over-responding in order to help a child put an event into perspective by giving an exaggerated response. Personifying ("That naughty door!") or exaggerating responses also can "defuse" frustrating or even explosive situations between peers.

Thus, these three strategies of initiating children's humorous interactions, facilitating children's learning ways to express humor, and increasing the humor level by being active responders to children's humor attempts can serve to help children develop their sense of humor.

By providing young children opportunities to laugh at the verbal, behavioral, and conceptual incongruities that they initiate and that adults, peers, and media present, teachers also are giving children opportunities for cognitive growth. Their beginning understanding of the multiple meanings in riddles and jokes are evidence of both intellectual and language development. Moreover, a climate of fun also can enhance emotional and social development as well as creative thinking. Although there are few studies of the effects of humorous teaching approaches on young children's learning, it is likely that humor use may improve young children's content learning as it does for older children and adults (Hill, 1988). Research is needed both on the effects of humor on learning in early childhood classrooms and on the strategies teachers can use to foster young children's humor development. Because human beings value a sense of humor in teachers as well as people of all ages, early childhood teachers' use of humor strategies may have a lasting effect on the children they teach.

References

Bergen, D. (1989). An educology of children's humour: Characteristics of young children's expression of humour in home settings as observed by parents. *International Journal of Educology, 3* (2), 124–135.

Bergen, D. (1990). Young children's humor at home and school: Using parents and teachers as participant observers. Paper presented at the Eighth International Humor Conference. Sheffield, England.

Bowes, J. (1981). Some cognitive and social correlates of children's fluency in riddle-telling. *Current Psychological Research, 1* (2), 9–19.

Bryant, J., & Zillman, D. (1988). Using humor to promote learning in the classroom. *Journal of Children in Contemporary Society, 20* (1), 49–78.

Canzler, L. (1980). *Humor and the primary child.* (ERIC Document Reproduction No. ED 191 683).

Freud, S. (1960). *Jokes and their relation to the unconscious.* New York: Norton.

Hill, D. (1988). *Humor in the classroom.* Springfield, IL: Charles C. Thomas.

Korobkin, D. (1988). Humor in the classroom: Considerations and strategies. *College Teaching, 36* (3), 154–158.

Krough, S. (1985). He who laughs first: The importance of humor to young children. *Early Child Development and Care, 20* (4), 287–299.

McGhee, P., & Lloyd, S. (1982). Behavioral characteristics associated with the development of humor in young children. *Journal of Genetic Psychology, 41* (2nd half), 253–259.

Okuda, N. (1990). *Humor, the missing element in Japanese education.* Paper presented at the Eighth International Humor Conference. Sheffield, England.

Sherman, L. W. (1975). An ecological study of glee in small groups of preschool children. *Child Development, 46* (1), 53–61.

Warnock, P. (1989). Humor as a didactic tool in adult education. *Lifelong Learning, 12* (8), 22–24.

Zajdman, A. (1990). *Humorous events in the classroom: The teacher's perspective.* Paper presented at the Eighth International Humor Conference. Sheffield, England.

D. Bergen

Inductive Model

Inductive teaching begins with the collection or introduction of data, continues with some type of data manipulation, and concludes with concept recognition, concept identification, conclusions, and/or decisions. The source of the original data can be the teacher, the students, books, surveys, experimentation and/or exploration. In contrast, deductive teaching begins with the naming of a concept by the teacher or text, and continues first with supervised and then independent practice. Deductive teaching concludes when the student can apply the concept in novel situations.

Bruce Joyce and Marsha Weil have identified several inductive teaching models, naming them for the persons who originally designed them. The Bruner model, also called the Concept Attainment model, presents students with both examples and nonexamples of a concept. The teacher invites the students to produce their own examples and nonexamples. A teacher of young children might say, "I'm going to open a shop. In my shop I will sell only certain things. Here is something I will sell in my shop (holding up a crayon). This is something I will not sell in my shop (holding up a cup)." The teacher continues identifying things that will be for sale in the shop (writing implements) and things that will not (nonwriting implements). After presenting examples and nonexamples, the teacher asks children to select things that would and would not be for sale in the shop. When the children can provide positive and negative examples, writing and nonwriting implements, the teacher might ask children to invent names for the shop.

In the Taba model, among the inductive models, children gather data directly. Students contribute, for example, to a list of words (or a collection of pictures or objects) about a topic, organize them into categories, and then develop statements describing their categories.

Inductive teaching has as its central activity the gathering, inspection, analysis, and interpretation of data. Discovery and inquiry teaching are types of inductive teaching. The more common deductive strategies situate the source of authority with the teacher or the textbook. Inductive teaching models rest some measure of authority with the learner.

Reference

Joyce, B., & Weil, M. (1972). *Models of teaching.* Englewood Cliffs, NJ: Prentice-Hall.

S. Greenberg

Learning Styles

The term "learning style" refers to the way learners concentrate on, absorb, and retain new or difficult information or skills (Dunn, 1983, p. 496). In the same way that each person looks and dresses differently, has personal preferences in music and art, and expresses himself/herself through a distinctive personality, each person has a unique style for learning, that is, "as individual as a signature" (Dunn, Beaudry, & Klavas, 1989, p. 50).

Early work on style conducted by psychologists Gordon Allport (1961), Carl Jung (1938), and Herman Witkin (1954), and others focused primarily on the cognitive domain. Witkin proposed the existence of different perceptual tendencies in persons depending on how they view and use their surroundings. He developed a two-dimensional model in which people are either field dependent or field independent. Gordon Allport was one of the first to use the term "learning style." He defined cognitive style as distinctive ways of living in the world. Carl Jung (1938) developed classifications of personality "types" in which individuals could be categorized based on predictable patterns of behavior. His types were based on how people view others and circumstances; some people view the world primarily through their senses, while others view the world primarily through their feelings or intuitions.

Building upon this early work, educators have begun to apply individual cognitive and affective style to the process of learning. A comprehensive model identifies 21 elements of style from the following 5 areas: environmental, emotional, sociological, physical, and psychological (Dunn, Dunn, & Price, 1981). Using a corresponding assessment tool, the Learning Style Inventory, teachers can obtain a computer-generated comprehensive learning style profile that identifies the suggested optimal learning conditions for each student. This inventory has been used extensively in research to investigate the nature and impact of style on learning.

Some elements of style are imposed at birth by genetic makeup, while others are developed as a product of experiences throughout life. One commentator contends that individual responses to sound, light, temperature, design, perceptual strengths, food and liquid intake, and mobility are biological, and inclinations toward certain sociological preferences, motivation, persistence, responsibility and structure are developed and modified through life experiences (Thies, 1979).

Studies (Carbo, 1983; Price, 1980) have shown that young children tend to be tactile (touch), kinesthetic (movement), and visual learners, and that there is a correlation between age and modality. In effect, the younger the child the greater the tendency toward tactile/kinesthetic learning. In most cases, the ability to learn easily through the auditory modality does not occur before grades five or six. A similar perspective holds that perceptual learning style preferences evolve for most students from the psychomotor (tactile/kinesthetic) to the visual and finally, as the learner matures, the aural (Keefe, 1979).

In addition to differences in perceptual style, younger students differ from older students in the areas of mobility, food intake, and time-of-day preferences. Research indicates that young students tend to want to eat and drink significantly more often than older students. Younger students also need to move around more than older students. Older students tend to prefer to read and study in the morning hours, whereas younger students seem to prefer the afternoon and evening hours.

Studies that have investigated the effects of matching individual learning styles to instructional methodologies have found significant positive results. One such study verified that youngsters with a strong preference for quiet achieved significantly better in reading in a quiet area, while those with a strong preference for sound achieved better in an environment with talking in the background (Pizzo, 1981). Another investigator found that formal and informal design can affect achievement; some students have a need for informal design and prefer to sit on rugs, pillows, or soft chairs while studying, while others prefer formal desks and chairs (Shea, 1983). Another

study concluded that matching students' lighting preferences also was important (Krimsky, 1982).

Recognition and understanding of learning style theory and application has important implications for early childhood curriculum decisions. One implication is that concepts should be introduced in using tactile (touch) and kinesthetic (movement) strategies. Auditory instruction should be minimized and augmented with visual aids. Students should be given choices in setting up and arranging their individual learning environments. Teachers should be sensitive to individual learning style needs and, when possible, accommodate those needs.

Instructional strategies should be incorporated that offer multisensory experiences such as language experience activities, shared journal development, drama, pantomime, and thematic teaching. These instructional strategies provide a framework on which students can receive and give information using their preferred learning styles.

References

Allport, G. W. (1961). *Pattern and growth in personality*. New York: Holt, Rinehart and Winston.

Carbo, M. (1983). Reading styles change between second and eighth grade. *Educational Leadership 40* (5), 56–59.

Dunn, R. (1983). Learning style and its relation to exceptionality at both ends of the spectrum. *Exceptional Children, 49* (6), 496–506.

Dunn, R., Beaudry, J. S., and Klavas, A. (1989). Survey of research on learning styles. *Educational Leadership 46* (6), 50–58.

Dunn, R., Dunn, K., & Price, G. E. (1981). *Learning style manual*. Lawrence, KS: Price Systems.

Jung, C. G. (1938). *Psychological types*. London: Kegan Paul, Trench and Truber.

Keefe, J. W. (1979). *School applications of the learning style concept: Student learning styles* (pp. 123–132). Reston, VA: National Association of Secondary School Principals.

Krimsky, J. S., (1982). A comparative study of the effects of matching fourth grade students with their learning style preferences for the environmental element of light and their subsequent reading speed and accuracy scores. (Doctoral dissertation, St. John's University, 1982). *Dissertation Abstracts International*, 43: 66-1A.

Pizzo, J. S. (1981). An investigation of the relationship between selected acoustic environments and sound, and elements of learning style, as they affect the reading achievement of male and female sixth grade students. (Doctoral dissertation, St. John's University, 1981). *Dissertation Abstracts International*, 42: 2475–6A.

Price, G. (1980). Which learning style elements are stable and which tend to change? *Learning Styles Network Newsletter, 1* (3), 1.

Shea, T. C. (1983). An investigation of the relationship among preferences for the learning style element of design, selected instructional environments, and reading test achievement of ninth grade students to improve administration determinations concerning effective educational facilities. (Doctoral dissertation, St. John's University, 1983). *Dissertation Abstracts International*, 44: 2004–7A.

Thies, A. A. (1979). A brain-behavior analysis of learning style. In *Student learning styles: Diagnosing and prescribing programs* (pp. 55–61). Reston, VA: National Association of Secondary School Principals.

Witkin, H. A. (1954). *Personality through perception: An experimental and clinical study*. Westport, CT: Greenwood Press.

R. L. Gull

Play

Early childhood educators have valued play as an essential educational medium through which young children develop their cognitive, linguistic, socioemotional, and physical abilities, and begin to learn essential competencies that serve as a basis for academic success. Almost any behavior can be playful or not playful, depending on the intentions of individuals players and on contextual factors in the environment.

A number of theorists have influenced how both researchers and educators think about play and its value in early childhood. For example, psychodynamic theorists view play as a means for helping children master social and emotional issues, and help educators understand such phenomena as why children take superhero and superheroine roles in fantasy play (Freud, 1961; Erikson, 1977). The cognitive view that play helps children construct knowledge in sequential stages such as practice play, symbolic play, and games-with-rules has helped both researchers and educators to describe the play they observe and relate it to children's stages of cognitive development (Piaget, 1962).

The work of early play researchers includes descriptions of types of play, related social interactions, and choices of play materials (Parten, 1932; Van Alstyne, 1932; Vance & McCall, 1934). Their work also influenced the curriculum and organization of many early childhood schools until the 1960s, when little new play research occurred.

In the past 20 years, researchers increasingly have sought to explain and describe play, as well as to relate play development to other developmental areas and academic learning processes. They have used observational, experimental, and self-report/performance methods (Bergen, 1987).

This research has implications for early childhood classroom practice. It concerns amount of space, kinds of toys (Ellis, 1973); sequence of stages and the effects of object realism on pretend play (Bretherton et al., 1984); role of television in imaginative play (Singer & Singer, 1973); methods of symbolic play training (Saltz & Dixon, 1974); relationships to cognitive skills such as fluency and problem solving (Pellegrini, 1984; Sylva, Bruner & Genoa, 1976) and language, reading, or mathematical skill (Isenberg & Jacob, 1985; Yawkey, 1981); adult-child interactive game play (Bruner & Sherwood, 1976); and types of adult role taking/pretense facilitation (Miller & Garvey, 1984). Practical ideas also arise from study of gender differences in play (Fagot, 1984) and the play of children who may be at risk or have handicapping conditions (Beckwith, 1985; Field, 1979).

Ensuring that play will have a place in the school experiences of children during the entire infant through primary years is an ongoing dilemma. University teacher education programs that include information on methods of studying play and involve teacher candidates and practicing teachers in play research can promote communication about the importance of play with parents, other teachers, and school administrators.

References

Beckwith, L. (1985). Parent-child interaction and social emotional development. In C. C. Brown & A. W. Gottfried (eds.), *Play interactions: The role of toys and parental involvement in children's development* (pp. 152–159). Skillman, NJ: Johnson & Johnson.

Bergen, D. (ed.). (1987). *Play as a medium for learning and development: A handbook of theory and practice* (Chapter 2). Portsmouth, NH: Heinemann.

Bretherton, I., O'Connell, Shore, & Bates. (1984). The effects of contextual variation on symbolic play: Development from 20 to 28 months. In I. Bretherton (ed.), *Symbolic play; The development of social understanding* (pp. 271–298). New York: Basic Books.

Bruner, J. S., & Sherwood, V. (1976). Peek-a-boo and the learning of rule structures. In J. S. Bruner, A. Jolly, & K. Sylva (eds.), *Play: Its role in development and evolution* (pp. 277–285). New York: Basic Books.

Ellis, M. J. (1973). *Why people play*. Englewood Cliffs, NJ: Prentice-Hall.

Erikson, E. (1977). *Toys and reasons*. New York: Norton.

Fagot, B. I. (1984). Teacher and peer reactions to boys' and girls' play styles. *Sex Roles, 11* (7/8), 691–702.

Field, T. M. (1979). Games parents play with normal and high-risk infants. *Child Psychiatry and Human Development, 10*, 41–48.

Freud, S. (1961/1920). *Beyond the pleasure principle*. New York: Norton.

Isenberg, J., & Jacob, E. (1985). Playful literacy activities and learning: Preliminary observations. In J. L. Frost & S. Sunderlin (eds.) *When Children Play* (pp. 17–23). Wheaton, MD: Association for Childhood Education International.

Miller, P., & Garvey, C. (1984). Mother-baby role play: Its origins in social support. In I. Bretherton (ed.), *Symbolic play: The development of social understanding* (pp. 101–130). New York: Academic Press.

Parten, M. (1932). Social participation among preschool children. *Journal of Abnormal and Social Psychology, 27* (3), 243–269.

Pellegrini, A. D. (1984). The effects of exploration and play on young children's associative fluency: A review and extension of training studies. In T. D. Yawkey & A. D. Pellegrini (eds.), *Child's play: Developmental and applied* (pp. 237–253). Hillsdale, NJ: Erlbaum.

Piaget, J. (1962). *Plays, dreams, and imitation in childhood*. New York: Norton.

Saltz, E., & Johnson, J. (1974). Training for thematic fantasy play in culturally disadvantaged children. Preliminary results. *Journal of Educational Psychology, 66* (4), 623–630.

Singer, J. L., & Singer, D. G. (1973). *Television-viewing and imaginative play in preschoolers: A developmental and parent-intervention study*. New Haven, CT: Yale University (ERIC Document Reproduction Service No. ED168576).

Sylva, K., Bruner, J. S., & Genoa, P. (1976). The role of play in the problem solving of children in 3–5 years old. In J. S. Bruner, A. Jolly, & K. Sylva (eds.) *Play: Its role in development and evaluation* (pp. 244–257). New York: Basic Books.

Van Alstyne, D. (1932). *Play and behavior and choice of play materials of preschool children*. Chicago: University of Chicago Press.

Vance, T. F., & McCall, L. T. (1934). Children's preferences among play materials as determined by the method of paired comparisons of pictures. *Child Development, 5* (3), 267–277.

Yawkey, T. D. (1981). Sociodramatic play effects on mathematical learning and adult ratings of playfulness in five year olds. *Journal of Research and Development in Education, 14* (3), 30–39.

D. Bergen

Questioning
(See **Discussion, Conversation, and Questioning: Critical Thinking**, above.)

Team Teaching
Team teaching, or collaborative teaching, means the sharing of responsibility for a group of children by two or more teachers. It offers an alternative to the self-contained classroom, in which one teacher works with one group of children, and to departmentalization, a model in which each teacher is responsible for one particular subject. In team teaching, each teacher is responsible for the full range of interdisciplinary subjects in a developmentally appropriate program for young children.

The advantages of team teaching include increased opportunities for individualization and enrichment for students. They get to know more children of their own age (and other ages, if interage grouping is present), as well as more than one teacher. Teachers have the opportunity to share ideas, teaching techniques, and materials. They feel less isolated, have increased incentive for risk taking, exploration and creativity, as well as help in problem solving and classroom management. The sharing of perspectives on students helps sharpen teacher awareness of individual children's strengths and problems. Parent conferences are therefore more informative and more effective. Parents like the increased communication and flexibility as well as the wider look at rationale, theory, and goals that collaboration implies.

The disadvantages of team teaching center around the fact that some teachers feel a loss of autonomy and privacy. Decision making and organization become more complex because of shared space and responsibility. Differences in values, approaches to teaching, and personality also can cause discomfort. When teachers collaborate in resolving issues, however, there is the potential to build upon each others' strengths and to model cooperative behavior for children.

M. Miletta

5.8 Field Trips

The articles that follow provide a sense of the varied opportunities available to young children from different regions. Within the diverse terrains of different regions of the United States, young children nevertheless may have parallel, but equivalent, kinds of experiences as they make trips beyond the classroom. There are subjects in each region for the study of social concerns and the arts as well as the physical and natural worlds.

Field trips define a range of experiences as diverse as exploring the workings of the building that houses classrooms and the spaces just beyond its walls that lend themselves to seasonal study, including plant and animal life, as well as issues such as moisture, absorption, and erosion. Field trips also include cultural and aesthetic concerns that define the social lives of children and their community, present and past.

The planning article that opens this section is useful to read in relation to each region because it outlines the considerations of moving beyond the classroom with young children. The article on the Northeast provides a context for considering the equivalence of human experience despite diverse environments, with some generic ideas for trips just beyond the classroom in most places. This piece also discusses the unique impact of urban life on young children's experiences at a time when many regions have been experiencing some urban growth. The discussion of the Midwest stands in contrast with its emphasis on agriculture, while it picks up a cultural strand from the Northeast that continues into the sections on the South, Southwest, and West. The distinctive survey of types of trips taken by different types of early childhood centers in the South provides an additional perspective about possible places to visit. What stands out about these discussions of field trips in early childhood, however, is the importance of using trips as part of an integrated curriculum that is appropriate to the development of young children and that provides for them the direct experiences by which their knowledge of content grows.

D. P. Fromberg

Planning Field Trips

Supervised field trips take place outside the early childhood classroom in order for young children to interact with various physical and social environments. Children can observe and study community resources while on trips. Later, they discuss the trip, extend their learning, or refine their conceptions. Mini–field trips, such as a walk around the neighborhood or a trip to the school nurse's office, are less complex to orchestrate, while trips requiring transportation need more advance planning.

In curriculum planning, teachers consider whether a trip is appropriate and worthwhile for the age, needs, interests, and previous experiences of the children. After teachers establish a trip's educational purposes, they also consider parent involvement; logistical planning; pre-trip, trip, and post-trip activities; and evaluation.

Trips can initiate or culminate a particular unit of study. Teachers can formulate and write a plan that incorporates the trip into the planned curriculum in a meaningful way and at a meaningful time. Places that are too novel and unfamiliar may not be the best ones for early childhood learning (Falk & Balling, 1982; Falk, Martin & Balling, 1978).

Parental involvement in trips may include such activities as providing transportation, being guides, and/or sharing relevant knowledge. They always should be informed in writing of the trip's purposes, times, and place. Chaperones will benefit from written instructions, including safety guidelines; names of children for whom adults are responsible, with a contact name and telephone number; travel/ parking directions; and ideas to assist children's learning. If a trip is complicated, the teacher and other adults can have a planning meeting beforehand.

With logistical planning, teachers consider time factors, such as distance of the site from school and duration of the trip, financing, and safety and liability issues. While on the trip, it is important to use name tags, do frequent head counts, or have adult leaders report at specified times.

Careful planning of pre-trip, trip, and post-trip activities help to maximize learning. Depending upon when the trip is scheduled within the curriculum, pre-trip activities may last a few days or several months. Possible activities include exploring classroom centers of interest that display related objects or books, as well as formulating questions that children might answer during the trip.

Adults accompanying children on the trip prepare in advance so that they can focus children's attention on points of interest and help them answer questions shared prior to the trip. Children can use individual "trip boards" depicting points of interest that they can check off as they see them. Taking photographs or obtaining free samples while on the trip also will enhance later enjoyment and learning.

Post-trip activities are important so that children can use and experiment with new concepts. Students can review questions raised before the trip, draw pictures, and/or write stories, or dramatize what they experienced.

Evaluation is the last step in a successful trip. Questions such as, "What did you like most/least and why?" promote higher level thinking and help teachers understand what children perceived. Teachers often record children's comments about the trip as well as the questions that remain for study, along with problems and suggestions. Evaluation and updating of field trip information is the best way to insure their continued educational excellence and success.

References

Falk, J. H., & Balling, J. (1982). The field trip milieu: Learning and behavior as a function of contextual events. *Journal of Educational Research*, 76 (1), 22–28.

Falk, J. H., Martin, W., & Balling, J. (1978). The novel field-trip phenomenon: Adjustment to novel settings interferes with task learning. *Journal of Research in Science Teaching*, 15 (2), 127–134.

C. H. Osteyee

Field Trips: Midwest

Field trips are an important part of the educational experiences of young children. Direct observation and hands-on activities enable children to develop a more vivid, richly detailed, integrated, and complete body of knowledge and understandings about a topic or theme. Field trips serve as a core experience around which to build many other related educational activities.

Generic themes or generic places of interest, such as farms, are frequent topics to study or sites for young children to visit. The midwestern states region, which includes Illinois, Indiana, Iowa, Kansas, Michigan, Minnesota, Missouri, Nebraska, North Dakota, Ohio, South Dakota, and Wisconsin, has many unique features of great interest to young children.

Farms: Leading Agricultural, Dairy, and Livestock Producers. Often referred to as "The Bread Basket" of this country, this region contains agriculture, dairy, and livestock, as well as food processing centers. Farms that are selected for a field trip could be ones that produce such commodities as wheat, corn, soybeans, navy beans, hay, carrots, beets, oats, peas, tomatoes, cherries, apples, blueberries, cranberries, maple syrup, hogs, beef and dairy cattle, and turkeys. The various types of barns, grain elevators, and machinery unique to this region also are noteworthy during trips.

Food Processing. Food production and distribution are among the studies of early childhood classrooms. The midwestern region is the leading area in the country for the conversion of agricultural goods into food products. Battle Creek, Michigan, for example, is known as "The Cereal Bowl" of this country. Milling wheat into flour and producing bread goods occurs throughout the area. Milk, cheese, and other dairy products are produced in great abundance. Vegetable and fruit processing is a major activity of great interest to children. There is also considerable meat processing that occurs. Viewing some aspects of the meat processing industry might not be appropriate for young children, but the later packaging stages might be of technical interest.

Farm Equipment. Serving the agricultural industry, the production and sale of farming machines, tools, and vehicles is prevalent. Young children are fascinated, particularly with farming implements.

Industrial Production. The midwestern region leads the nation in the production of automobiles, trucks, buses, airplanes, railroad cars, and heavy construction machinery. Numerous factories are present throughout the area, and visits to them enhance children's study of transportation vehicles and construction equipment.

There also are a number of interesting, unique factories scattered throughout the region, including a steel whistle factory and washboard company in Ohio, wooden shoe factory in Michigan, and corncob pipe factory in Missouri. The uniqueness of these products contribute to fascinating field trips.

Historical and Cultural Heritages. The 12 states in the region all have a rich Native American (American Indian) history, including the derivation of state names. Children enjoy learning about specific tribes and their unique features. Various small museums exist throughout the region that contain artifacts of former regional tribes. Hundreds of large, ancient Native American mounds are unique to this region and consist of such interesting shapes as those of a serpent, lizard, panther, bear, eagle, and person.

This region also celebrates a diversity of heritages through annual ethnic festivals. These special events offer authentic music, dance, crafts, and foods. Trips to these festivals enable young children to build understandings of various cultures as well as strengthen their own sense of identity.

References

American Automobile Association. (1989). *Tour Book* (Illinois, Indiana and Ohio; Iowa, Minnesota, Nebraska, North Dakota, and South Dakota; Kansas and Missouri; Michigan and Wisconsin). Heathrow, FL: Author.

Scholastic Book Services. (1987). *Our country today*, Scholastic Social Studies. Author.

World Book. (1989). *The world book encyclopedia*, Vols. 19, 11, 13, 14, 18, 21 (midwestern states). Chicago: Author.

R. McS. Becher

Field Trips: Northeast

The Northeast, although the smallest region in the United States in terms of land mass, is the largest in terms of population. It includes the New England states of Maine, New Hampshire, Vermont, Massachusetts, Rhode Island, and Connecticut, the Mid-Atlantic states of New York, New Jersey, Pennsylvania, Delaware, Maryland, Virginia, West Virginia, and the District of Columbia.

The Northeast region is considered predominantly urban because of its densely populated cities. The Northeast cities seem to flow from their central business areas into suburbs and then into other cities, creating one large urban area. Connected by major highway systems, bridges, and rail systems, this region has the highest concentration of traffic in the United States.

Nevertheless, there are rural areas in which about 40 percent of the population lives. Dairy farms, apple groves, and nursery and greenhouse farms are prevalent. Some mining and forest industries also exist, as well as commercial fishing. All of these endeavors are places that young children visit and from which they can learn about the economy as well as the natural world.

Children of the Northeast live lives vastly different from one another. The life of a child on a dairy farm in upper New York State differs greatly from that of a child on the Eastern Shore of Maryland. The lives of these children have little in common with those in New York City or the District of Columbia.

Environmental conditions affect children's lives in a number of ways. Beginning in infancy, the physical environment can affect children's developing locomotion, perception, and cognition. Children who live in high rise apartment buildings have been found to have less opportunity to play outside, or to explore their immediate neighborhood than do their counterparts in the rural areas who have greater freedom to explore and interact with the outdoor physical environment.

Diversity characterizes the urban areas of the Northeast. It is not uncommon for as many as 22 different nationalities and ethnic groups to be represented in many school systems. Children are affected by high density living socially as well. Some believe that in order for people to protect themselves from the overstimulation found in the cities, they distance themselves socially from others. Thus the bus driver, clerk, and letter carrier may be seen as providers of services rather than as individual people. With the need to separate from so many others, a ride on the New York City subway may become as isolating to children as a walk alone on the Appalachian trail. Despite the wide diversity of life in the Northeast, young children's lives are made similar by schooling. The environment of school offers children experiences that directly affect cognitive and memory development

(Stevenson et al., 1978). School appears to provide children with specific information and experiences that contribute to enabling them to develop similar skills, regardless of living area. Across cultural groups, living areas, and even social class, school attendance reduces the differences among and between groups of children.

Within the towns and cities, the school, neighborhood, and community become children's laboratory for learning, according to Lucy Sprague Mitchell (1971/1934). Field trips introduce children to new places and ideas within the neighborhood and community. Walking field trips in the many urban centers of the northeastern United States can be taken as follows:

- In the school, find out where the trash goes or where the water comes from. Observe food and other materials being delivered to the school. Identify the materials inside and outside of the school building. Find out how many machines in the office are used to communicate with others.

- On the playground, locate the children's classroom from the outside front, side, and back of the building. Try to find out how long it takes to stop a tricycle on rough or smooth, wet or dry surfaces. Identify the shapes of the school's windows, doors, and gutters.

- In the community, observe people building or tearing down a building, repairing electrical transmitters, or working under the street. Trips also may be taken to local stores and places of business to observe what goes on behind the counters or to make purchases for class projects.

Schooling thus serves to expand children's worlds. Curriculum content, including field trips, contributes to increasing children's knowledge of others and their environment.

References

Mitchell, L. S. (1971/1934). *Young geographers.* New York: Bank Street College of Education.

Stevenson, H. W., Parker, T., Wilkinson, A., Bonneavaux, B., & Gonzalez, M. (1978). Schooling, environment, and cognitive development:

A cross-cultural study. *Monographs of the Society for Research in Child Development*, 43 (3, Serial No. 175).

C. Seefeldt

nature. In these ways, field trips become an integral part of the early childhood curriculum.

C. Chaillé

Field Trips: Pacific Northwest

Field trips in the Pacific Northwest play an important role in providing opportunities for young children to connect their diverse experiences. Trips beyond the early childhood classroom have the potential to extend children's experiences as well as to serve as a catalyst for bringing into the classroom those interests that young children initiate once they have been exposed to some new experience outside the classroom.

Field trips that serve to extend classroom experiences in this region include those involving water and vegetation. After children study the movement of objects through water play and engage in activities with balls and mazes, they can visit a dam on the river where the movement of water and of salmon upstream in the fish ladders can bring to life the experiments in which they have engaged at the classroom water table or with mazes of various sorts. Other field trips can follow classroom experimentation with building structures and transforming materials, including block building and woodworking. These might include visits to a mill where trees are transformed into boards and sawdust.

Field trips that serve as a catalyst for experience include those involving local business and industry. A trip to a bakery can serve to inspire children to design and equip a dramatic center of interest that might involve play dough, water, and flour as well as the creation of their own scripts based upon direct experiences. A guided tour of a small airport can generate questions and subsequent extensive activities with paper airplanes and exploring ways to propel objects.

By capitalizing on resources and contexts available in different regions, field trips can add to children's cultural experiences and serve to stimulate thinking about local as well as global issues involving the community and

Field Trips: South

Mild weather, economic vitality in diverse areas, a rich, multiethnic historical tradition, and a history of celebrating the arts combine to provide a myriad of opportunities for field trips for young children in the South. These experiences often center around thematic studies with activities at school before the trip, carefully structured activities with provisions for adapting to unexpected opportunities, and follow-up activities that provide children with opportunities for integration and further exploration. A few suggested themes and related field trips follow.

Water. Almost every school in the South has either a creek, swamp, or wetland nearby where children can explore the properties of water and the animal and plant life that flourish there. Proximity to the Atlantic Ocean or Gulf of Mexico supplies opportunities for children to learn about waves, tides, and salt water life; collect shells to count, sort, and classify; and explore and build in the sand. Teachers often record children's constructions and observations with a camera.

Growing Things. The long growing season offers many gardens in which children observe and record growth and change. Several southern cities have botanical gardens. Children also visit farms where the region's industrial crops, such as peanuts, peaches, citrus fruits, and cotton, grow. Tifton, Georgia, is the site of the Georgia Agrirama, an outdoor living history museum depicting an 1890s town, forest, and farm.

Construction. The growing population in the region provides opportunities for children to watch buildings go up. Children visit sites in order to record the construction stages with photographs, drawings, and writings. Teachers arrange interviews with architects, contractors, and construction workers.

Writers. Many writers live in and have come from the South. Children listen to the stories and poems of an author, followed by a visit to his or her home. At Carl Sandburg's North Carolina home, children pet the descendants of the author's goats. At Joel Chandler's Atlanta birth place, children listen as storytellers continue his tradition. Children also visit a printing press where writers' words and pictures become books and magazines. Teachers follow up such visits by encouraging children to publish their own books.

Fine Arts. Crafts festivals abound with examples of regional crafts learned by one generation from another. Children watch artists at work and then explore the same media. Outdoor music festivals provide chances for children to picnic, play, and hear many styles of music.

Cultural Groups. The growing multicultural nature of the region provides opportunities for children to visit Native American (American Indian) settlements, museums, and mounds, at which children study groups such as the Cherokees or Seminoles, who were the region's original settlers. Many African-American, Latino, Cajun, Greek, Irish, and other groups celebrate cultural festivals and holidays that young children attend.

Civil Rights. Young children learn the story of the civil rights movements by visiting important historical sites in their communities. Among these are the Martin Luther King National Historic Site in Atlanta and the Dexter Avenue King Memorial Baptist Church in Montgomery.

M. L. McCloskey

A Survey Study of Field Trips in the South

A survey of 20 child care centers in a metropolitan area of the South found that 74 percent planned field trips for their educational value, with many field trips tying into class units or themes. Entertainment was the purpose of the remaining 26 percent of trips. All of the field trips at 6 percent of the centers were primarily for fun. Centers included those under church, hospital, university, govern-ment, for-profit chain, private, and corporate sponsorship.

Children most often travel to their field trip destination in center-owned vans or buses, and sometimes in car pools or rented buses. An admission fee for the trip's destination exists in 75 percent of centers, with no fee in the remaining 25 percent.

Children take field trips about once a month, with more frequent trips during the summer. Centers generally begin trips with three-year-olds and vary the destination with the children's age. The field trips listed in the chart on page 410 may represent only a portion of the field trips of those centers who responded to the survey.

R. L. Huss

Field Trips: Southwest

Texas, New Mexico, Arizona, and Oklahoma share the tradition of the West with emphasis on Native American (American Indian) legend, Spanish ancestry, and cowpoke lore. The frontier spirit of entrepreneurship reflected in the history of the region also is present in field trip opportunities. In Houston, for example, the National Aeronautics and Space Administration (NASA) center offers films, speakers, and simulated space flight. School groups can visit during a planned space launch. Teachers highlight contrasts and similarities between people in the past and present who explore new locations on land and in outer space with different technologies and systems of communication. Follow-up activities include language arts and creative writing, dramatizing space flights and sampling astronaut food; art, such as murals about the trip or imagined outer space; science study, through studying space rocks and weightlessness issues; and social studies, by considering group living conditions aboard the shuttle and other times and places.

In February and March, the annual Houston rodeo involves large numbers of people and presents images of life at earlier times. Riders on horseback and others in covered wagons converge on the city along well-pub-

Percentage of Type of Trip Taken by Each Type Center

	EDUCATIONAL TRIPS						
Sponsorship:	Church	Chain	Hospital	Univer.	Govt.	Priv.	Corp.
Animals zoo, pet store, game ranch	8	8	14	18	11	11	20
Outdoors nature center, botan. gard.	17	0	0	0	0	11	0
Science science centers	8	8	0	9	11	11	0
Food farmer's market, grocery store	0	15	0	18	11	11	0
Community library, hospital, fire station, airport	17	8	14	18	22	11	0
Museums historical, art	0	8	22	9	11	0	20
Cultural Events symphony, theater, puppet theater	17	23	14	9	33	22	20
	ENTERTAINMENT TRIPS						
Shows circus, ice capades, movies	8	0	14	9	0	11	20
Sports & Recreation gym, skating, swimming, bowling, parks	17	15	14	9	0	11	20
Restaurants McDonalds, pizza	8	15	8	0	0	0	0

licized trail routes. The riders range in age from preschool children to retirees, and represent various ethnic groups such as African-American cowpokes and Hispanic "Vaqueros." Local early childhood classes feature related activities during this time, such as parade viewing, square dancing, singing, and dramatizations. Children write original stories, read books about early life in the West, and cook regional foods.

Rich opportunities for field trips also exist in the New Mexico cities of Albuquerque, Santa Fe, and Taos. The Spanish influence in architecture, decor, and cuisine integrates existing Native American (American Indian) cultures. Working pueblos are sites for children to visit and observe artists and craftspeople making pottery, jewelry, weaving, and beading. Follow-up classroom activities have included art projects, such as bead-ing and clay work; social studies activities, such as recreating various habitats and dress; sampling Native American food and using tools; dramatic activities such as learning Native American dances and rituals; and language arts, such as writing accounts of trips as well as original stories.

In Oklahoma the history of the land rush exemplified by the Sooners as well as by Native American cultures are accessible by visits to individual tribal museums, and enhanced with field trips. Arizona also offers opportunities for such study through historical museums and old army forts.

D. L. Legro

Field Trips: West

Field trips in the western states reflect the geography, culture, and social life of communities that house early childhood programs. They also are influenced by the interests of teachers and families in relation to the age and ability of the children.

Teachers take children to nearby parks and zoos. They visit parents at work, local producers, merchants, and service organizations, such as the fire station and hospital.

Distinctly regional trips are possible because there are the following features:

- Great expanses of natural landscapes are easily accessible to land and ocean wildlife.
- Varied geographic features are accessible, such as the Pacific Ocean, beaches, mountains, lakes, deserts, badlands, and forests.
- Generally clement climatic conditions exist, particularly along the southern west coast and in the Hawaiian Islands.
- Few small, rural farms and communities exist.
- Relatively young cities are spread out with fewer historical sites and less heavy industry than other regions.

- Ethnic neighborhoods reflect recent immigrant groups including, Vietnamese, Laotian, Mexican, Filipino, Samoan, and Central American.

Prevailing attitudes among many teachers and parents include concern for preserving and maintaining close contact with nature and the environment. Teachers often plan trips in which children experience natural phenomena such as tidepools, redwood or bamboo forests, or mountain hikes. They visit communities that reflect cultural festivals, businesses, foods, and rituals.

It is common to expect young children to hike on trips, to take frequent trips, and to travel for an hour or more to reach a destination. Since climate is clement and community values encourage school trips, they are a common part of children's life in the western states.

E. Moravcik

Chapter 6

PERSPECTIVES ON EDUCATORS

Chapter *6*

PERSPECTIVES ON EDUCATORS

Introduction

There is a popular conception that anyone can teach young children, that no special abilities or preparation are needed beyond possession of a nurturing attitude. Research studies have found, however, that young children achieve better academically and are more socially competent when they have been in educational and caregiving situations with personnel who received special preparation in early childhood education and child development.

Teacher and caregiver preparation is effective when it includes the study of child development as well as early childhood education program development. Licensing bodies, including state departments of education and regional and national school and college accreditation agencies, as well as professional organizations, agree that these professional studies are essential. In addition, licensing providers increasingly are stressing the need for early childhood educators to be liberally educated individuals.

The unique variety of early childhood education settings and sponsorships are discussed in Chapter 3. The present chapter discusses the unique variety of caregiving and educational roles within the field of early childhood education. School administrators, professional teachers, paraprofessional teachers, aides, volunteers, parents, and maintenance, transportation, and support service personnel in different settings provide a rich variety of services to millions of children in this nation. The responsibilities of each position suggest the relevant preparation and ongoing staff development needed by these personnel.

The adults who function in a variety of roles all contribute to the education of young children. These roles are played out in the institutional setting of schools, centers, and hospitals as well as in homes and communities. This chapter considers the varied educational functions of adults engaged in early childhood education, including parents, other care providers, teachers, school administrators, and teacher educators.

These roles can be partly understood in the current setting of reformist literature concerning who should teach young children. The reformist literature focuses on the need to develop an educated citizenry who can work in a global economy that is moving increasingly into informational technologies. At the same time, there is recognition of the growing diversity of the country's population and the importance of improving the educational experiences of culturally varied children. In turn, teacher preparation and staff development programs need to take into account the varying teaching styles and ways of relating to children that have been influenced by teachers' cultural backgrounds. There also are differences in public and private sector programs that need consideration. Responding to societal needs and contemporary research findings, school-based educational programs increasingly are including provisions for extended child care services, and traditionally center-based child care programs are integrating educational components. While there is an ongoing tendency in these directions at this time, there is not yet a full convergence of education and child care functions.

In order to deal with the broadening roles of teacher/care providers, there has been a recommendation to increase the liberal arts backgrounds of prospective teacher/care providers and to require master's degrees. Another recommendation has been to increase the recruitment and retention of culturally diverse teacher/care providers. Many commentators suggest that requiring a master's degree for minimal entry into teaching will reduce the opportunity to include culturally diverse populations who have been underrepresented. Still another recommendation has been to increase the professional status of teachers in order to attract the most able candidates. There has been less attention to the preparation of educator/care providers for the preschool age child, an issue to which professional associations are turning their attention.

There has been a discontinuity between the experience of children in primary and preprimary grades no less than in the preparation of their teachers. The preparation of preprimary teachers often has included a strong emphasis on child development studies, whereas the preparation of primary and other elementary school teachers has tended to stress the pedagogy of teaching basic skills. In recent years the academic emphasis of the elementary school increasingly has influenced the education of younger children.

At the same time, there has been a growing trend in early childhood teacher education to consider wedding the use of developmental processes and subject matter content. Prospective teachers, however, dependent upon a student teaching model, often encounter field-based observation and practice in their preparatory program that contradicts their theoretical and research understandings. Increasingly, therefore, new teachers face the need to resolve the contradiction between what they say they believe rationally and what they feel comfortable doing in practice. Articles in this chapter, therefore, also discuss some ways in which teacher education strategies attempt to build professional resolve and deliberative action. Such preparation of reflective practitioners aims at developing a corps of professional educators.

Early Childhood Educator Professionalism

Professionalism reflects a level of practice in a field that requires a high level of knowledge and skill developed over a lengthy period of preparation. Originally, the term "profession" referred to the practices of law, medicine, and the ministry. Today it is applied more broadly.

Professions are established to maintain essential services related to an area of social need. Professionals possess a specialized body of knowledge and skills based on an undergirding theory that is gained over a protracted period of preparation. Professionals typically are organized into associations that support autonomous practice.

Questions have been raised about whether teaching in general, and early childhood teaching in particular, reflects a true profession.

Sometimes teaching is called a semiprofession since it manifests many but not all of the characteristics of a profession.

One way that professions maintain their high degree of professionalism is by controlling entry into the field and requiring high levels of preparation as well as a demonstration of required knowledge and competence, often through an examination. Completion of preparation and successfully passing the required examination lead to some form of license, often given by the state. Some states require continued professional development and behavior consistent with a code of ethics in order for the license to remain in effect.

In the field of education, such a license takes the form of a state teaching certificate. This teaching certificate usually is limited to a field of teaching and a range of ages or grades to which the certificate applies. While many states offer a teaching certificate in early childhood education, some provide an early childhood endorsement on an elementary teaching certificate instead. The age and/or grade range of the certificate or endorsement varies as well. Sometimes only a kindergarten endorsement is available or the certificate is limited to kindergarten through grade three, or it encompasses teaching children from birth through age eight. In order to receive a teaching certificate, individuals normally must have completed an approved program of teacher preparation. Most of these programs are at the bachelor's degree level, though some programs are at the master's level only, or require a full five years of preparatory study. Many states also require successful completion of an examination. In some states the examination covers the field of teaching or only basic academic skills.

While entry into public school teaching generally requires a state teaching certificate and a minimal completion of the bachelor's degree, this does not necessarily apply to teaching in nonpublic school. Many child care centers and preschools are sponsored privately, and the licensing and supervision of preschools generally is outside the domain of state departments of education. Requirements for practice also vary. Completion of a one- or two-year post-secondary program or the accumulation of a minimum number of credits in child care courses may be expected, or the requirement may be less rigorous, with experience serving in lieu of preparation.

Inasmuch as there is no teaching certificate available in many states for preschool or child care practitioners, the Child Development Associate (CDA) credential was developed as an alternative. Individuals attain this certificate by demonstrating competencies through meeting performance criteria. More than 27,000 CDA credentials have been awarded to date. This represents a small proportion of those who practice in the field and lack a teaching certificate. The credential presently is undergoing modification at a national level in order to become more available to practitioners. The National Association for the Education of Young Children has suggested that there be varying levels of professionalism for early childhood practitioners. *Early Childhood Teacher Assistants*, level one, would be entry-level practitioners who work under the direct supervision of professionals. They would be expected to have a CDA credential or its equivalent and to participate in professional development activities. *Early Childhood Associate Teachers*, level two, would implement program activities and be responsible for a group of children. They would be expected to have a community college two-year degree. *Early Childhood Teachers*, level three, would provide care and education for groups of children. They would have a bachelor's degree in early childhood education or child development. *Early Childhood Specialists*, level four, would supervise and train staff to design curriculum and, possibly, administer programs. They would be expected to have a master's degree in early childhood education or child development as well as early childhood work experience. *Early Childhood Teacher Educators*, level five, would prepare teachers and specialists in early childhood education. They would be expected to hold a Ph.D. or Ed.D. degree in an approved program.

Some early childhood educators have suggested that a career level plan be established for early childhood teachers, with practitioners able to start at the entry level and, through advanced training and experience, move to more responsible levels of professionalism. While this proposal generally has been regarded as a worthy one, there are a number of issues that remain to be resolved; and the proposal has never been implemented on any extended scale.

Early Childhood Teacher Educators

The literature on teacher education and early childhood education includes more discussion about the process of and content for teaching teachers than about teacher educators themselves. It is possible to view the role of the teacher educator as an extension of the role of the teacher with some important differences (Almy, 1975). In addition to an interest and desire to work with adults as well as with children, those who support the development of teachers need to have characteristics of effective teachers of young children, including warmth, nurturance, patience, energy, intelligence, and cultural sensitivity. Fascination with ideas and the ability to think conceptually as well as concretely, also are hallmarks of those who are successful in this role. These professionals should have the maturity that enables them to deal with the conflicts and ambiguities that often arise when one works with adults as well as children (Ibid.).

Teachers of teachers also are advocates for children and leaders in the field who create and disseminate new ideas and practices. Qualifications for early childhood teacher educators include successful professional experience as a teacher of young children and advanced education leading to in-depth knowledge of theory, research, and practice of early childhood education and child development. Those working in children's centers and schools should know the history and values of early childhood education. They should understand the role of play in children's development as well as how it is supported in an early childhood environment. They also need to remain current and professionally active in their field. In addition to these attributes,

those working in college settings must be able to engage in scholarly work that contributes to the knowledge base of the field.

Teacher educators need to be skilled in selecting and using effective teaching methods appropriate for adults. They can provide inspiration as well as practical guidance. Moreover, they need to know how to teach in ways that they want teachers to work with young children. As in all teaching, early childhood teacher educators must practice what they preach. This can take place when teacher educators also focus on the social and emotional as well as the intellectual development of their students, by starting where the learner is, and by providing opportunities for students to engage actively with materials and ideas and make meaningful choices regarding their learning (Jones, 1986).

In addition to these professional qualifications and skills, the personal qualities of teacher educators are important in enabling them to support their students' development as sensitive and caring teachers of young children. They need to be committed to helping others learn to teach; be able to create warm, nonthreatening relationships; and be respectful of the dignity and integrity of others. They should be tactful, understanding, and good listeners; able to share themselves and their professional experience; and able to provide their students with support and assistance in periods of confusion and discouragement. Like teachers of children, teacher educators need to be able to use feedback as a way to support professional growth. They also need to know when and how to enable learners to create their own ways of teaching and personal philosophy of education.

One of the issues faced by early childhood teacher educators is how to prepare professional educators who can effectively design educational experiences for young children that make a positive difference in their lives. Early childhood teachers often talk about adapting curriculum to children rather than having children fit into schedules or materials that limit growth, potential, and excitement about self-directed learning. In turn, teacher educators have been considering ways in which to work with prospective teachers and school administrators that is consistent with the philosophies, theories, research, and craft knowledge that they possess. In effect, teacher educators are attempting to adapt teacher and administrator education to the needs of prospective teachers and administrators who are expected likewise to adapt their teaching and administering to the development of children and teachers. The intent of this adaptation is to maintain the vitality of lifelong, self-directed, meaningful, and significant learning. In such deliberative scholar-educators lies the potential for professionalizing the broader field of early childhood education.

Parents as Early Childhood Educators. Teachers, school and center administrators, and care providers are not the only educators of young children. It is obvious that parents have an even more profound influence on children's growth and development through their day-to-day interactions with their children. While much of this interaction is informal or incidental, it is generally recognized that such interaction teaches as certainly as any planned learning experience carried out in a classroom or other deliberately educational setting.

Historically, the founders of the first kindergartens idealized parental influence. They believed that mother love was the purest expression of the divine in human nature (Froebel, 1909). Early educators came to view parents as possible beneficiaries of the new science of child behavior when the child study movement gained momentum at the end of the nineteenth century. Child development specialists expected that insights from child observations could be used to help guide parents in the many decisions involved in child rearing. Nursery schools and kindergartens influenced by "progressive" child study began to institute parent education programs that provided information on stages of child development and opportunities for parents, usually mothers, to discuss the common incidents of childhood.

Parent education programs tended to emphasize a flow of information from teachers or other specialists to parents, with some discussion around the chosen topics guided by the teachers or other group leaders. In settings such as parent cooperatives, however, parents assumed a more active role as teachers and administrators of early childhood programs. Here the flow of information was as much from the parents to the teachers as vice versa.

The Head Start program, beginning in the 1960s, defined parent involvement as having at least three aspects that included receiving information, as in the earlier parent education programs; volunteering as helpers in the classroom, periodically assuming the role of an aide or assistant teacher for special projects with individuals or small groups of children; and serving as program advisors to Head Start administrators. Policy makers thought that these activities would encourage parents to reinforce with their children at home the learning that was occurring in the schools or early childhood centers.

More recently, some programs have invited parents to assume a coinstructional role in classrooms, rather than the less demanding "helper" role that characterized earlier efforts. The parents participate in planning, carrying out activities, and evaluating their effects with their teacher team member.

Many early childhood programs today include several of these collaborative options for parent involvement, while others continue to favor the more traditional parent education approach.

This chapter consists of nine sections that examine the history of early childhood teacher education, present profiles of early childhood teachers and child care providers, identify major professional organizations and publications, explore salient professional issues, and describe preservice and in-service teacher education, teacher education policies, parent and community involvement in early childhood education, and the supervision and administration of early childhood programs.

References

Almy, M. (1975). *The early childhood educator at work.* New York: McGraw-Hill.

Froebel, F. (1909). *The education of man.* New York: Appleton.

Jones, E. (1986). *Teaching adults: An active learning approach*. Washington, DC: National Association for the Education of Young Children.

National Association for the Education of Young Children. (1990). *Draft model of early childhood professional development* (rev. ed.). Washington, DC: Author.

S. Feeney, D. P. Fromberg,
B. Spodek, & L. R. Williams

6.1 History of Early Childhood Teacher Recruitment, Certification, and Legislation

This section provides a historical overview of early childhood teacher education in the United States. The discussions in these articles include information on contemporary as well as continuing issues that help to define the field. These issues include finding a place for a culturally diverse population in the profession, the need for specific licensing in each state that supports quality early childhood education, and identifying the signs that point the way to professional status of the field of early childhood teacher education. The discussions also include the unique problems facing historically black institutions that prepare early childhood teachers.

The first two articles provide an overview. The third article, which focuses on the period from 1920 until the present, provides an opportunity to consider the status of the early childhood teacher education profession in a contemporary context. (See also Chapter 2 for legislative timelines.)

D. P. Fromberg

History of Early Childhood Teacher Education

The history of the kindergarten, nursery education, and child care movements continues to shape the history of early childhood teacher education in the United States.

The growth of the United States kindergarten movement in the late nineteenth century created a demand for teachers with specific training in the new kindergarten methods. Independent training schools grew and were supplanted by the growing number of normal schools designed to train elementary school teachers.

Professional kindergarten organizations recommended that kindergartens become part of the public school systems. Efforts of kindergarten educators to infuse modern kindergarten methods into largely inappropriate primary-grade curricula further cemented the association of kindergartens with primary-grade education.

With kindergartens in the public elementary school system, state departments of education increased regulation of kindergarten early childhood education programs as well as the institutional development of kindergarten early childhood teacher education programs by universities, colleges, and departments of education. In time, four-year baccalaureate degree programs for prospective teachers supplanted the three-year normal school teacher preparation programs, as teachers colleges evolved or were absorbed into universities.

Kindergarten education has become largely universal in the United States since the 1960s rediscovery of early childhood. Related to this trend, many state departments of education extended teacher certification standards to include kindergarten teachers. (See **Certification of Teachers**, in Section 6.7, below.) These requirements are incorporated in various ways by schools, colleges, and departments of education whose primary concern is the preparation of elementary and secondary school teachers.

In an effort to reestablish significant input into the preparation of kindergarten and primary-grade teachers, the National Association for the Education of Young Children (NAEYC, 1991) has developed four- and five-year teacher education program standards. NAEYC's standards have been accepted by the National Council for the Accreditation of Teacher Education as the standards for early childhood teacher education program accreditation.

The nursery school movement also continues to influence early childhood teacher education history. Emerging from early twentieth-century concerns for the physical health and social well-being of young children and their families, the nursery school movement developed a multidisciplinary perspective, including education, home economics, social work, psychology, nursing, and medicine. This movement has been strongly influenced by the methods and theories of child study and development.

Leading land grant universities and state university systems organized child development, family studies, and nursery education programs primarily within colleges of home economics. Inasmuch as only recently have public schools provided programs for three- and four-year-old children, nursery teacher education programs have not been required to meet many state department of education early childhood teacher certification standards. However, since 30 states now are providing some public early childhood programs for three- and four-year-olds, there is a beginning trend to revise state early childhood teacher certification guidelines and standards to conform more closely with NAEYC early childhood teacher education policies. These policies represent more of a child- and family-centered perspective than the standards usually associated with kindergarten and primary-grade education.

Feminist activism, social reform, economic hardship, and periods of war have affected the United States child care movement. Societal changes resulting from the civil rights and women's liberation movements, changing economic conditions, and concerns about early school success, have resulted in a staggering growth of preschool child care programs. As Head Start programs grew during the late 1960s, the shortage of large numbers of even minimally trained preschool early childhood teachers reflected the experiences of the Great Depression–era Works Progress Administration nurseries. In response, the Child Development Associate (CDA) credential was developed in 1973 as a training program to fill the need for Head Start and Follow Through teachers. Now under the auspices of NAEYC,

the CDA program provides basic training and certification for group child care teachers. Some state departments of human services also have established minimum teacher training standards, within their child care center licensing function, that are substantially less stringent than certification standards for public school early childhood teachers.

The kindergarten, nursery school, and child care movements' collective characteristics and developmental history will affect future early childhood teacher education. The current distinctions in preparation of primary/ kindergarten, preschool, and child care personnel are likely to influence the ongoing consideration of reasonable standards for different types and levels of professional responsibility. It is likely that early childhood professionals will become involved increasingly in establishing and revising certification standards, and in influencing external regulatory bodies.

References

NAEYC. (1991). *Early childhood teacher education guidelines.* Washington, DC: National Association for the Education of Young Children.

Office of Child Development (OCD). (1973). *The CDA program: The child development associate, a guide for training.* Washington, DC: United States Government Printing Office.

D. L. McLean & J. M. Johnston

Early Childhood Teacher Education at Black Colleges

Historically black institutions have been involved in the preparation of early childhood teachers since the late nineteenth century. Black early childhood teacher education programs emphasize diversity and help prospective teachers develop the necessary cultural competencies for working effectively with all children and their families. Students and graduates are able to respond to the same challenges as other early childhood teacher education graduates while helping to address specific needs and concerns in the black community.

As early as 1873, Hampton Institute in Virginia had a kindergarten program for five-year-olds and added a kindergarten training school in 1893. Tuskegee Institute operated a similar program at the turn of the century (Cunningham & Osborn, 1979). Early childhood education as a course of study was available at Howard University and Atlanta University, directed by Gertrude Ware, Superintendent of Kindergarten Training, in the early twentieth century (Ibid.).

Black women have recognized the importance of education in the early years throughout this century. The National Association of Colored Women (NACW), founded in 1896, established kindergartens for black children throughout the United States and Canada. Haydee Campbell, the first black to receive formal training in early childhood education, directed the NACW's kindergarten section (Ibid.).

Laboratory schools for preschool-aged children developed at colleges and universities in the early 1920s. The first black laboratory schools opened in 1929 and 1930 at Hampton Institute and Spelman College in Atlanta, respectively. Both programs became an early training ground for future leaders in early childhood education (Ibid.). Flemmie P. Kittrell was the first black to receive a doctorate in early childhood. She established a laboratory school at Bennett College in 1931, later was a dean at Hampton Institute, and went to Howard University in 1940 as the director of the laboratory school and head of the early childhood department (Ibid.; Corder & Quisenberry, 1987).

Most historically black institutions offer a bachelor's degree in early childhood education. The programs have had a strong parent and community focus. Students participate in a variety of field placements. At Norfolk State University in Virginia, for example, students in the B.S. and M.S. programs tutor and teach in the neighborhood housing projects throughout their course of study. Spelman College operates a laboratory school on campus and one in a housing project in Atlanta. Norfolk State University and Howard University, two of the largest historically black universities, offer exemplary master's degree programs in early childhood education. According to their university catalogs, both schools aim to prepare teachers to teach young children of diverse backgrounds, needs, and strengths from inner city and rural areas. Jackson State University in Mississippi is the only historically black institution with a doctorate in Early Childhood Education (Council for Early Childhood Professional Recognition, 1989).

Early childhood education at black colleges has been tied closely to the black community. Their programs have addressed the needs of black children and families. At the same time there has been an increasing enrollment of white students in these programs, adding to the multicultural training opportunities.

References

Corder, L. J., & Quisenberry, N. L. (1987). Early education and Afro-Americans: History, assumptions and implications for the future. *Childhood Education, 63* (3), 154–158.

Cunningham, C. E., & Osborn, D. K. (1979). A historical examination of blacks in early childhood education. *Young Children, 34* (3), 20–29.

Council for Early Childhood Professional Recognition. (1989). *National directory of early childhood training programs.* Washington, DC: Author.

M. W. Thornton

History of Early Childhood Teacher Licensure: 1920s–1990s

The history of early childhood teacher licensure from 1920 to the present can be understood best by focusing on two distinct groups—teachers who work with children from birth through four years of age and those that work with children from five through eight years of age. The reason to approach the topic from two viewpoints is that there is a general lack of certification or credential requirements for directors, teachers, care providers, assistant teachers, and teacher aides in early childhood programs that are not supported by public funds. Where credentialing requirements have existed, they have been part of center licensing standards that often are minimal.

Results of a survey of child care salaries and working conditions indicated that about one-third of the useable returns were from respondents who had no permits or credentials for doing their jobs (NAEYC, 1984). About one-third of those in teacher, lead teacher, or head teacher positions did not have a bachelor's degree or graduate work (Ibid.).

Studies have found, however, that the educational level of the early childhood teaching staff is a critical variable affecting program quality, although public policies regarding standards for teaching children under the age of five years are almost nonexistent (Ruopp, Travers, Glantz, & Coelen, 1979; Whitebook, Howes, Phillips, & Pemberton, 1989). Certification requirements for teachers who work with children five years of age and older have continued to change during the last seventy years. Licensing standards, however, have not always been based on existing knowledge about what teachers need to know in order to be successful with young children.

In the early 1920s, for example, 30 states had no certification requirement for elementary teachers, and no state required a college degree. Kindergarten and primary-grade teachers in these states could be hired without specific educational requirements related to working with young children. By the late 1960s, all but 4 states required a bachelor's degree for beginning elementary teachers and 42 states required teachers in publicly supported kindergartens to hold state certification.

What constitutes appropriate certification is a question that continues to cause disagreement. Certification requirements often have changed for political or economic reasons. The age range, title, and requirements for a specific credential often are based on school organizational patterns rather than on reasons of quality.

A 1988 survey found that 23 states and the District of Columbia have a clearly labeled Early Childhood certification (McCarthy, 1988; See also **Certification of Teachers,** Section 6.7, below). The most prevalent certification pattern is for teachers of children from three to eight years of age. There also were 11 states that had certification patterns similar to an early childhood certificate, but were labeled as prekindergarten, nursery–first grade, or other designations (Ibid.).

Many states offer an early childhood endorsement on an elementary certificate encompassing grades one to six or one to eight. In this approach, teachers major in elementary education and take additional courses in early childhood education. Requirements for an early childhood endorsement range from as few as two courses to as much as 15 to 18 semester hours plus a student teaching requirement (Ibid.).

All states now require that candidates for elementary or early childhood certification complete an approved teacher education program. Thirty-nine states require the successful completion of either the National Teachers Examination (NTE) or a state-developed examination. The purpose of these examinations is to assess the knowledge background of prospective teachers. The three, two-hour parts of the NTE include sections on communication skills, general knowledge, and professional knowledge. In some parts of the country there is also a required NTE Early Childhood Specialty Test section (Educational Testing Service, 1988).

Some states recently have required teachers to earn a baccalaureate degree in liberal arts and either minor in education or study education as part of a graduate program. Texas, Tennessee, and Virginia, for example, limit the number of undergraduate education credits to as few as 18 semester hours (Watts, 1989). This trend to reduce the number of education courses required for certification reflects a change during the past decade, according to a survey of 202 early childhood teacher education programs, in which 51 percent of the respondents reported increases in professional education course work (Spodek & Saracho, 1983).

The development of teacher induction programs is another trend in about one-third of the states (McCarthy, 1988). These programs attempt to support new teachers by utilizing some combination of help from experienced teachers, classroom observations, and assistance seminars (Huling-Austin, 1986; Medley, Rosenblum, & Vance, 1989).

Requiring the NTE, a baccalaureate degree in liberal arts and sciences, and teacher induction programs, are all examples of changes in certification policies within individual states. Two reports that support changes in these directions include *A Nation Prepared* (Carnegie Foundation, 1986) and *Tomorrow's Teachers* (Holmes Group, 1986). These reports suggest that many of the educational problems in the United States could be solved by improving the preparation of teachers.

The recruitment of early childhood teachers is an activity that has not received much public policy attention in the past. The lack of qualified teachers in the field who represent a broad range of the cultural groups in the United States, however, has fostered a variety of initiatives designed to attract such candidates who have been underrepresented. The number of culturally diverse teachers in the United States is declining while the number of black, Hispanic, and Asian school-age children is increasing (Brown, 1988). There have been suggestions that institutions of higher education adopt the recruitment and retention proposals of the American Association of Colleges of Teacher Education (AACTE) (Ibid.). The AACTE plan calls for active efforts to recruit culturally diverse teachers, and provide special support and counseling services, scholarships, and financial assistance programs (AACTE, 1989).

References

American Association of Colleges for Teacher Education. (1989). *Recruiting minority teachers: A practical guide.* Washington, DC: Author.

Brown, F. (January 1988). Minority teachers, human capital, and democracy and the educational reforms of the 1970s and 1980s. Paper presented at the NAEYC Colloquium on Early Childhood Teacher Education: Traditions and Trends. Miami, FL.

Carnegie Forum on Education and the Economy. (1986). *A nation prepared: Teachers for the 21st century.* New York: Author.

Educational Testing Service. (1988). *Guidelines for proper use of NTE tests.* Princeton NJ: Author.

The Holmes Group, Inc. (1986). *Tomorrow's teachers: A report of the Holmes Group.* Lansing, MI: Author.

Huling-Austin, L. (1986). What can and cannot reasonably be expected from teacher induction programs. *Journal of Teacher Education*, 37 (19), 2–5.

McCarthy, J. (1988). *State certification of early childhood teachers: An analysis of the 50 states and the District of Columbia.* Washington, DC: National Association for the Education of Young Children.

Medley, D., Rosenblum, E., & Vance, N. (1989). Assessing the functional knowledge of participants in the Virginia beginning teacher assistance program. *Elementary School Journal*, 89 (40), 495–510.

National Association for the Education of Young Children. (1984). Research report: Results of the NAEYC survey of child care salaries and working conditions. *Young Children*, 40 (1), 9–14.

Ruopp, R., Travers, J., Glantz, F., & Coelen, C. (1979). *Children at the center: Summary findings and their implications.* Cambridge, MA: Abt.

Spodek, B., Davis, M.D., & Saracho, O. (1983). Early childhood teacher education and certification. *Journal of Teacher Education*, 34 (5), 50–52.

Watts, D. (1989). NCATE and Texas eyeball to eyeball: Who will blink? *Phi Delta Kappan*, 71 (4), 311–314.

Whitebook, M., Howes, C., Phillips, D., & Pemberton, C. (1989). Who cares? Child care teachers and the quality of care in America. *Young Children*, 45 (1), 41–45.

M. D. Davis

6.2 Profiles of Early Childhood Teachers and Child Care Providers

People who care for and teach infants and young children outside the children's homes are known by numerous terms. The National Association for the Education of Young Children (NAEYC) agreed on four terms—*Early Childhood Specialist, Teacher, Associate Teacher, and Assistant*—to designate the level of professional education, experience, and responsibility of individuals who work with young children. Descriptions of these four NAEYC terms appear in the Introduction to Chapter 6, above. Other commonly used terms follow.

Certified Teacher refers to a person who is responsible for teaching a group of young children. This person holds a baccalaureate or master's degree and has fulfilled teacher requirements for the state. Certificates vary from state to state with regard to the span of ages of children for whom the teacher may assume responsibility.

Kindergarten Teacher refers to a certified teacher who teachers five-year-olds. In some states, this person may teach four-year-olds who might be known as prekindergarten children.

Early Childhood Special Education Teacher refers to a person certified in both early childhood and special education. This person teaches young handicapped children in schools or guides the treatment of handicapped infants by parents prior to the child's entry into the "least restrictive environment."

Montessori Teacher refers to an individual who has completed an authentic Montessori preparation program and received Montessori certification. Such certification may differ from state certification.

Associate Degree Teacher refers to a person completing a two-year program in a community or junior college child care program. Some unregistered preschools in the private sector employ such individuals as head teachers.

Child Development Associate (CDA) is a person who earned the CDA certificate through a nationwide program administered by the Council for Early Childhood Professional Recognition (see also, below.) Some or all of the CDA preparation may be part of a two-year community college program.

Head Start Teacher refers to a person who teaches in Head Start, the federally funded early childhood program for low-income young children. This individual typically has, at the minimum, a CDA certificate.

Teacher's Aide refers to an assistant to the teacher in a group of young children. Qualifications for this position range between a high school diploma to a diploma from a special-ized community college two-year program in early childhood education.

Caregiver or Care Provider refers to a person who cares for infants and young children, usually in a private home. The professional qualifications can vary widely from little or no education about young children to a professionally qualified person. Often these persons choose to stay home with their own children and provide family income by caring for children of other parents who work outside the home. Some states require them to register or qualify for a state license.

Nanny refers to an individual hired by a private family to care for their children. A nanny often lives with the family, beginning with newborns and infants. There are programs for preparing nannies, including some two-year college programs. Many who serve as nannies have no professional child development training.

V. Hildebrand

Career Development

Career development takes many forms, due to the varieties of sponsorship of early childhood programs, as well as the programs' diverse historical roots. Requirements and expectations also vary as a function of differing regulations among state and local agencies.

The growth of a sense of shared professionalism among early childhood educators is constrained by variations in the levels and the nature of preparation requirements in different programs. A person who works directly with children in a private preschool or child care center may carry a variety of titles, such as "teacher," or "child care worker." Depending upon state licensing requirements, this person's preparation may include as little as an interest in children to as much as undergraduate and graduate degrees in early childhood education. In-service requirements for child care and preschool staff often are minimal. Opportunities for in-service staff development often are limited, despite evidence that qualified staff is necessary for programs to have positive effects on children (see Section 6.1, **History of Early Childhood Teacher Recruitment, Certification, and Legislation**). Kindergarten/primary teachers typically have completed a bachelor's degree in elementary education or, less typically, in early childhood education, and generally are required to participate regularly in in-service professional development activities.

Head Start has provided a career ladder for many parents by encouraging them to move from volunteering in the classroom, to employment as paraprofessionals, to sometimes managing an entire program. A considerable portion of the annual Head Start budget is allocated to ongoing training and development of staff at all levels. Originally sponsored by Head Start, the competency-based Child Development Associate (CDA) credential was designed to provide a career development path alternative to traditional forms of higher education. The Council for Early Childhood Professional Recognition, an arm of the National Association for the Education of Young Children, now maintains the CDA process, and issues and renews the credential.

The provision of adequate compensation is a major determinant of a person's perception of himself or herself as a professional. Many young people complete early childhood preparation programs only to discover that the near minimum wage salaries are insufficient to maintain a reasonable standard of living and/or to nurture a sense of professionalism. The salaries of public school kindergarten and primary-grade teachers are considerably higher, although their status within the school systems often is quite low.

Public perception of the role of people who work with young children also limits the development of individuals and of the profession. The challenge facing the profession in the coming decades will be to increase public awareness of the importance of well-prepared and sufficiently compensated staff in child care centers and homes, preschools, and early primary units in elementary schools, in order to

enhance the professional and economic status of the teachers and to benefit children.

References

National Association for the Education of Young Children. (1991). *Early childhood teacher education guidelines.* Washington, DC: Author.

National Association for the Education of Young Children. (1984). NAEYC position statement on nomenclature, salaries, benefits, and the status of the early childhood profession. *Young Children, 40* (19), 52–55.

Ruopp, R., Travers, J., Glantz, F., & Coelen, C. (1979). *Children at the center: Summary findings and their implications.* Cambridge, MA: Abt.

Spodek, B., Saracho, O., & Peters, D. (eds.). (1988). *Professionalism and the early childhood practitioner.* New York: Teachers College Press.

H. A. Egertson

Early Childhood Teachers: A Profile

A typical public school early childhood teacher is a white female, about thirty-five years old, lives in the suburbs, has two children in school, and is satisfied with her work. She has probably been teaching in this setting for more than five years.

A typical center-based teacher for children under 5 is female, about 25 years old, may come from any ethnic background, and lives in an urban or suburban setting. She is new to the field and may not remain in this position for more than two years.

A typical family child care provider is a young mother with one or more children of her own who provides care for other people's children while caring for her own children at the same time. Although neither demographic statistics nor literature documents the educational background, gender, age, and ethnicity of early childhood teachers, there is common knowledge about who teaches young children. Literature on teaching and feminism coupled with practical knowledge of early childhood teachers and teaching patterns allows us to make such statements about the profession.

This descriptive piece profiles the backgrounds of those who teach young children.

Educational Background

Early childhood teachers come to teaching with varied educational backgrounds. Those who teach children over five in public school *must* hold a bachelor's degree and complete a certified teacher preparation program. Although requirements vary from state to state, a teaching credential is granted at the state level to those completing initial state requirements. Some states certify early childhood teachers with an N-3 certificate; some with a K-6 certificate; and some with a Pre-K/K endorsement to an elementary certificate.

Teachers of children under five, (e.g., child care providers, family day care providers, Head Start teachers, and preschool teachers) do not always need to meet standards of entry. Many of these teachers do not earn more than the minimum wage, perhaps because "the absence of certification standards is rooted in economic interests" (Spodek & Saracho, 1988, p. 63). Training and certification for teachers of children under five varies by state and is based upon licensing requirements of particular funding agencies. Trend data, however, indicate that more states are beginning to improve standards for these teachers.

One attempt at such improvement is through the Child Development Associate (CDA) credentialing program. This credential provides early childhood personnel the opportunity to demonstrate the skills and competencies in 16 areas such as health, safety, and learning environment necessary to work appropriately with young children. To date, "over 17,000 child care workers have been certified through the CDA program while 60 percent of the states mention it in their licensing requirements" (Jorde, 1988). In the 22,816 Head Start classrooms, 45 percent of the classroom teaching staff holds a degree in early childhood education or a CDA certificate (ACYF, 1989, p. 2).

Gender

It is common knowledge that women comprise the majority of teachers. The predominance of women in early childhood education is rooted in the traditional career paths open to women.

Literature on women's career identities describes them as having low career commitment and having more feeling than intellect (Bilken, 1987). It further describes women as failing to make their work an integral part of their identity. Such literature perpetuates the stereotype that teaching is merely an extension of women's work in the home and contributes heavily to the low status, pay, and reputation of early childhood teachers.

Contemporary literature on women, however, challenges these assumptions. It illustrates the similarities in men's and women's involvement with work, job satisfaction, and perceived balancing betweeen work and family issues. Women do take their work seriously, and, for most, it is an integral part of their identity (Bilken, 1987).

Although early childhood teachers are predominantly women, in 1984 there were between 50,000 and 150,000 men in early childhood who comprised about 5 percent of the early childhood teaching force (Seifert, 1988, p. 105). Literature on teachers indicates that both men and women are similar in their motivation and involvement with their work, job satisfaction, perceived conflict between work and home (Bilken, 1987), and personal and professional backgrounds (Seifert, 1988).

One area in which male teachers differ from female teachers appears to be in their long-term attitudes about early childhood education as a career. Research indicates that women remain in the profession longer than men either through choice or lack of alternatives (Sadker & Sadker, 1985). Men seek administrative work sooner and more frequently than do women and appear to become more easily frustrated with classroom work.

Attitudes and Job Satisfaction

A major outgrowth of these long held attitudes toward women has resulted in the low status and reputation of teaching in general and of early childhood teachers in particular (Feeney, S., Christensen, D., & Moravcik, E., 1987). Such low status has contributed "to women failing to identify proudly with their teaching role" (Bilken, 1987). Low salaries reflect the low value that society places upon early childhood teachers and the education of young children, and contributes to keeping men out of the field and high staff turnover in programs for under fives (Feeney, Christensen, & Moravick, 1987).

Given this situation, it is not surprising that many dedicated teachers and directors find themselves frustrated and experiencing low morale, job stress, and burnout. Many simply leave their positions to look for more lucrative and less stressful jobs (Jorde, 1988). Staff turnover in child care centers averages 30 percent to 40 percent a year, a rate far greater than in any other human service profession. Indeed, the Bureau of Labor Statistics reports that child care work is among the country's top ten job categories with the highest turnover (Ibid.).

Despite the political, sociological, and economic realities of the field, most early childhood teachers "feel strongly about the value and the work that they do . . . [believing it] . . . essential to the well being of children and society. Yet, it is difficult when they are not accorded the prestige and salary commensurate with those values" (Feeney, Christensen, & Moravcik, 1987, p. 32).

Those who are attracted to and remain in the profession over time demonstrate special qualities that provide the internal rewards necessary to sustain them in the field. Good early childhood teachers possess personal qualities that help them succeed in the field. They respect children, are open to new ideas, are nurturing, worldly, and physically healthy (Morrison, 1988; Spodek and Saracho, 1988).

Teachers of young children choose early childhood education for a variety of reasons. Most importantly, however, they exhibit the above mentioned characteristics and are attracted to the unique classroom teaching style of young children. Early childhood teachers enjoy initiating activities in response to children's interests and levels of development, providing choices to children, working closely with other adults in a team approach and working closely with parents.

References

Administration for Children Youth and Families (ACYF). (1989). Project Head Start Statistical Fact Sheet (p. 2). Washington, DC: ACYF.

Bilken, S. K. (1987). Women in American elementary school teaching: A case study. In P. A. Schmuck (ed.), *Women Educators: Employees of Schools in Western Countries* (pp. 223–243). Albany: State University of New York Press.

Feeney, S., Christensen, D., & Moravcik, E. (1987). *Who am I in the lives of children?* (3rd ed). Columbus, OH: Merrill.

Jorde, P. (1988). Early childhood education: Issues and trends. In Bauch, J. P. (ed.), *Early childhood education in the schools* (pp. 60–64). Washington, DC: National Education Association.

Morrison, G. S. (1988). *Early childhood education today* (4th ed.). Columbus, OH: Merrill.

Sadker, D. & Sadker, M. (1985). The treatment of sex equity in teacher education. In S. S. Klein (ed.), *Handbook for achieving sex equity through education.* (pp. 145–161). Baltimore: Johns Hopkins University Press.

Seifert, K. (1988). Men in early childhood education. In B. Spodek, O. N. Saracho, & D. L. Peters (eds.), *Professionalism and the early childhood practitioner* (pp. 105–116). New York: Teachers College Press.

Spodek, B., & Saracho, O. (1988). Professionalism in Early Childhood Education. In B. Spodek, O. N. Saracho, & D. L. Peters (eds.), *Professionalism and the early childhood practitioner* (pp. 59–74). New York: Teachers College Press.

J. Isenberg

Recruitment and Admission to the Profession

The field of early childhood education in the United States encompasses a variety of programs that have evolved during the past 160 years. As each program came into existence the nature of the program influenced the qualifications of the personnel deemed appropriate at that time. Tradition is often difficult to change, and there is a range of opinions regarding what kind of professional preparation and competencies different types of programs need. In addition, the low status of the early childhood profession, and the lack of funds to compensate personnel adequately, contribute to the ambivalence of professional organizations about specifying standards of performance.

Recruitment and admission to a profession under these circumstances develops within the context of understanding role expectations. The NAEYC (1984) guidelines for levels of professional roles provide the context for remarks that follow. Career awareness needs to develop for career role options within the field of early childhood education. Early childhood educators should develop career exploration programs for junior and senior high school students. Firsthand experiences such as part-time employment, volunteering, and adopt-a-center projects (e.g., making toys and games, assisting on field trips, conducting story times) would guide students in making an informed choice about their career goals. These experiences should be accompanied by reflective discussions that include self-evaluation related to teaching and alternatives for pursuing a professional education. Personalized, experience-based activities have the potential for identifying strongly committed and highly motivated teacher candidates from all ethnic and socioeconomic groups.

On-the-job recruitment is another way to encourage hesitant candidates who might have some interest in pursuing teacher education studies. Both recent graduates and midlife persons who might be ready to pursue a first career or make a career change might constitute other potential populations. For those who are ambivalent, employment in an early childhood program at level 1, Teacher Assistant, and participating in concurrent professional development activities might help to resolve questions about their personal goals. Professional colleagues might encourage a move to the next step of professional development, Teacher Associate.

Admission to the profession takes place within two categories of preparation, profes-sional and semiprofessional. Teachers in some child care programs and nursery schools demonstrate different levels of performance than do public school personnel. Candidates with professional preparation possess a theoretical base to guide their practice, whereas semiprofessionals have less theoretical and conceptual knowledge within their orientation to specific teaching skills (Howsam, Corrigan, Denemark, & Nash, 1976).

Professional status includes minimal completion of the bachelors degree from an institution of higher education. This requirement is a consistent standard among states. The National Council for Accreditation of Teacher Education also defines procedures that include screening for admission to teacher education and evaluation of candidates as they exit from programs. Thirty-nine states also require satisfactory completion of the National Teachers Examination (NTE) or another examination, which overrides all other judgments about a candidate's performance. At this writing, the NTE measures only academic knowledge rather than teacher effectiveness with children.

The regulation of semiprofessional personnel is an issue that government agencies and professional groups have not yet resolved. This situation affects a high percentage of personnel in nonpublic schools programs. The current state of these nonpublic programs indicates that it will be necessary to continue staffing them with many semiprofessionals. The importance of early childhood and the risks to young children, however, suggest that appropriate groups need to coordinate efforts in order to provide needed regulation of admission to employment.

References

Howsam, R. B., Corrigan, D. C., Denemark, G. W., & Nash, R. J. (1976). *Education as a profession.* Washington D.C.: American Association of Colleges for Teacher Education.

National Association for the Education of Young Children. (1984). NAEYC position statement of nomenclature, salaries, benefits, and the status of the early childhood profession. *Young Children, 40* (1), 52–55.

J. McCarthy

Support Services

Support service personnel work with teachers and children to provide a full range of services that affect the education of young children. They include specialist subject matter teachers and special educators as well as other professionals in the helping professions.

These services offer young children the greatest continuity when they take place in the context of children's classroom or family setting. When such integration is not possible, continuity can take place through the teacher or care provider who has primary responsibility for children's education. Mutual communication between teacher and support service staff, therefore, is critical.

To insure the most effective communication means that classroom teachers need short periods of time to meet support service personnel or prepare written communications for them. These arrangements require planning with the school administration and often, there are stipulations in collective bargaining agreements that support such efforts.

The use of specialist teachers, in particular, needs careful planning. They best serve children's educational needs when their activities are integrated with the classroom curriculum offerings, when teachers can plan together, and sometimes, team teach. The articles that follow in this section are arranged alphabetically.

D. P. Fromberg

Health Care Providers: Communication Linkages

Health care professionals, usually pediatric physicians and registered nurses experienced in the needs of young children in groups, play a vital role as consultants, supporters, and educators of early childhood professionals. They assist group programs for young children to develop and review health policies, plans, and emergency preparedness. They advise on sanitation and hygiene practices, prevention and management of infectious diseases, health record keeping systems, management of children with special health care needs and/or disabilities; and health and developmental screening. The consultant might provide immediate assistance or serve as a liaison between the individual health practitioner and the program, ideally in a flexible relationship as needed.

The key to successful communication among early childhood professionals, health care providers, and parents is the presence of a continuous communication loop among the three parties who care for the same child. Good communication begins with each party communicating critical information. Physicians complete required health forms with functional application to the classroom setting and ask parents about the child's regular care environment. Parents report accurately about their child's health development during the program intake process. During the intake process, program representatives outline and share health policies and procedures with parents and physicians.

After enrollment in a program, the child care providers, health care providers, and parents share responsibility for monitoring the health and development of the child in that setting. Examples of topics for discussions include the child's current health and nutritional status, including management of infectious diseases and handicapping conditions; growth patterns; hearing and vision functioning; patterns of development in each developmental area; adjustment to the program; and family program involvement. Information can be shared by telephone, progress reports, physicians' records, and personal conferences. Parental consent is necessary before the early childhood program initiates direct communication with the health care provider.

Health care providers also advocate for young children in policy forums. They may provide parent education, collaborate with licensing agencies to improve regulations, promote adequate funding and legislation, and join coalitions to improve and expand quality early childhood settings.

References

Deitch, S.R. (ed.). (1987). *Health in day care. A manual for health professionals.* Elk Grove Village, IL: American Academy of Pediatrics, Committee on Early Childhood, Adoption, and Dependent Care.

Kendrick, A., Kaufmann, R., & Messenger, K. (1988). *Young children: A manual for programs.* Washington, DC: National Association for the Education of Young Children.

A. Kendrick

Social Services

The Federal Interagency Day Care Requirements of 1980 define minimum caregiver qualifications, staff-child ratios, and other standards, and also consider the family and child's social and emotional needs. Social workers, child and family psychologists, and child psychiatrists usually provide support for social and emotional needs of the family. These professions are licensed by state regulatory boards, and therapists are certified by the national American Association for Marriage and Family Therapy. Usually these professionals offer part-time consultation to early childhood centers, or centers may refer families. Centers who specialize in working with handicapped children are more likely to utilize such services.

Social service professionals serve families who have serious problems such as alcoholism or divorce. They sometimes offer preventive mental health services such as parent support groups and education. A state agency social worker may help families whose care for children has fallen below acceptable community standards in cases of child abuse and neglect, and may work in varied ways to help parents resume wholesome child care.

Psychologists in a school system may focus upon more diagnostic evaluations rather than on therapeutic services. The latter are more likely to be offered by a psychologist in private practice. Professionals located in settings serving large numbers of people may focus upon short-term, highly structured services with specific goals, such as parenting skills classes or vocational guidance, whereas those in private practice will also offer services with broader goals, including family reorganization and long-term therapy.

The early childhood educator's effectiveness is enhanced when families use these services. Psychiatrists offer behavior- and emotion-altering medications that may support children's ability to learn. Psychologists can test children to identify specific cognitive and personality problems and create programs to enhance social skills, self-concepts, and parent-child communication. Social workers use community resources, such as rehabilitation funds, support groups, and job training, to support family functioning and optimal child development within early childhood learning centers.

R. Marcus

Special Education as a Support Service

Public Law 94-142, the legal basis for educating handicapped children in the United States, stipulates that school districts will provide opportunities for socialization with peers who are not handicapped. Public Law 99-457 extends the educational provisions to children beginning at birth. The law provides for necessary supplementary aids and services that include models for behavior.

Itinerant services and resource rooms are two forms that are used widely to provide these services in school settings. Personnel may serve children directly or act as consultants or facilitators to other staff or parents.

Resource settings usually exist where sufficient numbers of children receive services. Resource rooms may offer special services for one type of disability or for children with varying specified handicaps. The children remain the responsibility of the regular classroom teacher but are assigned to the resource room for most or part of the day.

The special educators, following plans with the regular teacher and parents, focus on skills such as tactile readiness, learning to read and write braille, auditory training, using multisensory approaches to learn to read, or working on speech sounds. Activities vary with children's needs, resources, and local policies.

Services may be available to children in homes as well as in schools and centers. The advantages of a separate room include space for special equipment usually not found in regular classrooms, the ability to use it without distracting others, and greater privacy in that small groups or individuals use the space. The advantages of serving children in the regular classroom are that teachers do not need to schedule around a particular child's leaving the room and special personnel can observe the child in the setting. In addition, the regular classroom teacher can observe the methods and equipment used by specialists. In this way, there can be a continuity of instruction.

References

Hart, V. (1981). *Mainstreaming children with needs.* Longman.

Lerner, J., Mardell-Czudnowski, C., & Goldenberg, D. (1987). *Special education for the early childhood years.* Englewood Cliffs, NJ: Prentice-Hall.

Peterson, N. (1987). *Early intervention for handicapped and at-risk children.* Love.

Thurman, K., & Widerstrom, A. (1985). *Young children with special needs.* Boston: Allyn and Bacon.

V. Hart

Specialist Teachers in Addition to the Classroom Teacher

School districts often employ specialist teachers who support and extend the work of the classroom teacher. Many specialist teachers offer skills in such areas as music, art, physical education, computers, reading, speech, science, or mathematics. They may provide direct instruction to children as well as provide classroom teachers with methods, materials, and specialized subject knowledge.

Some states require certain types of specialists. This practice is a result of the growing diversity among children as well as increasing public expectations for students and schools. Specialists sometimes overlap and schools with limited resources choose those who match their goals.

In utilizing the help of specialists, teachers consider that young children need continuity of contact with a limited number of people. Coping with too many changes can be "stressful" for young children (Bredekamp, 1987). Specialists serve best, therefore, when they are resources to the classroom teacher or part of a teaching team.

The reading specialist, for example, can offer in-service workshops about language acquisition and emergent literacy as well as insightful advice for dealing with children who have special learning needs. The school librarian, often a media specialist, can offer materials to supplement classroom study and fit an individual child's interests.

The Chapter I (Chapter I refers to a federally funded program) teacher is responsible for compensatory education for children whose basic subject development is slow. Questions have arisen recently about the effectiveness of out-of-classroom arrangements. Some research indicates that many reading pull-out programs that use a different teacher are not achieving their goals (Johnston, Allington, & Afflerbach, 1985).

Chapter I programs are being redesigned to provide both intensive help for individual children who have persistent difficulties along with cooperative assistance for their teachers. Resource room teachers of special education also function in these ways, and provide special-needs children with more opportunities for social integration. The goal is for the children to feel that they belong in the mainstream classroom group.

The guidance counselor also can advise teachers about children's social development and self-discipline, as well as work with parents. Some other specialists include the English as a Second Language (ESL) teacher, the school social worker, speech and language therapist, occupational or physical therapist, and the school nurse. The teacher who draws on each specialist's particular strengths, knowledge, and interests creates for children an environment enriched by the team at the same time that an emotional bond between teacher and child grows over time.

References

Bingham, R. T. (1987). Integrating the library into the curriculum. *Educational Leadership, 47* (7), 87.

Bredekamp, S. (ed.). (1987). *Developmentally appropriate practice in early childhood programs serving children from birth through age 8*. Washington, DC: National Association for the Education of Young Children.

Johnston, P., Allington, R., & Afflerbach, P. (1985). The congruence of classroom remedial reading instruction. *Elementary School Journal, 85* (4), 465-467.

H. Schotanus

Resource Room
(See **Special Education as a Support Service**, above.)

Unions and Early Childhood Education

Our society will provide universal, quality child development programs when unions, organizations of working parents, assume leadership on this issue. They did so in the last century to make universal free public education a right for all Americans. Unions have been involved in child development/early childhood education along two distinct avenues. Those unions having large numbers of women workers (CWA, AFSCME, SEIU, OPEIU, ACTWU, ILGWU, and UFCW, to name the most prominent) have been especially concerned with the desperate need of families for quality child care development programs at an affordable cost. Some have established committees to study the issue and educate other members. Some have negotiated joint union/management terms to initiate some form of child care assistance to employees. Such assistance has ranged from information and referral services to on-site child care facilities.

At present, the Coalition of Labor Union Women has been the main intra-union organization working with the various member unions and other child care organizations to advocate for family issues. CLUW nationally has adopted child care as one of their main concerns, sponsoring conferences, workshops, and demonstrations on this issue. The Los Angeles CLUW Child Care Task Force has provided speakers, workshops, and support and technical referrals for local unions seeking to agitate around this issue in their unions and negotiate child care in their contracts. The Task Force maintains a network of communication with child care activists in various unions for the purpose of educating members, lobbying, and letter writing in support of federal and state legislation for child care.

The second avenue of union involvement in early childhood has been through efforts to organize the workers in nursery schools, child care centers, preschools, and Head Start centers. Collective bargaining has had an important impact on center quality, compensation, and the training and retention of staff. In those areas where child development has come under existing public school or college collective bargaining agreements, or where the difficult task has been undertaken of organizing this very decentralized field, center by center, markedly higher standards and better morale has been documented (Child Care Employee Project, 1988). Unions that have organized workers in this field are AFT, AFSCME, SEIU, and UAW. AFSCME has chalked up great success in New York, as has AFT in California.

In the Greater Los Angeles area, the Early Childhood Federation Local 1475 AFT, AFL-CIO is the oldest union organization of preschool teachers. It began organizing in 1950 as the Nursery School Teachers Federation Affiliated with the United Office and Professional Workers union. The pioneers were cooperative nursery school teachers organized to provide mutual support and assistance toward professionalizing their work through better training and increased compensation. Considered little more than "baby sitters" at the time, they arranged the first "Core Curriculum in Early Childhood Education" at UCLA, and began negotiating agreements with their parent boards. They learned how to battle politically with city and county administrations for the right to conduct cooperative nursery schools in public parks.

Los Angeles union members worked in Head Start programs beginning in 1965. The Nursery School Teachers Federation, as it was then called, became the first union to sponsor a program focusing on low-income families when it formed a foundation to sponsor one of the then 13 Head Start/Preschool Agencies in the area. Local 1475 also began to organize and negotiate contracts with the agencies, one by one. Beginning in the late 1960s, the local grew, increasing its collective bargaining agreements to over a dozen large agencies and several smaller schools.

In addition to the traditional negotiations for wages, hours, working conditions, and the establishing of fair grievance procedures encoded in union contracts, the union often performed a valuable service in exposing byzantine administrations, misuse of funds, and violations of basic federal and state guidelines. The union was in a position to provide intra-agency communication and coordinate campaigns with parents to fight cuts in funding and quality standards. Members testified at hearings regarding federal and state quality standards, lobbied legislators for increased funding, marched when necessary in support of separating the Head Start program from a sinking poverty program, fought a landmark National Labor Relations Board decision reflecting the rights of child care workers to organize (the Golden Day Decision), and developed an exemplary career development salary schedule at the grantee level.

In human terms, organizing a union empowered this mainly female and minority work force through education in basic union rights and democratic procedures, and through providing opportunities for leadership in the various agency union chapters. Although salaries are low and the work with young children of poverty is very demanding, teachers and auxiliary personnel have remained in the field and studied to improve their skills, feeling themselves a respected part of the work team. The collective bargaining process has changed the administration of programs to emphasize cooperation and support for those closest to children, with a resulting rise in the quality of programs for children.

Reference

Child Care Employee Project. (1988). *Northern Alameda County Salary, Benefits and Working Conditions: Celebrating Caregivers.* Oakland, CA: Author.

R. R. Ungar

6.3 Glossary of Professional Associations and Journals

Professional associations that are relevant to early childhood teacher educators also may express the concerns of the broader profession of educators. Among such groups are those listed below.

The NAEYC, NAECTE, and some child care worker groups (also listed below) specialize in the concerns of early childhood education and early childhood teacher education. The scope of their combined efforts and the extent of their membership, as surveyed in the section below, suggests that these groups have the potential for creating and influencing important policies and practices to serve the early childhood profession and young children. As they appear below presented in alphabetical order, their scope and range of activities present powerful images.

D. P. Fromberg

American Association of Colleges for Teacher Education (AACTE)

In areas related to early childhood education, AACTE's Committee on Elementary Education has authored guidelines for elementary education programs, kindergarten to sixth grade. In 1990, the AACTE conducted a study on state requirements for the preparation of early childhood educators. AACTE collaborates with the major teacher organizations and with early childhood education organizations on general professional issues and in the area of accreditation.

AACTE is a national, voluntary organization of colleges and universities that prepare teachers and other education personnel. AACTE's primary membership consists of deans and chairpersons of education units in over 700 higher education institutions nationwide. The principal roles of the AACTE include professional development programs, representation before federal and state governmental bodies, participation in national accreditation of teacher education units, development of professional standards, information collection and analytical research, and publications on significant issues related to teacher preparation. In addition, AACTE has been associated with the ERIC Clearinghouse on Teacher Education. Both are located at the National Center for Higher Education in Washington, D.C.

AACTE serves as an information resource center on federal and state governmental issues related to teacher education; it publishes a semiannual compilation of legislative and regulatory actions in the states that affect standards for state approval of teacher preparation programs, standards for state licensure, and other areas of professional practice. AACTE has conducted and published several national surveys relating to recruitment and retention of minority teachers. AACTE conducts a continuing research effort (the RATE survey), based on a representative sample of teacher education programs, to provide annual data and analysis regarding teacher education institutions, faculty, and students. AACTE also operates, in conjunction with the National Council for Accreditation of Teacher Education, a Joint Data Collection System. This database provides annual information on productivity and accreditation standards. For additional information, contact AACTE, One Dupont Circle, Suite 610, Washington, DC 20202.

C. Smith

Association for Childhood Education International (ACEI)

Founded in 1892 as the International Kindergarten Union in Saratoga Springs, New York, the Association for Childhood Education International (ACEI), is one of the oldest educational organizations in the United States. The organization now has branches in every state and in 30 other countries. Among the early leaders were Susan Blow, Patty Smith Hill, Lucy Wheelock, and Susan B. Cooper (Snyder, 1972).

Childhood Education became the organization's official publication in 1924. The organization's name became Association for Childhood Education in 1930, and it merged with the National Council of Primary Education in 1931 in order to extend the principles of kindergarten education to the primary grades. The scope of work extended to include nursery, primary, and middle childhood ages when the word International was added to the organization's title in 1946.

Other publications of the organization include the *Journal of Research in Childhood Education*, the *ACEI Exchange*, and special publications, as well as position papers that make recommendations on major issues affecting children and their families. The organization also sponsors conferences, international study tours and branch meetings.

Membership in ACEI is open to students, teachers, administrators, parents, and anyone interested in the well-being of children from infancy through adolescence. For additional information, contact ACEI, 11141 Georgia Avenue, Suite 200, Wheaton, MD 20902; (800) 423-3563.

Reference

Snyder, A. (1972). *Dauntless women in childhood education, 1865–1931*. Wheaton, MD: ACEI.

S. Raines

Association for Supervision and Curriculum Development (ASCD)

The major focus of ASCD's work has been to assist school administrators, supervisors, teachers, and policy makers better to meet the needs of young children by intensifying their attention to the issues related to providing sound curriculum and quality instruction. Within the nationwide push to establish public school early childhood programs, the ASCD studied research demonstrating how schooling influences young children's intellectual and affective development. The result was the identification of early childhood education as one of five key areas for study in ASCD's 1985 five-year strategic plan.

ASCD attempts to influence educational decisions through its publications. Some of its early childhood publications appear in the references below. In addition, the organization offers annual in-service staff development events concerning early childhood, supports a network of special interest educators, and works with a consortium of 11 school districts who are establishing high quality early childhood programs. For additional information, contact: ASCD 1250 N. Pitt St., Alexandria, VA 22314, (703) 549-9110.

References

ASCD. (In production). *Developing a strong early childhood school program*. Alexandria, VA: ASCD.

Day, B. (1983). *Early childhood education: Creative learning activities*. New York: Macmillan.

Educational Leadership. (1986). *Special issue on early childhood education*. Alexandria, VA: ASCD.

Warger, C. (ed.). (1988). *A resource guide to public school early childhood programs*. ASCD.

C. Warger

Association of Teacher Educators (ATE)

Founded in 1920 for the purpose of improving teacher education for both school-based and campus-based teacher educators, ATE represents 3,000 members and 41 state groups, including over 650 colleges and universities, 500 major school systems, and the majority of state departments of education. Founded as the National Association of Directors of Supervised Student Teaching, the name changed to the National Association of Student Teaching in 1922 in order to reflect more accurately the activities of the organization. The organization was expanded in 1946 to include all types of institutions engaged in teacher education whose work was concerned with the organization and supervision of student teaching. Its constitution was completely revised in 1970 in order to permit wider participation

through a delegate assembly and the present name was adopted.

The organization's publications include a bimonthly newsletter, a quarterly journal, Action in Teacher Education, and special reports. In conjunction with the Macmillan Publishing Company, ATE publishes the *Handbook of Research on Teacher Education*. The Handbook synthesizes current research, developments, and issues in teacher education and staff development. A sample of recent publications appears in the references below. For additional information, contact the author (see **List of Contributors**).

References

Brooks, D. M. (1987). *Teacher induction: A new beginning, mirrors of excellence. Reflections for teacher education from training programs in ten corporations and agencies*. Washington, DC: ATE.

Haberman, M. (1987). *Recruiting and selecting teachers for urban schools*. ERIC/CUE Urban Diversity Series No. 95. Washington, DC: ATE.

Houston, R., Haberman, M., & Sikula (eds.). (1990). *Handbook of research on teacher education*. New York: Macmillan.

Orlosky, D. E. (1988). *Society, schools, and teacher preparation*. Washington, DC: ATE & Clearinghouse on TE.

Wittrock, M. C. (ed). (1986). *Handbook of research on teaching* (3rd ed.). New York: Macmillan.

E. Klugman

National Association of Early Childhood Teacher Educators (NAECTE)

A professional organization composed of early childhood teacher educators and researchers who primarily work in colleges and universities, the NAECTE was founded by a small group led by Michael Davis in 1977 at the NAEYC annual conference in Chicago. Membership has grown to more than 500, with 7 state affiliates.

The organization's goals include providing a forum for teacher educators, in institutions granting bachelor's and advanced degrees, who are concerned with early childhood teacher preparation; providing a communication network for teacher educators for the exchange of ideas about research and practice in the field of early childhood teacher education; and cooperating with state, regional, and national organizations to study about and advocate for young children.

NAECTE sponsors an annual conference in conjunction with NAEYC and publishes the *Journal of Early Childhood Teacher Education*. The organization cooperates with NAEYC on issues related to teacher certification, teacher training, and teacher education accreditation. This collaboration has included the establishment of guidelines and standards for early childhood teacher education programs.

NAECTE is governed by a 16-member governing board representing 10 regional areas in the United States. For additional information, contact the author (see **List of Contributors**).

J. B. Taylor

California Professors of Early Childhood Education

The California Professors of Early Childhood Education was founded in 1974 to (1) provide a forum for focusing attention on teacher education and preparation as well as the achievement of fullest possible professional development of teachers and professors active in the field of early childhood education; (2) provide a medium for exchange of information and the development of adequate standards concerning programs in the field of early childhood education; and (3) serve as a source of information, advice, and assistance to the public as well as public institutions concerning legislation and other developments in the field of early childhood education.

Membership in the organization is open to educators and other professionals interested in early childhood teacher education and preparation in four-year institutions of higher education within Region Nine of the National Association of Early Childhood Teacher Educators (NAECTE) (Arizona, California, Guam, Hawaii, Nevada, and Samoa). The organization is an affiliate of the NAECTE, although its existence predates the national organization. This affiliate publishes a newsletter, sponsors presentations at professional conferences, and its members represent the organization at public hearings. For additional information, contact the author (see **List of Contributors**.)

D. Smith

National Association for the Education of Young Children (NAEYC) and Regional Aspects

A nonprofit membership organization founded in 1926 as the National Association for Nursery Education, the NAEYC has worked to improve early childhood professional practice by providing professional development opportunities and by setting and promoting standards for professional practice. The organization also builds public understanding and support for high quality early childhood services through public policy and educational initiatives.

NAEYC publications include the bimonthly journal *Young Children*, and in conjunction with ERIC/EECE and Ablex Publishing Corporation, the *Early Childhood Research Quarterly*. More than 150 books, brochures, posters, and video training tapes communicate NAEYC's message about high quality early childhood services.

NAEYC's annual conference is the largest education conference in the country, attracting more than 20,000 participants. Conferees participate in hundreds of workshops, seminars, and speeches; exhibits of educational resources; tours of outstanding programs; and professional networking opportunities.

NAEYC has set and promoted standards for professional practice and program implementation. The organization's accreditation process recognizes programs that meet criteria of high quality. NAEYC definitions of developmentally appropriate practices for early childhood education establish the model for professional activity. Additional organization positions on such issues as professional preparation, licensing and regulation, early childhood legislation, and the need to improve quality, compensation, and affordability of programs have guided policy debates and administration of services.

NAEYC advocacy and public policy activities on behalf of young children have increased in recent years. The organization monitors federal legislation and prepares analyses of key bills for broad dissemination. Legislative alerts, briefing papers, testimony, and close communication with legislators and their staff help to promote NAEYC's views. NAEYC also strives to strengthen the advocacy efforts of members and affiliate groups through advocacy training.

NAEYC's publicized public education initiative is the Week of the Young Child in which local celebrations stimulate community involvement on behalf of young children. The organization also has prepared brochures on critical issues of child development and education for popular press audiences. These products are widely cited in the media, and members use them to communicate with parents, teachers, and community leaders.

NAEYC consists of a diverse membership, including persons with no formalized preparation as well as those with doctorates in the field; and those who work in centers, family day care, schools, formal settings such as vocational schools and advanced degree university programs, as well as regulatory and support service agencies. Programs in which members work may be nonprofit or for profit, sponsored by religious groups, government, social service agencies, colleges, public schools, or businesses.

Nearly all members join NAEYC through an affiliate group (see examples in articles below). The affiliate network consists of more than 375 groups nationwide and overseas. Community, state, and regional affiliate groups provide NAEYC members with additional, easily accessible opportunities for professional relationships and support in their community, state, and region in ways that can respond to local needs and resources. They also provide an evaluation and input system for the organization's activities.

NAEYC is governed by a 17-member elected board. Board members and officers serve a four year term on a rotating basis, with the exception of the president, who serves one year as president-elect, two years as president, and one year as past president. The NAEYC Board serves as the policy-making and decision authority for the Association. An executive director implements program policies. For additional information, contact NAEYC, 1834 Connecticut Ave, N.W., Washington, DC 20009.

J. McCarthy

California AEYC

An affiliate of the NAEYC, nine sections of the California Association for the Education of Young Children have a membership of almost 10,000 with several chapters comprising each section in the state. As membership increases, new chapters are formed.

The CAEYC State Board is composed of seven elected officers, the president, and a representative from each section, as well as the chairs of various committees. There are four governance committees, five program committees, and individuals responsible for the newsletter, public policy, employer-related child care, kindergarten practices, professional preparation, and a Peace Committee. Such committees change with program emphases. In addition, four members act as liaisons with the Academy, the California Child Development Program Advisory Committee, the California State Parent Teacher Association, and the NAEYC Governing Board. Chairs of the Conference Council, the Legislative Symposium, the Leadership Development Program, the Week of the Young Child, and the Public Policy Information Coordinator also serve on the board.

CAEYC and each section conduct affiliate activities related to conferences, workshops, membership, multicultural concerns, publications, and public policy. For many years, a statewide conference was conducted annually by each of the sections in rotation. In 1984 a statewide conference council was formed to coordinate the state conference with representation from the nine sections. The first conference under the council arrangement was held in Sacramento in 1988.

An annual legislative symposium takes place in Sacramento. For 13 years it has been designed to inform legislators of CAEYC positions on significant child-related legislation and to recognize individuals and organizations who have contributed to children's welfare. Ninety percent of state legislators or their representatives attend the recognition luncheon with CAEYC members from their constituencies.

The Leadership Development in Public Policy program was authorized by the CAEYC Board in 1984 to increase the number of child advocates in California. Under this program, as many as 15 interns from the nine sections participate each year in comprehensive advocacy and leadership training. The costs of residence in a week of intensive training, travel to the state conference and to the legislative symposium, registration, tuition, and incidental expenses are shared by CAEYC, each section, and the interns themselves.

E. Brady

Hawaii AEYC

The stated mission of the Hawaiian Association for the Education of Young Children is to promote, support, and expand quality and professionalism in early childhood programs and services for young children, birth to eight years of age, and their families. The supporting goals are to promote the implementation of high quality comprehensive educational programs and services for young children and their families; to facilitate the professional growth of the people working with and for young children; and to increase public understanding and to influence decision making related to early childhood issues.

The HAEYC is a statewide NAEYC affiliate initially chartered in 1972 with about 50 members. Membership now is between 700 and 800 annually. The affiliate is divided into seven chapters. These chapters focus on providing local early childhood personnel with educational workshops and support. Several are active in public policy.

An annual two-day Statewide Early Childhood Education Conference attracts more than 1,000 people. The first day, a Friday, focuses on issues of primary interest to program coordinators and administrators. The Saturday program features subjects of primary interest to teachers who work with children from infancy through primary grades. Funds raised at this springtime event support a small central office, a part-time office manager, and other organizational expenses.

Another major event is an annual dinner held early in June, which features presentations of awards to Teachers of the Year, one each for infant-toddler, preschool, and early elementary. A Community Service Award also is presented to someone employed outside the field of early childhood who has shown exemplary commitment to young children. This award has been presented to a Department of Human Services employee, a Department of Health employee, a legislator, and a media person. Beginning in 1990, a new honor will be offered to employers who have taken extraordinary steps to offer their employees child care assistance.

The HAEYC State Board takes leadership in public education and policy issues. Members and appointees are involved actively in serving on many boards, task forces, and committees for such entities as the state department and the state board of education, the Department of Human Services, the Office of Children and Youth, the State Strategic Plan, the State Commission on Family Literacy, and the Hawaii Children's Campaign. In this and other ways, the organization is involved in state decision making.

Another outreach attempt is through the sale of national publications at various conferences. In addition, a resource library of national publications is currently being amassed for use by policy makers and other interested persons.

Recently, a local foundation provided a $25,000 grant for the purpose of disseminating to the public information about how young children learn. Dissemination will occur through mass media and networking with key community organizations. For additional information, contact the author (see **List of Contributors**).

M. Rauch

Midwest AEYC

The Midwest Association for the Education of Young Children (MAEYC) began in 1926 as the Midwest Association for Nursery Education. During the 1965–1966 membership year, it became an affiliate of the NAEYC. Its current purpose and structure has evolved since 1968 into a regional linking group with automatic membership as a member of an affiliate AEYC group within a 12-state region, including Illinois, Indiana, Iowa, Kansas, Michigan, Minnesota, Missouri, Nebraska, North Dakota, Ohio, South Dakota, and Wisconsin. There are more than 18,000 members. Each state has one representative on the governing body, the Midwestern AEYC Council, with participation and governance accomplished through affiliate groups of NAEYC.

The purpose of the MAEYC is to encourage, coordinate, and activate efforts of diverse groups within the region as they strive to serve young children and their families. An annual spring conference is cosponsored with an affiliate group on a rotating basis, special project grants are awarded annually, and a leadership award is conferred. There are no dues. Funding comes from conferences and special activities. For additional information, contact the author (see **List of Contributors**).

J. Herwig

New England AEYC

Thirty NAEYC affiliates are organized as a regional group in the New England AEYC, with statewide groups in each of the six states, and local affiliates in Connecticut, Massachusetts, and Maine.

Public policy is the prime concern in some affiliates. As one of its major goals, the Connecticut AEYC nurtures policy makers among its local members. Through conferences, newsletters, and the provision of forums to discuss statewide issues, CAEYC has been active in influencing state funding policies, working with candidates for statewide office, and providing information through the local membership on developmentally appropriate practice for young children (M. Staggenborg, personal communication, 1991).

The Rhode Island AEYC sponsors policy and curriculum conferences in collaboration with other private and public agencies, engages in legislative advocacy, provides testimony at legislative hearings, disseminates the local RIAEYC newsletter to state legislators, and provides public policy alert information to affiliate members throughout Rhode Island (S. Connor, personal communication, 1991). Another state affiliate with a public policy emphasis, the Vermont AEYC, is active in the effort to bring national issues to the local level in a largely rural state.

Professional development is the primary focus in other affiliates in New England. Growing from an independent nursery school and kindergarten association in the 1940s, New Hampshire affiliated with NAEYC in 1965. The affiliate has long held successful conferences and has used its statewide affiliate newsletter as an effective form of communication between regional groups and members within those groups. Colleges and universities have played an important part in the development of the affiliate, both through the establishment of student chapters, and through attempts by many college instructors to identify individual professional growth with membership in the New Hampshire AEYC (T. McDonnell, personal communication, 1991).

Public visibility and service is the major mission of the Maine AEYC, which operates as a clearinghouse for information about young children and early childhood education in the state, and which promotes the status of early childhood practitioners. Responsive to the local affiliates, the Maine AEYC represents the early childhood community at all levels of local government (K. Sparks, personal communication, 1991).

The youngest of the statewide groups, the Massachusetts AEYC was established in 1987 to provide local affiliate members with a state-wide voice. In addition to representing members on public boards and committees of the commonwealth, MassAEYC is also a leading agency in providing the opportunity for early childhood practitioners to obtain continuing education unites (CEU's) outside of a traditional college and university structure. The organization works with state officials to approve alternative course offerings throughout the commonwealth, and this collaboration has been promoted nationally as a model of public and private cooperation.

This diversity of local interests finds a regional voice in the New England AEYC. This "affiliate of affiliates" has had a long, illustrious existence, numbering among its early presidents Abigail Eliot, founder of the nursery school movement in the United States. Profits from conferences held by the New England Association for Nursery Education (later NEAEYC) in the 1950s provided the seed money for the establishment of conferences on a national basis by the organization that became known in 1966 as NAEYC (J. Rustici, personal communication, 1991).

After a period of inactivity in the 1960s, the New England AEYC was reestablished in 1972 at a conference held at the University of New Hampshire with the purpose of providing leadership training for officers of local affiliate groups. The Delegate Assembly, consisting of two members from each of the region's other twenty-nine affiliates, is the governing board of NEAEYC. The organization provides leadership networking; public policy advocacy, information, and legislative lobbying; and input into the governance of NAEYC and communication with its national staff (E. Klugman, personal communication, 1991).

The relatively small size of the member states, the ease of communication and transportation links, and historical precedents dating back over three centuries emphasizing participatory government give the New England AEYC a strong public policy focus. Because of this close communication between affiliates in New England, participation as

members of NAEYC is strong. Although the region has only 5 percent of the total national population, 9 percent of the members of NAEYC are New Englanders. This cohesiveness, bred of diversity, is the outstanding feature of NAEYC affiliates in New England and has allowed those affiliates to take a strong advocacy, professional, and visibility posture in support of children and families both in the region and throughout the nation.

K. P. Counselman & G. Pedrini

Southern Association for Children Under Six (SACUS)

A professional organization of early childhood teachers, teacher educators, parents, researchers, child care workers and directors, and other individuals, SACUS is concerned about the care and education of young children and their families in the South. About 15,000 members and state affiliates (Alabama, Arkansas, Florida, Georgia, Kentucky, Louisiana, Missouri, Oklahoma, South Carolina, Tennessee, Texas, Virginia, West Virginia) unite in grassroots efforts to promote young children's developmentally based care and education.

SACUS grew out of a 1943 Nashville, Tennessee, meeting of concerned individuals and through several subsequent meetings that included the 1952 Louisville, Kentucky, organizational conference. From the beginning, SACUS advocated public kindergartens and health education standards for nursery and kindergarten programs. SACUS goals continue to focus on fine quality programs, the professional growth and status of individuals working with young children and their families, legislation impacting young children, and public understanding and support for developmentally based services to young children.

SACUS sponsors annual conferences, workshops, and numerous publications and materials, including the quarterly journal *Dimensions*. Advocacy efforts include the SACUS legislative platform, resolutions, position papers, fact sheets, participation in the Southern Governors' Conference, the Public Policy Institute, and numerous public policy activities. SACUS also networks with other professional organizations to promote quality in early childhood programs. For additional information contact SACUS, Box 5403, Brady Station, Little Rock, AR 72215.

K. Castle

Western States Leadership Network

Organized in 1982 in California as part of the NAEYC, the Western States Leadership Network's function is to bring together affiliate leaders of the 13 western states to share information, resources, and leadership techniques. These leaders represent the broad spectrum of all members of AEYC who work with or care about young children from birth through age eight. Participants identify, coordinate, and implement strategies to influence public policies related to young children, their families, and their educators, with emphasis on issues of common concern to AEYC leaders in the region.

This unique group has no elected officers, governing board, membership dues, or formal structure. It is in communication with the staff and board of NAEYC but functions independently. There is an annual conference where registrants learn organizational, political, and education skills in order to help their affiliate groups work more efficiently and productively.

The conference responsibility shifts to different volunteer host state AEYC organizations. Self-supporting, this conference seeks to maintain continuous and self-renewing ways of looking at leadership functioning.

At the conclusion of many of the conferences, a letter is sent to NAEYC outlining recommendations, requests, and concerns of the western states. A few specific outcomes of the conferences have been a comparative study of child care regulations in the region; a letter to the Idaho legislature urging establishment of licensing regulations, as Idaho was the only western state without child care licensing; and a letter to the Western Governors' Meeting regarding issues concerning the quality and standards of child care. For additional information, contact the author (see **List of Contributors**).

L. McKay

National Council for the Accreditation of Teacher Education (NCATE)

The NAEYC and the ACEI are constituent members of NCATE. In addition to providing financial support for NCATE, their representatives serve on one or more of NCATE's governance boards and on the Board of Examiners.

NCATE accredits professional education units at colleges and universities. These units are responsible for the initial and advanced preparation of all preschool through grade 12 professional school personnel, including teachers, counselors, school psychologists, and administrators. The standards with which units must comply are designed to ensure that units maintain programs, students, faculty, governance, and resources at a level of quality expected by the education profession.

Units that seek NCATE accreditation must meet ten preconditions before a review team conducts an on-site review. A five- or six-person review team is selected from NCATE's 400-member Board of Examiners to conduct an on-site review, in which standards are applied every five years in order to help determine whether accreditation is still viable.

A requirement of the preconditions process is that units respond to national specialty guidelines that have been approved by NCATE. Included in the approved guidelines are those for early childhood teacher education at the basic and advanced levels. If an institution offers early childhood teacher education programs or endorsements, a curriculum folio that responds to the guidelines of the NAEYC must be completed by the institution seeking accreditation. For additional information, contact NCATE, 2029 K Street, N.W., Suite 500, Washington, DC 20006.

D. Gollnick

Organisation Mondiale pour l'Education Pre-Scolaire (OMEP) (Worldwide Organization for Early Childhood Education)

Representatives from 17 countries and all 5 continents gathered in Prague in August 1948 for the first OMEP World Conference. This meeting included parents, teachers, physicians, social workers, architects, and others interested in preschool and family education. Their concerns stemmed from the suffering of young children during wartime. The purpose for the conference was to establish an organized international group that could remind national governments and international organizations of the needs of early childhood and to offer cooperation with intergovernmental organizations.

The original organizational goals continue to guide OMEP. They include the promotion of a general understanding of the importance of world peace, the child, and the home in the early formative years; the advancement of widespread development of nursery education in all countries; the formulation of progressive standards in regard to educational practices, health care, qualifications of teachers, buildings, gardens, and equipment; and the linking of representatives from voluntary associations and public agencies interested in early childhood education.

Each of the 52 member countries participates in a national committee. The United States National Committee includes approximately 500 members who are interested in promoting the goals of OMEP. Delegates from member countries assemble annually for a council meeting that is accompanied with either seminars or the triennial OMEP World Assembly. At each meeting the delegates agree upon issues to be addressed during the subsequent year. These issues provide the basis for each country's annual agenda. For additional information contact OMEP, 1718 Connecticut Ave., N.W., Suite 500, Washington, DC 20009.

J. McCarthy

Professional Journals Related to Early Childhood Education

Young Children, published by NAEYC and *Childhood Education*, published by ACEI, both address practitioners with articles about curriculum, management, and parent relations, as well as professional information, book and research reviews, and reader reactions. *Childhood Education* focuses on public school issues, and *Young Children*, on public policy issues.

Pre-K Today (Scholastic, Inc.) and *Teaching PreK–8* (Early Years, Inc.) provide short articles on similar topics for a lay audience.

Child Care Information Exchange (CCIE), for program directors, provides articles about staff management, funding, health, and marketing issues. These articles often are written by authors with a business background.

Early Childhood Research Quarterly (Ablex for NAEYC), the *Journal of Research in Early Childhood Education* (ACEI), and *Early Education and Development* (Psychology Press) offer articles with a research focus on both early childhood practice and child development. *The Elementary School Journal* (University of Chicago Press) includes research-based articles related to the primary grades. *Child Development* (University of Chicago Press) provides scholarly research reports on developmental issues regarding infants through adolescents.

Language Arts (National Council of Teachers of English, NCTE), *The Reading Teacher*, (International Reading Association, IRA), *Science and Children* (National Science Teachers Association (NSTA), and *Arithmetic Teacher* (National Council of Teachers of Mathematics, NCTM), often include articles centered on early childhood education topics.

For additional information, contact: Ablex, 355 Chestnut, Norwood, NJ 07648-9975; ACEI (see above); CCIE, P.O. Box 2890, Redmond, WA 98073-28980; Early Education and Development, Psychology Press, 39 Pearl Street, Brandon, VT 05733-1007; Early Years, 40 Richards Ave, Norwalk, CT 06854; IRA, 800 Barksdale Rd., Newark, DE 19714-8139; NAEYC (see above); NCTE, 1111 Kenyon Rd., Urbana, IL 61801; NCTM, 1906 Association Dr., Reston, VA 22091; NSTA, 1742 Connecticut Ave., N.W., Washington, DC 20009; Scholastic, Inc., 730 Broadway, New York, NY 10003; University of Chicago Press, 5801 Ellis Ave., Chicago, IL 60637.

A. G. Dorsey

6.4 Professional Issues

Certain issues of immediate concern to those who provide care and education for young children cut across many of the roles that have been discussed in the previous section. Foremost among these are issues of advocacy for teachers, compensation, professionalism, empowerment, professional ethics, and unionization of early childhood teachers and administrators. While those topics are treated in separate articles below, it is clear that they are highly related to one another and also permeate articles in the remaining sections of this chapter.

L. R. Williams

Advocacy for Teachers

For 30 years the early childhood education field has been seeking the critical determinants of good programs for young children. Just as professional consensus (National Academy of Early Childhood Programs, 1984) and empirical literature (Phillips, 1987) concur that good programs require teachers trained in child development and child-centered pedagogy, early childhood programs are unable to attract and hold onto such staff. It is clear that the problem exists for certain early childhood programs and not others. The question is "Why is the staffing crisis unevenly distributed across program types and what does this tell about solutions?"

Public schools are able to attract and retain trained early childhood teachers. Particularly because public schools are expanding prekindergarten programs, it is fortunate that public school teachers with graduate degrees in early education or related fields are increasingly common, and annual teacher turnover

for public school teachers averages only 6 percent to 8 percent. However, in non-public school programs, such as Head Start and private and publicly funded center-based child care, annual teacher turnover averages 30 percent to 40 percent. This difference between public school and nonpublic programs occurs because teachers with equivalent training and experience make better salaries and have better fringe benefits and more positive working conditions (e.g., paid breaks, shorter work days) in the schools.

There are several extant assumptions about why nonpublic school programs constitute a secondary labor market characterized by low pay and high turnover. Unquestionably such forces as gender discrimination in the marketplace, the belief that teaching young children requires few professional skills, and the relatively low income of parents of young children contribute to this situation. But each of these better explains uniformly low salaries for teachers across the field than the relative advantage of the public school programs. It is also not enough to say that public schools are funded by a broad base of tax levy dollars. Head Start and publicly funded child care programs also are supported by such monies, although admittedly at a lower annual cost per child than programs in the public schools. The factor that best explains the public school/nonpublic school difference is that almost all public school early childhood teachers are unionized, while almost all their colleagues outside the schools are not.

Unionization of any work force is controversial at the outset. In the early childhood field it raises fears about pitting staff against parents or placing teachers in conflict with directors. These are valid concerns, even though most unions that organize early childhood teachers understand the limits of parental incomes and adversarial bargaining. Acknowledging concerns like these does not mean that the present situation, in which hundreds of thousands of children are consigned to programs of tenuous quality, is acceptable.

Pragmatically, unionization in an industry that typically consists of thousands of small, independent businesses is difficult. This means that unionization will probably only occur in situations where there is a tradition of organized labor and where the funding of early childhood programs is fairly centralized. Therefore professional organizations such as the National Association for the Education of Young Children and its over 300 affiliates, child care and family day care associations, and other early childhood groups should assert a teacher advocacy agenda as the hallmark of their child advocacy efforts. Seeing advocacy for teachers as being synonymous with advocacy for children is an emerging trend, as the field accepts that research and practice have taught us that a program can only be as good for children as it is for the adults who work with them.

References

National Academy of Early Childhood Programs. (1984). *Accreditation criteria and procedures of the National Academy of Early Childhood Programs.* Washington, DC: National Association for the Education of Young Children.

Phillips, D. A. (ed.). (1987). *Quality in child care: What does research tell us?* Washington, DC: National Association for the Education of Young Children.

R. C. Granger

Compensation Issues

In any community newspaper there is likely to be a listing for several child-care teacher jobs, even during troubled economic times. While the qualifications required will vary because of differences in state regulations, the compensation package offered probably will not. Unless the job is being offered by one of a few well-subsidized public schools, universities, or corporate centers (or happens to be one of the 4 percent of the centers in the United States where teachers are protected by collective bargaining agreements), wages hover around $5 an hour with few, if any, benefits. Even those centers requiring teachers to have a bachelor's degree will probably offer salaries that are less than half the average paid to comparably educated people in the job market.

Because of these low wages, the chances are great that almost half of the teachers hired will be turning to the want ads again a year from now. In addition, two-thirds of those who leave the child-care field altogether, despite whatever investment they have made in child-related training. These are among the many troubling findings of the National Child Care Staffing Study (NCCSS), a comprehensive examination of the relationship between teacher characteristics and program quality in 225 center-based programs in five metropolitan communities across the country.

The Staffing Study found an average teacher turnover rate of 41 percent per year. Burnout and attrition contribute to turnover in any field, but the high rates in child-care centers stem directly from low wages. According to the Staffing Study, teachers' earning power plummeted over 20 percent between 1977 and 1988, and the turnover rate nearly tripled, up from 15 percent in this same time period. Teaching staff earning $4 an hour or less left their jobs at twice the rate of those earning $6 or more. Salary surveys conducted in three California communities this spring reveal turnover rates of 50 percent or greater.

Teacher turnover undermines the quality of care children receive and places children at-risk developmentally. The majority of classrooms observed by Staff Study researchers offered barely adequate care. Better quality classrooms were able to recruit better trained staff and retain them longer. Children attending poorer quality centers characterized by high turnover, low pay, and minimal staff training were found to be less competent in their language and social development.

The Staffing Study findings came as little surprise to most practitioners and advocates in the field who face the consequences of the staffing crisis each day. The findings provided the early childhood community not only with a disturbing self-portrait but also a vehicle to direct policymakers' attention to the issue of child-care quality and the necessity of upgrading child-care salaries.

Intensive lobbying has resulted in uneven federal government efforts. The 1990 Head Start Reauthorization Act included a "quality set-a-side," which explicitly reserves 5 percent of funds for salary enhancement and 5 percent for training opportunities for Head Start staff, which will continue for several years. The 1989 Military Child Care Reauthorization outlined the Caregiver Personnel Pay Plan, which has resulted in substantial salary upgrading linked to training requirements. Anecdotal reports from Army Child Care programs indicate a significant increase in child care work force stabilization.

The federal Child Care and Development Block Grant, which infuses several hundred million dollars into the child-care delivery system, takes a more equivocal stance in relation to quality enhancements and compensation in particular. While compensation is listed as one of five legitimate areas for the expenditure of dollars earmarked for improving quality, it is not a required activity. Furthermore, the regulations severely restrict the percentage of Block Grant funds that can be used for quality improvements, resulting in insufficient dollars for any meaningful impact on the staffing crisis. Federal funds through the Family Support Act and the At Risk Child Care Program restrict the reimbursement rate for services, thus insuring low salaries and high turnover.

Nonetheless, the precedent established by the federal government in recent years that public dollars can be spent to improve child-care compensation will likely generate even greater advocacy efforts. In particular, the federal Block Grant inclusion of increased compensation as a legitimate quality enhancement activity provides advocates in each state with a rally point for their efforts to address the problem. Their success will depend on the extent to which they can build a strong and unified voice for upgrading child-care work.

Exciting developments are underway. In Seattle, Washington, one of the five Staffing Study sites, the early childhood community has been diligently working to build a broad-based coalition to support their movement for "worthy wages." Strategies involve empowerment training for teachers, unionizing, parent education, and actions such as last year's city-wide one-day center closure and parade. In Wisconsin, teachers are participating in "taking action" workshops to raise consciousness about the impact of low wages and child-care quality and the role that each teacher must play to change the status quo. Simultaneously, parents are being educated about the "full cost of care" and the necessity for raising fees at least 5 percent annually above the increase in the cost of living.

At the heart of these efforts is the understanding that teachers are the agents of change. They must reject intolerable wages and working conditions and insist on levels of compensation that invite the emergence of a well-educated and stable child-care work force.

References

Child Care Employee Project. (1991). San Mateo Child Care Salary and Working Conditions Survey. Oakland, CA: Child Care Employee Project.

Morin, J. (1991). *Taking action: The role of child care teachers in improving compensation*. Madison, WI: Wisconsin Early Childhood Association.

Whitebook, M., Howes, C., and Phillips D. (1989). *Who cares? Child care and the quality of care in America: Final report National Child Care Staffing Study*. Oakland, CA: Child Care Employee Project.

M. Whitebook

Early Childhood Teachers and Professionalism

Historically, early childhood has been perceived as a field primarily for women, whose major role was to provide for the nurturance of young children rather than the development of children's academic knowledge. Since young children were not highly valued and had no power, teaching them was considered a low-status job that required no specialized knowledge or skill. This perception is still held by many today and has contributed to early childhood teachers undervaluing themselves and their positions. In spite of this low perception of self and position, and considering roles and range of titles that apply to early childhood practitioners (such as infant caregiver, state certified teacher, family day care provider, CDA certified teacher, untrained aide, child care center director, university professor or researcher), the field has achieved some degree of success in establishing itself as a profession. The many definitions of what constitutes a profession include certain elements that apply to the field of early childhood. One of these elements is that a specialized body of knowledge and skills served as the foundation of the profession. Early childhood derives its knowledge base from a variety of disciplines including developmental psychology, child development, and learning theory. Knowledge of pedagogical skill has been generated within the field through research and evaluation.

Another characteristic of a profession is a degree of commitment and continued involvement in professional development, measured by the intensity of interest and the quality of work done (Hamner & Turner, 1985). Most early childhood educators have a strong commitment to the field, as evidenced by their membership in early childhood professional organizations, particularly the National Association for the Education of Young Children (NAEYC) and the Association for Childhood Education International (ACEI).

Standards of performance for the profession and commitment to maintain professional standards also define a professional (Katz, 1987). NAEYC has been active in establishing standards for the profession, and currently has a model of professional development in process.

Another important element of professionalism is the sense of ownership and the decision-making power of its members. When practitioners experience collegiality and support from fellow members in professional endeavors, a growing sense of ownership develops within the profession. Early childhood practitioners have opportunities as individuals to make and implement curricular decisions determined by their knowledge base and their understanding of the learner. Selecting developmentally appropriate activities involves critical choices. Related to this is the decision making inherent in arranging the environment and choosing materials for enhancing the learner's potential. Additionally, early childhood practitioners have opportunities to speak in a collective voice through professional organizations to influence policy and legislation related to children, families, and education.

As the members of the early childhood profession continue to pursue scholarly activities, gain recognition as experts in the field, and build a strong sense of community, the status and dignity of its membership is enhanced, and professionalism is advanced.

References

Hamner, T., and Turner, C. (1985). *Parenting in contemporary society.* Englewood Cliffs NJ: Prentice-Hall.

Katz, L. (ed). (1987). *Current topics in early childhood education* (Vol VII). Norwood, NJ: Ablex.

Silin, J. (1985). Authority as knowledge—a problem of professionalization. *Young Children 40* (3), 41–46.

Spodek, B., Saracho, D., & Peters, D. (eds.). (1988). *Professionalism and the early childhood practitioner.* New York: Teachers College Press.

J. Moyer

Professional Empowerment, Supervision, and Educational Change

Teaching in the American public school has been described by some as a "semi-profession." Like medicine, law, and accounting, it requires specific academic preparation and credentialing through a state-sponsored licensing body for entry-level admission. Unlike these other professions, however, teaching offers little opportunity for professional growth. Entry into and exit from teaching are relatively easy. Salaries are static, showing little improvement relative to experience, education, or job performance. Furthermore, teachers do not have their own professional organization responsible for monitoring the conduct and practice of their membership.

A number of initiatives are currently underway to reform public school teacher preparation and to professionalize teaching. Reports by the Holmes Group and the Carnegie Forum have recommended restructuring of the undergraduate education major, including a strong liberal arts background as preparation for teaching; requiring graduate study for entry into the profession, and developing a national licensing board designed to set standards of professional practice. These initiatives could directly affect the preservice preparation of those who wish to teach in early childhood programs housed in publicly supported schools (Pre-K–3rd grade), and indirectly affect the professional identity and development of those teaching in private and federally supported child care facilities.

Implicit in these reform initiatives is the issue of teacher empowerment. Empowerment refers to teachers' roles as decision makers. Traditionally, the management of schools has been conducted from the top down, with decision making largely in the hands of school boards and school administrators. Teacher decision making has been confined to the conduct of the classroom. An expanded view of schools and other educational institutions in our society, however, has prompted analysis of the school as a workplace and of the school in relationship to the community (Berman and McLaughlin, 1978; Little, 1982; Sarason, 1982). From this work has emerged a picture of schools as social institutions in which collegiality, shared decision making, innovativeness, and common understandings of the school's mission characterize those settings that are most educationally effective and in which the staff are most professional. As a result, the model of top-down decision making has begun to change.

Both administration-oriented and teacher-oriented professional groups are investigating models of administration, supervision, and staff development that support collegiality and shared decision making in the provision of instruction and in the management of schools. In the area of supervision, models range from developmental approaches, in which the type of supervision provided by school administrators and/or supervisors is determined by a teacher's training, level of experience, and performance on the job, to peer coaching approaches in which teachers determine the goals of supervision and monitor one another's progress. In the area of school administration, models range from the Toledo Plan, in which the teachers' union shares with the district administration in monitoring the performance of teachers, to recent experiments in Minnesota and Florida, in which the role of school administrator has been delegated to the corps of teachers in individual schools. In these and other settings, the focus of change is on school improvement through teacher empowerment.

To bring teaching into the realm of the professions requires the involvement of teachers as decision makers in all aspects of their work—from professional preparation to school management and educational policy. "Teachers," wrote Henry Adams, "affect eternity; we can never tell where their influence stops" (Adams, 1931, p. 300). It is essential that their voice be heard clearly in the shaping of tomorrow's schools, particularly those that serve young children three through eight years of age.

References

Adams, H. (1931). *The education of Henry Adams.* New York: Modern Library.

Berman, P. B., & McLaughlin, M. W. (1978). Implementing and sustaining innovations. *Federal Programs Supporting Educational Change: Vol. viii* (R-1589/8-HEW). Santa Monica, CA: Rand Corp.

Carnegie Task Force on Teaching as a Profession. (May, 1986). *A nation prepared: Teachers for the twenty-first century.* New York: Carnegie Forum on Education and the Economy.

Holmes Group. (1986). *Tomorrow's teachers: A report of the Holmes Group.* East Lansing, MI: Holmes Group.

Little, J. W. (1982). Norms of collegiality and experimentation: Workplace conditions of school success. *American Educational Research Journal, 19* (3), 325–340.

Sarason, S. B. (1982). *The culture of the school and the problem of change* (2nd ed.). Boston: Allyn and Bacon.

F. O'C. Rust

Professional Ethics

Currently, early childhood education is an occupation striving to become a profession. A code of ethics is a hallmark of professionalism, conveying the field's own sense of its unique mission in society and responsibilities to it. Such a code is especially important in early childhood education because of the vulnerability and powerlessness of young children and because of the multiple constituents that early childhood educators serve, including children, parents, and agencies.

Early childhood educators often encounter problems of professional ethics in which their responsibilities are not clear or professional values are in conflict. An example is a situation in which a parent who needs to get up for work very early in the morning requests that a four-year-old be kept from taking his afternoon nap so that he will fall asleep earlier at night. Professional ethics develops from a shared process of critical, systematic reflection about the basic priorities of the field and the related responsibilities that practitioners assume in their roles as professionals. As fundamental commitments emerge, they are commonly articulated in a code of ethics that provides guidance to practitioners who find themselves trying to cope with situations in that their professional responsibilities are not clear.

A code of ethics for early childhood education, in one early view, would help to define and unify the field by moving decision making from an individual enterprise to a process based on consensus (Katz & Ward, 1978). In this view, a code of ethics would make it easier for teachers and administrators to behave ethically by providing more powerful justification for an argument or action. Practitioners who appeal to the provisions of a code would act, not as individuals alone, but as professionals governed by the common commitments to their field. A code would assure the public that practice in early childhood education met standards that reflect due regard for children, families, and the community.

The National Association for the Education of Young Children's (NAEYC) *Code of Ethical Conduct* was the culmination of a process begun in 1984 that involved early childhood educators from across the United States. The *Code* includes consideration of the results of surveys of association members that identified ethical issues most prevalent and problematic in early childhood education. The most commonly reported dilemmas included reporting child abuse and neglect; managing information, especially pertaining to issues of confidentiality; dealing with inappropriate program practices; dealing with issues raised by divorced or separated parents; providing for children with time-consuming special needs; and resolving the problems of parents and children whose interests may conflict, such as the situation of the parent who does not want the child to nap at school. This last category of "complex client" cases is especially troubling because it is not clear if the professional's primary responsibility is to the parent or to the child.

The central question, "What should responsible early childhood educators do and what should they refuse to do?" was the subject of reflection by groups of NAEYC members as they discussed issues identified by the survey respondents (Feeney & Kipnis, 1985). The *Code of Ethical Conduct* grew out of the shared reflection on professional responsibilities. It is organized into four sections that describe the obligations to children, families, colleagues, and community and society. Rather than provide formulas for dealing with every dilemma, the *Code* offers guidelines that can help guide practitioners to make responsible ethical decisions. Items in the *Code* are organized into ideals of the profession pointing to desirable and exemplary professional behavior, and principles of professional conduct that mark the line between acceptable and unacceptable behavior.

While the *NAEYC Code of Ethical Conduct* defines acceptable and unacceptable professional behavior, there is neither provision at present for supporting members who encounter difficulty acting in accordance with the *Code* nor provision for sanctioning those who violate it. The next step in professional ethics development for the field of early childhood education is to agree on procedures to insure that the *Code*'s provisions are observed. Such compliance procedures can further define the professionalism of the field.

References

Callahan, J. C. (1988). *Ethical issues in professional life.* New York: Oxford University Press.

Feeney, S., & Kipnis, K. (1990). Code of Ethical Conduct and Statement of Commitment. Washington, DC: National Association for the Education of Young Children.

Feeney, S., & Kipnis, K. (1985, March). Public policy report: Professional ethics in early childhood education. *Young Children, 40* (3), 54–56.

Katz, L., & Ward, E. (1978). *Ethical behavior in early childhood education.* Washington, DC: National Association for the Education of Young Children.

Kipnis, K. (1987). How to discuss professional ethics. *Young Children, 42* (4), 26–30.

S. Feeney

Union Relations

The unionization of early childhood teachers and administrators is still very much in its infancy. In the absence of an extensive research literature, interesting examples do exist of full-blown union recognition, affiliation, collective negotiations, and employee contracts, all dramatic exceptions to the rule that most employees in early childhood care and education are not currently engaged in union activity. Unions of early childhood professionals, as well as union-supported provision of child care through union contracts, are appearing very slowly across the nation.

A former child care director, for example, writes of the recognition of his staff as a union at the University of Wisconsin and their affiliation with the Wisconsin Childcare Union, District 65, United Auto Workers (UAW) (Morin, 1990). Likewise, the Harvard University Union of Technical and Clerical Workers (HUUTCW) negotiated a contract that "commits both the union and the university to developing a pilot project for a high quality, low cost, convenient child care center" (McEntee, 1990, p. 1). Whether this child care center's staff itself will be unionized is not yet clear, but the union contract is supporting these services. Even some child care directors are unionized in New York City, having joined the N.Y.C. Public School principals' and administrators' union, the Council of Supervisors and Administrators, AFL-CIO.

Growth in the interest in unions can be partly attributed to the dramatic increase in full-day, early childhood programs (i.e., child care) and the mounting recognition of this service as part of the educational system. Associated with this issue is a concern for stable professional relationships between young children and significant adults, opening the way for improving working conditions and reducing staff turnover. Thus, this article addresses the unionization of full-day "child care," the area in which collective negotiation is most active.

What is driving child care staff to form unions? It seems that unionization usually occurs under three related conditions—worker deprivation, legal rights, and institutional settings. Worker deprivation, actual and relative, is a force propelling early childhood educators to join a union (Morin, 1989). Research on child care teachers (Whitebook, Howes, & Phillips, 1988) often indicates poor pay (averaging $5.35 per hour in 1988, or $9,363 a year—below the official poverty level for a family of three), little or no benefits, and high turnover. Eighty-nine percent of child care teachers recommend "better salaries" to improve care; and 80 percent supports "improved benefits," both issues that unions traditionally address. In its recommendations, the National Staffing Study (Whitebook, Howes, & Phillips, 1988) stated flatly that unionization was important to meet the needs of these employees, or in the language of the report to "encourage child care teachers to join professional associations and unions committed to improving their compensation and working conditions" (p. 18).

Legal rights to bargain are usually prerequisites for unionization, since workers in all sectors have found most employers unwilling voluntarily to negotiate bilateral contracts.

Under the National Labor Relations Act (1935) and subsequent revisions and policies, child care workers in the private sector are protected in their request for bargaining, while publicly employed child care staff must depend on laws in 23 states that are are silent or deny public sector "teachers" the right to bargain.

Unionization works best in institutional settings where union organizers can appeal to larger groups of workers, and where employers tend to treat employees as "categories," not as individuals. (See Cooper [1980] and Cresswell, Murphy, and Kerchner [1980] on the unionization of public school teachers.) Thus, in other sectors, such as the public schools, it follows that if and when child care delivery becomes larger, more institutional, and a bigger target for union organizers, child care center employees will likely form or join unions, sometimes affiliate with "big labor," and pressure for improved conditions of work.

As it now stands, however, most child care staff are employed by very small centers (fewer than 30 employees), privately owned by lone entrepreneurs, or sponsored by churches, synagogues, or other nonprofit groups (Granger, 1989a; Granger, 1989b; Kagan, 1989). Two-thirds are "mom and pop" operations. Data on pay are indicative, however, of the nature of the problem (Whitebook, Howes, & Phillips, 1988). Of the four types of center auspices, the "chain, for profit" seems to have the worst pay (averaging $4.10 an hour) and concomitantly the highest annual turnover (74 percent); the "independent, for profit" are next, with $4.76 per hour, and 51 percent turnover; "non-profit, church/synagogue-sponsored" do better, with $5.04 per hour, and 36 percent turnover; and the "non-profit, non-affiliated" do best, with pay of $6.40 and an annual turnover of 30 percent—still poor remuneration by most standards.

Three exceptions do, however, exist: When child care is sponsored by public school systems where unionization exists, child care teachers occasionally enjoy some of the same rights and recognition, pay, and benefits as teachers or elementary and secondary educators (Mitchell, Seligson, & Marx, 1989); industrial child care employees, often on the site of a "union shop," usually engage in collective agreements as unions with their employers; and a few for-profit centers have recognized unions, though the "big two" (LaPetite and Kindercare) have not.

As unionization begins, early childhood education can anticipate some of the same developments in child care as have occurred in other sectors. Data from the 30-year history of public school teacher unions, for example, show four stages of development (Kerchner and Mitchell, 1988). The *Pre-bargaining phase* generally entails employees who are divided, exploited, and much concerned about deprivation, lack of status, compensation below a "living wage," and inadequate "conditions of employment" (retirement, health benefits, rights of grievance against job abuses).

In the *Meet and Confer phase*, employee committees often receive the right to "meet" with their employer, for purposes of working out problems and reaching some mutual agreements. This phase, however, breaks down when workers make demands that employers cannot or will not meet. The *Good-Faith Bargaining phase*, won through protests, strikes, adversarialism, and hard work, is when workers consolidate their power, gain recognition, engage in bargaining, sign contracts, and generally see their pay and benefits improve. It is reported that schoolteachers have made significant progress with collective bargaining, including a 21 percent improvement in pay within two years of their initial employment (Eberts & Stone 1984).

Finally, the *Professional Unionism phase* is when teachers and school management may eventually work together to solve professional problems, changing and augmenting the contract to meet new needs— an era of negotiated policy when "unions affect educational policy, and schools need to manage through their teacher organizations rather than around them (Kerchner & Mitchell, 1988, p. 230). Yet this final, cooperative stage of labor-management relations seems to come only after the storm and stress of earlier, adversarial unionization.

The future of labor relations for child care educators is not entirely clear at this point. Some signs point to the emergence of expanded collective bargaining, including the beginnings of union activity, union affiliation, and the pressure for better conditions of work. There is momentum to make early childhood education a recognized profession, one that questions the validity of unionization and its impact on the image of the field. Thus, with one distinct difference, the pattern emerging now in child care reminds one of the 1950s in the public schools, when teachers were struggling to balance their need for better conditions of work and their professional image. The difference is that the laws in the 1990s in 27 states protect the right of these employees to seek unionization. In the earlier period, public sector workers were totally unprotected in their efforts.

Yet, child care staff are a long way from extensive union negotiations. The organization of service delivery is still either highly private, small and proprietary, or not-for-profit, making real unionization difficult, though some interesting "consortia" of small center staff unions are beginning. Even the large corporate, for-profit employers, where unions are most likely to be present, have successfully fended off attempts to bargain. The Child Care Employee Project (Berkeley, California), however, has been a significant catalyst for increasing public awareness of the needs of staff in this field. The future of labor relations in the field will rest with continued demand for services; the spread of public, large-scale programs; and the activities of union organizers.

As one educator explained concerning the impact of unionization, "In terms of salaries, there's been some gain, but not a major difference. We're still talking about salaries between $5 and $7 an hour even in the unionized centers. To really affect [sic] any kind of change in working conditions, there needs to be a critical mass of workers and they need to be active in the larger advocacy effort to make high quality, affordable child care a reality" (Morin, 1990, p. 4).

References

Child Care Action Campaign. (1990). Examples of union involvement in child care. *CCAC Information Guide #5*, 330 7th Avenue, New York, NY, 10010.

Cooper, B. S. (1980). *Collective bargaining, strikes, and related costs in education: A comparative review*. Eugene, OR: ERIC Center for Educational Management, University of Oregon.

Cresswell, A. M., Murphy, M. J., & Kerchner, C. T. (1980). *Teachers, unions, and collective bargaining in public education*. Berkeley, CA: McCutchan Publishing.

Eberts, R. W., & Stone, J. A. (1984). *Unions and public schools: The effect of collective bargaining on American schools*. Lexington, MA: D.C. Heath.

Granger, R. C. (October, 1989a). The staffing crisis in early childhood education. *Phi Delta Kappan, 71* (2), 130–134.

Granger, R. C. (1989b). *What would it cost to solve the staffing crisis in early childhood programs*. New York: Bank Street College of Education.

Johnson, S. M. (1984). *Teacher unions in schools*. Philadelphia: Temple University Press.

Kagan, S. L. (February, 1989). Early care and education: Tackling the tough issues. *Phi Delta Kappan, 70* (2), 433–439.

Kerchner, C. T., & Mitchell, D. (1988). *The changing idea of a teachers' union*. Philadelphia: Falmer Press.

McEntee, G. (September–October, 1990). Work family issues: The union's response. *Child Care ActioNews, 7* (5), 1 & 6.

Mitchell, A., Seligson, M., & Marx, F. (1989). *Early childhood programs and the public schools: Between promise and practice*. Dover, MA: Auburn.

Modigliani, K. (March, 1988). Twelve reasons for the low wages in child care. *Young Children, 43* (3), 14–15.

Morin, J. (August, 1990). Learning to share: Directors, unions and power in the 1990s. *Child Care Information Exchange, 74*, 23–25.

Morin, J. (September, 1989). Viewpoint: We can force a solution to the staffing crisis. *Young Children, 44* (6), 18–19.

Whitebook, M., Howes, C., & Phillips, D. (1988). *Who cares? Child care teachers and the quality of care in America* (The National Childcare Staffing Study). Washington, DC: National Association for the Education of Young Children.

B. Cooper & S.G. Goffin

6.5 Preserve Teacher Education

Preservice teacher education is the subject of ongoing revision and national debate within the frame of reference of secondary and elementary education. As part of the larger field of teacher education, early childhood teacher education policies grow out of policies created by state departments of education as well as professional and accrediting organizations.

Understanding knowledge bases in a teacher education program is part of the movement for educators to make explicit their purposes and practices, and to engage in ongoing dialogue, development, and refinement of them. The articles in this section discuss issues connected with knowledge bases.

It is important to be aware of the controversy and confusion that surround the notion of knowledge bases. Controversy exists concerning the need to articulate shared bases for teacher education. Confusion exists concerning what bases teacher educators might share and about the need for ongoing scholarly dialogue in order to decide. Uneven state policies concerning teacher education sometimes further obscure knowledge base concerns and issues.

State variations in teacher education program specifications include requirements that teachers complete four-year, undergraduate degrees, both bachelor's and master's degrees in education, or liberal arts bachelor's degrees followed by master's degrees in education. A few states admit liberal arts bachelor's degree graduates to teaching positions who have not studied education or engaged in supervised field experiences. Some states limit the number of teacher education courses within an undergraduate degree program. In private sector preschools and child care centers, graduates of two-year colleges and others also teach groups of young children.

Within these varied program preparation patterns, student teaching or internships in early childhood education may or may not be present. Articles in the section below consider some student teaching policies and practices. In addition, there is a brief description of an

alternative form of preservice teacher education, the Child Development Associate (CDA) credential, which might bypass bachelor's degree programs for some recipients.

D. P. Fromberg

Knowledge Bases

There are three major professional tasks in early childhood education that are unique. These tasks are (1) bridging knowledge, (2) being acquainted with alternatives, and (3) understanding why and how to select from among them.

The unique aspect of early childhood teacher education, as contrasted with the body of teacher education in general, is the need to bridge the distance between adult conceptions of knowing and young children's ways of learning about conceptions of knowing. Prospective early childhood teachers study how to plan content based upon the conditions under which young children learn as well as the methods of inquiry of the adult fund of knowledge.

Prospective early childhood teachers ideally develop the power to select from among alternative activities, materials, and procedures in order to adapt their work to children. Among these alternatives is a particular attention to the study of research concerning the influence of play as one condition of early learning, as well as professional ways for teachers to provide for its inclusion in educational programs (Fromberg, 1987; 1990). This is essential in working with young children who have individual and special learning needs as well as children who bring diverse cultural experiences to school. It follows, further, that the prospective teacher needs to understand the rationales necessary in order to select from among these alternatives. In particular, prospective teachers who understand why decisions are made and how they value them, will be teachers who can communicate effectively with parents, administrators, and other adults.

Useful resources that are consistent with these three major tasks and extend these considerations for institutions of higher education appear in the following documents: *Elementary Education Guidelines* (Kindergarten–Grade Six) (AACTE, 1989); and *Early Childhood Teacher Education Guidelines* (NAEYC, 1991). These documents outline the importance of significant and relevant general education, specialty studies, and field experiences.

These documents represent the consensual work of specialists from various disciplines. At a time when educators and policy analysts have been debating the issue of the relation of liberal arts and professional education, the authors of these guidelines recommend that both liberal studies and professional studies are necessary backgrounds. They contend that this integration is necessary in the development of effective early childhood teachers. As generalists, early childhood teachers need to be broadly educated individuals with rich cultural interests. (See also **Liberal Arts Education**, below.)

Specialists also recommend that teachers need to understand the foundational philosophical, sociological, and historical issues that influence early childhood education. Prospective teachers learn about the diverse cultures and economic conditions that young children experience. Foundational understandings also help teachers to deal with reasons for policies and practices and the values questions that undergird them. These studies also form the basis upon which to consider socially committed concerns and ethical behavior; and to make decisions about advocacy for young children, their families, and the early childhood profession.

Child development as well as curriculum development studies are part of their recommendations. Supervised field experiences also are part of the recommendations of professional associations.

The unique ways in which young children think, learn, and behave, as well as their need for school continuity with their family experiences, makes the study of young children in the contexts of their families particularly significant for prospective early childhood teachers. Either understanding how children develop or having a repertoire of curriculum activities alone would be an incomplete preparation. Education in both of these background studies along with an understanding of social foundations, however, has the potential to create a corps of early childhood teachers who are capable of independent thinking, deliberative action, and innovative interaction.

The potentials for educational or social reconstruction, however, depend upon the distinctive knowledge bases that prospective teachers learn in a particular school of education. When consistently implemented within a preservice program, for example, each of the different behaviorist or constructivist or critical theorist positions encourages the development of teachers with different belief systems, practices, and social commitments. Therefore, faculties of education optimally engage in thoughtful dialogue about which kinds of knowledge bases to implement in their particular preservice early childhood teacher education program.

It is conceivable, for example, that early childhood teacher education programs exist that have developed over time with eclectic offerings. Often these offerings and policies show the effects of political decisions or just plain inertia. To offer an early childhood teacher education program with probity, however, requires ongoing discussion among responsible individuals who make thoughtful, ethical professional decisions.

Exemplary early childhood teacher education programs offer students opportunities to learn their profession through the processes of induction, coaching, and collaboration. Induction takes place when candidates have the opportunity to observe and participate in classrooms with several different teachers and to consider how their own belief systems emerge.

Coaching occurs when college supervisors and cooperating teachers provide feedback to candidates in relation to mutually discussed plans. Such coaching also emphasizes the importance of the candidate's capacity to make decisions based upon deliberative thought and self-awareness.

Collaboration takes place within the induction and coaching process, as well as in projects with other colleagues and parents of children.

Collaborative projects with colleagues might involve such activities as mutual data collection, sharing ideas and planning together, and engaging in peer coaching. Collaborative projects with parents might include such activities as planning community cultural events, sharing story themes, and building projects. These induction, coaching, and collaboration processes contribute to the creation of empowered professionals who have the opportunity to develop their practices and insights independently after graduation.

References

AACTE. (1989). *Elementary Education Guidelines* (Kindergarten–Grade Six). Washington, DC: Author.

Fromberg, D. P. (1987). *The full-day kindergarten.* New York: Teachers College Press.

Fromberg, D. P. (1990). Play issues in early childhood education. In C. Seefeldt (ed.), *Continuing issues in early childhood education* (pp. 223–243). Columbus, OH: Merrill.

NAEYC (1991). *Early Childhood Teacher Education Guidelines.* Washington, DC: Author.

D. P. Fromberg

Liberal Arts Education

Because young children want and need to know about everything, their teachers must have a broad understanding of all of the liberal arts, including art, music, social science, biological and physical sciences, mathematics, and language. Teachers also need to be able to make this knowledge accessible to young children. They must be able to extend and expand children's concepts with sequencing experiences that enable children to build meanings and relationships between ideas. They also need to be able to use the natural activity and play of children to teach content as an integrated, unified whole. This requires in-depth understanding of both child growth and development, and learning and content.

Inasmuch as teaching young children involves tremendous investment of self, it follows that knowledge of self is a part of the required knowledge base of early childhood teacher education. Self-understanding, knowledge of self, can also stem from an in-depth study of human development across the life span. With knowledge of human development as well as communication skills, teachers are better prepared to relate effectively with parents, other team members, or the community. They will also be able to more effectively advocate for children's rights.

How to provide prospective teachers with this necessary knowledge base is a matter of debate today. There is general agreement, however, that their preparation programs should instill in them the motives for lifelong learning in partnership with the children they teach.

C. Seefeldt

Historical Context of Student Teaching

Preservice student teaching placements and supervision have been part of teacher preparation programs in the United States since normal schools were established in the 1830s (Henry, 1989). Based on the notion of apprenticeship developed in Europe several centuries earlier, the concept of practice teaching offered students direct experiences in learning to teach by working in training schools. When many of the normal schools developed into teachers colleges in the 1900s, some opted to create on-campus laboratory schools and/or child study centers. Educators of the times expected these centers to be controlled settings with model classrooms that would provide ideal sites for practice teaching, as well as for observation, research, and experimentation. Laboratory schools were staffed by outstanding teachers who supervised preservice students and also taught courses in methods of teaching.

The recognition by teacher educators that future teachers ought to learn to teach in "real world" settings was one of several developments that precipitated a movement in the 1950s toward the increased creation of student teaching placements in off-campus settings. In the off-campus settings, students not only practiced teaching, but studied the teaching act (Golden, 1982). The classroom teacher who supervised the student teacher on-site was called the "supervising teacher" and later, the "cooperating teacher." A faculty member from the student's institution of higher education also provided supervision.

Problems that may arise in the administration of student teaching include level of agreement and commitment as well as effectiveness of communication between teachers at the student teaching school site and university faculty. Sometimes there is dissatisfaction with field placement sites or preparedness of student teachers.

Recent reports cite these and other concerns as reasons to reform teacher education programs (Holmes, 1986) and to increase collaboration between institutions of higher education and professionals who work in field settings. Increased influenced by cooperating practitioners could result from implementing such training partnerships.

The concept of student teaching is rooted in the belief that students learn from experience. During student teaching, prospective teachers confront problems to solve, have opportunities to test pedagogical approaches, and learn more about young children. They also become further socialized into the teaching profession. (See also **Student Teaching Placement and Supervision**, below.)

References

Golden, G. (1982). *Guiding clinical experiences in teacher education.* New York: Longman.

Henry, M. A. (1989). Change in teacher education: Focus on field experiences. In J. A. Braun, Jr. (ed.), *Reforming teacher education: Issues and new directions* (pp. 69–95). New York: Garland.

Holmes Group (1986). *Tomorrow's teachers: A report of the Holmes Group.* East Lansing, MI; Holmes Group.

J. J. Caruso

Student Teaching Placement and Supervision

Student teaching is part of an apprenticeship system in preservice teacher education. It is an opportunity for those who are preparing to teach young children to spend time working alongside a professional teacher in one or more school settings. During that time the teacher candidate is referred to as a student teacher. The professional teacher, usually called a cooperating teacher, serves as a model, coach, colleague, and collaborator.

The cooperating teacher is a model for the student teacher who follows the teacher's schedule for half or all of a semester. As a skilled practitioner model, the cooperating teacher works as usual with the children. In the best of worlds, the cooperating teacher discusses plans with the student teacher, invites suggestions and additions, and discusses what happened after working with the children.

The cooperating teacher also serves as a coach to the student teacher. Together, they discuss plans before the student teacher begins to work independently with children, first with individuals, then with groups of increasing size. After the teaching episodes, the cooperating teacher and student teacher discuss the relationship of the events to the plans, and ways in which the student teacher might modify interaction in the future. In this coaching process, sometimes called clinical supervision, the cooperating teacher encourages the student teacher to reflect on the personal dynamics of events.

Student teachers do not receive payment for their participation. Cooperating teachers sometimes, but not always, receive payment in the form of university course credit or a token amount of money. In some school districts where most teachers have completed master's degrees, the equivalent university course credits are shared by all the teachers in the district, based upon need. There are rare instances in which universities provide compensation by offering a course for cooperating teachers or a mentor teacher course.

The purpose of placing prospective teachers in working early childhood classrooms is to help them apply their study of the field to its actual practice, and to study their own teaching behavior. Sometimes, full-time (every day) student teaching takes place in two separate classrooms, for half a semester each. Inasmuch as early childhood education takes place in a great variety of settings, student teachers might have two separate placements in a preprimary setting and a primary setting; in a public and private school; or in a child care center and a public school. A comprehensive range of placements might include two or more part-time field placements and two student teaching placements that include work with primary, kindergarten, nursery school age and toddler/infant age children. A few schools offer a full year of student teaching with two to four placements.

Often, student teachers have engaged in other field experiences connected to courses offered before student teaching. In a child development course, for example, they might observe in a classroom and/or community setting and collect case study material on individual children. In a course in the teaching of reading or science education, they might spend a few hours each morning for a few months. During this time, they might teach a small group of children some aspects of language and reading or create or work in an ongoing classroom science center or in a series of projects.

The university offers support to the student teaching efforts by providing a weekly seminar for candidates, regular site visits by a university faculty member for coaching, and three-way conferences between cooperating teacher, student teacher, and university field supervisor. Some university supervisors make site visits at least three times during a semester. Most supervisors visit biweekly.

The National Council for the Accreditation of Teacher Education (NCATE) guidelines call for a minimum of ten weeks of full-time student teaching. Many states expect a minimum of 300 clock hours.

Policies concerning the placement of student teachers and their supervision differ between institutions of higher education and cooperating school districts. In order to prepare exemplary teachers, it is apparent that student teacher placements need to be in exemplary and culturally diverse settings. Some universities arrange placements through individual schools, requesting particular teachers who work in ways that are consistent with the university's philosophical knowledge base.

The NCATE expects accredited institutions to have consistency between the knowledge bases they use, their course of study, and their field work. Therefore, accredited schools of education communicate these requirements to school districts and limit their placements of students accordingly.

D. P. Fromberg

Child Development Associate (CDA) Credential

The National Association for the Education of Young Children, in its model of professional and career development, lists the CDA credential as the minimum requirement for entry into the early childhood profession. The goal of the CDA Program is to attest to the competency of child care personnel who do not hold formal degrees.

From its inception in the early 1970s, the CDA Program promoted a system of training and credentialing individuals based on demonstrated competency with children. A CDA is a person who is able to meet the specific needs of children from birth through five years of age and who, with parents and other adults, works to nurture children's physical, social, emotional, and intellectual growth in a child development framework. The CDA credential is awarded to child care providers and home visitors who have demonstrated their skill in working with young children and their families by successfully completing the CDA assessment process.

In 1985 the Council for Early Childhood Professional Recognition became the permanent site of the credentialing branch of the CDA Program. The Council conducts direct assessments for individuals who want only to be evaluated by the national office and operates a nationwide network of professional preparation programs.

Individuals who choose to become CDAs and who need training, enroll in a CDA Professional Preparation Program. This program offers one-year training for caregivers and deals with appropriate practices in early childhood education. During the first phase, individuals work in a child care setting and complete a self-study curriculum. During the second phase, while continuing to work in a child care setting, individuals attend a group seminar series, conducted under the separate auspices of a postsecondary educational institution that is under contract with the Council. During the third phase, individuals complete a performance-based assessment of their skills. For more information, contact the Council for Early Childhood Professional Recognition, Suite 500, 1718 Connecticut Avenue, N.W., Washington, DC 20009. (See also **History of Early Childhood Teacher Education,** above, and Section 6.2, **Early Childhood Teachers: A Profile.**)

R. W. Bouverat

6.6 In-service Teacher Education

In-service early childhood teacher education utilizes a variety of strategies (e.g., mentoring or coaching, self-study, collaboration, school-based management) and delivery systems (e.g., workshops, on-site seminars, professional conferences) that are utilized to enable teachers already employed in early childhood settings to acquire needed knowledge and skills or refine their existing, ongoing practice. In-service preparation also may be undertaken through college or university graduate programs that result in a master's degree or a professional diploma such as the CAS (Certificate of Advanced Study). In-service early childhood education graduate students are generally expected to be at least provisionally certified and to have had experience teaching in an early childhood setting prior to entry into the program.

L. R. Williams

Content and Providers of In-service Education Programs

Early childhood education programs are provided in a variety of settings by persons with various degrees of professional preparation. Diversity of training among early childhood

personnel can be healthy in many respects. Inadequate training or lack of training, however, can be problematic, since the amount of specific early childhood training has been shown to be the characteristic of early childhood teachers most closely related to program effectiveness (Ruopp et al., 1979). Of continuing concern in the early childhood field have been the twin issues of (1) providing in-service staff development focused on essential skills and knowledge to early childhood personnel with little or no training in the field *and* (2) providing in-service education designed to enable experienced personnel to maintain currency with curriculum, research, and practice. Other issues related to in-service education include type of training to be provided, the in-service teacher education curriculum, and views of empowerment as an aim of in-service education.

There are a number of in-service training programs currently in use, such as the Child Development Associate (CDA) credential, designed for use with child care workers, and the NAEYC (National Association for the Education of Young Children) model suggesting college-level preparation that includes a foundation in child development theory and research, training in developmentally appropriate instructional practices, and supervised teaching experience (NAEYC, 1982). The CDA Credentialing Program, initiated nationwide in 1971, provides child care workers with a competency-based program featuring the options of training through field work programs, work-study programs, or independent study programs that may or may not be associated with a college training program.

Staff development activities in early childhood settings are influenced by the local program's curriculum and its specific needs. In-service education generally takes place through university-sponsored courses, seminars, and workshops, as well as through professional organizations such as NAEYC. Local teacher resource centers also offer programs. Coaching is an emerging trend in the early childhood field. There are several coaching models, including (1) peer coaching in which teams of teachers are paired to provide feedback to each other, (2) mentor coaching in which an experienced teacher is paired with one or two new teachers, and (3) technical coaching in which consultants work with novice and experienced teachers in building new instructional strategies and theory into the classroom.

A useful device for pinpointing staff development needs in child care centers is the Early Childhood Environmental Rating Scale (ECERS). This seven-point assessment program generates a profile of strengths and weaknesses in center quality relating to personal care routines, furnishings and display, language and reasoning experiences, gross motor activities, creative activities, social development, and adult needs. Profiles developed from ECERS data may be used to identify staff training needs (Benham, Miller, Kontos, 1988).

While the ECERS is helpful in identifying staff development needs specific to individual programs, general concerns in the field of early childhood also determine the focus of in-service education. Today's early childhood professionals must know how to work with children of varying talents, abilities, and exceptionalities who come from diverse cultural, ethnic, socioeconomic, and religious groups. They must understand the sociology of poverty and be able to work with parents and community leaders to insure children's success. They need training in the skills of collaborative planning to insure that the transition of children from one setting to another is supportive, recognizing the needs identified and gains made in previous settings.

There is a well-documented need for effective in-service education for persons who guide children's early education. More research is needed on such issues as use of process consultants, mentors, and evaluators to improve in-service education; improvement of teacher supervision as a way of empowering child care workers and teachers; and improvement of the training of auxiliary personnel. Empowering early childhood educators through suitable in-service education will continue to be a serious challenge.

References

Benham, N., Miller, T., and Kontos, S. (1988). Pinpointing staff training needs in child care centers. *Young Children, 43* (4), 9–16.

National Association for the Education of Young Children. (1991). *Early childhood teacher education guidelines for four- and five-year programs.* Washington, DC: NAEYC.

Ruopp, R., Travers, J., Glantz, F., & Coelen, C. (1979). *Children at the center: Summary findings and their implications.* Final report of the National Day Care Study. Vol. 1. Cambridge, MA: Abt Associates.

Zigler, E., and Valentine, J. (eds.). (1979). *Project Head Start: A legacy of the war on poverty.* New York: Free Press.

E. P. Witty

Managing Change Through In-service Education

Educational innovation is the introduction of new personnel, processes, and/or materials into an educational setting with the intent of changing the operations of the setting. Educational change is a process that unfolds over time and is shaped by such contextual factors as the history of the setting, the people involved, institutional image, and methods of operation. Successful innovations are marked by strong leadership, broad-based commitment, and mutual adaptation, in that the innovation changes and is changed by the system.

Educational change evolves in a three-stage process of mobilization, implementation, and institutionalization. *Mobilization* describes those activities related to beginning the change process, including identifying the need for change, assessing the political climate, marshalling support (especially from the teachers and school administration), and developing strategies for implementation. In the field of early childhood, mobilization for change has clearly taken place in the areas of kindergarten, publicly sponsored early childhood programs, day care, professional licensure, child advocacy, and infant and family services.

Implementation follows the mobilization stage, and its outcomes are shaped by what has taken place. Community support is essential, but implementation generally takes place in a specific school setting and involves the faculty of that setting; it is only through sustained commitment to and interaction with practicing educators that innovations lose their newness and become a part of the fabric of the school, that is, *institutionalization* takes place.

In the field of early childhood, no group has been more profoundly affected by the extensive changes in the field than *in-service early childhood educators*, those who are and have been involved directly in the care and education of young children as service providers or indirectly as trainers of early childhood personnel. To enable in-service early childhood educators to develop and maintain currency with changes in their field and provide quality services to young children and their families, in-service education is essential.

In-service education describes a host of services ranging from consultant support to workshops that are made available to educators on site and are designed to enhance their practice and/or introduce them to new processes or materials. In-service education is integral to the implementation and institutionalization phases of the change process. In general, effective in-service education has the following characteristics:

- It is considered important to maintaining currency with changes in theory and practice in the field of education.
- It is provided for a reason, such as to introduce new methods and/or materials into an educational setting.
- It is coordinated by an individual or group who has financial and programmatic support from administration. In public schools, administration is the district office, the principal, and the school board. In other early childhood centers, administration is the director and governing board. Programmatic support refers to the commitment of time and personnel to introduce and familiarize staff with an innovation, followed by periodic workshops or consultant support to enable staff to make full use of their in-service work.
- It is sought after by those who will use it, and they are involved in planning for it.

- It is planned as a part of the workday, not as an add-on. In some cases this may mean providing alternate child care providers. In others, it may mean scheduling days when children do not attend.
- It is ongoing. It is not a one shot, once a year thing. There is a shared commitment to continuing education for all of a school's or center's staff.
- It is evident. In settings in which effective in-service education has taken place, it is clear that there is general understanding of the innovation, and that it has been adapted to the setting and adopted by the participants.

In-service education takes place within the context of the daily life of a setting. The design and implementation of a particular in-service education program should reflect not only the needs of the setting but also its climate, including its history, interpersonal factors, leadership style, programmatic focus, and schedule. What works in one setting may not work in another because of these factors. What works in one setting will almost always have to be adapted for use in another so that it fits the need and climate of the second setting.

The way in which educators respond to an innovation is critical to its implementation. They may simply reject it (nonimplementation); they may make it look as if they are using it but, in fact, change nothing (cooptation); or they may adopt it, changing it to fit the setting and changing themselves to accommodate to it (mutual adaptation).

Mutual adaptaton is essential to successful implementation. Effective in-service education is essential, also, to the institutionalization of change, for it is teachers' knowledge of, and willingness to use, an innovation that make it become a part of the day-to-day operations of a school or other educational setting. In the management of change, in-service education is an essential component.

References

Berman, P. B., & McLaughlin, M. W. (1978). Implementing and sustaining innovations. In *Federal Programs Supporting Educational Change: Vol.*

viii (R-1589/8-HEW). Santa Monica, CA: Rand Corp.

Lieberman, A., & Miller, L. (1984). *Teachers, their world and their work.* Alexandria, VA: Association for Supervision and Curriculum Development.

Loucks-Horsley, S., & Hergert, L. (1985). *An action guide to school improvement.* Alexandria, VA: Association for Supervision and Curriculum Development.

Sarason, S. B. (1982). *The culture of the school and the problem of change* (2nd ed.). Boston: Allyn and Bacon.

F. O'C. Rust,
with editorial suggestions from
S. Feeney & I. S. Stewart

Refinement of In-service Teaching Practice

When new teachers assume their first teaching position, they use the knowledge and skills and hold the attitudes they acquired in their preservice preparation, or through observation of experienced teachers with whom they had contact. During their first working years, many beginning teachers are faced with an immediate need for survival (Katz, 1971). They must expand their repertoire to include the content, strategies, and classroom activities that are expected within their current work assignment. They usually do not have the additional time or energy to think about how they might improve their teaching beyond that adaptation.

By their fourth or fifth year of teaching, however, many teachers are entering a time of renewal, when they feel a need to change, modify, or otherwise refine their existing teaching strategies (Katz, 1971). Some teachers have an open attitude toward self-improvement throughout their whole career so that they are constantly seeking ways to improve their practice. Such teachers generally strive toward a high standard of performance and are aware of the relationship between their own high performance and that of the children with whom they work.

The question that arises for many teacher educators is how can they help in-service teachers to refine their practice after the teachers have moved beyond the initial into the later stages of their professional development. Building on the work of Donald Schon (Schon, 1987), one answer in recent years has been to focus on promoting reflective practice with in-service teachers. Reflection in this context involves considering the origins and effects of one's actions, and devising alternative paths to desired ends, or even discerning alternative goals. Reflection in the form of interactive journals has been shown to be effective in enabling in-service early childhood graduate students to make desired changes in their practice (Williams, 1989).

Journaling has been popular for a number of years as a device for thinking about one's own teaching. Teachers may initiate the practice themselves in order to track the course of their own professional development or progress in use of a particular innovation. In-service teacher educators may use journals to carry on a dialogue with their students about specific elements of their practice. Through the medium of the journal, an intensive interaction can occur over time that may lead to refinement of practice in areas identified by the in-service teachers themselves.

Journaling is only one form of reflection. Other forms include participation in in-service discussion groups, use of autobiography to clarify an educational philosophy, and (by teacher educators) use of ethnographic interviews to enable teachers to see their own progress and work more clearly. (See following articles for description of other forms of reflection.)

References

Katz, L. (1971). *Talks with teachers.* Washington, DC: National Association for the Education of Young Children.

Schon, D. (1987). *Educating the reflective practitioner: Toward a new design for teaching and learning in the profession.* San Francisco: Jossey-Bass.

Williams, L. R. (1989). Some reflections on reflection: Comments on in-service teachers' journals as vehicles for refinement of practice. *The Journal of Early Childhood Teacher Education, 32* (10:3), 13–17.

L. R. Williams

Reflective Teaching

Reflective teaching brings awareness of the choices that teachers can make in practice, and demands that practitioners explore the values and beliefs on which they base their selection of actions. John Dewey (1910) warned that reflective thought is troublesome, not least of all because it leads to reflection on the broad consequences of beliefs. He proposed that teacher education needs to help students engage in reflective thought, which he viewed as a way of thinking that prevented inertia, replacing it with perplexity and a drive to inquire.

Certainly not widespread, reflective teaching is not cited in the index of the 1986 *Handbook of Research in Teaching* although there are multiple listings in the 1990 *Handbook of Research on Teacher Education.* There is a growing number of commentators who argue against the technical, skills-dominated apprentice model of teacher education and in favor of reflective teaching. One approach describes a teacher education program for elementary school teachers that prepares students to think in terms of educational, technical, and ethical criteria (Zeichner & Liston, 1987). The emphasis on reflectivity, which is not simply a set of techniques, is reflected in the whole teacher education program in which the staff models an inquiry approach to the curriculum and to their work. Conflicts can come into play if inquiry-oriented student teachers are placed in classrooms that resist such reflectivity. Students also may be unclear that experiences without reflection can be miseducative (Dewey, 1938), and consequently feel that reflection is a waste of time.

The teacher education literature describes a variety of approaches to developing reflective teaching. There is a renewal of interest in action research as one approach. Some approaches that support reflection for teacher candidates include keeping their own journals, writing biographies (Connelly & Clandinin, 1988), engaging in picturing (Hunt, 1987), and pursuing document analysis (Carini, 1982). Teacher candidates also can work with other professionals through writing letters, utilizing storytelling about their life experiences, acting as participant observers in classrooms, and carrying out teacher interviews (Connelly & Clandinin, 1988).

Biography or life narratives are valuable in helping teachers reflect on their values, beliefs, and practice, pointing out that such reflection can result in enhanced understanding and awareness of the role of choice (Ayers, 1988). In a collaborative inquiry carried out with a teacher and a student teacher, recorded observations and interviews about teaching revealed in some depth the underpinnings of practice (Yonemura, 1986). These records gave all in the study an appreciation of the complexities and surprises of teaching.

Some teachers (Ashton-Warner, 1964; Marshall, 1968; Pratt, 1948) also have written about their teaching, providing the profession with examples of reflective teaching in action, and demonstrating the impact of reflective teaching on the lives of young children, and its potential for ameliorating society.

References

Ayers, W. (1988). *The good preschool teacher: Six teachers reflect on their lives.* New York: Teachers College Press.

Ashton-Warner, S. (1964). *Teacher.* New York: Bantam Books.

Bellah, R. N., Madsen, R., Sullivan, W. M., Swidler, A., & Tipton, S. M. (1985). *Habits of the heart: Individualism and commitment in American life.* Berkeley: University of California Press.

Carini, P. F. (1982). *The school lives of seven children: A five year study.* Fargo: University of North Dakota Press.

Connelly, E. M., & Clandinin, J. (1988). *Teachers as curriculum planners: Narratives of experience.* New York: Teachers College Press.

Dewey, J. (1910). *How we think.* Boston: D. C. Heath.

Dewey, J. (1938). *Experience and education.* New York: Collier.

Goodlad, J. I. (1984). *A place called school.* New York: McGraw-Hill.

Houston, R. W., Haberman, M., & Sikula, J. (eds.). (1990). *Handbook of research on teacher education.* New York: Macmillan.

Hunt, D. E. (1987). *Beginning with ourselves: Practice, theory and human affairs.* Ontario: Ontario Institute for Studies in Education Press.

Marshall, S. (1968). *An experiment in education.* New York: Cambridge University Press.

Pratt, C. (1948). *I learn from children*. Cornerstone Library.

Schon, D. A. (1983). *The reflective practitioner: How professionals think in action*. New York: Basic Books.

Schon, D. A. (1987). *Educating the reflective practitioner: Toward a new design for teaching and learning in the professions*. San Francisco: Jossey-Bass.

Valli, L., & Tom, A. R. (1988). The knowledge base in teacher education: Criteria for a framework. In H. C. Waxman, H. J. Freiberg, J. C. Vaughan, & Weil, M. (eds.). *Images of reflection in teacher education*. Reston, VA: Association of Teacher Educators.

Wittrock, M. C. (1986). *Handbook of research on teaching*. New York: Macmillan.

Yonemura, M. V. (1986). *A teacher at work: Professional development and the early childhood educator*. New York: Teachers College Press.

Zeichner, K. M., & Liston, D. P. (1987). Teaching student teachers to reflect. *Harvard Educational Review*, 57 (1), 23–48.

M. V. Yonemura

Autobiography as a Means of Refinement of In-service Teachers' Practice

If teaching is conceived as a series of behaviors, methods, prescribed activities, and techniques, then the refinement of teaching practice can be thought of as straight-forward, top-down, and didactic. Teachers can improve simply by accumulating new methods, learning more techniques, taking on a wider range of behaviors. If teachers are essentially line employees, the education of teachers can be a training regimen akin to boot camp or assimilation into the society of the shop floor.

If, on the other hand, teaching is conceived as an intellectual and ethical enterprise, and teachers, therefore, as professionals and transformative intellectuals, the improvement and refinement of teaching practice is quite another matter. If teaching is assumed to be a voluntary, intelligent, collective activity that occurs in contexts that are often coercive, ignorant, and individualizing, then the education of teachers is a problem and a challenge, something neither simple nor settled.

Autobiography is one way into this more complex and holistic sense of teaching and the education of teachers. Autobiography is essentially the act of reflecting on one's pathway to teaching, bringing to consciousness one's own story and making it available for personal and perhaps public scrutiny. Autobiography is thinking about one's life, the constraints as well as the openings, the contexts not of one's making, and the choices freely made. Autobiography involves looking at what one has made of oneself and wondering why.

Teachers have a special responsibility for self-awareness because teachers, whatever else they teach, teach themselves. Autobiography—whether life-history writing, nonlinear activities, individual reflection, or collective efforts at consciousness raising—is an act of self-awareness, an act of self-examination. It is a way of exposing attitudes, beliefs, and preferences to serious scrutiny. Autobiography is a way for teachers to become clearer and more intentional in teaching choices.

References

Ayers, W. C. (1989). *The good preschool teacher*. New York: Teachers College Press.

Abbs, P. (1974). *Autobiography in education*. London: Heinemann Education Books.

W. C. Ayers

Ethnographic Interview as a Tool for Early Childhood Teacher Education

The ethnographic interview is a tool that can be used both for educational research and classroom practice. Rooted in the discipline of anthropology, the ethnographic interview is a questioning technique used to promote dialogue in the quest for greater understanding of the world views of others. The ethnographic interview requires the interviewer to seek out and put aside personal assumptions in an ongoing attempt to learn from others, the interviewees.

Like the traditional interview, the ethnographic interview begins with questions and responses. However, the course of the procedure is quite different. Rather than accepting the interviewee's response at face value and moving on to the next question, the interviewer clarifies responses and reformulates questions to insure that mutual understanding is achieved. Active listening, restatement of the response, use of body language, and statements of affirmation to encourage elaboration of a point and foster risk taking are all facets of the ethnographic interview. Interviewer and interviewee work as a team learning from each other as they negotiate meaning (Mishler, 1986).

Teacher educators can utilize ethnographic interviews as a means of modeling professional skills and developing those skills in their students. Using the ethnographic interview as a component of the advisement process or as a tool for determining admission to a program or limited-size class enables teacher educators to model methods of eliciting student needs and interests. Taking these needs and interests into consideration in the design of teacher education enables teacher educators to model the process involved in designing emergent curriculum and implementing course content relevant to the concerns of the students. In addition, the process helps preservice and in-service teachers to develop schema of professional collaboration, and confirms that who they are and what they think matters.

When preservice and in-service teachers are themselves taught to conduct ethnographic interviews, they begin to identify and internalize many of the attitudes and skills that are components of good early childhood education. One way to implement these procedures is through an interview exercise adaptable to the content of many teacher education classes. The class is broken up into dyads, and partners are asked first to interview each other and, then, to report their findings to the class at large. This exercise contributes to both the feelings of individual self-worth and to the sense of community that are fundamental to professional collaboration. It acknowledges a connection between previous experience and classroom life.

Participant responses to this interview activity are invariably diverse. Different kinds of information are sought by different dyads. Different styles and methods of eliciting and recording information are utilized. The exercise itself elicits different feelings in class members, such as pleasure or anxiety, that facilitate or impede the task performance. When the teacher educator articulates and reflects on these points, he or she provides concrete examples of the diversity of the classroom, examples that mesh with and extend the existent schemas of the participants. Moreover, through these reflections, the teacher educator is able to share attitudes and information that are fundamental to reflective teaching.

When ethnographic interviews are used as components of assigned projects, papers, or reports, a new dimension is added. Interviews with teachers in the field, colleagues in classes, and children in schools provide new insights for preservice and in-service teachers. In order to conduct effective interviews, teachers must clarify what they wish to know. To do so, they must reflect on their own philosophy and practice. The interview process leads the interviewee, teacher, or child to reflect on his or her own experience and validates that experience. Participants emerge from the process with new understandings and new respect for all involved. Teachers feel less isolated as they come to see that there are those who can serve as resources for them within the school itself. They themselves feel more professional as they see how extensive is the knowledge base of other teachers. They gain a new respect for the child and become more willing to implement child-centered classrooms as they learn that children are cognizant of and articulate about good classroom practice.

The importance of the ethnographic interview as a means of empowerment is not to be minimized. It is commonly acknowledged that early childhood teaching is traditionally women's work. As such, it is commonly construed to be intuitive rather than rational work, work that depends on "experts" outside the classroom for the definition of good practice. Many women who seek careers in early childhood education have been socialized to the role of silent service. Rarely have they been encouraged to identify their own personal and professional vision, and even more rarely have they been taught the skills to communicate this vision effectively. Ethnographic interview serves as a tool to give these women the skills to develop a voice, an awareness that there is someone who will listen to that voice, and an understanding that the teacher's voice is worthy of respect.

Ethnographic interviews also provide men with an opportunity to hear and understand what Carol Gilligan (1982) calls "a different voice." This strategy allows both men and women to engage in dialogue that enhances their own practice, leading to their own growth and development, and that of the children with whom they work.

References

Gilligan, C. (1982). *In a different voice.* Cambridge: Harvard University Press

Mishler, E. (1986). *Research interviewing.* Cambridge: Harvard University Press.

H. Freidus

Pathways to Career Development

Keeping abreast of current developments in the profession is especially challenging in the field of early childhood education, a field that employs professionals who are degreed and certified, as well as nonprofessionals with varying levels of training.

Opportunities for professional growth are available in a variety of settings for a novice or an experienced teacher. Active membership in a professional organization is beneficial. Regional, state, and local meetings, as well as the annual conferences of organizations (such as the National Association for the Education of Young Children and the Association for Childhood Education International) provide ample opportunity to discuss topics with other professionals and to hear presentations by leaders in early childhood. Professional journals of national, international, and regional organizations (see Section 6.3, **Professional Journals Related to Early Childhood Education**) provide more up-to-date information

than books, and they usually focus on current topics that are of general interest.

Universities often offer summer courses in early childhood or related areas that can provide current information and opportunities for practical applications. Correspondence courses, television, computer networks and bulletin boards, or telephone-based modes also are available.

Although career ladder programs are virtually nonexistent in early childhood settings, some public and private school systems sponsor them. University-based teacher academies, frequently sponsored in conjunction with state departments of education, and seminars sponsored by public or private sources enable participants to gain knowledge and strengthen skills in one- or two-day sessions. The National Association for the Education of Young Children is in the process of developing a model of early childhood professional development that includes an in-service component. Child care centers and schools often provide in-service sessions that incorporate teacher requests. The Child Development Associate credential, available to both professionals and nonprofessionals, is a program designed for on-the-job training to strengthen skills and to introduce current information. CDA is a viable solution to staff development and career advancement. (See Section 6.5, **Child Development Associate Credential**, above.)

State departments of education facilitate career development by publishing materials, conducting seminars and workshops, and providing consulting and technical assistance. Networking and study groups are other sources of professional support.

Networking is an informal system whereby individuals with similar interests and concerns meet in order to share ideas, discuss issues, and plan cooperative action. Networking has the benefit of helping professionals gain or maintain currency on issues of interest to them. Study groups, like networking arrangements, generally focus on particular topics relevant to the individuals involved or discuss professional readings. Teachers meet with other teachers for activities such as exchanging teaching strategies, sharing projects, reviewing curriculum materials, and evaluating assessment procedures. Study group meetings can be arranged for teachers who work with children the same age or adjacent ages. Mentoring, the support of new entrants by exceptional experienced teachers, is a growing practice. The future development of a national professional board, presently funded by the Carnegie Foundation, may provide an additional credential for exceptional teachers.

References

Briggs, P. (1985). The early childhood network—we work together for young children. *Young Children*, *40* (5), 54–55.

Clemson, R. (1987). Mentorship in teaching. *Action in Teacher Education*, *9* (3), 85–90.

Howes, C. (1988). *Keeping current in child care research: An annotated bibliography*. Washington, DC: NAEYC.

Klass, C., and Nall, S. (1989). Accessible professional development: A community-based program for early childhood educators. *Childhood Education*, *65* (4), 224–227.

J. Moyer

Career Ladders

The predominant career path that has surfaced as a result of the mid-1980s reports calling for educational reform has been the "career ladders" concept. The career ladders concept, an incentive plan that typically specifies three or four hierarchical levels of professionalism, may be of two types. One type is called the *differentiated assignment* approach. The other is the *quality-of-performance* approach. In each of these approaches, teachers are formally evaluated on their classroom performance and their pupils' progress. Movement up each step of the ladder is dependent upon having demonstrated outstanding classroom performance and consistently strong pupil progress, along with other criteria. In the *differentiated assignment* approach, teachers who move up to the higher levels usually teach children less and add responsibilities such as supervision, evaluation of other teachers, and possibly, curriculum development. In the *quality-of-teaching* approach, teachers are awarded more money and prestige as they move up the ladder, although they remain in the classroom and may become a mentor or master teacher for others to observe and emulate (Association of Teacher Educators, 1985).

Career ladder or incentive plans are currently operating in 25 states, with an additional 9 states in the beginning stages of development (Career Ladder Clearinghouse, 1988). While these plans impact primarily on public elementary, secondary, and college level teachers, their appropriateness for early childhood teachers is suspect. The public school models of evaluating classroom performance reward teacher-centered approaches and typically use standardized and criterion-referenced test results as evidence of pupil growth. These data sources do not reflect early childhood education standards of professionalism.

Due in part to diversity of settings and sponsorship, the field of early childhood education has not had a coherent system for career advancement. Thus, an individual could start and end a 20-year career in preschool education or in child care at relatively the same professional level and income. This situation reflects the lack of professional status accorded those who work with children under the age of five.

Currently, the National Association for the Education of Young Children is developing a model for early childhood professional development. Concurrently, states are grappling with policies designed to address differentiated staffing of early childhood services. As these efforts proceed, several questions regarding career ladders in early childhood will have to be addressed. These include the following:

- Will the career ladder concept encompass the differentiated assignment approach or the quality-of-teaching approach, or both?

- If performance evaluations and child progress are integral to the career ladder plan, how will these be conducted and who will do the evaluations?

• Given the diversity of individuals and settings associated with early childhood programs, how will movement up the ladder and compensation be determined?

Only when these questions have been answered will career ladders provide for higher salaries, promotion opportunities, and prestige within the early childhood teaching profession.

References

Association of Teacher Educators. (1985). *Developing career ladders in teaching*. Reston, VA: Association of Teacher Educators.

Career Ladder Clearinghouse. (Dec. 1988). *Is "paying for performance" changing schools?* Atlanta, GA: Southern Regional Education Board.

E. Surbeck

Graduate Degree Programs

Graduate degree programs in early childhood education have expanded rapidly in the United States during the past 25 years. Graduate level early childhood personnel are prepared in 272 programs listed in *Peterson's Guide* under the heading of Early Childhood Education, and an additional 84 are listed under Child and Family Studies (Peterson's Guide, 1988). Programs also may be found within departments of home economics and psychology. These programs lead to a variety of degrees at the master's and doctoral levels.

The diversity of the listings reflects the history of the field and often represents the substantive focus of the program content. Programs within colleges, schools, or departments of education tend to be oriented toward curriculum and pedagogy, while other programs are oriented toward understanding child development, developmental processes, and the family/early education setting relationship (Peters, 1978).

At the master's level, programs may be further differentiated into those professionally oriented programs, usually within education, that focus on the preparation of early childhood curriculum specialists, such as those in children's literature, kindergarten, or early childhood special education, supervisory personnel, or master teachers. These programs usually lead to specialist certification. Programs under the rubric of human development, child and family studies or the like, tend to focus on specialties in child care program management and administration, parent involvement, and programming, or school and home-based programs for special needs, developmentally delayed, or handicapped children and their families (Spodek, Saracho, & Peters, 1988).

The age range focused upon also may differ, with colleges or departments of education attending to the older portion of the 0–8 year old age span, and other units focusing on the younger portion of the age span. Colleges of human development and programs of child and family studies often have a second, research-oriented track within the master's degree (MS) for those seeking research careers or planning to continue studies through the Ph.D.

At the doctoral level, the distinction persists with the degree within colleges or schools of education directed toward preparation of senior administrative personnel, particularly for public school programs. Within Ph.D. programs, the intent is the preparation of researchers and scholars capable of generating new knowledge and assuming responsibility for the preparation of the next generation of early childhood personnel within colleges and universities. The distinction in this case lies between those who research curricular and pedagogical variables versus those with interest in the broader ecology of early childhood education (Peters, 1981).

References

Peters, D. L. (1978). Educational programs for preparing early childhood personnel. *Children in Contemporary Society, 12* (2), 11–14.

Peters. D. L. (1981). Up the down escalator: Comments on professionalism and academic credentials in child care. *Child Care Quarterly, 11* (5), 12–21.

Peterson's annual guides to graduate study: Graduate programs in the humanities and social sciences. (1988). Princeton, NJ: Peterson's Guides, Inc.

Spodek, B., Saracho, O., Peters, D. (1988). *Professionalism and the early childhood practitioner.* New York: Teachers College Press.

D. L. Peters

6.7 Teacher Education Policies

As demands grow for quality early education for all children, ensuring a sufficient number of competent early childhood teachers is a major challenge facing policy makers. Long-enduring issues concerning the recruitment, education, and retention of early childhood teachers can be viewed in context of the drive to professionalize teaching. Professionalization with its promise of greater prestige, higher standards, and improved working conditions would address some of the endemic problems of staffing early childhood programs by attracting and retaining better prepared teachers. While efforts to professionalize early childhood teaching are likely to meet more resistance than elementary and secondary teaching, policies regarding the recruitment, education, and retention of early childhood teachers will be affected by the current push to professionalize teaching.

Recruitment issues concern the relatively low status and compensation of early childhood teachers within the education profession and in relation to the established professions and the business world where opportunities are now more accessible to females and minorities—two groups of individuals who have disproportionately staffed early childhood programs in the past. Having lost its captive audience of competent females and minorities, early childhood teaching needs to be promoted as a viable career alternative, and working conditions have to improve to attract the number and quality of individuals needed to staff early childhood programs. Special incentives to ensure an adequate number of teachers, especially minorities, might involve specialized recruitment efforts, financial aid, and forgivable loans to encourage prospective and current early childhood teachers to complete college degrees, teacher certification programs, and continuing education requirements.

Policy issues related to the education of early childhood teachers are usually articulated through local, state, and national certification or accreditation requirements. While public school early childhood teachers must meet state or local certification requirements, other early childhood teachers must meet the requirements of professional associations, governmental agencies, religious bodies, or private groups. As states and localities extend the scope of certification requirements to include nonpublic institutions and younger ages, differences in requirements will need to be addressed. Issues of ensuring minimal competency versus instilling desired practices will undoubtedly create tension in the field.

External governmental requirements affect teacher education programs directly by prescribing admissions criteria (e.g., test scores, grade point averages), course content (e.g., child development, multicultural education, special education) and certification requirements (e.g., majors, credits, test scores, grade point averages, student teaching). As the teacher education reform movement continues, the trend is toward more rigorous entry requirements (e.g., higher grade point averages, academic majors, basic skills tests) and certification requirements (e.g., liberal arts tests, pedagogical knowledge tests, performance tests, professional portfolios, mandated internships, master's degrees, and periodic recertification). Now requirements are promulgated as needed to ensure a competent teaching force and to aid in the professionalization of teaching.

The teacher education reform movement, while promising to upgrade the teaching force, has provided some special dilemmas for early childhood teacher education programs, at the same time as it sidestepped some longstanding problem areas. For a field facing shortages of qualified teachers, the raising of entry and certification standards and lengthening of preparation time threaten to reduce the pool of qualified candidates even further. In addition, determining the appropriate knowledge base for early childhood teachers and devising valid measurement techniques, particularly in the critical area of practice, continue to challenge the early childhood field. Moreover, the longstanding issue of whether there should be distinct certification and separate preservice and in-service preparation programs for elementary and early childhood teachers becomes even more critical as preparation programs are lengthened and knowledge and performance assessments are mandated. Should early childhood preparation be required of all elementary teachers, exist as a separate self-standing program, or be a voluntary extension of an elementary program?

Additional preparation questions facing policy makers concern how best to prepare teachers to meet the needs of an increasingly diverse student population, how programs should be extended downward to include infancy, and how to address the issues related to the large number of nonpublic school early childhood teachers who may have neither college degrees nor adequate professional preparation. In some cases, the problem is to convince policy makers that teachers of young children need to be as well educated and professionally prepared as teachers of older children; in other cases, the problem is to convince them that teachers of young children need different and specialized preparation.

Policy issues related to retention of early childhood teachers concern mandated continuing education requirements, evaluation procedures, and the improvement of working conditions to keep competent teachers in the field. Professionalization of early childhood teaching calls for peer-defined standards of practice, increased accountability in exchange for increased autonomy, and the creation of professional working conditions. Such goals provide a challenge for policy makers and early childhood educators alike.

References

Carnegie Forum on Education and the Economy. (1986). *A nation prepared: Teachers for the 21st Century.* New York: Author.

Goodlad, J. (1990). *Teachers for our nation's schools.* San Francisco: Jossey-Bass.

The Holmes Group. (1986). *Tomorrow's teachers: A report of the Holmes Group.* Lansing, MI: Authors.

K. K. Zumwalt

Assessment and Evaluation of Early Childhood Teachers

The school reform movement of the 1980s saw increased demands for accountability from legislators, taxpayers, and the "expert" panels that were convened to examine the state of our nation's educational system (Carnegie Forum on Education and the Economy, 1983). Among recent trends in public schools have been the implementation of the National Teachers Examination (NTE) as a prerequisite for certification in many states, the institution of merit pay linked to student outcomes, and the increased reliance on students' standardized test scores as the major measure in teacher evaluations. Those trends have affected early childhood education differently due to the diverse nature of the field. Because public schools are not the sole system in which early childhood teachers are employed, these trends have had less impact on infant, toddler, and preschool teachers than on elementary and secondary school teachers. However, there has been a subtle influence that is cause for concern.

The trend toward use of standardized tests as the most influential measure of teacher accountability has naturally made standardized tests assume greater importance. High stakes testing is now a fact of life as early as kindergarten (Meisels, 1989). To the extent that assessment drives curriculum, the "accountability culture" of the schools has caused curriculum to be increasingly academic, inappropriate, and dictated by the skills that are easily measured on standardized tests (NAEYC, 1988; Shepard & Smith, 1988).

Another concern that has been raised is the negative effect of recent trends in teacher assessment on recruitment of teachers from culturally diverse backgrounds (Bowman, 1989). With the populations of our schools, particularly those in urban areas, including increasingly larger numbers of African-American and/ or Latino children, it is even more essential that students have teachers of their own ethnic or cultural background as role models.

Teacher assessment also has become increasingly important in other sectors of early childhood besides the public schools. For example, the Head Start program, traditionally the largest user of the CDA National Credentialing Program, has mandated that by 1992, every classroom will have a teacher who is qualified either by possessing a degree in early childhood education/child development or a CDA credential. Mandates such as these have resulted in unprecedented numbers of candidates seeking assessment by the Council for Early Childhood Professional Recognition, the agency that administers the CDA Credentialing Program.

Another manifestation of increased importance of teacher assessment in early childhood is the implementation of a national accreditation system for early childhood programs by NAEYC (1984). Although the accreditation is awarded to the program and not to individual teachers, the process relies heavily on observations of teacher practice in individual classrooms (NAEYC, 1985).

The challenge of the 1990s will be to develop more sophisticated measures of teachers' performance that are not overly dependent on students' standardized test scores. A positive sign on the horizon is the work of the National Board for Professional Teaching Standards, which plans to develop instruments and procedures to assess the knowledge, skills, and dispositions needed by master teachers to obtain professional certification such as that granted by the legal or medical professions. Their goal is to develop instruments that are professionally credible and that measure the art as well as the science of teaching.

References

Bowman, B. (1989). Self reflection as an element of professionalism. *Teachers College Record, 90* (3), 444–451.

Carnegie Forum on Education and the Economy. (1983). *A nation at risk: Schools for the 21st century*. New York: Author.

Meisels, S. (1989). High stakes testing in kindergarten. *Educational Leadership, 46* (7), 16–22.

National Association for the Education of Young Children. (1984). *Accreditation criteria and procedures of the National Academy of Early Childhood Programs*. Washington, DC: NAEYC.

National Association for the Education of Young Children. (1985). *Guide to accreditation by the National Academy of Early Childhood Programs*. Washington, DC: NAEYC.

National Association for the Education of Young Children. (March, 1988). Position statement on standardized testing of children, 3 through 8. *Young Children, 23* (3), 42–47.

Shepard, L., & Smith, M. (1988). Escalation of curriculum in kindergarten. *Elementary School Journal, 89* (2), 135–145.

S. Bredekamp

Certification of Early Childhood Teachers

State qualification standards for the certification of early childhood teachers vary considerably, despite evidence that specialized preparation makes a positive difference in the achievement of young children (Ruopp et al., 1979, p. 98; Schweinhart, Koshel, & Bridgman, 1987, p. 527; Warger, 1988, p. 112). For licensing purposes, different states define early childhood as nursery only or pre-kindergarten only; or kindergarten through fourth, third, or second grade; pre-kindergarten and kindergarten; nursery and pre-kindergarten; or nursery through kindergarten.

A 1991 survey of the present status of teacher certification in the United States reveals that seven states have no provisions for regular early childhood teacher certification (See Table 1, below.) A similar survey completed in 1988 found that 13 states had no regular provisions (Fromberg, 1989). This change suggests that a trend toward increasingly specialized preparation has occurred. Of the six states that changed, two provide a separate early childhood license (N–3; K–3), and four provide an endorsement (Pre–K; Pre–K, K.; and two K–3). An endorsement denotes some additional provision for early childhood preparation on the elementary teaching license. The elementary teaching license usu-

Table 1

Teacher Certification for Early Childhood Education in the United States

State	N	Pre-K	K	1	2	3	4	Sp.-Ed.	None
Alabama	+	+	+	+	+	+			
Alaska	E	E	E	E	E	E			
Arizona			E	E	E	E			
Arkansas			E					N–K	
California	+	+	E	E	E	E			
Colorado	E	E	E	E	E	E			
Connecticut	E	E	E	E	E	E			
Delaware	+	+	+	+	+	+			
Florida	E	E	E	E	E	E			
Georgia	E	E	E	E	E	E			
Hawaii			+	+	+	+			
Idaho			E	E	E	E			
Illinois	+	+	+	+	+	+			
Indiana		+	+	+	+	+			
Iowa		+	+						
Kansas	+	+							
Kentucky			E	E	E	E	E		
Louisiana	+	+	+						
Maine									—
Maryland	+	+	+	+	+				
Massachusetts	+		+	+	+	+		N–3	
Michigan		E							
Minnesota	+	+	+						
Mississippi									—
Missouri	+	+	+	+	+	+			
Montana									—
Nebraska			+	+	+	+			
Nevada								E/0–4 yrs.	
New Hampshire	+	+	+	+	+	+			
New Jersey	E	E							
New Mexico									—
New York									—
North Carolina	+	+							
North Dakota			E						
Ohio		+	+						
Oklahoma		+	+	+	+	+			
Oregon									—
Pennsylvania	+	+	+	+	+	+			
Rhode Island	+	+	+	+	+				
South Carolina			+	+	+	+	+		
South Dakota	E	E							
Tennessee			+	+	+	+			
Texas			E						
Utah			+	+	+	+			
Vermont	E	E	E	E	E	E			
Virginia	+	+	+	+	+	+			
Washington	E	E	E	E	E	E			
Washington, D.C.		+	+						
West Virginia		E	E						
Wisconsin	+	+	+						
Wyoming			E	E	E	E			

E = Endorsement on elementary certificate; + = Certification ally is kindergarten through sixth grade and, sometimes, kindergarten through eighth or ninth grade. Most public schools have a kindergarten through sixth grade organization, although there is a growing trend toward an organization of kindergarten through fourth grade elementary and fifth through eighth middle school grades. The National Association of State Boards of Education (1988) published a policy statement advocating the organization of public school early childhood centers, a slowly growing movement.

Twenty-five states have a separate early childhood license as contrasted with an endorsement on the elementary teaching license. Licensing of kindergarten teachers in these states requires special preparation. In the 25 endorsement-only states or no-provision states, practicing kindergarten teachers may have received no special preparation or supervised field work with young children.

Seventeen states have no provision requiring either an early childhood teacher certificate or an endorsement to work with children before kindergarten age. Three states specify teacher certification requirements for early childhood special education.

As increasing numbers of young children use group care and school settings, the debate about early childhood teacher certification continues and requirements are changing continually. While debate centers on such administrative and political issues as a school administrator's flexibility in reassigning teachers, and job protection in the event of funding cutbacks, scholarly agreement appears to center on the unique learning needs of young children and the efficacy of specially prepared teachers in meeting those needs. Resolution of political debate and scholarly agreement await future events.

References

Fromberg, D. P. (1989). Kindergarten: Current circumstances affecting curriculum. *Teachers College Record*, *90* (3), 392–403.

Ruopp, R., Travers, J., Glantz, F., & Coelen, C. (1979). *Children at the center: Summary findings and their implications*. Final Report of the National Day Care Study. Cambridge, MA: Abt.

Schweinhart, L. J., Koshel, J. J., & Bridgman, A. (1987). Policy options for preschool programs. *Phi Delta Kappan*, *68* (7), 524–529.

Warger, C. (ed.). (1988). *A resource guide to public school early childhood programs.* Washington, DC: Association for Supervision and Curriculum Development.

D. P. Fromberg

Entry-Level Testing of Teachers

Currently, 39 states mandate testing of teachers before granting certification. Of these, approximately half are legislative mandates, and the remainder are promulgated by the state boards of education. Six states use custom designed tests, three use a combination of custom designed tests and existing tests, and the remainder use existing tests. The National Teachers Examination (NTE) is the most commonly used.

States mandating the NTE tend to require the Core Battery, a series of three two-hour tests that include communication skills (listening, reading, and writing skills), general knowledge (knowledge of literature and fine arts, mathematics, science, and social studies), and professional knowledge (knowledge of the social and cultural forces that influence curriculum and teaching, and the general principles of learning and instruction).

In addition, a few states require the NTE Early Childhood Specialty Test that includes knowledge and understanding of the nature of growth, development, and learning in young children (aspects of development, factors that influence development, and contributions of major streams of developmental theory), and the ability to judge appropriateness of teaching behaviors, curriculum organization, and activities for children ages 3 to 8, as related to their growth, development, and learning (managing the physical environment, planning and implementing appropriate curriculum, evaluating informal and formal assessment and diagnostic procedures, knowing legal responsibilities and their implications, helping children to manage their own behavior, maintaining useful records of children's progress, maintaining effective interactions with parents, and understanding major streams of curriculum theory and development) (NTE, 1987).

It is generally accepted that teachers need both to be in command of a broad, basic education, and demonstrate mastery of pedagogical knowledge associated with their area of specialization. It is not accepted, however, that mastery of subject matter as measured by tests assures effectiveness as a teacher. Therefore, when a single criterion (a test) can override all other types of judgment, there is reason for concern. In early childhood education, for example, knowledge of child development that many argue should serve as the essential core for content, is not well addressed in the Core Battery. Yet the Core Battery of the test is the portion that is used by a majority of the states to determine the minimum competency for admission to the profession.

Another issue relates to whether tests that are normed to the dominant "Anglo" culture can assure equity to other ethnic groups whose language patterns and cultural orientation to the test may be considerably different. Testing, as one of many criteria for admitting teachers to the profession, may have some value when related to the expertise needed, and when designed to capture logical thinking and problem solving. Many early childhood educators believe that tests should not be the single criterion used to assess competence, however.

Reference

NTE programs: Description of the NTE tests. (1987). Princeton, NJ: Educational Testing Service.

J. McCarthy

Guidelines: NAEYC's Teacher Education Guidelines and NCATE

In 1982, the National Association for the Education of Young Children (NAEYC), the nation's largest organization of early childhood educators, developed *Early Childhood Teacher Education Guidelines for 4- and 5-Year Institutions* (NAEYC, 1991). These guidelines were developed in response to requests from some association members who, as teacher educators at NCATE-accredited institutions, were required to report how their programs used the guidelines of national specialty organizations. The guidelines also were developed to serve as a resource for early childhood teacher educators to justify program components during periods of budget reappraisal. Since early childhood programs were often the more recent additions to schools of education, they were also the first to be threatened during reorganization or retrenchment. An equally important rationale for development of the guidelines was to guide development of new programs and establish goals toward which existing programs could strive.

The guidelines were developed by surveying existing teacher preparation programs and involving members of the field. The guidelines address the following components of an early childhood teacher education program: curriculum, instructional practices, resources, faculty, enrollment, and evaluation and constituent responsiveness. The guidelines represent the consensus of the early childhood profession regarding the requirements of a program to prepare teachers to work with young children, birth through age 8.

Shortly after the guidelines were developed, the curriculum standards were approved by the National Council for the Accreditation of Teacher Education (NCATE). As a constituent member of NCATE, NAEYC has the right to submit guidelines for program curricula, to appoint a liaison to represent the association in NCATE activity, to appoint representatives to the Board of Examiners (individuals who are trained to serve on visiting teams), and conduct review of early childhood teacher education programs in institutions seeking NCATE accreditation (a process known as folio review).

Submission of folios is a precondition for accreditation. The appropriate professional organization reviews the folio and determines whether the program complies with the specialty guidelines. Compliance with specialty guidelines for each program area determines whether the unit is found to meet NCATE's

Standard 2.4, one of many standards on which an education unit is judged for accreditation.

The NAEYC guidelines require a broad base of knowledge of child development and learning throughout the age span and specialization in at least one developmental period (infants/toddlers, preprimary including kindergarten, or primary). In recognition of the diverse age groups and settings represented in early childhood programs, the guidelines also require that teacher candidates complete at least 150 hours of student teaching/practice in each of two different settings with two different age groups, one of which must serve preprimary age or infants/toddlers.

The NAEYC Governing Board appoints a Teacher Education Advisory Panel to serve as folio reviewers and to advise the association on action relevant to broad issues of teacher education. Each folio is reviewed by three people and a summary report is compiled by NAEYC staff. Programs that are found in noncompliance have the opportunity to submit a rejoinder or receive an on-site visit to obtain a positive review. A complete description of the development of the guidelines and their application in the NCATE process may be found in the references below.

References

Bredekamp, S. (1992). The development and application of professional standards for early childhood teacher education. In S. Kilmer (ed.), *Advances in day care and early education, Vol. 5.* Greenwich, CT: JAI Press.

Bredekamp, S. (1990). Setting and maintaining professional standards. In Spodek, B., & Saracho, O. (eds.), *Yearbook in early childhood education: Teacher education*, vol. 1. New York: Teachers College Press.

National Association for the Education of Young Children. (1991). *Early childhood teacher education guidelines for 4- and 5-year institutions.* Washington, DC: NAEYC.

Seefeldt, C. (1988). Teacher certification and program accreditation of early childhood education. *Elementary School Journal, 89* (3), 241–251.

S. Bredekamp

Legislation: Effect on Teacher Education

Major efforts have been undertaken during the 1980s to improve education. This effort has resulted from a public perception that teachers are not effective in fulfilling their roles. Because policy makers react to a nervous public, they have found it reassuring to their constituency to mandate testing with all its sanctions and rewards, restrict certification, and control funding. All levels of education, including teacher education, have been affected by this vision of educational policy.

Testing. There is a trend in the United States to require the testing of prospective teachers. Testing usually has concentrated on skills that are amenable to measurement and are designed only to assess rote knowledge associated in the public's mind with being an effective teacher. Teaching, however, is a human relations engagement that requires that teachers possess the ability to interact sensitively, creatively, and knowingly with children and their families. The potential impact of testing on teacher education programs is to narrow the curriculum and constrain teacher creativity and responsiveness to the needs of children.

Certification restrictions. Other legislative acts have been directed toward standards for certification that affect the content of teacher education programs. These mandates are associated with requiring more subject matter study and have reduced or eliminated pedagogical study. The impetus for such actions was primarily focused on improving secondary education. Broad requirements do not necessarily address the educational needs of diverse populations of children and the concomitant competencies of the teachers providing for their learning. State certification standards tend to be viewed by the public as maximal standards, even though they are minimal standards. In turn, resources in teacher education institutions are allocated to develop programs that are in compliance with state mandates. When students preparing to teach must concentrate their study in areas other than early childhood education in order to qualify for certification, the outcome can be a reduction of capacity to develop highly competent early childhood teachers.

Funding. Funding limitations also influence early childhood teacher education. Low salaries and insufficient compensation for individuals who pursue advanced study discourage teachers from developing master's level skills. Additionally, some schools discourage teachers' advanced study because they want to maintain a low operating budget and disallow recompense for additional degrees. Narrowing the pool of teachers who have the breadth of practical experience and advanced study in the field seriously limits the potential candidates for doctoral study who might become the researchers and teachers in higher education. There is a need to develop early childhood teacher educators who have the ability sensitively to link practice and theory in a meaningful way for future generations of early childhood teachers.

Reference

Jensen, M. A., & Chevalier, Z. W. (1990). I*ssues and advocacy in early childhood education.* Boston: Allyn and Bacon.

J. McCarthy

6.8 Parents, Parent Education, and Community Involvement

In the twentieth-century United States, parents are their child's first and foremost teachers. Within everyday parent-child interactions, young children develop concepts of self, attitude, values, behavioral patterns, and learn to understand language and to speak. By nature young children are curious, observing, exploring, and learning through play. Parents promote their child's learning and development as they provide opportunities for their child to explore—furnishing them with space, materials, and playmates, giving praise and encouragement, suggesting ideas and actively participating in experiences with their child.

This section explores some of the ways that families or parents have been recognized as educators in studies of family demographics and influence, design of parent education programs, and utilization of community members across a variety of early childhood settings. Issues in parent education and community involvement are highlighted in articles on underlying assumptions and ethics in work with families, parental views on bilingualism in their children, and family influence on children's literacy.

C. S. Klass & L. R. Williams

Families as Educators

It has been recognized increasingly that the family is a major educator. However varied the forms of the family may be, most children spend their earliest years in some kind of familial environment. It is during these early years that extraordinary educational feats are accomplished, such as learning language, and learning to sit up, crawl, and walk.

These early developmental and educational achievements are awe inspiring. We need not argue that the effects of the early years are irreversible to appreciate their educational importance. Although much recent research on life span development (Brim & Wheeler, 1966) suggest that human plasticity (and the possibility for making corrections and adaptations throughout life) is greater than had been assumed at one time, it remains important to recognize that the early years, the time generally spent in some kind of familial setting, are of profound educational importance (Bloom, 1976). For educators concerned with any stage of development from childhood to old age, an understanding of the family is important; for early childhood educators, however, such understanding is essential.

The family has recently become the focus of many studies that are explicitly concerned with education. Over the past few years, the growth of a special interest group (SIG) in the American Educational Research Association (AERA), entitled Families as Educators, is indicative of the potency of the topic.

The family has long been the subject of anthropological, sociological, economic, psychological, cultural, and historical inquiry; and indeed, research on families as educators has been considered in terms of a variety of disciplinary frameworks (Leichter, 1973, 1974, 1979, 1980). The family is often a focus of deliberate efforts at social change, and the forms that the family takes are closely associated with and may be regarded as a kind of barometer of the characteristics of the larger society.

Evaluations of the family vary widely, ranging from apocalyptic views of the decline of the family and society, to criticisms of the constraints that tightly knit, traditional families place upon their members. Evaluations of the family tend to be highly emotional, based in part on deeply held personal convictions and longstanding experience in one's own family. If evaluations of the family are to be adequate for purposes of educational policy and program planning, they need to take into account the great variety that exists in family forms and ties.

References

Bloom, B. (1976). *Human characteristics and school learning.* New York: McGraw-Hill.

Brim, O.G., Jr., and Wheeler, S. (1966). *Socialization after childhood.* New York: John Wiley & Sons.

Leichter, H.J. (1973). The concept of educative style. *Teachers College Record, 75* (2), 239–250.

Leichter, H.J. (Ed.). (1974). *The family as educator.* New York: Teachers College Press.

Leichter, H.J. (Ed.). (1979). *Families and communities as educators.* New York: Teachers College Press.

Leichter, H.J. (1980). A note on time and education. *Teachers College Record, 81* (3), 360–370.

H. J. Leichter

History of the Family in the United States

One might assume that our understandings of the history of families in the United States would be based on a long and rich tradition of scholarship focused on the evolution of family life throughout our history, but such is not the case. The best work on family history dates from the 1960s. Also, many of the pioneering scholars in the field emphasized the Colonial period and tended to limit their analyses to New England's Puritans and the Tidewater aristocracy. By contrast, recent studies have dealt more often with nineteenth-century family life, and the focus has begun to shift toward a broader regional representation.

Analysis of historical data reveals that almost from the start, Western European–American households have been essentially nuclear, rather than extended, in structure, but have often expanded and contracted in size and composition to match family life-course changes. At various points in time, many households included other relatives, unrelated persons, and large numbers of young children, many of whom contributed to the family income.

Although large families tended to be common throughout Colonial times and on into the period after the American Revolution, some regions, such as the Chesapeake Bay area, experienced relatively high rates of child mortality. Also, unlike the contemporary period, where divorce is a major cause of one-parent families, the death of one or both spouses often disrupted Colonial and early Republican families prior to the last children becoming adults. Often, spouses remarried relatively quickly. The modern period, from 1900 on, witnessed a sharply increased life expectancy on the part of family members.

During the early part of the nineteenth century, differences in regional economies contributed to marked variations in family circumstances. An almost exclusive reliance upon labor intensive agriculture heavily influenced southern family life. Intermarriage and cohabitation between African-Americans and Anglo-Americans was relatively high in the earliest part of the period, but the increasing dependence on large cash crops, such as cotton, and reliance upon the "peculiar institution of slavery" contributed to sharp differentiations between blacks and whites based on free and servile status. Although slave marriages were not legally recognized and often were disrupted by external economic circumstances, they maintained a surprising degree of solidarity.

Isolated families living in remote mountain and western frontier areas, including Native American families, differed considerably from those who lived in the villages and towns. In the latter, family life was closely tied to the community and its religious orientation. This was particularly the case for North American families across the country, as well as European-American families in New England and newly settled areas along the river valleys of New York and Pennsylvania.

Beginning in the East before the Civil War and continuing westward thereafter, Native American community, economic, and family life was progressively disrupted. As it did in the case of nearly every other sector of community existence, the Civil War exerted an enormous influence on family life. In the Border States, families often were divided by conflicting allegiances. Many families saw their sons and husbands sacrificed on the altar of battle, and many others suffered the loss of their lands and livelihoods.

The forces of industrialism and urbanization, as well as immigration, were key factors in changes that occurred in family life during the latter half of the nineteenth century. With the emergence of larger factories in the North and a substantial influx of new immigrant groups (such as the Irish and Germans, who came during the 1840s and 1850s, and, eventually people from Eastern and Southern Europe, as well as Asia, who arrived later on), family life in the United States began to diversify more sharply along social class as well as ethnic and racial lines.

The end of the nineteenth century and the beginning of the twentieth brought new concerns, most of which received expression in what has been called the Progressive movement. Seeking to ameliorate the harsh realities of urban family life in particular, the Progressives agitated for divorce reform, better child health, and the elimination of child labor. They also were involved in the first White House Conferences on Children and Families and the creation of the United States Children's Bureau. The subsequent emergence of "scientifically" oriented professions and academic disciplines (such as social work, psychology, and pediatrics, as well as philanthropically supported efforts to provide parent education), demonstrated an altered view of the citizenry with respect to the notion of family self-sufficiency.

Efforts to "save" the United States family and provide better care for children, as well as their elders, were aided as well as sidetracked by the Great Depression and the onset of World War II. In the wake of the overall prosperity of the late 1950s and early 1960s, the federal government launched a range of federal antipoverty programs that offered further assistance to low-income families.

The subsequent cutback of many of these supportive services and programs, reflecting an altered federal domestic policy in the 1980s, combined with economic dislocations and dramatic increases in the number of homeless families and low-income households headed by single parents, recently has created a dramatically polarized economic and social profile of families in the United States, and has sharpened marked differences between different age groups as well as ethnic and racial groups. As the nation faces the year 2000, the increasingly large proportion of children born into poverty and the devastating inroads in family life caused by the scourges of family violence, drug abuse, and AIDS present a picture vaguely reminiscent of that which the country faced at the beginning of the century. In some ways, the situation of families has become worse.

Readings in the history of the family in the United States can be found in a number of the books cited in the references, but much information also appears in family-related fields, such as women's studies and demographic history.

References

Coontz, S. (1988). *The social origins of private life: A history of American families, 1600–1900.* New York: Verso Publications.

Degler, C. N. (1980). *At odds: Women and the family in America from the revolution to the present.* New York: Oxford University Press.

Demos, J. (1986). *Past, present, and personal: The family and the life course in American history.* New York: Oxford University Press.

Gordon, M. (ed.). (1983). *The American family in social-historical perspective* (3rd ed.). New York: St. Martin's Press.

Gutman, H. G.(1976). *The black family in slavery and freedom, 1750–1925.* New York: Pantheon Books.

Hareven, T. K. (ed.). (1978). *Transitions: The family and the life course in historical perspective.* New York: Academic Press.

Mintz, S., & Kellog, S. (1988). *Domestic revolutions: A social history of American family life.* New York: The Free Press.

Pleck, E. H. (1987). *Domestic tyranny: The making of American social policy against family violence from colonial times to the present.* New York: Oxford University Press.

Ryan, M. P. (1981). *Cradle of the middle class: The family in Oneida County, New York, 1790–1865.* New York: Cambridge University Press.

R. S. Pickett

Characteristics of Families in the United States

Family characteristics in the United States today reflect and contribute to recent social and economic developments. Among these characteristics are demographics changing toward an immigrant society, extensive geographic mobility, and changes in the forms of economic activity shifting from an agricultural to an industrial and a postindustrial ("information") economy.

A particular set of economic and geographic circumstances may serve to strengthen certain family ties while disrupting others. Immigration and migration, for instance, may attentuate ties to those left behind, while at the same time foster mutual dependence among those that migrate together. (The early immigrants to the United States, for example, may have left behind family members that they never saw again and kept contact with only through correspondence, while at the same time the ties of language and ethnicity became more binding in the new country.) Even the most difficult conditions, for example, the upsurge of drug problems that devastate many inner-city homes, leaving some parents unable to care for their children,

may go together with strengthening the supports of other kin, such as grandparents.

There is great diversity of cultural traditions among families in the United States today stemming from periods of previous immigration and continuing immigration. Not only the fact of immigration from one society to another, or of migration from one area of the country to another, but the beliefs about the significance of maintaining or disengaging from cultural traditions must be considered. At times, an emphasis has been placed on acculturation, assimilation, and movement away from the traditions of the places or origin, and the acquisition of new values and beliefs of the new or dominant society. At other times an emphasis on the continuity of cultural traditions has been stressed.

Another characteristic of families in the United States today is wide disparity of income, seen in the recent exacerbation of homelessness, including homelessness of parents and children, and the devastating economic circumstances that face a significant portion of the population. Estimates of the number of children living in poverty (Edelman, 1989) make clear that considerations of familial education must include an examination of the social class and economic differentials among families, and the links of economic circumstances with child-rearing practices and possibilities.

There are several important demographic characteristics of families in the United States today. One is the variety of forms of household composition, with divorced, remarried, and single parent households being common forms. Another is the increasing number of women with preschool children going into the labor force outside the home full time, and the related need for day care facilities. Added to this is the dramatic increase in the proportion of the elderly individuals in the population. While many new kinds of facilities for the elderly have been created in recent years, models of the integration of persons of various age groups remain to be worked out, as well as solutions to the problems of the strain that may be placed upon a family where the mother is employed outside the home and at the same time also must deal with responsibilities of caring for children as well as elderly relatives. While critics have argued the need to "redesign the American dream" and examine the assumptions underlying various kinds of housing and community development (Hayden, 1984), the practical accomplishment of new designs (for example, those that will enable day care facilities to be in living areas, allow for new kinds of communal food preparation, and meet the needs of varying forms of households, not merely those of the conventional form of husband, wife, and children), remain to be accomplished on any large scale. Any more specific efforts to consider programs to assist families in educating their children should be based on a recognition of these larger societal settings that condition the child-rearing possibilities and problems of families.

References

Edelman, M. W. (1989). Economic issues related to child care and early education. In F. O'C. Rust and L. R. Williams, *The care and education of young children: Expanding contexts, sharpening focus.* New York: Teachers College Press.

Hayden, D. (1984). *Redesigning the American dream: The future of housing, work, and family life.* New York: Norton.

Vold, E. B. (1989). The evolution of multicultural education: A socio-political perspective. In P. G. Ramsey, E. B. Vold, & L. R. Williams, *Multicultural education: A source book.* New York: Garland.

H. J. Leichter

Parent Education in the United States, Emergence of

Parenting, the education of parents and community involvement in parent education, reflects the social, political, and economic state of society. Before industrialization, families worked together in home and field settings, and childhood was not seen as a separate stage of life (Aries, 1962). In early agrarian days, religious beliefs and institutions were the major source of parent education, supplemented by parents' daily contact with relatives, neighbors, and coworkers.

With nineteenth-century industrialization, mass immigration, and rapid growth of cities, a new family structure emerged. New laws barred children from employment, childhood was legitimized as a separate stage in life, and women took on familial roles of supervising children and creating a domestic haven from the workplace. These rapid changes brought a change from emphasis on moral training of children to a concern for their general well-being.

Since the late nineteenth century, the content of parent education has been determined in each period by prevailing ideas of the leading thinkers in child psychology. G. Stanley Hall was the first to popularize the idea that child study has the potential to revolutionize practices within the home. The first nationwide parent education organization, now known as the Parent-Teacher Association (PTA), held its initial meeting in 1897. It was grounded in Hall's ideas of play and freedom for the young child and was consistent with John Dewey's (1966) emphasis on nurturing children's interests and learning by doing (Schlossman, 1976).

Parent education was integral to the Progressive movement of late nineteenth- and early twentieth-century America. Settlement houses, committed to strengthening family life of the urban poor, emerged in cities. As immigrant mothers worked long hours in factories, wealthy women of leisure began day nurseries. These wealthy women promoted middle-class family values for these new immigrants as they regularly visited the children's homes and taught night classes in child care and homemaking skills. (Steinfels, 1973).

In the early twentieth century, the popular press promoted first Watson's behavioral psychology and then Freud's psychoanalytic psychology. Training children was replaced with an emphasis on understanding stages in children's development and allowing children to express their feelings. Each theory stressed the significance of early childhood and emphasized the family in determining how a child develops.

In the 1920s, with a decline in immigration and less public interest in social reform, parent education focused on instructing middle-class women in child rearing in accordance with the new discipline of psychology. Colleges, high schools, and even grade schools began offering parent education classes. Training schools for nursery school teachers and child development research grew. These nursery schools served middle- and upper-middle class families, and parent education was a central aspect of the programs (Weissbourd, 1988).

During the Depression, the first government-sponsored parent education emerged through government initiated programs operated by WPA workers; and parent education once again encompassed the underprivileged. Government-sponsored programs continued during World War II (Steinfels, 1973).

Government-sponsored programs had ceased by the 1950s, and organized parent education once again was limited to middle-class parents. The child-centered, permissive tradition of nursery schools became the taken-for-granted right of every child. This was an era of tremendous increase in popular magazines, parent books, and television shows that depicted the model nuclear family.

In the 1960s, federal involvement in parent education once again included the economically disadvantaged. The child development work of Jean Piaget, Benjamin Bloom, James McV. Hunt and Jerome S. Bruner gave convincing evidence that the first five years of life are the years of most rapid intellectual development and the foundation for children's school success. The emergence of this new research coincided with President Lyndon Johnson's antipoverty political agenda, the civil rights movement, and the new women's movement. Head Start was established, with family support as a central program component. The same research providing the basis for Head Start sparked middle-class parents' concerns for their children's cognitive growth and parental interest in early education.

The institution of marriage and the family remains a pivotal foundation of American so-ciety. Beginning in the 1970s, however, there have been fundamental changes in the family's structure and functioning, with accompanying profound changes in the context of childbearing. Unlike the idealized nuclear family of the 1950s, half of all marriages now end in divorce, single parenting is common, and, where both parents are in the home, both are likely to be employed. With these changes, family needs for support have become more widespread; and parent education programs have multiplied.

Since the 1970s, the traditional, didactic, parent education model has been extended to encompass a new approach—family support programs, which embrace an ecological approach; that is, they emphasize the family as a whole, and consider the child within the context of the family, and the family within the larger context of informal and formal social networks within their community. Family support programs are characterized by involvement of parent and child together as well as professionals working as partners rather than experts. Peer support is another feature of these programs. There is a belief in prevention rather than treatment, and the use of a health model that builds on each family's strengths rather than a deficit model aimed at remedying weaknesses.

There has been no single model of parent education in America. Rather, it has involved a wide range of strategies, including dissemination of parenting manuals, parenting courses, self-help and support groups, home-visiting programs, and television, radio, and magazine series. Parent education and family support programs have taken place in a variety of settings, and are sponsored by a wide range of community organization, such as nursery schools, day care centers, public schools, universities, health and mental health agencies, and civic and religious groups.

As we approach the twenty-first century, family structure and function in the United States will continue to change, as family mobility, employment of mothers, and serial marriages continue to increase. In turn, it is likely that new patterns of parenting, parent education, and community involvement will emerge to meet the needs of young children and their families.

References

Aries, P. (1962). *Centuries of childhood: A social history of family life.* New York: Vintage Books.

Dewey, J. (1966). *Democracy and education.* New York: Macmillan.

Hall, G. S. (1907). The content of children's minds on entering school. In T. L. Smith (ed.), *Aspects of child life and education.* Boston: Ginn & Company. (Essay first published in 1883.)

Schlossman, S. L. (1976). Before Head Start: Notes toward a history of parent education in America, 1897–1929. *Harvard Educational Review, 46* (3), 436–467.

Steinfels, M. (1973). *Who's minding the children? The history and politics of day care in America.* New York: Simon & Schuster.

Weissbourd, B. (1988). A brief history of family support programs. In S. L. Kagan, D. R. Powell, B. Weissbourd, & E. F. Zigler (eds.), *America's family support Programs*, pp. 38–56. New Haven: Yale University Press.

C. S. Klass

Parent Education and Involvement, Types of

Different types of parent education and involvement exist as a result of visions of family, and their goals for interaction of parents with their children. (See **Families and Schools: Underlying Assumptions**, under **Issues** below.) Some programs have focused on providing parents with information, or on teaching specific child-rearing or instructional skills. Other have sought to utilize parents' existing expertise in child-rearing situations or in informal or formal instructional capacities. The articles below describe some of the parent education programs and approaches that have been widely disseminated within child care and early education settings.

L. R. Williams

Mother-Child Home Program ("Toy Demonstrators")

The Mother-Child Home Program (MCHP) for two- to four-year-old children was designed to promote a parent-child support network in order to improve the educational opportunities of children disadvantaged by poverty. The study of this program began in 1965 as an outgrowth of the Verbal Interaction Project, developed by Phyllis Levenstein. The theory underlying the program is that ecological and socioemotional growth is fostered when child and parent/caregiver exchange rich language experiences focused around picture books and educational toys.

The method includes twice-weekly, half-hour home sessions in which trained "Toy Demonstrators" engage parent and child in reading the books and playing with the toys. Materials remain in the home along with guidelines that provide exemplary ways to stimulate formation of core concepts in the children.

The Verbal Interaction Project's research of the MCHP was approved by the federal Joint Dissemination Review Panel in 1978, thereby entering the program into the National Diffusion Network. The program has been cited by the U.S. Department of Education and by the U.S. National Institute of Mental Health as a model early childhood/parent education and family mental health intervention program.

Varied research methods have pointed toward its effectiveness. A longitudinal evaluation of the program's school effects was a Chapter I follow-up study of a Pittsfield, Massachusetts, MCHP replication. MHCP graduates met national academic norms through eighth grade, in contrast to the educational disadvantage of a comparison group. Correlations between mother-child preschool verbal interaction and MCHP graduates' first grade school competencies suggested that the model MCHP promoted a supportive parent-child network.

In 1989 there were 24 replications of the MCHP in 4 states, and in Bermuda and Canada. All participants were trained by a MCHP-specific method to be autonomous and creative but to follow the program's basic standards in order to attain the same effects as those in the model MCHP.

References

Levenstein, P. (1976). Cognitive development through verbalized play. In J. S. Bruner, A. Jolly, & K. Sylva (eds.), *Play—its role in development and evolution* (pp. 286–297). New York: Basic Books.

Levenstein, P. (1977). The Mother-Child Home Program. In M. C. Day & R. K. Parker (eds.), *The preschool in action* (pp. 27–49). Second edition. Boston: Allyn and Bacon.

Levenstein, P. (1979). The parent-child network. In A. Simmons-Martin & D. R. Calvert (eds.), *Parent-child intervention* (pp. 245–267). New York: Grune & Stratton.

Levenstein, P. (1988). *Messages from home.* Columbus: Ohio State University Press.

Levenstein, P., O'Hara, J. M., & Madden, J. (1983). The Mother-Child Home Program of the Verbal Interaction Project. In Consortium for Longitudinal Studies (ed.), *As the twig is bent.* (pp. 237–263). Hillsdale, NJ: Erlbaum.

P. Levenstein

Parent and Child Programs

Many Parent and Child (PAC) education programs for low-income families have replicated the Verbal Interaction Project, discussed in the preceding article. An example of such a program is an expansion of a Verbal Interaction Project program in 1978 by the public school districts of Great Neck and Manhasset, New York, and the Board of Cooperative Educational Services of Nassau County, New York. The expansion included a voluntary school-based experience where two-year-olds, parents, and grandparents share many experiences. The weekly PAC group offers parents an opportunity to observe their children as they interact with peers, share common concerns, learn about child development through examples of theory and practice, and just have fun during a regular routine sharing of music and stories with their children (Halbrooks, 1984). A parent-child program, whether located in a school, library, or community room, should meet the following criteria:

- A child-centered environment with many sensory motor activities, including sand, water, and pull and push toys;
- Enough materials for fine and gross motor development;
- Approximately one adult per three children;
- A heterogeneous grouping of parents with role models from different racial, ethnic, and economic backgrounds;
- Opportunities for parents to observe staff interacting with their children;
- A balance between parent-initiated activities and leader-initiated activities;
- An atmosphere in which parents can feel comfortable and laugh together, as well as engage in serious discussions; and
- Opportunities for former parents to return to the program as volunteers or paid aides, who become role models for new parents.

This exemplary program is open to children who participate in the home-based program as well as others on the waiting list. Transportation to the one and one-half hour weekly sessions is available.

Staff include trained volunteers and some paid aides. Volunteers, ranging in age from 21 to 80 years, come from different educational backgrounds and receive training before and during the intervention period. They must qualify as accepting, nonthreatening individuals who are knowledgeable about child development and capable of intelligent, nonjudgmental observations of children's behavior. The volunteer experiences flexibility within structure and an opportunity to be involved actively in the process of nurturing parents as well as children.

Staff meetings follow every PAC session to evaluate each child's progress, address parents' needs, and identify children with developmental delays. When parents are absent, a telephone call maintains close personal contact, which helps erase the sense of anonymity so prevalent among low-income families.

The total program offers important support for parents on their own turf (Levenstein, 1970, 1975; Lombard, 1973) and an opportunity for parents to feel less isolated by becoming part of a supportive group in the school setting. These components strengthen self-esteem and help bring about a stronger parent-school bond. Investigators have found that

100 percent of the parents in the PAC education program thought that the skills they had learned in the program would help their children to succeed in kindergarten (Townley et al., 1987).

References

Halbrooks, R. (1984). *Excellence in parenthood/child development education.* Detroit, MI: Kellogg Foundation.

Hausman, B. (1989). Parents as teachers: The right fit for Missouri. *Educational Horizons, 67* (1–2), 35–39.

Levenstein, P. (1970). Cognitive growth in preschoolers through verbal interaction with mothers. *American Journal of Orthopsychiatry, 40* (3), 426–432.

Levenstein, P. (1975). A message from home: Findings from a program for non-retarded low-income preschoolers. In M. J. Begab & S. A. Richardson (eds.), *The mentally retarded and society* (pp. 305–318). Baltimore: University Park Press.

Lombard, A. (1973). *Home instructional program for pre-school youngsters (HIPPY).* Center for Research in Education of the Disadvantaged. Jerusalem: Hebrew University.

Townley, K. F., et al. (1987). *Parent and child education program.* Conference on Education in Appalachia, University of Kentucky, Lexington, (ERIC Document Reproduction Services No. ED 300 189).

D. Kertzner

An Adapted Toy Lending Library

Play is an integral part of children's development, enabling them purposefully to interact with their environment. Because of limited motor ability, however, many children with disabilities are passive observers and are unable independently to play with toys. Their attempts to play can turn a potentially pleasurable activity into a frustrating experience.

In response to this problem, many schools and organizations have established toy lending libraries. Included in these libraries are a variety of battery and wind-up toys that have been adapted for use with interchangeable switches that can be used with any part of the body that has purposeful movement. Toys with mechanical adaptations, such as extension handles, knobs, and suction cups, allow the young child to play and experiment with toys while developing concepts and valuable social lessons. Many libraries also include developmental and educational toys, environmental control devices, adapted sports equipment, instructional VCR tapes and books appropriate for the children, their siblings, and their parents.

Rules for borrowing are similar to those in any library, with a specified number of toys and switches to be borrowed for a designated period of time. Late fees and rules for renewal are made at the discretion of each library.

When children borrow toys, they are taking home socialization tools. The toys provide children with an opportunity to develop a feeling of self-worth that can result from an ability to play actively and enjoy quality leisure time. Children with disabilities can truly experience the wonderful feeling of being a "handi-capable" person.

References

Boehm, H. (1986). *The right toys: A guide to selecting the best toys for children.* New York: Bantam Books.

Creating a toy library. (1987). New York: United Cerebral Palsy Association of Nassau County.

Directory of toy libraries in the United States. (1989). Evanston, IL: USA Toy Library Association.

UCP Nassau toy library. (1987). New York: United Cerebral Palsy Association of Nassau County.

S. Rosen

Parents as Teachers

The idea that parents are the first teachers of their children is not a new one. Both Pestalozzi's work in the late 1700s and Froebel's kindergarten in the mid-1800s honored the mother's role in children's subsequent development and learning (Weber, 1984). Over the past 100 years, parent education in the United States has rested on the premise that interaction between parents and teachers or parent specialists could improve child-rearing practices. (See **Parent Education in the United States, Emergence of,** above.)

It was not until the 1960s and early 1970s, however, that some educators began to view parents as teachers of specific school-related concepts and skills. New initiatives toward improving the educational outcomes for children from low-income homes encouraged psychologists, educators, and educational researchers to design programs that would prepare parents to teach their own children in their homes or at school, as a way of extending and supporting the schools' efforts.

Over the next decade, a wide variety of "parents as teachers" programs were created and field tested. Prominent among these were the Home Visitor Program, sponsored by the Demonstration and Research Center for Early Education (DARCEE) at George Peabody College in Nashville (Giesy, 1974) and Ira J. Gordon's Florida Parent Education Program, based at the University of Florida (Gordon, 1972). In each of these models, parents learned to work with their young children at home, using tasks and/or materials provided by home visitors or in specially designed parent meetings.

Other early childhood intervention programs soon incorporated strong parent-as-teacher components into their designs and documented the importance of parent involvement in the achievement of the program's educational objectives for the children. David Weikart, founder of the Perry Preschool Project and director of the High Scope Educational Research Foundation, identified the role of parents as teachers as a critical one in the success of three different preschool curricula (Weikart, 1981).

More recently, educators have urged parents to volunteer in the classrooms as teaching assistants or as leaders of special projects with the children. These efforts are extensions of the earlier idea that parents can directly contribute to their children's school success (Bearns, 1985).

References

Bearns, R. M. (1985). *Child, family community*. New York: Holt, Rinehart & Winston.

Giesy, R. (ed.). (1974). *A guide for home visitors*. St. Louis: CEMREL.

Gordon, I. J. (1972). Parents as teachers. *Theory into Practice, 11* (2), 145–201.

Weber, E. (1984). *Ideas influencing early childhood education*. New York: Teachers College Press.

Weikart, D. P. (1981). Effects of different curricula in early childhood intervention. *Educational Evaluation and Policy Analysis, 3* (6).

L. R. Williams

Parents as Decision Makers in Programs

Historically, parents have held decision-making roles in some early childhood programs. The Parent Cooperatives begun in the 1920s in the United States and continuing to the present day are examples of programs administered under parent governance. (See Chapter 3, Section 3.4, **Parent Cooperatives**.) Most privately sponsored early childhood programs invite parents to serve on their governing boards, and federally sponsored early childhood programs require that parents be a part of the programs' advisory councils.

Project Head Start has been especially influential in encouraging parents to assume decision-making roles within early childhood programs. The original directive on parent involvement, issued by the Office of Child Development in 1970, specified that parents were to be consulted in decisions affecting the education of their children; and subsequent federal programs have followed suit. Services to handicapped children provided under Public Law 94-142 also require direct parent participation in the preparation of Individualized Educational Plans (IEPs). It appears likely that an increased emphasis on parent involvement in a decision-making role will characterize early childhood programs in the future. (See also, Chapter 3, Section 3.5, **Head Start Policies** and **Special Education Policy**.)

L. R. Williams

Paraprofessionals and Volunteers

Paraprofessionals and volunteers are individuals who work with young children in a variety of settings. These individuals also are referred to as child care volunteers, day care aides, day care assistants, early childhood aides or auxiliaries, nursery school aides, preschool assistants, volunteer aides, and teacher aides.

Within the field of early childhood education the use of paraprofessionals has become commonplace. In the United States, elementary schools employ 1.5 million paid paraprofessionals and 6 million unpaid volunteers (Lambert, 1981).

Three concerns underlie the federal government's involvement in expanding the use of paraprofessionals. Policy makers in the 1960s wanted to raise educational outcomes in order to compete globally in a post-Sputnik era. The baby boom had led to serious overcrowding and teacher shortages. There was also greater awareness and pressure to alleviate the negative effects of poverty on educational outcomes. Programs like Head Start addressed the needs of preschool children and provided many low-income parents the opportunity to become paraprofessionals and volunteers.

Before the 1960s, paraprofessional positions tended to be part of a career plan. These individuals were often teachers in training or college trained adults. The paraprofessional of the 1960s was often low-income and/or a local community person. Becoming a paraprofessional meant gaining a footing on a career ladder that could possibly lead to a teaching credential (Howe, 1972). During the 1960s and 1970s, many schools were seen as having failed to meet the educational needs of children. The recruitment of paraprofessionals from the community served to support teachers in the everyday activities of the classroom, as volunteers had been doing since the early nineteenth century.

The duties and activities of paraprofessionals and volunteers may include, but are not limited to, directing small group activities, checking student work, preparing field trips, supervision and organization of outdoor activities, participation in the development of the general classroom environment, secretarial and housekeeping duties, and relating to students individually. The relationship between the teacher and the paraprofessional or volunteer is one in which the teacher establishes the educational program and the paraprofessional assists in implementing it.

The need for paraprofessionals in the 1990s can be expected to grow in order to meet the challenge for educating culturally diverse and low-income students, alleviating the teacher shortage, and providing for the children of the increasing number of mothers who work outside the home. The response to these challenges is likely to create a renewed interest in the utilization of career ladder positions for paraprofessionals. Volunteers, particularly senior citizens, again are being recognized as valuable resources to the educational community (Carney, Dobson, & Dobson, 1987; Taranto & Johnson, 1984).

References

Carney, J. M., Dobson, J. E., & Dobson, R. L. (March, 1967). Using senior citizen volunteers in the schools. *Journal of Humanistic Education and Development*, 25 (3), 136–143.

Howe, R. S. (1972). *The teacher assistant.* Dubuque, IA: Wm. C. Brown Company.

Kaplan, R. (1977). *From aide to teacher.* U.S. Department of Health, Education, and Welfare. Washington, DC: United States Government Printing Office.

Lambert, V. S. (1981). *Paraprofessionals working with young children.* Springfield, IL: Charles C. Thomas.

Taranto, D. E., & Johnson, S. O. (1984). *Educational volunteerism.* Springfield, IL: Charles C. Thomas.

L. M. Tannatt

Issues in Parent Education

A variety of issues continue to affect the design and conduct of parent education and other parent involvement programs. As parental influence on children's learning has been increasingly recognized, administrators, teachers, and care providers have had to reckon with the fact that parental values do not always reflect their own values. Administrators, teachers, and care providers have had to discover ways to respect parental beliefs and practices, while acknowledging their own, and (if necessary for children's emotional and physical well-being) while advocating for children. Parents likewise need to be self-aware and knowledgeable enough to advocate for their children against what they consider to be inappropriate educational practices.

The underlying assumptions governing the design of parent education programs have also come under scrutiny. Program designers and implementors must become increasingly responsive to the reality of shared initiation and shared power in the care and education of young children today. Finally, at a time when literacy in the United States as a whole appears to be declining, it is critical that policy makers recognize and address parental roles in fostering literacy. Aspects of each of these issues are addressed in the articles below.

L. R. Williams

Ethical Issues in Parent Education

The essential ethical dilemma for early childhood parent educators (those working professionally with families of young children) is how to raise basic ethical and moral questions without imposing the values of one group upon another. One confronts that dilemma if one considers that a fundamental right (within the constraints of the larger legal system) is the right to some degree of self-determination, and that the debate continues regarding families' and parents' rights to make educational "choices" for their children. At what point do the rights of parents determine the values and beliefs to which their children will be exposed educationally? And at what point do these values and beliefs run sufficiently counter to the larger standards and constraints that the society is justified in such measures as taking the child away from the parents, or requiring parents to comply with forms of schooling that run contrary to their most cherished views?

While the issues are extraordinarily complex, and it would be an oversimplification to suggest that their summary alone can offer guidelines, it is possible to suggest a number of issues to which parent educators (family educators) should themselves give attention.

At the very least, parent educators should be familiar with the basic legal cases in which the rights and responsibilities of families and the larger society (states, local community, nation) have been challenged. Such cases involve the right of parents to educate their children at home when available schooling violates their beliefs, and the right of families to choice of schooling, including the selection of school districts and determination of the boundaries of school districts.

Issues of the rights of parents to determine the education of their children hinge directly upon the confidence with which parents approach their educational efforts from the beginning of their parenthood. Some of the most basic issues for educating parents of very young children concern how to maximize the confidence of parents in educating their children.

Another fundamental ethical issue to which early childhood educators should give attention is the question of whether there are clearly established principles and procedures of child rearing that can be set forth as appropriate and superior for the education of young children. If there are such principles, it is necessary to ask how they can be conveyed and encouraged. Are there clear-cut right and wrong ways to approach the education of young children?

Social scientists have observed that in traditional societies, ways of rearing children were passed on from one generation to another; and particularly in the context of extended families, assistance in the details of everyday child rearing was given to young parents by members of the older generation. It also has been noted that the goals of parent education vary from one society to another; and it can be argued that the goals that may appear appropriate from the perspective of one society, may not be entirely in keeping with the adult personalities that can function best in another society. For example, fundamental ideas of how parents should handle emotional expressions (e.g., of anger and self-assertiveness) may vary from one society to another. These issues become especially complicated in a multiethnic, multicultural society, where the behaviors that one segment of the population may wish to encourage in young children are contrary to those that are most approved by other segments of the society.

Debates over educational timetables (i.e., the kinds of education that are appropriate at various developmental stages) offer other examples of issues of certainty of knowledge about young children and questions of imposition of views of one group on another. On the one hand, scholars such as Jerome Bruner (1961) have argued that anything can be taught to anyone of any age if one can find a developmentally appropriate manner in which to teach it. On the other hand, some educational theorists contend that particular educational activities are appropriate at particular stages. Some commentators counsel that early stimulation in a manner that might be described as "the more the better" is appropriate, while others argue that the developmental timetable of the child should guide the timetable of education.

Closely associated with ethical dilemmas that early childhood educators should consider in working with families is the question of how professionals may sustain confidence in their child-rearing recommendations, while at the same time retaining a healthy skepticism about the limits of certainty of child-rearing procedures. Confidence that one has a better vision of family life and knows how to create environments that will bring about the healthy growth and development of children is essential if one is to be able, with clear conscience, to suggest particular forms of child rearing to families. Yet, dogmatic certainties about uncertain issues, a certainty that preempts the need for empowerment, and the right of parents themselves to give reflective considerations to alternative ways of child rearing, may be counterproductive as overly qualified statements of the limits of existing knowledge.

Yet another set of ethical issues that early childhood parent educators must address is that of the linkage between the problems of particular individuals and families and those of the larger society. It may be argued that

families' problems concerning the care and education of young children derive as much from ignorance as from other factors. If this is the case, then efforts to reduce ignorance by specific education on how to care for young children are justified (e.g., the sort of presentation that T. Berry Brazelton offers on television in maternity hospitals, among other places).

Here again the issue of cultural variations of child-rearing advice arises. It is hard to imagine, for example, a contemporary hospital carrying televised advice from a Puritan handbook on child rearing or from a religious tract in which the fundamental assumption is "spare the rod and spoil the child." But where there is a gap in the transmission of child-rearing ideas (whether based on science or conventional wisdom), it is very possible that conveying basic ideas about how to care for and educate young children may fill a gap for parents, particularly for an increasing number of extremely young, teenage, and single parents.

Another dilemma concerns the criteria by which an educator can distinguish between ignorance and an alternative belief. At the very least, it should not automatically be assumed that a belief that differs from that of the professional stems from ignorance. An example is that of breast versus bottle feeding, where in the interest of modernization (and, one may argue, with the influence of companies that produce baby formula), mothers in developing nations have given up breast feeding because of the presumed benefits of the scientifically derived formulas.

Where the problems of child rearing derive from the failures of the larger society to provide minimum education, health, and social services (problems that stem from poverty, racism, sexism, ageism), those involved in early childhood education face a particularly complex ethical dilemma. If they argue for individual solutions or assume that the problems can be corrected by the reduction of individual ignorance alone, they may be undermining the very families and children that they seek to help. Through imposing ideas of child rearing and making suggestions that parents cannot achieve particular circumstances, they thereby further undermine the confidence and assurance of parents of young children; or, what is probably ethically even more problematic, through placing the blame on individuals and families, they direct attention away from the need to make improvements in the larger society. At the very least, parent educators of families with young children have an ethical obligation to educate themselves in the literatures that spell out the nature and extent of societal problems that impinge on the families of young children.

Finally, if one accepts the idea that in a democratic, multicultural society, one of the ultimate goals of lifelong education is to enable citizens to participate in a continuing debate about the means and aims of education, then early childhood educators need to consider when and how to begin educating for this debate.

References

Bruner, J.S. (1961). *The process of education*. Cambridge, MA: Harvard University Press.

Feeney, S. (1987). Ethical case studies for NAEYC reader response. *Young Children, 42* (4), 24–25.

Feeney, S. (1987). Ethics case studies: The working mother. *Young Children, 43* (1), 16–19.

Feeney, S. (1988). Ethics case studies: The aggressive child. *Young Children, 43* (3), 48–51.

Feeney, S. (1988). Ethics case studies: The divorced parents. *Young Children 43* (3), 48–51.

Feeney, S., and Kipnis, K. (1989). NAEYC code of ethical conduct and statement of commitment. *Young Children, 45* (1), 24–29.

Kipnis, K. (1987). How to discuss professional ethics. *Young Children, 42* (4), 26–30.

H. J. Leichter

Parents and Bilingualism

It is well accepted that parents are their children's first teachers. The role of parents as teachers is especially critical in the development of children's language. Children who experience a language-rich environment in the home generally enter school with a strong language foundation upon which to build and expand learning.

When the language of the school is different from that of the home, parents' opinions and reactions regarding the acquisition of two languages are varied. Some parents express great concern regarding the child's acquisition of the school language and insist upon its exclusive use in the home as well as at school, even when their own knowledge of that language may be limited. Other parents use their own language at home but insist that their children be schooled in society's dominant language. Still others opt for a bilingual approach to schooling with the thought that two languages will be acquired, learned, and used.

In spite of the different choices made by parents, many continue to fear that if the home language is used in school, children will not develop the language of the school and society and will therefore not be prepared for success. Parents are not monolithic in their opinions about bilingualism, but they all want their children to succeed.

There are a variety of factors that have an impact on how parents view bilingualism. One of the most powerful is the way that the dominant society perceives the home language and its related culture. If that perception is a negative one, parents may choose monolingualism in the "power language" over bilingualism. If the dominant society does not view language negatively, then parents may see bilingualism as a positive alternative. Even in cases where society perceives the home language as negative or nonprestigious, some parents will choose a bilingual approach to learning for their children as a way to maintain their own language and culture while incorporating the language and culture of the host country.

Recent research on the development of bilingualism in young children suggests that parental attitudes toward the two languages have an effect on children's attitudes and behaviors toward their acquisition (Fantini, 1985; Hakuta, 1986; Owens, 1986). In the case of minority groups, variables such as societal attitudes toward those groups also play a great role in how children react to the two languages. How schools support the development of the two languages, and how nondominant cultures are treated and reflected or not reflected in classrooms and learning materials, either help mitigate negative societal attitudes or reinforce them.

Although there are still questions regarding the best time to introduce a second language, researchers generally agree that the acquisition of a second language is not detrimental to the continued development of a first language (Cummins, 1979; Garcia, 1983, 1986). Bilingualism may be acquired simultaneously, or it may occur successively. Research suggests that when two languages are used in the home, the one parent–one language approach tends to be less confusing to young children (McLaughlin, 1984). This approach, however, is not always possible; and children do learn the two languages, albeit to different degrees, when two languages are used by both parents in the home.

Parents who do not know the dominant group language should continue to communicate in their own language with children in order to help them develop a strong foundation in that language. A strong foundation in one language will facilitate the learning of the second language (Cummins, 1986).

How the two languages are supported and emphasized by parents are among the key factors in the development of bilingualism in young children. It is evident that the child's affective and aesthetic associations related to each language will affect the child's motivation for its continued use. If one language is used solely for reprimanding, it will have negative associations for the child.

Parents who choose bilingualism for their children need to be aware that the majority language will probably become the dominant one for their children, because they will hear it and use it more frequently. They therefore need to provide a variety of positive experiences associated with the minority language, along with many opportunities for children to communicate in that language. Parents who consistently demonstrate positive attitudes toward the two languages, and who provide an environment rich with opportunities for language use, will encourage bilingualism in their children.

References

Cummins, J. (1986). Empowering minority students: A framework for intervention. *Harvard Educational Review 56* (1), 18–36.

Cummins, J. (1979). Linguistic interdependence and the educational development of bilingual children. *Review of Educational Research, 49* (2), 222–251.

Fantini, A. E. (1985). *Language acquisition of a bilingual child: A sociolinguistic perspective.* San Diego: College Hill Press.

Garcia, E. (1983). *Bilingualism in early childhood.* Albuquerque: University of New Mexico Press.

Garcia, E. (1986). Bilingual development and the education of bilingual children during early childhood. *American Journal of Education, 95* (1), 96–121.

Hakuta, K. (1986). *Mirror of language: The debate on bilingualism.* New York: Basic Books.

McLaughlin, B. (1984). *Second language acquisition in childhood: Volume 1, Preschool children.* Hillsdale, NJ: Erlbaum.

Owens, M. (1986). *Eithne: A study of second language development. Paper no. 15.* Dublin: Center for Language and Communication Studies.

Y. De Gaetano

Families and Schools: Underlying Assumptions

The relation of families to schools in the United States has sometimes been characterized by the implicit, if not explicit, assumption that one of the school's responsibilities is teaching the ways of the new country, or promoting acculturation and assimilation. This has been true with respect to both immigrant and Native Americans (American Indians), as Erik Erikson made clear in a classic description of how American Indian children were removed from their homes and sent to boarding schools in order to counteract the presumably negative influences of their families' cultures (Leichter, 1979).

These "assimilationist" views of family-school relationships are in contrast to views that family traditions and the "culture of the community" have an important place in the education of the child. In this alternative view, community values must be brought into the school, for example, through educators such as paraprofessionals from the community, who are recruited to bring schools and communities closer together culturally. In such models, representatives of the community, parents, and others become in a sense translators of family traditions. Planners of family education programs need explicitly to examine their underlying assumptions with respect to cultural traditions, and the links of cultural traditions with child-rearing practices and possibilities.

Scrutiny of assumptions with respect to social class, educational level, and child-rearing practices is also important. The possibility of class, as well as ethnic or racial prejudice regarding views on proper ways of rearing children, exists no matter how well intentioned the effort (Getzels, 1979). The presumption, implicit or explicit, that the child-rearing practices of the economically better off are inherently superior, or that they can be conveyed to those who lack basic economic resources, has characterized some efforts at parent education. When problems in child rearing stem from lack of information or knowledge, they presumably can be corrected by conveying this knowledge. But to the extent that they stem from other sources, information alone may be insufficient, or conceivably even damaging, if it sets up ideals of child rearing that are unattainable under particular circumstances such as serious poverty. It is possible that educational efforts may raise parental anxiety and guilt rather than modify parental behaviors in the presumably desirable directions (Bronfenbrenner, 1979).

References

Bronfenbrenner, U. (1979). Who needs parent education? In Leichter, H.J. (ed.), *Families and communities as educators*. New York: Teachers College Press.

Getzels, J.W. (1979). The communities of education. In Leichter, H.J. (ed.), *Families and communities as educators*. New York: Teachers College Press.

Leichter, H.J. (1979). Families and communities as educators: Some concepts of relationship. In Leichter, H.J. (ed.), *Families and communities as educators*. New York: Teachers College Press.

H. J. Leichter

Literacy, The Role of Parents in Promoting

Children from varying backgrounds have numerous experiences with written language before entering school, and these experiences support the children's efforts to become competent readers and writers. Reading and writing begins as children become aware that the writing they see around them makes sense. The most important feature of these events, regardless of the children's socioeconomic background, is that reading and writing is part of the social interactions within home and community (Heath, 1983; Taylor, 1983; Teale & Sulzby, 1988). Parents use written language as a social technique for dealing with everyday experiences, such as cooking, shopping, and writing and receiving letters. Children are part of these activities when observing the adult process and imitating or playing out events, such as pretending to read a menu, taking an order, and playing post office (Taylor, 1983).

Though all children have literacy experiences as part of their social interactions, not all children have the same quality of experiences in being read to or observing adults reading for pleasure. In contrast, children whose parents read to them tend to learn a great deal more about literacy, and evidence a stronger interest in reading and writing (Wells, 1986). A regularly designated time for reading, rereading stories and changing the way they are read, reading along with children, relating the reading to children's experiences, asking questions, encouraging children to ask questions, and responding to children's questions, are important ways in which parents support children's literacy development (Bloom, 1987; Teale & Sulzby, 1986).

Dolores Durkin's (1966) classic study of early readers found that these children usually had parents who provided a wide range of reading and writing materials for children to use and experiment with; who read and wrote a great deal themselves, thus modeling that reading and writing were valued activities; and who responded to questions and requests as children expressed a need to know.

Descriptions of parent/child reading and writing activities have appeared in case studies confirming the notion that children's literacy begins at home (Baghban, 1984; Bissex, 1980). Environments for these case studies have been professional or middle class, where children had many opportunities for interacting with a parent and peers in relation to various print materials.

References

Baghban, M. J. M. (1984). *Our daughter learns to read and write*. Newark, DE: International Reading Association.

Bissex, G. L. (1980). *GNYS AT WRK*. Cambridge: Harvard University Press.

Bloom, W. (1987). *Partnerships with parents in reading*. England: Hodder & Stoughton.

Durkin, D. (1966). *Children who read early*. New York: Teachers College Press.

Heath, S.B. (1983). *Ways with words*. New York: Cambridge University Press.

Teale, W.H. & Sulzby, E. (eds.). (1986). *Emergent literacy*. Norwood, NJ: Ablex.

Taylor, D. (1983). *Family literacy*. Portsmouth, NH: Heinemann.

Wells, G. (1986). Variation in child language. In P. Fletcher & M. Garman (eds.), *Language acquisition* (2nd ed.) (pp. 109–140). New York: Cambridge University Press.

N. H. Barbour

6.9 Supervision and Administration of Early Childhood Programs

This section consists of two articles concerning the supervision and administration of early childhood programs. The overwhelming body of professional literature about supervision and administration points to the important role of the building principal or director in creating a good learning climate. The first article addresses school climate directly and the second article addresses it indirectly through the national process of program accreditation.

In the consideration of school climate, this section underscores the central concern of early childhood education to create a good beginning learning climate for young children upon which they can build toward a lifetime of learning and participation as citizens. With all of these considerations, it is important for adults to keep in view the young child from birth through the first 100 months of life. Translated into months, the individual child's fragility stands out, along with adults' responsibilities to provide sensitive and intelligent caring.

D. P. Fromberg

Supervision and Administration of Early Childhood Programs

Supervision and administration of early childhood programs refer to the general oversight and management of these programs. Supervision relates explicitly to program staff and the quality of their interaction with children, while administration relates to all facets of program management.

In small centers, both supervision and administration often are performed by the same person, the program director. In larger programs, these tasks generally are divided. The program director or a head teacher might engage in supervision and an assistant administrator or secretarial person might handle program administration with oversight by the program administrator. In many early childhood centers, the program director and a board of directors share responsibility for general program policy and administration.

Administration of early childhood programs, even small ones, is a complex undertaking. Administration encompasses the obvious tasks of recruitment of both children and staff, budget, funding, accreditation and licensure, personnel procedures, public relations, maintenance of health and safety standards, and daily operations. It also encompasses the less obvious tasks of developing and implementing educational policy, maintaining good relations between the board of directors and school personnel, and between home and school, providing for staff development, curriculum oversight, program evaluation, and setting the "tone" of the center.

Supervision can complement program administration, for it is through supervision that the general educational philosophy of the program is articulated and staff development is achieved. In the field of early childhood, supervision refers to those interactions with program staff that focus on the content and quality of their interaction with children. Thus, supervision is highly personal and interactive.

An effective supervisor must be skilled in interpersonal relations, a good judge of teacher behavior, able to diagnose teacher and staff needs based on observations of program activities, knowledgeable about standards of practice among early childhood professionals, and able to work interactively with administrators, staff, and communities. At the same time, an effective supervisor must be broadly knowledgeable about child development and developmentally appropriate curriculum and practice.

Most administrators of early childhood programs learn on the job, often moving to the administrative role from a teaching position. In the private sector of early childhood education, there has not been a standard of professional preparation and licensure for supervisory and administrative personnel. Age, education, training, and experience are the most frequently mentioned criteria for choosing early childhood administrators (Seaver & Cartwright, 1986, p. 245). When education is required, a bachelor's or master's degree is generally specified rather than a specific field of study, such as developmental psychology, school administration, or early childhood education.

The National Association for the Education of Young Children (NAEYC) has begun to address the issue of qualifications for administrative and other educational personnel by developing standards for child care centers seeking accreditation by the National Academy of Early Childhood Programs. Under the NAEYC guidelines, professionals who supervise and train staff, design curriculum, and/or administer programs, are designated as early childhood specialists. They must have either an undergraduate bachelor's degree or graduate degree in early childhood education or child development, and at least three years of full-time teaching experience with young children. State education departments and other licensing bodies are considering similar standards of licensure.

A program's climate, the atmosphere or tone that characterizes the work setting, is directly affected by how supervision and administration are performed. Effective programs are characterized by collegiality, common goals, shared decision making, opportunity for professional growth, task orientation, a fair rewards system, and openness to change (Jorde-Bloom, 1988). Supervision and evaluation systems that are clear and appropriate and that have been developed by administration and staff together also tend to promote positive climate as well as strong student outcomes.

There are few factors that affect the quality of early childhood programs and thus the lives of the children whom they serve as greatly as their supervision and administration. It is important, therefore, that there be ongoing identification of the essential and unique skills and knowledge of the early childhood administrator and supervisor. The development of uniform standards for the preparation and licensure of early childhood administrators and supervisors is a next step in professionalization of the field.

References

Jorde-Bloom, P. (1988). *A great place to work: Improving conditions for staff in young children's programs.* Washington, DC: National Association for the Education of Young Children.

Seaver, J. W., & Cartwright, C. A. (1986). *Child care administration.* Belmont, CA: Wadsworth.

Wise, A. E., Darling-Hammond, L., McLaughlin, M. W., & Bernstein, H. T. (1984). *Teacher evaluation: A study of effective practices.* Washington, DC: Rand Corporation.

F. O'C. Rust and J. S. Delano

Accreditation of Programs

The National Association for the Education of Young Children (NAEYC) operates the only national, voluntary professionally sponsored accreditation system exclusively designed for early childhood centers and schools. The accreditation system, the National Academy of Early Childhood Programs, began operation in 1985 after almost four years of research and development. The first programs were accredited in 1986. During the first three years of operation, more than 1,000 programs from all 50 states achieved accreditation with more than 3,500 others in process.

The system includes any full-day or part-day group program serving children from birth through age five and/or school age children in before- and after-school child care. Accredited programs represent the diversity of the field of early childhood education. They include private, for-profit; community based, nonprofit; church-housed and sponsored; university sponsored; parent cooperatives; Head Start programs; and public school prekindergarten and kindergarten.

The goal of the Academy is to improve the quality of care and education provided for young children in group programs. The accreditation system achieves its goal by setting high quality standards and recognizing those programs that achieve substantial compliance. The criteria for quality address all components of the programs, including interactions among staff and children, curriculum, staff-parent interactions, administration, staffing, staff qualifications, physical environment, health and safety, nutrition and food service, and evaluation.

The three-step process of accreditation is designed to facilitate real and lasting program improvements. Programs conduct a self-study involving observations of classrooms, staff questionnaires, parent questionnaires, and the administrator's self-evaluation. The accuracy of the program's report of their compliance with the criteria is verified during an on-site validation visit. Then the results of the self-study and validation are reviewed by a three-person National Commission that makes the accreditation decision.

The accreditation process has benefited the individual programs that participate as well as the early childhood profession. Directors of accredited programs report that achieving accreditation improved staff morale, lowered staff turnover, and resulted in better communication and relationships with parents. The early childhood profession now has a consensus definition of what constitutes high quality practice for which to advocate at a state and national level. In addition, the accreditation system provides a positive focus for media attention and goals for public policy efforts.

References

Bredekamp, S. (ed.). (1984). *Accreditation criteria and procedures of the National Academy of Early Childhood Programs.* Washington, DC: National Association for the Education of Young Children.

Bredekamp, S. (ed.). (1985). *Guide to accreditation by the National Academy of Early Childhood Programs.* Washington, DC: National Association for the Education of Young Children.

S. Bredekamp

Index